Marital and Family Therapy

Peruvian Wedding by Filemen Leon, tapestry, 1983, private collection.

Marital and Family Therapy

Third Edition

Ira D. Glick, M.D.
Professor of Psychiatry,
Cornell University Medical College;
Associate Medical Director for Inpatient Services,
Payne Whitney Clinic,
The New York Hospital—Cornell Medical Center,
New York, New York,

John F. Clarkin, Ph.D.
Professor of Clinical Psychology in Psychiatry
Cornell University Medical College;
Director of Psychology
Westchester Division
The New York Hospital-Cornell Medical Center
Whie Plains, New York

David R. Kessler, M.D.
Clinical Professor of Psychiatry,
School of Medicine,
University of California, San Francisco;
Staff Psychiatrist,
Langley Porter Psychiatric Institute,
San Francisco, California

with Forewords by
Alan S. Gurman, Ph.D.
Professor of Psychiatry
University of Wisconsin Medical School
Madison, Wisconsin
and
Theodore Lidz, M.D.
Sterling Professor of Psychiatry Emeritus
Yale University School of Medicine
New Haven, Connecticut

Grune & Stratton, Inc.
Harcourt Brace Jovanovich, Publishers
Orlando   New York   San Diego   London
San Francisco   Tokyo   Sydney   Toronto

Grune & Stratton, Inc.
Orlando, FL 32887

Distributed in the United Kingdom by
Grune & Stratton, Ltd.
24/28 Oval Road
London NW1 70X

Library of Congress Catalog Card Number 87-081507
International Standard Book Number 0-8089-1878-8

Printed in the United States of America
87 88 89 90   10 9 8 7 6 5 4 3 2 1

To our families,
past and present,
personal and
professional

Contents

Tables and Figures

Acknowledgments

We wish to thank a variety of individuals and families who have helped to make this book possible.

First, our own families of origin, Bernard and Gertrude Glick, John and Helen Clarkin, and Benjamin and Thelma Kessler, who, in addition to steadfastly attempting to socialize us, provided us with our first major models of family structure and function. Second, our teachers, Theodore Lidz and Thomas Detre, at the Yale University Department of Psychiatry, Irwin Greenberg at Hillside Hospital, New York City, Alan Leveton at the Mt. Zion Hospital, San Francisco, Nathan Ackerman at the New York State Psychiatric Institute, and Olga Silverstein, Lynn Hoffman, and Peggy Papp at the Ackerman Institute, who by their concern and enthusiasm, first helped to stir our interest in family study and treatment and provided us with a family model of understanding human functioning. Third, our colleagues in family therapy, especially Henry Lennard and Jay Haley, who, by their stimulating and provocative comments, tried their best to keep us honest. Fourth, our trainees, with whom we have been privileged to work on the teaching-learning process in family therapy. It is they who have had the courage to ask the critical questions about the field, and it was for them that much of the didactic material in this textbook was formulated and used in courses we have taught both here and at other institutions.

Finally, a special word of thanks to those of our students, Carolyn Douglas and Jenny Havens, who took the time to read and comment on what was then a fairly raw first draft, and especially Peter Marzuk, who offered invaluable critical comments and suggestions for change. Of course, we take sole responsibility for the end results.

Special thanks are also due to the United States Public Health Service for support of Dr. Glick from July 1971 to June 1973 when he was a career teacher of the National Institute of Mental Health, MH-12450, and spent part of that time working on this book.

For the preparation of this editon we wish to thank Chris Hall, Lillian Conklin and Mary Ruth Goodley for a superlative secretarial job; residents of the Department of Psychiatry of the Cornell University Medical College for reviewing the manuscript; the members of our departments at Cornell and the University of California at San Francisco for extending help and cooperation; and both readers and reviewers of the first and second edition for their suggestions.

Most of all, we are indebted to the families whom we have treated. They have patently demonstrated the complexity of individual and family functioning and made it obvious that problems of families do not fit into any one theoretical framework.

Foreword

Alan S. Gurman, Ph.D.
Professor of Psychiatry, University of Wisconsin Medical School,
Madison, Wisconsin

Several years ago, a publisher asked me to review a proposal for an introductory text on family therapy. Although I recommended that they offer the author a contract for the book and the publisher did so, that "book" never saw the light of day. I suspect that many other plans for introductory family therapy textbooks have met a similar fate. Certainly, the field does not suffer from a shortage of authors of family therapy books, and there is clearly a market for them. So, why is it that there are no more than a handful of really credible introductory textbooks in family therapy? I have three closely related hypotheses: (1) very few family therapist authors can resist the temptation to try to write a book that is doctrinaire and pushes a rather singular "school" or point of view; (2) very few family therapists have the breadth of knowledge of the field to be able to even-handedly and comprehensively take on such a task; and (3) very few family therapists have had the *chutzpah* to think that they can surpass the quality of Glick and Kessler's first two editions of this volume.

The previous editions of this book have not only sold well, but also have been translated into several foreign languages. Why have these authors succeeded so well where others fear to tread? My own theory is that while other authors of introductory texts merely borrow the ideas of colleagues in the field, summarize their colleagues' work, and sew these patches together in quilt-like fashion, Glick and Kessler (and now, Clarkin) create a new fabric that is both stronger and more aesthetically pleasing than that of patchwork authors. Unlike other introductory family therapy texts, this third edition does not merely summarize where the field has been, but rather, sets the tone for where the field is going. And the field is going toward a more comprehensive view of couples and families, and toward the inclusion and coming together of what are often thought to be not only disparate, but fundamentally irreconcilably different points of view. In short, toward a greater respect for the multiplicity of useful perspectives on family functioning

xxiii

and the treatment of family dysfunction. When other authors take such a position, they often seem to do so in a perfunctory way, laden with the weight of social desirability; when Glick, Clarkin, and Kessler take this position, it is because they believe it.

So what emerges here is one of those rare volumes that combines exquisite scholarship with clinical wisdom.This is an unusual book, in which the systems perspective that purportedly informs all models of family therapy (yet in truth typically singles out the interactional domain for attention) is genuinely brought to bear. Respect for the power of social interaction is balanced with respect for the intrapsychic (cognitive and affective, conscious and unconscious) forces in family life, and with respect for the biological sphere.

Without being at all petulant, and in fact being quite polite, Glick and associates both implicitly and explicitly challenge many of the most basic clinical asumptions of scores of family therapists. Among the more controversial positions they take on matters of everyday clinical practice are the following:

- while the "symptoms" of individuals *may be* functional for family relationships, they are not always so;
- family therapy is *not* always the treatment of choice by itself, and *may* even be contraindicated at times;
- problematic interaction can be the cause *or* the effect of disturbed individual behavior;
- though there are many pathways to marital and family health, adjustment, and satisfaction, psychopathology is real, and clinical diagnosis is important;
- different types of clinical problems require different types of therapeutic intervention.

The quiet revolutionary notion in this book that family therapy is not a universal panacea for all problems brought to mental health professionals implies that family therapists sometimes don't know everything they need to know to be effective helpers. Despite the authors' unquestionable expertise in this field, there is a lovely and humble isomorphism between such views as expressed here and the structure of part of the book itself: rather than writing as if they "know it all" themselves, Glick and associates called upon over a dozen colleagues to co-author sections of a few chapters. Such humility-grounded-in-expertise is not only an impressive model for students of family therapy to emulate, but also a wise and mature stance for therapists themselves.

Foreword to the Second Edition

Theodore Lidz, M.D.
Sterling Professor of Psychiatry Emeritus,
Yale University School of Medicine, New Haven, Connecticut

Five years ago I had the privilege of writing the foreword to the first edition of this book and welcoming the first proper and much needed text in the relatively new field of family therapy. I recommended the book enthusiastically and predicted that it would enjoy a wide readership and many future editions as the field advanced. The book has not only been widely read but has become the standard introductory text for teaching family therapy. The field has advanced, and the new edition keeps pace with the latest developments and reflects the increased maturity of the field.

The preparation of a first text for a subject presents its authors with formidable problems of assembling material, organizing, selecting of topics, and so forth, without the opportunity to lean upon earlier authors and to crib from them. Drs. Glick and Kessler managed the task superbly, writing clearly and concisely and with a deceptive simplicity that reflected their mastery of the topic and an awareness of what students need to know and what they can assimilate before they have extensive clinical experience. Although it is a criticism I rarely make as I cherish conciseness, the first edition seemed too brief. Now the authors have not simply added new sections but have fleshed out their presentation with additional well-chosen clinical material. Other books about family and marital therapy have appeared in the past five years, including a few excellent works—Murray Bowen's *Family Therapy in Clinical Practice*, Minuchin's *Families and Family Therapy*, Napier and Whittaker's *The Family Crucible*, and Selvini's *Paradox and Counterparadox*—but these are works by innovators and are not always suited for the beginner. In *Marital and Family Therapy* we are offered a balanced and carefully planned approach. I found myself again admiring the authors' method of presentation, their selection of material, and their ability to remember that they were writing an introductory text and to forego the narcissistic gratifications of displaying their consummate knowledge of the field.

Some readers, probably more teachers than students, will consider the approach conservative. It does not promulgate innovative concepts or techniques; its creativity derives from the sorting out of diverse approaches introduced by persons of divergent training, ideologies, and personalities and from integrating them into a coherent presentation. The conservativism is not only appropriate in an introductory text but also needed in this therapeutic approach in which there has been a plethora of innovative techniques, some impractical, some unbridled, and some highly manipulative. Therapists have often impatiently sought shortcuts in promoting changes in personality functioning through changing family transactions without adequate appreciation of the strong forces that foster pattern maintenance in the family.

The authors properly do not consider methods and techniques alone but seek to establish an adequate foundation in family structure and dynamics for the future therapist. They recognize that the family not only forms a true small group in which the action of any member affects all, but that it has very special characteristics because of the prolonged and intense relationships between its members, because it is divided into two generations and two sexes, and because of the interrelated functions it serves for the couple who marry, for the children born into it, and for the society in which it exists. Although a marital or family therapist requires substantial knowledge of personality development and functioning on the one hand, and of larger social systems on the other, the authors confine themselves, as they must, to marriage and the family and assume that the student will have gained such knowledge elsewhere.

The authors take a broad view of marital and family therapy, rather than limiting themselves to the consideration of conjoint therapy. Taken in the broadest sense, family therapy can include any form of treatment that takes the import and impact of family transactions into account when considering the etiology and treatment of personality disorders. Only one person, the patient, a parent, or a spouse, may be in actual treatment, but the focus is upon changing the family interaction; or the various members of the family may each be treated individually; or all members of the family may be seen together in a group together with members of other families. However, the focus of the book is, as it should be, primarily on conjoint family therapy. It requires careful judgment to know when it is preferable to work with the designated patient and his or her internalizations of family members, when with the family or marital partner conjointly, and when with multiple couples or families in a group. The authors offer judicious, nondogmatic opinions that provide guidance for reaching such decisions.

The authors review the more widely used and most widely promulgated of the many different types of family therapy that have emerged, but rather than giving lengthy descriptions of a variety of techniques or promoting one above the other, they sensibly seek to instruct the student in three basic therapeutic strategies: the facilitation of communication of thoughts and feelings between family members; the attempt to shift disturbed, inflexible roles and coalitions; and the therapist's use of himself or herself as a family role model, educator, and demythologizer. Family therapy is a difficult therapeutic technique that has all too often been undertaken by persons with little, if any, experience in working with individuals or with meaningful groups. Inexperienced therapists can inadvertently promote disorganization of an individual or of a family because of their countertransference to a family member, their transference of their own family problems into the situation, their exasperation with the rigidities or lack of empathy of family members, their shock at the cruelties that may go on within a family, their narcissistic needs, or simply lack of recognition of their own limitations, as well as in still other ways. The book recognizes that any form of therapy that can promote significant change in the individual or family can also misfire and cause harm. It provides the basic knowledge the future therapist needs before entering into supervised work with couples or families, and it emphasizes the importance of supervised clinical experience in addition to didactic instruction. The field as a whole, as well as those entering it and those teaching it, has greatly benefited from the first edition of this well-tempered work, and this new edition will consolidate the book's position as the major basic text for teaching family therapy.

Preface

The three editions of this textbook of family therapy reflect the history and development of the family field, which has occurred rapidly in the past 20 years. The first edition was an outline about a field that was just beginning to grow and gain momentum. The second edition was a statement that the family field, which began in the minds of creative individuals in diverse settings (and often unknown to each other), was blossoming with great enthusiasm. In fact, the field had arrived with full gusto, and many clinicians were doing family work and clamoring for theoretical clarity and more training in this form of intervention.

This, the third edition, makes a statement, like its predecessors, about the current state of the art of family intervention. As we see it, the field has gone beyond its heyday of enthusiasm and advocacy of family intervention for every clinical condition, to a more sophisticated (and sober) time of differentiation. This differentiation is taking place on many levels (to list a few): when family therapy is indicated, and when it is not helpful; when the symptoms are under systems control and when they are more strongly determined by other factors, such as biological ones; how one evaluates in order to make *both* individual diagnoses and a family "diagnosis"; when the whole family is the patient and when the family is serving as co-therapist to help the individual with symptoms; when behavioral strategies of family intervention are more useful than systems strategies.

We hope that this edition adequately reflects this growing sophistication of the field. Since the publication of the second edition, it has been translated into Japanese, and parts into Chinese; it has been widely adopted in Italy, England, and other European countries. Clearly, the material in this text goes beyond charismatic leaders, who make most sense within their particular cultures. Our intent continues to be to provide the broad principles of theory and treatment that can be applied and adapted to all cultures and socioeconomic circumstances, and delivered by family therapists "regardless of their race, creed, color" or (even) gender.

Since the publication of the first edition of this book, we have been gratified by the response of both readers and many reviewers, as well as by its adoption by some teachers as the standard introductory text. Because of the growth and changes in the field, as well as suggestions received, we have decided that this is an opportune time to expand and rewrite the text. As such, there is a focus on the systems model to integrate and be the scaffolding (or glue) to hold together the most useful models (e.g., psychodynamic, medical, or experiential) utilized by experienced clinicians, teachers, and researchers. In doing so, we have completely rewritten most of the text, and to accumulate a large amount of new material, we switched to a "section" format, adding chapters and at the same time substantially revising others.

For this edition, we have provided a chapter on family life in its historical context, and throughout we focus on the new family forms such as single-parent and remarried families. We have expanded the section on evaluation, adding to material on process and content, as well as on how to use dimensions of functioning to plan goals and treatment. We have reorganized basic strategies and techniques around four models and expanded the chapter on resistance. Section V on "Marital and Couples Treatment" is completely new and includes material on gay, male couples and on families of professionals. Chapter 22, "Family Treatment in the Context of Individual Psychiatric Disorders," has been revised, in part, based on DSM-III-R, the American Psychiatric Association's third *revision* of the Diagnostic and Statistical Manual of Mental Disorders DSM-III.* There is a new chapter on family treatment in the context of other special problems, such as violence and chronic mental illness. The chapters on the family and the psychiatric hospital have been thoroughly rewritten to include material on psychoeducational approaches. Guidelines now include a "decision tree," expanded material regarding when to use family therapy based on recent outcome data, and the special modifications needed in the context of not only cultural and ethnic issues, but also those of gender. The section on the family model and other fields has been greatly expanded because of the positive response of nonfamily therapists—e.g., lawyers, doctors, school counselors, etc.—to the integration of this material to their settings. The chapters on research and training have been thoroughly rewritten and we have added a new chapter on ethical, financial, and professional issues. The number of clinical vignettes and examples continues

---

*American Psychiatric Association: Diagnostic and Statistical Manual of Mental Disorders, Third Edition, Revised. Washington, D.C.: American Psychiatric Association, 1987.

to expand. The references for each chapter have been updated, and suggested readings have been added.

Past readers have been very helpful and generous with their comments for revisions. We have added a third author, Dr. John Clarkin, a major teacher and researcher in family therapy, and have continued to include contributors who are well known in other areas of expertise. In the second edition, we invited readers to write with their suggestions. The response was not only astounding, but also helpful in improving the text. We offer the same invitation now in 1987, "so that we can continue to make this book as helpful and practical as possible."

A Guide for Using the Text

Since this book is intended to serve as a basic textbook for individuals at different training levels and orientations, complex clinical situations and their sequential management regimens have been oversimplified and compressed. We realize this may be a disadvantage for the more advanced therapist and so have included up-to-date references. The book probably will be most helpful when used with ongoing supervision or with an ongoing course, since most case examples and interventions are written in bare-bone detail in order to make one or two teaching points at a time. For the sake of clarity, some chapters reiterate concepts presented earlier in a different context. For example, goals are mentioned in the discussions of "evaluation," of the process of "setting goals before starting treatment" and of the "course of treatment."

Likewise, although there are a number of sections and short chapters that are (to our view) much too brief and superficial to be of value to the experienced family clinician, here too we opted to take the route of maximum breadth, with provision of the appropriate references to flesh out the material. We have also accumulated a list of suggested readings for the same purpose, and to guide the *instructor* of family therapy for his or her choice of assigned readings depending on class objectives. We believe that the alternative path, i.e., to be less inclusive and provide greater depth, would make this introductory text too narrow and less useful given the many situations in which the family model is now being utilized.

We recommend that the beginner read the text chronologically, although obviously the more experienced clinician initially may prefer to read particular sections or chapters only. The book is written for "reading," not as a reference to sit on a shelf. As such, core sections include I, II, III, IV, V, VII, and X. The remainder of the material (e.g., the chapters on *brief* family therapy or family intervention *in the hospital*, or the section on research and training) is more specialized and should be read as needed, or as appropriate, or as the reader's interest dictates.

The interested student may first want to turn to Chapter 33 on "Training." The reason is that different parts of the text are relevant depending on what the trainee is trying to achieve. This chapter gives an overview of goals and models—therefore it can guide the reader's priorities. For example, the learning needs of someone trying to master the family model at a family institute are quite different from a lay member of the community trying to learn the basics of the family model, and these are different from those of a psychiatric resident learning family therapy as one model among other competing models.

A note on the *teaching objectives*—there are two reasons for their inclusion: the first is that many fields in medicine and psychiatry/psychology are attempting to define the core knowledge and skill competencies required for a practitioner in that field. We do so in that spirit. However, a second and in many ways more essential reason is that the ground we cover is so broad and can be so confusing to the beginner that, by using the enabling objectives for each chapter as a road map, the trainee can use them to understand the logic, direction, and end-point for each topic. Our terminal objectives include, but are not limited to:

1. A general understanding of the underlying theoretical principles and hypotheses behind the family model.
2. An acquaintance with techniques, including an understanding of the advantages and limitations of such techniques, and a capability of drawing from the basic principles underlying any and all of them in the "process" of treatment.
3. Development of an appreciation, through experience, of one's abilities and difficulties in using such techniques.
4. An appreciation of the ethical issues involved in all areas of the practice of family intervention.

Contributors

Oliver J. W. Bjorksten, M.D.
Clinical Associate Professor of Psychiatry, Medical University of South Carolina, Charleston, South Carolina

Helen M. Blau, Ph.D.
Associate Professor of Pharmacology, Stanford University School of Medicine, Stanford, California

Ellen V. Bloch, M.S.
Genetic Counselor, Children's Hospital Medical Center, Oakland, California

Jonathan F. Borus, M.D.
Associate Professor of Psychiatry, Harvard Medical School; Director of Residency Training, Department of Psychiatry, Massachusetts General Hospital, Boston, Massachusetts

Audrey J. Clarkin, Ph.D.
Clinical Assistant Professor of Psychology in Psychiatry, Cornell University Medical College, White Plains, New York; Coordinator—Social Problem Solving Program, Scarsdale Public Schools, Scarsdale, New York

Suzanne Currie, O.T.R.
Nedlands, Western, Australia

Alvin I. Glasgold, M.D.
Chairman—Department of Otolaryngology, St. Peter's Medical Center, Middlesex General-University Hospital, Highland Park, New Jersey

Gretchen Haas, Ph.D.
Assistant Professor of Psychology in Psychiatry, Cornell University Medical College, New York, New York

Susan Haiman, M.P.S., O.T.R.
Assistant Director, Department of Therapeutic Activities, Payne Whitney Psychiatric Clinic, Cornell Medical Center, New York, New York

Beth Harris, R.N., M.A., C.S.
Patient Education Coordinator, New York Hospital-Cornell Medical Center, Westchester Division, White Plains, New York

Robert S. Hoffman, M.D.
Assistant Clinical Professor, Department of Psychiatry, School of Medicine, University of California, San Francisco, California; Clinical Instructor of Neurology, Department of Neurology, Stanford University School of Medicine, Palo Alto, California

Harvey S. Kaplan, M.D.
Chief of Pediatrics, Chope Community Hospital, San Mateo, California

Susan Matorin, M.S., A.C.S.W.
Director, Department of Social Work, Payne Whitney Clinic-New York Hospital; Senior Lecturer of Social Work in Psychiatry, Cornell Medical Center, New York, New York

John Patten, M.D.
Clinical Assistant Professor of Psychiatry, Cornell University Medical College, New York, New York

Jonathan Pesner, Ph.D.
Clinical Psychologist, Mt. Zion Hospital & Medical Center, San Francisco, California

Earl Pope, Architect
Professor of Design, Hampshire College, Amhurst, Massachusetts

Clifford J. Sager, M.D.
Clinical Professor of Psychiatry, The New York Hospital-Cornell Medical Center; Director of Family Psychiatry, Jewish Board of Family and Children's Services, New York, New York

Gail Saliterman, Ph.D., J.D.
Law Offices of Turner & Brorby, San Francisco, California

William A. H. Sammons, M.D.
Clinical Associate and Consultant in Child Development, Children's Service, Massachusetts General Hospital, Boston, Massachusetts

Thomas J. Stewart, Ph.D.
Chairman, Department of Health Services Administration, Medical
University of South Carolina, Charleston, South Carolina

Stuart Sugarman, M.D.
Associate Professor of Psychiatry; Director, Family Therapy Program,
University of Connecticut Health Center, Farmington, Connecticut

John A. Talbott, M.D.
Professor & Chairman, Department of Psychiatry, University of
Maryland, School of Medicine; Director, Institute of Psychiatry &
Human Behavior, UMMS, Baltimore, Maryland

Sanford R. Weimer, M.D.
Chairman, Department of Psychiatry & Mental Health, CIGNA
Healthplans of California, Los Angeles, California

Susan Lang Williams, M.B.A., O.T.R.
Vocational Consultant, Community Mental Health Services, San
Francisco, California

Section I

Family Therapy in Context

For family therapists, context is everything. Chapter 1 speaks to the issues of "What is family therapy?", "How did it develop?", and "What are the core concepts that every family therapist must know?" Finally, we distinguish in a very broad way the elements unique to family therapy from other psychotherapies.

Chapter 2 was placed early in the book to make the point that there is no way to understand and treat families without being aware of the changing social landscape *within which* the family is embedded.

Portrait of a Man and His Wife, artist unknown, late 5th Dynasty circa 2500 B.C., Egypt. Courtesy of Honolulu Academy of Arts, purchase, 1937.

1

The Field of Marital and Family Therapy: Development and Definition

OBJECTIVES

- To grasp the concepts of the historical development of family therapy as it influences theory and practice.
- To define family therapy and to begin to differentiate it from individual and group formats and strategies.
- To be cognizant of and be able to use the basic family system concepts in evaluation and treatment.

INTRODUCTION

Although the fields of marital and family treatment are relatively young, there is nothing particularly new about the overall significance of marriage and the family.[*]

---

[*]To avoid unnecessary duplication, the word "family" (as in "family therapy," "family system," and "family unit") will often be used instead of the more cumbersome term of "marital and family." In those instances in which we wish to refer to marital issues specifically, only the word "marital" will be used. Similarly, the words "family therapy" and "family treatment" generally also refer to the field of "family counseling," since the distinctions between the fields are not well-delineated and there seems to be considerable overlap.

4

It probably does not require any specific training or knowledge to perceive that these are important human systems and that they are different in several essential ways from other types of human groups and relationships.

Most people would likely agree that marriages and families perform vital tasks for the individuals involved, and for society at large. It has long been a commonsense view that we are all shaped in major ways by what we have experienced in our original families (see the reprinted example following this) and that what occurs in our current marital or family system is, for most people, the prime element in our general sense of well being and functioning.

Father Sentenced to Dinners. (Topsfield, Mass.) Oct.25 (UPI). The father of a 16-year-old accused shoplifter is serving a 30-day sentence—of dinners at home. A Salem district judge, Samuel E. Zoll, ordered the father of a Masconomet Regional High School student to be home between 5 and 7 p.m.every night. Their names were not released because a juvenile was involved. Judge Zoll said the father should "be at home for a meal where he could sit down and talk with the family."[1]

Clearly, individual family units are different from one another, and some seem to function better or are happier than others.* Many helping professionals in the past two decades have begun to examine, using fresh approaches, the processes and circumstances that lead to family distress. They have attempted to devise intervention procedures in order to alleviate problems and increase functioning. In the following chapters, we will discuss some basic concepts and techniques associated with family therapy. At this point, however, we offer a brief review of the emergence of the field, followed by a delineation of its scope.

DEVELOPMENT OF THE FAMILY THERAPY FIELD

Although exciting, innovative, and seemingly useful in helping families with problems in living, family therapy can be confusing at times. It may seem hard to understand the fundamentals of the field and to distinguish them from the personal styles of charismatic family therapists. Similarly, it may seem difficult to synthesize a coherent family theory from different fields, such as psychology, psychiatry, sociology, psychoanalysis, game theory, communication theory, Gestalt therapy, and the like. How did this state of affairs come about?

The significance attributed to the family's role in relation to the psychic and

---

*Throughout the text we use the broad definition of "family" to include both blood and nonblood relatives who may not be under the same roof, including what has been referred to as "significant others."

social distress of any of its members has waxed and waned over the centuries. The important role of the family in the development of individual problems was mentioned by Confucius in his writings, as well as by the Greeks in their myths. The early Hawaiians would meet as a family to discuss solutions to an individual's problem. For a long time in our own culture, however, what we now call mental illness and other forms of interpersonal distress were ascribed to magical, religious, physical, or exclusively intrapsychic factors. It was not until the turn of this century, however, that Freud delineated individual pschodynamics as determinants of human behavior. Although he stressed the major role of the family in the development of individual symptoms, he believed that the most effective technique for dealing with such individual psychopathology was treatment on a one-to-one basis.[2] At about this same time, others working with the mentally ill began to suggest that families with a sick member should be seen together and not "as individuals removed from family relationships."[3] Also psychiatric social workers in child guidance clinics, who often saw one or more parent individually or together, began to recognize the importance of dealing with the entire family unit.

In the 1930s a psychoanalyst reported his experience in treating a marital pair.[4] In the 1940s, Fromm-Reichmann postulated that a pathologic mother (called the "schizophrenogenic mother") could induce schizophrenia in a "vulnerable" child.[5] This speculation led other psychoanalysts, such as Lidz, to study the role of the father.[6] This work suggested that the father also plays an important role in the development of psychopathology. At the same time, Mittelman began to see a series of marital partners in simultaneous, but separate, psychoanalyses.[7] This approach was quite innovative, because psychoanalysts previously believed that this method of treatment would hinder the therapist from helping the patient, since it was thought that neither spouse would trust the same therapist and consequently would withhold important material. Therefore, the other marital partner was usually referred to a colleague.

Outside the field of psychiatry proper, marital counselors, ministers, and others have been interviewing spouses together for some time. In the early 1950s the first consistent use of family therapy in modern psychotherapeutic practice in the United States was apparently reported simultaneously by several different workers.[6,7] Ackerman began consistently utilizing family interviews in his work with children and adolescents,[8] and Lidz and associates,[9] as well as Bowen,[10] began an extensive series of investigations of family interactions and schizophrenia. Bateson and associates[11] and Wynne and associates[12] began an intensive study of family communication patterns in the families of schizophrenic patients and others.

It was not until the early 1960s, however, that these ideas were integrated into a general theory of family interrelationships and that the modern field of family therapy began to take shape.[8,13] Various schools of thought developed and journals (most notably *Family Process*) were established. Many mental health professionals became interested in learning about family therapy and in utilizing its techniques. As a matter of fact, a 1977 poll taken of California psychologists who practiced psychotherapy showed that, as expected, 90 percent were using individual therapy, but more than 60 percent were by that time using family therapy; only 30 percent were doing group therapy.[14] These statistics well illustrate the rise in the growth of the family therapy field.

During the 1970s the range of family therapy was expanded to include application to a "broad range of psychiatric problems with families differing widely in socioeconomic origin," but results were poor until crisis-oriented and short-term methods were developed to meet the needs of these families.[15] Family researchers have begun more controlled studies on what actually transpires within families[16,17] and on the outcome of family therapy.[18,19] Further discussion of research into family treatment outcome and family process can be found in Chapters 31 and 32, respectively.

For many mental health professionals, family therapy seems to be the "right" treatment at the "right" time. For example, a study carried out to determine the reasons people seek help for emotional problems reported that marital concerns ranked first, followed by other family problems.[20] Another survey revealed that 50 percent of the patients requesting psychotherapy did so mainly because of marital difficulties, and that another 25 percent mentioned problems related to marriage. In 1979, a major national organization was formed called the American Family Therapy Association. The American Association of Marital Counselors has changed its name to the American Association of Marriage and Family Therapists (AAMFT). Recently new training programs have been created and others expanded. In addition to these developments, there are now many substantive journals originating in countries all over the world exclusively devoted to family issues.

In the 1980s, we see a major change from early polemics and enthusiastic faith in a new-found orientation to a more finely honed set of techniques for differential application to family and marital problems and the familial context of individual illnesses. For instance, the early history of the family movement included a preoccupation with the communication patterns of the family as an etiological agent in serious psychiatric disorders. The family movement still has a great interest in schizophrenia, but with a changing focus and emphasis. In the intervening years, it has become relatively clear that there is an important genetic component in the etiology of schizophrenia, and psychopharmacological treatment is mandatory. One no longer thinks of family therapy as the primary treatment for schizophrenia, but as one important component of a multimodal intervention. With the extremely helpful research on expressed emotion, it is now possible to design family interventions specifically addressing those noxious influences that seem directly related to the exacerbation of a thought disorder. *As such, this example illustrates a current objective of using techniques of family intervention with methods based on the biological model.*

The health of the family movement is in its diversity, however, and other target populations are being investigated and treated (for instance, families disrupted by divorce). At the same time, there is also a movement toward specificity, as also noted in the development of classification systems for families (Section III) and in the development of selection criteria for the application, focus, duration, and intensity of family and marital intervention(Section VII).

While treatment techniques have become more differentiated, so that one can speak of major orientations such as systems, behavioral, and psychodynamic, there is, we believe, a need for integrating such techniques into a treatment package that is flexible and meets the needs of individuals and family units alike. Now, in the late 1980s, the family therapy field is fortunate in having so early in its history a body of outcome research, with its promise of further addressing the questions of which techniques work best with specific problem areas. This research is growing, and is becoming more sophisticated in design and execution. The findings indicating that family therapy has demonstrated positive results with specific family problems are encouraging.

DEFINITION OF MARITAL AND FAMILY THERAPY

Family therapy is distinguished from other psychotherapies by its conceptual focus on the family system as a whole. In this view, major emphasis is placed on understanding individual behavior patterns as arising from and inevitably feeding back into the complicated matrix of the general family system. Beneficial alterations in the larger marital and family unit will therefore have positive consequences for the individual members, as well as for the larger systems. The major emphasis is placed upon understanding and intervening in the family system's current patterns of interaction, with usually only a secondary interest in their origins and development.

Vonnegut has beautifully illustrated one interpretation of the family systems concept.

Your parents were fighting machines and self-pitying machines. Your mother was programmed to bawl out your father for being a defective money-making machine, and your father was programmed to bawl her out for being a defective housekeeping machine. They were programmed to bawl each other out for being defective loving machines. Then your father was programmed to stomp out of the house and slam the door. This automatically turned your mother into a weeping machine. And your father would go down to a tavern where he would get drunk with some other drinking machines. Then all the drinking machines would go to a whorehouse and rent fucking machines. And then your father would drag himself home to become an apologizing machine. And your mother would become a very slow forgiving machine.[21]

Marital and family treatment can be defined as a professionally organized attempt to produce beneficial changes in a disturbed marital or family unit by essentially interactional, nonpharmacological methods. Its aim is the establishment of more satisfying ways of living for the entire family and for individual family members.

In many families, the members may be "selected" as "symptom bearers." Such individuals will then be described in a variety of ways that will amount to their being labeled "bad," "sick," "stupid," or "crazy." Depending on what sort of label such individuals carry, they, together with their families, may be treated in any one of several types of helping facility—psychiatric, correctional, or medical. On the other hand, there may not always be an *identified patient*. Occasionally a marital or family unit presents itself as being in trouble without singling out any one member. A marital couple may realize that their marriage is in trouble and that the cause of their problems stems from interaction with each other and not from either partner individually.

There is a continuum between the intrapsychic system, the interactional family system, and the sociocultural system. Different conceptual frameworks are utilized when dealing with these systems. A therapist may choose to emphasize any of the points on this continuum, but the family therapist is especially sensitive to and trained in those aspects relating specifically to the family system—to both its individual characteristics and the larger social matrix.

Family therapy might broadly be thought of as any type of psychosocial intervention utilizing a conceptual framework that gives primary emphasis to the family system and which, in its therapeutic strategies, aims for an impact on the entire family structure. Thus any psychotherapeutic approach that attempts to understand or to intervene in a family system might fittingly be called "family therapy." This is a very broad definition and allows many differing points of view, both in theory and in therapy, to be placed under one heading.

Although many clinicians agree that there is faulty interaction in families containing an individual with gross disturbance, it is not always clear whether the faulty interaction is the cause or the effect of the behavior of the disturbed individual. Although somewhat digressive, these points may be part of a central issue bearing on the definition of family therapy. They were summarized by the Group for the Advancement of Psychiatry in 1970.

Some practitioners continue to perceive and treat as the central issue the disequilibrium in the intrapsychic apparatus of the individual, viewing the contextual social matrix of development and adaptation and most particularly the family as adding an important dimension to their conceptualization and treatment. Others see and treat as the central issue the disequilibrium in the family, viewing balance of intrapsychic forces and counterforces in an individual to be of secondary or even of inconsequential relevance to the task of the helping professional.[22]

For the present there is no reason to believe that both views may not be important. Pending further research and experience in this area, it seems prudent for the student *to evaluate each clinical situation carefully, attempting both to understand the phenomena and to select intervention strategies designed to achieve the desired ends.*

CORE CONCEPTS

Like other developing fields of knowledge, the family field has needed to generate its own terminology. While concepts for individual behaviors and individual psychodynamics have had a long history, family therapists, until recently, have noted a dearth of concepts and terms to describe specific interactions among people. Family therapy is based upon a new (and developing) theory and data base and a *systems view of interactions*. Thus, there is a need at the beginning of this text to delineate the basic concepts underlying the recent developments in family intervention. These concepts are not numerous, but their paucity belies the profound shift in focus that occurs when progressing from concepts about the individual to describing a system and its functioning. Therefore, close attention to these concepts is basic to fuller understanding of the remainder of this text.

Von Bertalanffy is credited as being the first to introduce principles that provide an organismic approach to understanding biological beings. These concepts were given the title *general systems theory*.[23] He felt that the reductionistic mechanistic tradition in science was insufficient to explain the behavior of living organisms, since that kind of approach depends upon a linear series of stepwise cause and effect equations. In contrast, Von Bertalanffy developed general principles, which he used to explain biological processes that include tremendous complexity and levels of organization. Gray, Duhl, and Rizzo[24] describe general systems theory as a "new approach to the unity of science problem which sees organization rather than reduction as the unifying principle, and which therefore searches for general structural isomorphisms in systems." Thus, a systems approach puts an emphasis on the relationship between the parts of a complex whole, and events in the context in which they are occurring rather than on an isolation of events from their context.[25] A living system is (1) organized, (2) possesses control, (3) adaptation, and (4) possesses and utilizes energy. Let's see how these notions apply to families.

Any living system has a high degree of *organization*; that is, a consistent

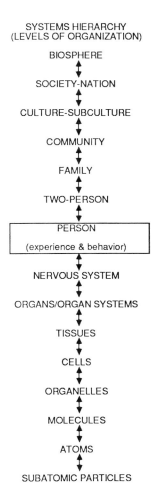

Fig. 1-1. Hierarchy of Natural Systems. (From Engel G: The clinical application of the biopsychosocial model. Am J Psychiatry 137:535-544, 1980.)

relationship between the elements or parts of the organism. The systems concept implies that the organism or entity is greater than the sum of the separate parts. No single element in the system can be thought of as acting totally independently.

In order to protect its organization, the living system must have boundaries (Figs. 1-1 & 1-2). The membrane around a cell defines the boundary or outer limit of that functional unit. The cell membrane, while it does create a boundary between itself and the outside, also provides through its permeability an interactional relationship between the inside and outside of the cell, by selectively allowing transfer of chemicals across its membrane. In analogous fashion, the organized family system has a "membrane" or boundary between itself and the surrounding neighborhood and community. This boundary is functional by the implicit or explicit rules by which the family keeps the information and activities to itself or allows outside information and contact with people in the neighborhood and the

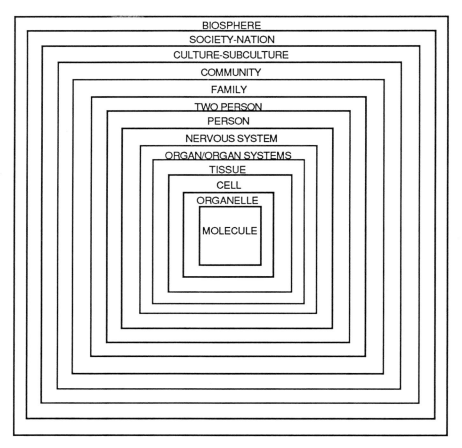

Fig. 1-2. Continuum of Natural Systems. (From Engel G: The clinical application of the biopsychosocial model. Am J Psychiatry 137:535-544, 1980.)

community. Minuchin,[26] among others, has stressed that for a family to be functional, it must have boundaries, and for subsystems within the family such as the marital subsystem to function, it must have a boundary that separates it from other subsystems such as the sibling subsystem.

Minuchin has described boundaries on a continuum where poles range from being overly permeable to being overly rigid, while normal families are in the middle with clear boundaries (see Figure 1-3). There is not a one-to-one correlation between extremes of boundary functioning, such as enmeshment/distantiation, and symptomatology, but extremes are seen as more likely to lead to pathological behavior in one or more members of the family system. Recognition of the existence of subsystems within the family system relates to another notion about organization, and that is *hierarchical organization*. The system itself is or-

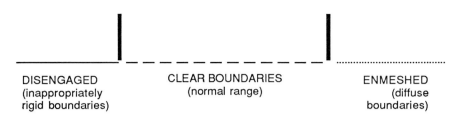

Fig. 1-3.   Minuchin's description of the boundaries of the family system.(From Minuchin S: Families and Family Therapy. Cambridge, MA, Harvard University Press, 1974, p 54.)

ganized on one or many hierarchical levels entailing systems or subsystems (again see Figure 1-1 & 1-2).

In addition to organization, a functional living system must have some means of *controlled adaptation onto the environment*. In 1939, Walter Cannon,[27] a physiologist, introduced the term *homeostasis* to describe mechanisms within the neuroendocrine system that provide a constancy of the internal environment of the organism. In 1948, Wiener[28] introduced the notion of cybernetics (from the Greek word meaning Steersman) as a branch of science dealing with control mechanisms and the transmission of information. Wiener pointed out the similarities between the mechanisms or internal control and communication in an animal and in machines. A key concept in cybernetics is that of *feedback* and the *feedback loop*. In such a circular sequence of events, element A influences element B, which influences element C, which then in turn influences element A. For example, if the temperature in a room becomes too low, the thermostat kicks off a mechanism which turns on the furnace, which in turn raises the temperature in the room, which registers on the thermostat, which then signals the furnace in turn to shut off once again. Such mechanisms serve to control the state of the organism or environment. These control concepts such as homeostasis and feedback have been used by family theorists to understand and change family systems.[29,30]

By way of illustration, corrective feedback (or "negative feedback," in the language of general systems theory) results in a sequence of events that returns a person to a previous, more modulated state.[31] For example, in the P family, a young father with schizoaffective disorder, noted that as he became more hyperactive at home his wife would say things like, "Why don't you slow down? I'll help you with the chores." This intervention appeared to help the subject regain control of his activity level. A key concept for the beginner is that *despite the fact that to an outside observer some behavior appears "crazy" or self-defeating, this is assumed to be the family's best solution to their problems*. Just as an individual utilizes defense mechanisms to cope, so too the family organizes around idiosyncratic patterns of behavior that allow them to function. The term "homeostatic" is used in family work as a way to describe the way families maintain function within the family, not the way it is used in physiology.

A third key concept relevant to living systems is that of *energy and informa-tion*. Living systems are "open" systems in which energy can be transported in and out of the system. Instead of a tendency toward entropy and degradation of energy, which happens in nonliving systems, living systems have a tendency toward increased patterning (families have routines) and organization. In human open systems such as the family, *information* (meaning knowledge from outside of the family) acts as a type of energy that informs the system and can lead to reduction of uncertainty.

To summarize, a theoretical framework commonly utilized by family therapists is the "*family systems approach.*" Understanding of families is *ecologi-cal*, in that the capabilities of the family are greater than an arithmetic sum of its parts. Each person is viewed in interactive relations with the other family mem-bers, all functioning to maintain the family system coherently but also striving for their own unique goals. The family system is maintained by its members so as to preserve its essential traditions, myths, patterns, identities, and values. Often it returns to an apparent *steady state*, but it must always deal with the inevitable changes that time and biological development bring. Sometimes it responds with creative novelty, but at other times with stagnation. The notion of the evolution of families as life events occur (e.g., a child goes away to college) differentiates this view of coherence from that of a fixed homeostasis. Indeed, it can be said that the critical issue for families is which homeostasis to evolve towards—what to preserve of the past (in order to manage the present competently) and to look for-ward to the future. Hoffman[32] has developed a useful diagram (Fig. 1-4), which she calls a *time capsule*, to illustrate the concepts of (1) how the family (and treat-ing team) interface with the community and with its internal dynamics and (2) how each family has a long history ("mythic times"), and is constantly evolving. She describes it as follows:

The figure presents a diagram of this construct, sometimes still referred to by me as my Cosmic Sausage, because so much depends on where you cut it. In this case, we will assume that the cable's outer skin ends at the boundary of that imaginary entity called the family. The cuts in the cross-section correspond to different dimensions of time: present time, onset time, historical time, mythic time, and future or hypothetical time. At each posi-tion depicted by the Time Cable, "difference" questions work to clarify family alignments in relation to the problem, by revealing five aspects:

1. family alignments as they relate to the problem in the present
2. family alignments as they relate to onset
3. family alignments as they furnish a historical matrix for the problem
4. the effect on family alignments if the problem were to change
5. family alignments related to paradigmatic values that the problem metaphorically represents

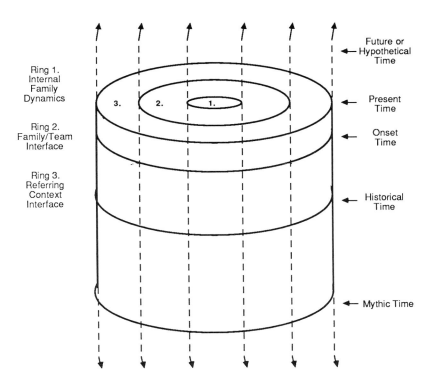

Fig. 1-4.   The Time Capsule. (From Hoffman L: A co-evolutionary framework for systemic family therapy. In Hansen & Keeney (Eds): Diagnosis and Assessment in Family Therapy, The Family Therapy Collections. Rockville, MD, Aspen Publications, 1983, p 42.)

Information thus gathered can be used both to build a hypothesis and to suggest a positive connotation of the problem in whatever temporal context seems most relevant.

The cable also contains subcylinders: Rings 1, 2, and 3, indicated within the cross-section, in the present. The idea of the rings is to show that there are several systems interfaces one might have to consider in targeting an intervention, and there seemed to be an order of priority, too. Interface dynamics within the family took second place to team/family dynamics, and both were usually outranked by the interface between the team/family system and professionals from the referring context. As I said before, the interface that seems most important in any interview can be called the "presenting edge."

DIFFERENTIATION OF FAMILY THERAPY
FROM OTHER PSYCHOTHERAPIES

Family therapy as a format of treatment can be distinguished from other psychotherapies by its *goals, focus, participants,* etc. (Table 1-1). First, the term "family therapy" connotes a format of intervention that attempts to include many (or most) of the nuclear family members (or *significant others*). The presence of all members of the nuclear family is considered crucial to addressing the goal of family treatment, which is the improved functioning of the family as an interlocking system and network of individuals. This format allows a focus on the family system as a whole in order to understand current individual behavior as rising from, and inevitably feeding back onto, the complicated matrix of the general family system. The group format poses a superficial similarity between family and group therapy. However, the fact that the "group" in family treatment is consanguineously related, and often live in the same home, makes for a profound difference.

However, family therapy is not exclusively synonymous with the family together format. Some theorists (e.g., Bowen[33]) suggest that the goals of family treatment can be achieved by intervening with a *single* family member, often the healthiest one, who can be instructed and helped in such a way so as to change behavior and thus enable the whole family to change. Likewise, some therapists work with the whole family but utilize the healthiest member as *change agent*.

Both the final goals and intermediate goals of the family format are different from the individual and group formats. The final goal of the family model is improved family functioning, and this is reached by intermediate goals of (for example) improving family communication and decreasing family conflict. Thus, the focus of the family model is on the current family interactions with the various coalitions, boundary malfunctions, etc. In contrast, the final goal of the individual model is personality, symptom, or behavior change in one particular individual. In order to reach such a final goal, the focus of individual intervention format is often on the individual's behaviors, unconscious conflicts, thoughts, and wishes. With this focus and goals, the intermediate goals of individual intervention (depending upon the particular therapeutic strategies) include insight into intrapsychic conflicts or interpersonal interactions with others, or knowledge of one's individual behaviors and a progressive change therein. The group format has as its final goal improved individual social functioning. The focus (somewhat similar to family treatment) is on current group interaction and intermediate goals, but would include the individual sharing with the group and manifesting an improved relating skill with other group members.

The strategies and techniques of family therapy (Chapter 12), whether insight-awareness, strategic, behavioral, experiential, or supportive, overlap with these same techniques as they are used in individual and group formats, but take

Table 1-1

Family Therapy Format Compared with
Other Types of Psychosocial Therapy Formats

Therapy Format	Intermediate Goals	Final Goals	Focus	Participants	Length of/Frequency of Sessions	Mean Overall Duration of Treatment
Family	Improve family communication; decrease family conflict	Improved family functioning	Family intervention: family coalitions and roles	Nuclear family unit: extended family: 1–2 therapists	1½ hours, 1x/wk	3 months—2 years
Individual	Insight into intrapsychic conflicts; insight into interaction (transference)	Individual personality/symptom change	Unconscious conflicts: individual's thoughts, wishes, and behaviors	1 patient—therapist	1 hour, 1–5x/wk	2 months—5 years
Group	Sharing with group; improved relating skills in group	Improved individual social functioning	Group participants and feedback	6–8 patients—1–2 therapists	1½ hours, 1x wk	6 months—2 years

on added dimensions in a family session. For example, in individual insight-oriented psychotherapy, the therapist may make an interpretation to an individual about his interaction with his wife as it relates to his earlier developmental interaction with his mother. The individual patient, hearing this alone, may integrate this in such a way that his behavior toward his wife changes. If such an interpretation were made in a marital or family session, in the presence of the patient's spouse, such an intervention can also have further impact on the spouse—for better or for worse—such that the spouse may further change by helping new behaviors to arise with interpretation, or alternately, can use such information and insight into the spouse's behavior by using it as a weapon against him. Comparable alterations in behavioral approaches can arise in these techniques as used in a family setting. For example, in the treatment of acting-out adolescents,[34] parents can be taught to use behavioral rewards and punishments with the adolescent. Thus, the behavioral techniques are not just used between therapist and patient, but in this case, the parents are using such techniques with the adolescent, and with full knowledge by the adolescent that such is going on.

The model of psychopathology underlying family treatment is quite different from other forms of intervention. The family model is based on the assumption that personality development, symptom formation, and therapeutic change result, at least in part, from the family's function as an *interdependent transactional unit*. The individual psychopathology model is based on the view that these factors are largely determined by the dynamic, intrapsychic function *of the individual*. If one takes a psychodynamic point of view (or a biological point of view), the individual has been the major focus of attention. In contrast, Schatzman[35] states in his critique of the individual model that, although this model is helpful, it is ultimately inadequate for understanding how people effect each other. He believes that,

Psychoanalytic theory cannot render intelligible someone's disturbed experience or behavior in terms of disturbing behavior by someone else on that person. In order to comprehend a relationship between two individuals—husband and wife, mother and child, or father and son—we must take into account that each individual experiences the world and originates behavior. Of course, psychoanalysts know that other persons' experiences act upon their patients and that certain persons who dealt with their patients as children influenced them greatly by their behavior. But insofar as psychoanalysts speak of object relations, their theory does not adequately account for this influence.

We will return to the discussion of family therapy as compared to other psychotherapies in Chapter 16. For now, let us go to the context of marriage and family.

SUGGESTIONS FOR FURTHER READINGS

Hoffman L: **Foundation of Family Therapy.** New York: Basic Books, 1981.
This book is hard-reading, but an excellent summary of general systems theory and the cybernetic paradigm as applied to the family. It places important figures such as Minuchin, Bowen, Whitiker, Haley, Ericson and Palazzoli in historical and theoretical perspective.

Paolino TJ, and McCrady BS: **Marriage and Marital Therapy.** New York: Brunner/Mazel, 1978.
This edited book provides chapters that contrast theory and therapeutic strategies from the psychoanalytic, behavioral, and systems perspectives.

REFERENCES

1. Father sentenced to dinners. New York Times, October 26, 1975
2. Sander FM: Marriage and the family in Freud's writing. J Am Acad Psychoanal 6:157-174, 1978
3. Smith ZE: Discussion on charity organizations. Proceedings of the National Conference on Charities and Correction, 1890, p 377
4. Oberndorf CP: Folie a deux. Int J Psychoanal 15:14-24, 1934
5. Fromm-Reichmann F: Notes on the development of schizophrenia by psychoanalytic psychotherapy. Psychiatry 11:267-277, 1948
6. Lidz R, Lidz T: The family environment of schizophrenic patients. Am J Psychiatry 106:322-345, 1949
7. Mittelman B: The concurrent analysis of married couples. Psychoanal Q 17:182-197, 1948
8. Ackerman NW: Treating the Troubled Family. New York, Basic Books, 1966
9. Lidz T. Cornelison A, Terry D, et al.: Intrafamilial environment of the schizophrenic patient. VI. The transmission of irrationality. Arch Neurol Psychiatry 79:305-316, 1958
10. Bowen M: A family concept of schizophrenia. In Jackson DD (Ed): The Etiology of Schizophrenia. New York, Basic Books, 1960, pp 346-372
11. Bateson G, Jackson DD, Haley J, et al.: Towards a theory of schizophrenia. Behav Sci 1:251-264, 1956.
12. Wynne L, Ryckoff I, Day J, et al.: Pseudo-mutuality in the family relations of schizophrenics. Psychiatry 21:205-220, 1958
13. Satir VM: Conjoint Family Therapy: A Guide to Theory and Technique. Palo Alto, CA, Science and Behavior Books, 1964
14. Zimet CN: NIMH backs up on its forward plan and the National Register survey of licensed/certified psychologists. Psychother Bull 10:1-3, 1977

15. Zuk GH: The three crises in family therapy (Editor's Introduction). Int J Fam Ther 1:3-8, 1979.
16. Reiss D: Individual thinking and family interaction. III. An experimental study of categorization performance in families of normals, those with character disorders, and schizophrenics. J Nerv Ment Dis 146:384-404, 1968
17. Reiss D: Individual thinking and family interaction. IV. A study of information exchange in families of normals, those with character disorders, and schizophrenics. J Nerv Ment Dis 149:473-490, 1969
18. Gurman AS, Kniskern DP: Research on marital and family therapy: Progress, perspective and prospect. In Garfield SL, Bergin AE (Eds): Handbook of Psychotherapy and Behavior Change: An Empirical Analysis (2nd Ed). New York, Wiley, 1978
19. Wells RA, Dezen AE: The results of family therapy revisited: The nonbehavioral methods. Fam Process 17:251-274, 1978
20. Gurin G, Veroff J, Feld S: Americans view their mental health: A nationwide interview survey in Joint Commission on Mental Illness and Health, Monograph Series 4. New York, Basic Books, 1960
21. Vonnegut K, Jr: Breakfast of Champions. New York, Dell 1973, pp 256-257
22. The Field of Family Therapy, Report No. 78. New York, Group for the Advancement of Psychiatry, 1970, p 534
23. Von Bertalanffy L: General Systems Theory. New York, George Braziller, 1968
24. Gray W, Duhl FJ, Rizzo ND: General Systems Theory and Psychiatry. Boston, Little Brown, 1969, p 7
25. Towards the differentiation of a self in one's own family. In Framo JL (Ed): Family Interaction: A Dialogue Between Family Researchers and Family Therapists. New York, Springer, 1972, pp 111-166
26. Minuchin S: Families and Family Therapy. Cambridge, MA, Harvard University Press, 1974
27. Cannon W: The Wisdom of the Body. New York, Norton, 1939
28. Wiener N: Cybernetics, or Control and Communication in the Animal and the Machine. Cambridge, MA, MIT Press, 1962
29. Jackson DD: The question of family homeostasis. Psychiatr Q Suppl 31:79-90, 1957
30. Minuchin S, Baker L, Rosman B, et al.: A conceptual model of psychosomatic illness in children. Arch Gen Psychiatry 32:1031-1038, 1975
31. Strauss JS, Hafez H, Lieberman P, et al.: The course of psychiatric disorder. III. Longitudinal principles. Am J Psychiatry 142:289-296, 1985
32. Hoffman L: A co-evolutionary framework for systemic family therapy. In Hansen JC & Keeney BP (Eds): Diagnosis and Assessment in Family Therapy, The Family Therapy Collections. Rockville, MD, Aspen Publications, 1983, p 42

33. Bowen M: Family Therapy in Clinical Practice/Murray Bowen. New York, Jason Aronson, 1978
34. Patterson GR: Coercive Family Process. Eugene, OR, Castalia Publishing Co, 1982
35. Schatzman M: The Schreber case. Fam Process 14:594-598, 1975

Family in Tenement by Lewis Hine, New York City, 1910. Courtesy of the International Museum of Photography, in the George Eastman House, Rochester, New York.

2
Family Life in Historical and Sociological Perspective

with Oliver Bjorksten, M.D., and
Thomas J. Stewart, Ph.D.

OBJECTIVES

- To place the development of present day family structure and function in historical context
- To understand recent changes in the family and in marriage
- To suggest clinical implications of the current social context of the family
- To share speculations about the future of the family

INTRODUCTION

Now that we have some notion of the genesis and meaning of the term "family therapy," this information should be placed in the larger context of an historical, cultural, and sociological perspective. Our bias is that it is crucial for all mental health professionals (not just family therapists) to have a thorough understanding of current and evolving norms, patterns, and trends in family life. This chapter offers an overview and synthesis of contemporary, American familial trends in an historical context, as well as a discussion of their clinical implications.

In the past, marital status was usually viewed as binary, that is, either one was married or not, and the state of marriage, once assumed, was regarded as essentially permanent. Today, it appears that there are frequent shifts in *companionship status*: cohabitation, marriage, divorce, remarriage. This marital "pool activity" makes the understanding of marital phenomena complex, since it is impossible to obtain an accurate picture from individual statistics, such as the divorce rate, alone. In this review we attempt to integrate statistics in both an historical and functional fashion.

HISTORICAL AND CURRENT TRENDS IN STRUCTURE AND FUNCTION OF THE AMERICAN FAMILY

The Past

Professor Stephen Fleck[1] has emphasized that as fault ridden and problematic as the nuclear family (i.e., parents and children) may be, no one has come up with a better alternative to it. Perhaps this lack of alternatives can be best explained by recent anthropological data, which suggests that the origins of man may lie, not (as commonly thought) in the development of a material culture or as a result of bipedality, but *in the development of the nuclear family*. Family evolution may have resulted from man's most unique characteristic, that is, his intelligence, which would, in part, account for the need for social and sexual relatedness (including intensified parenting and social relationships), monogamous pair bonding, and specialized sexual reproductive behavior.[2]

Throughout history, the structure of the family has altered to conform to the social mores of the times. The particular roles and tasks of individual members of the family have also varied from one time period to another. For example, during colonial days the family was a self-sufficient economic unit that produced more of its daily sustenance than did that of the family in later periods. During this time there was a greater emphasis on the economic basis of marriage than there was on romance. Traditional roles for husbands and wives were fixed and accepted with little possibility of role and task rearrangement. There was little recognition given to the separate needs of children and adolescents. Family members who were as young as seven years old were treated as junior-sized adults and were expected to work. Throughout most of history, children (and women) were seen as chattels, producing income or salable merchandise, and existing solely to help fulfill a parental (or family) need. Only recently have most families been concerned with providing for the creative and developing needs of their children.

Over the years there has been a decline in infant mortality as well as in birth rate, thereby enabling women to have more time and freedom. Parents are now able to give more attention to each individual child, and the family itself is moving toward developing the maximum potential of each of its members as it begins to decrease the rigidity of gender roles and increase overall sexual freedom.

Lasch believes that there has been a gradual erosion of the private life of the family ever since the eighteenth century, when the family was a self-contained unit providing for the emotional, financial, and daily needs of each of its members,[3] and Davis suggests that, "the preindustrial family performed a variety of economic, religious, educational, and welfare functions that have since been assumed, for good or ill, by other institutions."[4] Later, in the nineteenth century, the focus of work moved from the home to the factories, and the family was suddenly no longer providing for all of its needs. In the twentieth century the family has been invaded by outsiders who now fulfill its needs—including teachers, social workers, doctors, and other professionals.

The Changing Model of the Family

The current state of the family is well described in the following editorial concerning the changing family.

The family is the basic unit in all societies regardless of cultural diversities. Families everywhere consist of men, women, and children united by ties of kinship and mutual obligations. Within its capacity, the family is expected to meet the basic needs of its members for food, shelter, and clothing, and to provide the intangible needs for affection and a sense of belonging. It helps to transmit from one generation to the next the traditions and the cultural, moral, and spiritual values unique to each society. Inevitably, in each era there are changes, large or small, gradual or abrupt, which may alter or transform family patterns. Foremost among the forces influencing family life today is the rapid pace and nature of social change. First, the effect of national development is to change the economic, social, and physical environment, possibly to open up new horizons and opportunities, certainly to pose challenges for the family, if not to impose additional burdens on it. Second, development almost invariably involves adjustment within the family itself, in the roles and responsibilities of family members, and in relationships among the generations. Because of their complete dependence on adults, children are the first to suffer or benefit from changes affecting the family. Throughout the developing world, the past few decades have witnessed dramatic changes. The gradual awakening of women to their rights and dignities, the rapid rate of urbanization, population pressures, increasing education, and technology are factors that are affecting the family in countless ways. Change is a continuing and inescapable reality in today's world.[5]

Heated discussion continues concerning the extent to which the family is changing and whether or not the family is dying altogether. The traditional model of the "average" family—one that is made up of husband-breadwinner, wife-homemaker, and two children— has been questioned,[*] but there are other models of living together in a continuing intimate relationship whereby adults are involved in "family" functions. Also, some writers think of a much broader definition of the system, which Pattison and associates[6] call the "kinship model." By kinship they mean the variety of individuals, extended families, the community, and the neighborhood who are seen as "the family." Sociologists call this new version of the family unit "the modern nuclear family," in contrast to the "traditional, extended family" in which several generations of a family all lived under the same roof. The "old" nuclear family had two parents and several children and relied on relatives for economic and emotional support, as well as for childrearing. Until recently the modern nuclear family was considered an undesirable adaptation to the increased mobility of family members, thereby making the modern family more vulnerable to instability, isolation, and stagnation.

Although an extended family may have been adaptive to the life styles of the past, it did, however, have its disadvantages. Roles were rigid and the restrictions on individuals and individuation were greater. Intergenerational conflicts were more intense. On the other hand, the ideal modern version of the nuclear family does allow for freedom from some of these constraints, with the hope of finding a mutually satisfying balance between restraint and permissiveness.

Because there are many possible and workable types of family organization, family therapists need to be careful not to project, knowingly or unknowingly, their own, and perhaps inappropriate, ideals of family structure and function when they are treating their patients. From the initial contact with a family, the therapist should pay special attention to the actual structure of that family: its goals, resources, and potentialities. Only after understanding the specifics of a particular family can the therapist begin to think about treatment.

Contemporary observers from both the political right and left, refer to the happy, extended multi-generational families of bygone times as the ideal to which we should aspire and lament the current "dismal state of family life" as though we have somehow "fallen from grace." While some attribute this fall to moral decay, others blame governmental intrusion into private and family matters. Both agree, however, that things were seemingly better in the past and that family life today is "deteriorating." Frequently, the increasing divorce rate is taken as a single measure of this family disintegration and portrayed as a sign that marriage is no longer important to Americans. Until recently, television portrayals of family life have facilitated this mythical image by portraying families in the past as long-lived, multigenerational, geographically stable, and healthy. Men and women are portrayed as being family oriented. Although still true, most people would agree

---

[*]The model has been challenged for not representing the statistical mode and for its stereotyped role allocations.

that women are less interested than in past centuries in becoming married and certainly much less interested in bearing children.

An historical review of marital data reveals the above characterizations to be largely inaccurate. One of the most striking findings of such a review is that a number of marital patterns that were common in the past *continue* to be prevalent today. The nuclear family, including two generations, continues to be the basic family unit in European and American societies as it has been over the last several centuries. Laslett,[7] Shorter,[8] and Demos[9] have demonstrated this constancy in Western Europe and this country. In the past, (the 1800s) very small numbers of American families (about 7–8 percent) had more than three generations living in the same household, and this percentage has remained constant. Thus, the multigenerational extended family represented only an *ideal*, which in fact occurred in only a small minority of our population. Factors such as the migration to frontier lands, high mortality rates, and economic conditions have all adversely affected the availability and stability of multi-generational families. Indeed, substantial numbers of three and four generation families are a phenomenon primarily of this century due to recent increases in longevity. Aging and historical mortality information are discussed below.

One of the most significant marital constants is the percentage of women who choose to marry and who become mothers. Women born in the 1936–1940 period marry and have children with approximately the same frequency as women born 100 years earlier. Regardless of enormous cultural changes, the vast majority of women continue to enter marriage and bear children, thus demonstrating the viability of marriage as an institution. Over the past century the overall marital dissolution rate (the sum of widowhood (death) plus divorce and desertion) has remained remarkably *constant*. While the divorce rate has substantially increased, this trend has been offset by the dramatically falling death rate, leading to an overall marital dissolution rate of approximately 34 per 1000 existing marriages (Table 2-1).

Table 2-1
Annual Marital Dissolutions by Death and Legal Divorce, and Rates per 1000 Existing Marriages, 1860–1970

Year	Dissolutions per Year		Dissolutions per 1000 Existing Marriages			Divorces % of Total Dissolutions
	Deaths	Divorces	Deaths	Divorces	Combined	
1860–1864	197,200	7,170	32.1	1.2	33.3	3.5
1900–1904	390,800	61,863	26.5	4.2	30.6	13.7
1970	903,200	715,000	19.3	15.2	34.5	44.0

Adapted from Davis K: The American family in relation to demographic change. In Westoff CF, and Parke R (Eds): Demographic and Social Aspects of Population Growth, Volume 1. Washington, D.C.: U.S. Government Printing Office, 1972, p 256.

A key concept in the myth of the "golden era of family life" is that of geographic stability. We developed the rather dubious image of a three-generation family living in a little house with a white picket fence. Geographic mobility has been and continues to be a way of life with Americans. The movement from rural to urban areas has been an important migration of this century, and migration patterns continue today, primarily to the west and south.

Thus, while some things remain strikingly constant (e.g., percentage of women who marry and have children, rate of marital disruption, geographical mobility), there are important and striking changes in various aspects of family life.

Aging of the Population

The most important single change in American society is the aging of the population. Life expectancy in the United States has increased substantially: in 1900 the average life expectancy from birth was 49.2 years, but by 1983 it had climbed to 74.6 years. As death rates fall, there is usually a secondary decline in birth rates due to changes in the perceived value of having many children and the wish to maintain the high quality of life that is often threatened by large families.

As life expectancy improves, larger cohorts of individuals remain alive into their later years. By the year 2050, over 20 percent of the population will be over the age of 65 and approximately 30 percent of the population will be under the age of 25. One of the major impacts of life expectancy on family life is on the composition of families, so that today we expect more multi-generational ones than existed in the past. Men and women in the 50 to 60 age range may be expected to spend time taking care of their elderly parents. Childhood dependency will give way not only to adult autonomy and independence, but, in the future, will continue on to a caretaking role for the elderly as well.

Increased Status of Women

One of the most significant historical trends has been the gradual increase in the status of women, evidenced by at least two clearly measurable phonemena: employment and education. At the end of the last century and early in this one, most employed women were single. In general, a single woman would get a job only to quit upon marriage, and usually would not re-enter the labor force. By the end of World War II, a reversal had taken place so that the majority of working women were married. This suggests that although single women continue to work, their married compatriots rejoin the labor force later on. Today, women work prior to and often during the early years of marriage, leaving the labor force temporarily during the childbearing and childrearing years, only to rejoin it later on.

The educational status of women has been improving dramatically. In 1980, 50.6 percent of all college enrollments were female, up from 34.5 percent in 1960. The proportion of college or advanced degrees earned by females was 47.5 percent in 1980, up from 24.4 percent in 1950. The major implication of the increased education and employment status of women is that they are able to support themselves and thus are increasingly independent. *This strongly suggests that women will feel less constrained by unwanted marital relationships and will be more capable of altering them.*

Patterns of Sexual Behavior

With the sexual revolution in America, which occurred from 1960 until the present, many of the "radical" attitudes and behaviors of the 1960s have gradually come to be incorporated into everyday life. For example, premarital intercourse is commonplace today, as is cohabitation. Recent surveys of adolescents indicate that there is a lifetime prevalence of premarital intercourse of 31 percent for white and 63 percent for black youths. According to a report by the National Center for Health Statistics, the proportion of women who delayed sexual intercourse until marriage declined from 48 percent among women who married in 1960–1964, to 21 percent among women who married in 1975-1979.[10] Because people are more sexually experienced when they enter marriage, they will probably have higher expectations of sexual satisfaction from their marital partners. Sexual gratification alone is no longer a reason for getting married, as it once was.

Women seem to be adopting an attitude of increasing control over their own reproductive functions. For example, in 1965, 64.9 percent of all married white women between the ages of 15 and 44 used some form of contraception, while by 1976 this percentage increased to 68.7 percent. In 1973, there were 744,600 legal abortions, while in 1978 this number had almost doubled.

Cohabitation has become increasingly accepted in the United States. It is very difficult to accurately determine the number of individuals who are cohabitating; however, it has been estimated that approximately 2.3 percent of all man-woman couples living together in the same household in 1978 were not married, representing a total of 1.1 million couples.

Women and Children

The vast majority of women continue to become mothers, although it appears that increasingly larger numbers of them *delay* childbearing and prefer to have *fewer* children. In 1900, the average woman bore approximately six children, while today she usually has between one and two.

One of the most profound changes in the evolution of marriage in the United States is the substantial modification of the life cycle of women. Women born at mid-points in the 19th and 20th centuries marry at roughly the same time (with modern women marrying at a slightly younger age). However, women born in the mid-19th century spent 12.5 years of their lives from the birth of the first to last child (because more children were born per family). Modern women, on the other hand, experience a corresponding period of only 2.5 years. The brevity of time from birth of first to last child coupled with the fact that they (the mothers) also experience greater longevity, defines a rather extensive period in which they will have no childrearing responsibilities and an opportunity to spend more time in other pursuits.

Today, it seems reasonable to think of essentially two phases of a marriage using this conceptual life cycle for men and women. The first might be referred to as a "family oriented phase" in which children are present, and the second, a "post-childrearing phase" after the children have left home. The adaptations and skills necessary for a successful family oriented marriage cannot be assumed to necessarily apply in the post-childrearing one with its greater intimacy and couples' orientation.

Contemporary Living Arrangements

There is no one dominant family form of marital and family living arrangements in the United States today. Single breadwinner nuclear families, the usually idealized concept of the "family," comprise only 13 percent of the population. The most prevalent form of household composition today is one in which people live in a child-free or post-childbearing marriage (23 percent), followed by single, widowed, separated, or divorced persons (21 percent), single parent families (16 percent), and dual breadwinner nuclear families (16 percent).

Impact of Dual-Career and Working Women

The related phenomena of working women and dual-careers in a family are subjects of much contemporary marital and family research. Recent extensive surveys[11,12] indicate over half of one sample felt there was a negative effect on the family of the dual career arrangement; 9 percent of the children involved cared for themselves following school and prior to the time one or both parents returned home from school (so called "latch-key children"). Waite[13] found that time management was one of the most critical matters faced by both men and women.

It is clinically significant that general marital satisfaction studies have found that working wives report greater happiness than those who act as full-time housewives. There does not seem to be substantial differences in regard to marital conflict or greater reporting of strain or stress when comparing the traditional with the working couple.

In summary, current trends in the modern family include: increased latency to childbearing, fewer children per family, use of alternative childrearing facilities (such as daycare centers), and high divorce rate.

THE CHANGING MODEL:
THE CYCLE OF
MARITAL ACTIVITY

Categories of marital status, such as singlehood, marriage, divorce, widowhood, etc. are frequently conceived of as stable and discrete states. This view is no longer accurate. A much more dynamic picture of marital activity in which a *larger number of people shift between various marital statuses* is more accurate (Fig. 2-1). Though most Americans still marry prior to age 30, demographers and marital researchers have noted a general delay in marriage, with more marriages occurring in the age range of 25–44.

The extent of divorce activity in the United States is frequently referred to as an indicator of general decline in the importance of marriage and family living in the United States. Divorce has increased markedly in America in this century; however, it is important to appreciate several caveats and contextual matters. As mentioned earlier, the divorce rate has increased markedly and the death rate has declined, thus offsetting each other, so that *the total rate of marital dissolution has remained stable for well over 100 years.* Perhaps the most useful divorce data is not the divorce rate, but cohort studies that essentially track the marital and divorce history of selected subpopulations. For both first marriages and remarriages, by the time the fiftieth anniversary occurs for a couple, only slightly over one-half of the couples will still be married. Of interest is that remarried people seem to divorce sooner, but with about the same frequency as people in first marriages. Thus, a remarriage has about the same probability of success as first marriages.

As expected from the proportion of individuals having children and the great extent of divorce activity, most children today are very likely to experience a divorce. There is a concomitant substantial increase in the number and proportion of single parent families and with remarriage, stepfamilies or blended families. It has been estimated that stepfamilies make up 10-15 percent of all households in the United States.[14]

Until recent decades, remarriage was primarily a phenomenon for widowed

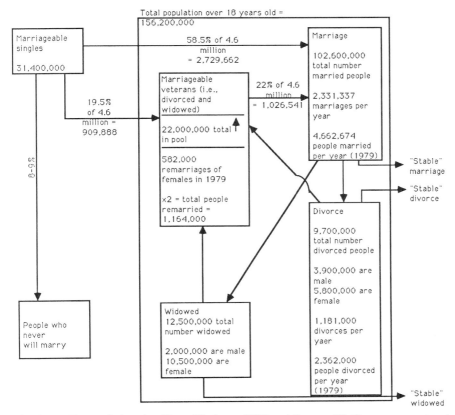

Fig. 2-1.   The marital cycle. (From Bjorksten OJW, and Stewart TJ: Contemporary trends in American marriage. In Nadelson CC, and Polonsky DC (Eds): Marriage and Divorce: A Contemporary Perspective. New York: Guilford Press, 1984.)

individuals. In 1979, 41.5 percent of all marriages involved at least one partner who had been previously married. Using 1980 data, it was estimated that following a first divorce, almost 80 percent of the partners will remarry. Following a second divorce, almost 90 percent of the partners will remarry.

It is the purpose of this section to consider the impact that current demographic trends will have on the family therapist and mental health practitioners in general. We will consider how the current social context may influence marital adjustment, pathology, and the overall treatment situation. The clinical implications of current marital trends fall roughly into two categories: first, our concepts of marital "normality" and "reality," and second, the manifestations of marital problems.

Traditional Marriage

Over the last several generations, major changes in marital style have occurred from a "traditional" to a "companionate" pattern. Traditional marriages can be viewed from a structural perspective in which marital roles and duties were prescribed, non-negotiable and well defined. The focus of marriage was "functional," in that each partner was expected to fulfill role obligations. Marital "failure" was synonymous with role failure, which was easy to determine since there was good cultural agreement about what husbands and wives "should" do. These marital roles were closely associated with sex role stereotypes, so that men were reluctant to perform women's duties and visa versa. It was these sex role stereotypes that connected marital role behavior with individual identity, and thus related marital and individual pathology. These relationships served as the rationale for the individually oriented psychotherapy approach for the treatment of marital problems.

The key concepts in traditional marriage were "duty" and "responsibility." "Duty" implied a known set of role functions that one accepted upon marriage; if a person did not want to perform them, then he or she would not marry. Thus, in this sense traditional marriage was "binary." Once married, each partner was "responsible" for his or her role functions, i.e., was expected to perform them. If love occurred at all in traditional marriage, it grew after marriage, and was by no means a requirement in the decision to marry; rather, one appraised a potential partner in terms of his or her ability to perform role functions; i.e., "will he be a *good provider*?" or "will she be a *good mother*?"

Companionate Marriage

The traditional marital style began to shift with the onset of industrialization in the latter part of the 19th century, but did not really give way to the companionate style until the post-World War II era. The companionate style of marriage can be viewed from a "process" perspective (i.e., meaning how they work), since it has an emotional focus in which roles evolve through negotiation and are often variable and vague. Communication and negotiation skills are vital in this style of marriage, and it is important that each partner have the maturity to know what he or she wants from the marriage. In contrast with the traditional style, in the companionate marriage, roles are "created" by the partners so that role competency is difficult to evaluate and marital failure is synonymous with "poor relationship" rather than role incompetency. Partners in traditional marriages must tolerate the stresses of *adaptation* to marital roles, whereas in the companionate form, they must tolerate role *ambiguity*.

The key concepts in companionate marriage are "love" and "choice." The raison d'etre for these marriages is that people *want* to be together because they love each other and *expect* to obtain *fulfillment* from their *relationship* with their partner. The actualization of this romantic ideal is a historically new phenomenon that implies a level of prosperity sufficient to release people from a survival orientation, and a degree of equality between partners hitherto unknown because of inadequate birth control, short life expectancy, and lack of economic opportunities and education for women. In short, the increased status of women has been a major factor in the rise of "love," i.e., companionate marriages.

The concept of marital choice implies not only choice within the marriage, but also *of* the marriage. The freedom of *both* partners to choose to marry each other is a recent historical phenomenon and now appears to be an ongoing matter after marriage, since divorce is relatively easy to obtain. We take for granted that women can leave marriage as easily as men, but this has only become possible in recent years when women have joined the work force and have achieved the economic freedom that makes this option possible.

The partners in companionate marriages have high expectations of their partners and of the relationship. They expect to remain "in love" and be "happy." These expectations often lead to disappointment when romance settles into routine and the relationship is no longer exciting. This has led to the development of "marital enrichment" workshops designed to help partners achieve more "fulfilling" marriages.

The concept of "the increasing status and freedom of women" is not meant as a vague or philosophical term but rather, as a description of demographic trends, supported by increasing employment rates of women, increasing educational achievement (e.g., over 50 percent of college enrollments in 1980 were women), fewer children per woman, increased latency to childbearing, curtailed childbearing years, and increased utilization of daycare facilities, to name a few. With this increased status has come increased freedom of choice regarding intimate relationships. Although this has permitted more love marriages, it has probably also contributed to a much higher divorce rate.

Traditionally, the marital agenda usually focused on the development of a family (i.e., children) and the acquisition of property (i.e., home). This agenda usually implied a high degree of stability so that "roots" could be established. Thus, psychiatric appraisal of marriage used these criteria, among others, to judge whether or not a marriage was working. Today, mental health professionals are faced with a much more difficult dilemma in evaluating companionate marriages. Since the focus is on love and the relationship itself, rather than on children or property, the evaluation of marital success is based much more on the subjective appraisal by the partners than on external objective criteria. Couples may view their marriage as very successful, even though they have no children and move frequently, suggesting a "rootless quality," and seem, to the psychiatrist, to be quite "unstable." So what are the criteria for evaluating such a marriage? An answer is, for the couple, "it works."

The currently high remarriage rate has several important clinical implications: first, it suggests that people are committed to the *institution* of marriage but may want to "adjust it" on an individual basis by changing partners. Second, attitudes about divorcees have changed in a direction of increased acceptance. Third, women are not disadvantaged in their remarriage prospects if they have children. In fact, the older a divorced woman with children is, the greater her remarriage prospects, i.e., the *absence* of children seems (for reasons unclear to us) to reduce older women's remarriage prospects. Fourth, the prevalence of divorce and remarriage suggests that these changes in marital status may be of less psychiatric significance than was previously thought. Finally, since on the average, one child is associated with each divorce, and most divorcees remarry, large numbers of "reconstituted" or "blended" families are being formed each year.

MARITAL STYLE AND DYSFUNCTION

The traditional and companionate marital styles each lead to different views regarding marital pathology. In the structural/traditional model, since marital roles were prescribed and could not be easily changed, marital pathology was usually related to *role adaptation*. Adaptational pathology usually took several forms. In the "trapped wife syndrome," one of the best known forms of marital pathology, women were so constrained and bored by the repetitiveness and demands of childrearing and household duties that they became resentful, depressed, angry, and usually felt unfulfilled. One of the most common aspects of this syndrome was the increasing discrepancy between women's personal development and that of their partners. The most common clinical manifestation of the trapped wife syndrome was depression, for which many women sought the assistance of mental health professionals.

Rebelliousness represents another form of role adaptation pathology. Some partners develop a negative or counterdependent identity characterized by a sense of self defined by defiance, i.e., "pushing" against known or prescribed rules. This can best be seen in rebellious adolescents who define themselves by their disobedience. If this form of identity is perpetuated into adulthood, it can lead to difficulties in accepting a marital role. This is usually manifested either by people who blatantly break marital rules, as for example, *severe* philanderers, or those who covertly "cheat" on their marital responsibilities as, for example, people who gamble with the household finances.

Finally, role incompetence is another form of adaptational difficulty in which, for whatever reason, a person is incapable of performing his or her marital role functions. This can be caused by mental illness, inadequate preparation for the responsibilities of marriage, or many other factors. Thus, it made eminent sense for a traditional future father-in-law to be sure that his prospective son-in-law had a good job and seemed to be a competent person before the marriage took place.

Psychiatric treatment for role adaptation pathology usually took the form of individual psychotherapy aimed at helping the patient adapt. Treatment might be continued until the patient accepted his or her marital role and/or developed sufficient competence in it. This therapeutic concept had validity only as long as there was good cultural agreement about what normal marital role behaviors consisted of for men and women.

In contrast with traditional marriages, companionate marriages, with their process orientation, lead to different kinds of problems. Since their focus is on emotional fulfillment, often role functions are not carefully considered during courtship, so that marital difficulties may manifest themselves in terms of marital role definition, and include role ambiguity, power struggles, communication problems, and disappointed expectations.

Marital partners today are free to determine their own style of marriage, that is, to determine who will do what in the relationship. On the one hand, this reduces much of the "coercion" that many partners experienced in traditional marriages, but on the other hand, it leads to problems in determining marital roles. Since partners are free to engage in a variety of marital roles, which ones they settle on depends on what they *want* and their ability to negotiate. In early marriages, many partners are not sure which roles they really do want or should engage in. If they do decide, it is usually in a tentative fashion. This leads to a feeling of role ambiguity, that is, uncertainty about what to do in the marriage and how to do it. More importantly, many partners are unsure which of the following criteria to use to decide role behaviors: what they feel at the moment, what is "best," what their parents suggest, or what their friends are doing. This dilemma usually heightens the already present anxiety. Each partner may look to the other for help, but neither is really capable of helping so both usually feel frustration, disappointment, and anger.

Since roles are not clearly defined in companionate marriage, each partner must fend for himself or herself, which may lead to "power struggles," that is, conflicts over which partner's preference will prevail. Negotiation requires a degree of maturity, tolerance, fairness, good faith, and clarity of one's own desires. Many partners develop a "win at any cost" mentality that may be successful in the short run but seldom works well in the long run. They often develop the idea that "losing" a disagreement means their wishes will always be subjugated to their partner's. Gradually, partners assume an adversarial stance and can no longer see themselves in the common endeavor of marriage. One of the earliest signs of this is when partners begin to keep a mental "ledger" of who "won" or of whose turn it is to give in.

It would be misleading to suggest that marital competition for power is new. In Teutonic marriages in the Middle Ages, each partner attempted to place his or her hand on top when asked to join hands during the marriage ceremony. Occasionally this led to such turmoil that the minister had to settle it, usually by putting the man's hand on top, thus symbolizing his supremacy in the marriage.

Although the struggle for marital power may have always occurred, in the past there was little doubt about who was "right" or "wrong" in the matter. Today, there is little consensus about who "should" be dominant, and most people advocate either equality (i.e., symmetry) or parity (equivalent power but in different areas).

Communication problems are one of the most common manifestations of a variety of marital problems. They are usually the *result* of difficulties and in turn cause further ones, rather than being the initial cause of problems. Communication difficulties are of particular importance in companionate marriage, since in many ways communication is the sine qua non of love and is required for role negotiation. It is difficult to imagine love without it. Thus, when communication begins to deteriorate, most people either view their marriage as becoming routine, or as being problematic.

Companionate partners expect to feel love for their marital partners as well as receive it. When problems of role definition arise and partners feel frustrated and angry, their difficulties are often accentuated by their disappointment in "not feeling love." Since marriage and love are equated, when other feelings interfere with love, the marriage itself is called into question, thus rendering companionate marriages very "fragile" during problematic times.

Although we discuss clinical issues of marital therapy in greater detail in Section V, let us digress briefly here in order to make illustrative linkages between the historical/sociological prospective and diagnosis/treatment issues. Problems of role definition in companionate marriage are best treated by conjoint therapy focusing on improving the relationship so that it is fulfilling for each partner. Treatment continues until partners are able to alter their relationship and/or interpersonal behaviors enough to be rewarding for each. While either partner may have his or her own difficulties requiring individual psychotherapy, the endpoint of the marital therapy is defined by both members of the couple. If conjoint therapy is unsuccessful, some couples will divorce and try again.

Occasionally couples seem to have the kinds of role pathology common to both traditional and companionate marriages. They are usually old enough to have been socialized in a traditional mode but had problems adapting to it. When their children leave home and they anticipate many post-childbearing years together, they may experience problems of role definition. While they have societal encouragement to "develop the potential of their relationship," they may never have developed the communication and negotiation skills necessary to accomplish companionate goals. An educational approach to the marital therapy of these couples can be very helpful, as can "marital enrichment" approaches.

Although divorce is now socially accepted, it still represents a major stressor. Divorce is usually accompanied by some social isolation and depression and is associated with increased morbidity and mortality. Since people seem to experience diminished physical "resistance" after divorce, it may be important for physicians to be especially vigilant for illnesses that are concomitant with immunosuppression, stress, and depression. While the depression associated with divorce is common and usually only requires reassurance, on occasion it can be severe and prolonged, requiring treatment with antidepressants and/or psychotherapy.

Since, on the average, one child is associated with each divorce, a need for custody arrangements is the norm. Divorce is becoming increasingly less adversarial today, so that "no fault" concepts of divorce are being applied to custody as well. Increasingly, joint custody arrangements are established and are frequently favored by the courts. Probably the most important single factor in the success of co-parenting is good communication between the members of the divorced couple. It seems paradoxical and thoroughly modern to suggest the idea that divorced people should communicate well, yet this is usually the case in the majority of couples that have joint custody of their children.

THE FUTURE OF THE FAMILY

A recent editorial in *Science*[15] and a 1977 conference entitled, "The Family: Dying or Developing,"[16] were both concerned with the future of the family. The writer noted that the percentage of married households (out of total households) has declined so drastically that it is questionable whether or not we will have any married households left within a generation or so from now.

Family form has changed remarkably toward a kinship model. Students of the family predict even more changes in life style, peer and power relationships, social and intellectual competence, health patterns, and family values. There will be an increase in dual-career and single-parent families in the future, and although there will be a leveling off of single-parent families, there will be more largely female-headed families.

With all these shifts within the structure of the family, it is only natural to ask: Is the family, as an institution, disintegrating, or is it only changing? What happens to the children of divorce? What should roles be for males and females, and how should these roles differ in single-parent homes and dual-career marriages? What do lasting or satisfying marriages have in common? How do public policy, societal attitudes, and educational efforts influence these attributes?[15]

We prefer to view the family as evolving and developing rather than as dying. In contrast with the past, there are increasing numbers of options for women, men, and children. Individuals are no longer forced to work at an early age and can thus develop their creative potential. Society now allows men to take a "supportive" as well as "constrictive" role. They can become involved in the nurturing of younger children and not merely in "limit setting." The family itself has more options. Because we have moved to an extended kinship model (father, mother, grandparents, relatives, housekeepers, ex-spouses), each individual may provide support in various ways for the other members.

It is not at all clear that being in a one-parent family, as an alternative style, is necessarily detrimental.[17] There may be advantages in terms of certain options that allow individual growth for both the child and the adult that the two-parent families are unable to foster.

Eisenberg believes that, "In a full human society, the goal of social institutions should be to maximize the possibilities of personal choices for women and men."[18] Rather than a rigidly prescribed distribution of roles, individual differences in family units should be the determining factor in deciding who fulfills what role.

Finally, Sussman has made a number of predictions of trends for the future.[19]

1. The divorce rate will continue to rise with a corresponding drop in the marriage rate. Between one-third and one-half of all marriages in 1977 are likely to end in divorce, the majority occurring during the first three years of marriage.
2. A continuous rise in singlehood is expected. This is a consequence of increasing decisions not to marry, increased rates of cohabitation—basically a nonlegal marriage form—and a longer postponement of remarriage among the divorced.
3. There will be a continuous increase in the incidence of child-free marriages, with major efforts to sanction this union as a socially approved form. The costs of having and supporting children, increasing emphasis on equitable dyadic relationships, the importance of the marital health of couples, and the increasing incidence of sterilization—which, incidentally, is the preferred form of contraception in the United States and world-wide—are reasons for the rising number of childless marriages.
4. Political and legislative efforts will be made to "stabilize" the family of the future. The "White House Conference on the Family" was one such beginning effort. Will family pluralism be used as its conceptual base or will there be efforts to reestablish a nuclear family with a traditional role structure?
5. Increasingly, the "everyday" family or focal family will become the significant primary group for the individual, perhaps even eclipsing the legal, both psychologically and socially. This is the group of individuals who may or may not be related by blood or marriage and who provide intimacy, emotional

support, companionship, role models for children, and help when in need. These are the persons one can count on, with whom one has free and easy access, and with whom one likes to spend free time.

Additional trends have been suggested by others:

1. Offspring will increasingly rely on peers and the media (especially television) for role models, with decreasing reliance on parental models.
2. There will be an increasing sense of dislocation, alienation, and confusion of marital partners and parents as to their appropriate roles and functions, with increasing numbers turning for help and guidance to outside sources.
3. On the horizon lie such possibilities as increased availability and utilization of abortion, pregnancy for single individuals by use of artificial insemination and other "laboratory" means, and changes from passage and implementation of statutes similar to the Equal Rights Ammendment.

Based on these trends, Sussman[19] also suggests the following:

1. An organized policy and program for childbearing
2. Divorce insurance
3. Utilizing the extended "everyday" family as caretakers
4. Training people to deal with bureaucracy
5. A qualifying test for marriage.

RELEVANCE FOR THE FAMILY THERAPIST

The family has maintained itself as an institution throughout history and through all recognized cultures. In various subtle and major ways it has also changed with respect to specific ways of carrying out its functions. The family therapist needs to examine the particular family to see to what degree it has carried out its functions and to what extent other intrafamilial people and institutions are available to help the family continue to do so.

We have discussed the past, present, and the future of the family. In the following chapter we look at how families function.

SUGGESTIONS FOR FURTHER READINGS

Shorter E:**The Making of the Modern Family.** New York: Basic Books, 1977.
   The history of courtship, the mother-child relationship, the boundary be-

tween the family and the community, as influenced by the industrial and sexual revolutions.

Murstein B: **Love, Sex and Marriage Through the Ages.** New York: Springer, 1974.
   A delightful peak at sex and love from the Old Testament to the future.

Reiss D, Hoffman H (Eds): **The American Family: Dying or Developing.** New York: Plenum, 1979.
   The influence of history, social class, ethnicity, and divorce on the family.

Segraves RT: Marital status and psychiatric morbidity. In Bjorksten O (Ed): **New Clinical Concepts in Marital Therapy.** Washington, D.C.: American Psychiatric Press, 1985.
   Excellent review of the existing data relating marital status to psychopathology.

REFERENCES

1. Fleck S: A holistic approach to family typology and the axes of DSM-III. Arch Gen Psychiatry 40:901-906, 1983
2. Lovejoy R: The origins of mankind. Science 211:341-350, 1981
3. Lasch C: Haven in a Heartless World. New York: Basic Books, 1977
4. Davis D: The American family and boundaries in historical perspective. In Reiss D, and Hoffman HA (Eds): The American Family: Dying or Developing. New York: Plenum, 1979, pp 13-33
5. Editorial: Coping with change. UNICEF News 89:3, 1976
6. Pattison EM, DeFrancisco D, Wood P, et al.: A psychosocial kinship model for family therapy. Am J Psychiatry 132:1246-1251, 1975
7. Laslett P: Social developing and aging. In Bienstock R, and Shanas E (Eds): Handbook of Aging and the Social Sciences. New York: Van Nostrand Reinhold, 1976
8. Shorter E: The Making of the Modern Family. New York: Basic Books, 1977
9. Demos J: The American family in past time. In Skolnick A, and Skolnick J (Eds): Family in Transition (2nd Ed.). Boston, Little Brown, 1977, pp 59-77
10. Premarital sex trends. New York Times, April 17, 1985
11. House and Garden Louis Harris Study. How the baby boom generation is living. New York: Conde Nast, 1981
12. General Mills American Family Report, 1980-1981. Families at work. New York: Louis Harris Assoc, 1981

13. Waite L: Women at work. Population Reference Bureau 36(May):1-44, 1981

14. Espinoza R, Newman Y: Step-parenting (DHEW ADM #78-579). Washington, D.C.: U.S. Government Printing Office, 1979

15. Etzioni A: Science and the future of the family. Science 196:487, 1977

16. Reiss D, Hoffman H: The American Family: Dying or Developing. New York: Plenum, 1979

17. Schulman GL: The changing American family: For better or worse. Int J Fam Ther 1:9-21, 1979

18. Eisenberg L: Changes in family life have medical implications. JAMA 230:1241-1247, 1974

19. Sussman MB: Actions and services for the new family. In Reiss D, and Hoffman HA (Eds): The American Family: Dying or Developing. New York: Plenum, 1979, pp 213-237

Section II

The Functional and Dysfunctional Family

Our bias is that to treat families, the student must understand not only how families function, but also the development of dysfunction. To further complicate matters, traditional as contrasted to new family forms are different in how they function—and "being different" does not mean bad, or dysfunctional.

Although there is not a generally accepted model of function and dysfunction, our intent is to provide the information on what *is known*, so that the student can formulate a working model for use in clinical situations.

Spirit of Life by Robert Russin. Courtesy of Robert Russin and the Palm Springs Desert Museum.

3

Understanding the Functional Family: The Traditional Family Form

OBJECTIVES

- To understand the concept of the traditional family as a functional system
- To list and characterize the phases of the traditional family life cycle
- To list and understand primary family tasks
- To list and understand characteristics of the functional family

INTRODUCTION

In the opening sentence to *Anna Karenina*, Tolstoy[1] declares, "Happy families are all alike: Every unhappy family is unhappy in its own way." Although one hesitates to disagree with Tolstoy, the next three chapters describe the ways in which functional families are alike, and also quite diverse, and the ways in which dysfunctional families are alike and yet quite unique.

There is probably little need to stress the general importance of marriage and the family. These institutions have existed throughout recorded history in all places and at all times. Even in late twentieth-century America—despite the talk in some quarters about the death of the family—family and marital relationships, although changing, are clearly very much with us and undoubtedly will continue to be so in the foreseeable future. Well over 90 percent of all people in the United

States still live in (some form of) family and, except for early adulthood, human beings live in families most of their lives.[2]

It is also certainly true, however, that marriage and the family have carried different assignments and expectations at various places and times. This variability appears when we compare the traditional American family with the radical modifications of this pattern. The current lack of a generally accepted pattern for marriage and the family is a cause for uncertainty, instability, and distress for many people. On the other hand, this diversity offers a multiplicity and richness of solutions for both individual and societal situations that a more rigid, unchanging pattern could not.

Birdwhistell has suggested that the "average American family" is organized around idealized, nonachievable goals (for example, romantic love).[3] Failure to live up to such family myths is a cause of conflict and distress for all family members (see Chapter 5). As we pointed out in Chapter 2, there is a great diversity of family types and styles related to a variety of demographic and psychological variables. All families have conflicts: their feelings toward each other are mixed, their love is not always constant, and so forth. Furthermore, the completely well functioning, growing, long-term marriage is a rarity (estimated at about 5 percent).

The frame of reference provided in this chapter for understanding the family is not intended to be exhaustive or complete. No such final statement about the family can be made. Instead, our model is intended to be supplemented by those frames of reference that apply to individual and sociological models. Exclusion is not meant to imply that the other models are not important, only that they are not in keeping with the general tenor of this book—that of presenting ideas of particular interest or use to the family therapist. Undoubtedly the richness, complexity, and variety of marriages and families will not be completely described or explained by our categories, nor will all of the categories fit precisely into every specific family system. It is hoped, however, that this material will offer a useful structure for thinking about all families, including those members in distress, who present themselves in one way or another to professionals for help.

In the next two chapters, we consider the *family as a system*, and its life cycle, tasks and functional characteristics as they relate to traditional and new family forms. In the chapter after those two, we describe how dysfunctional families, who often have symptomatic members or members with problem areas, operate in these three dimensions. And, finally, in Section III we discuss the assessment of families.

Since this is both a long chapter and a key one, we first provide an outline to it to guide the reader:

The Family As A System

THE FAMILY AS A SYSTEM

Marriages and families differ from other human groups in many ways, including duration, intensity, and type of function. For human beings, the family constitutes the most important group in relation to individual psychological development, emotional interaction, and maintenance of self-esteem. For many of us, the family is a group in which we experience our strongest loves and our strongest hates, and in which we enjoy our deepest satisfaction and suffer our most painful disappointments.*The characteristics of the family (or of marriage) as a unit are different from the mere sum of its components.* Knowing the attributes of all the individuals in the family is not the same as understanding the family system as an entity. The family has a history and function of its own, the specifics of which differ from those of its individual members.

Marriages and families need to be thought of as *interactive milieus* in which transactions between component parts are continually taking place. Thus the action of one member will affect the entire family. A ripple set off anywhere internally or externally that impinges on the family will reverberate throughout. There is a basic, underlying consistent homeostasis in every family that is used to maintain each member's identity, defined as the sum of the individual's internal and external patterns of adjustment to life. The family is a system in dynamic equilibrium. Stresses and strains of family existence inevitably affect each family member. At times, these reactions may be of such a nature as to cause them to be labeled as symptoms. For example, when a father and mother stop communicating (a change in homeostasis), the father may begin to drink (a symptom) or the mother may become depressed (a symptom).

The family is usually bound together by intense and long-lasting ties of past experiences, social roles, mutual support and needs, and expectations. There are factors constantly at work, more or less successfully, to keep the family system in equilibrium and to keep it from undergoing a too severe or rapid change. This, too, has been referred to as family homeostasis. These equilibrating mechanisms often have to do with maintaining a continuing system of symmetrical and complementary relationships.

As we have pointed out, family homeostasis refers most generally to the concept of the family as a feedback system designed to maintain a relatively stable state so that when the whole system or any part of it is subjected to a disequilibrating force, the system will operate to restore the preexisting equilibrium. As we will see, it is often functional to move to a new equilibrium. Family therapists have noted that changes in one member of the family often bring about changes in other members. For instance, the onset of illness in the family member identified as the patient (for example, a child becoming schizophrenic) can cause another member to decompensate (become depressed). As the child improves, the other member may improve, and, concurrently, the marriage may deteriorate.

If one thinks of characteristic *patterns* of achieving equilibrium for the family, then families can be thought of as having personalities or styles analogous to those of individuals, for example, "isolated" families or "musical" families or "tragedy-prone" families. A more recent scientific approach to this issue is to categorize families by their cognitive and problem-solving styles. A generally accepted system of family typologies is not available (although badly needed), but there is a general recognition of differences in family patterns of thinking, feelings, interacting, and of the types of coping mechanisms used to deal with stress, as well as the kinds of "myths" or "scripts" that families seem to act out (see Chapter 6). All marriages and families are subject to stress, disequilibrium, and crisis, and they all develop habitual techniques to deal more or less successfully with these situations. The issue is how functional or dysfunctional are these techniques.

THE FAMILY LIFE CYCLE

Overview

Although stability and homeostasis are important elements of marital and family sytems, inevitably there are also other forces that are continually changing the family, pushing it in the direction of development and differentiation. Some of these forces constitute the growth pattern known as the family life cycle. This can be thought of as the expectable events that most families go through in a fairly standard sequence. Other stresses can be thought of as traumatic or unexpectable in that they are extraordinary; they are not necessarily experienced by most families or they occur outside of the normal sequence. Thus each family finds its own balance between those forces that tend to keep it stable and those that encourage change.

Given that life is a series of "ups and downs" for all people and all families, the family unit has to continually cope with the unavoidable changes that time inevitably brings. This notion is contrary to the popular romanticized version of life and of marriage.

The longitudinal view of the family's development has been referred to as its life cycle (Fig. 3-1) and is analogous to the individual's life cycle. Also various authors have studied the specific tasks for each phase in an individual's and in a family's life,[4-9] and in Table 3-1 psychosocial models of adult development are juxtaposed with family stages.[10,11]

As in individual development, the family evolves through *expectable* phases. These phases include: (1) *the beginning family* (engagement, marriage, and honeymoon); (2) *the childbearing family* (birth of the first child); (3) *the family with school children*; (4) *the family with teenagers*; (5) *the family as a launching center* (the offspring's marriage and separation from home); (6) *the family in its middle years* (one or both spouse's retirement); and (7) *the aging family* (eventual death of a spouse).

There are also the *unexpected* or traumatic stresses on the family. Sometimes these consist of one of the normal phases coming out of turn, such as the death of a spouse or parent at an early age. Other such stresses are the illness or incapacitation of a family member and financial reverses. These traumatic changes involve either someone's entering or leaving the family (actually or imminently) or a threatened or actual role change for a family member (such as a job change or loss).

The family's ability to pass successfully from one specific developmental phase to another will depend to a considerable extent on how prior stages have been mastered. There are various phase-specific psychosocial tasks that need to be worked out at each stage. The extent to which this is accomplished will depend on the flexibility and functionality of the family as a whole and as individuals.[12]

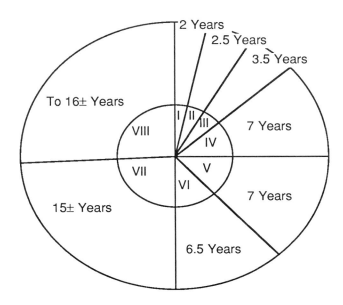

Phase	Family Phase	Family description
I	Beginning family	Married couple without children
II	Childbearing family	Oldest child, up to 30 months
III	Families of preschool children	Oldest child, 30 months to 6 years
IV	Families with school children	Oldest child, 6-13 years
V	Families with teenagers	Oldest child, 13-20 years
VI	Families as launching centers	First child gone to last child leaving home
VII	Families in the middle years	Empty nest to retirement
VIII	Aging families	Retirement to death of both spouses

Fig. 3-1. The Family Life Cycle.

Even if one phase goes badly, another may go well; for example, a young couple may be at odds in the childrearing stages of a marriage, but function quite well during the empty-nest phase.

A competent family self-destructs; children grow up, leave the nest; parents grow old, and having failing function, die. Adaptation to these stark realities is successful only to the degree that individuation is complete. In such evolved people, a sense of capability does not depend on unchanging relationships. There is an ability to accept the future, to acknowledge and adapt to the great changes brought about by growth and developing, aging, and death. A family member can then operate with respect for his own dignity and that of others. He can have joy in encountering a loved one, even though that very encounter brings awareness of the implications of loss and passage of time. When individuation is incomplete, separation is resisted and family pain and functional difficulty increase.[13]

Table 3-1

Comparison of Psychosocial Models of Adult Family Development

| | | Author of Model | | |
| | | | | |
Age	Erikson	Gould	Levinson and Associates	Duvall
18–20		Getting away from parents	Leaving the family	—Beginning family
20–25	Intimacy versus isolation			—Childbearing family
25–		Working on the business of living	Getting into the adult world	—Families with preschool children
30–		Questioning what life is all about	"Should I make a change?" (unstable period)	—Families with school children
35–	Generativity versus ego stagnation		Settling down	—Families with teenagers

Age				
40–		Awareness of time squeeze—turning toward family	Becoming one's own man	—Families as launching centers
			Disparity between what I've got and want (unstable period)	
		Growing satisfaction with marriage and friends		—Families in the middle years
50–	Ego integrity versus despair		Restabilization period outcome of mid-life transition	
55–		Mellowing and reviewing what life is all about		
60–				—Aging families

Reprinted with permission from The American Journal of Psychiatry 135:677, 1978 (©1978, the American Psychiatric Association), and from Duvall EM: Family Development (4th Ed.), Philadelphia, Lippincott, 1971, p 121.

In this section on the family life cycle, we first discuss tasks involved in the *beginning family*, and then those concerning the *adult life cycle as they relate to the traditional family form.*

Marriage
THE ENGAGEMENT PHASE

Rapoport states that there are three tasks involved in the *intrapersonal* preparation for marriage.[14,15] They are: (1) making oneself ready to take over the role of husband or wife; (2) disengaging (or altering the form of engagement) of oneself from especially close relationships that compete or interfere with commitment to the new marital relationship; and (3) accommodating patterns of gratifications of premarital life to patterns of the newly formed couple (marital) relationship.

Rapoport also states that completion of these tasks leads to consideration of the second major group of engagement tasks, namely those involved in the couple's *interpersonal* preparation for marriage.[14]

1. Establishing a couple identity.
2. Developing a mutually satisfactory sexual adjustment for the engagement period.
3. Developing a mutually satisfactory system of communication between the pair.
4. Establishing a mutually satisfactory pattern with regard to relatives
5. Developing a mutually satisfactory pattern with regard to friends.
6. Developing a mutually satisfactory pattern with regard to work.
7. Developing mutually satisfactory patterns of decision making.
8. Planning specifically for the wedding, honeymoon, and the early months of marriage that lie ahead.

In the honeymoon phase, the work seems to involve both interpersonal and intrapersonal tasks including the following:[11]

Intrapersonal Task I : Developing competence to participate in an appropriate sexual relationship with one's marital partner.

Intrapersonal Task II: Developing competence to live in close association with the marital partner.

Interpersonal Task I : Developing the basis for a mutually satisfying sexual relationship.

Interpersonal Task II: Having a mutually satisfactory shared experience as a basis for developing a later husband-wife relationship.

Let us discuss some issues that arise in the marital life cycle, both with regard to the ages when people decide to marry, as well as what happens after the people (in these age ranges) marry.

AGES 18 THROUGH 22

Marriage in this age group often represents a search for a substitute parent in the spouse. This is because the partners usually have not yet been able to effectively separate themselves, physically or emotionally, from their parents to define themselves as competent individuals. These early marriages may actually interfere with the further individuation of the partners.

Before the recent rise of women in the labor force, it was more difficult for women to master the task of individuation, for they were not afforded access to the vocational competency that is often necessary to help individuals to define themselves as worthwhile and autonomous. For many women, a job role, other than that of being a wife and mother, has not been as readily acceptable as it has been for men. Thus, many women have felt prematurely arrested in their potential, both by general cultural patterns and by an early marriage.

THE MID-TWENTIES

The accepted myth is that people in their mid-twenties marry for love. A closer examination reveals, however, that first marriages are often a matter of conforming to social expectations; regularizing sexual outlets; wanting to be dependent on a parent substitute; getting away from home; or that of filling some psychological void. Marital satisfaction is greatest in the first year and soon begins to decline, reaching a low point in the late thirties before starting to ascend again. The seventh year of marriage is often a critical one with many divorces occurring at that time.

AGES 28 THROUGH 34

Many men (and women) go through their twenties *and thirties* feeling that success in their careers is their main task. These are the people who may become workaholics and locked into their jobs with the often unexamined idea that vocational achievement will offer a continuing sense of security. For this end they may sacrifice other aspects of their lives, most noticeably their husbands, wives, and families. There are other people who drift through their twenties without firm commitment, which for them may not come until the thirties or, rarely, later.

For noncareer women during the same period, the feeling is that a dependent role as wife will make them a whole person. As some women become increasingly disillusioned with this role, they may become more passive, angry, and depressed. Husbands may begin to look outside the marriage for their satisfaction and indicate that they want their wives to become more assertive, as long as the wives do not overdo it and disrupt the marital equilibrium. Divorce may be seen as the way to eliminate the problems for either the husband or the wife or for both.

THE MID-THIRTIES

For women with other goals, it may nevertheless not be until age 30 or 35 that they are able to work out a satisfactory amalgam of career and family responsibilities.

Most women, up until very recently, have taken on the role of care-givers, marrying by their early twenties and seeking their major satisfaction via their husbands and families.

By the mid-thirties, the average mother has sent her last child off to school and has been re-entered into the labor market for years as a contributor or sole provider of the family income. It is the most common time in which the wife runs away and the divorced woman remarries, since in both cases the woman feels free to try a new life-style.

THE FORTIES

Individuals in their forties are subject to important re-evaluations of their basic attitudes with the realization that their remaining years are limited. For the man this may involve his coming more in touch with his own tender and care-giving qualities, which have been relatively neglected over the preceding years. His wife may often become more self-assertive and self-concerned, his children more independent, and his work more routinized and stultified. The wife may be feeling freer at the time her husband may be feeling more entrapped. As they examine themselves and their partners, couples often sense the need for a re-evaluation of their marital contract. This process is often accompanied by communication difficulties and marital separations on the basis that the partner no longer "fits."

According to Gould, if this period goes well then, "marital happiness and contentment with the spouse continues to increase, along with renewed interest in friends and social activities . .." although, ". . . friends and social activities are not substitutes for concern with one's own children, which continue at a very high level."[8]

THE FIFTIES AND BEYOND

Marriage in this age group has not yet been well studied. In general, parents may be seen by children more realistically and as less blameworthy for their own problems. Levinson feels that, "In the fifties, the data indicate that one begins to feel less responsible for one's children and begins to look for the children's approval, as a meaningful concern to be ranked as co-equal with self-approval and the spouse's approval. The concern with health increases during the fifties. There is a certainty that time is running out."[4] Having an orientation toward the future with specific goals in mind is helpful in maintaining not only physical health but also mental health.

When a loss (through death, separation, or relocation) occurs in the family, healthy families are able to cope with the mixed feelings about the lost member. In dysfunctional families the occasion is used to even old scores as in the following example.

The R. family consisted of Mr. and Mrs. R., two older sons in their thirties, and a daughter age 20. There was a 70-year-old grandmother. When she committed suicide, the family reacted. The mother became severely depressed; she cried incessantly and was unable to work. The father drank continuously from the time he got home until the time he went to sleep; and the two older boys accused their mother of "killing grandmother." The mother used the occasion to berate the boys for not achieving all that she and her husband had expected of them.

FAMILY TASKS

We will now discuss the following family tasks: *Provision of Basic Physical Needs: Food, Shelter, Clothing; Development of a Marital Coalition; Personality Development of Offspring;* and *Development of Sibling Coalition.*

Provision of Basic Physical Needs: Food, Shelter, Clothing

The essential life-maintaining tasks of the family group may at times be overlooked by middle-class therapists treating middle-class families. Those who have come into contact with family systems for which these basics have not been provided become much more aware that there is a fundamental biological requirement for all families. All of the more complex functions of the family will be affected in one way or another and become distorted or deficient, depending upon the extent to which these needs are adequately met or dealt with in an idiosyncratic fashion. A therapist must pay attention to the basic reality factors and, where indicated, the major, or at least the initial effort, may have to be to help the family deal more adequately with its basic needs. A family system already overwhelmed by gross deficiencies in basic needs will not usually be motivated or sensitive to more sophisticated or symbolic considerations.

Development of a Marital Coalition

The core of the family is the marital coalition. This term implies that the spouses have been able to loosen their ties appropriately from their families of origin and have been able to develop a sense of their own individuality and self-worth. Marriage is not merely a joining together of two individuals; it is also a distillation of their families of origin, each with its own experiences, history, life style, and attitudes. *One marries not only an individual, but also the family context in which the individual lives.* Actual members of these original families often play important roles in the new family. Some individuals may come to a marriage hoping to gain families they never had, such as the child who spent many years in foster homes, essentially without parents.

If grandparents are alive, they may be involved very clearly and specifically in the daily operations of nuclear families. They may take sides, comment on childrearing practices, or live next door. In healthy families, in-laws can provide a good deal of cohesion and finanical and emotional support to make a new family function more efficiently. In-laws can also be a destructive force, however. This can happen, for example, when the mother-in-law tries to reform or control her daughter-in-law, or when the husband reacts unrealistically toward his mother-in-law, unthinkingly seeing her as a carbon copy of his own mother.

Even when the extended family is not physically present, however, the patterns experienced by the spouses in their original families inevitably influence their current marital and family interactions. In its extreme the *"three generation hypothesis"* refers to the notion that influences may be passed down from grandparents to grandchildren. Therefore a therapist must constantly bear in mind the presence of these third parties.

The couple must be able to work together toward common goals and to establish both complementary and symmetrical relationships that are mutually functional and satisfactory. A *complementary relationship* occurs when two people exchange different sorts of behavior (for example, giving and receiving). A *symmetrical relationship* occurs when two people exchange the same behavior (for example, passivity).When a couple is unable to form either of these relationships, the marriage in that context may be restricted.

The process of working out a satisfactory marital relationship involves shared agreements, largely undiscussed, between the two people involved. These agreements may consist of explicit rules, implied rules (which the couple would agree to if they were aware of them), and rules that an observer would note but that the couple itself probably would deny. Seen this way, conflicts in marriage arise when there are disagreements about the rules of living together, about who is to set those rules, and about who is to attempt to enforce those rules that are mutually incompatible. For example, there may be disagreements as to whether the husband or wife should wash the dishes, but there may be further disagreements as to who should make this decision. More complex still is the situation in which one spouse forces the other to agree "voluntarily" to wash the dishes.

Another convenient and useful way of understanding marital or dyadic (two person) relationships involves assessing three critical dimensions.

1. *Power:Who is in charge?* There are some subtleties in this category, for example, an apparently "weaker" or "sicker" member may conquer by means of this very "weakness" or "sickness." Also, leadership need not be all or none—the father can be leader in deciding which car to buy and the mother can be leader in deciding what food to serve.
2. *Intimacy:* Partners struggle with their need for and fear of closeness.
3. *Inclusion and Exclusion: Who else is considered to be part of the marital system?* This question applies not only to actual relatives and other persons, but also to time allocations for career, recreational interests, and so on.

The ways in which these dimensions will be handled will depend on the intrapsychic characteristics of the individuals, the marital and family styles that have evolved, and the phases of the marriage at the time in question. Dysfunctional couples tend to be less flexible and more static and rigid. One of the core issues of marital therapy and marriage is the meshing of individual needs with the needs of the relationship.

Berman and Lief indicate that, "Issues that appear to be purely individual or purely dyadic are often actually a result of a complicated interaction between marital and individual crisis points (especially at ages 30 and 40).[16]

At this point is may be worthwhile to review and elaborate on the concepts discussed thus far. Table 3-2 compares the stages of development for individuals and for marital systems including phases, specific tasks and conflicts, and how these dimensions of marital relationships emerge during the marital life cycle. (The reader is also referred to the earlier, more basic discussion of some of these issues, centered around Fig. 3-1 and Table 3-1.)

Table 3-2 should be carefully studied, since no attempt will be made to repeat in narrative form all the details contained therein. As an example of how the information may be helpful, however, we can consider the case of a marital couple coming for treatment, both partners of whom are in their late thirties. Referring to Table 3-2, under Stage 4, the therapist can, at a glance, focus on what the expectable individual and marital tasks and challenges of this period are likely to be, and guide the evaluation and treatment accordingly. By shifting to earlier

Table 3-2
Individual and Marital Stages of Development

Item	Stage 1 (18–21 years)	Stage 2 (22–28 years)	Stage 3 (29–31 years)	Stage 4 (32–39 years)	Stage 5 (40–42 years)	Stage 6 (43–59 years)	Stage 7 (60 years and over)
Individual stage*	Pulling up roots	Provisional adulthood	Transition at age 30	Settling down	Mid-life transition†	Middle adulthood	Older age
Individual task	Developing autonomy	Developing intimacy and occupational identification: "getting into the adult world"	Deciding about commitment to work and marriage	Deepening commitments: pursuing more long-range goals	Searching for "fit" between aspirations and environment	Restabilizing and reordering priorities	Dealing effectively with aging, illness and death while retaining zest for life
Marital task	Shift from family of origin to new commitment	Provisional marital commitment	Commitment crises; restlessness	Productivity: children, work, friends, and marriage	Summing up: success and failure are evaluated and future goals sought	Resolving conflicts and stabilizing the marriage for the long haul	Supporting and enhancing each other's struggle for productivity and fulfillment in face of the threats of aging

Marital conflict	Original family ties conflict with adaptation	Uncertainty about choice of marital partner; stress over parenthood	Doubts about choice come into sharp conflict; rates of growth may diverge if spouse has not successfully negotiated stage 2 because of parental obligations	Husband and wife have different and conflicting ways of achieving productivity	Husband and wife perceive "success" differently; conflict between individual success and remaining in the marriage	Conflicting rates and directions of emotional growth; concerns about losing youthfulness may lead to depression and/or acting out	Conflicts are generated by rekindled fears of desertion, loneliness, and sexual failure
Intimacy	Fragile intimacy	Deepening but ambivalent intimacy	Increasing distance while partners make up their minds about each other	Marked increase in intimacy in "good" marriages; gradual distancing in "bad" marriages	Tenuous intimacy as fantasies about others increase	Intimacy is threatened by aging and by boredom vis-a-vis a secure and stable relationship; departure of children may increase or decrease intimacy	Struggle to maintain intimacy in the face of eventual separation; in most marriages this dimension achieves a stable plateau

Table 3-2 (continued)

Item	Stage 1 (18–21 years)	Stage2 (22-28 years)	Stage 3 (29–31 years)	Stage 4 (32–39 years)	Stage 5 (40–42 years)	Stage 6 (43–59 years)	Stage 7 (60 years and over)
Power	Testing of power	Establishment of patterns of conflict resolution	Sharp vying for power and dominance	Establishment of definite patterns of decision making and dominance	Power in outside world is tested vis-a-vis power in the marriage	Conflicts often increase when children leave, and security appears threatened	Survival fears stir up needs for control and dominance
Marital boundaries	Conflicts over in-laws	Friends and potential lovers; work versus family	Temporary disruptions including extramarital sex or reactive "fortress building"	Nuclear family closes boundaries	Disruption due to reevaluation; drive versus restabilization	Boundaries are usually fixed except in crises such as illness, death, job change, and sudden shift in role relationships	Loss of family and friends leads to closing in of boundaries; physical environment is crucial in maintaining ties with the outside world

Reprinted with permission from The American Journal of Psychiatry 132:586, 1975 (©1975, the American Psychiatric Association).
*From Levinson and associates.[5]
†For some individuals, this stage may run throughout their forties.

and later stages, one can get a sense of how adequately previous periods have been handled, and of the capacity of the marital dyad for dealing with the future.

The extent to which these issues—involving family rules, roles, and coalitions—are satisfactorily clarified and developed, and the manner in which the process occurs, are related to the couple's style of communicating thoughts, feelings, and attitudes. Partners who are experienced in expressing themselves (and are permitted to do so) about relevant, meaningful, interpersonal issues will stand a better chance of coping competently with the challenges of family living. If the marriage is one in which the members are not free or accustomed to indicate their concerns and needs, then the members will be hampered in dealing productively with the inevitable stresses that will befall the marriage. Each of these two styles may be self-reinforcing, so that "virtuous" and "vicious" cycles, respectively, may be set up.

For the spouses, the marriage will present an opportunity for them to deal with their sexual needs. It may offer, in part, a relationship of friends in which there is mutual sharing of feelings, interests, activities, availability, and emotional support. As we mentioned, historically, marriages were based to a large extent on economic considerations. This continues to be the case today, but for the most part not as prominently so. Marriage offers a fairly practical and acceptable way to conceive and raise children. Marriage seems to offer a sense of stability, continuity, and meaningful direction into the future. For some, marriage is a response to a variety of social pressures that sanction and reinforce it as an institution. For any two individuals, marriage may afford the opportunity for the meshing of particular psychological traits and needs.

The marital coalition over the entire course of the family cycle is marked by changing circumstances. Usually the spouses have a period of time alone together as husband and wife before the arrival of offspring. Later they must accommodate to being a father or mother as part of a *parental dyad,* in addition to being either husband or wife as part of a *marital dyad.* With the passage of time the parental role decreases in functional significance and the marital partnership becomes the primary, perhaps almost the exclusive, dyad once again.

If the marital interaction has atrophied while the children were being parented, it will be difficult to let the children go. A major readjustment will be necessary when the two partners find themselves alone in an empty house after the children have grown, since they will have to renew their roles of husband and wife. Figure 3-1 makes clear that the average family life cycle will find the marital partners alone together for about half the total lifetime of the family after the children have left home. For about half of this latter period the breadwinner often is no longer working (thereby losing another important role function and self-esteem support) and the two marital partners are physically together more than they were in previous years.

Individual roles and views of the relationship may contribute to the couple's problem.[17] With the shift in marital expectations, increasing attention must be paid to individual developmental goals. Even the individuals of a well-functioning couple can grow apart or distinct from each other. As goals, values, and expectations change, marital interaction may cease to be gratifying or rewarding. The individual adaptive changes, which disturb the balance of the relationships itself, may cease to be functional if complementary shifts are not possible or if they are not strongly desired by another partner.

Marital conflict arises from many sources, including differences in information, beliefs, interests, desires, and values, as well as competition between the partners. One can distinguish between productive and destructive conflicts. Productive conflicts may be characterized by mutual recognition of different interests, open and honest communication, and trusting attitudes that allow both partners the possibility of finding creative solutions. Destructive conflicts may be characterized by tendencies to rely on strategies of power and on tactics of threat, coercion, and deception—all of which lead to mutual suspicion and lack of communication. With a dysfunctional marriage the therapist must elucidate the patterns that have resulted in the predominance of destructive conflicts in the marital interaction.

What factors make marriages successful?[18] Not surprisingly, there are no simple answers. Some positive relationships consist of a matching of individuals with complementary styles, while others are of a pairing of individuals with symmetrical styles. The one finding that seems constant is that of "interest in each other as companions." These people are "not boring and they are not bored within their marriages." Are the two people capable of being friends, in addition to being compatible with respect to sex, money, social class background, and the like?

Computer matching of potential couples tends to use the variables of socioeconomic class, which usually amounts to education and income, religious, ethnic, and racial backgrounds, political and social attitudes and values, avocational interests, and others, with the notion that the closer the two individuals are on these parameters, the greater the chance for a successful match. Dissimiliarity or complementarity of personality styles may actually enhance a partnership, as might other subsidiary interests. Two people matched with this set of variables would be capable of being friends, as well as marital partners.

Personality Development of Offspring

Families are thought of as crucial in socializing offspring in relation to a particular culture. The degree to which parents are physically responsible for determining the outcome of the nature of their children varies from one culture to another, as well as from one family and one offspring to another. Our own present-day American culture seems to offer a variety of norms for families in this respect, and enculturation is also strongly influenced by peer groups, schools, and television.

It is our bias that what we call "personality," is each person's adaptation to the biological equipment inherited at birth interacting with the demands of the family and the external world.

UTILIZATION OF AGE-APPROPRIATE CHILDREARING TECHNIQUES

Both parents should have at their disposal the techniques for childrearing and the emotional capacity for relating appropriately to the offspring at each phase of development. Given the qualifications mentioned earlier, early experiences may be critical in intellectual and emotional development. (It has been shown that differential rearing can even affect the actual structure and chemistry of brain tissue. Progress is now being made toward ascertaining the specific effects of rearing conditions on brain and behavior, properties of the environment that contribute to these effects, and developmental periods in which brain tissue is most sensitive to environmental modification.[19])

Each stage of childrearing provides opportunities as well as pitfalls. The decision to have a child; the period of pregnancy, birth, and the immediate neonatal period; the varying and insistent demands of the infant and the growing child; and then the demands of the school years, adolescence, and further independence; the culminating period in which offsprings leave home and form their own families; and then the relationship to offsprings as co-adults—all constitute a process that is amazingly complex and challenging.

It is not surprising that families experience many difficulties along the way. For many individuals, parenthood will be one of the most fulfilling roles in their lives, but for others it will seem painful and unrewarding. Marital partners may be relatively unsophisticated and ignorant with respect to appropriate techniques and cultural expectations relating to various developmental phases. They may have particular difficulty in some specific phase, perhaps because of what they experienced in their own families of origin. They may find it difficult to move from one stage to another, and may find themselves "hanging on" inappropriately to a phase that is past. For example, some couples seem to be particularly comfortable with infants and children, and do a good job in raising them, but have a stormy and troublesome time with adolescents.

Mr. and Mrs. Z. were in their late thirties and had considerable experience in raising puppies and violets. Only after several years of marriage did they decide to have a child. They had done quite well when their son was an infant, enjoying diapering, feeding, and so forth; but as soon as he became autonomous and had desires of his own, they found that he upset the routine they had worked out over many years, and they began increasingly to fight with one another. Patterns that had been set for the past 13 years suddenly were no longer available.

Families may become so rigid that they are unable to move successfully from one phase to another. For example, it is the job of the family, among other tasks, to make sure that during late adolescence the children are appropriately emancipated from the family. This will be a difficult task for families in which the spouses do not have a gratifying marital relationship to fill the void created when the children leave the family. Such parents may refuse to let the adolescents out of the house to date or to spend time with their own peers.

MAINTENANCE OF THE PARENTAL COALITION

The arrival of children signals the need for the marital partners to broaden their roles to include those of being parents. The task is to form an appropriate parental coalition with respect to childrearing practices. It is beneficial to have parental agreement and consistency in these areas, with a sharing of responsibility and mutual support. Children may become confused if they do not know what is expected of them, or if they receive continually conflicting messages from each of the parents. Clearly, parents cannot agree on everything, and there may be danger in attempting to present a facade of agreements that is in fact only pseudo-agreements. On basic important matters, however, it is preferable that parents have some sort of mutual, consistent childrearing guidelines, rather than not being able to form a working coalition.

Mr. and Mrs. L. were only children who married in their late twenties. They both had been favorite children in their respective extended families. They found in the early years of their marriage that whenever a decision had to be made (as it did some 30 to 40 times a day), decision making was accomplished by one partner "winning" and the other "losing." When they had children, this pattern continued and was accentuated by the children's own desires. The children quickly found that they could get what they wanted by aligning themselves with one parent or the other. The couple sought treatment at the point where they were unable to communicate and agree about anything, because discussion exploded into throwing pots and pans with the children "cheering them on."

Are two parents required? It is believed that the parent of the same sex as the offspring serves as a role model for identification, while the parent of the opposite sex provides the basic love object. In a family in which the parents do not form a workable coalition, the child may have difficulty in development.

In a family with one parent absent (through death or divorce, for example), personality defects of various types may be formed at certain periods in the child's development, unless the remaining parent or parent-surrogate is able to fill the role of the absent one.[20] A critical factor in this situation seems to be the quality of the parental relationship prior to the loss of the parent. If the parents get along well, then the loss of one of them may be much less significant for the child than if they did not get along well. The remaining spouse is able to encourage positive, rather than negative, identification with the lost parent.

The relationship that existed between the lost parent and the child is also of crucial importance to the child's adjustment following "parental deprivation." The term "parental deprivation" is popularly used to connote the belief that loss or deprivation is etiological in a child's deficiencies. This view is not always justified by the data. If parent and child get along well before the separation, then there is a much greater likelihood of the child's continuing to do well after the separation. In one case, a father often took his 7-year-old son fishing, put him to bed every evening, and participated in most childrearing decisions. After the loss of his father, the son showed no decline in functioning.

Parents may be able to maintain a reasonable coalition with their children and be relatively good parents, even though in other areas there may be considerable marital disharmony. This is sometimes seen in the extreme case in which the spouses have been divorced but are able to maintain positive parental functioning. In other families the opposite can also be seen, for even though the marital relationship functions fairly adequately, the two spouses seem unwilling or unable to devote the requisite amount of time, energy, and interest to the parental role. They are good marital partners, but relatively poor parents. This is sometimes the case with immature, selfish, or narcissistic parents.

In a family in which there are children who are seriously disturbed, the parents, instead of forming a workable coalition, may (1) deprecate each other in a hostile manner; (2) become rivals for the child; (3) equate the child's loyalty to the other parent with rejection of themselves; (4) indicate to the child that growing up to be like the other parent is unacceptable; or (5) promote unhealthy parent-child dyads. The child may respond by (1) trying to bridge the gap between parents; (2) feeling responsible for the parents' problems (the scapegoat role); or (3) supporting the parent whom the child feels the need to cater to the most.

Often the child who is considered disturbed is the bond that holds the marriage together, for the parents in many ways can become dependent on the child's problems to keep the focus off their own relationship. Improvement in the child may then be expected to cause disruption in the parental relationship.

MAINTENANCE OF GENERATION BOUNDARIES

Broadly speaking, parents must act like parents and children like children. The nature of the generation boundary changes at various stages of the family life cycle. The nurturing role of parents in relation to their children is different when the child is one week old from when the child is 40 years old. Parents should not be emotionally dependent on their immature children but, rather, should look to one another for support and reinforcement.

The R. family consisted of father, mother, older daughter, and two sons. Mr. R. was barely able to hold a half-time job while Mrs. R. stayed at home, alternately complaining of various bodily ailments and crying hysterically. In this family the daughter planned and cooked the meals, the two sons both worked to supplement the family income, and the three children together did the planning of family activities each week. When major decisions had to be made, the older son would call the family together; the parents would be brought in to the room and would then sit passively while the three children made the decisions, such as how to finance a family house.

In the B. family, the father had been killed in an automobile accident soon after the third daughter was born. Mrs. B. found herself overwhelmed by having to raise her daughters and had turned over this job to the eldest daughter. This daughter had become overly rigid in enforcing limits, not allowing either of her two younger sisters to date. Consequently, the two younger sisters were at war with her. The eldest sister, at the age of 19, felt deprived of her own chance to have fun.

In the P. family, both father and mother were brilliant physicians. The couple was thought to have an ideal marriage, and both seemed to be functioning successfully. They had three children. The mother suffered a severe automobile accident in which she was brain damaged. The father's reaction to this was to spend less and less time with the family. He turned the responsibility of running the family over to the older son. The older son was told that he was responsible for the mother because he was the man of the house. The older son actually did assume responsibility; for example, he paid the bills, did the shopping, and took care of younger siblings. The father spent less and less time at home and the older son spent most of his hours with the mother. Eventually he began to have several fights with the younger siblings and the mother's condition took a turn for the worse. The father accused him of killing the mother because she had become upset over the fighting. The older son's solution was to get out of the house (that is, to go *away* to college), but he had many misgivings and much guilt over his decision to do so.

The maintenance of generation boundaries tends to lessen role conflicts that follow the blurring of roles and the ambiguity this fosters. A totally "democratic" family in which all members, regardless of age, responsibility, and experience have an equal voice in all decisions seems wholly unrealistic. Far from being something to be decried, a "generation gap" between parents and children is an absolute necessity, if we mean by the term a difference in responsibility, role, maturity, and often of attitude. It should not, however, consist of a deficiency in communication. Recognition must be given to the different affectional relationships that need to exist between parents and between parent and child.

Emotional room must be left for the child to learn, for the child to interact with peer groups, and for the child to develop an identity.

In a seriously disturbed family, parents may exist in a childlike dependency on one another; may be rivals for the child's affection; or may be jealous of the child. Incestuous feelings may become pronounced, and parents may leave the task of decision making to the child rather than appropriately assuming that responsibility themselves.[21] Other parents may be dissatisfied with their own lives and become jealous of their offspring and thus compete with them. Parents in a disturbed family may also feel inadequate in their parental role (perhaps because of unfortunate experiences in their own family of origin) and may be inappropriately and unrealistically permissive, abdicating many of the duties and responsibilities that revolve around the role of the parent. In some instances, because of economic or other realistic pressures, an older child may be called on to fulfill a parental role for the younger siblings and thus may never have the opportunity to experience and master the developmental tasks of childhood or adolescence.

Unlike the unrealistically permissive parents, overly dictatorial parents at least offer their offspring a clear model (if only one to revolt against), although they often may be using the child to attempt to master some of their own unresolved issues. Often such parents find it extremely difficult to let go of their offspring and admit that they have become autonomous after a certain stage in their development. The parents should recognize that they have done the best they could and need no longer feel responsibility for their children; instead they should deal with them as fellow adults.

Special problems exist in a society such as our own, which is extremely youth oriented and in which the rate of change is constantly accelerating. In such a society, it is hard for parents and children to feel that what the parents have to offer is relevant. Children are bombarded by the outside influences from the communications media (notably television). The age-peer group may prematurely come to be a dominating influence. Parents (and their children) may become confused, and as a consequence some may throw up their hands in permissiveness, whereas others put their foot down in authoritarianism.

ADHERENCE TO APPROPRIATE SEX-LINKED ROLES

The sexual identity of the offspring is an important factor in personality formation. Appropriate sex-linked role attributes do not develop merely by the accident of biologically male or female birth; they are acquired by role allocations starting in infancy and continuing with role assumptions and identification as the child grows older. The crucial factor in determining one's basic *sexual identity* (that is, whether one regards oneself as basically a male or female) is that of how our parents deal with us in this respect. This factor will be dominant even if it contradicts every known biological gender indicator. Even clearer are the environmental influences in *gender role* (how masculine or feminine we consider ourselves to be and what the components of this identity are).

Lidz has written that clear-cut reversals with respect to gender role functioning and task divisions lead to important distortions in the child's development.[12] This traditional view holds that the female should be the expressive-affectional gender and the male should be the instrumental-adaptive gender. Furthermore, a cold, nonaffectionate mother would be relatively more harmful to the offspring, especially to female offspring, than would a cold, nonaffectionate father. A weak, ineffective father, on the other hand, would tend to be more damaging to the offspring, especially the male offspring, than would a weak, ineffective mother.

These traditional, idealized gender roles have been increasingly challenged in recent years, viz. through changes in sex-appropriate grooming and dress and in the emergence of changing attitudes of women. In fact, children raised by a lesbian parent are psychologically healthy and do not become homosexual when evaluated in their teens.[22] An increasing number of people are becoming more free to explore whatever potentialities exist within themselves without being constrained by the gender stereotypes imposed by society. Many men are more comfortable being "expressive and empathic," and many women are feeling less threatened by being "capable and logical." The negative aspect of this development in theory lies in the fostering of greater gender role confusion.

One of the current areas of conflict in families is that of *role assignments*. Women have been assigned to roles and tasks that place them in a submissive position to the husband and give them little gratification. Men, as fathers, have been found to be as significant in a child's development as women are as mothers.[20] There is a gradual changing of role assignment, and a more egalitarian sharing of tasks. Clinicians have noted that changes in role disrupt families in which a dominant-submissive pattern exists.[23] Vital family tasks need to be performed, although who should perform them might best be decided on the basis of mutual accommodation, rather than cultural gender stereotypes.

ENCULTURATION OF THE OFFSPRING

It is one of the tasks of parents to teach the younger generation the basic adaptive techniques of their culture. It is necessary for them to transmit instrumentally valid ways of thinking, feeling, and acting. Of course, many of these "enculturation" tasks are now assumed by extrafamilial systems.

Communication skills are basic for any type of successful and gratifying social interaction and personality growth. Parents usually play the major role in the children's proper development of these skills. They are models for the children in behavior, and in the appropriate, and effective methods of expressing thoughts and feelings. Children need to be given the proper labels and comments with respect to what and how they feel and think. A child who is clearly angry needs to have this feeling recognized and labeled, rather than having a parent consistently deny, overlook, or misinterpret such feelings. Children need to be given leeway to experience their own feelings as valid and not be restricted to those of their parents.

In pathological families, various difficulties in these areas of psychological development may be noted. Members of dysfunctional families may show particularly intrusive, projective, tangential, concrete, or bizarre thinking. There may be considerable ambiguity and vagueness, with a prevailing feeling of meaninglessness. Some investigators have noted these difficulties especially in families of schizophrenic patients (see Chapter 22). In some families the children's emotions may be distorted because the children are consistently denied, contradicted, ignored, or punished. For example, in some families, sadness or disappointment cannot be expressed by the child because it "upsets" the parents.

Certain families seem to have difficulty teaching their children socially acceptable techniques of behavior, and these children seem to grow up with either a deficient or a distorted repertory of social-behavioral skills. Both overly authoritarian and overly permissive attitudes in the parents may lead to inflexible, maladaptive patterns in the children.

How are childrearing tasks dealt with by different socioeconomic classes?* There are certain practices that do seem "typical" for each class. The higher the parents' social class position, the more likely they are to value characteristics indicative of self-direction and the less likely they are to value those of conformity to external authority. Working-class parents are consistently more likely to employ physical punishment and to live in the present and in terms of an action orientation and early gratification of impulses. Middle-class families rely more on "constrictive" practices, such as reasoning, isolation, and appeals of guilt (and other methods of involving the threat of loss of love); they are future-oriented; deal more with words (and often symbolic process); and repress and delay gratification. When some families move up the socioeconomic ladder they adopt the parental practices of their new class; others, however, still raise their children the way they themselves were raised.

Development of a Sibling Coalition

The history of developmental theory has largely neglected the role of siblings in families. There has been greater emphasis on dysfunctional than functional relationships. For example, disproportionate attention has been paid to sibling rivalry hostility. Family theory has stressed the important role that siblings

---

*By socioeconomic classes we mean the classification of families according to a given educational and occupational status.

play in normal family functioning. Each sibling has a crucial role in the maintenance of homeostasis for that particular family system. Siblings often work together when their parents are continually at odds, or have divorced, or one or both parents have severe mental illness. That bond is often the link to keep a family functional when one or both parents cannot carry out parental roles.

Issues of loyalty, attachment, and bonding are felt by family therapists to be important and useful in changing dysfunctional patterns. Dysfunctional families often have dysfunctional sibling relationships. For example, siblings may mimic the parental relationship, i.e., always bickering in the same way the parents bicker, or one being dominant.

Family treatment is based upon these models of sibling functioning. Treatment using older siblings as change agents, or where there is sibling conflict, using forgiving rituals, are important. When one parent has died, siblings are important in maintaining the family homeostasis in coping with the parental loss.

CHARACTERISTICS OF THE FUNCTIONAL FAMILY

Tolstoy notwithstanding, most authors would argue that there is not one, but many paths to healthy family adjustment and effective functioning. The functional family is seen as having at its disposal a range of skills including *communication skills, problem-solving skills, skills in dealing with anger and negotiating disagreements*. Most families seem to deal with a similar range of problems but, whereas effective families solve their problems, ineffective families do not deal with (at least some of) theirs.

Behavioral, marital, and family therapists utilizing a social learning model have suggested that *conflict resolution skills* are quite critical in a successful marriage. Communication skill level, even defined variously, differentiated between satisfied and dissatisfied couples more strongly than most other types of relationship behavior.[24,25]

The functional family in the McMaster[26] model is seen as having good *problem-solving skills* and effectively addressing problems rapidly and without extensive consideration. The optimal family has clear and direct communication—the more masked and indirect the family communication, the more ineffective family functioning becomes. Through effective *role assignment and fulfillment*, the effective family carries out necessary family functions such as the provision of food, clothing, and shelter; nurturance and support; sexual gratification; life skills development for the children; maintenance and management of the family systems involving leadership, decision-making, etc. Members of a functioning family have the *ability to respond to a range of stimuli* with the appropriate quality and quantity of feelings (affective responsiveness) and show empathic interest in the activities of other family members (affective involvement). Finally, the effective family is seen as *controlling the behavior* (behavior control) of its members in physically dangerous situations (e.g., seeing that a child does not dangerously run out into a road) and in situations involving meeting and expressing psychobiological needs or drives (e.g., eating, sleeping, sex, and aggression) and interpersonal socializing behavior.

Lewis et al.[13] extensively studied a group of white, middle-class families to investigate the differential characteristics of functional and dysfunctional families. The families with *severe dysfunction* often had members with schizophrenia and/or psychopathy. *Mid-range families* had members with reactive psychoses or behavior and/or neuroses disorders or neuroses. *Healthy families* exhibited no evidence of psychiatric disorder and displayed effective functioning. The functional families exhibited an open affiliative attitude to others, a high respect for individuality and autonomy, open clear communication, a firm parental correlation; utilized flexible control by negotiation; showed highly spontaneous interaction with considerable humor and wit, high levels of initiative by family members, and encouragement of uniqueness and difference. In a more recent study, it has been found that healthy low-income families from *different races* have functional characteristics that are *similar*.[27]

From an object relations point of view, a functional or healthy marriage would include: *differentiated partners* with voluntary dependency on each other; spouses who *come to terms with their own irrational expectations of marriage and of their spouse* as derived from experience with their family of origin; *empathic understanding* of the mate; *meeting each other's realistic needs* in the face of differences; clear and open *communication*; *flexibility* in dealing with situational stresses and crises; and a *realistic appraisal of mature and idealized love*.[28]

While the global encompassing systems of the McMaster group, Olson, and Lewis and Beavers are extremely important, it may be that another way to advance the notion of optimal functioning versus dysfunctional family functioning is to explore such functioning in very specific population groups. Research data on families who have members with specific psychiatric diagnoses will be reviewed in later chapters (Chapters 31 and 32).

SUMMARY

The functional family possesses many of the following characteristics:

1. *Accomplishment of basic family tasks:* provision of basic resources such as food, clothing, shelter and money; provision of nurturance and support for the children; sexual gratification of the marital partners; life skills development for the adult as well as the children, including assisting the children in starting and getting through school, assistance in the

adults'pursuits of careers and vocational interests, and each individual's personal development; enculturation of the children; crisis coping; emancipation and postnuclear family adjustment.

2. *The functional handling of systems issues:* the establishment and maintenance of proper system boundaries and sub-boundaries; ego boundary, generation boundary, and family community boundary permeability.

3. *Individuation:* individual members able to separate from family group and function on their own as well as function within the group; individual members progressing in individual personality development according to age norms; respect for and sensitivity of the differences and subjective world of others; individuation of spouses from family of origin with adequate resolution of early developmental tasks.

4. *Communication skills:* this involves day-to-day communication skills, problem solving skills, and conflict of resolution skills.

5. *Family cognition:* image of self and family congruent with reality.

6. *Affectivity:* adequate interpersonal communication and expression of warmth, enjoyment, humor, wit, tenderness, and empathy; consonance between emotional expression and stimuli in the environment.

7. *Effective responsiveness to change:* crisis coping.

8. *Behavior control:* monitor and control of families' behaviors in physically dangerous situations, e.g., child running on the road, meeting and expressing psychobiological needs or drives such as eating and sleeping, sex, aggression, and control and shaping in interpersonal socializing behavior.

SUGGESTIONS FOR FURTHER READINGS

Lewis JM, Beavers WR, Gossett JT, and Phillips VA: **No Single Thread: Psychological Health in Family Systems.** New York: Brunner/Mazel, 1976.

Minuchin S: **Families and Family Therapy.** Cambridge, MA: Harvard University Press.
   This volume includes two transcribed interviews with "normal" functioning families of different cultural and ethnic backgrounds. They give the reader a sense of how an expert family therapist assesses a family, and the variety of normality in a young family.

Walsh F (Ed): **Normal Family Processes.** New York: Guilford Press, 1982.
   The best single collection of papers on the normal family, its functioning and development.

REFERENCES

1. Tolstoy L: Anna Karenina. New York: Bantam, 1960, p 1
2. Family life in America (editorial). N Engl J Med 274:1209, 1966
3. Birdwhistell R: The idealized model of the American family. Social Casework 5:195–198, 1970
4. Levinson DJ: The mid-life transition: A period in adult psychosocial development. Psychiatry 40:99–112, 1977
5. Levinson DJ: Eras: Anatomy of the life cycle. Psychiatric Opinion, September 1978, pp 10–48
6. Levinson DJ, Darrow CN, Kelin EB, Levinson MH, and McKee B: The Season's of a Man's Life. New York: Alfred A. Knopf, 1978
7. Lowenthal MF, Thurnher M, and Chiriboga D: Four Stages of Life: A Comparative Study of Women and Men Facing Transitions. San Francisco: Jossey-Bass, 1975
8. Gould R: The phases of adult life: A study in developmental psychology. Am J Psychiatry 129:33–43, 1977
9. Sheehy G: Passages: Predictable Crises of Adult Life. New York: EP Dutton, 1974
10. Stein SP, Holzman S, Karasu TB, et al.: Mid-adult development and psychopathology. Am J Psychiatry 135:676–681, 1978
11. Duvall E: Family Development. Philadelphia: Lippincott, 1967, pp 44–46
12. Lidz T: The Family and Human Adaptation. New York: International Universities Press, 1963
13. Lewis JM, Beavers WR, and Gossett JT: No Single Thread: Psychological Health in the Family System. New York: Brunner/Mazel, 1976
14. Rapoport R: Normal crises, family structure and mental health. Fam Process 2:68–80, 1963
15. Rapoport R, Rapoport RN: New light on the honeymoon. Human Relations 17:33–56, 1964
16. Berman EM, Lief HI: Marital therapy from a psychiatric perspective: An overview. Am J Psychiatry 132:583–592, 1975.
17. Nadelson CC, Bassuk EL, Hopps CR, and Boutelle WE: Evaluation procedures for conjoint marital therapy. Social Casework 56:91–96, 1975
18. O'Brien P: Marriages That Work. New York: Random House, 1977
19. Wallace P: Complex environments: Effects on brain development. Science 185:1035–1037, 1974
20. Block J: Lives Through Time. Berkeley, CA: Bancroft, 1971 *p.69*
21. Coe WC, Curry AE, and Kessler DR: Family interactions of psychiatric patients. Fam Process 8:119–130, 1969
22. Green R: Sexual identity of 37 children raised by homosexual or transsexual parents. Am J Psychiatry 135:692–697, 1978

23. Silverman J: The women's liberation movement: Its impact on marriage. Hosp Comm Psychiatry 26:39–40, 1975

24. Markman HJ: Application of a behavioral model of marriage in predicting relationship satisfaction of couples planning marriage. J Consult Clin Psychology 47:743–749, 1979

25. Jacobson NS, Waldron H, and Moore D: Toward a behavioral profile of marital distress. J Consult Clin Psychology 48:696-703, 1980

26. Epstein NB, and Bishop DS: Problem-centered systems therapy of the family. In Gurman AS, and Kniskern DP (Eds): Handbook of Family Therapy. New York: Brunner/Mazel, 1981, pp 444–482

27. Lewis JM, and Looney JG: The Long Struggle: Well-Functioning Working Class Black Families. New York: Brunner/Mazel, 1983

28 Framo JL: The integration of marital therapy with sessions with family of origin. In Gurman AS, Kniskern DP (Eds): Handbook of Family Therapy. New York: Brunner/Mazel, 1981, pp 133–158

La Familia by Isabelle Bernal, 1984.

4
Understanding the Functional Family: New Family Forms

OBJECTIVES

- To understand structure and function of the new family forms: (i.e., the separated family, single-parent family, remarried family and dual-career families) as compared to the traditional family form
- To delineate the functional (as compared to dysfunctional) methods of coping of these new family forms

INTRODUCTION

This chapter describes the family system, life cycle, and functional characteristics of new family forms, i.e., alternatives to the traditional marital form. These are the families resulting from frequent shifts in companionship status: (1) cohabitation and serial relationships, (2) marital separation, (3) divorce, (4) remarriage, or (5) living as a single-parent.

The notion that at the age of 20 one will have selected his or her partner for the next 60 years seems a bit unrealistic. Some individuals choose marriage and then never divorce; others marry and then divorce and choose a series of relationships; and others choose never to marry at all, preferring serial relationships. People may need different types of partners at different stages of their lives, and this has sometimes been referred to as the "seven-year switch." The data described in Chapter 2 documents the changing roles of companionate status. These data have been used to forecast the "death" of the family, but they can be seen as indicators of alternatives to the traditional pattern, i.e., *new family forms*.

SERIAL RELATIONSHIPS

When we look at the family life cycle, we note a marked change from the notion of the "couple together *forever*" to a model based on *serial or sequential relationships*. Traditionally, the typical life cycle has included a long courtship and a long-term marriage. This pattern is based on a belief that the best way to self-fulfillment is through marriage. It is still the one that most people strive toward.

The new life cycle is one of sequential relationships. Marriage may or may not be included in this series of relationships. The cycle includes creation and destruction of two or three family units. It is a cycle of courtship, then marriage, then separation, then divorce, and finally remaining single or remarrying. The notion among couples is that there is not one ideal way to do it. It is also based on the assumption that most relationships have a predetermined "half-life," rather than the notion that all relationships have to be forever.

MARITAL SEPARATION[1]

Separation is a relatively common crisis of marital life. Although it is emotionally traumatic for the individuals involved, it can serve as a time for reassessment of the marital contract and of individual goals. Depending on what phase of the marriage is involved, different precipitants will have brought about the separation, and therefore different issues may need to be addressed.

Separation in the early stages of a marriage may be caused by the partners coming down from their infatuation "high," with subsequent disillusionment and eagerness to flee from the task of working things out. For those who got married under the gun of pregnancy, later recriminations or second feelings about the reasons for the marriage may bring about a stormy period.

Some people get married to get away from their parents' home or in desperation about their inability to ever attract anyone else who will be seriously interested in them. When these underlying motives lose their force, the foundation of the marriage may be undermined. Spouses whose children are grown and have left home may not easily become accustomed to living alone together as a marital couple. With the parental role diminished or absent, there may be little emotional or functional viability left in the marriage.

Although it is natural to think of marital separation as an unfortunate event, the tendency to do so must be avoided in order to view it as *symptomatic of the marital-system problems* needing attention. In this sense, separation and its subsequent resolution can be considered as offering the potential for growth and change for the better.

Trial separations can be useful to provide a "cooling-off" period for couples whose difficulties seem insurmountable. It offers them the opportunity to examine more objectively their relationship. At the same time the individuals can test their ability to adapt to living alone. This separation, together with new life experiences of various sorts (which may not have taken place had the couple stayed together) will often enable the husband and wife to change their behavior and feelings toward each other by the time they attempt a reconciliation.

Often enough, however, one spouse may use a separation as an attempt to manipulate the other spouse, or to have that spouse experience defeat and humiliation. In such cases little or no objectivity or growth occurs. An individual may become fixed in an angry or depressive posture, either of which positions, if adhered to rigidly, will prove self-defeating.

About half of those couples that separate go back together; of those couples, about half divorce later on.

We must make a short tangent in order to discuss "separation." A recent study found that there are notable differences between men and women that are precisely the opposite of the traditional stereotypes.[2] For instance, a woman's love appeared to predict better than that of a man's the direction in which the relationship would continue. Either as a prelude or a consequence, women fell out of love more quickly and easily than did men. Usually the partner least involved in the relationship was more likely to initiate the break up. A woman who was more committed but felt less reciprocity in the relationship was the partner who was more likely to break up the relationship. Men less commonly withdrew unilaterally from their relationship when they were over-committed and involved. Overall, women seemed more realistic than men in appraising the future of their relationships. Predictably, the rejected partner was more distressed than the partner who introduced separation, and men were generally more distressed by the ending of their relationship than were women. Even the women who were the more involved partners had greater equanimity after the break up than did men in comparable situations.

DIVORCE

As was indicated in Chapter 2, the divorce rate in most developing countries has been rising, although in the mid-1980s, it shows signs of leveling off. Weiss states that, "*Divorce is an essential adaptation to the conflict between the value we place on commitment to a mate versus the value we place on self-realization.*"[1] If the relationship has been long standing, divorce is one of the most painful experiences in anyone's life. The ambivalence that ex-spouses feel about each other is probably more extreme than that in any other human relationship.

A number of authors[1,3-5] have delineated stage models of the divorce process. In summary, the stages would include the following: a pre-divorce phase involving growing disillusionment and dissatisfaction with the marriage and arrival at some consideration of divorce; the separation and divorce itself involving depression, geographic relocation, and filing for divorce; an immediate post-divorce period, which would include finalizing the divorce, undertaking new activities, and stabilizing new systems patterns; and a remote post-divorce phase in which the divorce is a painful memory.

Usually the rejected party feels enormously wounded and hurt, while the rejector often reacts with guilt. Later reactions may include playing out earlier parental conflicts with both partners with the intent of "getting even." Postmarital fighting is often predicated on realistic issues (such as those of custody and money and on what went wrong in the marriage), and sometimes offers a way of staying in contact with the other spouse. Each spouse tends to develop a version of what went wrong in the marriage. This serves the function of re-establishing their intrapsychic equilibrium, since the social network of marital partners is often disrupted, with one partner usually retaining most of the friends. The process of re-establishing a social and sexual network usually takes from one to three years. Regardless of how bad the marriage was for both spouses, many divorced people find that the transition to living alone is excruciatingly painful.

What about the children of divorce? Contrary to popular belief, most children of divorce do not appear to be permanently damaged. As with any other crisis, divorce can offer a potential for growth. Children in this situation may be forced to cope with separation, issues of self-reliance, and change. Over 80 percent of divorced children live with their mothers and if the father remains involved, empathic, and warm, the adjustment of the children is thought to be better than if the father showed no interest at all.

REMARRIAGE AND THE REMARRIED FAMILY (REM)
with Clifford J. Sager, M.D.

As suggested in Chapter 2, concurrent with the change in divorce rate (nearly one million people get divorced every year) is the increase in the number of people *remarrying* (four out of five divorced people remarry).

The REM family is created by the marriage (or living together in one domicile) of two partners, one or both of whom had been married previously and was divorced or widowed, with or without children who visit or reside with them. The couple and the children (custodial or visiting) comprise the REM family system. The metafamily system is composed of the REM family plus former spouses, grandparents, aunts, uncles, and others who may have significant input to the

REM system. The children are part of each of their bioparents' household systems. Both the REM system and the metafamily system have now become permanent variations of family networks because of the high divorce rate.

Structurally, the membership in a nuclear family usually is well defined and has boundaries with visible demarcation between external and internal; that is, who does or does not belong to them. There is input from significant others, but this input does not usually endanger the system's functioning. For the nuclear family, the expectations, rules, roles, tasks, and purposes are clear, with generational boundaries and sexual taboos defined by society. In contrast, membership in the REM system is open to interpretation: some members may belong in two systems, or feel they do not belong at all in the unit. The system has permeable, (i.e., open) boundaries[6] and input from significant others in the metafamily; not only former spouses, grandparents, and children, but institutions can have a marked impact on the REM family's viability and functioning.

Marital and family therapists are confronted with a set of problems not seen previously.

The old assumption in the psychiatric and sociological literature was that people tended to recreate the same patterns they had in their first marriages. With further study, this assumption appears not to be always true. The reasons for first marriages (true love, getting away from parents) appear to be quite different from the reasons for second marriages. The first marriage is seen as a training school for the second. Following breakups of first marriages, both partners are usually quite "depressed and devastated." New relationships seem to produce a "rebirth." However, there is a complex intermixing of past families and present families. These create problematic situations for spouses, children, and old and new families.[7]

These individuals find that the second marriage is more egalitarian and happier than the first. Remarried people usually marry a different kind of person with a different personality structure. They find that they value friendship and companionship more than they did when they first married. And yet, 59 percent of second marriages, but only 37 percent of first marriages, end in divorce. The meaning of these statistics awaits clarification, but suggests that people look for the "best fit" of personalities. Alternatively, this may represent a "distillation artifact," that is, one keeps distilling out a higher percentage of people who are unhappy and prone to remarry.

THE FUNCTIONAL DUAL SINGLE-PARENT FAMILY

One of the most dramatic social statistics of the decade is the increase in single-parent families (see Chapter 2). They are defined as units in which there is only one parent at home by reason of death, divorce, separation, or births outside of marriage. There is usually another parent around—which is why we use the term "dual." About 10 percent of all families are now one-parent families. About 90 percent of these families are headed by females.

The single-parent family can be viewed as an alternative form of family life. When the role of the absent parent is taken by the remaining parent or by someone else, the homeostatic forces may operate essentially as they do for a two-parent family. With the exception of the marital coalition phases, the family life cycle may be the same as for the two-parent families.

Most of the interesting differences between one-parent and two-parent families exist in the area of family tasks. Many single parents find themselves much closer to their children than they were when the other parent was also present. They consciously compensate for the absent parent. In other cases the single parents may spend less time with the children than they did previously because of a need to work to support the family, and also because they are involved in dating and social activities outside the home.

Being the only parent creates family issues that may include:

1. Social isolation and loneliness of the parent.
2. Possible awkwardness in dating and jealousy from the children.
3. Demand by small children for the continuous physical presence of the one parent.
4. Children fending for themselves and carrying a greater share of the domestic responsibilities because the sole parent is working.
5. Children feeling different from other children because they are a member of a single-parent family.
6. Less opportunity for a parent to discuss pros and cons of decisions and to get support and feedback when decisions are made.
7. Crises and shifts caused by the introduction of a potential new mate or lover or companion, or a combination of these.[8]

Evaluation of the impact of an absent spouse on the rest of the family unit must take into account the phase of family development in which the absence occurred and the total length of the absence, the feelings of the remaining family members about the nonpresent member, and the mechanisms the family has utilized in coping with its different constellation. The remaining spouse may have to be both mother and father to the children. At first all of this may seem overwhelming. After a time, however, the family unit may have reorganized itself and may have reached a new equilibrium, utilizing the potentialities that were not readily apparent earlier. Single-parent families in which the father is the head of the household appear to do just as well as those in which the mother is the main figure. The effectiveness of parenting depends not on the sex-stereotypic role but on the qualities of the specific parent. Despite this reassuring fact, however, one report concludes that it is still preferable to have a two-parent family:

> In those families without one parent, or those who have had a child die, the incidence of childrearing failure increases. A whole family is generally better than part of a family. Identity formations seem more difficult without family role models and opportunities to observe adults of both sexes functioning intimately within a framework of mutual commitment.[9]

Mother-Headed, Dual Single Parent Families

Some of the stresses of mother-headed families include task overload, financial stress, social isolation and loneliness, and a need for "time out." These stresses may be greater for mothers than for fathers, if the mother has custody. They are greater for divorced women than for women who are widowed (in part, because widowhood is more socially accepted).

In such families potential problems for developing children may include defects in cognitive performance, e.g. mathematics. Children growing up in mother-headed families may show deficits in such abilities, especially in cases in which children lost their fathers at an early stage of their development. The effects of such a loss on children may be cumulative and may not appear until they reach grade school. A father with low participation or low warmth in his relationship with the family may be just as detrimental to his child's intellectual growth as one who is totally absent. Therefore, the mere presence of a father is not the important variable; rather, it is the type of participation that a caring father can provide. A warm father (or stepfather) may substitute successfully, as will an achievement-oriented mother.

A second problem area can be in the social and emotional development of the offspring. Recent research seems to indicate, contrary to popular thinking, that in terms of sex-role typing the presence of a father can be more important than the presence of the mother—not only for development of the boys but also for girls.[8] In mother-headed families, boys, but not girls, demonstrated some difficulties in sex-role typing when the separation from the father occurred before the age of five. Other areas of potential risk for the child exist in the development of heterosexual relationships and self-control.

In general, the developmental disruptions that do occur "seem to be attributable mainly to father absence, but also from stresses and lack of support systems that result in changed family functioning for the single mother and her children."[8] When the mother is able to handle her role effectively, such disruptive patterns need not occur.

It is not clear from the above what factor that is absent is causing the developmental disruption. The study by Kellam and associates on the risk of social maladaptation and psychological ill health in children of Chicago black ghetto families suggests that (1) mother-alone families entail the highest risk; (2) the presence of certain second adults has an important ameliorative function—mother-grandmother families being nearly as effective as mother-father families, with mother-stepfather families similar to mother-alone families with regard to risk; and (3) the absence of the father was less crucial than the aloneness of the mother in relation to risk.[10] This study suggests that having another adult to share the tasks and responsibilities of childrearing is helpful to child development.

Father-Headed, Dual Single Parent Families

Father-headed families consist of only about 10 percent of single families, but this statistic is climbing, since more divorced men are demanding the right to have custody of their children. "Close to 900,000 American children under the age of 18 (nearly 50,000 of them preschool age) now live with their male parents and the numbers are going up."[11] With many more men taking over important instrumental roles in parenting, fathers are arguing that they are just as capable and as indispensable to a child's development as are mothers. Usually fathers get custody when mothers prefer to pursue their own careers or other relationships.

Men of father-headed families have problems and concerns that are different from women of mother-headed families. In general, most fathers are much less comfortable in assuming custody of children than are mothers. This is due to the fact that up until the last decade, childrearing and domestic roles have been parceled out to mothers. After the initial period of apprehension, however, fathers seem capable of assuming the nurturing role with equal effectiveness as the mother. They do it in their own style and in their own way, with their own set of values, which may be different from those of the mother. The father needs to develop not only a set of childrearing and domestic skills, but also a method of coping with the mother's feelings about his role—her beliefs about gender and role (the stereotype being, "only women can raise children"). To the extent that both parents can achieve collaboration (although living apart), the adjustment of the children will tend to be positive.

Joint Custody, Single Parent Families

A good and functional arrangement for custody appears to be when both parents can collaborate on decisions involving the children and can spend the necessary time with their children. Although the psychiatric literature shows some bias against joint custody, more couples are electing this route.

There are many ways to set up joint custody, such as, when geographically feasible, to have the children alternate the weeks or the days in which they can visit either parent. Despite the usual objection that such an arrangement will confuse and upset the children, it appears easier for children to adapt to a new life style than it is for adults. The most important issue for the children may be to have ongoing regular contact with each of their parents; this advantage may outweigh the disadvantages of their having two homes.

Women are thought to be more capable of being nurturing figures for their children than are men, and therefore they are usually awarded custody. This belief may have been true in the past and is probably still true in the traditional family setting; but this belief certainly does not pertain to all men and women, nor to family systems and role allocations of contemporary college graduate families. Within these systems there appears to be more flexibility. Women are permitted to be career oriented and men to be relatively more nurturing and "maternal" with children. In fact, Friedman has pointed out that "improvement in the father-child relationship "is a possible outcome in many divorces. Particularly if the children are young, divorce increases the possibility for an intensified parental bonding experience with the father having the opportunity to do direct nurturing."[12] Therefore, in these cases, the factors to be considered when awarding custody should include the personal qualities of each parent, as well as the age, sex, and particular needs of the offspring. Probably more careful evaluation by judges, lawyers, and other professionals would be beneficial.

The family therapist, by virtue of interest and expertise in the family system, brings a new viewpoint to the evaluation and outcome of custody and other childrearing issues. In critically assessing the parents, the family therapist should not be guided by societal biases and prejudices against granting custody to one parent and not the other merely on the basis of sexual preference, especially in the cases in which both parents are involved in childrearing and the family therefore has suitable, adaptable, and workable options. The family therapist brings new and relevant viewpoints and techniques to increase the function and happiness of single-parent families.

DUAL CAREER FAMILIES

As we indicated in Chapter 2, dual career families are markedly increasing. By tradition, such relationships were thought doomed to failure. Not so! Members of such relationships have worked out special rules in order to be functional, such as special emphasis on communication. This issue seems to overshadow many others, and as such, couples in defining roles set up a household-communication system (using a household calendar to inform each other of social commitments and work schedules), set a lower priority for housework, pay special attention to *avoid* bickering over housework and allocation of tasks equally. In addition, such couples set aside time to get away alone (to aid communication and intimacy).

FAMILY VIGNETTES

Harvard and Radcliffe Universities publish annual reports of its graduates 25 years postgraduation. The following four nicely encapsulate some of the concepts like life style, tasks, and systems discussed in the last three chapters.

Case 1

For years I had a dream of a fulltime career, which I tempered with responsibilities to family. I now have full time to devote to my challenging career as a tenured professor. The biggest disappointment since college was my bitter divorce from my college sweetheart. He ran off with my best friend after 14 years of marriage and it was a very low point for me. He was threatened by my desire for a career. He wanted a housewife. I found the women's movement, and went through consciousness-raising, a life-saving experience. I will be eternally sad that my children are from a broken home, but I found a second chance at a marriage. I have a successful and satisfying career, two wonderful daughters, a loving husband and good health. Isn't life wonderful?

—College professor, California

Case 2

After having gone wife-mother-homemaker and getting dragged (kicking and scream-ing) into the fight for legal tender (thanks, Jackson Browne), I am paying more attention to me.

I have zigged and zagged from pinnacle to crisis on an erratic path that has come to seem less strange as time passes. I look around and see some of my friends disabled by dis-ease or injury, or psychologically wounded while fighting the good fight. Divorce, death, bankruptcy, business reverses, alcoholism, diet pills, ennui—they're all the great levelers. I pinch myself, sometimes, and find that I'm still intact in all important ways. There is no single, grandiose disappointment, just a series of broken dreams and unrealistic expec-tations.

—Advertising executive, Arizona

Case 3

Like many of us, I suspect, I work too hard. From the beginning of my career at a big Wall Street firm all the way up to the present at the New York City practice I started with my two present partners 15 years ago, I regret having spent too much time working and not enough enjoying my beautiful wife and two wonderful daughters. I wish that I hadn't found it so consistently necessary to do all the things that kept me away from them.

I'm glad that many lawyers care about the problems of I.B.M. and A.T. & T., but I confess that the presence of a close human relationship is most important to me. As a result, most of my clients are friends with whom I have shared some significant experience. I've incorporated their dreams, sat on their boards, negotiated their deals, sold their stock, created their trusts, and probated their wills. It's been grand, and it's getting better.

It's also been grand watching my wife transform herself from housewife and mother without a clue about the nature of a debenture into a highly sophisticated investment banker. In fact, although neither of us are where we thought we'd be 25 years ago. We're both delighted and immensely grateful for our healthy, beautiful children and our busy but interesting lives together.

—*Attorney, New York*

Case 4

I stand on my 20th Anniversary Report, which I attach. The last five years have been icing on the cake.

Chapter 1: I got married. I went to Harvard Law. I dropped out and (in consequence?) I got disowned.

Chapter 2: I starved. I wrote television commercials. I began to make money and (in consequence?) I got divorced.

Chapter 3: I ran away to Japan. I led a dissolute life. I traveled for years and (in consequence?) I returned broke.

Chapter 4: I met a Japanese woman. I married her. I made more money and (in consequence?) I retired.

Chapter 5: We lived on a mountain top. We had marble bathrooms and horses. We lived the idyll of kings and (in consequence?) I got cancer.

Chapter 6: I was given six months to live. We sold the mountain, canceled the idyll. We cried, we suffered, we prayed and (in consequence?) we did not die.

Epilogue: (The writer) is happier, healthier and just a little bit wiser than he has any right to be.

—*Retired advertising executive, Texas*

We further discuss "new family forms" in Chapter 19. Our focus there is on dysfunction and its treatment, in contrast to a focus on function here.

SUGGESTIONS FOR FURTHER READINGS

Sager CJ, Walker E, Brown HS, et al: Improving functioning of the remarried family system. Journal of Marital and Family Therapy, 1981 pp 313.

Sager CJ, Brown HS, Crohn H, et al: **Treating the Remarried Family.** Brunner/Mazel, New York, 1983.

Gurman A, Kniskern D (Eds): **Handbook of Family Therapy.** New York: Brunner/Mazel, 1981.
  Each of the authors in this edited volume describe their theory of family functioning and dysfunction.

Wallerstein JS, Kelly JB: **Surviving the Breakup.** New York: Basic Books, 1980.
  Based on data from a longitudinal study, this is an excellently written description of parents and children who have lived through a divorce.

REFERENCES

1. Weiss RS: Marital Separation. New York: Basic Books, 1975
2. McDonald MC: On the matter of love. Psychiatric News, April 15, 1977, pp 41-42
3. Bohannan P: The six stations of divorce. In Laswell ME and Lasswell TE (Eds): Love, Marriage and Family: A Developmental Approach. Illinois: Scott, Foresman & Co, 1973
4. Kessler S: The American Way of Divorce: Prescription for Change. Chicago: Nelson-Hall, 1975
5. Salts CJ: Divorce process: Integration of theory. J Divorce 2:233-240, 1979
6. Messinger L: Remarriage between divorced people with children from previous marriages: A proposal for preparation for remarriage. J Marr Fam Counsel 2:193-200, 1976
7. Westoff L: Two-time winners. New York Times, Magazine Section, August 10, 1975, p 10
8. Hetherington EM, Cox M, and Cox R: The development of children in mother-headed families, in Reiss D and Hoffman HA (eds): The American Family: Dying or Developing. New York: Plenum Press, 1979, pp 117-156
9. Lewis JM, Beavers WR, and Gossett JT: No Single Thread: Psychological Health in the Family System. New York: Brunner/Mazel, 1976
10. Kellam SG, Ensminger ME, and Turner RJ: Family structure and mental health of children. Arch Gen Psychiatry 34:1012-1022, 1977
11. Molinoff DD: Life with father. New York Times, Magazine Section, May 22, 1977, pp 12-17
12. Friedman HJ: The father's parenting experience in divorce. Am J Psychiatry 137:1177-1182, 1980
13. Ideas and Trends: The Class of '61 Offers Some Dissertation on Itself. The New York Sunday Times, July 13, 1986

The Interrupted Marriage by Rigaud Benoit, 1972. Courtesy of Selden Rodman, from *The Miracle of Haitian Art* by Selden Rodman.

5

Understanding the Dysfunctional Family

OBJECTIVES

- To understand the components of dysfunction in the family system, family life cycle, family tasks, and family myths
- To understand the theories of how one individual member becomes the identified patient
- To understand theories of the development of family dysfunction

INTRODUCTION

The preceding chapters describe the organization and behavior of the functional family discussing the concept of the family as a system with its own life cycle, as well as the relation of family tasks to functional family units. In this chapter (and again in Chapters 17, 18, and 19, with special emphasis on dysfunction and what to do about it), we focus on the disturbances in these same areas and the ways in which families become dysfunctional. We discuss the family life cycle, the inability of the family to accomplish family tasks, dysfunctional family myths, types of disturbances manifested by the dysfunctional family systems, and the particular family member manifesting those disturbances.

THE DYSFUNCTIONAL FAMILY SYSTEM

How do problems become problems? What leads to symptoms? Who begins to realize that a problem is bad enough to need outside intervention? These are issues that intrigue family theorists (and individual theorists before them) and will plague the family therapist as he or she goes into the assessment of the family (Section III).

It is interesting to note (briefly) Freud's explanation of the development of symptomatology so that one can contrast it with that of more recent family theory. Freud focused on data obtained from the verbalizations of patients about their internal thoughts, feelings, and experiences. He saw psychopathology as relating to internalized conflict, conflict between wishes and desires, and the control mechanisms within the psyche. The emphasis was on the individual patient and the focus was on internal experience, which was thought to have its roots in the early history of the individual. Current biochemical views of psychiatric illness, which in some ways Freud anticipated, also focus on the individual, but instead of the mind, they examine the individual's neurological synapses and neurotransmitters in order to relate psychobiological changes to changes in mood and thinking.

Many, but not all, family theorists eschew the medical model, with its emphasis on etiology and a "linear" view of causality of illness (that is, bacteria "x" gives disease "y" and is treated with drug "z"). Instead, there is an emphasis on a *circular causality*[1] in which symptomatology is thought of as arising (just as all communications and behaviors) from many circular feedback loops within the family. It is argued that with living systems, one cannot assign one part of the system as having a causal influence on another part. As pointed out by Wynne and colleagues,[2] there is no empirical evidence to support an exclusive attention upon circular causality. It seems quite likely to us that circular feedback loops in family interaction are an important factor in the etiology, maintenance, and exacerbation of symptomatology. However, there is strong evidence to suggest that other causes (such as biochemical ones) are also often active in at least some types of symptomatology, e.g., like dopamine metabolic dysfunction in schizophrenia. The ultimate answers lie in future research.

SYMPTOMS FROM A SYSTEMS PERSPECTIVE

Freud's microscope was focused on the individual and the individual's inner life. We need also to move the lens back and look at the same phenomena from an interpersonal and systems perspective. We will not go into the history of the family systems view of symptoms—as that has been done elsewhere[1]—but simply note a few crucial steps along the way. One of the early interactional concepts about symptomatology was Bateson's 1956 paper,[3] "Toward a Theory of Schizophrenia," in which the double-bind concept was enunciated. The term *double bind* described a communication impasse between individuals in a relationship system, which hypothetically gave rise to responses in one individual that were called "schizophrenic." These authors presented the double-bind concept as a communicational theory of the origin and nature of schizophrenia. The necessary ingredients for a double bind in a situation between two people were: (1) two or more persons, (2) repeated intense experience between these two people, (3) the giving of a primary negative injunction in the form of, "If you do this, I will punish you," (4) a primary injunction followed by a secondary injunction conflicting with the first at a more abstract level, (5) a third negative injunction prohibiting the victim from escaping from the impossible situation. The authors suggested that this interaction occurs not only between the pre-schizophrenic and his mother, but also in normal relationships. In such situations, people respond defensively in a manner similar to the schizophrenic, and confuse literal and metaphoric communication.

In furthering the ideas of the Bateson group, of which he was a member, Haley[4] described a *control theory* of schizophrenic interaction by making an analogy between the governor in a mechanism that controls the range of movements within it, to an individual who acts to control the range of others' behavior in the family. Since the double-bind situation in effect disqualifies meanings of the communications and thus controls someone else, people put in such a situation would become as adults very sensitive to having their behavior controlled by others.

Bowen[5] was one of the first of a number of family theorists who emphasized a triadic or triangular interaction in the causality of pathology. According to Bowen, when confronted with stress, a two-person emotional system brings in a third person or thing, and thus, "*triangulates.*" Tension between the original twosome caused by the stress is thus shifted to a third person or thing. While it is hypothesized that all families function in triangulated fashion, pathology is associated with those families in which there is a rigidity about such triangles under change or stress. This triangulation may spread to the entire family and even peripheral family members and outsiders as the emotional contagion grows.

The R. family consisted of a father in his late forties, a mother in her early forties, and a son, Sam, in his early twenties. Sam was the identified patient. The parents, although seemingly close, had given up sexual relations and attending social functions together. Sam had dropped out of school and was staying in the house, playing his guitar and watching television. The mother was perfunctory in her housework, eventually intending to clean up her closet and to study gardening. The father managed his work as a salesman by routinely following the same pattern he had for many years and was barely eking out a living. The family never seemed to disagree with one another on anything. Individual members seemed unable to allocate separate time for themselves but always did everything "together." They were afraid to deal with differentness. There was a pervading sense of emptiness: the mother spent much of her time in bed, the father complained of not getting satisfaction from his work or his family, and the son felt hopeless.

Later, Haley's thinking about pathology shifted from the communication level to the structural level of the family.[6] Here, Haley emphasized the function of deviant behavior or symptomatic behavior when other members of the family are in conflict. From this point of view, the first hypothesis is that the deviant or symptomatic member is *needed* by the family in order to help keep the family in some form of balance, even in one spouse's fantasy world. Thus, unhappiness, and then, of course, pathology such as acting out, depression, etc., is thought to result because a desired and needed relationship in the inner world of one spouse is not fulfilled by the spouse. Individual human beings with their needs and fantasies constitute the theoretical background, but the focus of perception and treatment is the system of interacting personalities (which leads to the collusion).

THE SOLUTION AS THE PROBLEM

All families are faced with "problems," that is, situations that most observers would say cause consternation, assessment, and some action on the part of the individuals involved. It is plausible to think that the family as a task group would bring out their characteristic ways of acting when confronted with what they consider to be a problem. This may or may not be true. At any rate, many family theoriticians have noted that when faced with what they consider a problem, some families proceed to act and develop patterns of behavior around the original "problem" in such a way as to compound emotional upset and behavioral excesses, sometimes involving psychiatric symptoms. Watzlawick, Weakland, and Fisch[7] refer to this as *"more of the same,"* or *"when the solution becomes the problem."* According to these authors, this mishandling occurs when (1) a solution is attempted by denying that a problem is a problem and nothing is done, (2) change is attempted for something that is unchangeable or nonexistant, (3) or action is taken at the wrong level of the problem.

The original "problem" that creates the nexus for the ill-conceived family problem-solving efforts could be one of a multitude of things. They may include things that others would not even consider a problem, e.g., a minor cold in a child who is then told to stay home from school and becomes school phobic. It may include a normal life stress that is perceived as a crisis. Hill[8] has speculated on what disposes families to relate to normal life stage events as crises. The problem may be a serious and real one, such as dealing with cancer in a family member. It may be helping a seven-year-old son who has learning disabilities to study. Or for that matter, quite relevant to the mental health professional, it could be how the family copes with a mental illness in one member that has biological and genetic components, such as Major Affective Illness and Schizophrenia. Leff and Vaughn[9] have described in human terms the effective ways families cope with a schizophrenic family member. The families who cope well with this most serious mental disorder in a loved one seemed to be most characterized by a mature sense of flexibility. They respond to the patients' demands for either greater closeness and support or distance. They recognize the legitimacy of the illness, and adjust expectations accordingly. They have an emotional equilibrium that allows them to take the illness seriously, but can also be dispassionate and even humorous about it at times.

For now, the family therapist's task is to make their best judgment of the relative weight of the family variables on development of dysfunction.

THE LIFE CYCLE OF THE DYSFUNCTIONAL FAMILY

Although some families will be plagued by minor generalized problems throughout their existence, others will have trouble at specific periods. Most episodic family difficulties may be related to (1) an inability to cope adequately with either the tasks of the current family phase, or (2) the need to move on to a new family phase or (3) the stress of traumatic, excessive, and out-of-order events in the family developmental cycle, or (4) all three problems.

The stress and difficulties may be those attendant on the normal, expectable family life crises. The marriage or family may be unable to cope adequately with the current phase in its life cycle and any particular phase of the family cycle may be affected, depending on a variety of factors relating to the adequacy and availability of the family members' resources for accomplishing the tasks inherent in their current stage.

For example, as indicated in Chapter 3, two people optimally need to have reached a certain stage in their own personal development, as well as in their relationships with their family of origin, before being ready as two independent individuals to consider marriage. To the extent that this and other prior stages have not been successfully mastered, the individuals and the marital unit will be hampered in dealing with current challenges. This concept applies to each of the family phases.

Everyone is familiar with the young married couple who find it difficult to break away from their own families to establish a successful independent unit.

On their wedding night, Mr. and Mrs. W. found that they were unable to have intercourse because of Mrs. W.'s nausea and vomiting. Mr. W. became so depressed that the couple had to return from the honeymoon after one night. Soon after this, both husband and wife found themselves spending so much time with their own parents after work that they had very little time for each other, and "sex just never seemed to get off the ground." Each partner developed a feeling of anger and resentment toward the other and their communication became markedly decreased. At the same time, their social life became more restricted and they were unable to plan any events together. They came to therapy at the point where they were considering divorce.

A couple may feel compelled to get married because the woman has become pregnant ("the shotgun marriage"). The two people become instant marital partners and parents, perhaps involuntarily. In this situation, various developmental phases are skipped altogether or are drastically condensed.

Mrs. V., age 18, came for treatment following a suicide attempt. She had married a boy, age 19, whom she had known for four months, after discovering that she was pregnant. Although she did not really care for him, she married in order not to disgrace the family. Week nights were spent with her mother, who prepared supper for the couple. On weekends Mrs.V. went shopping with her mother while Mr. V. played ball with his friends. He preferred not to waste time around the house since his in-laws also lived there, and since he had never gotten to know (or like) his new father-in-law. Soon after the wedding, sexual relations ceased and screaming fights eventually culminated in Mrs.V.'s suicide attempt.

Families may find it extremely stressful to move into the next appropriate phase of marital development. Families may have chronic difficulty attempting to deal with the requirements of a particular phase; they may appear to cope quite successfully until a threatened transition plunges them into distress and dysfunction. Change is difficult, and modifying or abandoning old familiar roles and patterns of interaction and taking on strange new ways is not easy. The "empty-nest syndrome" refers to one such difficult phase.

The J. family had four teenage children; the youngest was 16 and the oldest 20. All of the children lived with their parents and were forbidden to date. On the occasions when the family did go out, they went together to "noncontroversial" movies. The family was referred by the juvenile court for treatment after the oldest child had run away several times. Inquiry revealed that both parents, although insisting that they wanted their children to grow up and be on their own, were quite frightened about the prospect of being together in the house without the children. They thought that they had probably lost interest in each other, having focused their relationship on taking care of the children.

Unusual or unexpected events in the family life cycle may overwhelm the coping capacities of family systems to handle developmental changes. Common examples of such events are those of separation, illness, accident, violent crime, or death in the family.

The Q. family consisted of the father, an engineer, the mother, a housewife, and an infant daughter, age 3. The father suddenly was sent to work in Alaska, 3000 miles from home. The mother felt lost and abandoned. She found great difficulty in taking care of the house and her daughter. The daughter was the identified patient, referred by the pediatrician because she was setting fires. It became clear that the mother was so depressed that she would go to bed early, leaving the daughter to play by herself for a couple of hours. During this time, the daughter managed to climb up to the stove and ignite a piece of paper. The father was brought home to be with his family. The fire setting stopped as mother found new meaning to her life as a woman, mother, and as a spouse.

TASK PERFORMANCE IN THE DYSFUNCTIONAL FAMILY

Various deficiences in carrying out the family's functions will lead to strains and distortions in family life. The major family tasks, as discussed earlier, are:

1. To provide for the basic physical requirements.
2. To develop a working marital coalition.
3. To rear the offspring.

In the dysfunctional family, these tasks are either not handled, or handled differently, and less adaptively, than in healthy families. In Chapter 3 some of these processes and outcomes are detailed for both the functional and dysfunctional family.

In pathological families, various difficulties in these areas of task performance may be noted. Members of dysfunctional families may show particularly intrusive, projective, tangential, concrete, or bizarre thinking. There may be considerable ambiguity and vagueness, with a prevailing feeling of meaninglessness. Some investigators have noted these difficulties, especially in families of schizophrenic patients (see Chapter 22). In some families the children's emotions may be distorted because the children are consistently denied, contradicted, ignored, or punished. For example, in some families sadness or disappointment cannot be expressed by the child because it "upsets" the parents.

In raising children, we believe that an important issue is the "goodness of fit" between child and parents. The difference between functional and dysfunctional childrearing may, in part, result from the fit among (1) parental temperment, (2) child temperment, and (3) their interaction.[10] This view has important implications in working out, and implementing, a strategy for changing a "poorness of fit" to a "goodness of fit" (of temperment).   On the other hand, the question may be asked, does having problems as a child doom an "identified patient-child" to adult difficulties? The answer is "no"—there is a discontinuity between childhood and adult psychopathology.[11] In fact, the most important predictors of adult maladjustment are not diagnosis or psychopathology, but rather, the degree of impairment of childhood social adjustment (higher is worse), IQ, and parental socioeconomic status (lower is worse). "Acting out" type of symptoms, as an early developmental difficulty, is also associated with poor outcomes.

Development of Family Dysfunction

Marital and family systems, like individuals, have characteristic patterns of coping with stress. The family's first line of defense is usually to evoke, strengthen, and emphasize characteristic adaptive patterns that the family unit has used in the past. If these are inappropriate or maladaptive, the type of disturbance resulting therefrom may be similar to the rigid inflexible character of an individual with a personality disorder.

If such characteristic adaptive mechanisms are not available or fail to deal adequately with the situation, however, one or another family member may develop overt symptoms. These symptoms in the family member may cause the individual to be labeled "bad," or "sick." The appropriate social helping institutions may become involved with that individual in an attempt to deal with the particular symptomatic expression. The individual then takes on the role of the "identified patient." More often than not, the family context from which the individual's symptoms emanate will be overlooked entirely, deemphasized, or inadequately attended to. The "bad," "sick," "stupid," or "crazy" individual family member will be treated and either will be found intractable or "improved." If "improved," he will soon become symptomatic again when returned to the family context or may cause another family member to become symptomatic. The underlying family disturbance will have to be dealt with.

A major tenet of family therapists, therefore, is that the symptomatic family member is often thought of as being indicative of widespread disturbance in the entire family system.[3,12-15] For a therapist to overlook or deal inadequately with the more general family disturbance would cause at least one family member to continue to be symptomatic.

In the X. family, Mr. and Mrs. X. found that over the course of 12 years of marriage their sexual relationship had become more and more unsatisfactory. They contemplated divorce. At about the same time, their son began to do poorly in school and they sought help for this problem. Concurrently, they felt less concerned about the unsatisfactory nature of the marriage. As the boy's school work improved, the marital problem returned to the fore.

Dr. B. brought Mrs. B. for help because she had "headaches again." Her headaches always followed problems he had with his patients. Dr. B. was a hardworking but rigid person who firmly believed in male superiority. Things had gone well for them in the early years of their marriage until Mrs. B. became dissatisfied with the role of "number two" in the marriage and pressed for equality. At that point Dr. B. intensified the authoritarian approach and rather than fighting back, Mrs. B. became depressed.

The patterns of interaction within a family cannot always be clearly related to any specific dysfunction. The reasons why a specific type of disturbance is manifested in a family system or family member are not understood clearly at the present time, but certain innate tendencies and life circumstances probably favor the development of one or another symptomatic expression in a particular instance.

Similarly, the reasons why one family member rather than another becomes symptomatic have not been definitively settled. A number of reasons, however, have been described to account for this phenomenon. They are as follows:

1. *Individual susceptibility, that is, genetic predisposition.* For example, an individual who was born brain damaged and is under family stress is likely to become symptomatic. Genetic temperamental differences may contribute.[10] Chess and associates,[16] who have studied activity levels of infants, have suggested that the more phlegmatic babies have a greater tendency toward developing schizophrenia, whereas active, awake, exploring babies have a greater tendency to become delinquent.
2. *The situation in the family at the time of birth.* For example, a parent whose own parent died around the time of the birth of a child might use the newborn infant to work out his feelings about his own dead parent.
3. *Physical illness of the child.* A child who is chronically ill may have family problems projected on him whenever he has an acute episode.
4. *Precipitant in the external family.* Accidents or a death that relates somehow to one child more than another (an eldest daughter who was with her grandmother the day the grandmother had a heart attack) may make one family member the focus for family problems.
5. *Sex of a child may correspond to a particular difficulty of the parent.* For example, if a father feels particularly inadequate with other males, his son may become symptomatic.
6. *Birth order of siblings.* The eldest child may get the major "parental loading," whereas the youngest child is often "babied" and kept dependent.
7. *Family myth attached to a specific individual.* Certain people in families are known as the "stupid" one, the "smart" one, the "lazy" one, the "good-looking" one, the "ugly" one. First names of children and nicknames may reveal these myths. Children are sometimes named after godparents or other people significant in the parents' past and, in turn, carry along a myth attached to that person. Girls are sometimes given names of somewhat ambiguous gender: for example, Lee, Dale, Marion, Frances, Glenette, Alberta, Carol, as though to indicate parental displeasure at

having a girl. This is also true for males. Sometimes assigned names are grossly inappropriate for the gender of the child.

It has been suggested that:

In less than optimal families, the mother is the first to suffer from the system's inadequacy. She is most often the first to become dissatisfied, distressed, or symptomatic. At increased levels of family system dysfunctioning, a child may also begin to experience distress and become symptomatic. Frequently, he will then become an identified patient. The father, with more in the way of outside sources of esteem, is often the last family member to become symptomatic.[17]

The symptomatic family member may be the family scapegoat and may have family difficulties displaced on him or her or may be psychologically or constitutionally the weakest, the youngest, or the most sensitive family member, unable to cope with the generalized family disturbance. The identified patient may be the family member most interested or involved in the the process of changing the family. For example, there are teenagers who want to "save" their parents because they are not getting along with each other. One hypothesis about family functioning is that these children may begin to steal in order to get caught, so that the entire family can be referred for help.

Robinson[18] has summarized the literature on the family theory of the development of family dysfunction:

Family theory views symptoms as connected with the conflict located at the transactional interface between the natural developmental strivings of an emerging individual and the distorted relational objectives of the dysfunctional family system. A dysfunctional family is one whose organizational peculiarities cause it to mismanage those aspects of family interaction associated with individuation, distance, and closeness in such a way that the social maturation of family members is impaired or arrested. This impairment is caused by . . . forces that seek to maintain the parent-child relational axis as the principal determinant of family organization. Symptoms are an expression of the conflict between the inherent strivings of the individual to establish himself as an adequate member of his own generation and the opposing pressures generated by a dysfunctional family motivated to maintain the status quo. For example, if the marital relationship is underdeveloped as the center of parental need satisfaction, the chances that the parent-child relationship will become overdeveloped are increased. In such families the child is inclined to develop a preoccupation with his role and the problems of his parents. He may be emotionally trapped by the dynamics of the family whether he accepts or rejects the roles designated for him by the family system. Acceptance . . .means that the child attempting to leave the family is inadequately prepared for separation and faces a concealed but active opposition. He is therefore likely to experience high levels of anxiety and guilt and to collapse in his efforts toward independent living. Rejection of the roles and values of the dysfunctional family may result in a premature breaking away from the protective functions of the family and the child being forced to sustain himself in the outside world. The parents in these families are therefore participants in the conflicts underlying individual symptom formation because they suppress individuation and separation in order to protect the family's triangular bigenerational base.

FAMILY MYTHS

Individuals and families have systems of belief that determine their feelings and behavior. These attitudes, largely unexpressed directly, run below the surface of the family's interactions and help to shape its general outline and specific features. These subterranean structures have been referred to as "family myths." They are often found to be important roots of family difficulty, and family therapists must be aware of them if they are to understand family behavior that might otherwise seem inexplicable.

Ferreira defines family myths as "a series of fairly well integrated beliefs shared by all family members, concerning each other and their mutual position in the family, which go unchallenged by everyone involved, in spite of the reality distortions which they may conspicuously imply."[19] The implications of Ferreira's definition involve very personalized and specific myths for each family in which individual family members are singled out for particular slots, roles, or self-fulfilling prophecies, such as "mother is the emotional one in the family" or "our son misbehaves continually."

Although we discuss these types of specific family myths in various parts of this book, at this point, however, we turn instead to generalized myths having to do with a family's overall view of itself as a system with its own "philosophy" of life. In discussing some of the important and frequent myths that seem to cause difficulty, we include those that seem most prominent in the experience of family therapists. Not everyone will agree with the value judgments about the myths that are expressed here. Each therapist must work out his or her own values with respect to these issues. The therapist must be sensitive to, and deal appropriately with, those attitudes and beliefs that seem to be deleterious to a family's functioning and, conversely, must understand that some myths aid functioning.

If life has not worked out well for you as an individual, getting married will make everything better.   No matter how unfortunate one's life experience has been in terms of relationships with parents, peers, career choice; or how satisfactorily one is living alone; or how dissatisfied one is with one's genetic endowment, social and economic situations—getting married will make things much better.

This myth is often shared not only by the individual who had the myth but, more surprisingly, by the spouse. If the marriage does last, each spouse bears the resentment that the other feels for not making it a happy one and for not overcoming all the obstacles that existed prior to the marriage. What happens is that many of these same problems get played out between spouses.

Marital and family life should be totally happy, and each individual therein should expect either all or most gratifications to come from the family system.
This romantic myth dies hard in some quarters. Many of life's satisfactions are found outside the family setting. There is a whole range of gratifications that families need to work out to fit their own particular components.
The "togetherness" myth. To what extent will merely remaining in close proximity or jointly carrying out all activities lead to satisfactory family life and individual gratification? Again, there will probably be great variation from one family to another, but surely this cannot be an ideal pattern for all families under all conditions. One should be able to be separate and autonomous; otherwise any relationship will be potentially distorted.

Marital partners should be totally honest with one another at all times. In its modern guise, this idea may be derived from experience with "encounter groups" in which people are encouraged to express their feelings freely (especially negative ones, it seems) and also from the concept that what is suppressed will of necessity damage us eventually. In fact, full and open frankness in feeling, action, and thought may cause at least as much harm as good. Also, "honesty" can be enlisted in the service of hostility or it can be a constructive, problem-solving approach. Many people feel that a degree of interpersonal sensitivity will often mitigate this concept of "total honesty" and that many hurtful statements, especially regarding factors that cannot be changed, are perhaps best left unspoken.

A happy marriage is one in which there are no disagreements, and when family members fight with one another it means that they hate each other. It seems inevitable that family members will have differences with one another and that these will often lead to overt disagreements. These arguments, in turn, may lead to "fights" or arguments. If they are dealt with constructively, clarification and resolution can be found without anyone suffering loss of self-esteem. Many families, however, seem afraid to disagree and therefore cover up differences by pseudoagreement. On the other hand, there are families that fight all the time about almost every issue, but seemingly are unable to resolve any disagreements; instead, they seem to resort to personal attacks on each other's motives and veracity.

The marital partners should see eye-to-eye on every issue and should work toward being as identical in outlook as possible. The first part of this statement is just about impossible to achieve, and the second part is of questionable benefit. Open recognition of the inevitable differences may be helpful and constructive. Many married couples seem either unwilling to accept or incapable of recognizing their inevitable differences with respect to past experience, basic attitudes, and personality styles. Instead, there often seems to be a marked projection of one's personality attributes, both positive and negative, onto the partner with relatively little ability to see the partner realistically.

Marital partners should be as unselfish as possible and give up thinking about their own individual needs. Most successful marriages seem able to reconcile the needs of the separate individuals with those of the needs of the family unit. Some individuals, however, unsuccessfully pretend that they do not have personal needs and satisfactions, but are rather merely satellites or undifferentiated masses attached to the larger family system. For example, a mother may live only for the sake of the family. Successful family units recognize the differential allocations and satisfactions to be derived from one's role as an individual human being, as a marital partner, and as a parent.

When something goes wrong in the family, one should look around to see who is at fault. At times of stress, many people react almost reflexively by blaming themselves or others. This is often not a useful response; instead, it may be more productive for them to look toward other frames of reference. When things go wrong in nongratifying family interactions, it may be in relation to the interactional properties of the entire system, which can be examined with a problemsolving approach in a relatively nonpersonalized, nonblaming manner. Each family member can be encouraged to assess his or her own role in the situation and in the solving of the problem. When two pieces of a jigsaw puzzle do not seem to fit well together, which of the two pieces is to blame?

When things are not going well, it will often be of help to spend a major part of the time digging up past as well as present hurts. Arguments that involve endless recriminations about past disappointments and difficulties may serve to give temporary relief by allowing the parties to air their resentments. This can often lead to futile escalation of the argument with a sort of "Can you top this?"discussion. Besides usually making things worse rather than better, this detracts from any constructive attempts at problem-solving. Often one of the first jobs of the family therapist is to act as a kind of "traffic cop" in stopping these nonproductive family maneuvers. Nothing can be done to change what has happened in the past. "Crying over spilt milk" rarely, by itself, does much good unless it leads to increased understanding and modification of present patterns.

In a marital argument one partner is right and the other is wrong, and the goal of such fights should be for the partners to see who can score the most "points."

Obviously this is not the case. When one marital partner wins a fight, it is usually the marriage as a whole that loses. Competitiveness in the marital relationship is not usually preferable to a cooperative working together in which neither marital partner necessarily scores points, but in which the outcome is such that the individuals and the marriage itself stand to gain.

A good sexual relationship will inevitably lead to a good marriage. Everyone has seen examples of individuals who married when they were physically infatuated with one another, but who woke up after the honeymoon to discover that in respects other than physical, they were relatively poorly suited to one another. A good sexual relationship is an important component of a satisfactory marriage, but does not necessarily preclude the presence of difficulties in other areas.

If the marriage is satisfactory in other respects, sex will more or less take care of itself. The sexual relationship in a marriage may need specific attention. It cannot automatically be taken for granted that a good marriage and good sex go together. Difficulties in the sexual sphere do seem to lead to difficulties in the rest of the marital relationship. Specific sex therapy for the couple may be indicated, following which other basically secondary difficulties may diminish.

Marital partners increasingly understand each other's verbal and nonverbal communications, so there is little or no need to check things with one another. This may certainly be the case in functional, nonproblem families, but it is often strikingly untrue for families in trouble. Marital partners and other family members may assume that what they have said or done was clearly understood. They may also believe that they are able to read someone else's mind or know what someone else really means. When they are encouraged in therapy to specifically check some of these assumptions with one another, they are often shocked at their own misperceptions and misinterpretations.

Positive feedback is not as necessary in marital systems as is negative feedback. Many marital couples have gotten out of the habit of reflecting back to their partner when he or she has done something pleasing. However, there is often less hesitancy in commenting on something that has caused hurt or disappointment. Positive reinforcement of desired behavior usually serves to increase its occurrence and is usually a much more effective behavior-shaping technique than is negative feedback or punishment.

"And then they lived happily ever after." A good marriage should just happen spontaneously and should not need to involve any work on the part of the participants. This is perhaps another carry-over of the romantic idea of marriage as some type of blissful, dream-like state. The sad but realistic truth, however, is that

marriage involves day-to-day and minute-by-minute interaction of the people involved, as well as constant negotiation, communication, and solving of problems. Members of dysfunctional families may spend only a few minutes a week talking with one another about anything meaningful.

Any spouse can (and should) be reformed and remodeled into the shape desired by the partner. In many marriages an inordinate amount of time and energy is spent in the often mutual effort to mold the spouse to a desired image. This is commonly done with little or no recognition of the fact that basic personality patterns, once established, are not easily modified. Attempts to do so lead mainly to frustration, anger, and disillusionment, although certain characteristics may be moderated or even rechanneled, and partners can be made to be more sensitive to each other's reactions. But even though the "reform movement" marriage may work out satisfactorily as long as both partners consent to play the requisite roles involved, it may still lead to futile arguments about personal qualities and lack of cooperation. Therefore, it would be better for a spouse to look inward in order to assess which personal characteristics should be modified to best profit the marriage.

A stable marriage is one in which things do not change and in which there are no problems. To be alive is to face continual change. Those systems that attempt to remain fixed in some unchanging mold will sooner or later come to be out of phase with current needs. Systems do have a tendency toward a dynamic equilibrium in which certain patterns and interactions repeat themselves, giving a sense of continuity and stability. At the same time the entire system is moving inevitably onward.

Everyone knows what a husband should be like and what a wife should be like. This statement may have been truer in the past than it is now. There is increasingly less agreement on this subject, with a constant flood of conflicting messages. The lack of a preconceived or defined notion of marital roles presents a possibility of greater confusion, but it also offers an opportunity for much greater development of each partner's and the marriage's actual potential.

If a marriage is not working properly, having children will rescue it. Although the arrival of children may often temporarily make the spouses feel somewhat more worthwhile and give them a new role (that of being parents), children are not the cement that will hold poor marriages together. What often happens instead is that children become the victims of marital disharmony.

No matter how bad the marriage, it should be kept together for the sake of the children. It is not necessarily true that children thrive better in an unhappy marriage than they do living with a relatively satisfied divorced parent. If the marriage partners stay together, the children may bear the brunt of the resentment that the partners feel for one another, with the parents feeling they have martyred themselves for their children's sake.

If the marriage does not work, an extramarital affair or a new marriage will cure the situation. Although on certain occasions this is true, what may often happen is that the new partner is uncannily similar to the rejected one, and the same non-gratifying patterns begin all over again; only the names of the players have been changed.

Separation and divorce represent a failure of the marriage and of the individuals involved. This almost always has been the traditional view of marital partners, family members, friends, and professional counselors. Individuals in a marital union, however, may grow apart or be poorly matched at the outset. At different phases of one's family life cycle, different partners may be desirable. Separation or divorce (or both) may represent a creative and positive step rather than a failure for the family members.

A dysfunctional family seldom has the internal resources to change due to the unwritten rules by which it operates. If it were to have these resources, then it could change and the family would therefore not be dysfunctional. A member of the family may ask for external help for himself or another family member or may try to harm himself or someone or something and thus come to the attention of an external agency. To take the "identified patient" at face value and to deal only with that person, without seeing the rest of the family, would represent a very distorted and limited perspective of the dysfunction inherent in the family.

GENERAL SCHEMES OF FAMILY PATHOLOGY

In a general scheme of family adjustment proceeding from optimal and adequate families, to *mid-range* borderline, and *severely disturbed* families (see Table 5-1), the Lewis et al.[17] study that we referred to in Chapter 3 indicates the qualities and interactional aspects of these pathological families. *Mid-range families* who often have offspring with neurotic and behavior disorders have relatively clear communication. However, they exhibit constant effort at control. Living means controlling. There is much distancing with affect such as anger, anxiety, and depression, and ambivalence is handled by depression. In *borderline families*, which often have severe obsessive offspring or borderline offspring, there is shifting from chaotic to tyrannical control efforts. Boundaries fluctuate from poor to rigid. These families experience distancing, and affect is often that of depression

Table 5-1
Family Qualities Important in the Development of Healthy Individuals*
(Derived from Studies of White, Urban, Intact Middle-Class Families)

	Severely Disturbed Families	Adequate (Mid-range) Families	Healthy Families
1. Power Structure	Chaotic	Rigid	Flexible: shared power, with benign and generous leaders; clear, flexible family rule system
A. *Parental Coalition*	Absent: father has little power	Weak: one member dominant	String: father as leader; high degree of marital complementarity
B. *Generation Boundaries*	Broken: frequent overt mother-son coalition	Blurred: occasional covert parent-child coalition	Intact: children share in decisions
Affiliative vs. *Oppositional Style*	Behave as if encounters will be oppositional (dominant or submissive)	Intense conflict: 1. overt (producing competitive, explosive behavior disorders) 2. covert (producing depressive, compulsive, or neurotic characters)	Behave as if encounters will be affiliative
II. Degree of Family Individuation	Individuation incompatible with acceptance by others; "group think," "undifferentiated ego mass" (Bowen); "pseudomutuality,"	Coherent individuation but with rigidity and guilt	Separateness with closeness

A. *Autonomy (ability to express and take responsibility for separateness)*	Failure to take responsibility for own feelings, actions, goals; unclear communication; indirect use of power—control of interaction without clear statement of own feelings, thoughts, or responsibilities, via: 1. asking questions 2. evasions or shift of meaning 3. diffuse attacks on others' positions 4. hostility, sarcasm, ridicule	Commonly statements relate to others' behavior or are negative statements about one's self; control; difficulty with ambivalence	Autonomous interaction, relatively conflict-free; comfortable with uncertainty, ambivalence, and disagreement; trial and error without loss of self-esteem; freedom in communication, spontaneity, permission to think and feel freely
B. *Respect for another's Differentness*	Invasiveness; "mind-reading"	Attempts to control others' thoughts and feelings as well as actions; frequent criticism; scapegoating inside or outside of family; many "shoulds" or blaming of others	Respect and sensitivity to subjective world of others; tolerance of uniqueness; infrequent scapegoating, projection, blaming, or denial
C. *Ability to be Responsive and Open to Others*	Impermeability: lack of acknowledgement; no negotiations	Members talk in turn, but children often ignored by parents, or several people talk at once	Open, receptive; acknowledging; skill in negotiations, agreements result from inventive compromise ("respectful negotiation")

111

Table 5-1 *continued*

	Severely Disturbed Families	Adequate (Mid-range) Families	Healthy Families
III. Acceptance of Separation and Loss	Fantasy and denial as defenses against loss	Offspring still in conflicted relationships with parents, or unable to grieve a dead parent successfully; recreate old relationships with parents in current relationships	Able to accept separation and loss of loved ones; strong marital and wider community relationships; transcendant value system extends identity beyond family
IV. Perception of reality			
A. *Family Mythology*	Incongruous, shared family myths maintained by denial and obliviousness	Distorted, most evident in area of feelings	Myths flexible, closely related to reality
B. *Time Binding*	Sense of timelessness	Passage of time distorted, but not obliterated	Real sense of time's passage
V. Affect (Prevailing Mood, Degree of Expressiveness, Quality of Empathy)	Hostility or depression	Unpleasant, constricted; world view: humans basically evil	Humor, tenderness, warmth, hopeful, caring; conflicts open without lingering chronic resentments

*Adapted from Chapter 3 of Beavers WR: A theoretical basis for family evaluation. In Lewis JM, Beavers WR, Gossett JT, et al.: No Single Thread in Psychological Health and Family Systems. New York: Brunner Mazel, 1976, pp 46–82.

112

and outbursts of rage. Finally, in the *severely disturbed families*, in which one finds "sociopathic" or schizophrenic offspring, there are poor boundaries. Communication is often confused and there is a lack of shared attentional focus. Affect includes despair, cynicism, and denial of ambivalence.

In Olson's model of family functioning,[20] the dimensions of family cohesion, adaptability, and communication are central. Dysfunctional families are likely to exhibit extreme levels of cohesion, disengagement or enmeshment, similar to Minuchin's schema.[21] In terms of family adaptability, extremes of rigid and chaotic handling of change are seen as more pathological. And finally, in terms of family communication, dysfunctional families would exhibit more negative communication such as double messages, double binds, and mutual criticism.

In the McMaster's model of family functioning,[22] psychopathological families are likely to exhibit (1) poor problem solving, (2) masked and indirect communication, (3) inadequate family functions (or the allocation of an accountability around family functions are not maintained), (4) affective responsiveness is on a very narrow range involving only one or two affects, and (5) the amount and quality of affect responsiveness is distorted (given the context, affective involvement that is symbiotic or, in the other extreme, the lack of involvement, and behavior control that is chaotic rather that flexible). This model has had relatively wide acceptance in the family field and we therefore use it extensively to evaluate dysfunction (Chapters 7 & 8).

There is a growing body of research on the specific interactional patterns observed in dysfunctional families as opposed to functional ones. This research is reviewed in Chapters 31 and 32.

SUMMARY

Both the functional and the dysfunctional family unit can be examined in terms of three areas: the family as a system, the family life cycle, and family tasks. The issues are:

1. How dysfunctional is the family *system*?
2. How well are *life cycle* issues being coped with by the family?
3. To what degree are *family tasks* accomplished?
4. How close are *family myths* to family reality?

It is important to note that when an individual in the family has a diagnosable disorder, which at this state of our knowledge appears to have a major biological causative factor (e.g., schizophrenia, major affective disorder), there is no good reason to assume that the family is ipso facto dysfunctional. It is quite conceivable that a family with a schizophrenic member functions well systemically, handles life cycle issues with adequate coping, and does an adequate job of accomplishing the basic family tasks. On the other hand, there are families that have a member with a diagnosed psychiatric illness who are dysfunctional either around the illness and/or more generally, behaving in such a way as to maintain or exacerbate the individual's symptoms. At the present state of our knowledge, this situation would be best exemplified by families (marriages) in which there is one member with schizophrenia or major affective illness.

Although techniques for measurement of family dysfunction are not yet sensitive enough to clearly demarcate the differences between functional and dysfunctional families, clinicians have observed that in healthy families there is a sense of ongoing cooperation, communication, and togetherness that can best be described by using the following analogy.

A functional family is like an orchestra playing a beautiful symphony: each of its members plays a different instrument, but together they add up to an overall configuration of harmony that is effective and fulfilling. Conversely, in a dysfunctional family there is a lack of this congruence, as well as a pervasive negative mood of unrelatedness.

A dysfunctional family is like a poker game in which each player holds certain cards, yet no one will put them on the table. Therefore, the same old game keeps being played. No one will risk losing (or winning) by playing a new card, so in effect no one wins and no one loses and the game becomes a pointless exercise; or one player may win the same hollow victory repeatedly and another may indeed always be identified as the loser.

SUGGESTIONS FOR FURTHER READINGS

Dicks HV: **Marital Tensions.** New York: Basic Books, 1967.
   A must for anyone interested in the dynamics of marital interaction.

Pincus L and Dare C. **Secrets in the Family.** London: Faber & Faber, 1978.
   An excellent discussion of the interaction of individual and family models.

REFERENCES

1. Hoffman L: Foundation of Family Therapy: A Conceptual Framework for Systems Change. New York: Basic Books, 1981, p 7
2. Wynne LC, Gurman A, Ravich R, and Boszormenyi-Nagy I: The family and

marital therapies, in Lewis JF and Usdin G (Eds): Treatment Planning in Psychiatry. Washington: American Psychiatric Association, 1982

3. Bateson G, Jackson D, Haley J, and Weakland J: Toward a theory of schizophrenia. Behav Sci 1:251-254, 1956

4. Haley J: Toward a theory of pathological systems. In Zuk GH,and Boszor-menyi-Nagy I (Eds): Family therapy and disturbed families. Palo Alto, CA: Science and Behavior Books, 1969

5. Bowen M: Family Therapy in Clinical Practice. New York: Jason Aronson, 1978

6. Haley J: Toward a theory of pathological systems. In Watzlawick P and Weakland J (Eds): The interactional view. New York: WW Norton, 1977

7. Watzlawick P, Weakland J, and Fisch R: Change: Principles of Problem Formation and Problem Resolution. New York: WW Norton, 1974

8. Hill R: Families Under Stress. New York: Harper & Bros., 1949

9. Leff J and Vaughn C: Expressed Emotion in Families. New York: Guilford Press, 1985

10. Thomas A and Chess S: Temperament and Development. New York: Brunner/Mazel, 1977, p 270

11. Cass LK and Thomas CB: Childhood Pathology and Later Adjustment: The Question of Prediction. New York: Wiley-Interscience, 1979, p 259

12. Ackerman NW: Psychodynamics of Family Life, Diagnosis and Treatment in Family Relationships. New York: Basic Books, 1958

13. Bell JE: Family group therapy. Public Health Monograph No. 64. Washington, DC: Department of Health, Education and Welfare, Public Health Service, 1961

14. Carroll EJ: Treatment of the family as a unit. Pennsylvania Medicine 63:57-62, 1960

15. Counts R: Family crisis and the impulsive adolescent. Arch Gen Psychiatry 17:74, 1967

16. Chess S, Thomas A, and Birch H: Your Child Is a Person. New York: Viking, 1965

17. Lewis JM, Beavers WR, Gossett JT, and Phillips VA: No Single Thread: Psychological Health in Family Systems. New York: Brunner/Mazel, 1976

18. Robinson LR: Basic concepts in family therapy: A differential comparison with individual treatment. Am J Psychiatry 132:1045-1048, 1975

19. Ferreira AJ: Family myths and homeostasis. Arch Gen Psychiatry 9:457-463, 1963

20. Olson DH, Porter J, and Bell R: FACES II: Family adaptability and cohesion evaluation scales. Family Social Service, University of Minnesota, St. Paul, Minnesota, 1982

21. Minuchin S: Families and Family Therapy. Cambridge MA: Harvard University Press, 1974

22. Epstein NB and Bishop DS: Problem-centered systems therapy of the family. In Gurman AS and Kniskern DP (Eds): Handbook of Family Therapy. New York: Brunner/Mazel, 1981, pp 444-482

Section III

Family Evaluation

Once the trainee understands family function and dysfunction, the task is to formulate an evaluation of what is wrong, and what (if anything) can be done about it.

To this end, this section examines the process of doing the evaluation, what areas to cover, i.e., the content, how to formulate the case and finally, how to plan the therapeutic approach and establish a treatment contract. A case example illustrates the outline. The section concludes with supplementary techniques which can be useful depending on the clinical situation.

Andean Family by Hector Poleo. Courtesy of the Museum of Modern Art of Latin America (OAS), Washington, D.C.

6

The Process of Evaluation

OBJECTIVES

- To be able to gather historical data
- To be cognizant of the progression and choice points of the evaluation interview
- To understand the role of individual and of family diagnoses in gathering data

INTRODUCTION

Evaluation of a marital couple or family should be understood as a continuing process, begun at the first contact but not necessarily completed at any particular point. Some initial formulation is useful to the therapist to help with the marshalling of data and forming of hypotheses, but in a larger sense, the evaluation is often an inextricable part of the therapy itself.

As data are gathered, the therapist forms hypotheses based on one or another conceptual frame of reference. *The therapist attempts to assign priorities and weight to the variety of contributory variables and then sets up an overall strategy with particular intervention tactics designed to lead to certain desired goals.* (This strategy and its tactics are described in subsequent chapters on family therapy techniques.) In this process further data are obtained that serve to confirm, modify, or negate the original hypotheses, strategies, and tactics. These later formulations are then tested in the matrix of the family sessions as further data are obtained.

ROLE OF HISTORICAL MATERIAL

There are several points of view regarding the type and quantity of the evaluative data to be gathered. Some family therapists begin with a specific and detailed *longitudinal history* of the family unit and its constituent members, which may perhaps span three or more generations—i.e., the genogram. This procedure has the advantage of permitting the family and the therapist to go over together the complex background of the present situation. The therapist will begin to understand unresolved past and present issues, will usually gain a sense of rapport and identification with the family and its members, and may then feel more comfortable in defining problem areas and in planning strategy. The family, for its part, may benefit by reviewing together the source and evolution of its current condition, which may prove to be a clarifying, empathy-building process for the entire family. The good and the bad are brought into focus, and the immediate distress is placed in a broader perspective. Sometimes a family in crisis is too impatient to tolerate exhaustive history gathering and therefore, in acute situations, lengthy data gathering must be curtailed.

Other therapists do not rely heavily on the longitudinal approach, attempting instead to delineate the situation that has led the family to seek treatment at the time and to obtain a *cross-sectional view* of its present functioning. This procedure has the advantage of starting with the problems about which the family is most concerned, and is not as potentially time-consuming nor as seemingly remote from the present realities as the preceding method. The therapist, however, may not emerge with as sharp a focus on important family patterns, since much of the discussion may be negatively tinged because of a preoccupation by the family with its current difficulty.

More experienced (and perhaps more courageous) therapists may severely curtail past history gathering and may also minimize formalized discussions of the family's current situation. They may begin, instead, by dealing from the onset with the family's important characteristic patterns of interaction as they are manifested in the interview setting. They may tend to utilize primarily, or exclusively, the immediate "here and now" observable family transactions, understanding these to be characteristic of the family. They may clarify and comment on these, intervening in a variety of ways. This approach has the advantage of initiating treatment immediately, without the usual delay of history gathering. There is often a heightened sense of emotional involvement, which may cause more rapid changes to occur. Sometimes families are overwhelmed by such an approach, however, feeling threatened and defensive. Also, when specific information and patterns are allowed to emerge in this random fashion, the therapist does not always have the same degree of certainty as to whether the emerging family patterns are indeed relevant and important. (Such a procedure is not usually recommended for beginning therapists.)

To a considerable extent these differences in technique may mirror differences in the therapists' training, theoretical beliefs, and temperaments. Most therapists, however, probably use combinations of these approaches as the situation warrants, for there is no evidence of one technique being superior to the others.

WHOM TO INCLUDE IN FAMILY EVALUATION

An early and strategic question is what members of the family to include in the evaluation sessions. From the very first contact, often by phone call, the therapist is often talking to one individual who represents the family and presents the problem. Sometimes the problem is presented as a family problem and other times the problem is presented as an individual's problem that is disturbing other family members. We assume here that from the very first phone call or contact by a family member that the therapist is considering the possibility of family intervention or other types of intervention such as individual intervention, either alone or in combination. Thus, the question arises of who to include in the evaluation sessions. Most family therapists would agree that it is important from the very first session to include all members of the family in the evaluation sessions. This usually means all members of a nuclear family, that is, mother, father, and children who reside under the same roof. It is obviously impractical and often unnecessary to include, for example, a son who is 32, living 2000 miles away from his mother, at least for the first sessions. In addition to nuclear family members, and especially in new family forms, *significant others* must be included.

Clinical experience suggests that it is easier to include all family members for evaluation sessions *at the beginning* rather than waiting until later to do so. If one begins with all family members, including the marital subsystem and the children subsystem, than one can have subsequent sessions with one subsystem while excluding the other.

There may be particular circumstances when one would not want to include the whole family in the evaluation sessions. For example, a couple who present having sexual difficulties may be seen as a couple without their children for at least the first evaluation session. Likewise, the couple may be seen alone for what they identify as marital difficulties without involving the children, again at least for the first evaluation session. Specialists in the marital field will sometimes see both spouses together in an initial evaluation session, followed by individual sessions with each spouse alone. While some would say such a situation encourages one spouse telling secrets to the therapist, others suggest that the only way for a therapist to proceed is to have all information at the beginning. Some would utilize individual sessions with each spouse but indicate before the session that all material is privy to the couple sessions, thus precluding the forming of coalitions and yet possibly discouraging the full disclosure of information.

A practical consideration that often arises is the issue of evaluation sessions to which one or more central family members are absent. We believe that often such missing family members are crucial in the problem and the absence must be discussed and their presence brought about. Napier and Whitaker[1] give an interesting clinical illustration of a family in which the initial evaluation session is not continued because of a missing son and his presence is brought about by maneuvers of the therapist by the second session. It is probably not an uncommon practice of family therapists to refuse to go on with the evaluation until the missing member is present.

PROGRESSION OF THE FAMILY EVALUATION INTERVIEW

Several authors[2,3] have discussed the sequential progression of the family evaluation interview. Most would suggest that the first interview task is to greet each of the family members, and to begin to accommodate to the family. This is accomplished by noting the power system of the family, acquiescing to it, and utilizing the family vocabulary that surfaces. Next, the interview can proceed to some delineation of the family problem as each family member sees it.

Reiss[4] has provided a helpful analysis of the choice points that a clinician faces in the initial assessment of a family. He distinguishes substantive or theoretical choice points from technical choice points.

The first *substantive* choice point is whether to focus on the cross-sectional (current functioning of the family), or to give more attention to the developmental history of the family unit and its individuals. We discussed this earlier in this chapter. A second choice point is whether to focus on the family as the central shaping force or to focus on the environment or community(e.g., its forces and properties) that influence the family. The latter would include focus on the network of kin and friends, the school, etc. A third choice point concerns crisis versus character orientation. The former is a focus on the current immediate concrete problem or symptom that brings the family in, while the later is a focus on the more enduring patterns of self-protection, cognitive and affective style, and deficits that the family manifests. Another choice point is whether to focus on the pathology or the functional competence of the family unit. A fifth choice point concerns the basic theoretical understanding of the evaluator and his/her emphasis

on finding family themes versus looking at concrete behaviors and their consequences. In the psychoanalytic tradition, there is an emphasis on discovering the
thematic or underlying (conscious or unconscious) structures that give family life
and behavior its meaning and thrust. In contrast, therapists with a behavioral
orientation focus on the problem behaviors and their antecedent and consequent
events.

The first *technical* choice point concerns the pacing of the assessment. Some
advocate a thorough assessment before beginning treatment with a clear marker
between, while others emphasize that assessment and treatment merge, especially
as assessment involves making interventions and assessing how the family
responds. A second choice point involves individualized measurement of the
family (emphasizing the uniqueness of the family) or standardized measurement
of the family focusing on major dimensions that are relevant to all families. Chapter 8 discusses another choice point involving assessment, the issue of dimen-
sionalizing the data (how does the family rate on "communication" for example)
or typologizing the family (the enmeshed family, for example). A final technical
choice point is the clinician's perspective of being inside or emphatically feeling
what it is like to be with this family versus observing as objectively as possible
(as an outsider), how the family performs and carries out functions.

These decision points are not "either/or" situations, of course, and the
evaluation will emphasize different areas on the polar dimensions depending upon
the situation. But they are indeed choice points that in a time-limited setting of
doing evaluations must be faced.

ROLE OF INDIVIDUAL AND FAMILY DIAGNOSIS

In deciding who to include, the question arises of, "include for what purpose?" This text has the bias that both the family as well as the individuals in the
family unit can be important in the diagnostic equation.

In psychiatry, there is an imperfect relationship between individual diagnosis
and treatment planning, as often the diagnosis itself does not give enough information to plan the interventions. This imperfect relationship (between diagnosis
and treatment planning) is even confounded in the area of family therapy, where
one must have enough information to give an individual diagnosis (especially if
there is a clearly identified patient) and also make a family diagnostic statement.

The first implication is that in assessing families one must obtain enough individual information to be able to give individual DSM-III-R[5] diagnoses to members with significant pathology. There is no place in DSM-III-R for family
pathology. And DSM-III-R clearly has a narrow limit of usefulness for many
family therapists. However, the lack of any emphasis in the classification of
family pathology in DSM-III-R was probably necessary given both the *purpose*

and *individual orientation of DSM-III-R* and the current *lack of research evidence* supporting various methods of classifying family pathology. It will be important in DSM-IV to have some research data enabling family classifications to be made. DSM-III-R makes only passing reference to disordered family functioning. There's only one section in DSM-III-R in which *parent/child* or *marital problems* are mentioned, and this section is titled, "Conditions not Attributable to a Mental Disorder that are a Focus of Attention or Treatment," known as V Codes. Axis IV, the rating of psychosocial stressors, may be most helpful in indicating patients for whom family stress is prominent. At the present time, while there are many proposed typologies of family functioning, we think that family typologizing is premature. Rather, the family diagnosis should consist of dimensional statements concerning the family and its functioning as outlined in the family diagnostic outline in the next two chapters.

We discuss these issues again in Chapter 8 as they relate to formulation of a case and in Chapter 22 in the context of discussing the family and individual psychiatric disorder.

SUGGESTIONS FOR FURTHER READINGS

Haley J: **Problem-Solving Therapy.** San Francisco: Jossey-Bass, 1976.
A good chapter on the evaluation interview that provides an interesting list of criteria a supervisor could use to evaluate a trainee's family evaluation.

REFERENCES

1. Napier A, Whitaker C: The Family Crucible. New York: Harper & Row, 1978
2. Haley J: Problem-Solving Therapy. San Francisco: Jossey-Bass, 1976
3. Minuchin S: Families and Family Therapy. Cambridge MA: Harvard University Press, 1974
4. Reiss D: The Family's Construction of Reality. Cambridge MA: Harvard University Press, 1981
5. American Psychiatric Association: Diagnostic and Statistical Manual of Mental Disorders, Third Edition, Revised. Washington, D.C.: American Psychiatric Association, 1987

Family Portrait. Photograph by Baron von Stillfried, from *Once Upon A Time: Visions of Old Japan* (1984).

7

The Content of Family Evaluation

OBJECTIVES

- To be aware of the information needed for each category in the outline for family evaluation
- To be aware of the salient content areas of family evaluation

INTRODUCTION

We have indicated that there is more than one potentially useful way to evaluate a family, depending on the situation. The procedure offered in the evaluation outline below (Table 7-1) combines useful aspects of the two approaches discussed in the last chapter. In addition, the reader is provided with other evaluative techniques (Chapter 9). These approaches combine both verbal and nonverbal techniques for obtaining information. (The process of gathering information over the course of therapy is discussed in greater detail in Chapter 13).

Since one cannot evaluate *everything* about a family without getting lost in details, both the trainee and the experienced family therapist need an outline, analogous to the outline for assessing an individual patient that is engraved in the head of every resident (Chief Complaint, Present Illness, etc.) that indicates not only *what* to evaluate but the *priorities* of evaluation. The theory of family functioning and its relationship to the cause and maintenance of pathology in an individual family member should guide and prioritize such an evaluation.

128

Table 7-1
Outline for Family Evaluation

I. Current Phase of Family Life Cycle
II. Explicit Interview Data:
   A. What is the current family problem?
   B. Why does the family come for treatment at the present time?
   C. What is the background of the family problem?
   D. What is the history of past treatment attempts or other attempts at problem solving in the family?
   E. What are the family's goals and expectations of the treatment? What are their motivations and resistances?
III. Formulating the Family Problem Areas:
   A. Rating important dimensions of family functioning:
      1. Communication
      2. Problem solving *abilities*
      3. Roles and Coalitions
      4. Affective responsiveness and involvement
      5. Behavior control
      6. Operative family myths
   B. Family Classification and "Diagnosis"
IV. Planning the Therapeutic Approach and Establishing the Treatment Contract = *Goal*

*In developing this outline, we adapted material from three major sources: Gill M, Newman R, and Redlich F: The Initial Interview in Psychiatric Practice. New York: International Universities Press, 1954; Group for the Advancement of Psychiatry: The case history in the study of family process. Report No. 76. New York: Group for the Advancement of Psychiatry, 1970; and the McMaster Model (Epstein NB and Bishop DS: Problem-centered systems therapy of the family. In Gurman AS and Kniskern DP (Eds): Handbook of Family Therapy. New York: Brunner/Mazel, 1981, pp 444-482).

DIMENSIONS OF FAMILY PATHOLOGY

Family theoreticians and researchers have delineated the various dimensions of family pathology. If one examines these existing schema and looks for redundancy and consensual validation across systems, one can arrive at the dimensions of family functioning that seem salient by consensus.[1]

Because of its thoroughness, operational definitions, congruence with the major areas of family functioning or dysfunctioning mentioned above, teachability, and relevance to treatment planning, we recommend a modified version of the McMaster model of family evaluation.[2] In this model, there are five dimensions of family functioning that must be assessed, dimensions that are congruent with the concepts of functional and dysfunctional families (enumerated in previous chapters), and congruent with the consensus areas of importance across family models mentioned in the previous paragraph. These dimensions are: communication, problem-solving, roles and coalition, affective responsiveness, involvement, and behavior control.

OUTLINE FOR FAMILY EVALUATION

Drawing heavily from the McMaster evaluation model and integrating other aspects, we developed the evaluation outline presented in Table 7-1. This outline offers a practical alternative to either gathering an exhaustive history or plunging into the middle of the family interaction. Although far from exhaustive in scope, this outline does provide some anchoring points for initial understanding and planning. It is not meant to be inflexible or unchangeable, and it certainly can be expanded or contracted as the situation warrants. Each topic of the outline is discussed in greater detail in this chapter (content of the family evaluation) and the next chapter (formulating the family problem areas).

CURRENT PHASE OF FAMILY LIFE CYCLE

Identifying the current phase of the family life cycle can readily be accomplished by ascertaining the ages and relationships of those family members living under one roof. Knowing each stage the family has reached in its developmental cycle is an important criterion for a basic understanding of the family's structure and functioning, in both the actual and optimal sense. (This is discussed at greater length in Chapters 3 and 5.) Each stage of the family life cycle has unique stresses, challenges, opportunities, and pitfalls. By being alert to these, the therapist is in a position to observe and explore those particular tasks, roles, and relationships that are phase-specific for the family. The therapist can also ascertain to what extent the family members clearly recognize and are attempting to cope with actual issues relevant to the family's current stage of development. For many marriages and families, the basic difficulty underlying the need for professional help can be related to their inability to cope satisfactorily with their current developmental phase.

The J. family, mentioned in Chapter 4, is a good example of the type of problem arising in a later stage of marriage—the "empty-nest" syndrome—in which the parents could not cope with the separation of their children from the home because of their fear of being alone as husband and wife.

EXPLICIT INTERVIEW DATA

What is the current family problem? The interviewer asks this question of each family member, in turn, with all family members present. The question is thrown out on the floor. The interviewer attempts to maintain the focus on the *current family problem*, rather than on one or another individual, or on past difficulties. Each family member receives an equal opportunity to be heard, without interruption, and to feel that his or her opinions and views are worthwhile, important, and acknowledged. The interviewer will begin to note what frames of reference are delineated by the family members in discussing their difficulties. It will be determined whether there exists a family or an individual problem, which individuals seem to be bearing the brunt of the blame, how the identified patients deal with their role, what are the alliances in the family, who seems to get interrupted by whom, who speaks for whom, who seems fearful or troubled about expressing an opinion, who sits next to whom, and so forth.

The nonverbal communication of families is a gold mine of information. Because nonverbal communication is not dependent on words, a family evaluator must train himself to observe other signals. Videotaping a family interaction is one way to closely observe nonverbal communication, which may be expressed by a child who twiddles his thumbs in the same way as his mother, a father whose facial expression and bodily movements indicate the opposite of what he is actually saying, or a parent who stares off into space when his adolescent son yells. All of these observations are of as much or more value than some of the verbal comments that the family may make to the interviewer.

Why does the family come for treatment at the present time? The answer to this question helps to shift the focus of difficulty even closer to the current situation and also provides an opportunity for further specifying the kinds of factors that lead to family distress. The kinds of "last straw" situations usually present the important patterns of family interaction in a microcosm.

In the L. family, a son, Tom, age 25, had symptoms of paranoid schizophrenia for many years. The parents "allowed" Tom to sleep in their bedroom at night. On the day after he moved out, Mr. and Mrs. L. began to blame each other for the son's behavior and sought attention because their son was "out on the streets where anything could happen." The son had maintained an uneasy balance between the parents by staying in the parental bedroom at night, thus obviating their need for intimacy or sex. It was only when he moved out that the parents' problem came into sharp focus.

The answer to the above question also helps alert the therapist to any acute crisis situation that may need either the therapist's or the family's immediate intervention. The answer will be relevant, too, in assessing the goals the family has in mind for the therapy and the degree to which it is motivated for help. Until recently it was usually the wife who requested psychotherapy. This may have reflected the wife's greater involvement in the family, rather than her having a greater degree of intrapsychic disturbance.

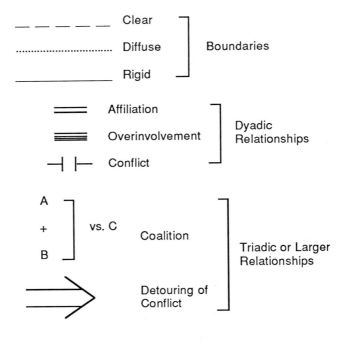

Overall family pattern (characterized by boundaries):

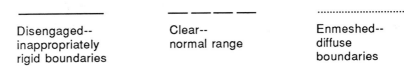

Disengaged--   Clear--   Enmeshed--
inappropriately   normal range   diffuse
rigid boundaries   boundaries

Fig. 7-1. Symbols for mapping family structure (adapted from Minuchin, 1974). From Levant RF: Family Therapy: A Comprehensive Overview. New Jersey: Prentice Hall, 1984, with permission.

What is the background of the family problem?

1. *Composition and characteristics of the nuclear and expanded family, including age, sex, occupation, financial status, medical problems, and so on.* A genogram can be used. It is a graph of the patient and several generations of the patient's family, noting important dates (births and deaths, marriages, separations, etc.), occupational role, and major life events such as illness. Levant has provided a glossary of symbols for a genogram (Figure 7-1). A good example of a genogram can be found in Figure 7-2. For the sake of clarity, it is drawn without symbols:

2. *Developmental history and patterns of each family member.* Individual family member's life histories are evaluated in terms of patterns of adaptation, in-

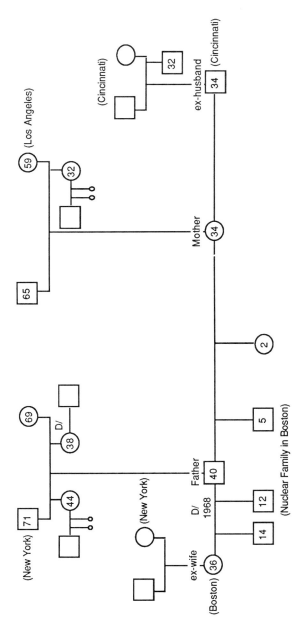

Fig. 7-2. Example of a genogram. From Levant RF: Family Therapy: A Comprehensive Overview. New Jersey: Prentice Hall, 1984, with permission.

cluding an impression of how the individual manages affects, frustration and disappointment, self-image, personal values and goals, and role and identity outside the family. Although somewhat outside the scope of a family therapy text, our bias is that the evaluator should not underestimate the importance of individual styles of adaptation, the use of defenses and resistances, tolerance of stress and ego strengths, signs and symptoms of any mental disorder, and the capacity of each person to be supportive and empathic to his or her partner.

3. *Developmental history and patterns of the nuclear family unit.* The longitudinal course of the family unit is explored with reference to the role of the spouses' individual expectations, values, goals, and conflicts in their relationship; the effect of each partner's adaptive patterns on the other partner; the need for control by one partner or the other, including how control is obtained and maintained; the existence of mutual trust and ability to share; the importance of individual and mutual dependence issues; and the family's ability to deal effectively with its earlier life phases.

4. *Current family interactional patterns (internal and external).*[2] Is the power structure flexible, rigid, or chaotic? Are the generation boundaries intact, blurred, or broken? Is there an affiliative or oppositional style? What degree of individuation is noted? Is there clarity of communication; tolerance for ambivalence and disagreement; respect for others' differentness versus attempts at control or intrusiveness; responsiveness to others; ability to deal realistically with separation and loss? Are the family myths close to reality or are they gross distortions? What is the overall family affect: that of warmth, humor, caring, hope, tenderness, and the ability to tolerate open conflicts, or that of constricted, unpleasant, hostile and depressive or resentful behavior?

This part of the evaluation—the background of the family problem—lends itself to expansion or contraction depending on the circumstances. For example, an intensive examination of a particular sector of the family's current functioning or past history might be thought relevant in a particular instance. In another situation only a relatively brief amount of background data might be gathered initially, with the feeling that more would come out as the treatment sessions proceeded. In any event, the therapist would always want to recognize the important participants in the family's current interactions, the quality of the relationships, and the developmental patterns of the family unit over a period of time.

What is the history of past treatment attempts or other attempts at problem solving in the family? It usually is illuminating to understand the circumstances that have led a marital couple or family to seek assistance in the past, from what sort of helpers this assistance was elicited, and the outcome of the expectations, experiences, and results of this assistance. Experience in previous help-seeking efforts serves to illuminate more clearly both the family processes and the possible therapist traps and often delineates useful strategies. Past help-seeking patterns are often useful predictors of what the present experience will be in both family therapy as well as in other therapies.

The B. family came into treatment presenting the complaint that they could not get along with each other and were contemplating divorce. They gave a history of being in family therapy several years before. They had had some 20 sessions, which "of course led to nothing." In discussion with the couple and the former therapist, it was discovered that the couple had spent most of the sessions blaming each other and attempting to change each other, rather than making any change in their relationship or in themselves. In addition, Mr. B., who was quite authoritarian, had persuaded the therapist to line up on his side and say that his wife was quite unreasonable. This treatment had been unsuccessful. The strategy in this case was to go over, in detail, the past problems in treatment, suggest that the present therapist would not be a judge, and that the focus was to be on the couple's relationship rather than on what the other partner would have to do.

Often one spouse has been in intensive individual psychotherapy or psychoanalysis and has been seeking help with the marital relationship. When this has proven unsuccessful, both therapist and patient may blame the failure on the spouse not in treatment. This may exacerbate the difficulty and lead to separation or divorce.

Mrs. P. came into treatment because she felt her husband was inadequate. Her own life had been replete with difficulties, starting from the time she had lost both her parents in an automobile accident when she was two years old. She had lived in various orphanages, had had two marriages by the time she was 22, and had periodic bouts of alcoholism and depression. She felt that her present marriage of five years was "okay" until she had children. She felt that although she had some difficulty in raising the children, the real problem was in her husband. She went into individual psychotherapy three times a week, and in the course of this began to "see quite clearly what a loser he was." Although her therapist at first struggled valiantly to point out her own difficulties, he, too, began to see the difficulties in the husband. The husband himself was never called into therapy, and after two years of treatment the couple was still experiencing the same problems and they were contemplating divorce. A consultant suggested marital therapy.

What are the family's goals and expectations of the treatment? What are their motivations and resistances? Some families come to treatment for short-term goals, such as making final an already fairly well decided separation between husband and wife. Others come for more long-term goals, such as making a basic change in how the family functions. Other families come because of "mother's depression" (an individual-oriented goal), whereas still others come because "the family isn't functioning right" (a family goal). In a case in which the goals are individual-oriented, the therapist's task is to translate for the family the relationship between the symptoms and the family process. Goals are, at times, unclear or unrealistic. In such instances the therapist and the family must work out from the beginning an appropriate and clear set of goals (see Chapter 11).

The marital couple and family presumably will have certain types of positive hopes and motivations for seeking help, but at the same time will have some hesitations, doubts, and fears about this very same help. One of the therapist's jobs is to explore and reinforce the positive motivations, to clarify them and to keep them readily available throughout the process of therapy, which at times may be temporarily stormy and stressful. In marital therapy the motivation of each partner for conjoint therapy should be evaluated, and the evaluation should include stated commitment to the marriage, the evaluator's opinion of their commitment to therapy, the reality of their treatment expectations, and the secondary gain for each spouse that the marital distress may represent.

It is the positive expectations, goals, and motivations that keep the family members in treatment, and every effort should be made to ensure that each family member will benefit from the family therapy sessions as individuals, and also as concerned members of the family. It has been found helpful to work out these expectations explicitly, so that both the family members and the therapist understand them in order to avoid the situation wherein one of the family members has the feeling that he or she is not attending the sessions as an individual, but only to help some other member of the family.

Ideally it would be desirable for each involved family member to know clearly what positive reasons there are for his own participation, as well as to understand what the more general family system goals may be. At the same time the therapist must be aware of individual and family resistance to treatment and, where appropriate, try to make explicit these obstacles and negative feelings before they undermine either the successful utilization of treatment or its actual continuance. Clinical judgment will suggest when such fears and resistances need immediate attention and when they need only to be kept in mind as potentially major obstacles.

Such resistances may be of various sorts. Although some may be specific to particular families, many are commonly seen. Among these is the feeling that the situation may be made worse by treatment; that some member of the family will become guilty, depressed, angry, or fearful as a result of the treatment; that a family member may go crazy; that the family may split up; that perhaps there is no hope for change and it is already too late for help; that shameful or damaging "family secrets" may have to be revealed; or that perhaps it would be better to stick to familiar patterns of family interaction, no matter how unsatisfying they may be, rather than attempt to change them in what may be unknown and hence frightening directions. (Chapter 14 is devoted to a more detailed review of resistance to treatment.)

In the newlywed Q. family, the wife felt that to continue in marital treatment after her recovery from an acute psychotic episode might mean that she would go crazy again. She believed that she would have to explore with her husband their unsatisfactory marriage and that this might lead to separation or divorce. She also felt that she would have to be strong and powerful to prevent her husband from committing suicide in the same way that his own father had committed suicide, presumably in relation to having a weak, nonsupportive wife. The husband, for his part, had a very obsessional personality structure with little interpersonal sensitivity or emotional awareness. He felt angry at psychiatrists and was insecure and threatened by the therapist as a male role model.

SUGGESTIONS FOR FURTHER READINGS

Epstein NB and Bishop DS: Problem-centered systems therapy of the family. In Gurman AS and Kniskern DP (Eds): **Handbook of Family Therapy.** New York: Brunner/Mazel, 1981, pp 444-482
Good description of a basic, down-to-earth, practical outline of family functioning and evaluation.

REFERENCES

1. Clarkin JF, Frances A, and Perry S: Family classifications and DSM-III. In Wolberg LR and Aronson MR (Eds): Group and Family Therapy 1983. New York: Brunner/Mazel, 1983, pp 220-237
2. Epstein NB and Bishop DS: Problem-centered systems therapy of the family. In Gurman AS and Kniskern DP (Eds): Handbook of Family Therapy. New York: Brunner/Mazel, 1981, pp 444-482
3. Group for the Advancement of Psychiatry: The case history in the study of family process. Report No. 76. New York: Group for the Advancement of Psychiatry, 1970

Family Group by Henry Moore. Courtesy of the Hakone Open-Air Museum, Hakone, Japan.

8
Formulating an Understanding of the Family Problem Areas

OBJECTIVES

- To detail the clinically significant dimensions of family functioning and dysfunction in order to formulate an evaluation of the family
- To examine the process of treatment planning and establishing the treatment contract
- To be able to apply the concepts of treatment planning to a clinical case
- To formulate important problem areas in preparation for planning and choosing the therapeutic approach

INTRODUCTION

Meeting with the family, the therapist experiences its patterns of interaction and uses the data obtained in order to begin *formulating a concept of the family problem.*[1]

Data for these formulations may come from historical material, but just as important will be what the therapist has observed in personal contact with the family. This will help to form a basis for hypotheses and therapeutic strategies. The data gathered from the outline provided should permit the family therapist to pinpoint particular dimensions or aspects of the family functioning and its members that may require attention. In addition, the data assist in laying out a priority system, so that the therapist can decide *which* areas of the family problem should be dealt with first and in *what order*. The data also make possible greater clarity about therapeutic strategy and the tactics indicated for the particular phases and goals of treatment.

RATING IMPORTANT DIMENSIONS OF FAMILY FUNCTIONING

Utilizing the explicit interview data (Chapter 7), and drawing heavily from observation of the family in interaction during the evaluation sessions, the therapist is in a position to summarize and rate, either formally or informally, the important dimensions of family functioning. (These dimensions are discussed in greater detail in Section IV from the point of view of treatment strategies.)

Communication

The major focus here is on the quality and quantity of exchange of information among the family members. Can they state information clearly and accurately? Is that information listened to and perceived accurately by the other family members? Can some family members do this, while others are unable?

Problem-Solving

Every family is faced with problems, and one difference between non-distressed and distressed families is that the latter do not come to effective agreement and action on problems, which then accumulate. The family has ostensibly come for evaluation with at least one problem, and by asking about current and prior attempts at solving this problem, the interviewer gets a sense of how effectively the family can proceed to solve problems. Many authors[2,3] have delineated the steps of effective problem-solving, and some have made teaching of these problem-solving steps a major ingredient of family intervention (e.g., Falloon's[4] approach to schizophrenia and the family, detailed in Chapter 22). In the assessment, it is important to note which of the steps in the problem-solving sequence the family is capable of: stating the problem clearly and in behavioral terms, formulating possible solutions, evaluating the solutions, deciding on one solution to try, assessing the effectiveness of that solution).

Roles and Coalitions

As detailed in Chapters 3 and 4, there are basic tasks that must be done in the family unit, including provision of food, clothing, shelter, money, nurturance and support, and sexual gratification of the marital partners. The notion of roles refers to the recurrent patterns of behavior by various individuals in the family through which these family tasks are carried out.

Furthermore, as the individuals in the family carry out their functions, how do they coordinate and mesh with others in the family? Who assumes leadership, especially around issues of decision making? To what extent does the family seem fragmented and disjointed, as though made up of isolated individuals? Or does it rather appear to be one relatively undifferentiated "ego mass"? How are boundaries maintained with respect to family of origin, extended family, neighbors, community? To what extent is the marital coalition functional and successful? To what extent are there cross-generational dyadic coalitions that are stronger than the marital dyad? How successfully are power and leadership issues resolved?

Affective Responsiveness and Involvement

Here the clinician assesses the family's ability to generate and express an appropriate range of feelings. To what extent does the family appear to be emotionally "dead" rather than expressive, empathic, and spontaneous? What is the level of enjoyment, energy, and humor? To what extent does there appear to be an emotional divorce between the marital partners? To what extent does the predominant family mood pattern seem to be one of depression, suspicion, envy, jealousy, withdrawal, anger, irritation, and frustration? To what extent is the family system skewed around the particular mood state or reaction pattern of one of its members? Are the emotions expressed cosonant with the behaviors and context?

Affective *involvement* refers to the degree of emotional interest and investment the family members show with one another. This could range from absence of involvement, to involvement devoid of feelings, to narcissistic involvement, empathic involvement, overinvolvement, and symbiotic involvement.[5]

Behavior Control

Behavior control is the pattern of behavior the family utilizes to handle physically dangerous situations (e.g., child running onto a road, reckless driving), expression of psychobiological needs and drives (e.g., eating, sleeping, sex, aggression), and interpersonal socializing behavior. Control in these areas can range from rigid, to flexible, to laissez-faire, to chaotic.

The single most important initial assessment and intervention involves the prevention of physical harm to the family members or to the therapist. Abused children, battered wives, and sometimes battered husbands, as well as abused grandparents, are all too common. The therapist must also be aware that violence directed toward therapists is not uncommon, particularly with patients who are angry, paranoid, alcoholic, or impulsive. Neither the family nor the therapist can work on other issues when they are afraid. Remember, too, that most families are afraid of psychotic individuals, even when there has been no violence or threat of it.

In these cases, the array of community resources must be considered and employed when appropriate. Encouraging family members to call the police when threatened, to seek shelter when abused, and to inform the appropriate authorities of child abuse should be regarded as the beginning of family therapy and as necessary for its success. Nothing can be accomplished when family members act from fear rather than from love and understanding.

Operative Family Myths

Some individuals in families are "selected" to be "bad, sick, stupid, crazy," and often these roles constitute a kind of self-fulfilling prophecy. Families as well as individuals function with a set of largely unexamined fundamental attitudes that have been termed "myths." These markedly influence the family's manner of looking at and coping with itself and the world.

FAMILY CLASSIFICATION AND "DIAGNOSIS"

There is currently much ferment in the family field to generate a common method of reliably giving the family a classification (or typology), somewhat analogous to the DSM-III-R classification of the individual. Instead of creating a family typology, others[6] have suggested that the best approach is for family therapists to agree on a few, common, important, dimensions of family functioning (as we have done in the previous sections of this chapter), and generate reliable rating scales for each of these. Secondarily, "types" of families could emerge from these ratings. (Table 8-1 summarizes family styles and typologies that may be helpful depending on the circumstances.[7]) We think this is the most sensible approach, and in the following chapter, we provide the clinician with some self-report instruments and rating scales that assess the dimensions in our therapy assessment outline. Needless to say, there is much research to be done in this area.

As a first step, most family therapists use a fairly heuristic scheme[8] like:

1. Families *with problems*—i.e. a systems problem such as marital conflict.
2. Families *with a problem person*—i.e., one who is sick, disabled or deviant (such as bulimia, schizophrenic disorder, learning disability, etc.) and the systems dysfunction is consequent to that problem.

Table 8-1
Family Typologies

Classification 1: Based on rules for defining power
    1. The symmetrical relationship
    2. The complementary relationship
    3. The parallel relationship

In *symmetrical relationships*, both people exhibit the same types of behavior (which minimize the differences between them), role definitions are similar, and problems tend to stem from competition.

In *complementary relationships*, the two people exhibit different types of behavior, and this is found most often in the so-called traditional marriage. This form maximizes differences and tends to be less competitive and often highly workable. Unless role definitions are agreed on, however, serious problems can result.

In *parallel relationships*, the spouses alternate between symmetrical and complementary relationships in response to changing situations.

Classification 2: By Parental Stage
The move from the dyadic marital configuration to the larger, more complex one involving children tends inevitably to bring with it the potential for increased activities. Possible subcategories under this classification are as follows:

    1. *Couples.* Couples are not families. They are entered into by choice and can be left by choice. They may not be composed of equals, but clearly a couple has only one generation present and thus is more equal than another family form. There are no parental responsibilities between members of a couple to each other.

    2. *Families with young children.* These families almost always come for help with a child. If a child is not the problem, they come as a couple. When they come as a family, while the parents often do not agree as to means, they do agree that they would like the child to be helped.

    3. *Families with seriously disturbed young adults or a sick member.* This is the area where this particular classification may overlap with the previous idea. The problem is often to make the correct decision: namely, is this illness or problematic interaction? Unfortunately, in the family field this decision is usually made ideologically and on the basis of theory rather than empirically.

    4. *Adults.* Much family work is done with youngish adults who desire to work out a different relationship with their parents, and much family theory is devoted to this issue. Whether the work here is a family therapy or an enlarged form of individual therapy is an open question.

Classification 3: By Level of Intimacy
    1. *The conflict-habituated marriage* is characterized by severe conflicts, but unpleasant as it is, the partners are held together by fear of alternatives.

2. The *devitalized marriage* has less overt expressions of dissatisfaction, with the marital partners conducting separate lives in many areas. This interaction is characterized by numbness and apathy, and seems to be held together principally by legal and moral bonds and by the children.

3. The *passive-congenial marriage* is "pleasant" and there is sharing of interests without any great intensity of interaction. The partners' level of expectation from the relationship is not very high, and they derive some genuine satisfaction from it.

4. The *vital marriage* is intensely satisfying to the spouses in at least one major area, and the partners are able to work together.

5. The *total marriage*, which is very rare in the investigators' experience, is characterized by similarity to the vital marriage except that the former is more intense and satisfying in the whole range of marital activities.

Classification 4: By Personality Style[1]

1. *The obsessive-compulsive husband and the hysterical wife.* Conflicts of intimacy often become of major importance.

2. *The passive-dependent husband and the dominant wife.* Power is the central theme of this system.

3. *The paranoid husband and the depression-prone wife.*

4. *The depression-prone husband and the paranoid wife.*

5. *The neurotic wife and the omnipotent husband.* Power is the primary conflict area. The wife's resentment is expressed through depression and a variety of other symptoms.

These marital styles often work very satisfactorily if the needs of the two partners are met and if they are not overly inflexible in their application. Problems arise only when the cost of keeping the system going is too high—when one spouse changes, thereby upsetting the system, or when one partner indicates the desire to change the "rules."

Classification 5: By Descriptions of Families in Treatment[6]

No overall concept or model underlies the following six clusters; they are descriptive in nature. Because they were derived from families referred for treatment, the clusters imply a generally maladaptive tendency.

1. *Constricted.* Characterized by excessive restriction of a major aspect of family emotional life, such as expression of anger, negative affect, or ambivalence. These emotions become internalized into anxiety, depression, and somatic complaints. The presenting patient is often a passive, depressed child, or young adult.

2. *Internalized ("enmeshed").* Characterized by a fearful, pessimistic, hostile, threatening view of the world, leading to a constant state of vigilance. Such a family has a well-defined role structure, high family loyalty, and a pseudo-mutual bond between parents.

3. *Object-focused.* Characterized by overemphasis on the children (*"child centered"*), the outside community, or the self (*"narcissitic"*). Motivation for treatment depends on the willingness of the marital couple to form an effective coalition.
4. *Impulsive.* Characterized by an adolescent or young adult acting out anger toward a parent onto the community or expressing his or her parents' difficulties in a socially unacceptable way.
5. *Childlike.* Characterized by spouses who have remained dependent on their own families or on the community, based on either inadequacy or immaturity.
6. *Chaotic.* Characterized by disintegration, lack of structure, chronic psychosis and delinquency, and low commitment to the family unit.

Classification 6: By Relational Mode
1. *Dominance versus subordinancy*
2. *Cooperation versus antagonism—dominant-cooperative (active-dependent).*
3. *Dominant antagonistic (active-aggressive).*
4. *Submissive versus cooperative (passive-dependent).*
5. *Submissive antagonistic (passive-aggressive).*

But a more detailed approach is needed, we believe. This involves asking the following questions:

1. What is the phenomenology for the family? Here it is necessary to review the *dimensions* of functioning to determine if the family fits criteria for one of the Vcode diagnoses like *Marital Problem* or for a particular family typology.
2. What is the phenomenology for the individual? (Does the individual fit criteria for a DSM-III-R Axis I, II, or III diagnosis?)
3. How can the phenomenology best be explained?
   a. Is the family involved?
   b. Can systems concepts help understand the phenomenon?
   c. Can individual psychodynamic or behavioral concepts help understand it?
   d. How do (b) and (c) interact?

Since there is no one way of classifying the complexity of marital and family life styles that is universally applicable, Table 8-2 presents the way we organize the data, i.e., the answers to the above questions. This method is based on the research demonstrating that a *combination of clinically identified problems and DSM-III* is the best guide to treatment.[9] The steps are:

1. Formulate the family problem areas into a "diagnosis," that is, a *broad understanding* of the family's problems.
2. Dissect this concept using a family systems model, *both* dynamic (i.e., what is the problem and how did it happen to come to be this way), and descriptive

Table 8-2
A Comprehensive Evaluation Schema

	Type of Formulation	For the Family	For the Individual(s)
	Systemic and/or Dynamic	A system formulation	e.g., Behavioral or individual psychodynamic model of understanding problem
Diagnosis	Descriptive	DSM-III-R, conditions not attributable to a mental disorder that are a focus of attention or treatment, e.g., parent-child problem, family typology	DSM-III-R Classification for each family member on Axis I, II & III as appropriate

(e.g., for the family, a diagnosis of "parent–child problem" is made or for an individual a member may have "Schizophrenic Disorder"). Our assumption is, that in respect to etiology, we believe in both a family systems approach (in its broadest sense) and a family genetic approach (also in its broadest sense). We believe that both dynamic and descriptive models interact.

3. Do this for both the family and for its individuals where appropriate. Make a judgment of whether the family is significantly involved in (or contributory to) family pathology. Once that decision is made, then go into detail in order to best understand both the family and its individuals.

This schema, albeit imprecise, is our best judgment of the state-of-the-art of evaluation and its implication for goals and treatment. *To reemphasize, just as individual, psychodynamic theories maintain that symptoms are the result of internal forces, dynamics, and fantasies; so family theories maintain that symptoms are the result of, or maintained by, the properties of an interaction or the functioning of a family system and the characteristics of the individuals involved.*

The key task is to determine which and how much of these theories contribute to an understanding of the development, and maintenance, of the problem and *even more important, what approach is most likely to foster change?* A purely physical symptom, such as postmyocardial infarct invalidism, can be maintained by the way family members treat the patient, and a problem, such as difficulties in shared decision-making, can be the result of individual dynamics. If you decide that the family contributes to the problem, and you believe that intervening with them may be productive of change, then discuss this with them and agree on a contact for meeting.

PLANNING THE THERAPEUTIC APPROACH AND ESTABLISHING THE TREATMENT CONTRACT

After the evaluation data have been gathered, and formulated into *diagnostic hypotheses*, goals regarding important problem areas can be formulated (Table 8-3). Note in the chart how we line up "goals" to follow "evaluation." The therapist is then ready to consider what therapeutic strategies will be appropriate. (This subject is discussed in Chapters 6-8.)

At this point, a definite, clearly defined contract with regard to goals and treatment should be established. This should include who is to be present; the location, times, estimated length, and frequency of meetings; the fee and contingency planning with respect to absent members and missed appointments. For some families, treatment will be very brief and crisis-oriented, lasting only one or two sessions, whereas for other families treatment may continue for years.

At this point, the therapist should make a concise, explicit statement of the family problems(s) using language the family can understand. Such a statement can be used as a springboard for discussing the treatment plan. For example, the therapist might say, "I think your drinking has to do with some of the feelings you and your wife have about each other. Perhaps it has to do with your feeling that she is trying to limit your 'fun.' From her point of view, she feels that you do not understand how hard she has to work. I think we should meet together to see how we can change things in the family and explore what has happened."

As mentioned earlier, if it appears from the initial family *evaluation* that one (or more) member of the family is suffering from a diagnosable psychiatric disorder, this must be noted and taken into account in the *formulation* and treatment planning. In fact, most often the way a family gets to the family therapist is through an individual. Common situations include those in which one spouse has a diagnosable depression or phobia, one or more family members appears to have a severe personality disorder, there is serious substance abuse in one or more members, schizophrenia is present in one of the young adults living in the parents home, there is childhood and adolescent antisocial behavior. The initial suspicion of a diagnosable disorder in one individual may necessitate further evaluation either in the family setting or individually in order to assess carefully the nature and extent of the individual symptoms as enumerated in DSM-III-R. Our assumption then is that there are important components of *both the individual model and the biological model*, which interact, and the family model.

Case Example Illustrating the Outline

The following case example illustrates the use of the outline for family evaluation.

Table 8-3
Setting Goals After Evaluation

	Type of Formulation	For the Family	For the Individual(s)
Diagnosis	Systemic and/or dynamic	A system formulation	e.g., Behavioral or individual psycho-dynamic model of understanding problem
	Descriptive	DSM-III-R, conditions not attributable to a mental disorder that are a focus of attention or treatment, e.g., parent-child problem. Family style or typology may also be used.	DSM-III-R classification for each family member on Axis I, II & III as appropriate
Goals	Based on Diagnosis	Specify for each problem	Specify for each problem

I. Current Phase of the Family Life Cycle.

The therapist notes that the identified patient is Mrs. R., a 44-year-old white female. Her husband, Mr. R., is 55, and there are three children ranging in age from 17 to 22 years. This family is approaching the empty-nest phase, in which the parents will have to face being alone together. The therapist begins to wonder and to ask to what extent the couple has emphasized the parental role rather than the marital relationship, and to what extent they have encouraged the development of the children's ability to move out of the house and complete their maturation and separation from their parents.

II. Explicit Interview Data

A. What is the current family problem? The oldest son said that the family problem was his mother, because she had recently stopped using barbiturates on the advice of her doctor and subsequently began having ideas that people in the family were trying to harm her. The father added that his wife had always been the "problem." He was joined in these sentiments by the daughter, age 17, and by the younger son, age 20. The mother, however, said that the problem was that nobody would help her and that she could not get any cooperation from the family members around the house.

The therapist then asked the family to think in terms of what the current family (not individual) problem was. The younger son said he thought that maybe the problem was not the mother, but the fact that nobody in the family was communicating or was happy.

The oldest son had been living in a room by himself in some other part of the house. Seven days prior to the first therapy session, he had indicated that he was moving out to live with his girl friend.

B. Why does the family come for treatment at this time? The family reported that about the time the older son announced that he was going to move out, the parents' quarreling intensified. The mother went to a family doctor for a tranquilizer. The doctor said that she appeared confused and suggested she stop taking the barbiturates she had been using. She then became even more suspicious and had a fight with her husband in which they both threw pots at each other. At this point, everybody felt that she should see her family physician, who recommended admission to an inpatient psychiatric unit.

C. What is the background of the family problem?

1. *Composition and characteristics of nuclear and extended family:* The identified patient was a 44-year-old white housewife. Her husband was a 55-year-old white male who was a manual laborer in a shipyard. The older son was 22 and worked part-time in a record store; the younger son was 20 and a part-time student at college; there was a 17-year-old daughter.

2. *Developmental history and patterns of each family member:* Mrs. R.'s father was manager of a cemetery, and she described her mother as being sick all the time. Her parents' relationship revolved around the father's taking care of the mother through much of the marriage, because of her sickness. Mr. R.'s father was well liked, but his mother was "an overprotective bitch," and the father essentially catered to his wife.

   Mrs. R. gave a history of being chronically sick. She had been born prematurely and developed sinusitis and asthma at an early age. She was the younger of two siblings, having an older brother.

   Mr. R. was the oldest of four and took care of two younger siblings who were always sick. He also had physical problems. He never quite lived up to his parents' expectations. He quit college, did not want to move out of the house, and dated very little.

3. *Developmental history and patterns of the nuclear family unit:* The wife and husband were introduced by relatives. Most of their courtship was involved with family social events, and there was very little intimacy during the courtship period. Mrs. R. described the marriage as somewhat disappointing. She indicated that she had married for stability, whereas he had said that he thought she would provide some of the spark that he lacked. Both partners

stated that they had no knowledge of contraception, and a child was born early in the first year of the marriage. They had very little experience being alone together as husband and wife. After they had the other two children, Mr. R. began spending more and more time at work. Mrs. R. found herself becoming more sick with various respiratory and other ailments. They both had to turn to their own mothers, his for financial support, hers for help in raising the children and taking care of Mr. R.

4. *Current interactional patterns:* At the time of the referral the situation had progressively worsened during the past two years. Husband and wife found themselves drifting farther apart and spending less time together, barely talking to each other. Mr. R. was working much more, which made Mrs. R. suspicious that he was chasing around. Mrs. R. continued to complain of physical symptoms, to take more medications, and to become less able to perform childrearing or housekeeping tasks. The older son began to experiment with the use of psychedelic drugs, the younger son had difficulty with his grades, and the daughter attended school less frequently and did poorly when in class. The two mothers-in-law fought over who was helping the family more, each placing the blame for the family problems on the other's child.

D. What is the history of past treatment attempts or other attempts at problem solving in the family? The mother had been seeing the same internist over the past 15 or 20 years. The doctor had frequently suggested psychiatric treatment, but she had refused. She went for individual psychotherapy over a three-month period but quit, saying, "It didn't make my husband better." They also consulted their local family clergyman on several occasions, and he counseled tolerance and patience. Both Mrs. R. and the family had not found past treatment helpful since it did not get to the heart of the problems in the family and because she seemed to be developing all kinds of "phony insights."

E. What are the family's goals and expectations of the treatment? What are their resistances? The family's expectations at first were to help the mother so she could get better. During this evaluation interview, when the therapist opened up some channels of communication that were not previously available, it became apparent that the father had abdicated his role as a parent and a spouse. The marital coalition was almost nonexistent; instead the daughter and father were on one side and younger son and mother on the other. The older son had in many ways withdrawn from the battle by using drugs to blot it all out of his mind.

The primary resistances that existed during this evaluation interview were the family members' scapegoating of the mother and a reluctance to change themselves, the latter quite evident in the father's saying he could not get to treatment sessions because of his job, no matter what time was suggested for the meeting. Although it was less apparent than the resistance, each person in the family did seem to recognize that there was something wrong with the overall functioning of the family and with its individual members and that this problem could be worked on.

III. Formulating the Family Problem Areas

A. Important Dimensions of Functioning

Communication.   There was little or no spontaneous interaction or communication between husband and wife. The children seemed somewhat at odds but were united, however, in a struggle to prevent their parents from taking power. Even when the therapist tried to get them to talk to each other, it was impossible, as the wife felt that the husband never listened to her, and the husband felt his wife was always complaining and could not do anything. There was very little communication followup from one to the other, thus leaving them without continuity of communication or closure. The family seemed to be five unrelated people, each pulling in a different direction from the others.

Problem solving.   The family had difficulty agreeing on anything, even the making of a laundry list. The topic of the laundry list led to various arguments involving many members of the family.

Roles and coalitions.   Mrs. R., who was currently a daughter, wife, and mother, had been unable to move out of her family of origin to her present family. She seemed almost child-like in her presentation and her functioning. She seemed to be overly involved as a daughter and less involved as a wife and mother. The husband was likewise very involved with his family of origin. He had essentially given up his role as husband and turned over the role of father to the older son, who had been managing the family finances, bringing in extra money, and making the kinds of family decisions that Mr. R. used to make.

There had been a reversal of generation roles, with the daughter running the household and doing the cleaning and cooking. The daughter also fulfilled part of a spouse's role, in that father and daughter frequently went to the movies together, whereas the identified patient stayed home with her headaches. The strongest coalition in the family appeared to be a father-daughter instead of the more usual husband-wife.

The main alignments and communication patterns pitted the father and daughter against the younger son and mother, with the older son being a neutral mediator. In his role as mediator, the son was the center of all communication. All fights seemed to be resolved in his "court." This seemed to be taking a toll on him, as he "had not found himself" and was having great difficulty in making a job decision or career choice. It became clear that this son's leaving home would be a grave crisis for the family.

The parental coalition was mainly nonverbal. It consisted of the mother's clutching her stomach, grabbing her heart, and rolling her head back, as though she were about to have a stroke or a heart attack, at which point the father would move his chair farther away from everyone in the family.

Affective responsiveness and involvement. The therapist noted that the general emotional tone of the family was one of anger and frustration. Any sign of positive emotional expression between members was lacking.

Behavior control. There seemed to be no difficulty in this area, as there was no inappropriate expression of aggressive or sexual impulses.

Operative family myths. In this family it appeared that the mother was "sick" and the father was "helpless"; the daughter was a "pest," the older son a "mediator," and the younger son "noninvolved."

The family operated under the myth that a happy marriage is one in which there are no disagreements. Mrs. R. lived under the fantasy that everything should be rosy and that any flaws or problems were to be avoided and not to be discussed. Mrs. R. also felt that both marital partners should be as unselfish as possible and that she had sacrificed her life for her children and husband.

On the other hand, Mr. R. felt that he had worked himself to the bone to bring home the money to keep the family going, sacrificing everything for everyone else. Both parents were bitterly resentful of the nonresponse of the rest of the family to their sacrifices.

Mrs. R. was the scapegoat in the family. Whenever anything went wrong, everyone turned on her. If what she had done did not seem to be an adequate explanation of the problem, an explanation was found taking into account her past transgressions.

Positive feedback had been virtually abandoned in this family for years. Most importantly, Mrs. R. had felt all along that things would work out if she could just remake her husband into a handsome Prince Charming instead of the small, rotund, shy, withdrawn man that he was.

B. Family Style or Typology

Classification 1: Based on rules for defining power: this is a dysfunctional complementary relationship.

Classification 2: By parental stage: this is a family in the empty-nest stage.

Classification 3: By level of intimacy: this is a conflict-habituated marriage.

Classification 4: By personality style: this is a dependent husband and a hysteroid-dysphoric wife.

Classification 5: By description of families in treatment: this family can be described as child-like.

C. Individual Diagnoses

The wife met criteria on Axis I for Barbituate Abuse (304.1). Both wife (histrionic) and husband (dependent) met criteria for personality disorder features on Axis II.

IV. PLANNING THE THERAPEUTIC APPROACH AND ESTABLISHING THE TREATMENT CONTRACT

The first decision was to approach this family's problem from a family standpoint rather than by treating Mrs. R., the identified patient, as an individual, isolated from her family. The family seemed to be in a crisis, facing the imminent departure of the older son, the family mediator. The parents seemed unable to handle this separation; i.e., they could not cope with the empty-nest phase. The father seemed to be chronically weak and ineffective, and both parents' relationship with their own families of origin was still a dependent one. The basic strategy was to strengthen the marital coalition by increasing interaction between the marital dyad, by attempting to decrease the inappropriate interaction between these two people and their families of origin, and by attempting to decrease the cross-generational ties between these two people and their children.

The therapist treated the family as a unit, and he also met with only the marital dyad together for many of the sessions; for a time, the children were consulted alone without the parents. The considered decision was made to exclude the parents' in-laws from treatment and to encourage the marital dyad to take over the parental role that they had abrogated not only to the older son, but also to their own parents. In those sessions in which just the marital dyad participated, positive attention was given to reinforcing communication patterns between husband and wife. They were taught to pick up emotional cues and to respond to each other, rather than to withdraw or to somatize.

The mother was encouraged to reassume the maternal role and the father was encouraged to start making some decisions after discussing them first with his wife. The older son was steered toward his girl friend and a career choice, letting his father make the decisions the son had once made. The daughter was encouraged to improve her failing schoolwork and to stop doing the housekeeping and the cooking.

SUGGESTIONS FOR FURTHER READINGS

Wynne LC (with Gurman A, Ravich R, Boszormenyi-Nagy I): The family and marital therapies. In Lewis JM and Usdin G (Eds): **Treatment Planning in Psychiatry.** Washington, DC: American Psychiatric Association, 1982, pp 225–286.

Excellent, current discussion of information needed to plan a family intervention.

Fleck S: A holistic approach to family typology and the axes of DSM-III. Arch Gen Psychiatry 40:901–906, 1983.

Excellent discussion of the ways of assessing and understanding families.

REFERENCES

1. Mandelbaum A: Diagnosis in family treatment. Bull Menninger Clin 40:497-504, 1976
2. Jacobson NS: Behavioral marital therapy. In Gurman AS and Kniskern DP (Eds): Handbook of Family Therapy. New York: Brunner/Mazel, 1981, pp 556-591
3. Epstein DB and Bishop DS: Problem-centered systems therapy of the family. In Gurman AS and Kniskern DP (Eds): Handbook of Family Therapy. New York: Brunner/Mazel, 1981, pp 44-482
4. Falloon IRH, Boyd JL, McGill C: Family Care of Schizophrenia. New York: Guilford Press, 1984
5. Wynne L: Personal communication
6. Berman EM and Lief HI: Marital therapy from a psychiatric perspective: An overview. Am J Psychiatry 132:583-592, 1975
7. Cuber JF and Harroff PB: Sex and the Significant Americans. Baltimore: Penguin Books, 1966, pp 43-65
8. Grunebaum H: Personal communication
9. Longabaugh R, Stout R, Kriebel GW, et al.: DSM-III and clinically identified problems as a guide to treatment. Arch Gen Psychiatry 43:1097-1103, 1986

Ceremony Possession by Wilmino Domond. From *Haiti: The Black Republic: The Standard Guide to Haiti* by Selden Rodman. Courtesy of Selden Rodman.

157

9
Tools for Evaluation Including Rating Scales and Tests

OBJECTIVES

- To understand the family genogram and its use in evaluation
- To indicate when, and how, to use special evaluation techniques such as structured interviews, psychological testing, and home visits
- To be able to prescribe clinical self-report instruments and rating scales for family dysfunction as an aid to evaluation

INTRODUCTION

As we discussed in the previous chapter, there is a working consensus about the most important areas of family functioning that must be assessed for effective family intervention. This chapter examines those rating scales, self-report instruments, and tests that assess some aspect of those dimensions. These in contrast to purely verbal techniques may be useful for the family that is not verbally facile or may use words as a smokescreen. What families say, and what they actually feel, and do, may often be quite different. Verbal techniques rely on both a family's ability to give information and the therapist's ability to elicit it. There may be great variance in the information given from interview to interview. The family therapist, therefore, may use more than one technique to gain information.

158

Table 9-1
Instrument and Area of Assessment in Family Pathology

Instrument	Dimensions of Family Functioning				
	Communications	Problem-Solving	Roles/Coalitions	Affectivity	Behavior Control
1. Dyadic Adjustment Scale (DAS)	X			X	X
2. Family Cohesion and Adaptability Evaluation Scale (FACES)	X				
3. The Beavers-Timberlawn Rating Scale(BT)	X	X	X	X	
4. Family Assessment Device (FAD)	X	X	X	X	X
5. Family Assessment Measure (FAM)	X		X	X	X

THE FAMILY GENOGRAM

Some family therapists choose not to utilize a comprehensive assessment scheme such as our Family Evaluation Outline and prefer a family genogram, which is exclusively focused on family issues. The family genogram, developed by Murray Bowen,[1] can be used in this section. Usually the genogram information is taken during the beginning phases of a treatment, and serves many process as well as content purposes: (1) it provides the patient, family and family therapist with a structure from which to explore current difficulties and their background, (2) it gives the therapist background information from which to put current difficulties in context, (3) the process of gathering the information may give the patient some conception, distance, and control over the emotional tugs and pulls created by the family, (4) it can be used later in the therapy to dispell fantasies of problems disappearing magically and set realistic goals for dealing with the emotional strains of the family system in the future. Meyer[2] provides a very useful clinical illustration of the use of the genogram in assisting a 24-year-old single female in coping with anxiety at the point of graduating from college.

MEDICAL EXAMINATIONS

In order to rule out physical problems as the cause of family dysfunctions, medical examinations need to be done for each family member when indicated.

> Mr. G. who was a successful musician in his late forties, was noted to become progressively paranoid and quarrelsome. His family therapist felt that his paranoia was related to his wife's love of dancing (sometimes with his friends), her younger age, and to the reality of the children's leaving home. Even with excellent family therapy over three or four months, however, Mr. G. began complaining of headaches and double vision. A neighbor suggested that he consult a physician, who, after a medical workup, discovered a brain tumor. When the tumor was removed, Mr. G.'s paranoia decreased dramatically, and so did the problems between him and his wife.

Major psychiatric illness should be evaluated using traditional history-taking and mental-status examinations.

HOME VISITS[3-5]

Many family therapists visit the family in its own home, with as many family members present as possible. Sometimes this is done only once during the evaluation period. Some family researchers, however, have lived with a family for a period of several weeks, much as an anthropologist might do in an unfamiliar culture. Home visits can be considered at any time when the therapist senses a gross discrepancy between the interactions observed in the office sessions and the reports of what is taking place at home. The timing of the visit can vary depending on its purpose, but it should always be discussed with the family and agreed to in advance.

Home visits enable the therapist to see the family on its own turf and may lead to a better understanding of its interactional patterns. The family may feel more comfortable being seen in their own home. Some families have the feeling that the therapist is more interested when he is willing to make a home visit. The family, however, may see the visit as an intrusion or may try to convert the therapy into a purely social situation. In such cases, the time consumed may be uneconomical. On balance, we recommend home visits whenever possible.

FAMILY TASKS

Techniques utilizing the entire family in a structured task have been developed. For example, the family plans a picnic together or furnishes a room together, using hypothetical furniture and a fixed amount of money. Such techniques give the family therapist useful ways of evaluating families in which verbal interventions are not the common communication method. In such situations, games are a most useful way of obtaining information.

FAMILY RATING SCALES

We will review here some useful rating scales and instruments for family and marital assessment (see Table 9-1). Although most clinicians do not employ these instruments routinely, they may be useful in two situations:

1. At the beginning of therapy to pinpoint deficiencies and the focus of family therapy.
2. During the middle stages of treatment to assess progress.

Self-Report Instruments

There are a number of brief and useful self-report measures of overall marital adjustment and satisfaction, and family functioning, that can be quite useful to the practicing clinician as the instruments are filled out by the patients at home and can be brought to the session.

The Dyadic Adjustment Scale[6] is a 31-item self-report measure intended to assess the quality of marital or dyadic relations. It measures the specific dimensions of satisfaction, cohesion, consensus, and affectional expression. A more extensive albeit lengthy (280 items) self-report instrument, the *Marital Satisfaction Inventory*, was developed by Snyder.[7] There are two forms of the inventory, one for couples with children and one for childless couples. The scale is notable for its inclusion of a measure of how socially desirable a couple may be, a virtue that the frequently used *Locke-Wallace Marital Adjustment Test* does not have.

The Self-Report Measure of Family Cohesion and Adaptibility. Olson and colleagues[8,9] have developed a promising family typology around two major dimensions: family cohesion and adaptability. Family cohesion is defined as the emotional bonding between members of the family, and relates to such issues as independence, autonomy, coalition, boundaries, pseudomutuality, undifferentiated ego mass, and other concepts central in the family theory literature. Family adaptability is the capacity of the family when confronted with situational or developmental stress to change its rules, power structure, role relationships, and styles of negotiating.

With the self-report instrument, the Family Cohesion and Adaptability Evaluation Scales (FACES), individual family members are asked to report on family cohesion and adaptability. Several studies (e.g., reference 10) suggest that in contrast to functional families, pathological families score on the extremes of cohesion and adaptability.

The clinician can also utilize the observations of each spouse in order to complete the assessment of marital interaction. While it can be argued that the spouses' observations might be inaccurate, it is eminently useful for the clinician to know in what areas the spouse's observations seem biased and distorted. Thus, comparing each spouse's observations with the other and with that of the clinician is quite helpful in planning for treatment focus. The following tests examine this area.

Developed by the Oregon Group,[11] the *Spouse Observation Checklist (SOC)* covers 12 categories of behavior including companionship, affection, considera-tion, sex, communication, coupling activities, child care and parenting, household responsibilities, financial decison making, employment-education, personal habits and appearance, and self and spouse independence. Each spouse is told to check all behaviors emitted by the spouse during the previous 24 hours and indicate only those behaviors that were experienced as either pleasing or displeasing. The data can be used to pinpoint displeasing behaviors, provide a baseline for pre-therapeutic efforts, and focus interventions aimed at increasing positive behavior.

The Areas-of-Change Questionnaire (A-C)[11,12] asks each spouse to list be-haviors of the mate in which change would be desirable. It asks for an indication of major areas for change including a prediction of what change the partner will desire. The *Areas-of-Change Questionnaire* score is highly correlated with the *Locke-Wallace Marital Adjustment Test* and provides information on target areas of treatment.

The Marital Precounseling Inventory (MPCI)[13] was developed to elicit from both spouses material on an extensive range of marital issues: identification of target problems, common interests, satisfaction with communication, rules for decision making, reinforcement power, general satisfaction, and optimism regard-ing the future. This self-assessment packet is quite extensive and is seen as one of the most comprehensive and thorough self-report packages for behavioral marital intervention.[14]

The McMaster Family Assessment Device (FAD)[15] is a screening instrument to assist in the initial process of evaluation of a family for intervention. Each family member (over age 12) fills out a paper and pencil questionnaire on the family functioning in six areas: problem solving, communication, roles, affective responsiveness, affective involvement, and behavior control. The instrument is easy to give (takes 15–20 minutes to complete) and provides a face-valid measure of areas of family function/dysfunction that could be targeted for intervention.

The Family Assessment Measure (FAM)[16] is another self-report pencil and paper instrument that can be used to assess the whole family. Based on a model of family functioning quite similar to the McMaster model, the instrument provides scores on task accomplishment, role performance, communication affective expression, involvement, control values and norms, and a general overall rating of family functioning. The instrument takes approximately 30 minutes to complete and can be done by all family members 10 to 20 years of age and older.

Marital and Family Interaction Instruments (Rated by the Therapist)

The Beavers Timberlawn Rating Scales (B-T)[17] is a rating by an outside observer of the family functioning across a number of areas including: overt power, parental coalitions, closeness, mythology, goal-directed negotiation, clarity of expression, responsibility, invasiveness, permeability, range of feelings, mood and tone, unresolvable conflict, empathy, and a global health/pathology rating.

In the clinical assessment of marital interaction, Jacobson, Elwood, and Dallas[14] suggest giving the couple a problem solving task with the therapist as observer, and rating the couples on a variety of dimensions relevant to communication effectiveness as codified in, for example, the Marital Interaction Coding System (MICS).[12] Simply reviewing the dimensions of the MICS is helpful in assisting the clinician in pinpointing the specific couple's difficulties.

As another alternative, it has been recommended[14] that the practicing clinician utilize the Verbal Problem Checklist (VPC).[17] As the observer of marital interaction, the clinician can rate the 49 categories of verbal behavior (e.g., fast talk, slow talk, obtrusions, excessive question asking, etc.).

For the clinician who wants a view of the actual ecology of the family, it has been noted that the family meal time is a microcosm of the family in sociological and dynamic terms.[18] Direct observations of family meal time planning, preparation, and consumption can be made. Alternatively the family therapist can ask the family to draw a diagram of the seating at a typical family meal. Sometimes family members will not eat together. Children rather than parents may prepare the meals. An adolescent who is angry with his parents will often take his meals alone—if the parents allow this. One particular child might be used as a mediator between the parents and be asked to sit between them, whereas the other siblings are not so involved in the parental drama. In a situation in which one parent cannot function (for example, a drinking father), that parent may take meals in the bedroom. Such observations are often helpful in determining the family patterns.

A few investigators have adapted several projective tests, the Thematic Apperception Test[19,20] and the Rorschach Test[21] (originally designed for individual use), for family evaluation. The entire family, meeting together, is, for example, asked to look at a Rorschach card, discuss their percepts with one another, and try to arrive at a common story or interpretation. As in individual testing, the process by which the family arrives at its interpretation is as carefully noted as the content of the interpretation itself. Notable success has been reported in being able to predict the nature of the identified patient's clinical psychiatric symptomatology from an examination of the psychological test protocols of the patient's parents, tested jointly, with the patient absent.[22]

Marital Assessment Packages

Several authors recommend a particular combination of instruments for assessment of the marital relationship. For example, the pretreatment assessment at the University of Washington Psychology Clinic utilizes the *Areas-of-Change Questionnaire*, portions of the *Marital Precounseling Inventory*, the *Marital Status Inventory*, the *Marital Activities Inventory*, the *Dyadic Adjustment Scale*, and the *Sexual Interaction Inventory*.[14]

Weiss and Margolin[23] describe the assessment package utilized by the Oregon group: self-report instruments (*Locke-Wallace, Areas of Change Questionnaire,* the *Marital Activities Inventory*, the *Marital Status Inventory*, 28-item problem checklist, *Pleasing and Displeasing Spouse Observation Checklists*) and two-minute samples of problem-solving behavior rated by the MICS.

SUGGESTIONS FOR FURTHER READINGS

Wynne LC (with Gurman A, Ravich R, and Boszormenyi-Nagi, I): The family and marital therapies. In Lewis JM and Usdin G (Eds): **Treatment Planning in Psychiatry**. Washington, DC: American Psychiatric Association, 1982.

Jacobson NS, Elwood RW, and Dallas M: Assessment of marital dysfunction. In Barlow DH (Ed): **Behavioral Assessment of Adult Disorders**. New York: Guilford, 1981.
    Marital assessment from a behavioral point of view, with use of several self-report instruments.

REFERENCES

1. Bowen M: Family Therapy in Clinical Practice. New York: Jason Aronson, 1978
2. Meyer PH: Between Families: The Unattached Young Adult. New York: Garland Press, 1980
3. Fisch R: Home visits in a private psychiatric practice. Fam Process 3:114-126, 1964

4. Friedman AS: Family therapy as conducted in the home. Fam Process 1:132-140, 1962

5. Henry J: The study of families by naturalistic observation. In Cohen IM (Ed): Family Structure, Dynamics and Therapy. Psychiatric Research Report No. 20. New York: American Psychiatric Association, 1966, pp 95-104

6. Spanier GB: Measuring dyadic adjustment: New scales for assessing the quality of marriage and similar dyads. J Marr Fam 38:15-28, 1976

7. Snyder DK, Willis RM, and Keiser TW: Empirical validation of the marital satisfaction inventory: An actuarial approach. J Consult Clin Psychology 49:262-268, 1979

8. Olson D, Russell C, and Sprenkle D: Circumplex model of marital and family systems. VI. Theoretical update. Family Process 22:69-83, 1983

9. Olson DH, Portner J, and Bell R: FACES II: Family adaptability and cohesion evaluation scales. St. Paul: Family Social Science, University of Minnesota, 1982

10. Spenkle D and Olson D: Circumplex model of marital systems. IV. Empirical study of clinic and non-clinic couples. J Marr Fam Counsel 4:59-74, 1978

11. Patterson GR: Some procedures for assessing changes in marital interaction patterns. Oregon Res Instit Bull 16(7), 1976

12. Weiss RL, Hops H, and Patterson GR: A framework for conceptualizing marital conflict, technology for altering it, some data for evaluating it. In Hamerlynck LA, Handy LC, and Mash EJ (Eds): Behavior Change: Methodology, Concepts, and Practice. Champaign, IL: Research Press, 1973

13. Stuart RB and Stuart F: Marital Precounseling Inventory. Champaign, IL: Research Press, 1972

14. Jacobson NS, Elwood RW, and Dallas M: Assessment of marital dysfunction. In Barlow DH (Ed): Behavioral Assessment of Adult Disorders. New York: Guilford Press, 1981

15. Epstein N, Baldwin L, and Bishop DS: The McMaster family assessment device. J Mar Fam Therapy 9:171-180, 1983

16. Skinner H, Steinhauer P, and Santa-Barbara J: The family assessment measure. Can J Community Mental Health 2:91-105, 1983

17. Thomas EJ: Marital Communication and Decision-Making. New York: The Free Press, 1977.3

18. White SL: Family dinner time: A focus for life space diagrams. J Clin Social Work 4:93-101, 1976

19. Winter WD, Ferreira AJ, and Olson JL: Hostility themes in the family TAT. J Projective Techniques and Personality Assessment 30:270-275, 1966

20. Winter WD, Ferreira AJ, and Olson JL: Story sequence analysis of family TATs. J Projective Techniques and Personality Assessment 29:392-397, 1965

21. Willi J: Joint Rorschach testing of partner relationships. Fam Process 8:64-78, 1969

22. Jackson DD, Riskin J, and Satir V: A method of analysis of a family inter-
    view. Arch Gen Psychiatry 5:321-339, 1961
23. Weiss RL and Margolin G: Assessment of marital conflict and accord. In
    Ciminero AR, Calhoun KD, and Adams HE (Eds): Handbook of Behavior
    Assessment. New York: John Wiley & Sons, 1977, pp 555-602

Section IV

Family Treatment

Once the therapist achieves some understanding of what is wrong, the next issue is to set treatment goals (Chapter 10). Before doing that, however, it is necessary for the student to understand the competing models of understanding and treating family disorder—each with its unique mediating and final goals. These are reviewed and compared to each other in Chapter 11.

Finally, we get to the nitty-gritty of how to do family treatment (Chapter 12) and what treatment looks like over time (Chapter 13), including a special detour to describe the modifications necessary to do a very common brand of family work—brief family therapy. Chapter 15 reviews problems, i.e., the resistances that can occur during a course of treatment.

We close this section by covering ground rules—the issues that are of interest to beginning therapists—who to include, what about co-therapy or teams, where and how to see and schedule families, setting fees, keeping a record of treatment and current treatment packages, including family therapy in combination with other treatments (e.g., drug treatment), and helping agencies.

167

Reclining Chiricahua Mother by Allan Houser. Courtesy of the artist and the Gallery Wall, Inc., Phoenix, Arizona

10
The Major Schools
of Family Therapy

OBJECTIVES

- To outline (in broad strokes) the major schools of family therapy
- To differentiate the strategies, techniques, stance, goals and data base among schools

INTRODUCTION

An observer of the general psychotherapy scene has recently stated, "In picking up the textbook of the future, we should see in the table of contents not a listing of School A, School B, and so on—perhaps ending with the author's attempt at integration—but an outline of the various agreed-upon intervention principles, a specification of varying techniques for implementing each principle, and an indication of the relative effectiveness of each of these techniques, together with their interaction with varying presenting problems and individual differences among patients/clients and therapists."[1] Indeed, we agree wholeheartedly, but this seems like an ideal to be striven for, rather than a full possibility at the present time.

However, in the spirit of the above quote, we present in this (and the following) chapter, the general schools* of family intervention by focusing, not primarily on their originators, *but on their mediating and final goals and related strategies of intervention.*

---

*"Schools" is used interchangeably with "models" in this chapter.

Much has been written about the diverse schools of family intervention, often formed around charismatic leaders such as Minuchin, Haley, Bowen and Ackerman. There are different classifications of the schools, each with their own assumptions about the origin and maintenance of pathology; goals, strategies and techniques for intervention; and indications for utilization. It is necessary for the beginning student of family intervention to have some general conceptual understanding of these schools, their history, and the personalities involved (Table 10-1).

INSIGHT-AWARENESS MODEL

The insight-awareness orientation has also been known as the "historical," the "psychodynamic," or the "psychoanalytic school." In a real sense, this is the oldest school of family therapy, since it grew naturally out of the psychoanalytic tradition. One of the earliest family therapists was a child analyst, Nathan Ackerman, who utilized his analytic background to inform and lend substance to his approach and understanding of families. One has only to read the transcripts of his sessions to appreciate the influence that analytic thinking and techniques had upon his work with families and couples.[2]

By changing the transference distortions, correcting the projective identifications, and infusing insight and new understanding into the arena of interpersonal turmoil and conflict, this school of family therapy attempts to change the functioning and interrelationships of the various members of the family or marital system. The data base is derived from historical material of the current and past generations, from transference/countertransference phenomena, unconscious derivatives, and resistances. A basic assumption is that intrapsychic conflict, interpersonal problem foci, and defensive and coping mechanisms are modeled and taught within the family system. Portions of the data base that are of paramount interest to the practitioners of this model are dream and fantasy material, fantasies and projections about other family members, and transference distortions about other family members and the therapist. Understanding the history and mutations over time of these dynamics is considered crucial to understanding current dysfunction.

A broad use of the terms "transference" and "countertransference" is used here. Such phenomena can be understood in terms of transference on at least five levels: (1) man to woman; (2) woman to man; (3) woman to therapist; (4) man to therapist; (5) couple to therapist. Just as there are multiple transference reactions, there are multiple countertransference responses. It is assumed that understanding of unconscious derivatives and their resistances is usually necessary to effect change.

Table 10-1
Models of Family Treatment

Treatment Approach ("School")	Representative Therapists	strategies and Techniques	Stance	Goals	Data Base
1. Insight-awareness (a.k.a. historical, or psychodynamic or psychoanalytic)	Ackerman Nagy & Spark Paul Nadelson	1. Observation 2. Clarification 3. Interpretation	1. Listener 2. "Therapeutic distance" 3. Therapeutic stance of technical neutrality	Foster understanding and insight to effect change	1. History 2. Unconscious derivatives 3. Transference
2. System-structural (a.k.a. systems, communications or structural)	Palo Alto Group (Jackson, Bateson, Haley, Satir) Sluzki Bowen Minuchin M. Erickson Palazzoli	1. Strategies to alter family structure and behavior 2. Observe and transform using directives	Therapist observes and moves in and out of process	Change structure, communication pattern and roles, which change perception and behavior	1. Sequences 2. Communication 3. Rules 4. History

3. Behavioral	R. Weiss N. Jacobson G. Patterson I. Falloon	1. Communication teaching 2. Problem solving skills 3. Contingency contracting	Therapist is collaborator in the development of interpersonal skills	Eliminate dysfunctional behaviors and learn to utilize new and more effective interpersonal behaviors	1. Observation of overt behaviors 2. Functional analysis of problematic behavioral sequences
4. Experiential-existential	Whitaker Bowen Nagy	1. Therapist designs and/or participates with family in the emotional experience 2. Empathy	Therapist offers himself for interaction to minimize distance between family and himself	1. Change ways family members experience (and presumably react to) each other 2. Growth and differentiation	1. Observed verbal and non-verbal behavior 2. Shared feelings (including the therapist's feelings)

The theoretical underpinnings of this model are the familiar ones of psychoanalytic thinking, including especially topographical concepts of conscious, preconscious, and unconscious; constructs of the id, ego, and superego; and concepts that focus on the interaction of individuals, such as secondary gain, transference, and projective identification. While early analysts, who opted for a more interactional model (for example, Nathan Ackerman), criticized this model for its lack of attention to, and language for, interactional data, more recent authors in the analytic tradition of object relations (for example, Henry Dicks[3]) have applied these concepts to the understanding and analytic treatment of these interactional problems.

The major therapeutic techniques of this model include clarification, interpretation, exploration of intrapsychic as well as interpersonal dynamics, and development of insight and empathy. Using such analytic techniques with an individual in the presence of a spouse or other family member represents a unique development. At the very least, it is possible that while the therapist is addressing an interpretation to one individual, the other members of the family can utilize the interpretative method to explore their own conflicts and difficulties, as well as to begin to understand the family member more fully with the input from the therapist. The goal is to foster understanding and insight in order to effect change in individuals as well as in the family unit.

THE SYSTEMS-STRUCTURAL MODEL

The orientation that is unique to the family movement and that has given it impetus is the systems understanding of family function and dysfunction. The family systems approach uses the metaphor of communication theorists such as Gregory Bateson and the computer metaphors of our modern age, such as feedback loops, communication exchange, and so forth. These explanatory concepts lead the practitioner to focus on a data base composed of repetitive interchanges between individuals in a marriage or family that occur in the here and now (as opposed to the interest in the history of the relationship in the psychoanalytic model), and that define, limit, and structure the behavior and experience of the individuals in the system. *While the assumption of the psychoanalytic model is that individuals in a family group can perceive and distort the working of the group, the assumption in this model is that the group is greater than the individuals who comprise it, and that the individual is governed and regulated by this greater entity (the family or the marital dyad).* This model works on the assumption that there is no such thing as nonbehavior—even silence is a means of communication. There is a focus on syntax (ways of communicating), semantics (the meanings of communicative arts), and pragmatics (the practical effects of communication). The ultimate goal of the model is not insight but to change structure and function. These are changes that presumably alter perception of the other members of the system.

The treatment techniques (or strategies) in this model include: (1) changing family transactional patterns; (2) marking boundaries; (3) escalating stress; (4) assigning tasks both within and outside of the therapy sessions; (5) focusing on, exaggerating, deemphasizing, or relabeling symptoms; (6) reframing; (7) manipulating mood; (8) clarifying communication; (9) interrupting repetitive interactional patterns; and (10) prescribing paradoxical injunctions.[4-6] We say more about these techniques in the next four chapters, but for now, the student should understand that in one way or another, the techniques are intended to interrupt current repetitive interpersonal behaviors and introduce new interactional patterns that will result in the creation of new and more mature, or less symptomatic, interactions and inner states.

THE BEHAVIORAL MODEL

The behavioral model grows out of the behavioral orientation that has historically flourished parallel, and in reaction, to the psychoanalytic tradition. The data base for this orientation is quantifiable, measurable behavior, whether internal (thoughts) or external (actions). Explanatory concepts are those of the learning theories traditions; for example, stimulus, response, and concepts of such as classical conditioning, operant conditioning, schedules of reinforcement, and so forth. With the behavioral model becoming increasingly applied to interactional systems such as the family, other concepts have been introduced to expand the model into the interpersonal sphere. Perhaps the most influential has been the *behavior exchange model* of John Thibaut and Harold Kelley,[7] in which it is postulated that there is a benefit and cost ratio for each individual in an exchange situation (for example, marriage). What that ratio is has a major influence on the course and outcome of that relationship. For example, if one spouse receives (what is perceived as) only a little benefit for a lot of effort, it would increase the risk of the marriage failing.

The goal in this model is to effect change in discrete, observable, measurable behaviors that are considered problematic by the individuals seeking assistance. As opposed to the psychoanalytic model, which often seems to have more ambitious goals of character change and "insight," this model tends to focus more on discrete problem areas defined by clear behavior patterns. Thus, treatment in this model tends to be briefer and more circumscribed. Emphasis is placed not on pathology but upon behavioral deficits and excesses that are to be changed. If undesired behaviors are eliminated (for example, husband hitting wife), it is not assumed that more social behaviors will necessarily spontaneously emerge, but

rather that the therapist might be required to teach new and more adaptive behaviors to the spouses or family members.

Techniques include helping family members learn means of effecting the
desired behavior in another member. Some of the major tactics utilized are behavioral contracting based on good faith or *quid pro quo* agreements ("if you do
this, I will do that"), training in communication skills, training in effective
problem solving, and combining positive reinforcement with a decrease in
destructive interchanges.

The stance of the therapist is quite active since he sees his job as a means to
introduce behavior change into the repertoire of the family members. Although
behaviorists have written little about how they handle individual and family resistance to their suggestions, making them sometimes appear somewhat naive to the
experienced clinician, they are increasingly paying more attention to resistance
and at times suggest the use of paradoxical injunctions more typically enunciated
by the systems theorists. Indeed, it has been suggested that there is a congruence,
if not a growing similarity, between the techniques of the behaviorists and the systems interventionists.

This school of family therapy avoids the traditional techniques of individual
therapy. It does not concentrate on eliciting historical material, it is not particularly interested in fostering increased awareness or expression of buried
feelings, and it does not engage in interpreting psychodynamics. It does not consider understanding and insight to be important or essential in producing change.
Instead, this group of family therapists manipulates variables such as the participants and rules of therapy by active suggestion and direction.

The ultimate goal of this orientation is not so much to foster understanding
and insight as to change family behaviors, such as communication patterns,
problem solving skills, etc.

THE EXPERIENTIAL-EXISTENTIAL MODEL

This school believes that it is vital for the therapist to be aware of and take
into account not only the experience of each member of the family, but also the
therapist's experience as an outsider entering the family.[8] Empathy is the key
here—that is, the ability of the therapist to experience what a particular family
member feels at any given moment in the context of the family. The data base is
not only what the therapist sees, but what he and/or the family *feel*.

This data base is derived from situations that the therapist designs, permitting
him to participate with the family in an emotional experience. If a subject cannot
be discussed, the therapist brings it up. His use of empathy enables him not only
to understand what an individual family might be feeling but allows him sometimes to serve as a model for identification. He may be a role model for a family

or an advocate and help the family achieve something. If a family is starving, the family therapist helps change the family by going with them to get food stamps.

Thus, in this form of therapy the therapist offers himself as a real person in order to minimize the distance between himself and the family. He is always on the side of the family, but his behavior is different from any other family member and is designed to promote more functional behavior.

The goal is to change the way family members experience and presumably react to each other. A secondary goal is growth and differentiation of family members.

CONCLUSION

Currently there are various strategies for treating families. Each may emphasize different assumptions and types of interventions. Some therapists prefer to operate with one strategy in most cases, whereas others intermix these strategies depending on the type of case and the phase of treatment. At times the type of strategy used is made explicit by the therapist, whereas in other instances it remains covert; but irrespective of whether a therapist specializes in one or another approach or is eclectic, some hypotheses will be formed about the nature of the family's difficulty and the preferable approach to adopt.

Some therapists emphasize reconstruction of past events, whereas others choose to deal only with current behavior as manifested during the therapy session. Some therapists favor verbal exploration and interpretation, whereas others are more in favor of utilizing an action or experiential mode of treatment, either in the session itself or by requiring new behavior outside the interview. Some therapists think in terms of problems and symptoms and attempt to decode or understand possible symbolic meanings of symptomatology, whereas other therapists focus on the potentials for growth and differentiation that are not being fulfilled. Some therapists utilize one or a very limited number of methods in dealing with a whole range of "problems," but others are more eclectic and attempt to tailor the treatment techniques to what they consider the specific requirements of the situation.

With the therapeutic focus on one person, the emphasis is often on the individual's perceptions, reactions, and feelings, and also on the equality of status between the individual and the therapist; when two people are the operative system, attention is directed to interactions and relationships. Therapists who think in terms of a unit of three people look at coalitions, structures, and hierarchies of status and power. The number of people actually involved in the interviews may not be as important as *how many people are involved in the therapist's way of thinking about the problem.*

SUGGESTIONS FOR FURTHER READINGS

Gurman AS and Kniskern DP (Eds): **Handbook of Family Therapy.** New York: Brunner/Mazel, 1981.

The editors asked authors representing the major schools of family therapy to describe theory, assessment, and intervention strategies and techniques for their school of work.

Hoffman L: **Foundations of Family Therapy.** New York: Basic Books, 1981.

A very good discussion of the theoretical underpinnings of the major schools of family therapy.

REFERENCES

1. Goldfried M: Toward the delineation of therapeutic change principles. Am Psychologist 35:997-998, 1980
2. Block D and Simon R (Eds): The Strength of Family Therapy: Selected Papers of Nathan W. Ackerman. New York: Brunner/Mazel, 1982
3. Dicks HV: Marital Tensions. London: Routledge & Kegan Paul, 1967
4. Minuchin S: Families and Family Therapy. Cambridge, MA: Harvard University Press, 1974
5. Minuchin S and Fishman HC: Family Therapy Techniques. Cambridge, MA: Harvard University Press, 1981
6. Selvini-Palazzoli M, Oscolo L, Cecchin GF, et al.: Paradox and Counterparadox: A New Model in the Therapy of the Family in Schizophrenic Transaction. New York: Jason Aronson, 1978
7. Thibaut JW and Kelley HH: The Social Psychology of Groups. New York: Wiley, 1959
8. Napier AY and Whitaker CA: The Family Crucible. New York: Harper & Row, 1978

A Ride for Liberty by Eastman Johnson. Courtesy of the Brooklyn Museum.

11
Family Treatment:
Goals

OBJECTIVES

- To be able to set the mediating and final goals of family treatment
- To be able to individualize treatment goals
- To relate the goals of treatment to strategies and interventions
- To relate the goals of treatment to process and content of treatment issues

INTRODUCTION

Now that you are familiar with the four schools of family therapy, and realize that each school has somewhat different goals, let us examine the issue of goals from five prospectives:

1. Mediating and Final Goals
2. Individualizing Goals with the Family
3. Goals and Their Relation to Process and Content Issues
4. Mediating Goals and Their Related Strategies
5. Goals and Related Strategies Common to All Family Therapy Schools

MEDIATING AND FINAL GOALS AS THEY RELATE TO SCHOOLS

One convenient way to conceptualize types of treatment goals is to distinguish the *final goals* (the ultimate results desired) from the *mediating (or inter-*

180

mediate) goals that must precede the final results. While one would conceptualize unique and specific goals for each individual family, more general mediating and final family therapy goals are presented below. These are relatively broad areas that allow for considerable flexibility according to the specifics of each particular family or marital unit, and they are not mutually exclusive but often intertwined. These broad categories help clarify the therapist's idea of what is to be achieved, and they suggest potential treatment strategies and timing of interventions.

The Most Common Mediating Goals

1. *Establishment of a working alliance.* It is likely that patients and families size up therapists very quickly and those early attitudes are likely to persist. Thus, the early connection between family therapist and each family member is quite crucial to the ultimate outcome of the work. Setting up such an alliance in individual therapy seems relatively simple in comparison to setting up an alliance with the multiple members of a family, who themselves often do not get along with each other.
2. *Specification of problem(s).* This would include a detailed delineation of family members behaviors around the symptoms or problems that brought the family to treatment.
3. *Clarification of attempted solutions.* It is very likely that many families have attempted solutions to their problems before coming to the conclusion that they need outside intervention. Almost by definition these are solutions that failed so the therapist should determine what did not work, (as indeed, some would say that problems are simply ordinary situations to which poor solutions were applied).[1]
4. *Clarification and specification of individual desires and needs as they are expressed, mediated and met in the total family/marital environment and network of relationships.* It is the lack of clarity and conflict, either overt or covert, around such needs and desires that leads to or constitutes family pathology itself.
5. *Modification of individual(s) expectations or needs.*
6. *Recognition of mutual contribution to the problem(s).* While therapists differ in how much they think this recognition must come early in the therapy or how explicit it must be, the very acceptance of the family intervention format (most or all family members coming to most sessions) implies some recognition of mutual contribution to the problem or at least to solutions.
7. *Redefinition of the problem(s).* Redefining a problem as an asset or redefining it into various parts, some of which are problematic and others not, are all steps to possible solutions.

8. *An improvement in communication skills,* including listening and expressive skills, diminution of coercive and blaming behavior with increase in reciprocity, and effective, pleasant problem solving and conflict resolution behaviors.
9. *A shift in disturbed, inflexible roles and coalitions.* This may include helping to improve the autonomy and individualization of family members, to facilitate the more flexible assumption of leadership by any particular family member as circumstances require, and to facilitate general task performance by one or more members.
10. *Increased family knowledge about serious psychiatric illness.* In families that have one or more members with serious Axis I pathology such as schizophrenia or recurrent affective illness, a common mediating goal is to increase family information about the illness, its course, and its responsiveness to environmental, including familial, stresses.
11. *Insight* regarding historical factors related to current problems or insight about current interaction patterns. This mediating goal may be relatively important in psychodynamically-oriented family or marital work, and be totally absent in other orientations.

The Most Common Final Goals

1. *Reduction or elimination of symptoms, or symptomatic behavior, in one or more family members.* These symptoms may include major or minor symptoms of mood and affect (anxiety and depression), thought disorder, disruptive behaviors in children and adolescents, marital conflict and fighting, and sexual disorders.
2. *Resolution of the problem(s) as originally presented by the family.*
3. *Increased family/marital intimacy.*
4. *Role flexibility and adaptability within the family matrix.*
5. *Toleration of differentness and differentiation appropriate to age and developmental level.*
6. *Balance of power within the marital dyad, with appropriate sharing of input and autonomy for the children.*
7. *Increased self-esteem.*
8. *Clear, efficient, and satisfying communication.*
9. *Resolution of neurotic conflict, inappropriate projective identification, and marital transference phenomena.*

The problems of families and the goals specific to them, both mediating and final, should determine the strategies of the therapy. Table 11-1 sequentially follows Tables 8-1 and 8-2 in making this concept clear, and the assumptions embodied in this table are central to the rest of the text.

Table 11-1
Deciding Strategies After Goals are Set

	Type of Formulation	For the Family	For the Individual
Diagnosis	Systemic and/or dynamic	A system formulation of problems	e.g., Behavioral or individual psychodynamic model of understanding problem
	Descriptive	DSM-III-R, Conditions not attributable to a mental disorder that are a focus of attention or treatment, e.g., parent–child problem. Family style typology may also be used.	DSM-III-R Classification for each family member on Axis I, II & III as appropriate
Goals	Based on diagnosis	Specify for each problem	Specify for each problem
Strategies	Based on goals	Specify for each goal	Specify for each goal

Too often, unfortunately, the theoretical background and convictions of the therapist with his predetermined set dictate the techniques utilized. As research specifies the behaviors that cause or maintain a problem or specific symptoms, the mediating goals of the treatment can be further specified. Several examples come to mind from recent research. Since prolonged contact between an individual with schizophrenia and a family member who is hostile and critical leads to the reappearance of symptoms and often rehospitalization, one specific goal of treatment with such an individual and his or her family would be the reduction of such stress. In another area, research suggests that antisocial behavior in adolescents is related to coercive behavior exhibited by parents who lack parenting skills.[2] Treatment in such situations would, therefore, involve mediating goals of reducing parental coercive behavior, and instigating parental behaviors of appropriate punishment and boundary setting. These two illustrations are meant only as indications of the kinds of research that will specify needed mediating and final goals in order to change symptomatic constellations. In such a way, so-called "schools" of family intervention will give way to specified mediating goals that require the utilization of proven strategies to accomplish the desired goals.

INDIVIDUALIZING GOALS WITH THE FAMILY

Now that we have set the stage by providing background about the main "schools" of family therapy—and discussing the concept of mediating and final goals—let us again return to the issue of setting goals within the clinical situation, i.e., with a family.

The therapist forms a concept of the family's difficulties based on the evaluation of the family's history and interaction (see Section III). The treatment often begins with the issues that seem to be most crucial to the family; the treatment at the outset helps the family to deal with an immediate crisis situation. Only after some stability and rapport have been achieved is it possible for the therapist to begin to help the family in areas that will also be beneficial. The work is often slow and gradual; sudden or miraculous major shifts in long-standing family patterns are not likely to occur. When such rapid changes occur, they may prove to be mirages, as well as harbingers of later difficulty.

In setting goals it is helpful to think not only of the family as a whole and of the various interpersonal dyads and triads, but also of the individuals who make up the system. Each individual will have a history, a personality, and a set of coping mechanisms. A thorough knowledge of individual personality theory and psychopathology is essential for knowing what to expect from the individual atoms as well as from the family molecule.

At times it will be necessary to provide specific treatment for, or to direct specific attention to, the needs of an individual family member (for example, when a family member is floridly psychotic) with individual sessions, somatic treatment, and sometimes hospitalization (see Chapter 24).

Even under ordinary circumstances, however, a thorough understanding of the strengths and weaknesses of each family member (basic personality patterns, reactions to stress, and so on) will help to determine the goals and techniques of the family therapy.

The goals of family treatment must be in some way congruent with what the family members seem to desire and what they are realistically capable of achieving at any particular point. The therapist's views of the appropriate therapeutic possibilities, however, may differ from those the family members initially envision. Overall goals encompass the entire family system as well as its individual members. Ideally, the entire family should function more satisfactorily as a result of family therapy, and each family member should derive personal benefit from the experience and results of the therapy. The family therapist, for example, should not be in the position of taking the focus off a scapegoated member (saying, for instance, "It's not Dad's drinking that is the problem") only to consistently refocus on one or another family member ("It's Mom's yelling") as the cause of the family's difficulties.

Families traditionally enter therapy because of gross symptomatic difficulty. This is often related to one family member. A marital partner may blame the spouse for causing his or her distress or may feel guilty because the children are not behaving properly. A child may be singled out as the only problem in the family. One member, therefore, may have already been labeled "the identified patient."

Less commonly, family members talk about system difficulties as "marital troubles" or "family unhappiness." One family member may have instigated the seeking of help, or, even less frequently, the family as a whole may have discussed the difficulties and may have agreed to seek professional assistance. Families may come into treatment on their own with varying levels of motivation and expectations or they may be referred by other agencies or individuals.

Some families today are seeking professional help, not for these more traditional reasons, however, but rather for clarification of family roles and as a *growth-enhancing experience.* In such cases, a *problem-solving model* seems less appropriate than a growth-development model.

The goals of treatment will be related to what has been learned during the initial evaluation period, as well as to whatever develops as the therapy progresses. All specific mediating and goals need not be clearly spelled out at the onset of treatment; sometimes goals are left somewhat vague, with details being clarified only later, or perhaps never being discussed explicitly. The particular areas to be dealt with, as well as a determination as to the priority in dealing with them, must be carefully considered. Some family therapists are relatively comfortable with allowing goals to develop as the therapy proceeds. Such treatment sometimes appears as a sequence of short-term problem resolutions. Other therapists attempt to delineate major goals early in the course of treatment or to get the family to cope better with problems that cannot be reversed, such as the death of a family member.

GOALS AND THEIR RELATION TO PROCESS AND CONTENT ISSUES

The relative importance of the treatment *process* as compared with its *content* is an issue sometimes raised by family therapists. The more traditional view tends to favor substantive content issues, whereas the newer holistic view looks more closely at the characteristic patterning in an interpersonal network, with less emphasis on the subject matter. In some ways this may be an artificial dichotomy. For example, the communication process may become the most important subject matter of the therapy. Any attempt to deal with a specific content issue inevitably brings process issues to the surface.

The C. family requested help because their 19-year-old son, T., was very angry at his mother, and the parents were having difficulty in controlling him. The trouble started when he became engaged a year prior to treatment. In sessions T. would talk angrily all the time and the mother would complain about him whenever he did stop talking. It was clear after seeing this pattern repeatedly that an initial goal was to facilitate a wider range of communication possibilities between them. All the family members agreed to this goal. The content of what the mother and T. talked about was irrelevant and emotionally charged; the context and pattern of the communication was the key.

The therapeutic interventions were to stop T. from talking all the time, to get T. to listen to his mother, to stop the mother from complaining, and to get the others to express their feelings toward T. A younger brother was used as a spokesman for T. to answer mother in a way T. might have. Thus, all family members had a chance to observe and interact in a new way.

Sometimes major emphasis is placed on a particular process technique and goal, such as clarifying a family's communication patterns,[3] or helping family members deal with their feelings.[4] Family therapists may see such process goals as being primary, either on ideological grounds or because of the appropriateness to a particular family, with the family being encouraged to deal with content issues as they arise now that the family has the general process tools to do so. Other family therapists, perhaps because of differing conceptual bases applicable to different types of family goals, will tend to work in the other direction—i.e., from the more specific content issues toward the more general process issues.

Trainees often feel uneasy about setting goals for family therapy, since they are afraid of being too authoritarian by taking away from the family their right to set their own goals. Indeed, families should be encouraged to set their own goals to the greatest extent possible. It is with disorganized families that the therapist will need to be more active.

MEDIATING GOALS AND THEIR RELATED STRATEGIES

The intersection of appropriate mediating goals with the most efficient therapeutic strategies and techniques at the most propitious moment and in the right sequence is by definition the art of psychotherapy. Future research will help specify such combinations, but clinical skill and creativity will always play a role. For heuristic and instructional reasons, Table 11-2 presents such a general schema of family intervention mediating goals as related to strategies. In later chapters we delineate more fully the specific techniques of family intervention.

Table 11-2
Mediating Goals of Family Therapy and Their Strategies

Strategies	Mediating Goals
1. Supporting adaptive mechanisms	Increased knowledge, decreased guilt, redefinition of problems, increased use of adaptive coping mechanisms
2. Expanding emotional experience	Appropriate emotional experience and communication
3. Development of interpersonal skills	Use of communication skills, problem-solving skills, parenting skills
4. Reorganizing the family structure	Clarification of boundaries setting of appropriate boundaries between familial subsystems and family of origin
5. Increasing insight	Insight regarding current transactions and historical factors, decreased conflict

GOALS AND RELATED STRATEGIES COMMON TO ALL FAMILY THERAPY SCHOOLS

Although repetitive with material presented earlier, we think it is useful to conceptualize the broad strategies of intervention that cut across the various schools of thought, as in practice strategies are combined in different ways to treat the individual family. There are various ways to conceptualize overall strategies of family intervention,[5,6] and we summarize them here.

1. *Strategies for supporting adaptive mechanisms.* There are a number of ways to assist families in utilizing existing strategies and developing new strategies for coping. Providing the family with information (psychoeducation) about illnesses in family members, about parenting skills, etc., are several examples. Supportive advice and encouragement of existing coping mechanisms are also included here.

2. *Strategies for expanding emotional experience.* Many therapists utilize fantasy, humor and irony, direct confrontation, family sculpting, and choreography to open up new areas of immediate emotional experiencing for the family.

3. *Strategies for the development of interpersonal skills.* By a multitude of techniques, including modeling of intent listening to others, insisting that only one person speak, at a time, questioning the exact meaning of what others are saying and wishing to communicate, and explicit instruction in communication skills, the family is brought to a better communication level. This improvement in communicational levels can be an end in itself, or can be used to solve specific problems that brought the family to treatment in the first place.

4. *Strategies for reorganizing the family structure.* Reframing of the problems as presented by the family, enacting the family problems with their attendant interactional sequences, marking of boundaries, and restructuring moves can all be used to change the structured family behaviors that are judged to be causing or contributing to the family distress. Paradoxical interventions can be used for families that are resistive or at an impasse.

5. *Strategies for increasing insight.* Traditional techniques of psychodynamic psychotherapy, such as clarification, confrontation, and interpretation either in the here and now or of genetic material, can be used in the marital and family treatment formats in order to bring underlying conflicts to the fore and reduce conflict-laden interactions.

Each of these strategies entails the use of a repertory of intervention tactics designed to produce the desired goals. These strategies are not based on any generally agreed upon theory of family structure, function, and therapy, but represent ad hoc attempts by clinicians to deal with the kinds of problems with which they are presented. Some family therapists believe strongly in one or another of these strategies and their underlying concepts, and utilize the same basic strategy with every family. Others feel that one strategy may be particularly suited to one type of family, whereas a different strategy is more appropriate for another family. Still other therapists move flexibly from one to another of these strategies as the situation in any one family at any one time seems to require.

SUMMARY

There are short-term goals (see Chapter 13) and long-term goals. The beginning therapist, however, is cautioned against trying to produce instantaneous behavioral change that may only prove to be evanescent. The chronicle of non-conventional therapies is replete with claims of being able to change behavior in the short term. In contrast, family therapists should aim for a more permanent, long-term change in family structure and function.

These differences in outlook and practice can be bewildering to the inexperienced therapist who is not aware of the underlying rationales and guidelines. Given the current state of the field, with no unifying theory of family pathology, nomenclature, or even of treatment, each new situation represents an "experiment" in which the therapist is required to clarify and test hypotheses.

Examples of goals can be found in the case of the R. family presented in Chapter 8 and in the S. family in Chapter 35, and goals with different types of families are discussed in Chapter 22.

SUGGESTIONS FOR FURTHER READINGS

Gurman A, and Kniskern D(Eds): **Handbook of Family Therapy.** New York: Brunner/Mazel, l981.

> *An attempt to survey under one cover the major schools of family intervention and compare their assumptions, style of assessment and intervention, and current research support.*

REFERENCES

1. Watzlawick P, Weakland J, and Fisch R: Change: Principles of Problem Formation and Problem Resolution. New York: W.W. Norton, 1974
2. Patterson GR: Coercive Family Process. Eugene, Oregon: Castalia Publishing Company, 1982
3. Satir V: Conjoint Family Therapy: A Guide to Theory and Technique. Palo Alto, CA: Science and Behavior Books, 1964, pp 162-167, 175-176
4. Paul NL: The role of mourning and empathy in conjoint marital therapy, in Zuk GH and Boszormenyi-Nagy I (Eds): Family Therapy and Disturbed Families. Palo Alto, CA: Science and Behavior Books, 1967, pp 186-205
5. Glick ID, Kessler D, and Clarkin JF: Different approaches to family therapy, in Arieti S and Brodie H (Eds): American Handbook of Psychiatry, Vol. VII. New York: Basic Books, 1981, pp 388-407
6. Wynne LC, Gurman A, Ravich R, and Boszormenyi-Nagy I: The family and marital therapies, in Lewis JM and Usdin G (Eds): Treatment Planning in Psychiatry. Washington: American Psychiatric Association, 1982, pp 225-285

Birth of a Notion by Susan Kay Williams, private collection.

12
Family Treatment: Strategies and Techniques

OBJECTIVES

- To understand the common elements of psychotherapy as they apply to family treatment
- To become familiar with the general strategies of family therapy and their related techniques.
- To become familiar with existing treatment packages for specific situations/disorders

INTRODUCTION

Before describing "what to do" in treating families, we must first examine family therapy in the general context of the strategies and techniques of "psychotherapy." We conclude the chapter with reference to current "treatment packages" for various diagnostic and/or problem situations that families face.

GENERAL ELEMENTS OF PSYCHOTHERAPY AND THEIR RELATIONSHIP TO FAMILY THERAPY

There are at least seven elements that most schools of psychotherapy share in common:[1]

1. A good patient-therapist relationship
2. Release of emotional tension
3. Cognitive learning
4. Operant reconditioning of the patient toward more adaptive behavior patterns by explicit or implicit approval-disapproval cues and by a corrective emotional relationship with the therapist
5. Suggestion and persuasion
6. Identification with the therapist
7. Repeated reality testing or practicing of new adaptive techniques in the context of implicit or explicit emotional therapeutic support

Family therapy, too, involves all of these elements, but does so in the context of the whole family, with the goal of improving the overall functioning of the entire group. The particular mix of therapeutic elements will vary with the specific needs of the family. There is hardly any specific technique utilized in other therapy formats (individual and group) and orientations (psychodynamic, cognitive-behavioral, strategic, experiential-humanistic) that could not in some way be adapted for use in family intervention.

BASIC STRATEGIES OF FAMILY INTERVENTION

Since there is much overlap in the schools of family intervention (both in theory and techniques) and since our bias is that the field must advance beyond parochial schools to basic principles of change, at this point we present *our* choice of *basic strategies of family intervention*. We also provide a description of the techniques that are utilized in each of the strategies. Basic to family therapy are strategies for:

1. Supporting adaptive mechanisms, including imparting new information, advice, suggestions, etc., the so-called psychoeducational approach.
2. Expanding individual and family emotional experience.
3. Explicit development of interpersonal skills, e.g., communication skills, parenting skills, problem-solving skills.
4. Reorganizing the family structure.
5. Increasing insight and fostering conflict resolution.

Even these strategies abstractly stated in terms of their aim or goal in the treatment are not mutually exclusive. To some extent, they represent different frames of reference for understanding and dealing with the same family phenomena. Nevertheless, each strategy seems to offer something unique in its conceptualization and execution.

As listed, the five basic strategies are in an order reflecting a certain increasing depth of involvement with the family and its individuals.The earlier techniques are simpler, less involved with the family, and if they work they should be used alone. As the family problems are more complex, complicated, and the family shows resistance to change using simpler techniques, the more involved techniques in the latter half of the list might be needed. Of course, there are some cases when one might want to use less "ambitious" techniques or goals even if there are complicated problems.

In a clinical situation, the therapist will be hard put to remain a purist. A therapist's efforts to clarify communication may produce shifts in family coalitions or initiate an exploration of family myths that may lead to a considerable outpouring of previously concealed affect.

Although some specific therapeutic strategies are listed, there is no one magical phrase or technique that will "cure" the family. Interventions are instead a series of repetitive maneuvers designed to change feelings, attitudes, and behavior. If the overall goals and strategy are kept in mind, specific interventions will suggest themselves and be modified by the particular circumstances and the therapist's own style.

What is unique in family therapy is not so much the specific technique utilized but rather the overall focus and strategy that aims to evaluate and produce a beneficial change in the entire family system.

Techniques for Supporting Adaptive Mechanisms

First and foremost, the therapist utilizes many techniques to support the active or latent positive coping mechanisms that the family has at its disposal. Every family has some health, and that should be acknowledged and actively encouraged. Empathic listening and concern, positive feedback about the use of adaptive defenses (such as healthy denial in the face of terminal illness), and education about poorly-adaptive defenses, and well-timed advice are all helpful to the family in distress.

The therapist is constantly in the role of a teacher, either directly or indirectly. Without saying a word, he is modeling mood, tempo, and interpersonal acceptance. The therapist also teaches values, often implicitly. For example, in structuring the treatment so that only one person in the family speaks at once, he is modeling good communication, but also indicating implicitly the value of respecting the thoughts of every person in the family.

More recently there has been a growing emphasis on providing *explicit* information that might be helpful to families in their coping.This approach has been most obvious in the psychoeducational strategies used with families who have a member with diagnosed schizophrenia.[2,3] Information can be communicated through written material, lectures and discussions in family groups, and in workshop format. Anderson and colleagues[3] have described a day-long "survival skills workshop," which the family attends without the patient. Information is provided on the nature of schizophrenia (its history and epidemiology, biology, personal experience), medication and psychosocial treatments, and the role of the family (family reactions to the patient and the illness, coping with the condition).

Of course, the educational approach need not be limited to situations in which there is a clear diagnosis of a condition that has biological components in its etiology. For example, Patterson[4] provides information to parents with antisocial children so that they can improve their family management skills. Likewise, in some situations, there are families who function relatively well for whom the therapist gives "advice." This may include discussing parenting alternatives (like discipline styles) or helping the family to make difficult decisions, e.g., should a child go away to school or stay at home.

Techniques for Expanded Emotional Experience

Techniques that are used to help individuals and family units expand their experience repertoire tend to focus on the here-and-now experience in the sessions themselves. These techniques are designed to help the individual family members to quell anxiety, slow down their reaction process and maximize the emotional and cognitive experience of the moment, experiences that may have been denied, defended against, and missed in the past. These techniques would include the following:

1. *Gestalt techniques.*[5] In adapting Gestalt techniques to family problems, the therapist stresses that the only real time is the present, and he does not rehash the past. He stresses that each individual is responsible for his or her own behavior, and the symptoms and conflicts are seen as here and now expressions of unfinished situations of childhood that can be finished in treatment. Significant attention is paid to nonverbal behavior.
2. *Weekend family marathons.*[6] Weekend family marathons have been reported in which one or several entire family units get together for extended periods (anywhere from 8 to 12 hours or longer) with leaders or "facilitators" for a variety of intensive types of encounters, usually including affect catharsis and nonverbal experience. Self-help groups, often led by clergy, also utilize such weekend experiences to foster marital satisfaction.
3. *Role playing.* Role playing techniques have also been used to help families enact problems and work out new patterns of adaptation. They are especially useful in nonverbal families.[7] In role playing or reverse role playing, one

partner either plays himself in a hypothetical situation or takes on the role of his partner, often switching roles back and forth (role reversal) and commenting on the observations, feelings, and behavior elicited. Role reversal is believed to be useful, especially for developing empathy in family members. We have used role-playing scenarios for families in which one member takes antidepressant medication. The family acts out (for the therapist) how they function when the identified patient is on and off medicine.

4. *Guided fantasy.*[8] With the technique of guided fantasy, the therapist helps the individual share his internal system of fantasies and thoughts with other family members. The rationale is that "daydreaming" can provide people with a powerful tool for their growth and problem solving. It is important to have each member share his or her inner thoughts with the rest of the family, so that they can be empathic in helping the individual grow.

5. *Family sculpture.*[9] Family sculpture is a technique in which the therapist asks one or all of the members of the family to create a physical representation of their relationships at one point in time by arranging their bodies in space. Alliances and estrangements can be concretized by such an exercise. The technique can be used as part of the diagnostic work-up to generate hypotheses or to represent a concept being worked on concretely during the course of therapy. Both the content of the "sculpture" and the way the "sculptor" (i.e., family member) uses mass and form are examined. It is an excellent technique for nonverbal families.

6. *Mourning and empathy.*[10] With the technique of mourning and empathy, the therapist elicits unresolved grief in a family or family member for a parent, child, or relative in order to effect change. This technique is, in part, borrowed from Gestalt therapy, in which there is an attempt to release long-hidden feelings, expectations, and emotions.[11]

Techniques to Develop Interpersonal Skills

Many families and marital units do not utilize basic skills of communication, parenting, and general problem solving, either because they have never learned such skills due to poor or absent parental modeling or because of interpersonal conflicts that interfere with the utilization of such skills.

The therapist is an expert in communication and thus can help the family members express their thoughts and feelings more clearly to one another. The therapist tries to promote open and clear communication, emotional empathy, and positive rapport betwen family members, being aware that disturbed families often have major problems in this regard. Although it is impossible *not* to communicate in a family, nevertheless many troubled family members spend very little time talking meaningfully with one another. Not only thoughts but feelings, too, are distorted, hidden, negated, or blurred.

The therapist supplies an arena for family discussion, being cognizant of the different levels of meaning in messages and how these influence and sometimes contradict each other. The therapist does not allow anyone to monopolize a session or to speak for someone else. At the same time, the therapist attempts to encourage interpersonal sensitivity and empathy and tries to help each person become more aware of their own thoughts and feelings.

The therapist encourages family members to be specific, to state who did what to whom (for example, "Dad hit me with a stick," rather than "He did it"). The therapist stresses that individuals are held accountable for their actions. He fills in gaps in communication, points out discrepancies, and deals with nonverbal communication.[10] The therapist points out nonproductive verbal and nonverbal family communication patterns and tries to identify the implicit, unstated patterns or attitudes that may be causing trouble. Through his efforts, the covert is made overt; the implicit is made explicit. Blocked channels of communication and feeling are opened up.[9] The therapist counsels that good communication includes listening. Often three or four family members are heard talking at exactly the same time during a session, presumably to avoid hearing thoughts and feelings other than their own. The therapist, in such a situation, may function as a communications traffic cop or referee.

The behaviorally oriented family therapists have organized the steps that a therapist can use to teach communication, parenting, and problem-solving skills. This would include the following:

1. Providing the informational content of communication skills by verbal instruction and modeling via role playing (e.g., therapist taking the role of one spouse and role playing with the other spouse).
2. Rehearsal of the new communicational behaviors by the couple in the session.
3. Descriptive and not interpretive feedback by the therapist on the couple's performance of the communicational behaviors.

Marital and family life, is filled with problems, large and small. Distressed families have no more problems than non-distressed families, but non-distressed families utilize effective problem-solving techniques so that problems are handled and do not multiply. Distressed families can be taught problem-solving methods by the following techniques:

1. Teaching problem definition.
2. Teaching generating problem resolution alternatives.
3. Teaching making decisions about the best problem solution.

In addition to the communication and problem-solving skills needed by a

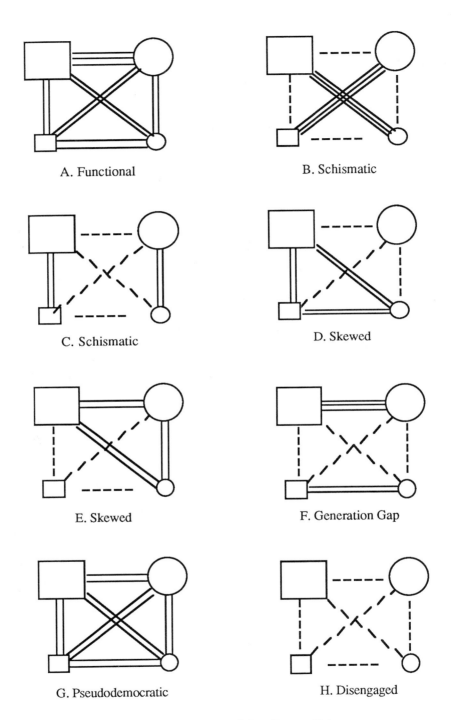

A. Functional

B. Schismatic

C. Schismatic

D. Skewed

E. Skewed

F. Generation Gap

G. Pseudodemocratic

H. Disengaged

Fig. 12-1. Types of family coalitions.

marital dyad, there are additional skills needed to raise children effectively. Patterson[4] has referred to these as family management skills, and he has devised techniques for teaching these skills to families with an antisocial child. The family management skills that can be taught include rule setting, parental monitoring (detection and labeling), and parental sanctions including the appropriate use of positive reinforcement and punishment. Each of these skills must be carefully taught, role played and supervised.

In the social learning theory tradition, Stuart[11] has outlined a behaviorally oriented marital therapy package that begins with assessment, and proceeds through "caring" days (i.e., people caring for each other) techniques organized to increase small, high-frequency, conflict-free behaviors; communication skills; contracting procedures; training in problem-solving skills; training in conflict containment; and strategies for maintaining the changed interaction. He gives (as a clinical example) a "holistic agreement" (several behaviors by one spouse are exchanged for several by the other, with no requirements that the offerings by one exactly match those of the other), an agreement arrived at by Sam and Jane negotiated and put in writing by the two. Jane would like Sam to wash the dishes, mow the lawn, initiate lovemaking, take responsibility for balancing their checkbooks, etc. Sam would like Jane to have dinner ready by 6:30 nightly, weed the rose garden, call him at the office daily, etc. It is contracted and expected that each will do as many of the above things requested by the other as is comfortably manageable, ideally at least three or four times weekly.

Strategies and Techniques for Changing Structured Family Behaviors

In many ways, the unique contribution of the family orientation *is* the recognition of structured (repetitive and predictable) behavioral sequences in family groups that contribute to the etiology and/or maintenance of symptomatic behaviors. A graphic representation of some family coalitions is provided in Figure 12-1. A "typical" four-member family is taken as the unit, with the squares representing the males and the circles the females. The larger symbols stand for spouse/parent, and the smaller symbols represent the offspring/siblings. The solid straight lines joining these symbols are intended to represent positive communicational, emotional, and activity bonds between the individuals involved, in a semi-quantitative fashion, according to the number of straight lines utilized. Dotted lines, on the other hand, are used to represent the relative absence or negative quality of the interactions.

In example A, the *functional family*, the marital coalition is the strongest dyad in the family, the generation boundary is intact, and all other channels are open and about equal to one another in importance. In contrast to this are the various types of dysfunctional families that follow.

In example B, the marital coalition is relatively weak or absent, and instead there are strong alliances across the generations and sexes—between father and daughter, and mother and son—with a relative absence of other effective channels. In example C there are cross-generational alliances between same-sexed parent and child. Examples B and C can be thought of as representing types of the *schismatic family* (see Chapter 3).

Examples D and E depict *skewed families* in which one family member is relatively isolated from the other three, who form a fairly cohesive unit. Example F represents the *generation gap family*, in which the marital unit and the offspring each form a fairly cohesive duo, with little or no interaction across the generational lines. Example G represents the *pseudodemocratic family*, in which all channels seem to be of about equal importance, with the marital coalition and the parental role not being particularly well differentiated. Example H, the *disengaged family*, offers the representation of an extreme case in which each family member is pretty much cut off from every other member, and in which one would expect very little sense of positive interaction, feeling, or belonging to a family unit.

Clearly these representations are highly oversimplified and are pictured only for a two-generation, four-member family. Infinite variations could be added to the list. Such representations enable the therapist to conceptualize more clearly the nature of the coalitions in a particular family and to begin planning a strategy to bring those coalitions into a better functional alignment, presumably more closely approximating example A. In example B, for instance, the therapist might give attention to activating the marital coalition, the coalitions between parent and offspring of the same sex, and those between the offsprings themselves. Also, an attempt might be made to attenuate the force of the existing cross-generational, cross-sexed interactions.

The tactics and strategies of family therapy, viewed in this light, might include changes in the marital coalition (very commonly the case), as well as in the parent-child dyads. Although triads are not considered to any great extent in this discussion, an isolated family member might be brought into interaction with the rest of the family unit. Looking outside of the nuclear family for a moment, it is important to consider the appropriateness of encouraging extrafamilial contacts with outside peers, both for the parents about to face the "empty nest," as well as for children and adolescents. At times, when such outside interactions, especially those with in-laws, seem maladaptive, modifications might have to be considered. Temporary triads, incorporating the therapist, are often purposely formed in order to produce structural change.

Techniques that enable the family therapist to interrupt and change such structured family behaviors are central to this understanding.[12,13] The techniques include the following:

1. *Reframing.* Each individual "frames" reality from his own unique perspective. When the therapist perceives and understands the patients or family's frame, and then counters this frame with another, competing view, this is called a "reframe."[14] Such a therapeutic move can be sudden, dramatic, and/or humorous, and model a more relaxed, less conflicted view of the world and the nitty gritty of family life.

2. *Enactment.* It is one thing for a family to describe what has happened, and it is another thing for them to enact it in front of the therapist. Enactment is the technique of eliciting the playing out of interpersonal problems the family complains of in the therapeutic hour. Probably one of the most dramatic stories of enactment in the family therapy literature is Minuchin's[15] description of a session in which he required an anorexic young woman and her family to eat a meal, with the injunction to the mother and father to get her to eat. Enactment enables the perceptive therapist to observe the interpersonal behaviors in the problem sequence, rather than hearing the typical censored version offered by each participant in a canned rendition of what goes on.

3. *Focusing.* The individual therapist is flooded with a multitude of data from the patient. With the recent developments in brief therapy, literature has accumulated on the patient ability and therapist factors in focusing the sessions. This multiplicity of data is compounded in family therapy by the number of individuals in the action. For there to be organization, highlighting, and progression in the treatment, someone must focus the attention of the group. From multiple inputs, the therapist must select a focus and develop a theme for the family therapy work.[13]

Haley's strategic approach to families[16] provides a good example of how a clinician uses a theoretical rationale for focusing a whole sequence of interventions toward a defined goal. He states that the typical child problem involves an overintense parent–child dyad that alternatively includes and excludes the other parent. The alignment is the focus of intervention. In one clinical illustration provided by Haley, a five-year-old boy had never been toilet trained, and several times a day had a bowel movement in his pants. The mother was overinvolved with the child and benevolently tolerated him. The father was a studious and serious engineer who hovered on the periphery. By the end of the first session, the family therapist began to wonder (aloud) what unwanted consequences would occur if the boy changed. In the second session the parents could think of no adverse consequences, so the therapist suggested (focusing on the mother–child dyad) that perhaps others could not tolerate their (the parents) being successful with their child. The manuever is conceptualized as supporting the mother (in the idea that she can stand being successful), but challenging her to prove it. The therapist wondered aloud if the mother could tolerate being more successful than her own mother, and what she would do with all her free time if the problem were solved. And the therapist proceeded: could the father tolerate success, what would happen to the mother–father relationship if there were no distracting child problem? By the fourth scheduled session, the couple reported that the boy was regularly using the toilet every day, and indicated they enjoyed being without the problem.

According to Minuchin and Fishman,[13] there are three major techniques to challenge the structure of the family:boundary making, unbalancing, and complementarity.

4. *Boundary making.* Boundary-making techniques are ways of focusing on and changing the psychological distance between two or more family members. A common example is a mother who speaks for the daughter, countered by a therapist who marks a boundary by commenting that mother is helpful in the way she reads her daughter's mind and speaks for her. In triadic interactions, a typical situation is one in which the unresolved conflicts between the parents are acted out by the misbehavior of a child who then sides with either mother or father or becomes a judge or go-between for the two of them. The therapist can intervene by distancing child from the mother-father dyad.The therapist can make boundaries by verbal reconstructions, giving tasks, spacial rearrangements in the sessions, non-verbal gestures and eye contact.[13]

5. *Unbalancing.* The family therapist uses unbalancing techniques in order to change the hierarchical relationship of members of a family system or subsystem.[17] There are three basic ways of unbalancing the existing family hierarchy and power distribution: affiliating with certain family members, ignoring family members, or entering into a coalition with some family members against others. A therapist unbalances the family's existing power system by, for example, allying with a family member low in the power hierarchy.

6. *Complementarity.* By use of mainly cognitive interventions, the family therapist attempts to help the individuals in the family perceive and understand the workings of their mutual interdependence and membership in an entity (the family) larger than themselves. Members of a family generally perceive themselves as acting and reacting to one another, rather than seeing the larger picture of the family dance over time.

There are three areas in which the family therapist challenges the family's usual rhetoric (formulation): the family notion that there is only one identified patient, the notion that one person is controlling the family system, and the family's time-limited vision of their interactions. Even if one person is obviously symptomatic, the therapist introduces the notion that family interactions are probably helping maintain the problem. Secondly, the therapist counters the idea that one person controls the system with the conception that each person provides the context for the other. Symptoms in one person are maintained by the interpersonal context. Finally, the therapist helps the family achieve a conception of the interactions over a large time-frame so that they can perceive the family "rules" that transcend the individual family member.

7. *Paradoxical techniques.* Paradoxical techniques are related to unbalancing, mentioned above. For example, a therapist may ally with a dominant member of the family, creating what is called a runaway, in which the family member's habitual way of reacting is pushed to its limits. Symptom prescription has been called the most powerful form of problem resolution. Watzlawick, Weakland, and Fisch give a number of examples, including prescribing less of the same, making the overt the covert, advertising instead of concealing, utilizing resistance, etc.

As a clinical illustration we repeat the case of Antonella, a 17-year-old daughter of Italian parents treated by Palazzoli.[18] The adolescent had suddenly become anorectic, connected to her being forbidden to date a boy strongly disapproved of by the family. While seemingly blase about the daughter's condition, the mother became visibly upset when asked about how much pain the situation caused her mother (Antonella's grandmother). The family game, according to Palazzoli, was that Antonella must forget the boyfriend and must recover in order not to make grandmother suffer. The therapeutic team decided to attack the triangle of the three women (the patient, her mother, and her grandmother) first via a prescription that was read to the family. The prescription indicated that if Antonella were to recover, she would start meeting her boyfriend again, and grandmother would suffer even more than if Antonella would die of her illness. During the next session this danger threatening grandmother would be discussed.

At the next session two weeks later, Antonella reported that she had begun to eat and gain weight. After the previous session, the girl had run to show her grandmother the written prescription, to which grandmother responded that, of course, she wanted Antonella to eat. Grandmother was invited to the next session, and she was treated respectfully. The next injunction to the family excluded grandmother, and was to be read aloud every night. Father's message was to thank Antonella for not eating because it will keep mother close to home and him. Mother's message was to thank Antonella for refusing to eat, for it would assure grandmother that she was taking care of Antonella.

After the therapist "orders" the family members (or individual) to intensify the occurrence of the symptoms, the symptoms begin to lose their autonomy, mystery, and power. Whereas they previously seemed to have been out of control, they now appear to come under the therapist's control. The participants in the behavior become more conscious of them, and often the disruptive behavior lessens or disappears. A marital couple that has engaged in nonproductive arguing now finds that the therapist has asked them to continue fighting and even to increase it; the couple is told to fight about the menu before dinner, so that they can enjoy the food. This injunction jars the continuing process, and they may rebel against the outsider's orders (which is often a necessary step to change).

The therapist is obligated to follow through to make sure that the directions have been followed in the way that was intended. The therapist does this by seeing the family in his office on an ongoing basis, by asking more than one family member what changes have taken place, or by visiting the family at home.

Other therapists write a family prescription after the initial session, telling the members they will receive a message about what the therapist thinks is wrong with the family and what needs to change.[7] This gives the therapist time that is not available in the heat of the session and creates an opportunity for a more accurate formulation of the family's problems. The prescription is a typewritten letter sent separately to each family member. It may describe just what the family is doing and ask each member to continue doing it.

For example, the therapist agrees with Joe (the identified patient) that he should not move out of the house at present. His parents, however, should continue to vacillate in alternately supporting his moving out and undermining it. This prescription was sent to a family with a 32-year-old son who kept "messing up" each time he left home and then had to return to the family. The prescription had the effect of making Joe angry, of shifting him out of the house, and of identifying what his parents were doing. For some families there is something quite powerful about a well-thought out message that is "official" and to the point.

Techniques for Insight and Conflict Resolution

While the experiential and psychodynamic schools of psychotherapy have different goals, both have in common the use of techniques to further the emotional-cognitive horizons of the patient(s), with the assumption that such expansion will lead to behavior/character change. In expressive dynamic therapy, the therapist uses the context of therapeutic neutrality to employ such techniques as clarification, confrontation, and interpretation, either with the individual or the marital dyad or family unit.

1. *Clarification.* In utilizing the technique of clarification, the therapist asks the patient(s) to elucidate his or her (their) understanding and/or emotional reaction to present and past events.
2. *Confrontation.* Confrontation is the pointing out of contradictory aspects of the patient's behavior, often between verbal and nonverbal behavior.
3. *Interpretation.* Interpretation is the elucidation by the therapist of links between present contradictory behavior and present or past distortions that are out of the awareness of the patient. In making interpretations, often immediately preceded by clarifications and confrontations, the therapist is providing a conceptual link for patient and family. It should be timed so as to maximize cognitive and emotional impact, between *current* behavior (as dis-

torted or guided by internal templates) and *past* experiences (distorted by anxiety and defense mechanisms).

Interpretations can be made in the here-and-now interaction between family members, or between therapist and family member(s), or interpretations can link present behavior to past history. Probably the former are of more use in family intervention. Ackerman[20] was a pioneer in utilizing dynamic techniques (along with a multitude of others) in a family therapy format in order to interrupt intrapsychic conflicts being played out in the interpersonal sphere. Dicks[21] has more than any other author spelled out the use of dynamic techniques in the intervention with marital couples.

Dicks[22] describes the brief marital therapy case of H., a 45-year-old man, married 20 years to W. The couple had three adolescent children. The presenting complaint was H.'s sexual impotence of ten years duration, depressive moods, and irritability, especially at his wife and children, all of which threatened his marriage.

In the initial diagnostic interview with H. alone, he was asked about his early sexual attitudes. In the process of responding, he recalled dealing firmly but kindly with a scoutmaster who made mild homosexual advances toward him. His associations then shifted to his parental home and its atmosphere, noting that his sulking did not work as it did for his father, as he knows it is wrong. This was followed by an interpretation by the therapist: there seemed to be a similarity between attacking passively and sexual withdrawal. The patient's next association was to his wife, whom he saw as having her own way as to times for intercourse. He then described the many talents of the wife in contrast to himself. Another interpretation was offered: You feel inadequate in comparison to W., as if she has all the potency, much as it was in your parents' case.

In the diagnostic interview with W., she described a strong bond to an idealized father who died when she was 17, and a scarcely concealed hostility toward a weak mother.

In the first conjoint marital session, it appeared that the couple had a stereotyped and unvarying pattern of attempting intercourse while simultaneously anticipating failure, followed by some symptomatic behavior on the part of the wife. In the second conjoint session, W. suggested that they discontinue sleeping together, as the strain left her without sleep and constantly tired. An interpretation was made: Her symptoms showed her emotional frustration, which might reflect her disappointment that H. was not the strong, potent man she expected. She had tried to improve him, and H. had met this with anxiety and resistance. H. conceded that he left the office cheerful, but when he entered the home he felt depressed, nagged, and belittled. W. responded by saying that it was not she but the children who got the brunt of his moods. She described her husband's belittling and sarcasm toward the children. Another dyadic interpretation was given: There is a vicious circle around power and control. H. feels W. is trying to control him, while he is feeling a great need to control the family through the children. W. becomes anxious and resentful because she would like to run things her way. This battle has invaded their relationship, and the struggle to contain the urges to dominate has produced mutual strain and pushed out affection. The wife responded to this interpretation by conceding that she is driven to control, and sees how H. responds by becoming controlling with the children. At this point the therapists suggest that this pattern may relate to earlier experiences in their families of origin. W. recalled that she felt a lack of support from her mother and a devotion to her prematurely deceased father, a need to support and control the weak mother, a desire that in marrying H. he would make up for it all. An interpretation was made that she must feel very complicated about H.'s sexual difficulty and his feelings as the weak one. She now saw him not as the interested, inspiring father for her children in whom she saw her own needs mirrored. This interpretation was followed by a show of great feeling on the part of W., in which she recalled that the father was not only loving, but had also been very demanding and sarcastic, the latter so intolerable to her in H.'s behavior toward their children. Another interpretation: Perhaps W. had not seen the similarity before between her feelings for H. and for her father, with great disappointment that like her father H. had weaknesses that she must control, since she could not bear them. H. responded with some emotion about how as a child he had been very strong-willed and strove to compel his mother to give in to him. This was followed by a final dyadic interpretation: It was the strong-willed part of H. that W. liked. Because of his fear of weakness, the failure in sex, which could have happened to anyone under the circumstances, when it did, was quite disproportionately seen by H. as an utter failure, with a compensatory need to control in the home. W., attaching her aspirations for strength and success on him, felt disproportionately disappointed in him because it destroyed her fantasy that he was like her father. Her reaction to disappointment, both in the past and now, was to take control.

By the third session, the couple reported that their general relationship was much improved, and the husband had been completely potent on a number of occasions.

TREATMENT PACKAGES

Recent clinical work and research, especially in the areas of marital therapy and enrichment,[23] divorce therapy and mediation,[24] family treatment of schizophrenia,[3] antisocial adolescents,[4] sexual dysfunctions,[25] and reconstituted families,[26] suggest that so-called "treatment packages," which contain a combination of techniques delivered in some specified sequential fashion, are effective with targeted patient populations. These treatment packages will include prescribed use of various techniques from the major strategies enunciated above. These manuals add to an abstract listing of strategies and techniques by indicating the overall goals, mediating and final, of the treatment for the targeted families, with a rationale for the timing and sequencing of the techniques of intervention. The interested reader should consult the indicated reference for details.

The field of psychotherapy research, in general, is in an era of research investigation of treatment packages (that is, the combination of a series of defined intervention techniques delivered in some prescribed order), as they are applied to specified disorders.

INDICATIONS FOR DIFFERENTIAL USE OF THE FIVE BASIC STRATEGIES

It is no wonder that trainees always ask when to use the various strategies and techniques differentially. This is an unresolved area, not only in the field of family therapy, but in all psychotherapy. In their clinical zeal for their own favorite set of strategies and techniques, clinical writers usually do not discuss when their techniques are indicated and when not. Clinical research that has pit one set of therapy techniques against another indicates that by and large no one technique is clearly superior. It remains for future research to clarify the differential application and effectiveness of the various techniques. However, in the interim, clinical decisions about the thrust of strategies in family intervention must be made on every case and in every session.

It is clear that some strategies of family therapy have received research support for their effectiveness while others have been the focus of very little if any research. In a recent review, Gurman, Kniskern, and Pinsof[27] conclude that the following have shown probable or established effectiveness: behavioral family therapy with schizophrenia, substance abuse, anxiety disorders, juvenile deliquency, conduct disorders, and marital discord; psychodynamic/eclectic family therapy with substance abuse; and structural family therapy with substance abuse and psychosomatic disorders.

Patient diagnostic issues are for the first time beginning to be important for the type of family therapy techniques that are recommended. Patients with serious axis I pathology, such as schizophrenia and manic depressive disorder, and their families, should probably receive at least some psychoeducation about the illness and how to cope with it. It has also been argued that since the individual with schizophrenia is by the nature of the disorder vulnerable to cognitive and emotional overload (and this seems more true of males than females), family therapy strategies that stir up family emotional conflict should not be used, at least during certain phases of the disorder.[28]

Beutler[29] has probably given the most thoughtful framework for suggesting when to use certain therapy techniques, based upon non-diagnostic patient characteristics. Although Beutler was discussing individual therapy, the principles can be applied to the family treatment format. If the problem is a "neurotic-like" disturbance, therapy aimed at conflict resolution is needed, whereas problems determined by habit formation and disorders can be approached by narrow-band, behavioral approaches. Second, one must consider characteristic defensive style. Defenses that lead to impulsive, emotional activity need externally focused treatments. On the other hand, those with ruminative anxiety magnifiers need treatment focused on cognitive control and refinement of internal cognitive structures. Finally, those with little emotional awareness need assistance with emotional arousal and awareness in the treatment. Third, one must consider the reactive level of the patient, that is, the degree to which the patient is open to external influence or those who seek their own personal control and tend to reject assistance from others. The former will take a directive therapeutic approach, while the latter need a relatively nondirective therapist.

It remains to be seen whether or not family classification schemes and typologies can be useful in guiding not only whether or not to use the family therapy format but also which strategies and techniques should be used in the family treatment format.

Since most of the therapy research has substantiated little differential effect for the various treatment strategies and techniques, some have argued[30] that elements common to the various strategies are most important. This would include careful assessment, focus as negotiated by the therapist, a reasonable rationale for proceeding, the generation of hope that intervention will help, and orientation to a goal. From this point of view, it is the organized approach of the family therapist that is more important than the specific strategies and techniques. One clinical application of this notion is that the family therapist should not be eclectic in strategies to the point of shifting constantly from one set of strategies to another. A clear focus on the central family pathology with a combination of a limited set of strategies is probably more efficient, less confusing to the family, and more effective. This is congruent with the fact that negative outcomes in family therapy are associated with a lack of therapist structuring and guiding of early sessions, and use of frontal confrontations of highly affective material early in treatment.[31]

BEYOND TECHNIQUES

It has been wisely noted that a therapist, not unlike an artist, spends years of hard practice acquiring and honing techniques. Once acquired, they become relatively invisible.[8] This is the era of outcome research in which manuals are written to carefully describe treatments, and therapists are taught to perform as the manuals describe. And, yet, with this careful attention to scientific rigor, researchers have noted that the same technique in the hands of a "pro" and a "neophyte" (despite years of practice) can have quite different effects on the patients (personal communication, M.Weissman).

SUGGESTIONS FOR FURTHER READING

Munichin S, and Fishman HC: **Family Therapy Techniques.** Cambridge, MA.: Harvard University Press, 1981.
> *A masterful summary of structural techniques with informative clinical examples.*

Paolino T, and McCrady B(Eds): **Marriage and Marital Therapy.** New York: Brunner/Mazel, 1978.
> *Excellent chapters on psychodynamic, behavioral, and systems techniques (Chapters 3, 5, 7), accompanied by a scholarly comparison of the three by Alan Gurman (Chapter 9).*

Haley, J: **Uncommon Therapy: The Psychiatric Techniques of Milton H. Erickson, M.D.** New York: W.W. Norton, 1973.
> *The art of paradoxical techniques brought to its zenith in the hands of Milton Erikson.*

REFERENCES

1. Marmor J: Marmor lecture. Psychiatric News, November 5, 1975, pp 1-15
2. Falloon IRH, Boyd JL, and McGill C: Family Care of Schizophrenia. New York: Guilford Press, 1984
3. Anderson C, Reiss D, and Hogarty G: Schizophrenia and the Family. New York: Guiford Press, 1986
4. Patterson GR: Coercive Family Process. Eugene, OR: Castalia Publishing Company, 1982
5. Leveton A: Elizabeth is frightened. Voices 8:4-13, 1972
6. Landes J and Winter W: A new strategy for treating disintegrating families. Fam Process 5:1-20, 1966
7. McKinney J: Adapting family therapy to multideficit families. Social Casework 51:327-333, 1970
8. Friedman PH: Outline (alphabet) of 26 techniques of family and marital therapy: A through Z. Psychotherapy: Theory, Research and Practice 11:259-264, 1974

9. Simon R: Sculpting the family. Fam Process 11:49-58, 1972

10. Paul NL: The role of mourning and empathy in conjoint marital therapy, in Zuk GH, Boszormenyi-Nagy I (Eds): Family Therapy and Disturbed Families. Palo Alto, CA: Science and Behavior Books, 1967, pp 186-205

11. Stuart RB: Helping Couples Change: A Social Learning Approach to Marital Therapy. New York: Guilford Press, 1980

12. Minuchin S: Families and Family Therapy. Cambridge, MA: Harvard University Press, 1974

13. Minuchin S and Fishman HC: Family Therapy Techniques. Cambridge, MA: Harvard University Press, 1981

14. Watzlawick P, Weakland J, and Fisch R: Change: Principles of Problem Formation and Problem Resolution. New York: W.W. Norton, 1974

15. Minuchin S, Rosman B, and Baker L: Psychosomatic Families. Cambridge, MA: Harvard University Press, 1978

16. Haley J: Problem-Solving Therapy. New York: Harper, 1976, p 142ff

17. Minuchin S and Fishman HC: op cit p164

18. Hoffman L: Foundation of Family Therapy: A Conceptual Framework for Systems Change. New York: Basic Books, 1981

19. Selvini Palazzoli M, Cecchin G, and Prata G et al.: Paradox and Counterparadox. A New Model in the Therapy of the Family Schizophrenic Transaction. New York: Jason Aronson, 1978

20. Ackerman N: The Psychodynamics of Family Life. New York: Basic Books, 1958

21. Dicks, HV: Marital Tensions. London: Routledge and Kegan Paul, 1967

22. Dicks HV: op cit p 237ff

23. L'Abate L: Skill training programs for couples and families, in Gurman AS and Kniskern DP (Eds): Handbook of Family Therapy. New York: Brunner/Mazel, 1981, pp 631-661

24. Kaslow FW: Divorce and divorce therapy, in Gurman AS and Kniskern DP (Eds): Handbook of Family Therapy. New York: Brunner/Mazel, 1981, pp 662-696

25. Heiman JR, LoPiccolo L, and LoPiccolo J: The treatment of sexual dysfunction, in Gurman AS and Kniskern DP (Eds): Handbook of Family Therapy. New York: Brunner/Mazel, 1981, pp 592-627

26. Sager CJ, Brown HS, and Crohn H et al.: Treating the Remarried Family. New York: Brunner/Mazel, 1983

27. Gurman AS, Kniskern DP, and Pinsof WM: Research on the process and outcome of marital and family therapy, in Garfield SL and Bergin AE (Eds): Handbook of Psychotherapy and Behavior Change (3rd Ed). New York: Wiley, 1986, pp 565-624

28. Heinrichs D and Carpenter W: The coordination of family therapy with other treatment modalities for schizophrenia, in McFarlane W (Ed): Family Therapy in Schizophrenia. New York: Guilford Press, 1983, pp 267-287

29. Beutler LE: Eclectic Psychotherapy: A Systematic Approach. New York: Pergamon Press, 1983
30. Hoberman HM and Lewinsohn PM: The behavioral treatment of depression, in Beckham EE and Leber WR (Eds): Handbook of Depression: Treatment, Assessment and Research. Homewood, IL: Dorsey Press, 1985, pp39-81
31. Gurman AS and Kniskern DP: Deterioration in marital and family therapy: Empirical, clinical and conceptual issues. Fam Process 17:3-20, 1978

Supper by J. F. Willumsen (1918). Courtesy of J. F. Willumsens Museum, Denmark.

13

The Course of Family Treatment

OBJECTIVES

- To acquire techniques for gathering history
- To become familiar with some of the processes of each stage of family treatment and the various opportunities and interventions appropriate to each stage

INTRODUCTION

Trainees frequently request to be shown an entire course of treatment. We have responded to this need by including a transcript of a case from beginning to end in our final chapter. In this chapter, we review the stages of a typical course of treatment—somewhat arbitrarily dividing them into *early phase*, *mid phase*, and *termination phase*.

EARLY PHASE

This, always the most difficult for trainees, is divided according to the following outline.

- what are the objectives of this phase
- how to get started
- how to distribute time

214

- how simultaneously to gather history and build an alliance
- when is evaluation also treatment

Objectives

Some of the primary objectives of the early stage include the following:

1. Detailing the primary problems and nonproductive family patterns.
2. Clarifying the goals for treatment.
3. Solidifying the therapeutic contract.
4. Strengthening the therapeutic relationship.
5. Shifting the focus from the identified patient to the entire family system. In the early stages, the therapist may give directives designed to reorganize alignments of structures in the family that quite often serve to take the focus off the identified patient. As soon as this is accomplished, the relationship between the marital partners may become the core of the treatment, and in the middle stage most of the work may be devoted to seeing only the marital couple together, often with the identified patient.[1] If there are offspring, they are seen little, if at all.
6. Decreasing guilt and blame.
7. Increasing the ability of family members to empathize with one another.

Strategies to Get Started

Before describing in some detail the specific techniques that enable the therapist to achieve the final goals of family intervention, it is important to note the general strategies used in beginning work with the family. These skills are basic, assumed by all orientations, and crucial for the neophyte to master. Without such skills, family drop-out is likely, precluding any further possibility of change.

1. *Accommodating to and joining the family.* The family is a biological-psychological unit that over time has evolved set rules (overt and covert), procedures, and customary interactional patterns. The therapist must come "in from out of the cold" and join this group by letting them know he understands them and wants to work with and for their better good.[2] Every family therapist will use his own unique personality, combined with sensitivity and warmth, to join with the family in distress.
2. *Interviewing various subgroups, extended family, other networks.* Family therapy is by definition a therapeutic approach that emphasizes the tremendous power and influence of the social environment upon the individual. This social environment includes immmediate family, family of origin, extended

family, neighborhood, school, and community. One crucial decision that often takes place early in treatment is the decision about which parts of the social environment to include directly in the treatment. Various groups of individuals can be included for assessment only, or more involved in the ongoing treatment. This is discussed further in chapter 16.

3. *Negotiating the goals of treatment.* The family or couple usually come to treatment with their own goals in mind. Unlike individual therapy, however, where one individual comes with his own goals, the family comes with a few individuals having specific goals, often for other people (not themselves) to change, and some individuals not wanting to be there at all.

Distribution of Time

If one is engaged in short-term crisis intervention, 30 minutes may be all the time that is available for evaluation. In a training setting, with no fixed time limit for treatment, one may be able to allot more time for thorough evaluation. Some clinicians take the time at an initial phone contact to gather detailed biographical and historical information. This leaves the evaluator much freer in the initial interview to ask selective questions, to stay more in the here-and-now, and to conduct the session in a more dynamic way.

The Process of Building a Treatment Alliance with the Family

Styles and techniques of gathering history are very much related to the crucial task of building a treatment alliance with the family. These techniques vary as to which *phase* of the treatment is operative. This ground was covered earlier, but some of it will be repeated here in the context of course of treatment.

A beginning therapist may want to obtain a fairly extensive history, perhaps mainly in the opening session, whereas a more experienced practitioner may rely on only a few bits of historical data, working more with what happens in the session and gathering longitudinal data only as needed during the course of the meetings.

The therapist may decide to hear from each family member in turn on certain important issues or may let the verbal interaction take its own course. A decision may be made to call on one parent first, then the other, and then the children in descending chronological order, or it may appear more advantageous to call on the more easily intimidated, weaker, or passive parent (or spouse) first. The therapist may decide to use first names for all family members to help put everyone on an equal footing, or he may prefer to be more formal in addressing the parents in order to strengthen relatively weak generational boundaries and parental functioning. Some therapists may encourage the family members to talk with one another, whereas others may focus the conversation largely on themselves, at least during the first sessions or at times of stress or chaos.

The assumption (*not* always true) is made that the family's behavior in the office and at home is similar, although perhaps modified in some ways in the office by the presence of the therapist. At this point the therapist is somewhat the outsider, whose main function may be to allow everyone to be heard, including the weakest members of the family. Some family members will often be on the attack, whereas others will be defensive during the initial period. An identified patient who is an adolescent will often demand changes at home, because those in this age group are frequently the ones most interested in change. An angry, frustrated spouse will demand that the marital partner change. Some therapists may point out that they will not be decision makers for the family but will help the family members clarify their problems and help them with their decision-making processes. Such therapists may act as referees or traffic cops when necessary, making sure that one person speaks at a time, that no one person is overwhelmed by attacks during the sessions, and that nongratifying family patterns are not allowed to continue unchallenged during the therapy sessions. They create an atmosphere that encourages the verbal expression of feelings toward constructive ends.

Therapists indicate that in an unhappy family everyone hurts and therefore everyone wants to get something positive out of the sessions. A therapist conveys the feeling that all the family members are doing the best they can and that one needs to understand the motives of oneself and of others. The family therapist explains that well-intentioned attitudes and actions are nevertheless sometimes less than totally positive in their outcomes.

Families vary considerably in their readiness to move from a discussion of the current crisis situation to an exploration of their patterns and histories. Therapists will follow the family's lead in these respects. For example, a therapist may be willing to start the sessions even though the father is absent and may sense that the family members need some time to talk about the "badness" of one of the offspring.

It is important that a therapist gets an idea of the family's mode of operations in order to convey a sense of respect for and understanding of the family's initial point of view. At the same time, the therapist will need to guard against being so passive and accepting that nothing new will be added to the equation. The family's experience in the therapy hour should not be merely a repetition of the nongratifying interactional patterns for which they originally sought help. It may be helpful to indicate to the family that individual problems often are related to family problems and that they all need to find our more about the family as a whole, in order to enable each member, and the family as an entity, to benefit from the treatment.

As we discussed in Chapter 6 speaking of "choicepoints," it may be desirable to move on to a longitudinal, chronological narrative of the family's history (perhaps through three generations) or instead to begin with a cross-sectional inventory of how the family currently functions. Which of these areas will be elucidated first depends on the therapist's predilections, the family's distress, and the nature of the difficulty. The major longitudinal data to be gathered will refer to the parents' period of courtship, engagement, marriage, honeymoon, early years of marriage prior to the arrival of children, and the changes in the family as a result of the first child and each subsequent child and so on through the family cycle.

One may start with the courtship period (which is, in part, predictive of marital patterns), move on to the marriage, and then work backward, with each partner going back to his or her original family. One can discuss the life history prior to the marriage for each partner, including any previous marriages. In going back to the parents' families of origin, one gets a picture of the functioning of those previous families that serves as a foundation for understanding the present family and its problems. Careful attention must be given not only to recollections of the past and to expressions regarding attitudes and values, but also to overt behavior. For example, gross difficulties in sexual adjustment should be carefully delineated by taking a thorough and complete sexual history. It is the authors' experience that this is something still done all too rarely in the field of family therapy, as though sexual problems were regarded as only secondary to other interpersonal difficulties.

A short digression here: primary difficulties in sexual adjustment, however, will often sour the rest of the marital relationship. Sometimes sexual difficulties are the major area of difficulty for the married couple and perhaps the one most difficult for them to deal with. There are couples who appear to need and who will benefit from specific therapy directed toward improving their sexual adjustment. To the extent that this can be done satisfactorily, other areas of marital and family interaction may then markedly improve. The sexual adjustment of the marital pair should be evaluated as carefully as other areas of marital and family interaction. It is not safe to assume that any sexual problems are secondary and will resolve themselves more or less spontaneously when other areas of family difficulty have been overcome.[3]

Another area often overlooked or slighted in the evaluation phase is that of the family's dealings with money. The authors have found this to be an important issue in marital and family friction. As with sexuality, this is not always merely secondary to other marital problems. Some marital couples have never been able to work out a satisfactory way of managing money as a marital pair. Any other marital problem may be reflected in fights about money, just as they may be reflected in sexual maladjustment.

The amount and type of data to be assembled will be strongly influenced by the current phase of the family life cycle. It is appropriate to concentrate on material relevant to issues pertaining to that particular phase of family life. The relative emphasis, as well as some of the specific content of the history to be gathered, would be quite different if one were dealing with a couple in the first year of marriage or a family whose last offspring is preparing to leave home.

Should the family present the history or should the therapist structure the history with an outline? Most therapists seem to combine both approaches. It is often helpful to let the family members talk until they run "dry." On the other hand, the therapist presumably has expertise in helping families with problems and can help them in structuring a history. What is excluded by the structuring usually will emerge as time goes on, but what is missed by not structuring (for example, not taking a sexual history) may never be revealed.

History gathering requires complex skills. Excellent references on methodology for getting a family history include works by Satir,[4] Bell,[5] and the Group for the Advancement of Psychiatry.[6] There are also training films on family therapy, parts of which demonstrate history taking.[7-10]

Evaluation Versus Treatment

For clarity of presentations we have separated family evaluations and family treatment. In practice this rarely happens and is not particularly desirable. A process of continual evaluation and hypothesis testing takes place throughout the course of therapy, with the therapist constantly checking his perceptions. At the same time, every session should have some beneficial outcome. The more skillful and experienced the therapist, the less rigid the approach and the more total the blend of evaluative and therapeutic aspects and the more extensive the use of improvised variations, condensations, and extensions on some of the themes.

Mr. and Mrs. G., a young couple in their early twenties, came for treatment because their marriage was in trouble. An evaluation was done (using the format described in Chapter 7). At the onset of the session the following week, the therapist asked the couple what had happened since the evaluation. Mr. G. said he realized that they were not communicating, although they had made it a point to increase communication during the week. Mrs. G. said that she thought the session had not done anything, but she had recognized for the first time that there was a communication problem.

During the early phase, the therapist comes to a better understanding of the life of the family, making contact and promoting empathy and communication. Some major nonproductive patterns are spotlighted and scapegoating is neutralized. The painful shift begins to move away from the identified patient and attention is directed to the entire family system.

MIDDLE PHASE

The middle stage is often considered to be the one in which the major work of change takes place. Since chapters 11, 12, 14, and 15 are devoted to these specific issues, less will be said here regarding this stage. What the therapist does during the middle stage will vary, depending on the goals that have been singled out as being of primary importance. Common examples of persistent, nongratifying interpersonal patterns and attitudes, preferably drawn from recent or here-and-now interactions, are discussed repeatedly. Old non-functional coalitions, rules, myths, and role models are challenged, and the possibility of alternative modes is presented. New habits of thinking, feeling, and interacting take time to develop, and much repetition is often required. At the same time resistance to change comes to the fore, and must be dealt with accordingly (Chapter 14).

The initial focus may be on the identified patient, but the focus then moves to the family. *Often the identified patient may improve before the family does.*

A crisis often develops when the problems that have been hidden away or have been too painful to face are brought to the conscious awareness of the family members.

In the T. family the identified patient was Mr. T., who had chronic schizophrenia. Mrs. T. was a long-suffering housewife. There were two young children. Mrs. T. had been doing most of the childrearing. The couple socialized very little. When the family was brought together, Mr. T. talked about his wife's chronic hostility to him. She responded by saying, "Look what I put up with." This gradually accelerated until they were talking about divorce. This crisis was used to change the patterns of childrearing on the part of both parents. Mr. T. shared some of the family tasks, such as getting the kids to school on time and helping them do their homework. Mrs. T. had more time for herself. She returned to work as a biochemist. Feeling better about herself, she suggested to her husband that they go out to movies and concerts.

In this stage, the situation may appear to worsen, rather than improve. Symptomatology may accelerate, new symptoms may arise, and families may talk about quitting treatment. This upheaval usually is related to the family's barely perceived awareness that for things to get better, some member will have to change. Rather than change, a family member may accentuate or exaggerate symptoms. Family therapy changes have to be made sequentially. A family cannot let go of an offspring until the marital couple has found increased satisfaction in their own lives and in their relationship.

TERMINATION PHASE

In the closing phase the therapist reviews with the family which goals have been achieved and which have not. It is often useful to review the entire course of therapy, including the original problems and goals. A useful technique is to ask each family member to say what they would have to do in order to make the situation the same as it was at the onset of treatment. For example, father would have to yell at mother, who would have to yell at daughter, who would have to stop going to school. In essence, the family reconstructs the sequences leading to the pathology. Videotape playback may be helpful at this time, so that the family can see what it looked like at the start of treatment, compared to its present stage.[9] It is important to acknowledge that some behavior cannot be altered and that life will continue to change—i.e., will have unexpected and periodic problems. The family should be provided with the skills for solving future conflicts and challenges.

What are the criteria for suggesting termination of therapy? If the original goals have been achieved, the therapist may consider stopping. Even if the goals have not been achieved but have been worked out to the best capabilities of therapist and family, therapy can stop. When the treatment has been successful, new coping patterns and an enhanced empathy by family members for one another will have been established. There will come recognition that the family itself seems capable of dealing satisfactorily with new situations as they arise. There may be little to talk about during the sessions and little sense of urgency. Nonproductive quarreling and conflict having been reduced, the family will be freer to disagree openly and have methods of living with and working out its differences and separateness. The family will seem less inflexible in its rules and organization and appear more able to grow and develop. Individual family members will be symptomatically improved, and positive channels of interaction will be available between all family members. There will be improved agreement about family roles and functions.

Families often cannot or do not recognize changes that have occurred during therapy. A therapist should carefully check for any change and amplify it, giving positive reinforcement. If a family can produce a small change, then this may be an indication that bigger changes are possible. With some families, no change may occur until the therapy is completed.

During this end phase there may be an exacerbation of presenting symptoms. A son may begin hallucinating again coincident with father's reduction in communication with the mother. These eruptions are usually short lived and may represent a temporary response to the anxiety of terminating treatment, rather than being a sign of treatment failure. It is thus part of the separation process, which is always a key issue to be worked on in termination and which in some theoretical orientations may represent the major theme of the entire therapy.

SUGGESTED READINGS

Napier A and Whitaker C: **The Family Crucible.** New York: Harper and Row, 1978.

A very readable description of the whole treatment of a family by two expert therapists.

Papp P (Ed): **Family Therapy: Full Length Case Studies.** New York: Gardner Press, 1977.

Enjoyable look at the work of others.

REFERENCES

1. Berman EM and Lief HI: Marital therapy from a psychiatric perspective: An overview. Am J Psychiatry 132:583-592, 1975
2. Minuchin S and Fishman HC: Family Therapy Techniques. Cambridge, MA: Harvard University Press, 1981, p 31
3. Masters W and Johnson V: Human Sexual Response. Boston: Little, Brown, 1966
4. Satir V: Conjoint Family Therapy: A Guide to Theory and Technique (2nd Ed). Palo Alto, CA: Science and Behavior Books, 1967
5. Bell JE: Family Group Therapy. Public Health Monograph No. 64. Washington, D.C.: Department of Health, Education and Welfare, Public Health Service, 1961
6. Group for the Advancement of Psychiatry: The Case History Method in the Study of Family Process. Report No. 76. New York: Group for the Advancement of Psychiatry, 1970
7. Ackerman N: The Enemy and Myself. 16mm black and white sound film, 50 min. New York: The Family Institute
8. Kessler DR: Family in Crisis. 16mm color sound film, 48 min. San Francisco, CA: Langley Porter Neuropsychiatric Institute, University of California, San Francisco Medical Center
9. Glick ID and Marshall GJ: Family Therapy: An Introduction. Videotape and 16mm black and white sound film, 43 min. New York: Cornell University Medical College, Payne Whitney Clinic
10. Ackerman N: In and Out of Psychosis: A Family Study. 16mm black and white sound film, 120 min. New York: The Family Institute

Reconciliation of the Family by Jean-Baptist Greuze, courtesy of the collection of the
Phoenix Art Museum.

14
Family Treatment:
Resistance to Change

OBJECTIVES

- To be aware of and understand family resistances to treatment and change
- To understand those therapist reactions to the family that interferes with progress in treatment
- To identify strategies for countering resistances

INTRODUCTION

In family intervention, the primary focus is on *interactional change. Patterns and transactions that prevent or impede change can be thought of as resistances.* There may be multiple factors underlying specific resistance maneuvers. Family members fear change, but at the same time want relief from their problems. The family is often reluctant to change because, even if the present family system is working poorly, these known patterns may be better than anything else the family can envision.

DEFINITION

The term resistance (an analogy to the physics of two objects rubbing against each other and impeding movement) has a long history in the theory of individual psychopathology and treatment. Family theorists have an ambivalent attitude toward the concept of resistance, especially those who eliminated this concept

224

along with other psychodynamic concepts in their reaction to the notion of pathology as an individual affair.[1] While some family theorists are beginning to welcome back the concept and adapt its meaning to the family system, all practicing family therapists will tell you many tales of struggles with resistant families. Thus, in this chapter we define the concept as it applies to family intervention, describe the characteristic types of resistance encountered in practice, and provide clinically useful antedotes to resistance.

Resistance in family therapy has been defined broadly as any force or forces that impede the therapeutic system.[1] Resistances to family intervention can be conceptualized according to their *source* (family or therapist of treating system), or in what *phase of the treatment* they occur (initial evaluation and structuring of treatment, or during ongoing treatment).

RESISTANCES AT EVALUATION AND EARLY IN TREATMENT

The first task of the therapist is to set the structure within which the family intervention can occur, and during this process of negotiating the structure with the family, many resistances can surface. In contrast with individual therapy, family or marital therapy necessitates the attendance of a number of people, most who do not have overt symptoms. Getting fathers into and involved in family therapy has been classically seen as the most difficult task,[2] especially for inexperienced therapists.[3] In their description of a family therapy involving mother, father, and three adolescents, Napier and Whitaker[4] describe their approach in doing family therapy while insisting that the whole family be present. In the very first session the adolescent son did not come. The therapists refused to begin the psychotherapy without him despite the fact that the parents were fearful that an adolescent daughter was suicidal. The suicide potential was assessed, and judged not to be significant, and the parents were told to return for the second session with the whole family.

Strategies for getting father (and/or other important members of the family) to sessions include the following: reassuring the missing member of his importance, pointing out that changes depend upon his presence, noting that his absence can sabotage therapy, flexibility in scheduling, and spacing appointments.[1,5] Stanton and Todd[6] generated a number of principles to ensure attendance in starting family intervention with drug addicts and their families that are probably appropriate for other symptom groups as well: The therapist and not the family should decide which family members will be included in the treatment; whenever possible, family members should be encouraged to attend the evaluation interview; the index patient alone should not be given the task of bringing in the other members of the family; the therapist should obtain permission from the index patient and personally contact the family (fathers especially should be contacted personally); the therapist should contact the family with a rationale for family intervention that is non-pejorative, non-judgmental, and in no way blames the family for the symptoms and problems of the index patient.

In the F. family Mr. F. was the identified patient, with a long history of unipolar depression. Once his depressive episodes had been regulated with medication, he told the therapist that his wife was unhappy with their relationship. The therapist suggested marital therapy. He stated that this was his cross to bear because she would not come in for therapy. The therapist suggested that he again try talking to her about this. Mrs. F. surprisingly appeared for the next session and stated that she was unhappy with the relationship but had never been asked to come in for therapy. Mr. F. stated that he had asked her but admitted he might have "mumbled the invitation."

Families in which there is a member who exhibits current self-destructive behaviors (e.g., suicidal threats, gestures, and attempts; anorexia and/or bulimia; drug abuse; physical violence) present special issues in the initial structuring of the therapy. Clinicians vary in how they address these behaviors in the early structuring of the treatment. While there is little research evidence as to the most efficacious approaches, it is our clinical opinion that from the beginning, even in the very first session, the family therapist must address his or her responsibilities and the family's responsibilities if and when these destructive behaviors occur. The therapist must often spell out in great detail what he or she will and will not do when these behaviors occur. The therapist can also help the family members enunciate how they will behave.

Another area of potential resistance and deadlock in the early phase is disagreement about the goals of treatment. The family members themselves may disagree about the problem and the goals of treatment. For example, the family of an index adolescent patient may see the adolescent as the only problem, while the adolescent sees no problem in himself or herself and sees the parents as authoritarian, narrow and hostile. In marital therapy, covert disagreement about the problem and especially the goals of intervention occur when one spouse wants the marriage improved, while the other secretly wants out, and is intending to leave the spouse with the therapist for assistance in the break-up. Strategies to overcome family differences about the problem include searching for a *new definition* of the problem with which all family members agree, labeling the disagreement as part of the problem, and asking the family to give up notions about truth and reality. Covert goals can be approached by encouraging family members to say what has remained silent. Disagreement about goals of intervention can also occur between the therapist and the family. This seems most prominent when the therapist sees the problems of the index patient as related to the interactions of the family, while the family sees no contribution of their own and wants the index patient "changed" or cured. The therapist can approach this problem by initially accepting the family's view of the problem or at least not challenging this view, or by broadening the family's definition to include other aspects of interaction.

When working with families who have a member hospitalized for the first time with the initial emergence of psychotic symptomatology subsequently diagnosed as either schizophrenic or affective in nature, a common resistance of the family is to deny either the presence of an illness or its severity. If such denial persists, the family is in danger of avoiding follow-up care for the patient and family and continuing expectations for the index patient that are unrealistic and thus cause stress for the vulnerable individual.

A particularly troublesome resistance for the beginning family therapist, especially if a psychiatric resident, psychology intern, or social work student, is the family's attack on the therapist's competence or personal characteristics (e.g., age, sex, race, socioeconomic level, etc.). These resistances can come in subtle barrages ("You're so good for a youngster, but you probably don't know much about older people") and not so subtle barrages ("This is probably you're first case, and we are not making any progress. Have you talked to your supervisor about this?"). Contact with an experienced and level-headed supervisor is most helpful in these situations. The therapist, *if able to see the remarks in the context of resistance*, can explore the meaning of the questions about competence by empathizing with the family's concern. With equilibrium and, at times, humor, the therapist can admit differences and limitations (youth, relative inexperience) and appeal to the family for their assistance and help, and ask for a period in which to give the therapy a chance of succeeding.

RESISTANCES IN ONGOING TREATMENT

Once treatment has gotten past the initial evaluation and structure-setting phase, and the family or couple have settled down to some negotiated common goals and work, other resistances can emerge that can threaten the treatment with mid-phase stalemate. Anderson and Stewart[1] have listed a number of interactions that threaten the treatment: a family member who is consistently too talkative and dominant; a family member who refuses to speak; chaotic and disruptive children; use of defenses such as intellectualization, rationalization, and denial; constant focus by one or more members placing blame on others. Overly talkative members can be limited by the therapist or by other family members encouraged to do so by the therapist. Parents of chaotic children can be educated by words and the model of therapist to set controls in the sessions. In addition, the therapist can point out the function of the children's disruptions in the sequences of events in the session.

There are a number of techniques for handling defenses, not unlike those one might use in individual or group therapy. To counteract intellectualization and rationalization, the therapist can go with the theme by emphasizing the intellectual aspects of the therapy and/or giving intellectual explanations. Relabeling of feelings as facts may help. A denying family can be slowed down so as to emphasize aspects before they are glossed over. Non-verbal and experiential techniques can also be used to get to denied material.

Family Secrets

Individuals in the family often have "secrets" that in most cases are known but not acknowledged by other family members. They may involve overt behaviors, such as marital infidelity, that one marital partner feels he or she has been able to conceal from the other; or they may involve thoughts, feelings, and attitudes that family members believe others are not aware of. For example, parents may not realize (or may deny) that children pick up the general emotional tone existing between mother and father. They may act as if marital discord is hidden from their children and may want to keep that discord "secret."

Secrets can also be kept hidden from the therapist by the family.

The X. family consisted of a hospitalized adolescent, the parents, and two older siblings. For ten weeks, the family therapy seemed to be bogged down. The family stopped treatment. Two months later the family therapist discovered a secret that the entire family already knew—that is, the identified patient was having sexual relations with a ward nurse. The patient had told his siblings, who told the parents, who then signed the patient out of the hospital. The secret served the purpose of denigrating the hospital staff (including the family therapist) and effectively halting the family therapy.

Helping the family bring these pseudosecrets into the open usually results in a clearing of the air and eventually leads to a sense of relief and greater mutual understanding. Interestingly, it is commonly the children who talk openly in the family sessions about what was thought by others to be a secret. The therapist should, however, be prepared to deal with acute shock waves at the time the secret first emerges. When an individual in a family requests an individual session for the purpose of revealing a secret, the therapist may listen and try to explore the consequences of discussing the issue within the family setting. If, for example, one of the spouses has an incurable illness and the other spouse does not know about it, the reasons for the secrecy would be examined and the spouse would be encouraged to share the information with the whole family. If the secret does not seem crucial, the therapist might take a more neutral stance. The therapist must guard against being trapped into becoming a repository of secrets. At times a family member may insist on total honesty, either because of emotional insensitivity or as an active way of hurting another family member. For example, a parent might report to a child every negative feeling that crosses his or her mind in the guise of honesty.

MODELS FOR COUNTERING RESISTANCE

In the family field there are currently at least four different models for dealing with families who present difficulties in forming a therapeutic alliance.

The Medical Model

In the medical model, it is assumed that the index patient has an illness such as schizophrenia or major affective disorder and that the family is not the only, *ADD* nor necessarily the principal factor, in etiology of the illness. With this assumption, the major strategy in reducing family resistance to treatment is psychoeducation for the family, in which they are taught about the symptoms, etiology, and course of the illness. In this model it is emphasized that the family did not cause the illness, thus reducing the family guilt and resistance to meeting with the therapist. The family therapist takes on the role of a teacher who instructs the family about the illness and what the family can do to ensure optimal coping.

The Coaching Model

Therapists who work in both individual and family formats utilizing behavioral techniques tend to ignore the concept of resistance in their writings. Instead, they emphasize that individuals in families must learn certain basic skills for harmonious interpersonal interactions, such as communication skills, social skills, and problem-solving skills. It is not assumed that individuals lack these skills because of conflict, but rather show these deficits because of lacunae in prior learning. In this model the therapist is a coach and rational collaborator, who elicits the cooperation of the patient and family in learning skills that are missing. Resistances in learning these skills—such as failure to do homework, diverting attention in the session from learning the skills, etc.—are met by rationale ("You need to learn these skills in order to function"), encouragement, and positive reinforcement for approximation ("You did the first step in the homework and you did that extremely well"). More recently, behaviorists are beginning to discuss patient resistance to behavioral intervention. Patterson[7] has noted that a subgroup of families interact in sessions in such a way as to condition and shape the behavior of the family therapists as opposed to the other way around.

The Conflict Model

In a continuation of the psychodynamic tradition, the conflict model assumes that particular individuals in the marital or family system may exhibit resistance to intervention and change based upon their own internal conflicts and defense mechanisms. In this model the family therapist, like the individual dynamic therapist, uses techniques of confrontation and interpretation of the here-and-now interaction, especially negative interactions that might destroy the therapeutic relationship and the very survival of the therapy itself.

The Systems Model

A unique contribution of the family field is its theoretical position regarding the strength of a pattern of family interactions that shape and mold the behavior and psychopathology of an individual member of that group. In this orientation, it is assumed that family systems in homeostasis, even when the homeostasis involves psychopathology, will resist change. When faced with resistance of a whole system, the therapist must use strategic interventions to change not individual behaviors but a pattern of systems behaviors.

Minuchin and Fishman[8] give a clinical example of using the technique of unbalancing to overcome a family's resistance. The mother and father present with a four-year-old girl who acts as an uncontrollable monster. The mother is seen as an ineffective person, and the father is perceived by the mother as authoritarian and potentially violent. Minuchin unbalances the system by allying with the father and supporting his flexibility, his accepting manner, and his non-authoritarian behavior. The mother challenges these statements by re-enunciating her perception of the husband as a potentially violent man, but the therapist persists in expanding a perception of the man as potentially warm and supportive and reduces the myth of the father's potential violence by exploring concretely and factually how little he has ever done that is violent.

Probably the most dramatic therapeutic attempt to counter systems resistance is the work done by Palazzoli and colleagues.[9] When the family is not motivated for treatment, but coming mostly by the authoritarian force of a referring physician, interventions are used to immediately put the family in a crisis. On the other hand, when the family comes on its own initiative in crisis, in the first session the therapist *prescribes the symptoms* to the identified patient, positively connotes the symptom (e.g. therapist says, "Father is showing his love by *yelling* at everyone in the family") and allies with the family's homeostatic tendency.

THERAPIST REACTIONS TO THE FAMILY

The therapist, like the family, may develop unrealistic and inappropriate reactions, and these likewise may be of such intensity and nature as to present difficulties in treatment. For example, the therapist may behave toward the patient and family as though they were the therapist's own family, either past or present. When this occurs, the therapist must recognize and deal with the situation.

In individual therapy there is a one-to-one therapist-to-patient relationship. In the family or marital setting, the relationship is even more complicated. The therapist can act out feelings with any one member of the family, but must bear in mind that intense affect and interaction is appropriately often activated in both families and therapists during the session. The family's feelings about the therapist and the therapist's feelings about the family may be intensified, rather than diluted. Keeping distance and avoiding being drawn into dysfunctional interactions and special alliances are at the essence of family therapy. These may be most difficult for the beginning therapist.

In the early phase of treatment, the therapist may have the tendency to try to overhaul the family totally. There may be much blaming. In the middle phase of treatment, the therapist may become overly identified with various family members. In the late phases, the therapist may have difficulty in separating from those members.[10]

Certain psychiatric syndromes lend themselves to particular inappropriate reactions by the therapist. For example, in families with a member who has schizophrenia, the mother (by her apparent overindulgence) may be the therapist's target, whereas in families with a delinquent member, the target may be the father by his absence.

An important issue in the treatment of families and the training of family therapists is the problem of blaming the family. Appleton[11] has pointed out a number of crucial areas in which therapists inappropriately blame parents for the pathology of the children. The notion of more than one causal influence on psychopathology is difficult for the neophyte therapist, who may still be hoping for simple answers. Patterns of blame have been related to traditional notions of sex roles and sex-role stereotypes. It is assumed that the father is responsible for psychopathology relating to stereotyped masculine behavior. Where there is not clear-cut, sex-role stereotype, the mother is usually blamed. Many theories of psychopathology place major emphasis on the common sense but untested notion that the crucial family relationship is the one between mother and child.

As in individual therapy, the therapist must avoid being drawn into a role that confirms the reality of the patient's and family's misconceptions. The therapists' attitudes to such matters as family, marriage, and money, for example, must be open to introspection and worked through so as not to interfere with the therapy. Many therapists find that in working with families, unresolved personal issues are stimulated to the degree that they affect the therapist's own personal relationships. Having personally undergone therapy may be of help, and this includes both individual psychotherapy and especially family therapy. The ability of family therapists to work with difficult families may be directly in proportion to their ability to know their own families.

The question is often raised about a match between the family's stage of development and the therapist's own stage. Although the accepted dogma is that such a match counts for little in the ultimate outcome, clinical experience in family therapy has led us to at least question this assumption. Common sense indicates that the more the therapist has in common with the family, the better the likelihood of a positive relationship; for example, both being of the same gender, class, race, or sexual orientation would appear to have implications for a greater chance of working together successfully (more on this issue in Chapter 27). In the course of family therapy training, the therapist should be helped to recognize the implications his or her own particular life stage and family experience has on therapeutic work. For example, there might be serious therapeutic blind spots when a newly wedded 25-year-old therapist begins working with a couple who have been married for 25 years and are undecided about whether to stay married.

A FINAL NOTE

Doing family therapy is very different from doing individual treatment. Therapists are usually apprehensive at first, but as they gain experience they are excited by the challenge and fascination of work with natural units. Many therapists find themselves uncomfortable doing family work and should not force themselves to undertake it. In some ways, the experience for the therapist is like sitting in the middle of the couple in *Who's Afraid of Virginia Woolf?* or the family in *Long Day's Journey into Night*, or like sitting in the middle of a three-ring circus. One has to pay attention not only to individuals in the family system, but also to the family unit, and at the same time be aware of one's own feelings toward the family. The task is to stay focused on the objective to be achieved with each family unit.

SUGGESTIONS FOR FURTHER READINGS

Anderson CM and Stewart S: **Mastering Resistance: A Practical Guide to Family Therapy.** New York: Guilford Press, 1983.
> *A very practical guide with a catalog of resistances to family treatment, and helpful techniques to overcome them.*

Palazzoli MS, Boscolo L, Cecchin G, and Prata, G: **Paradox and Counter-paradox.** New York: Jason Aronson, 1978

Grunebaum H and Glick ID: The basics of family treatment, in Grinspoon L (Ed): **Psychiatry Update, Vol. II.** Washington, D.C.: APA Press, 1983, pp 185-203

REFERENCES

1. Anderson C and Stewart S: Mastering Resistance: A Practical Guide to Family Therapy. New York: Guilford Press, 1983
2. Forrest T: Treatment of the father in family therapy. Fam Process 8:106-109, 1969
3. Shapiro R and Budman S: Defection, termination and continuation in family and individual therapy. Fam Process 12:55-67, 1973
4. Napier A and Whitaker C: The Family Crucible. New York: Harper & Row, 1978
5. L'Abate L: Pathogenic role rigidity in fathers: Some observations. J Marr Fam Couns 1:69-79, 1975
6. Stanton MD and Todd TC: Engaging resistant families in treatment. Fam Process 20(3):261-293, 1981
7. Patterson GR: Coercive Family Process. Eugene, OR: Castalia Publishing Co., 1982
8. Minuchin S and Fishman HC: Family Therapy Techniques. Cambridge, MA: Harvard University Press, 1981, p 169ff
9. Palazzoli MS, Boscolo L, Cecchin G, and Prata G: Paradox and Counter-paradox: A New Model in the Therapy of the Family Schizophrenic Transaction. New York: Jason Aronson, 1978
10. Whitaker C, Felder RE, and Warkentin J: Countertransference in the family treatment of schizophrenia, in Boszormenyi-Nagy I and Framo JL (Eds): Intensive Family Therapy. New York: Harper & Row, 1965, pp 323-342
11. Appleton WS: Mistreatment of patients' families by psychiatrists. Am J Psychiatry 131:655-657, 1974

La Familia by Lorenzo Homar, 1967. Courtesy of the artist and the Division of Education of the Committee of Puerto Rico.

15
Family Treatment:
General Considerations

OBJECTIVES

- To understand the common elements of psychotherapy as they apply to family treatment
- To become familiar with the general strategies of family therapy and their related techniques.
- To become familiar with existing treatment packages for specific situations/disorders

INTRODUCTION

By this time the reader should have some understanding of how families function and how their difficulties may be conceptualized. In addition, material has been presented relative to evaluating troubled families and to setting appropriate treatment goals. The following discussion considers more general features of marital and family treatment, namely, the participants, the setting, the scheduling of treatment, and the use of family therapy in combination with other treatment methods and helping agencies. Finally, we compare family therapy with other therapy formats.

236

FAMILY PARTICIPANTS

In practice it is often preferable to begin treatment by seeing the entire family together. The family can broadly be defined to include all persons living under the same roof; all those persons closely related to one another, even though they do not live together; or even more broadly, all persons significant to the family, even though not related to them (friends, "caretakers," or "social network").[1,2]

Sometimes family therapy is carried out with the same therapist meeting with the whole family and with each family member individually. This is termed *concurrent family therapy.* At other times two therapists who maintain some contact with each other, but who do not work jointly, may each see separately one or more members of a family in what is known as *collaborative family therapy. Conjoint family therapy* has been defined as family therapy in which the participants include at least two generations of a family, such as parents and children, plus the therapist, all meeting together. Conjoint marital therapy is limited to the two spouses plus the therapist meeting together.[3]

Although it often seems desirable to meet with all family members present, in actual practice this may be impossible or even contraindicated. For example, it would usually seem more appropriate when discussing the sexual adjustment of the parents that the children not be present. This issue is discussed more fully in Chapter 18. Often, too, the therapist will be involved with incomplete families, either because the family itself has experienced divorce or death, or because one or more family members temporarily or permanently refuse to participate. In the latter case a decision will have to be made, either at the outset of treatment or following the evaluation, as to whether it is worthwhile and possible, to continue working with the incomplete family. Hard and fast rules as to *when* it is "worthwhile" are not easy to give, but our bias is that if the pros and cons are about equal it is better to give treatment a try even if the family is incomplete.

At times individuals will feel uncomfortable talking about certain topics in front of the other family members. In such instances the family therapist will have to use his or her judgment as to when individual interviewing might be indicated. This might be done, for example, with the goal of eventually bringing the material from the individual session to the entire family group. It must be recognized that there may be family secrets that cannot be productively shared with other family members and that should be kept private between an individual family member and the therapist. (This issue is discussed more fully in Chapter 14). On this issue, too, no rigid guidelines can be established.

An example of an unshared family secret comes from a family in which a 20-year-old girl was the identified patient.* The patient's mother had had a postpartum psychosis following the patient's birth, during which she had jumped in front of a train, resulting in bilateral amputation below the knees. The patient's grandmother had also had a postpartum psychosis after the birth of the mother. The patient had not known about these secrets. The story was revealed by the father in a family session that did not involve the identified patient. The patient was never informed of her mother's psychosis based on the judgment of all concerned that she was not psychologically capable of dealing with this material at that time.

The family concept can be extended to cover nonrelated people who have an impact on the individuals in treatment. These might be friends, neighbors, professional helpers, or custodians. Such people often do not have the same kind of emotional impact and influence that the natural family unit has, but at any one particular time these groups of "significant others" may be quite important.

Many experienced family therapists hold to the view that the probability of improvement increases as the number of nuclear family members involved in treatment increases. We agree.

Extended Family and Significant Others

Family therapists include grandparents or in-laws as participants when they seem to significantly influence the family difficulties (see Chapter 12).† Grandparents and other extended family members play vital roles in many families. For some they may provide important help financially and functionally in carrying out the family's tasks. They may be a repository of emotional support and warmth, available in times of crisis and need. Their contributions and participation may at times be viewed as interference or infantilization. They may create or demand obligations in return for their involvement. The grandparents may provide money with strings attached, which may be in the form of rules and regulations concerning the rearing of their children; such aid may also imply an obligation that the family visit the grandparents on a prescribed schedule.

The question of whether or not a friend, fiance(e), boyfriend, or girlfriend should participate in a therapy session is occasionally raised. Such individuals should be included if their involvement is judged to be important to the progress of the therapy. Such outsiders are less motivated to change than are family members, however, and are hence more likely to drop out of family therapy.

---

*We are indebted to Pamela Ingber, M.D., for this example.

†An excellent example of a family in which a child may feel much closer to a grandparent than to his father or mother is provided in the 1976 movie, *Lies My Father Told Me*. In this film, a seven-year-old boy is being raised by a mother who is totally devoted to a rather insensitive, chronically inadequate spouse. The boy spends most of his time with his grandfather, who acts as a father substitute.

Caretakers

Caretakers (e.g., baby-sitters or housekeepers) are playing an increasingly important role in the function of families, especially those in which both parents work. They are often usefully included in treatment.

In the G. family Mr. and Mrs. G. were separated. Mrs. G. had great difficulty functioning as a person and mother. Mr. G., therefore, had custody of the children. Care of the children, ages 14, 12, and 10, was left to a baby sitter, who was the 21-year-old sister of Mr. G.'s current girl friend. Feeling despondent, Mrs. G. made a suicide attempt. It was at this point that attempts at family therapy were initiated, but Mr. G. refused to attend because he was angry with his wife. At the onset of family therapy, Mrs. G. complained that she was unable to get the children to attend. They were on Mr. G.'s side. The children refused to attend when the therapist called them, saying the baby-sitter would not let them travel to the sessions. The baby sitter was, of course, on the father's side. Furthermore, once the children began to attend therapy, the sitter would, after each session, belittle the mother to the children. They would then in turn berate their mother, who would again become suicidal. It was only after both the husband and the baby sitter were included in family therapy that this sequence of interactions could be understood and modified.

Pets

Pets often serve important functions in the family.[4]

1. As safe, faithful, intimate, noncompetitive, nonjudemental love objects and friends.
2. As substitute children for childless couples or for those whose children have left home; couples planning to have children may find that practicing their parental skills first on pets is desirable.
3. As ways of compensating for personal deficiencies by identification with the pet's strength, courage, assertiveness, attractiveness, size, playfulness, directness, animality, dependence, or independence.
4. As scapegoats or allies in intrafamily conflicts.
5. As a means for children to learn responsibility and compassion.

Ms. P. was from a family based on dyads (mother-father, older sister-younger sister). The "confidant" for this person during her emotional crisis was her dog. When she left home to attend school, the dog developed a rash and lost his hair. He manifested the symptoms during the beginning of his empty-nest syndrome. There was also a family crisis that revolved around who should take care of the dog.

In the G. family, Mr. G. was unable to express any affection to his wife, son, or daughter, but he spent long hours caressing, talking to, and grooming his five dogs.

Veterinarians have observed the relationship between the neurotic behaviors of pets and those of their owners. One veterinarian has recently taken a family approach, stating that, "You can't change a dog's behavior without changing the dog owner in terms of how he relates to the dog."[5]

The family therapist may want, at least temporarily, to include a pet as part of the therapy to observe and discuss the role of the pet in the family system. A pet may be used as a more neutral way of getting into the family's dynamics, because it may be easier to talk about the pet than to talk about the problems involving the human beings in the family.

THERAPIST COMBINATIONS

Co-therapy

Most family therapists work alone. A number of therapists, however, prefer to work with a *cotherapist* to help monitor the complexity of the transactions and as a check-balance on the other therapist. For training purposes, a student therapist can work with either a more seasoned veteran or with a student of another discipline. Cotherapists can present an experiential model of a two-person interaction that is similar to a marital dyad by openly dealing with their own differences and by providing models for healthy communication. If, on the other hand, the cotherapists feel that they need to present a united front or that they need to be identical in their attitudes and interactions with the family members they are jointly treating, the family will then be provided with a very unrealistic model.

Cotherapists are usually of the opposite sex. This gives each family member someone of the same sex with whom to identify and to use as a model. Often cotherapists are or become personally intimate.

Cotherapists may come to be seen as parents or as husband and wife by the family and may therefore be the recipients of the typical patterns, feelings, and attitudes that the family has toward people in these roles. The cotherapists may find themselves in danger of being split and having to take sides between one family member and another, in a manner very similar to what takes place in the actual treatment family. The cotherapy team must avoid falling consistently into this trap. A solution is for one cotherapist to be sensitive to a family member who is in distress and who may need support, while the other therapist focuses on someone else. A cotherapist may either complement or synergize with the other therapist.

It is necessary to consider whether or not a therapist can work effectively with a cotherapist and if cotherapy is the best use of each therapist's time. A recent study suggests that therapist satisfaction with a cotherapist decreases as experience in family therapy increases.[6] Furthermore, some authors have found that a cotherapist causes problems that can impede family progress. For example, if the male cotherapist has had significant problems with his mother and is in the process of treating a family that has a "difficult" mother, he might have difficulty working effectively with a female therapist. Another obvious reason for the more common use of a single therapist is that it costs less.

In order to make cotherapy a successful experience, the cotherapists should know and like each other. They should have worked together, so that they are able to appreciate each other's therapy style and attitude. They should have time to discuss together what has been going on in their therapy sessions and to have a chance to work out their mutual roles with respect to the family and each other. Ideally, cotherapists should meet together prior to each session in order to review their objectives and ideas. Cotherapists should meet after each session for a review of what went on and to plan for the next session.

Another technique of family therapy is to use more than two therapists—one for each individual family member and one for the whole family together. This method has been used as part of multiple impact therapy (MIT).[7]

An innovative approach is the use of cotherapists from different disciplines, which, as stated, is a desirable approach for beginning therapists. This technique has the advantage that each therapist may complement the other, since each discipline has different training and may bring its own areas of expertise. This method requires the use of extra staff time, however, and to justify it, one would have to prove its differential effectiveness over family therapy as it is usually practiced.

One report has noted the use of the therapist and his or her family to treat the identified patient and his or her family.[8] This method must be considered experimental at this time.

Working as a Team

Several groups have experimented with using a treatment team (3-4 therapists) to work with the family.[9,10] Typically, one or two therapists are in the treatment room with the family, while the rest of the treatment team is behind a one-way mirror. The team communicates with the therapist in the room by telephone, or by having a conference (without the family) either during or toward the end of the therapy hour. The team assists the therapist by: (1) providing directives to the therapist-trainee, (2) by helping formulate messages and tasks, including paradoxical tasks that will be conveyed to the family by the therapist.

One central technique in this approach is to have the two cotherapists play out in explicit detail the implicit conflicts within the family. For example, with a family where one member has schizophrenia, one team member will take the extreme position that "schizophrenia is an individual illness, patients are responsible for their own behavior and illness, and that Mom and Dad should not only back off, but enjoy their freedom from responsibility for their children in order to maximize the potential for the marital dyad." The other team member takes the position that, "schizoprehenia is an illness that realistically makes the patient dependent upon the parents, that given the psychotic process, it is impossible for the patient to control his behavior and comply with treatment, and the family must take over." *The task for the team is to reconcile the discrepant family position.* This is possible to varying degrees.

While expensive in therapy manpower, the team approach has the advantage of many heads being better than one, and utilization of outside observers that are not enmeshed in the family interaction. It seems clear that with a number of team members, the team must generate its own smooth systems functioning, including clear leadership, cooperation, etc.

SETTING

Family therapy has been carried out in settings such as child-guidance clinics, psychiatric hospitals, emergency rooms (walk-in or crisis clinics), outpatient clinics, juvenile probation offices, domestic relations courts, private offices, schools,[11] social welfare services,[12] and many other places. There have been cases in which entire families have been hospitalized for treatment[13] and for research purposes.[14] Other therapists have carried out treatment in the family's own home. In fact, in Italy, most treatment contacts at some Community Mental Health Centers are made in the home. (Advantages and disadvantages of home visits are discussed in Chapter 9).

TIME, SCHEDULING, AND FEES

Most family therapists will see a family once a week for a duration of 45 to 90 minutes. In Italy, many sessions are two hours or more. In outpatient settings, a minority of therapists see a family more than once a week. In inpatient settings, family sessions may be scheduled more frequently. There is nothing sacred about once-a-week scheduling. In fact, since the frequency of sessions is somewhat arbitrary (once a week is the commonest), meeting less frequently may be strategically better for some families. Palazzoli meets with a given family in treatment once a month. She mails the family a "prescription" between sessions.[15] In multiple impact therapy, families are seen on an intensive basis and in different combinations—marital couple, mother and son, whole family, individuals, and so on—over a two- or three-day period by various members of a therapy team, consisting of psychiatrist, psychologist, social worker, and vocational counselor. Techniques focus on bringing about rapid change in the family during this time period, because its members have come for therapy from distant locations. A variant of this technique is the one employed by Masters and Johnson[16] in their sex therapy, which consists of a two-week treatment course of multiple daily sessions with one male and one female cotherapist.

The decision as to the overall duration of treatment would, in part, depend on the goals of treatment. On the average, family therapy is a short-term method compared to individual or group psychotherapy or psychoanalysis. Other ground rules:

1. *Missed appointments* should be rescheduled that week.
2. *When one member of the family comes late,* the therapist starts the clock at the arranged time and proceeds with whoever is present. He may role-play for the absent family member(s).
3. *What can be done if one member of the family will not come to treatment?* Often the resistance is not just from the member who will not come, but from the other members of the family who covertly (or overtly) encourage such an absence. They may be unaware of their collusion, however, and often ask for help to get the reluctant member to participate.
4. *Fees* are set (usually) by time, i.e., the length of the session, not by number of members of the family present.

KEEPING A RECORD OF TREATMENT

Opinions differ as to the value of keeping written notes on the course of family treatment. Such a record may be useful both in monitoring goals and also in recording changes. The problem-oriented record modified for families provides a concise overall picture of the identified patient and the family, and outlines problems, goals, and strategies.[17] Ongoing progress notes record significant family developments, enable goal achievement to be measured, and provide a record of treatment and modalities used for achieving these goals. Referrals to other agencies are also noted. Such a system has a definite advantage over the traditional practice of keeping a separate record for each family member.

Many therapists focus on the process rather than the content of the sessions and therefore believe that there is no need to write down the "facts" of what goes on. Records are often very helpful for training purposes. Many family therapists prefer not to keep any records of treatment to protect themselves against the possibility of their being subpoenaed. (This issue is discussed in Chapter 30). Our bias is to keep succinct relevant records.

FAMILY THERAPY IN COMBINATION WITH
OTHER PSYCHOSOCIAL THERAPIES

At present the differential effectiveness of family therapy alone as compared with its use in combination with other therapies is just beginning to be studied (see Chapter 31). During the 1980s, the use of family therapy in combination with somatic, individual, and group therapy has incresed and is now common.

A minority of family therapists uses conjoint family therapy alone. All contacts are kept strictly within the joint family setting, and the therapist will not communicate even by telephone with individual family members. No other treatment is used, including individual therapy. This is done to avoid any type of coalition derived from material shared by the therapist and any part of the family system.

It is becoming more usual for the same therapist to employ individual psychotherapy and family therapy.[18] The therapist here has the advantage of knowing both the individual and the family. This combination, however, changes the nature of the therapy as follows: (1) the patient in individual therapy feels that what he or she reveals in the one-to-one situation may in some way (either overtly or covertly) be communicated to the family by the therapist; (2) family members may be reluctant to deal with sensitive issues in the conjoint sessions, preferring to reveal them in individual sessions; and (3) transference in individual sessions does not develop as fully, because the patient can directly express his or her feelings about his or her family in the family therapy. This may present an insurmountable obstacle to the individual therapy. Inexperienced therapists may tend to identify with the individual patient, thus seeing the family from the patient's point of view. The therapist may see all problems as resulting from "this cold, passive, authoritarian father and smoldering, double-binding, rejecting mother" and from what they have done to the "poor patient." This may make it extremely difficult to work conjointly with the whole family.

In addition to conjoint family treatment, individual therapy has simultaneously been carried out with only one patient, or with both parents in separate sessions.

In the C. family the identified patient was the son, Henry, who had chronic schizophrenia. He was 20 when he was brought for treatment because he had not gone out of his room for a year. The mother and father were bringing him his meals in bed, and he had stopped attending school. History revealed that there were two older sisters who were functioning well. Mother and father had met 25 years before. The father was shy and withdrawn. The mother was overbearing, domineering, and brought in most of the money. She worked as a cashier. Life for them had been good up until the birth of the youngest child—the identified patient—at which point mother and father stopped having sexual relations (the previous frequency had been about two times per week). The mother said that she was "uninformed" about contraceptive methods and that since she did not want any more children, the only way she could think of was to stop having sex. Since the father was a noncommunicative person, this had not been discussed for 19 years, up until the time that the patient returned to the hospital.

Treatment intervention was initiated with somatic therapy for the identified patient's schizophrenia. Once his symptoms (negativism and autistic thinking) began to clear, treatment was directed toward his rehabilitation. In order to do this, and to place the patient in a work setting, the parents had to let him "out of the nest." Family meetings were held with the mother, father, sisters, and the identified patient. Mother and father were also seen separately to help them rebuild their marital relationship. A series of progressive behavioral exercises markedly improved their sexual relations, which resumed with a satisfactory frequency. Once all this had occurred, the parents helped to find a halfway house for the son.

A major shift in the 1980s has been the notion of using different formats over different stages of time. A common sequence of treatment is the couple that presents with a sexual problem. Sexual therapy solves the problem. At this point, marital problems often come to the fore. Marital therapy is then employed and the marital relationship improved. Following this, one, or both, members of the couple may decide they want to explore different aspects of their own growth and development; therefore, individual therapy is prescribed. Numerous variations on this concept are possible and *the important issue for the beginner to understand is that this kind of sequencing is an increasing trend*.

Sugarman[19] describes some rules of thumb in making decisions about combined therapy:

... (1) It is useful if it appears that different modalities would help significantly in different dimensions, such as the biological, social, and psychological; (2) if it appears that a given modality is either not helpful or of limited usefulness without an additional modality; (3) if there is significant motivation on the part of the individual or family to combine modalities; and (4) if the modalities are synergistic and enhance each other. On the other hand, the following reasons would be contraindications to combining modalities: (1) The epistemological foundations of the various modalities are often based on contradictory assumptions. Since the goal of clinical work is to provide a coherent cognitive ordering of the world, combining modalities can at times be unproductively confusing for the patient system. (2) The additional time and money involved may be unnecessary. A single modality is often powerful enough to accomplish what is therapeutically necessary. (3) Different modalities can dilute the potential cathexis available for each separate therapeutic involvement. To the extent that there is meaning to the concept of psychic energy, it could be divided between the various modalities with not enough available in any one for the "critical mass" necessary to accomplish therapeutic work. This is similar to the concept of "diluting the transference" in psychoanalytic thought.

Individual treatment as a supplement to conjoint family therapy has also been carried out with mother and/or child. Individual sessions supplemented by conjoint sessions for all family members is an approach employed commonly in child psychiatric practice (see Chapter 26).

Family therapy has been prescribed in combination with group therapy[20,21] and with behavioral therapy.[22,23] It has been used in conjunction with hospitalization for one member (usually the identified patient) or for all members of the family in both inpatient[14,24] and day hospital[25] settings; in conjunction with psychiatric medications[26] and electric-shock therapy, which are used to control the identified patient's acute symptoms. In one case, one of us (IDG) found that marital therapy was possible, and effective, only after both marital partners had been treated for their depressions (which predated the marriage) with antidepressants.

Family therapy has been prescribed as an adjunct to individual therapy[27] and psychoanalysis. In these situations it may be useful for diagnostic purposes to correct distorted perceptions and to shorten treatment.[28] (See Chapter 1 and later in this chapter for indications for, and comparisons of, several types of psychosocial treatments.)

FAMILY THERAPY IN COMBINATION WITH OTHER HELPING AGENCIES

The family therapist often finds himself in the situation of using family therapy at the same time that other helping agencies are also exerting influences on the family. This may create unwanted complications.

Commonly, families have multiple problems that involve a wide variety of agencies: welfare, probation, school, housing, and so on. These agencies may be pulling the family in different directions. The need is often to open up communication among the various agencies and to allocate areas of responsibility. It then becomes necessary to coordinate the work of the various agencies in the service of the family's goals, thus avoiding much duplication and wasteful contradictory efforts.

In some families there is simultaneous treatment by the therapist and physician of one or more members of the family, and this may exert a significant influence.[29] For example, one family member may be receiving cortisone for rheumatoid arthritis, which may make that person euphoric. He or she may be difficult for the family to live with. The family therapist will have to be in continuing contact with the family physician to coordinate treatment in such cases.

Family members may play one agency against the other in the service of their needs. For example, the family members may need to have the identified patient remain dysfunctional so that they can get welfare or disability payments;

Table 15-1

Comparison of Therapy Formats and Strategies

Therapy Format	Strategies		
	Insight-Awareness	Strategic-Behavioral	Experiential
Family	Confrontation of the family interaction: clarification of inter-action: interpreta-tion of conflict	Psychoeducation: assign-ment of task: marking boundaries	Empathic contact: explore present family experience
Individual	Confrontation: clarification: interpretation	Assignment of indiv-idual task: cognitive restructuring: role playing: desensiti-zation	Empathic contact: explore present individual experience
Group	Confrontation of group interaction: interpretation of group and individual transference	Role playing: behavioral rehearsal: assignment of tasks	Empathic contact: explore present group experience

but they simultaneously experience the distortions in the family system that this may produce. In another case a spouse who is not getting along with her husband may suggest to the probation worker that the husband has been violating his parole and should go back to jail, whereas she tells the family therapist that she is trying to work out their problems in order that they may stay together.

COMPARISON OF THERAPY FORMATS AND STRATEGIES

Finally, now that we have presented the techniques of family therapy, let us again compare family therapy to individual therapy and to group therapy—only this time (compared to Chapter 1) by type of strategies utilized. Table 15-1 is an expansion of Table 1-1. It reveals the relevant similarities and differences, but the main issue is to note the most obvious difference in the unit that is being worked with by the therapist in individual therapy, an individual; in family therapy, mem-bers of the same family (broadly defined); while group therapy is conducted with persons who are not members of the same family.

SUGGESTIONS FOR FURTHER READINGS

Bodin AM: Family therapy, in Karasu TB (Ed): **The Psychiatric Therapies**. Washington, D.C.: American Psychiatric Association, 1984.
The when, why, and how of family intervention.

Gurman A (Ed): **Questions and Answers in the Practice of Family Therapy**. New York: Brunner/Mazel, 1981.
The everyday, clinical questions that one runs into with to-the-point answers from experts.

REFERENCES

1. Speck RV and Rueveni U: Network therapy: A developing concept. Fam Process 8:182-191, 1969
2. Speck RV and Attneave C: Network therapy, in Haley J (Ed): Changing Families. New York: Grune & Stratton, 1971, pp 312-332
3. Cutter AV and Hallowitz D: Diagnosis and treatment of the family unit with respect to the character-disordered youngster. J Am Acad Child Psychiatry 1:605-618, 1962
4. Feldman B: Pets soothe their owners' hang-ups. San Francisco Examiner, November 20, 1977
5. Campbell W: Owners cause dogs' mental problems. San Francisco Chronicle, October 29, 1975, p 45
6. Rice D, Fey W, and Kepecs J: Therapist experience and "style" as factors in co-therapy. Fam Process 11:227-238, 1972
7. MacGregor R, Ritchie AM, Serrano AC, et al.: Multiple Impact Therapy with Families. New York: McGraw-Hill, 1964
8. Landes J and Winter W: A new strategy for treating disintegrating families. Fam Process 5:1-20, 1966
9. Montalvo B: Aspects of live supervision. Fam Process 12:343-359, 1973
10. Hoffman L: Foundation of Family Therapy: A Conceptual Framework for Systems Change. New York: Basic Books, 1981
11. Moss S: School experiences as family crisis. J Int Assoc Pupil Personnel Workers 15:115-121, 1970
12. Morris R: Welfare reform 1973: The social services dimension. Science 181:515-522, 1973
13. Abrams G, Fellner C, and Whitaker C: The family enters the hospital. Am J Psychiatry 127:1363-1370, 1971
14. Bowen M: Family psychotherapy. Am J Orthopsychiatry 31:40-60, 1961
15. Palazzoli M, Boscolo L, Cecchin G, and Prata G: Paradox and Counter-

paradox: A New Model in the Therapy of the Family Schizophrenic Transaction. New York: Jason Aronson, 1978

16. Masters W and Johnson V: Human Sexual Response. Boston: Little, Brown, 1966

17. Deming B and Kimble JJ: Adapting the individual problem-oriented record for use with families. Hosp & Comm Psychiatry 26:334-335, 1975

18. Greene BL (Ed): The Psychotherapies of Marital Disharmony. New York: Free Press, 1965

19. Sugarman S (Ed): Interface of Individual and Family Therapy: Family Therapy Collection. Rockville, M.D.: Aspen Publications Inc., 1986

20. Leichter E and Shulman G: The family interview as an integrative device in group therapy with families. Int J Group Psychother 13:335-345, 1963

21. MacGregor R: Group and family therapy: Moving into the present and letting go of the past. Int J Group Psychother 20:495-515, 1970

22. Fine S: Family therapy and behavioral approach to childhood obsessive-compulsive neurosis. Arch Gen Psychiatry 28:695-697, 1973

23. Coe W: Behavioral approach to disrupted family interactions. Psychotherapy: Theory, Research and Practice 9:80-85, 1972

24. Fleck S: Some general and specific indications for family therapy. Confin Psychiatry 8:27-36, 1965

25. Zwerling I and Mendelsohn M: Initial family reactions to day hospitalization. Fam Process 4:50-63, 1965

26. Cohen M, Freedman N, Englehardt D, et al.: Family interaction patterns, drug treatment, and change in social aggression. Arch Gen Psychiatry 19:1950-1956, 1968

27. Szalita A: The combined use of family interviews and individual therapy in schizophrenia. Am J Psychother 22:419-430, 1968

28. Szalita A: The relevance of the family interview for psychoanalysis. Contemporary Psychoanal 8:31-44, 1971

29. Anthony E: The impact of mental and physical illness on family life. Am J Psychiatry 127:138-146, 1970

Encounter by Naomi Gerstein, private collection.

16

Brief Therapy: Telescoping the Course of Treatment

OBJECTIVES

- To be aware of and understand the indications for brief family therapy
- To describe the course of and techniques of brief intervention

INTRODUCTION

In the last ten years there has been much clinical and research attention on the duration of therapeutic intervention. Brief therapy has been viewed (in contrast to longer, open-ended treatments) as a legitimate form of intervention. The focus on brief therapies has come about from a multitude of factors. Economic limitations of patients and clinics helped press for an intervention package that was time-limited and cost effective. Long waiting lists at clinics with patients expecting assignment to therapists also pressured clinicians to consider and experiment with shorter forms of intervention. Another reason for increased use was the need for research on psychotherapy, coupled with the realization that to research ten sessions of therapy was much more practical than observing and recording a therapy that spanned some years. And, most importantly, some clinicians began to formulate the theoretical advantages of a short, preplanned intervention and linked it to the historical roots of the beginning of psychotherapy, pointing out that Freud's initial work, for example, was brief.[1]

Family therapy is a relatively recent newcomer to the therapeutic scene, and thus it was not encumbered with an emphasis on longer and "deeper" therapies. Family therapy arrived not too much earlier than the brief therapy beginnings. In this context it was natural for family intervention to be brief, or at least, not have an exclusive emphasis on long-term work. Gurman[2] has even commented that to call family or marital treatment brief is redundant, as the typical family intervention is approximately 15 to 20 sessions. Gurman suggests some interesting hypotheses as to why marital therapy tends to be brief. For the non-insight awareness models, the therapist focuses on the current problem, rather than relating to the historical antecedent involving dynamics of the problem. Most of the patients who enter marital therapy have shown themselves capable of having at least one (more or less) meaningful relationship judged by the very fact of their being married, and thus these individuals are likely to constitute a selected good-prognosis population. In addition, the interpersonal and/or transferential aspects of the problems are not only talked about, but also exhibited in the therapy sessions themselves, since both parties are present. Finally, the loss of the therapist at the termination of the treatment is not as threatening as the ending of an individual treatment, because the partners leave with each other as company.

INDICATIONS FOR BRIEF FAMILY INTERVENTION

Indications for when to utilize planned, brief family or marital intervention would include the following:

1. *When there is a current, relatively focused family (or marital) conflict.* Examples include the need to separate from the family of origin[3]; to establish marital commitment; to resolve ambivalence over intimacy and dependency; to establish modes of conflict resolution, decision making and negotiation in the marital dyad[4]; to clarify role expectations; to develop channels for expression of positive and negative feelings; to explore the decision to divorce or gain assistance in negotiating a separation or divorce that is least harmful to spouses and children involved.
2. *When there is evidence that family members are currently contributing to an identified patient's focused symptom or problem complex.*
3. *When family cooperation must be mobilized as an induction to another mode of therapy.*
4. *When the family situation is baffling, and brief therapy is chosen in part as an extended evaluation and in part as therapy.*

It is not only the specific focused problem area that is important in indicating brief family intervention, but also the specific capabilities of the family members for focused brief work that are decisive in the decision to use this mode of treatment. These *patient/family enabling factors* for brief family or marital work include the ability of the family to meet together without uncontrollable fighting, family agreement and ability to focus on specific problems, and motivation of the significant family members for the participation needed. For the most part, these factors need be less present in longer family work.

COURSE OF TREATMENT

The initial referral contact and evaluation interview can be used to set the stage for the brief family treatment. The therapist in collaboration with a family can focus on specific issues, clarify the goals and expectations, and channel the interactions in ways suited to short-term, focused work. For example, if the family situation fits one of the types of problems discussed above, then the evaluation data gathering will focus on material and processes relevant to that category and its goals, and other types of data will be given less attention.

Before the end of the first session, the therapist will have made a contract with the family outlining the goals and duration of treatment. There may also be an agreement as to what goals will not be pursued. Anything else that is made explicit to the family about the process of treatment may vary, but the therapist should have a blueprint in mind.

As the therapy proceeds, the therapist will actively keep the family on the track and discourage derailments of various sorts. Depending on the type of treatment involved, the family will be rewarded for continuing in the necessary stepwise sequence or for gaining mastery in a more adaptive way of dealing with an old pattern. The therapist will be conductor, traffic cop, referee, mentor, and model utilizing a knowledge of individual and group dynamics, as well as family processes.

The family will be reminded of the limited nature of the treatment. The therapist will be aware of the possibility of termination anxiety, with re-emergence of distress as the end of the treatment approaches, even when positive gains have been made during the earlier phase of treatment. The therapist will resist attempts to prolong therapy beyond the agreed time and will deal with the family's fear of being unable to cope and its pull toward dependence instead. The family members will be helped to summarize the gains they have made during treatment and to rehearse their future problem-solving efforts.

TECHNIQUES

In this section, specific techniques are discussed that have been established as especially useful in brief, focused family evaluation and treatment. Although the list is by no means exhaustive, it is meant to be extensive enough to give an adequate idea of the variety of therapeutic options available. There is no necessary and absolute connection between any one technique and the five general strategies outlined in Chapter 12, although some techniques obviously lend themselves more easily to one strategy than to another.

Experienced therapists are most likely to be flexible in what they do, from case to case and from minute to minute. The following categories, then, should be thought of as freeing the therapeutic imagination, rather than restricting it into a straightjacket.

Setting Limited Goals and a Definite End Point

When brevity is not part of the agreed-on contract, the reasons for therapy often remain vague and ambiguous. Sessions are likely to continue with no fixed termination agreed to in advance and with changing goals and directions as treatment proceeds. Symptomatic and behavioral progress is not taken as a sign of the possibility of ending treatment, but rather as confirmation of the positive effects of the treatment and the desirability of continuing it.

It is essential in brief therapy that the therapist be clear as to the focused and limited goals of treatment. The therapist in every session must keep clearly in mind that the amount of contact with the family will be limited and will have a definite end point, either in terms of number of hours or in the achievement of a specific goal. The therapist's concept may be centered on the least that needs to be done to help the family to continue on its own, rather than on more ambitious, if not grandiose, notions of what the family's potential might be.

The focused goals of the treatment should be stated and discussed with the family in the first few sessions in concrete and specific detail. The family can be asked to specify in concrete terms how family life would be six or ten weeks from now if interactions were better around the problem area. This approach can both flush out grandiose and unrealistic goals on the part of some family members, vagueness on the part of others, and resistance to visualizing any change on the part of others. Stated in concrete and observable terms, the goals can then stand as barometers to be observed during the course of treatment and at the termination to assess the progress, thus reinforcing the efforts of successful families and challenging the more resistant families.

The content of the goals will, of course, vary according to the situation. If the evaluation indicates that the family has been functioning satisfactorily until a recent crisis, efforts will be made to restore the pre-existing equilibrium as quickly as possible. For example, crisis intervention techniques may be utilized in a family in which the 22-year-old son, living with his parents, has had an exacerbation of positive symptoms in his chronic schizophrenic condition. The parents panic, demand hospitalization of their son, as well as his permanent removal from the home. With ventilation, attention to what triggered the upset, support, symptomatic relief for all concerned, and a setting that allows for daily visits to the therapist, brief but intensive therapy may avoid hospitalization and quickly restore the family's ability to cope.

If the family's distress seems more related to long-lasting patterns of interaction, some attempt can be made to set goals in one or two crucial areas in a way that will open up new possibilities for the family to grow and develop on its own, without further reliance on the therapist. For example, when a wife's suicide attempt seems related to chronic unspoken doubts about the viability of the marriage, the therapist will work toward the goal of getting the husband and wife to express more openly to each other the extent of their current needs, disappointments, and frustrations. As soon as they are able to engage satisfactorily in these transactions, the couple may be ready to carry on without the therapist's presence.

Setting a fixed number of sessions with the family at the beginning of treatment is often desirable, as it makes explicit and concrete the limited time in which the goals are to be achieved. It is essential that this commitment to terminate be adhered to, in spite of various attempts the family may make to undermine it. The essence of such treatment may actually consist of helping families begin to understand how they do not keep agreements and how they sabotage attempts at changing dyfunctional patterns.

Active Focus: Reinforcement of Family Strengths, Reconceptualization

The therapist will be alert to the need of staying on target during the course of the treatment and will continually help the family to stick to the one or two primary goals that have been agreed on. Other issues that emerge can be conceptualized as relating to the core issues in some important ways or as resistances to dealing with those issues. Alternatively, "extraneous" matters can be noted as important, but not germane to the current focus, and perhaps they can be left for the family to deal with later, on its own. Whatever treatment focus has been selected will benefit from underlining and positive reinforcement from the therapist whenever possible.

Family therapy requires the active contribution of the therapist, possibly more so than in some other formats of therapy. In brief family therapy, *even more* therapist participation is usually needed. Passivity and indecisiveness only tend to activate the family's dysfunctional repetitive patterns.

Existing and emerging family strengths should be reinforced and supported, as should the concept that all members of the family are doing the best they can. Especially in brief therapy, in which there is little opportunity for the gradual development of rapport, the therapist must be nonblaming and encouraging and must indicate that an attempt is being made to understand the situation from each member's, as well as the whole family's, vantage point. Especially for effective brief therapy, each family member needs to feel understood and accepted by the therapist. Informal moments before, during, and after sessions are invaluable for the therapist to add a personal touch of contact with each family member.

Successes in substituting more functional patterns during the course of the therapy should be rewarded. Indications that the family can change should be highlighted, and the important idea that the therapist is there to catalyze the changes and help the family learn how to carry on this process alone should be emphasized. The therapist may temporarily be extremely active and directive, but always with the end in mind that the family needs to learn how to monitor and direct itself. The therapist discourages any long-term reliance on outside "experts" and challenges and educates the family to take charge of itself in more gratifying ways.

Active Exploration of Alternatives: Behavioral and Emotional Rehearsal

Sometimes families need to be given permission and encouragement to consider alternative patterns to those they have been living with or feel they will be facing in the future. The mere raising of such an issue can be a liberating experience. A middle-aged couple, facing the oncoming empty-nest syndrome in which their parental role will be sharply curtailed, may find it exhilarating to consider the idea of rethinking their marital contract and marital roles. Once such a door has been opened by the therapist, the couple may quickly find that they are able to proceed on their own.

Couples who have secretly thought about separating but have never dared to make such ideas explicit may at first feel threatened by a therapist who openly suggests this as one way out of their situation. With a skillful therapist such a couple can come to face ideas and feelings they have been too afraid or guilty to express before.

During the therapy sessions, family members should be given the strength to express themselves more openly to one another than before. The therapist should make it safe for them to do so but then should also explore with the family the subsequent consequences of such openness. Repeated rehearsals of possible consequences may be required before more open communication can be established as being safe.

When a child is the "problem," rehearsals aimed at strengthening the *paren-*

tal coalition may be essential. The parents may be undermining each other's authority, and this is often related to weaknesses in their marital relationship.

Homework and Family Tasks

For therapy to be effective, changes must be noted outside the treatment sessions. To speed up this process, and to maximize the effect of the limited number of available sessions, family members can be asked to carry out "homework" assignments. These should be relatively simple and achieveable and should bear on those crucial problems that are the focus of treatment. They may involve, for example, various types of marital and/or familial communication exercises. Husband and wife may be requested to practice the negotiating of differences at home. They can be told to make explicit to one another their position on a given issue, with the expectation that the partners repeat to one another their understanding of each other's position.

Interaction and behavioral exercises are often helpful. For example, two estranged family members can be asked to jointly plan and carry out a dyadic activity that they would enjoy and to report about it at the next treatment session. Negative injunctions, such as prohibition of recriminatory dredging up of the past, can be used.

Sometimes a family member can be aided to clarify or modify an important outside relationship, such as with that member's family of origin. A wife who has felt squeezed between her love for her husband and her mother's disapproval of him can be asked to start talking to her mother about this in an attempt to resolve the issue.

To encourage rapid transactional changes, explicit contracts between family members can be negotiated by the therapist. The mother, for example, may be asked to agree to let her teenage daughter stay out until midnight on weekends in return for the daughter's having all her homework completed by then. Such contracts can bring a temporary halt to bickering, can offer a model for mutually satisfying negotiations, and can allow the family sessions to get on with other issues.

THE PROBLEM ORIENTED SCHOOL OF BRIEF THERAPY

There is a school of brief therapy based on the notion that change can be accomplished by identifying the problems and changing the family's solution to it.[5] The model ignores virtually all historical material. The rationale is that the families' attempted solutions maintain and compound the problem. The therapeutic intervention then is to intercept and redirect the families "solution."

In the Q. family the presenting problem was that the adolescent son got into fights with his single-parent mother. The mother's solution had been to reason with her son as to why she couldn't fulfill his demands. Her solution actually escalated the problem. Taking as an example the son's demands for her always to prepare meals despite her busy work schedule, she was instructed to tell the son simply that she wouldn't be able to get supper every night because "she is not a good enough mother." After eight sessions, mostly with the mother, the son began to be more helpful and his fighting outside the home stopped completely (as determined over a one-year followup period).

CRISIS INTERVENTION

In one sense, the extreme form of brief intervention is crisis intervention needed when a family is in acute distress that threatens the very life of an individual, the family unit, or non-psychotic adjustment. This would be analogous to a serious medical emergency in which primary efforts would be directed toward maintaining vital body functions, stopping any loss of blood, and providing for supportive conditions until the system stabilizes. At such a time, no definitive reconstructive or elective procedures can be undertaken.

For family emergencies, attention must be given to the carrying out of necessary family tasks, including the basic provision of food, clothing and shelter. Physiological needs, such as sleep, may require professional intervention, and outside sources of help (relative, friends, and other agencies) may need to be utilized. Behavioral controls and at least a modicum of emotional stability should be sought while an evaluation is made of the "last straw" that resulted in the acute family disequilibrium. Every effort should be made to eliminate, contain, buffer, understand, or conceptualize this factor, so as to allow the family to return quickly to its former level of adjustment.

After the acute crisis has passed, further intervention may not be needed or desired. Often, however, a new contract (or referral) can be made for ongoing treatment with new goals.

SUGGESTIONS FOR FURTHER READINGS

Budman, S (Ed): **Forms of Brief Therapy.** New York: Guilford Press.
   Excellent chapters on brief therapy with children, marital therapy and other formats of brief intervention.

DeShazer S, Berg IK, Lipchik E, et al.: Brief therapy: Focused solution development. Fam Process 25:207-222, 1986.
   A very recent review of the issues involved in doing brief family therapy.

REFERENCES

1. Malan DH: A Study of Brief Psychotherapy. London: Tavistock, 1963
2. Gurman AS: Integrative marital therapy: Toward the development of an interpersonal approach, in Budman S (Ed): Forms of Brief Therapy. New York: Guilford Press, 1981, pp 415-457
3. Haley J: Leaving Home: The Therapy of Disturbed Young People. New York: McGraw-Hill, 1980
4. Jacobson N and Margolin G: Marital Therapy: Strategies Based on Several Learning and Behavior Exchange Principles. New York: Brunner/Mazel, 1979
5. Watzlawick P, Weakland J, and Fisch R: Change: Principles of Problem Formation and Problem Resolution. New York: WW Norton, 1974

Section V

Marital and Couples Treatment

Although there is much overlap in the theory and practice of both marital therapy and of family therapy, for heuristic purposes we separate out certain issues relevant to the former in this section. Accordingly, Chapter 17 reviews the theory and therapy for dysfunction in the "traditional" marriage, while in Chapter 19 we do the same for new marital forms. Although it is somewhat pedagogically awkward to do so, the reader must keep in mind the material from Chapters 2, 3, and 5, which is more focused on marriage as it relates to the nuclear family. Likewise for didactic reasons, we separate out sexual issues in a chapter focusing on marital and sexual therapy. Issues for gay, male couples are quite different from both the traditional and new marital forms, and they are reviewed in Chapter 20. Likewise, working with physicians (or other professionals) and their families presents special problems and challenges, which are discussed in Chapter 21.

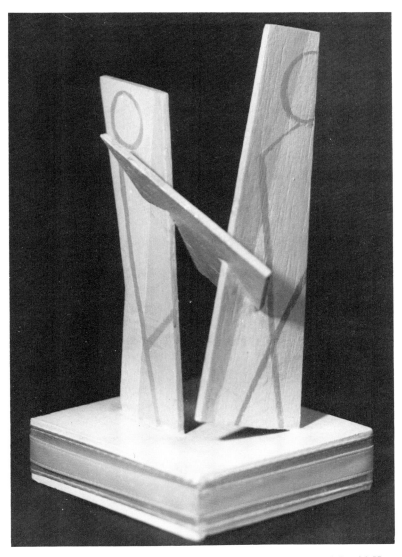

Bride and Groom (ornament for wedding cake) by Emily Chang and David Humphrey, 1983, private collection.

17

The Dysfunctional Marriage and Marital Therapy in the Traditional Marital Form

OBJECTIVES

- To understand marriage and marital therapy in historical context
- To describe common marital stressors, conflicts, and their evaluation
- To outline strategies and techniques of marital therapy

INTRODUCTION

Husband and wife form the essential subsystem of the nuclear family. How this subsystem functions and copes will, in large measure, determine how the family will progress over time. Chapters 3 and 4 considered how *families* function (and introduced the idea of dysfunction) with a special focus on how the *marital coalition* arises from the family of origin. That material, while pertinent to the marital subsystem, is not repeated here. Instead, this chapter starts with an historical perspective on marriage, and then considers specific *dimensions and patterns of dysfunction in the marital dyad* in order to then formulate marital therapy goals and strategies. We consider the "traditional" marriage, somewhat arbitrarily defined, as a marriage between two spouses who have not had previous marriages and who are on some continuum of commitment/failing commitment to this marital union.

264

MARRIAGE IN ITS HISTORICAL CONTEXT*

Marriage is seen by some as a romantic ideal, by others as a contract of convenience, by some as a thing of the past, by others as an object of derision, and by still others as a sacred state that is the pillar of society. Marriage has meant different things throughout the centuries in various cultures.[1,2] Modern marriage can be defined as a two-person, social system with legal, emotional/behavioral and biologic definitions. All three interact to stabilize and enhance the relationship, or, under less than ideal conditions, these forces may act to destabilize and produce distress.

From the anthropological point of view, marriage has been (up-to-now) an important institution in every culture. It is a mandate (in almost all cultures) that the individual road to adult status involves successful mating, marriage, and procreation. In many societies it provided an essential mechanism for the transfer of property and privilege, for the establishment of alliances and making of truces. The more primitive the society, the more highly regulated marriage arrangements were—that is, individual preferences for any particular mate were not at all considered. The political, economic, and social needs of the clan were the primary factors determining the marital fate of any individual. Even so, the bond of marriage, once established, became the strongest of all individual social bonds.

Through the middle ages, the marriage contract became more individualized. What evolved was the "modern European marriage," with the gradual disappearance of the classic, "socially-arranged marriage" of two families (vide infra).

The modern version of marriage is characterized by four features:

1. Freedom to choose a spouse (although there are still some prohibitions attached to this freedom).
2. Equality of the sexes—in terms of the vows of marriage.
3. Emancipation from relatives and the *individualization of the marriage contract.*
4. An increased emphasis on intimacy. An intimate relationship not only fulfills a strong human need, but also buffers the individual from depression[3] and probably other stresses and strains of life. Intimacy is probably an ingredient and/or byproduct of the functional family skills described in Chapter 3, self-disclosure and healthy development of object relations.[4] The ingredients of commitment, intimacy, and passion change over time (Fig. 17-1). The major clinical point for the therapist is the concept that the range of intimacy varies from couple to couple—there is no absolute. Pushing a couple to more than they can tolerate is a common mistake.

---

*I am indebted to E. Kovacs, M.D., for some of the material in this section.

Commitment, Intimacy,
and Passion Over Time
in Long-Term
Relationships.

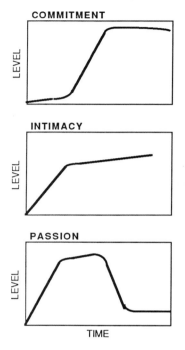

Figure 17-1. From Goleman D: Patterns of love charted. The New York Times, September 10, 1985.

This individualization of the marital contract must be viewed in its historical context. Marriage is a state of being, which the vast majority of people have entered (and will enter). It is a social state, which has existed for reasons that have transcended the individual—and as such, it has had a life and momentum of its own. Chapter 3 has more fully described the functional marital system, life cycle, and tasks. Now let us look at marital *dysfunction*.

MARITAL DYSFUNCTION

There are a number of theories, not mutually exclusive, that attempt to explain why marriages (which often begin in bliss) become conflicted, dissatisfying, and indeed extremely painful, to the point of dissolution. In our view, the most developed theories and the ones that seem most clinically applicable, are the exchange model of Thibaut and Kelly,[5] the object relations model of Dicks,[6] and systems concepts that apply to the marital subsystem both within and in relation to the other subsystems of the family.[7] None of these theories is totally adequate, but from them come some guiding notions and hypotheses of dysfunction in marital dyads that are clinically useful. The material should also be considered in the context of the clinical issues raised in our discussion of marriage in Chapter 2.

In the current interaction:

1. Distressed couples engage in fewer rewarding (positive reinforcement) exchanges and more punishing (negative reinforcement) exchanges than nondistressed couples.
2. Distressed couples are more likely to reciprocate the partner's use of negative reinforcement. These individuals are immediately reactive to the negative (actual or perceived) stimuli of the partner, and respond in kind.
3. Distressed couples are likely to attempt to control the behavior of one another through negative communication and the withholding of positive communication. Unhappy couples tend to strive for behavior change in the other by aversive control tactics, that is, by strategically presenting punishment and withholding rewards.

From a systems point of view:

4. Distressed systems are characterized by intense, binding coalitions, e.g., mother and child are close at father's expense.
5. Covert coalitions often exist that cross generational lines.
6. Third parties are used to interfere and deflect conflict or closeness between the marital pairs.

From a dynamic point of view:

7. Individuals who need assistance with marital conflict seem to have a rigidity in their personalities that forces them to deny or be blind to the existence of certain aspects of themselves. If they are confronted with a similar aspect of the partner's personality, this will be ignored or not accepted.
8. Many tensions and misunderstandings between partners seem to result from the disappointment that one or both feel, and resent, when the other fails to play the role of spouse after the manner of a preconceived model or figure in their fantasy world.
9. Individuals may persecute tendencies in their spouses that originally

caused attraction. The partner is perceived unconsciously as a symbol of "lost," that is, repressed aspects of the subject's own personality.

From a developmental point of view:

10. The preponderence of secure, loving outcomes of reality testing and conflict resolution in early developmental years creates a reservoir of relational potential that is brought to the marriage. In less fortunate cases, however, there will remain unresolved needs and demands on parent figures invested with deeply ambivalent feelings of love and hate.
11. In the process of mate selection, the partner is attractive because he or she promises a rediscovery of an important lost aspect of the subject's own personality, which owing to earlier conditioning has been recasted as an object for attack or denial.

Mental Disorder in One Spouse

Having a spouse with a serious Axis I disorder, such as depression or mania, phobias, alcoholism, or schizophrenia puts understandable strain on the marital relationship. The marital interaction prior to, during, and following the onset of the symptoms in the spouse is influenced by numerous factors and is quite variant across dyads. It is false to assume that in all cases the interaction between the spouses brought on, or caused, or even helped trigger, the mental disorder and symptoms in the other. Whatever the symptoms in one spouse, the relationship of symptoms to the marital interaction could take any one of the following forms:

1. The marital interaction neither caused, nor stressed, the spouse who is vulnerable, either by biological factors or prior learning, to the symptoms.
2. The marital interaction did not stress the vulnerable individual, but following onset of symptoms, the marital interaction declined and became dysfunctional, thus causing more distress.
3. The marital interaction was a stressor that contributed to the onset of symptoms in a vulnerable spouse.
4. The symptoms can be explained totally as under the control and function of the interactional patterns between the spouses.

Research is needed to delineate further the nature of the marital interactions as it relates to various symptom complexes in one (or both) spouse. Two areas that have received some interesting attention are phobias and depression in a marital partner, and these are reviewed in Chapter 22. While the data is currently sparce, it suggests that the diagnosis and symptom picture of the spouse and characteristics of the other spouse are related to the symptoms in the marital interaction and should, therefore, influence the planning of intervention. For example, if one spouse has a non-endogenous, unipolar depression with no clear precipitating stressful life events, the marital interaction could be a chronic stressor and contibutor to the condition. Marital therapy in this situation could well be a preferred mode of intervention. On the other hand, if the spouse is suffering from a bipolar illness, manic episode, and the marital interaction has been good prior to the episode, psychoeducational intervention with the couple may be in order with little or no attention to the ongoing marital interaction.

MARITAL THERAPY

Marital therapy is a format of intervention involving both members of a marital dyad in which the focus of intervention is the dysfunctional and displeasing interactional patterns of the couple. Its similarities to family intervention are so numerous that often the differences have been overlooked.

The focus of marital therapy is on the marital dyad and its intimate emotional and sexual aspects, whereas family therapy is usually focused on issues involving behavior of a child or adolescent and the interactions between parents and children. In family therapy, one can discern triangles involving various family members, whereas in marital work triangulation in the here-and-now interaction (as there are only two family members present) must involve the therapist. In marital therapy, while the children may be called in during the initial assessment or later for specific issues, the sessions are usually attended by only the spouses.

Evaluation

With the obvious modification of focusing mainly on the marital dyad, the outline for family evaluation (Chapter 7) can be used for the evaluation of a marital pair seeking assistance with their troubled relationship. This involves obtaining data on the current point in the family and marital life cycle, why the couple comes for assistance at this point in time, and each of their views of the marital problem. In formulating the marital difficulty, the evaluator will want to summarize his or her thoughts around the couple's communication, problem-solving, roles, affective expression and involvement, and behavioral expression, especially in sexual and aggressive areas. The clinician should ascertain if there is a diagnosable condition, especially Axis I, in either or both partners.

There are several areas, imbedded in the above general categories, that deserve special evaluation attention. This would include each spouse's commitment to the marital union, and the sexual expression of this commitment and/or lack thereof. This can become clinically difficult when one or both partners are ignorant of the commitment and extramarital sexual activity of the other. Both conjoint and individual assessment interviews with each of the partners may be needed.

Each spouse's commitment to the marital relationship will have profound effects on the subsequent course of any marital therapy. In some situations, one spouse expresses commitment to the relationship at the beginning of therapy, but is secretly carrying on an affair and plans to leave the relationship once the final attempt at therapy asked for by the spouse is tried. This scenario can waste the time of the therapist and the couple. In many of these situations, the spouse who secretly plans to leave wants the therapist to support the "left partner" when the separation occurs.

The complicated issue of how the therapist can get the information about degree of commitment and ongoing extramarital affairs is handled in various ways. We recommend that in every marital evaluation, where these might be issues, the therapist hold both conjoint and individual evaluation sessions with each spouse. While that position may seem somewhat extreme, at the very least we recommend that periodic review of each members' commitment be made. In the individual evaluation sessions, the spouse is told that anything discussed will be held in confidence. Some therapists will not proceed with marital treatment unless a spouse actively engaged in an extramarital affair end the affair immediately. The rationale is that infidelity (regardless of the family dynamics) has the potential for very destructive consequences for the family unit. This is probably more because of the power of the secret alliance to subvert the trust inherent in the marital coalition, than the actual sex involved.

Related to the issue of assessing the commitment of each couple to the relationship, is the assessment of the *nature* of this commitment. We agree with Sager[8] that the therapist must assess the existing *contract*, i.e., "the deal," both overt and covert, between the couples. One way to do this is to have each spouse make a list of five goals they want from the marriage and five, in exchange, they will give. Each spouse does this separately without consulting the other, and lists are discussed in the next session.

Grunebaum, Christ, and Neiberg[9] have provided a practical and clinically informed "decision tree" guideline to assist the clinician in deciding whether or not to use marital therapy as opposed to other forms of intervention. Three parameters must be assessed. The first involves the evaluation of whether the couple's problems are marital or not and the extent to which the couple are committed to one another and able to work on them. The second diagnostic nodal point involves an evaluation of whether the focus of the problem is primarily within the marriage or involves *both* the marriage and outside activities and relationships. The third evaluation point is the extent to which the problems are acute and ego alien (i.e., seen as a problem) versus chronic and ego syntonic (not seen as problem) to both members. These authors recommend marital treatment for couples (1) presenting with marital problems, (2) who are committed to one another, and (3) who have acute ego alien symptoms within the marriage. Concurrent individual psychotherapy for each of the partners by the same therapist is recommended for those individuals who have symptoms both inside and outside of the marital relationship. We further discuss guidelines for marital therapy in Chapters 25 and 26.

Grunebaum and associates suggest from their own clinical experience that there are two types of couples who apply for marital treatment but who probably should be treated in another therapy format. The first group is comprised of couples in which both partners are immature and dependent, often recently married, with developmental difficulties and intense relationships with their own families of origin. The second group is one in which the spouse is psychotic.

Goals

The mediating goals of marital therapy include specification of the interactional problems, recognition of mutual contribution to the problems, clarification of marital boundaries, clarification and specification of each spouse's needs and desires in the relationship, increased communication skills, decreased coercion and blame, increased differentiation, and resolution of marital transference distortions. Final goals of the marital intervention involve resolution of presenting problems, reduction of symptoms, increased intimacy, increased role flexibility and adaptability, toleration of differences, improved psychosexual functioning, balance of power, clear communication, resolution of conflictful interaction, and improved relationships with children and families of origin.[10]

Marital therapy need not, but is often, conceived of as a relatively brief therapy, usually meeting on a once-weekly basis, with a focus on the marital interaction. There are times when bringing in one or both spouse's parents may be beneficial for cutting through issues that are affecting the marriage.[4] Although we discuss guidelines in Section VII, for now the major indication for marital intervention is the presence of marital conflict contributed to by both parties, but may also include symptomatic behavior in one spouse such as depression, agoraphobia, etc. Marital treatment is contraindicated, even when the above conditions are present, when the two parties would use treatment disclosures to injure the other. (We return to this in our discussion of "legal issues.")

Strategies and Techniques of Intervention

Like family therapy in general, marital therapy utilizes strategies for imparting new information, opening up new and expanded individual and marital experiencing, psychodynamic strategies for individual and interactional insight, communication and problem-solving strategies, and strategies for restructuring the repetitive interactions between the spouses.

As the divisive spirit of the era of the earlier schools of psychotherapy recedes and there is a growing pluralism and clinical pragmatism, clinicians will attempt to integrate the various strategies into a coherent treatment approach that can be adapted to the individual case. Gurman[11] has formulated an integrative marital therapy model based on psychodynamic thinking that utilizes psychodynamic, behavioral, and structural-strategic strategies of intervention.

This model assumes that effective marital treatment does not artificially dichotomize individual and relationship change, and thus focuses on both. The model assumes that not all behaviors of the spouse are under the interactional control of the other, and even behavior with obvious relationship to the marital interaction is not completely under relational control. Furthermore, the author asserts (rightly in our view) that adoption of a systems perspective does not preclude attention to unconscious aspects of experience. In fact, self-perceptions are the mechanisms that power the behavior—maintaining aspects of interpersonal reinforcement.

Treatment Goals and Assessment

The goals of assessment are to evaluate the functional relationships between the antecedents and consequences of discrete interactional sequences; to evaluate the recurrent patterns of interaction including their implicit rules; and to evaluate each spouse's individual schemata for intimate relationships.

EARLY PHASE: ALLIANCE AND INTERVENTIONS

Alliances must be developed early between the therapist and each marital partner, with the therapist offering empathy and warmth. The therapist must also ally with the couple per se and learn their shared language. The therapist must ally with the individual differences between husband and wife, their different problem-solving styles and attitudes.

MID-PHASE ISSUES

The focus should be primarily on the transference distortions between husband and wife, and not on the couple-therapist transference. However, negative transference distortions toward the therapist must be addressed quickly and overtly.

There are three strategies in this focused, active treatment of marital discord:

1. The therapist interrupts collusive processes between the spouses. The in-

teraction may involve either spouse failing to perceive aspects of the other that are clear to an outsider (e.g., being very jealous or stingy) or when either spouse behaves in a way aimed at protecting the other from experiences that are inconsistent with the spouse's self-perception, (e.g., husband working part time views himself as bread winner, but wife works full time and manages checkbook to shield husband from reality of their income and finances).

2. The therapist links individual experience, including past experience and inner thoughts to the marital relationships.

3. The therapist creates, and gives tasks that are constructed to (1) encourage the spouses to differentiate between the impact of the other's *behavior* versus (the other's) *intent*, (2) to bring into awareness the concrete behavior of the partner that contradicts (anachronistic) past perceptions of that partner, and (3) to encourage each spouse to acknowledge their *own* behavior changes that are incompatible with the maladaptive ways each has seen themselves and has been seen by the marital partner.

The last (3) is most important. In fact, we insist in the initial stage of marital treatment that each partner focus on what they want to change in themselves, not how they want the other spouse to be different.

Behavioral techniques, including tasks, communication training, and problem-solving training, are used to facilitate the process of helping marital partners reintegrate denied aspects of themselves and of each other. However, the focus is not on behavioral change alone, as overt behavior is seen as reflecting the interlocking self-perceptions of each spouse. An emphasis on enhancing communication and self-disclosure would come in later sessions, only after collusive defenses that contradict such behaviors are addressed.

The next chapter reviews issues of sex therapy and marital therapy separately and in combinations.

SUGGESTIONS FOR FURTHER READINGS

Dicks HV: **Marital Tensions.** London: Routledge and Kegan Paul, 1967.
   A brilliant and thought-provoking look at marriage and its perversions from an object relations point of view.

Stuart R: **Helping Couples Change.** New York: Guilford Press, 1980.
   A thorough, well-organized account of marital therapy from a social learning theory perspective.

Grunebaum H, Christ J, and Neiberg N: Diagnosis and treatment planning for couples. Int J Group Psychotherapy 19:185-202, 1969.
   An excellent overview of the process of treatment of couples.

REFERENCES

1. Murstein B: Love, Sex, and Marriage Through the Ages. New York: Springer, 1974
2. Shorter E: The Making of the Modern Family. New York: Basic Books, 1977
3. Brown GW and Harris T: Social Origins of Depression: A Study of Psychiatric Disorders in Women. New York: Free Press, 1978
4. Framo JL: The integration of marital therapy with sessions with family of origin. In Gurman AS, Kniskern DP (Eds): Handbook of Family Therapy. New York: Brunner/Mazel, 1981, pp 133-158
5. Thibaut JW and Kelly HH: The Social Psychology of Groups. New York: Wiley, 1959
6. Dicks HV: Marital Tensions. London: Routledge and Kegan Paul, 1967
7. Minuchin S: Families and Family Therapy. Cambridge, MA: Harvard University Press, 1974
8. Sager C: Marriage Contracts and Couple Therapy: Hidden Forces in Intimate Relationships. New York: Brunner/Mazel, 1976
9. Grunebaum H, Christ J, and Neiberg N: Diagnosis and treatment planning for couples. Int J Group Psychotherapy 19:185-202, 1969
10. Gurman A: Contemporary marital therapy: A critique and comparative analysis of psychoanalytic, behavioral and system therapy approaches. In Paolino TJ and McCrady BS (Eds): Marriage and Marital Therapy. New York: Brunner/Mazel, 1978, pp 445-566
11. Gurman A: Intergrative marital therapy: Toward the development of an interpersonal approach. In Budman S (Ed): Forms of Brief Therapy. New York: Guilford, 1981, pp 415-457

Study for "Dance in the Country" by Pierre Auguste Renoir (1841-1919), France. Courtesy of the Honolulu Academy of Arts, purchase, 1937.

18

Sex, Marriage, and
Marital and Sex Therapy

OBJECTIVES

- To point out the connections between sexual problems and other family problems
- To make clear the relationship between marital therapy and sex therapy
- To describe techniques of combining family therapy and sex therapy as well as other psychotherapies

INTRODUCTION

It has been estimated that 50 percent of American marriages are beset with sexual difficulties. According to Masters and Johnson,[1] there is no uninvolved partner when one member of a couple presents with sexual inadequacy, which they define as problems with potency or ejaculation in the male and with orgasm or intercourse in the female. In 44 percent of the couples referred to them, both partners had a sexual dysfunction. The majority of marital units with sexual dysfunction seen by Masters and Johnson had no evidence of a primary relationship problem other than the specific symptoms of sexual dysfunction. The sexual dysfunction, therefore, may not be a symptom of a disturbed marriage, but the core issue itself. Sexual dysfunction need not be a symptom of a mental disorder; rather it is often caused by ignorance of sexual anatomy and physiology or by negative attitudes and self-defeating behavior. Although sexual functioning is not the sum total of any marital relationship, it is thought that few marriages can exist as effective, complete, and ongoing entities without a comfortable component of sexual exchange.

There has been a marked shift in the general attitude toward female sexuality in recent years. Women are increasingly expecting not only to receive pleasure from sexual activities but more specifically to achieve orgasm. They also expect to participate in a more assertive way, since they have had their sexual interests and activities legitimized. Men have become disturbed and sometimes dysfunctional because of the changing and increasingly assertive sexual role of women. Men at times feel that they have failed if their partner has not reached orgasm. Each partner should decide how much they are responsible for the other's pleasure and how much for their own.

Sex therapists have to assess the capabilities of each partner in giving and receiving sensual and sexual pleasure. The notion of sex as recreation, rather than as a marital obligation or an exclusively procreative function, is receiving increasing attention. It has long been obvious that sexual activity is mixed with a variety of motives such as power, hostility, dependence, and submission. The traditional equation of sex and love has come into question. The blurring of stereotyped gender roles has led to additional complexities in sexual relationships. Hostility and mystery may be more important components of sexual attraction than many are willing to admit.

A recent study of sexual complaints from couples, who believe that their marriages are working reasonably well, has revealed that, although 80 percent of the couples reported their marital and sexual relations were happy and satisfying, 40 percent of the men reported erectile or ejaculatory dysfunction, and 63 percent of the women reported arousal or orgasmic dysfunction. In addition, 50 percent of the men and 77 percent of the women reported difficulty that was not dysfunctional in nature (for example, lack of interest or inability to relax). The women were not only probably experiencing greater dysfunction, but were more willing to admit their dysfunction. It was learned that husbands underestimated their wives' dysfunction. The therapists noted that the partners' actual sexual performance seemed less important to them than the feelings they had for each other. In summary, sexual dysfunction and marital distress can operate independently of each other.[2]

RELATIONSHIP BETWEEN SEX THERAPY AND MARITAL THERAPY

Heiman and colleagues[3] reported that approximately 80 percent of the couples they have seen in sex therapy also had significant marital problems.

Sager[4] estimates that 75 percent of couples seeking marital therapy have a mixture of marital discord and sexual problems.

A careful evaluation of their total interactions needs to be done by therapists. When it appears that the basic marriage is a sound one, but that the couple suffers from specific sexual difficulties (which may also lead to various secondary marital consequences), the primary focus might be sex therapy per se. In many cases, however, specific sex therapy cannot be carried out until the relationship between the two partners has been improved in other respects; indeed the sexual problems may clearly be an outgrowth of the marital difficulties. When marital problems are taken care of, the sexual problems may readily be resolved. It may be difficult to disentangle marital from sexual problems or to decide which came first. The priorities for therapy may not always be clear.

Healthy sexual functioning can be thought of as resulting from relatively nonconflicted and self-confident attitudes about sex and the belief that the partner is pleased by one's performance. In this type of situation, a reinforcing positive cycle can be activated. One of the fundamental principles of the new sex therapies is to reduce performance anxiety, while at the same time building communication, relieving guilt and other restrictive attitudes, and utilizing specific sexual techniques in a learning and training atmosphere.

When either partner has doubts about his or her sexual abilities or the ability to please the other, his or her sexual performance may suffer. This morbid self-absorption and anxiety will characteristically produce a decrease in sexual performance and enjoyment and can lead to impotency and orgastic difficulties. Marital and individual difficulties of various sorts might then follow. A vicious cycle may be activated, with worries being increased, leading to increasingly poor sexual performance.

Couples who continue in marital or individual treatment for long periods of time can resolve some of their marital problems, but can still suffer from specific sexual difficulties in their marriage. It is also true that specific sexual problems may be dramatically reversed after relatively brief periods of sex therapy, which utilizes some of the new techniques, even though such problems may have proven intractable following long periods of more customary psychotherapy.

Usually when a marital couple has a generally satisfactory relationship, any minor sexual problems may be only temporary. Resolution of sexual problems in a relationship, however, will not inevitably produce positive effects in other facets of a relationship as well.

Marital and sexual problems interact in various ways:

1. *Sexual dysfunction producing secondary marital discord.* Specific strategies focused on the sexual dysfunctions would usually be considered the treatment of choice in these situations, especially if the sexual dysfunction occurred in relationships other than the current one.

2. *Sexual dysfunction secondary to marital discord.* In such situations general strategies of marital treatment might be considered the treatment of choice. If the marital relationship is not too severely disrupted, however, a trial of sex therapy might be attempted, because a relatively rapid relief of symptoms could produce beneficial, motivational effects on the couple's interest in pursuing other marital issues.

3. *Severe marital discord with sexual problems.* This situation would probably not be amenable to sex therapy because of the partner's hostility to each other. Marital therapy would usually be attempted first, with later attention given to sexual dysfunction.

Mr. and Mrs. L. had both been raised in traditional backgrounds. Mrs. L. had been taught that sex is dirty and should not really be discussed. Having fantasies about other men was strictly taboo.

Mrs. L. had problems during adolescence, dating "men who my mom didn't like." Through twice-a-week individual psychotherapy, she had worked through these problems, married Mr. L., and had a child. Two years after the marriage, marital problems developed, focused around sex. Frequency and enjoyment of sex for both partners was markedly decreased. Mrs. L. refused to have sex, saying that she was too upset.

Whereas at one time individual psychotherapy might have been the treatment of choice, the therapist decided to use both marital therapy and sex therapy. Marital therapy helped to open communication between the couple. It was discovered that Mrs. L. was using the tactic of sex refusal because she was angry at her husband for not helping with childrearing responsibilities. In addition Mrs. L. felt that sex was wrong and was upset by her fantasies of having sex with other men.

The couple was encouraged to deal more directly with their differences and with the disappointments underlying their anger. Issues related to each partner's family of origin were brought up. Roles were restructured—Mr. L. took over more of the childrearing responsibilities. As the marital relationship improved, their sexual problems were addressed.

Because of the interrelatedness of these two problem areas, therapists who undertake to treat couples should become competent in both marital and sex therapy. Therapists should be in a position to move freely from one of these areas to the other (also see Chapter 33 on training). If they are not, they should refer such a couple for either the marital or the sex therapy that they themselves may not feel able to offer.

TAKING A PSYCHOSEXUAL HISTORY

Guidelines for clinical evaluation preceding treatment of both the family and the marital couple are provided in Section III. The taking of an intimate sexual history of husband and wife should, of course, not be done in the family setting and is detailed here.

What type of vocabulary should be used when discussing sexual topics? Some authorities advise against the use of terms that would be offensive or uncomfortable for either the therapist or the couple. Care must be taken, however, to avoid using bland generalities and ending up with no specific sexual information at all.

In questions and discussions about sex, the therapist should assume that everyone has done everything. Rather than phrasing the question, "Have you ever had any homosexual experiences?" the therapist should ask, "What kinds of homosexual experience have you had?"

Euphemisms should be discouraged and frankness encouraged. When there is vagueness, the therapist should feel free to use follow-up questions.

The therapist should use simple language or use the simplest technical sexual term that the patient is comfortable with. Some patients will misunderstand technical terms. For others the use of the vernacular by the therapist may be inappropriate. The problem faced in the choice of language is itself an indication of our general cultural discomfort with sexuality. The therapist's own use of a particular sexual vocabulary can be a model to help the marital partners feel comfortable in communicating with each other more openly.

Adolescents, racial and ethnic subgroups, gays and lesbians, and others may have specialized sexual argots that they use. The therapist's ability to use this language in a comfortable and knowing manner may serve to enhance rapport and reduce communication barriers.

Specific methods have been devised for eliciting a sexual history and for evaluating sexual functioning. Descriptions of techniques in sex therapy have been thoroughly described in the literature.[5,6] The marital therapist should become familiar with these ideas and obtain experience in their utilization. Some marital therapists still are not well informed about their clients' sexual histories. This presumably arises from their own discomfort about such material and from their lack of a conceptual frame of reference to help them utilize the sexual data they might obtain.

STRATEGIES SPECIFIC TO SEXUAL DYSFUNCTIONS

While the term "sex therapy" has arisen, we do not conceptualize it as a distinct therapy, but as one more instance of conjoint treatment focused on a specific problem area, utilizing a range of techniques that in form can be used for many problem areas (see Chapters 10–12 for general strategies). Both the format (individual, marital, marital group) and the techniques of therapy can vary depending upon the specifics of the case.

PSYCHOSEXUAL DISORDERS AND THEIR TREATMENT

The types of sexual problems that have lent themselves to the new sex therapy techniques have been those that fit into a task-oriented, symptom-removal model. These problems include:

1. Inhibited sexual desire.
2. Inhibited sexual excitement.
3. Inhibited female orgasm.
4. Inhibited male orgasm.
5. Premature ejaculation.
6. Functional dyspareunia.
7. Functional vaginismsus.

General techniques for these problems may involve joint sexual history taking and discussion, joint "sexological" examination, educational and desensitization techniques, and encouraging improvement of verbal and nonverbal communicational techniques between the couple. In addition to these general aspects of sex therapy, more specific techniques involving the assignment of behavioral tasks, homework, and use of mechanical equipment have been developed to deal with each of the problem areas. A gratifyingly high proportion of couples with uncomplicated sex problems have been helped rapidly by these methods. These techniques can be tried with the expectation that a fairly short-term course will show dramatic improvement.

In those couples who did not do well, three factors were found, either singly or in combination, when they returned for additional treatment after a standard two-week sex therapy program.[7] These were categorized as having difficulties in the areas of pleasure, intimacy, and cooperation. A variety of additional therapeutic interventions may be required to deal with these issues, supplementing the standard sex therapy techniques. With such couples, treatment using behavioral-experiential techniques, individual psychotherapy, and family therapy techniques are needed.

Other factors that have been cited as relative contraindications to successful sex therapy include situations in which the marital problems outweigh the sexual problems and certain psychiatric disorders, such as antisocial behavior, schizophrenic disorder, paranoid disorder, and severe personality disorder.

Patients who have a sexual phobia have been successfully treated with a combination of antipanic medication, sex therapy, and marital therapy when indicated.

Sexual ennui, another type of psychosexual disorder, may actually be "marital ennui" and may not lend itself to specific sex therapy (see Figure 17-1). Some of the more general techniques used in the sex therapies, however, such as sensate focus, mutual massage, and permission for sexual fantasies of various kinds, may serve to improve this situation. More often a general examination of the state of the marriage is indicated.

For treating general sexual inhibition, techniques similar to those utilized in the preliminary aspect of the therapy of sexual disorders may be useful, as outlined in the previous paragraph. Wherever possible we recommend that couples be treated by the marital therapist. If that is not possible, or indicated, then referral to a sex therapist is necessary.

OTHER SEXUAL CONCERNS

Homosexuality or Bisexuality in Either Partner or Offspring

The fear of or actual presence of homosexual behavior in either partner may present various types of marital difficulty, although marriages can work successfully even with overt homosexuality in one partner. When such issues emerge in marital treatment, the therapist needs to discover in what specific ways they are a problem, and to whom. If the homosexual orientation has been a "secret" or has only recently come into the affected partner's awareness, there may be questions as to whether the marriage should continue, whether "conversion" or "reversion" treatment should be undertaken, or whether some current marital or other dissatisfactions have temporarily produced a "pseudohomosexuality".[8]

If the situation has progressed to actual sexual dysfunction in the marriage, the couple may present themselves for therapy with one partner being unaware of the other's underlying agenda. For some couples the bisexuality of one partner has been an established and agreed on part of the covert marital arrangement, but questions may emerge when children are born or the affected partner becomes more flagrant in his or her homosexual behavior. Concerns may arise about the effects on the children or whether the marriage has become untenable. Marital therapy might then be indicated.

Many parents worry about the possibility of one of their children growing up to be homosexual. Such concerns are often unrealistic, and even if they are based on good evidence, dispute exists as to what course to pursue with an adamantly homosexual offspring. Books have been written to help parents try to forestall homosexual tendencies in their children on the premise that they are undesirable.[9] Such thwarting actions, however, are highly questionable and may cause more harm than good. Some work dealing with the life history of homosexual patients has implicated the family system as contributing to the individual's homosexual development.[10] There is reason to believe, however, that the causes of homosexuality are much more complex and variable.[11] At the very least, recent research suggests that sexual orientation is familial.[12]

Similarly *transvestism, transsexualism*, and other sexual variants have been ascribed to particular patterns in the family of origin. Whether they are amenable to one or another type of preventive family intervention is an open question.

Family treatment may be important in helping to deal with these often extremely difficult issues once they have surfaced into the family's awareness. Some families may be aided in understanding and accepting life styles that cannot be changed without disrupting positive and important relationships.

Sexual Problems after Medical Illness

Couples often raise the question of sexual intercourse after a myocardial infarction in one of the spouses. "Coitus is infrequently associated with sudden cardiac death."[13] Sometimes the spouse's coronary is used as a weapon in the family interaction to prevent emotional closeness.

Total abstinence is unjustified. Sexual intercourse, with some limitation of the amount of activity, might be justified on psychological (rather than physiological) grounds. For those couples who feel that they are informed as to the risks versus the benefits, there is no reason medically to prohibit such activity.

Sexual Problems in the Elderly

With the rapid growth in the number of elderly people, there has been an increased interest in their psychiatric and sexual problems. In couples over 60, many of the primary problems that exist are sexual, which may be one reason why fewer couples are staying together. Contrary to popular belief, however, sexual activity does not have to decrease once couples pass their forties. The family therapist can help couples realize the following.

1. Advancing years are not a contraindication to sexuality and sensuality.
2. It is perfectly acceptable for the couple to have less frequent intercourse.
3. Older men may achieve erection and orgasm more slowly and may not necessarily ejaculate each time they have intercourse, and older women may have a shorter excitement phase, and their orgasms may be less intense, with slower vaginal contractions. Both partners, however, can still have a regular ongoing sexual life.

Even after an elderly patient has had a severe disability, such as a stroke, his or her sexual life can still be maintained. The couple can be aided in adjusting to changes of sexual functioning by using a variety of sexually stimulating techniques available to them.

Rape

With the recent emergence of the Women's Movement, there has been a new understanding of rape. No longer is the woman seen as a provocateur and the rapist as an emotionally frustrated, psychologically intact male. In fact the rapist has been found to be a psychologically damaged individual, and rape is viewed as aggression—a violent crime—rather than a sexual process. The term "rape" is more accurately a legal one with different implications for the lawyer than for the family therapist and the family.

"An important aspect in response to rape, to be considered by those caring for the victim, is that it may affect relations with the family and among friends."[13] In contrast to most personal crises in which sharing is usually beneficial, there is a real possibility that rape will alter the marital and family relationship in a disruptive way.[14] Families often prefer to avoid discussion because of their own anxiety and because of the difficult feelings they may stir up. This avoidance reinforces the victim's guilt and prevents successful coping with the experience. The family therapist must cope with one's own feelings and biases toward rape, and help the victim and family to deal effectively with the event in reestablishing the marital and family homeostasis.

SUGGESTIONS FOR FURTHER READINGS

Kaplan H: **The New Sex Therapy: Active Treatment of Sexual Dysfunction.** New York: Brunner/Mazel, 1974.
Kaplan is a leader in this area.

Kaplan H: **Disorders of Sexual Desire.** New York: Simon and Schuster, 1979.
Beyond simple sexual difficulties, and into the more relevant clinical situations in which individual dynamic and interactional difficulties disrupt sexual functioning.

REFERENCES

1. Masters W and Johnson V: Human Sexual Response. Boston: Little, Brown, 1966

2. Hartman LM: The interface between sexual dysfunction and marital conflict. Am J Psychiatry, 137:576-579, 1980

3. Heiman J, LoPiccolo L, and LoPiccolo J: The treatment of sexual dysfunction. In Gurman A and Kniskern D (Eds): Handbook of Family Therapy. New York: Brunner/Mazel, 1981, pp 592-627

4. Sager C: The role of sex therapy in marital therapy. Am J Psychiatry 133:555-558, 1976

5. Masters W and Johnson V: Human Sexual Inadequacy. Boston: Little, Brown, 1970

6. Kaplan H: A New Sex Therapy: Active Treatment of Sexual Dysfunction. New York: Brunner/Mazel, 1974

7. Levay AN and Kagle A: A study of treatment needs following sex therapy. Am J Psychiatry 134:970-973, 1977

8. Masters W and Johnson V: Homosexuality in Perspective. Boston: Little, Brown, 1979

9. Wyden P: Growing Up Straight. New York: Stein and Day, 1968

10. Brown D: Homosexuality and family dynamics. Bull Menninger Clinic 27:227-232, 1963

11. Tripp CA: The Homosexual Matrix. New York: McGraw-Hill, 1975

12. Pillard RC and Weinrich JD: Evidence of familial nature of male homosexuality. Arch Gen Psychiatry 43:808-812, 1986

13. Cobb LA and Schaffer WE: Letter to the editor. N Engl J Med 293:1100, 1975

14. Nadelson CC: Rapist and victim. N Engl J Med 297:784-785, 1977

Untitled photograph by Francisco Alvardo-Juarez. Courtesy of the artist.

19
Treating Couples and Families in the New (Nontraditional) Marital Forms

OBJECTIVES

- To examine the principles of diagnoses and treatment of new, non-traditional marital forms
- To examine the treatment goals and techniques with such family forms

INTRODUCTION

In chapter 4 we discussed both the function and some of the common difficulties that non-traditional families (i.e., separated, divorced, single parent, reconstituted families) suffer and cope with. Some families, either because of the multiplicity of stressors, or poor coping, or psychopathology, are not able to deal with the situation and come for help. In this chapter we discuss the assessment and treatment of these non-traditional couples in difficulty.

SEPARATION

With separated (and even divorced or single-parent) families in trouble, the therapist needs to evaluate the relationship between parent(s), other caretakers,

288

and the children. The deficits noted in family functioning should be altered, based on the needs of the family. One immediate resource is the psychosocial kinship system, i.e., grandparents, step-parents, etc.

When a couple is separated, the family therapist can help uncover the problems that prevent some people from living together successfully on a sustained basis. Maintaining a lasting relationship is often more difficult than forming a new one, although some people hold onto a relationship in order to avoid change. *For this reason the family therapist can, quite reasonably, err on attempting to hold a marriage together rather than breaking it up.* Not everything can be changed, and the therapist needs to be realistic in helping the husband and wife to accept parts of themselves that cannot be changed. When emotions are high, separate individual therapy for one or both partners, or group therapy, may be indicated to "cool" a contentious relationship so that joint therapy can be initiated.

If children are involved, no matter what their ages, the reasons for separation or divorce should be discussed openly, honestly, and in a way that the children are able to understand, given their age level. Parents need to make clear that the separation or divorce is taking place because they cannot get along with each other and not because of any primary problems with the children. The children should be aware that both parents are still interested in them and love them. Bodin[1] suggests the following when talking to children in these situations:

1. "We are getting a divorce."(Explain divorce.)
2. "You didn't cause it."
3. "You couldn't have prevented it."
4. "I'm still your Mommy." "I'm still your Daddy."
5. "We both still love you." (Cannot be emphasized enough.)
6. "We always will."
7. "You don't have to choose between us." (Explain living arrangements.)
8. "People should be able to be fairly happy in marriage. If we had stayed together you would have had to look at a bad marriage still longer and your view might have been set against marriage as having any possibilities for happiness."
9. "We don't understand everything about the reasons for the divorce ourselves, but as we find out more we will try to explain more to you." "What do you think the reasons were?"
10. "As time goes on, Mom and Dad may need to talk more about the divorce and you might need to talk about it too. Anytime you have any questions or feelings you want to talk about we'll always be ready to listen. Just don't make it the main topic of conversation when we have company."
11. "It's OK to tell your friends." "It's not a secret."

It is important for children to realize that at the time of their birth their parents loved one another, and that they were "wanted children"; this knowledge can help alleviate the fear that they were in some way responsible for the divorce. Financial and living arrangements must be thoroughly explained; even though the children may be quite young they need to know that they are not going to be abandoned, and that regardless of the living arrangements, the absent parent will continue to love them.

The parents should consider being together when they discuss the above points with the children, unless the animosity between them is too great. Parents should not use children as hostages or as ammunition to support their arguments. They should not denigrate each other to the children. Unfortunately, one parent often accuses the children of growing up just like his or her spouse and even blames them for the divorce. What constitutes good parenting varies with the developmental needs of children, and each parent does not necessarily provide the optimal degree at each stage of his or her child's life. The family is not a static system; therefore, its needs, expectations, desires, and abilities do change over time.

DIVORCE AND POSTDIVORCE TREATMENT

Family conflict escalates in the year following divorce, and the parenting skills of the ex-spouses decrease as the parents become inconsistent, less affectionate, and exert less control over their children.[2] Statistically the risk of delinquency is much greater if the parents separate or divorce than if a parent dies.[3] Parental quarreling and mutual denigration can lead to the child's questioning of a previous positive evaluation of the parents.[4,5] Criticism of the absent father by the mother can lead to disruption of sex-typing for boys[6] and disruptions in heterosexual relations in adolescence for girls.[4] Custodial mothers are likely to develop a mutually coercive interaction with the children, especially with a son.[6] As the parents begin to date, the children (and particularly pre-adolescents and adolescents) become more aware of their parents as sex objects and some develop precocious sexual behavior.[7]

The *fact* of divorce should not lead one to think of only pathological sequellae, as a conflict-ridden intact family can be more detrimental to a child than a stable home in which the parents are divorced.[2] As such, *divorce can be a positive solution to a destructive family situation*. This seems to be especially true in the presence of a rejecting, demeaning, or psychiatrically ill father.[7]

The parameters of marital discord that seem most toxic for the children are prolonged marital disputes, especially those that involve the child, parental pathology that impinges on the child's functioning, and lack of a good relationship with even one parent.[3] Most encouraging is the fact that the condition of the child is not irreversible but will improve with an improvement in family relations.

The acute phase of the divorce process is commonly a period of disruption and crisis in which the parenting skills decrease as the divorcing parties give maximal attention to their own needs, with concomitant emergence of symptomatic behavior in the children. (For the sake of treatment planning, we include in the acute phase of the divorce process both the pre-divorce turmoil and the immediate post-separation period.) The common treatment alternatives at this phase include no formal clinical treatment (but support in the school and community) versus formal clinical treatment such as divorce counseling, brief individual or brief family treatment, or the initiation of longer term individual or family treatment.

Divorce therapy is a time-limited (usually 6–15 sessions) intervention, with the child and one or both parents in which the goal is to provide advice, information and counseling concerning the common alternatives, problems, and emotional upsets involved in the divorce process.[7,8] In this therapy, it may help to keep in mind the tasks the child has to accomplish in relation to the divorce process. In addition, there are divorce mediation and counseling systems[9,10] that are of potential benefit in effective divorce. Goldman and Coane[11] have utilized a brief family intervention with the task of redefining the family to include all members, firming generational boundaries and reducing parentification of the child/adolescent, experiencing a replay of the history of the marriage with the goal of correcting developmental distortions, and helping the parents divorce emotionally. When symptoms pre-existed in a child or adolescent or spouse, but are exacerbated by the acute divorce process, the clinician may be more inclined to entertain longer term intervention, either family or individual.

It is important to note that selecting participants for family therapy is more difficult and requires more strategic planning and tact with families of divorce than with intact families. Family therapy in this situation does not mean that all members of the parental and child generations should be at all sessions. The therapist will often wish to meet alternately with various subsystems of the family. Goldsmith[12] has outlined goals of the therapeutic interventions with the family of divorce for the co-parental (divorcing spouses), custodial parent-child subsystems, and noncustodial parent-child subsystems. Involvement in therapy of former spouses with each other can be quite threatening to a new mate of one of the former spouses. Alternately, involvement in therapy of a spouse with a new mate and the children can be quite threatening to the former spouse. In both cases, the therapy can be met with hostility and resistance. In this situation, it is important and helpful to point out to the adults, as aptly suggested by Goldsmith,[12] that reuniting the spouses is not the goal, but rather the re-equilibrium of the children and the establishment of a non-spousal parental coalition.

REMARRIED FAMILY UNITS
with Clifford Sager, M.D.

Remarried (REM), also called step or reconstituted families, have another set of problems, potentials, and options, with which they may need professional help. Just by the sheer number of such families, they vie numerically with intact nuclear families and must be recognized as a viable form of a new, commonplace American family. Acceptance of this reality is a necessary orientation for therapists working with REM families.

There are special concerns of REM families that need to be addressed; for example, roles of step-parents vis a vis the children and vice versa, relationships with the former spouse, financial arrangements, and child custody and visitation, which all too often are determined by courts.

Once divorce has taken place and remarriage is being considered by either spouse, the caretaking system takes another jolt when a step-parent enters the system as new spouse and co-parent. Former spouses have to continue their remaining responsibilities to each other and to their children while one (or both) enter into a second marriage. At this juncture there often is a recrudescence of old feelings of injury and anger just at the time when it is particularly important not to fall back into adversarial positions. Both bioparents do best to make efforts to be as constructive co-parents for the children while accepting the need for the co-parenting step-parent.

Goals include ensuring that (1) children have access and ongoing relationships (rather than mere visitation) with both their parents and their families, in order to define their own identity and identifications; (2) parents and children remain emotionally attached and responsible to each other; (3) guilt and anger are reduced for parents and children; (4) the noncustodial parent's participation is increased; (5) pains are taken by bioparents not to stimulate loyalty conflicts in the children; (6) children can gain by experiencing two father and mother images and two different family cultures.

Common treatment goals with REM families include many that are premised on acceptance and enhancement of the effectiveness of the *metafamily system*. For example, an early goal may be to stop scapegoating a child. This might be approached by helping former spouses and their own biofamilies (grandparents, etc.) to eschew fixing blame for the termination of the former marriage. This then makes it easier to work through anger to more readily bypass it for the children's needs. Guilt or retribution for past acts is not utilized as motivation for current action, thus allowing bio and stepparents to share some of the responsibility for childrearing. A reasonably functioning metafamily can help to free each REM or the two single-parent household systems to grow and function more effectively in its childrearing responsibilities as well as to serve the other needs of the adults.

Other goals may be:

1. To consolidate the REM couple as a unit and their authority in the system; helping the two adults to understand and develop a modus operandi to further their romantic love requirements and their necessity to parent.

2. To consolidate the parental authority in the system among bio and step-parents with the formation of a collaborative co-parenting team.

3. As a corollary to item 2, to help children deal with and minimize the continuance and exacerbation of loyalty binds between their two bioparents and the bioparent and ipsolateral step-parent.

4. To facilitate mourning of the nuclear family, former partner, old neighborhoods, friends and way of life. A period of mourning prepares the way to accept and to grow with the new reality of REM.

5. To be sure there is a secure place for the child's development and to maximize the potential within both family systems. Hopefully the two systems can be synergistic at the same time the child learns that there is not just one way of dealing with many life situations.

6. To accept and integrate the child's need for individuation from both families and for more peer involvement. A corollary to this is the child who prematurely develops great peer involvement when it was not possible to find appropriate love and nurturance in either bioparents' household system. One approach may be to strengthen the bond and acceptance of the child in one if not both family systems.

7. To help family members accept and tolerate their differences from some idealized intact family model. These include differences such as: (a) lack of complete control of money and income; (b) shared responsibility for children, some lack of control must be given up, (e.g., when child is in other parent's home); (c) the reality that children may neither like nor love a step-parent and vice versa; (d) the difference in feeling (the REM family will not feel the same to a participant as did his/her former nuclear family; there are different levels of bonding and different characters playing different if seemingly similar roles; these latter roles need clarification for all involved); (e) children may need help in accepting the different rules and expectations that are likely to exist in the two homes (flexibility is necessary for the child to navigate situations that are not precisely to his or her own wishes); (f) it is not as easy to live in a REM family structure— sometimes it is more complex, more persons are involved, models and guidelines less clear and every REM family is, in a sense, a pioneer family; (g) however the REM family system can be regarded and promoted as an enriching one enabling the child to avail himself of more diverse parental and interactive models.

The primary therapeutic process is to refocus and redefine the problem with the family in terms of the whole system and its subsequent needs and responsibilities. In REM, the therapist helps the family understand the expanded system: its differences from a nuclear family; the appropriate significance and role, if any, of the metafamily non-household members and how they all may affect one another. This process facilitates de-scapegoating children, who often are blamed for the REM family's troubles. When tasks are used we are concerned with any resistance to carry them out and the feelings evoked by them as well as the actual effects on individuals and the system. The reasons and feelings that are surfaced by an incompleted task are often of great therapeutic inport.

Key treatment questions with REM include the issues of whom to include in the therapeutic program. The therapist, after the assessment period, has to be clear when to include which metafamily members and for what purposes, and which treatment modalities to use, when, and for what ends. There are no hard and fast rules, and sensitive timing is of the essence. Familiarity and ease in working with a variety of modalities is helpful. It is easier to begin the first session by trying to include all members of the metafamily system who are involved in the problem and then work down to pertinent subunits, than it is to begin with the microsystem (for instance the child or only one bioparent's unit) and try to include others later.

If the REM couple's relationship is the presenting problem and the children are not involved, but there is clearly unfinished business with the prior partner, then a few couple sessions with the divorced pair, or individual sessions with the REM partner may be held to further the completion of the divorce, while at the same time moving into couple's work with the current partners. It is rarely necessary to include all metafamily for REM members in every session, but we try to keep in mind the different subsystems and how the present parts fit into the entire dynamic mosaic. The capacity for both flexibility and activity on the part of the therapist is crucial: successful treatment of REM depends on the therapist's comfort with moving in and out of the different parts of the system easily, and with treatment in different modalities that can include family, couple, individual, and child, as indicated. Since emotions in REM families often run high, the therapist must be comfortable in being active and able to take charge of the sessions. These abilities are particularly necessary when the session includes the former spouse, when there is a psychotic individual, when members are manipulative or there is an alliance to defeat the therapist, or when the family's underlying feelings of hopelessness and despair are rampant. We prefer working within a system framework, keeping in mind where each individual and subsystem is in his/her or its life cyle, and the dynamics of each individual. We summarize this as being constantly aware of systems, cycles, and psyches.

COHABITATING PARTNERS

One new form of relationship is the unmarried, cohabiting heterosexual couple. As noted in Chapter 2, it has been estimated that by 1978, there were 1.1 million cohabitating couples in the United States. Cohabitation has probably increased even more since then, and they are coming to "marital" therapists for help. Couples may live together for years while not marrying for one reason or another. They may feel there are tax and other financial reasons for remaining unmarried. There may be some lingering doubts about the long-term viability of the relationship. As long as there is no desire for children, they may see marriage as unnecessary. There may be dynamic reasons why they stay unmarried, such as the fear that the official and public act of marriage brings boredom, loss of sexual excitement, a sense of confinement, etc., that was exemplifed in their parents' marriages.

Dysfunction and Evaluation

In working with cohabitating partners, the therapist should not take the simplistic view that since they do not marry there must be pathology. When such couples present themselves to a marital therapist, it is important to assess and focus the intervention around the area for which the couple wants help. Some couples come seeking an improvement in their relationship (with no interest in current or eventual marriage) of a general nature (e.g., conflicted communication) or a specific nature (e.g., sexual dysfunction). Others come with a question of whether or not to remain as a couple, and this often proceeds just like such a situation in which the partners are married. Others come with a major question about the future of the relationship. After some years of cohabitation, some couples question the relationship and begin thinking of "divorce." In some situations, one partner begins to want marriage and/or children, and the other partner is resistant or heavily conflicted.

Treatment

Above all, the goal of the couples intervention is neither marriage nor separation, but assistance in the movement of a relationship that is stalemated or in conflict. Strategies and techniques of intervention are synonymous with those of marital therapy in general.

SERIAL RELATIONSHIPS

There are a growing number of individuals in our society who go from relationship to relationship (either cohabitating relationships or those involving marriage) in serial fashion. The sociological factors in our current society discussed at length in Chapter 2 provide the context for serial relations: geographic mobility, increased life expectancy, improved employment status and education of women, convenient methods of birth control, etc. Function and dysfunction in these couples is somewhat different from those discussed earlier in this chapter, and accordingly are discussed as a separate category.

Dysfunction

Of course, psychological factors in addition to the above mentioned societal factors can also play a prominent role in a history of serial relationships. Nature and degree of defensiveness, fear of intimacy and commitment, and a need for novelty and stimulation may all combine to foster serial relationships.

Assessment

General principles of assessing couples should be utilized. The focus of the assessment will be determined in part by the presenting problem that brings the couple for evaluation at this time. Often these couples are seen at a point when one or both members are thinking of dissolving the relationship. Assessment of the nature and pattern of prior serial relations may shed much light on the present conflicts.

Treatment

All strategies and techniques of marital treatment are useful in treating these individuals. If one partner has been involved in serial relations and the other has not, one might consider individual therapy with the former individual if it is felt that the major pathology and reasons for current conflict reside with that person.

SUGGESTIONS FOR FURTHER READINGS

Paolino T and McCrady B (Eds): **Marriage and Marital Therapy: Psychoanalytic, Behavioral and Systems Theory Perspectives.** New York: Brunner/Mazel, 1978.
> *An excellent comparison of different theoretical and strategical approaches to marital dysfunction.*

Dicks HV: **Marital Tensions.** London: Routledge and Kegan Paul, 1967.
> *A brilliant and thought-provoking look at marriage and its perversions from an object relations point of view.*

Stuart R: **Helping Couples Change: A Social Learning Approach to Marital Therapy.** New York: Guilford Press, 1980.
A thorough, well written examination of marital treatment by an articulate behaviorally-oriented marital therapist.

Wallerstein JS and Kelly JB: **Surviving the Breakup.** New York: Basic Books, 1980.
An extremely well written account of parents and children who have lived through a divorce.

Sager C, Brown H, Crohn H, Engel T, Rodstein E, and Walker L: **Treating the Remarried Family.** New York: Brunner/Mazel, 1983.
The best summary of clinical work with individuals in several family systems—the predivorced one and the remarried one.

REFERENCES

1. Bodin A: Divorce: Suggestions for talking with your child(ren). Am Fam Ther Assoc Newsletter 7:10, 1982
2. Hetherington EM, Cox M, and Cox B: The aftermath of divorce. In Stevens JH Jr and Mathews M (Eds): Mother-Child, Father-Child Relations. Washington, D.C.: National Association for the Education of Young Children, 1977
3. Rutter M: Separation, loss and family relations. In Rutter M and Hersov L (Eds): Child Psychiatry: Modern Approaches. Oxford, England: Blackwell Scientific Publications, 1971, pp 47-73
4. Hetherington EM: Effects of father absence on personality development in adolescent daughters. Dev Psychology 7:313-326, 1972
5. Tessman LH: Children of Parting Parents. New York: Jason Aronson, 1978
6. Hetherington EM: Divorce: A child's perspective. Am Psychologist 34:851-858, 1978
7. Wallerstein JS and Kelly JB: Surviving the Breakup. New York: Basic Books, 1980
8. Wallerstein JS and Kelly JB: Divorce counselling: A community service for families in the midst of divorce. Am J Orthopsychiatry 47:4-22, 1977
9. Coogler OJ: Structured Medication in Divorce Settlement. Lexington, MA: Lexington Books, 1978
10. Grandvold DK and Welch GC: Intervention postdivorce adjustment problems: The treatment seminar. J Divorce 1:81-91, 1977
11. Goldman J and Coane J: Family therapy after the divorce: Developing a strategy. Fam Process 16:357-362, 1977

12. Goldsmith J: The post-divorce family system. In Walsh F (Ed): Normal Family Process. New York: Guilford Press, 1982, pp297-330

Seated Couple, courtesy of the Metropolitan Museum of Art. Gift of Lester Wunderman, 1977. Wood and metal sculpture, Dogon tribe, Mali, African. XIX-XX century.

20
Gay Couples

OBJECTIVES

- To describe relationship patterns among gay male couples
- To be familiar with treatment issues with gay couples

INTRODUCTION

It is no longer news that gay people come in a variety of shapes, sizes, and colors, and that they are not all hairdressers or ballet dancers, and that many are still hiding in the closet. In the last decade there has been a considerable increase in the amount of reliable information available concerning gay people.[9] This, together with their growing visibility, has helped to make family therapists more aware of the range and diversity of the homosexual population.

We believe this material is of importance to the marital and family therapist for two reasons. First, there are special issues relevant to the understanding and treatment of gay couples. Second, understanding these kinds of couples sheds light on the more traditional kinds of couples that marital and family therapists are likely to see in the course of their practices—in particular, as they relate to such issues as gender roles, sexuality and relationship styles.

Unfortunately, we do not have as much material on lesbian couples as we do on gay men. Our clinical experience is limited and the literature is meager.

300

Table 20-1
Comparison of Non-gay and Gay Couples

	Non-gay Couples	Gay Couples
Societal models and support	present	absent
Involvement of extended family	present	absent
Offspring	present	absent
Rapport (producing closeness and affection) CLASSICAL STEREOTYPE	low	high
Contrast (producing complementarity and sexual interest)	high	low
Traditional masculine/feminine roles	present	absent
Equality of partners CLASSICAL STEREOTYPE	absent	present

RELATIONSHIP PATTERNS

One area of gay male life, however, that is only now beginning to be studied is that of relationship patterns.[12,13,15,16] The realities of gay male couples have been submerged because most homosexuals in our society continue to lead a covert and vulnerable existence.

The process of commitment to a gay relationship requires intrapsychic and interpersonal shifts similar to those in non-gay couples. For the individuals involved, self-awareness has to be reconciled with concern for the partner and for the couple as an entity. Superficial playfulness has to make room for emotional intimacy, and physical passion has to be joined by caring and tenderness. There will be a need to reallocate previous involvement with family and friends.[4]

These factors exist for both gay and non-gay couples. For gays, however, there are, in addition, all those issues related to being a member of a despised group, and to the acquisition of a positive and open gay identity. Given the profound and pervasive anti-homosexual bias in our society, these transitions are fraught with considerable psychological and social hazards (Table 20-1).

Committing oneself to living as a same-sex couple requires coming to terms with the idea of being gay. Although one may earlier have been reluctant to admit to oneself the true nature of one's sexual orientation, and may even have actively engaged in fighting against it, joining in a gay relationship implies having admitted gayness and having to some degree accepted it. It usually also means "coming out" not only to oneself but to the gay community as well.

A gay couple becomes recognized as an entity in whatever gay subculture exists in a particular locality. It may be much more difficult to pass as "straight" with colleagues at work after one has settled down with a gay lover. A common way of coping with this problem is to compartmentalize completely one's work and social contacts, with a profound distancing by gay couples from other people who may not be aware of or may not be accepting of the couple's homosexuality.

We will outline some of the old myths about gay male relationships, discussing them in the light of more recent findings. Comparisons will be offered with lesbian and heterosexual couples, and there will be a brief discussion of the implications of the new data for clinical practice.

MYTHS ABOUT GAY COUPLES

Myth: Gay relationships don't last, and are doomed to failure. This false idea arises from many sources. All gay males are thought to be sexually promiscuous and hedonistic, and basically incapable of anything other than superficial, if not totally anonymous, relationships. Many people know little about gay life except for the singles bar scene and take that to be the prototype for all gay male existence. There may be some deep-seated doubts that any relationship would continue were it not for societal sanctions, traditional gender roles, and the presence of children. Gay males who have settled down with one another tend often to be much less visible to the general community. This allows for much greater projection by some non-gays of their own desires for greater freedom and joyfulness when they feel constrained or trapped in their marriages.

It is instructive to compare the structure and functioning of gay couples with that of their non-gay counterparts. For gay couples there is strikingly less societal and institutional support for the maintenance of continuity and fidelity in their relationships. Religious, legal, and tax considerations do not serve to stabilize the gay couple as they do the non-gay one.

Cultural guidelines about how gay couples can operate are only rarely available to gay people. We have (mostly) all, gays and non-gays alike, grown up in non-gay families, and this is the cultural pattern we are familiar with. Since one of the outstanding features of gay existence has until recently been its invisibility, it has been rare for gay people to know any gay couples. This has left them with the options of adapting, or sometimes caricaturing, the model of the heterosexual couple, or otherwise experimenting with innovative, non-traditional patterns.

Because there tends to be little or no involvement of the extended family members in the relationship or the social structure of the gay couple, gays tend to be much more dependent on an extended friendship network instead. Because of the relative weakness of societal reenforcers, for gay couples mutual commitment to one another and to their relationship often takes longer to establish.

The promise or actuality of offspring helps keep non-gay couples together, provides them with community involvements (neighbors, schools), and helps move them from an orientation to the self and to the present to one that involves others and the future. The absence of offspring in most gay households weakens these opportunities. Here, as in other aspects of gay male existence, the individual's mind set and expectations are all important. If one has come to believe, on the basis of internalized cultural homophobia, that as a gay male one is destined to be emotionally unstable and unhappy, such an attitude will have negative consequences for establishing a successful relationship.

Nevertheless, the fact is that there is nothing inherent in male homosexuality that precludes the establishment of meaningful and continuing partnerships.[6] Such relationships exist in large numbers. For example, recent studies indicate that almost all gay males had been involved in at least one continuing physical/emotional relationship. Of gay men in their 20's, 40 percent were currently involved in such a coupling that had lasted an average of 2–3 years.[13]

Although one might expect that "closeted" gay couples do better than those that are open, the findings are not completely conclusive. There are couples who appear to do well irrespective of the degree of their closetedness. However, there is reason to believe that gay males who are "out" feel better about themselves and that gay couples of this sort mix more comfortably in the general community. They are thus able to gain outside validation for their status as a gay couple. They do not have to push their beds apart when their parents came to visit, nor do they have to pass as mere roommates at social functions.[8,15]

Myth: The fact that a gay couple is composed of two "homosexuals" is more important than that it is composed of two men. Actually, in many respects an individual's relationship attitudes and behaviors seem more highly correlated with his or her background and gender role as a male or female than with a particular sexual orientation.

Coming from a stable family and having a history of good psychosocial functioning, including previous successful relationships, are probably more crucial indicators of one's potential as a partner than is one's rating on the Kinsey scale. While it may be true that gay men find it easy to engage in sexual acts without emotional commitment—that is, they can separate sex from love—is this because they are gay, or because they are *males*? In contrast, for lesbians, romantic involvement much more often precedes any genital contact, but isn't that true for American women generally?[7]

It has been said that compatibility in a couple's relationship requires both rapport and resistance. Rapport is a similarity of response and outlook, and is important for closeness and affection. Resistance, consisting of tension, distance, and dissimilarity, is the matrix for complementarity and sexual interest.

According to this view, non-gay couples would tend to be low on rapport (or similarity) and high in resistance (or contrast). In male-female relationships there is a greater social sex-role differentiation between the partners. Problems for these

Table 20-2
Comparison of Gay Male and Lesbian Couples

	Gay Male Couples	Lesbian Couples
Individuation	high	low
Fusion, clinging	low	high
Sex/Intimacy	S precedes I	I precedes S
Sex/Love	often unrelated	usually related
Fidelity	open relationship	monogamy
	or unattached	

couples often stem from a lack of empathy, and from excessive differentness, which leads to major collisions.

For same-sex couples, on the other hand, one would expect a high level of rapport and a low level of contrast. Such a configuration results in an easy initiation of gay relationships, but also an early detection of possible mismatch. Satisfying sexual intimacy can be established early, but the same factors would also predispose toward early sexual boredom. The excessive similarity of many gay couples may produce relational "fatigue," i.e., a feeling of being bored in a relationship. It therefore often takes gay couples longer to establish emotional commitment to one another than it does for non-gay couples, and many gay relationships have "burned out" before reaching this stage.

In couples composed of two *men*, each partner has undergone a socialization process leading to his adopting a predominantly traditional masculine *social sex role*, even though his *sexual preference* may be atypical. Males have been socialized to be competitive, independent, unemotional, unaffectionate, and more goal- than process-oriented. These traits are not conducive to committed intimate relationships, and must be modified considerably if two males are to live together successfully.[3]

In our culture it is usually the woman, rather than the man, that tends to keep a marriage together. Traditionally women have been thought of as the nest builders, and the men as explorers. In this regard, it is interesting to contrast the relationships of lesbian couples with those of gay males (Table 20-2). When two women come together in a lesbian relationship, their union tends to last longer, on the average, than does that produced by the joining of two gay males. This is true, even though the sexual activity of the lesbian couple tends to decline earlier than that of their gay male counterparts.[13]

In contrast to male couples, female relationships characteristically show less individuation in each partner, and more clinging and "fusion." Sex tends much more often to be equated with love. Sexual monogamy is much more valued than in gay males. Lesbian relationships tend to be more closed and inbred. There is a greater tendency toward a sticky "triangulation," in which someone, typically a former lover, becomes enmeshed in the couple's relationship. Bell and Weinberg's[9] "close-coupled" style is modal for lesbians, whereas the "open-coupled" style is modal for gay males.[9] Some observers have attempted to account for these dissimilarities by pointing out that in the lesbian couple both partners have been socialized into the female role.[1,11,14]

Myth: Gay male couples engage in stereotypical "husband-wife" role-playing. This is a commonly held idea, perhaps related to another false belief that gay males take either "male" or "female" sexual roles. In their sexual activity, gay males exhibit a considerable degree of variety and variability. Although any one individual may prefer one or two types of sexual activity, gay males are often able to accommodate to a partner's wishes as well.[10]

The situation is similar to gender role allocation in the non-sexual aspects of the partnership. For example, in long-lasting gay male couples, each partner is able to be active in some areas and passive in others. Each seems to choose the chores he likes and is able to compromise on the others. Chores are more likely to be assigned according to preference and ability.

In reality, most gay couples reject the models of traditional marriage and social sex roles. Their relationships, as do those of lesbians, more closely resemble those of best friends, with the added ingredients of romance and erotic attachment. There is a marked tendency toward egalitarianism, with sharing of power, responsibilities, and tasks. They do not, as a rule, support each other financially, and they tend to be dual-career households. These partnerships demonstrate that non-traditional models can be effectively utilized as the basis of love relationships.

Sex-typed role-playing is much more typical of heterosexual than homosexual couples. Amongst homosexuals, such role-playing is most common in those who are male, older, and of lower socio-economic status.

Myth: Sexual exclusivity helps bind gay couples together, whereas infidelity destroys these relationships. In reality, the prohibition against "open" (meaning nonmonogamous) relationships is much more important for heterosexuals, and perhaps lesbians, whereas for gay men happy and stable long-term partnerships are characterized by such "openness."

Long-lasting couples of whatever gender or sexual orientation are involved in an ongoing process requiring continual adjustments, with phase-specific tasks and difficulties. At times and for certain functions the partners operate more closely together, whereas at other times and for other reasons they are more differentiated and seem more like two separate individuals.

Recently, (in the 1970s) 156 gay male couples who had been together for periods ranging from 18 months to 30 years were studied.[2,8] In the early phases of their partnerships, they were more likely to be monogamous than later on. In fact, not one of the couples who had been together for over five years maintained a sexually exclusive partnership. Successful couples found that as time went on sexual exclusivity didn't work, and outside sexual relationships seemed to enhance the quality of their mutual sexual attraction. The exploration of sexual fantasies external to the primary relationship seemed to lead to their later incorporation into the couples' own sexual contacts. Far from destroying relationships, in the past, sexual infidelity seemed actually to be a necessary ingredient of keeping relationships together. This involved putting a different meaning on "fidelity." Rather than sexual exclusivity, fidelity came to be defined as emotional commitment.

Such an open system is workable to the extent that outside sexual contacts do not encroach on other important aspects of the relationship. Gay males utilize several mechanisms to minimize this possibility. For some couples, there is an implicit recognition that outside sex may be taking place but it is not a topic to be discussed. Partners will participate in such activity on their own time, when the other partner is not around, and in such a way as not to bring the matter to the other's attention.

For other couples the agreement allowing outside sex is explicit, but such sexual partners are not brought into the home, the contacts are limited only to sex, and specific sexual adventures may not be shared openly between the partners. Still other couples may seek outside sexual activity together as a couple, either inviting someone to their home for three-way sex, or going out to the baths together.

Myth: "And they lived happily ever after." The idea still persists that enduring relationships stem from an early period of erotic infatuation, and that such a state of "enthrallment" persists unchanged in successful, long-lasting relationships.[7] This romantic notion is simply contrary to experience for both gay and straight relationships. Indeed, its presence in gay couples may signal that they have bought into an extensive collection of heterosexual marital myths. It unrealistically denies the concept of differentiated stages in a relationship, related to the life cycle of the individual and the couple, with phase-specific stresses that require adjustment.

Gay couples who stay together for long periods had known each other longer initially before ever becoming lovers, and the partners are more likely to have met in a non-sexual setting. They decided to settle down with one another as a couple not primarily because of their sexual attraction to one another but for other reasons, such as mutual compatibility.[10]

In long-lasting couples, people are not living with their fantasy "type." In one recent study of gay couples, 90 percent did not live with their ideal sexual partner. The early intense sexual passion typically wanes, and as the members of the couple get to know each other better and get to live in increasing harmony, their sexual interest in one another often declines dramatically.

In successful couples, the ability to work on a relationship and to communicate and negotiate successfully are of utmost importance. For example, the issues of autonomy and attachment may be continually in flux over the course of a couple's living together.

ISSUES IN THE THERAPY OF GAY COUPLES

Inevitably two gay male partners will face many of the same kinds of issues seen in any other type of couple.[2] These challenges may be thought of as involving communication, role allocation, power, sex, money, and so on. A gay male relationship has to confront these issues, but perhaps with the differences in style and context described above, including the fact that two participants are both males.

For example, many gay relationships come to grief on the question of sex with outside partners (despite some degree of acceptance, discussed earlier). For many gay men this is just as unacceptable an idea as it is for non-gay individuals. On a personal level, individuals may feel too threatened, insecure, possessive, and jealous to tolerate a partner's having sex with someone else, and may feel that they themselves have little or nothing to offer aside from sex. In a broader sense, many people, gay and non-gay, have difficulty modifying the traditional beliefs concerning sexual fidelity in marriage. This despite the fact that sexual interests between marital partners often decline markedly with the passage of time, and that infidelity can actually help stabilize a relationship. For a gay man, still operating on our culture's double-standard of sexual fidelity for men and women, the subliminal expectation may exist that his male partner should adhere to the monogamous conduct he has been programmed to think appropriate for a female.

There are, however, some themes that are unique to a gay relationship and will not be met with in non-gay couples. These concern attitudes toward being homosexual and the homosexual's relationship to the straight world.

The principal factor has to do with how the couple itself and important aspects of the surrounding subculture feel about homosexuality. To the extent, for example, that the partners themselves feel negative about being gay, clearly their feelings about themselves, the other, and their relationship will suffer. To the degree that they feel isolated as a couple due to the societal homophobia around them, the two partners may feel forced to become almost totally dependent on each other, causing considerable strain on their alliance.

Two partners who are at different stages in their self-acceptance as homosexuals, and are at different points in their "coming out" or "going public" process, may produce a very unstable equilibrium. Gay couples who unthinkingly accept traditional heterosexual models as molds for their own relationships may fall into an unnecessarily restrictive set of options.

ACQUIRED IMMUNE DEFICIENCY SYNDROME (AIDS) with John Patten, M.D.

A gay couple or their extended families should be aware of the effects of AIDS on the relationships. Initial impressions are described below.

As of September 1986, almost 25,000 Americans have been diagnosed with AIDS; half of that number are dead. Seven times that number have ARC, Aids Related Complex, a prodrome of AIDS. Effects on those high risk populations, principally gay men and intravenous drug abusers, have been profound and surprising. The pressure on gay men to couple has increased dramatically, and they have had to deal with issues of intimacy rather than having more superficial relationships around sex. Yet the fear of contamination has altered feelings about having sex, which has had (for some) negative effects on gay relationships. Families of gay men, some of whom did not know prior to diagnosis about their sons sexual preference, are polarized in their reactions and ability to deal with a catastrophic illness. For some families, it is the perfect excuse to "write off" a family member they see as aberrant. Other families become closely involved and form new close relationships with "son and his life."

Drug abusers serve a central role in the context of the homeostasis of their families. Once they get AIDS then they no longer have the sort of problem that is useful to this homeostasis. Their role in the family becomes much less central, and often they are unofficially abandoned to die.

Because of the lack of AIDs knowledge and "safe sex" education, the potential for carriers (HIV +ve) to spread the virus by an intravenous or a sexual route is great. Many women who themselves (or their spouses) are former or current abusers are having babies who have AIDS/ARC.

In the "middle class," many men, gay or intravenous drug users, are turning up who are antibody +ve. This may be a blood donor who is found in routine testing, a hemophiliac, or an army recruit who doesn't seem to fit into any high risk group. Being antibody +ve has enormous implications; more and more families are living with this secret.

REFERENCES

1. Krestan JA and Bepko CS: The problem of fusion in the lesbian relationship. Fam Proc 19:277-289, 1980
2. McWhirter D and Mattison A: Psychotherapy for gay male couples. J Homosex 7(2/3):79-92, 1981/1982

3. Morin SF: Male sex role and gay male couples. Paper presented at the meeting of the American Psychological Association, 1977

4. Morrison C: Made in heaven: Coupling (and uncoupling) the gay way. Blueboy, November 1980

5. Peplau LA: What homosexuals want in relationships. Psychology Today, March 1981, pp 28-38

6. Silverstein C: Man to Man: Gay Couples in America. New York: William Morrow & Co, 1981

7. Tennov D: Love and Limerence. New York: Stein and Day, 1979

8. McWhirter DP and Mattison AM: The Male Couple. Englewood Cliffs, NJ: Prentice-Hall, 1984

9. Bell AP and Weinberg MS: Homosexualities: A Study of Diversity Among Men and Women. New York: Simon & Schuster, 1978

10. Tuller NR: Couples: The hidden segment of the gay world. J Homosex 3(4):331-343, 1978

11. McCandlish BM: Therapeutic issues with lesbian couples. J Homosex 7(2/3):71-78, 1981/1982

12. Peplau LA: Research on homosexual couples: An overview. J Homosex 8(2):3-8, 1982

13. Mendola M: The Mendola Report: A Look at Gay Couples. New York: Crown, 1980

14. Tanner DM: The Lesbian Couple. Lexington, MA: DC Heath, 1978

15. Symposium on homosexual couples. J Homosex 8(2):1-83, 1982

16. Duffy SM and Rusbult CE: Satisfaction and commitment in homosexual and heterosexual relationships. J Homosex 12(2):1-24, 1985/1986

Death in the Sick Chamber by Edvard Munch, 1893. Courtesy of Nasjonalgalleriet, Oslo.

21
Marital and Family Therapy for Career-Oriented Marriages: Troubled Physicians and Their Families*

with Jonathan F. Borus, M.D.

OBJECTIVES

- To understand the family system problems experienced by male physicians and their families
- To be able to apply these concepts to a clinical case
- To summarize the treatment issues with this population

INTRODUCTION

As clinicians, we have been impressed with the frequency with which troubled physicians are part of a disturbed family system. Initial distress in a physician's spouse or other family member also often seems linked to the person and role behavior of the physician. But physicians are notoriously difficult to treat. The family model is often crucial in this situation. We have found that inclusion of the spouse in the evaluation and treatment processes can have beneficial effects on both understanding and improving the troubled physician's (and family's) problems.

Because our experience has included few female doctors, we have focused exclusively on the family dynamics of male physicians. Further study of the individual and family problems of the growing number of female physicians is

---

This chapter has been adapted from Glick ID and Borus JF: Marital and family therapy for troubled physicians and their families. JAMA 14:1855-1858, 1984.

sorely needed. Suffice it to say, the issues we discuss here increasingly have large overlap to female physicians, especially as they attempt to balance the needs of career and family. We believe that much of what we describe here for doctors is generalizable to other professionals such as lawyers and politicians, investment bankers, etc. We must leave to the reader the work of extrapolating to these groups.

FAMILY SYSTEM PROBLEMS FOR PHYSICIANS

Male physicians tend to engage in "selective recruitment in seeking a marriage partner, with the aim of finding someone who will fit into the singlemindedness of the doctor's lifestyle" (G. Deckert, M.D., personal communication, 1979). Until the last few decades, many women saw the physician as a "good catch," worthy of the trade-off of postponing or abandoning her career to meet the needs of her husband's profession. When such marriages occur during the rigorous days of residency training or the initial years of practice building, much of the burden of family and home responsibilities usually falls on the spouse, and she must delay many personal and material gratifications. During this period, she often builds high expectations of the positive changes she hopes will occur at the end of training. Therefore, the physician finishing his training in his early to mid-30s is often under great family pressure to settle down and devote more time to being a husband and provider. Concurrently, emerging from years of patterned, structured training, the physician is eager to explore his professional opportunities and wants to devote his energies to his practice.[1] This disparity frequently leads to major family conflicts, and long-delayed expectations of realignment of roles and reward for delaying gratification in the service of training are frustrated when the practicing physician continues to work hard in his profession and to depend on his wife to "run the family."

The homeostatic balance between demands, responsibilities, and rewards in the physician's family is often delicately maintained and easily disrupted throughout his career. Communication decreases if the physician's work keeps him excessively away from home, and the more he becomes involved professionally, the less available he is to tend to his spouse's needs and to help her with family tasks. Over time, the spouse often feels neglected and painfully aware of a lack of individual personal meaning in her life. This may lead to anger and withdrawal on her part, or an attempt to carve out a separate identity. Such changes may result in physician-spouse conflict, causing the physician to have difficulty in his work or to develop symptoms that bring him to seek psychiatric treatment.

Like most couples, marital conflict between the physician and his spouse arises most frequently around role, status, power, and priority issues. Role issues concerning the division of time between professional and family tasks often get rigidified rather than renegotiated by the physician and his wife during the length of their marriage. Although a role split that was comfortable during training or the early practice stage of marriage may no longer be satisfying to either partner, there may be little time or communication devoted to altering these early roles. The physician's status in the community and in his professional world is often in sharp contrast to that of his spouse, who may feel "one down" as the losing competitor in the marriage. The troubled physician may have difficulty allowing his wife to have independent areas of competence outside of her family roles. Power issues are expressed through the physician's greater flexibility and control over money and other resourses, while his wife's power is often expressed in her ability to configure family relationships and in her control of intramarital sexual relationships.

In dual-career couples, in which the wife either maintains or reestablishes a working life outside the home, determining who comes first at a particular stage of professional and marital life is an especially prominent cause of conflict. Both partners are pressed during professional growth-spurt periods to pursue their careers full tilt if they are to "get ahead," and neither has much time for the marital relationship or family life. Such conflicts are further "complicated" by children, and child care responsibilities may be shunted from one spouse to the other. Indeed, as in most marriages, the very setting of life's major priorities concerning work, money, power, sex, and family responsibilities is the meat of family conflict between, and family therapy with, the physician and his spouse.

Such family issues may first come to psychiatric attention with different presentations related to the age of the couple. Young physician's spouses (aged 25 to 35 years) today are often being less willing to trade-off or delay their careers to defer to their husbands' needs. They do not want to be "mere shadows" of their husbands or "just the doctor's wife"; the culture tells them that they are failing if they don't have independent careers and some level of financial independence from their husbands. With so many young physicians' wives not accepting the notion that they should devote time to family matters at the expense of their own careers, there is often no one at home "minding the family store" while the young physician is heavily engaged in his training or early practice. Competition over career priorities and insufficient devotion of time to the marriage by both partners may produce dissatisfaction in both, leading to an incident (often the exposure of infidelity) that precipitates the request for therapy.

Midlife spouses (aged 35 to 50 years), who initially accepted giving up their career for their husband, are also affected by the current culture that implies that they were foolish to do so. Some become depressed, thinking their lives have passed them by, while others try to reenter the work force in a career that will increase their independence. Depression in the spouse or problems in their adolescent children are often the first symptomatic expressions of medical marriage disequilibrium in midlife couples seeking treatment.

Although also aware of the recent cultural changes in women's roles, older physicians' spouses (50 years or older) are often more strongly committed to the role of the "doctor's wife" who takes care of the home and family. When their grown children leave the home, they may feel acutely alone while their husbands continue working, and the couple may find they have little left in common if the physician decreases his work load or retires completely. Impulsive behavior or depression in one partner, or constant bickering between them, may precipitate the request for professional help.

CASE EXAMPLES

One

A couple in their early 30s came for treatment when the spouse insisted that they either seek help for their marriage or dissolve it. The spouse complained that her husband, a senior infectious disease fellow, was self-centered, overinvolved with his work, paid little attention to the couple's three-year-old son, and expected home and family life to revolve around his needs. The physician was critical of his wife's profession (college teaching), and their marital disharmony first surfaced when their move to a new city for fellowship had dislodged the wife from a full-time position in which she had held major administrative responsibility. The wife was angry that her husband expected her to earn money but belittled her work and refused to assist her in child care during her professional busy periods.

Marital therapy focused on increased communication between the couple, role realignment, parenting issues, and the couple's anxiety about the changes attendant to the physician's imminent transition from training to practice. Early in the treatment the husband acknowledged his anger, sadness, and feelings of failure that his son did not want to be with him and would not listen to him. He said that he felt shut out at home and therefore retreated into his work at the office, often leaving before his son awoke and working through dinner until his son was in bed. The spouse, in turn, acknowledged that she had compensated for the husband's absence by becoming overly close to her son in an attempt to obtain the companionship from him that her marriage lacked. The therapy helped the physician devote more time to his wife and son, helped the wife give her son enough room to establish a relationship with the husband, and structured couple time together to discuss the decisions about their future.

With ten months of weekly therapy, the partners were getting along much better and were sharing in the decision making about the potential jobs that the husband might take to enter practice and their attendant family changes. The physician had devoted specific time each day to being with his son, they had established an independent relationship, and the spouse had gained a more appropriate distance from her child. The therapy terminated when the couple moved to a new city so that the husband could begin practice; a six-month follow-up from a third party indicated that the family had maintained their improved level of functioning.

Two

A couple in their early 30s came to treatment at the point at which the spouse was considering having an affair. Evaluation indicated that although the couple had known each other since their teens, she had always felt "one down" in the relationship, had sacrificed her career, believed that he placed his professional work as a radiologist ahead of her, and treated her like "one of the boys." Marital therapy was recommended.

Therapy in this case was focused on their roles and patterns in dealing with each other. The couple had functioned in a typical "one down" model, and the spouse felt demeaned and withdrew from her husband. She had the fantasy of initiating an affair, had told her husband about it, but he was patronizing and aloof in response. Marital therapy forced the physician-husband to evaluate the effect of his behavior on the spouse (negative and resulted in her withdrawing from him) and forced him to increase communication, which previously had been perfunctory and focused on her meeting his needs. She was encouraged to take a job that gave her some satisfactions outside the home.

After one year of weekly sessions, there was marked improvement in the marriage and in each partner individually. Six-month follow-up showed that "they were closer than ever before" and were planning to have a child.

Three

A couple in their 40s came to treatment when they felt unable to control their five children, aged 2 to 13 years. The precipitant was the worsening of the spouse's back problem, which prevented her from running the household in the highly efficient way she had previously. Her husband's reaction to this change was to withdraw from the family into his work. At age 13 years the oldest daughter had taken over much of the household and parenting responsibilities with disastrous consequences, ranging from fights with her 11-year-old sister, rebellion on the part of the three younger siblings, despair and depression in the mother, and further withdrawal by the father. History showed that both spouses had functioned fairly well before and in the early years of their marriage, and that neither was particularly psychologically minded. Family therapy and marital therapy were suggested, with an emphasis on the former in the stages of treatment. Treatment goals were aimed at increasing family communication, helping the husband and wife share responsibility for family life and helping the 13-year-old give up some of her power over and responsibility for the rest of the children.

The treatment initially focused on the lack of communication between husband and wife. For the spouse to get her husband's help, she often became histrionic to force him to deal with the problem of the children. His reaction was to withdraw from the family, saying there was "really no problem" and that his wife was just a chronic complainer. The older children took over to fill the power vacuum. The young children would engage in a variety of dysfunctional behaviors such as breaking things, screaming, or, in the case of the four-year-old, holding her breath until cyanotic. The presence of the entire family in the session literally forced the physician to face the frustration he felt in having to deal with so many children (the expressed wish to have the children was his wife's). It also allowed him to discuss and cope with the problems he was having with his partners in his practice. The outcome was a "role realignment," with the husband taking over some of the parenting roles and spending fewer hours at work.

After one year of treatment with all seven family members and concurrent marital treatment with the couple, there was marked improvement in the physician (he reported functioning better in his practice and as a husband and father), the spouse (she had moderate relief from her backpain, as she was now "free" to seek appropriate medical attention and did not have to carry the burden of the house), the older children (they were able to withdraw from the role of parent substitutes), and the younger children (they improved in school and were better able to accept limits).

THERAPEUTIC ISSUES

Principles of treatment are for the most part the same as described in other parts of this text. But we have encountered specific therapeutic dynamics in the treatment of physician-spouse couples that merit discussion. First, the physician and his spouse may both expect the two physicians (physician-patient and psychiatrist-physician-therapist) to ally with each other since they have similar professional roles and considerable overlap in professional training and socialization. The spouse suspects that the therapist will side with her husband and attend more to his needs because he is the professional and she is "just the spouse." A second common dynamic pulls in the opposite direction when the physician-patient sees the therapist as his competitor. Coming to a psychiatrist as a patient often makes the physician feel "one down," stimulating a need to prove his competence and deny his problems to the other physician in the room. This stance is often fostered by a third common treatment dynamic, that of the "good doc-bad doc" split. In this situation, the spouse may idealize the therapist as the good physician who treats her in a much more caring, communicative way than her spouse does. The therapist's attempts to explore the difficulties that the couple has in ordering family and professional roles, and his suggestions of ways to improve the marital situation, may provoke each marital partner to believe that the therapist is on the other partner's side. To minimize the solidification of any particular dyad in what must remain a triadic therapeutic relationship, the psychiatrist has to walk a careful, impartial line between his two patients and make extra ef-

forts to ally with both partners as a couple. The therapist must be able to com-
miserate with the physician in terms of understanding the professional demands
on him, but also point out the temptations inherent in the physician's role to
neglect family needs and seek gratification in work efforts. He should discuss the
normal need to reassess and revise family roles at different points in the marriage
and help the couple find an agreeable complimentarity that does not denigrate
either partner.

Individual therapy for the troubled male physician has been reported to be
difficult and often ineffective because of the physician's narcissism and heavy use
of the reaction formation and denial.[2-7] Families seldom have been involved in the
treatment.[8] Concurrent individual therapy for the physician and his spouse may be
indicated initially when the relationship is too emotionally charged for the couple
to be seen together. However, our data and that from another (two-case) clinical
report suggest that the treatment of choice for the troubled physician may be
marital or family therapy, based on the rationale that family structure and function
must change for the physician-patient to change.

Such an approach is helpful for both the physician and his spouse. We
hypothesize that the presence of the spouse forces the physician to confront
problems rather than deny them, offers them an alternative view to the physician's
narcissistic image, serves as a control to inhibit a troubled physician's self-
destructive behavior, and provides a persistent motivation for change (e.g., a
spouse's statement that she will separate if "things don't improve"). At the least,
such an approach almost always increases communication between the couple and
clarifies the problems they share.

REFERENCES

1. Borus JF: The transition to practice. J Med Educ 57:593-601, 1982
2. Waring EM: Psychiatric illness in physicians: A review. Comp Psychiatry
   15:519-530, 1974
3. Scheiber SC: Emotional problems of physicians. I. Nature and extent of
   problems. Arz Med 34:323-325, 1977
4. Scheiber SC: Emotional problems of physicians. II. Current approaches to the
   problem. Ariz Med 35:336-337, 1978
5. McCue JD: The effects of stress on physicians and their medical practice. N
   Engl J Med 306:458-463, 1982
6. Waring EM: Medical professionals with emotional illness. A controlled study
   of the hazards of being a 'special patient.' Psychiatr J Univ Ottawa 4:161-164,
   1977
7. Coombs RH: The medical marriage. In Coombs RH and Vincent C (Eds):

Psychosocial Aspects of Medical Training. Springfield, Il: Charles C. Thomas, 1971, pp 133-165

8. Krell R, Miles JE: Marital therapy of couples in which the husband is a physician. Am J Psychother 30:267-275, 1976

Section VI

Family Treatment When One Member Has A Diagnosable Psychiatric Disorder Or Other Special Problem

How is the family different when one member has a psychiatric disorder? What special modifications of techniques are needed for special situations such as the common and problematic family in which aggressive, homicidal, or suicidal behavior are frequent? The differences in evaluation and treatment made necessary by these situations are presented in this section. In a similar way, family behavior can be organized around acute or chronic mental illness. We believe it is crucial for the trainee to be aware of the typical patterns and responses of families in these situations.

Finally, we discuss treatment in settings in which these problems are often managed from a family perspective (or should be), such as the psychiatric hospital and the community mental health center.

Quarrels between Mr. and Mrs. Latimer, and Brutal Violence between Them, Were the Natural Consequences of the Too Frequent Use of the Bottle, from "The Bottle" by George Cruikshank, 1847. Courtesy of the Quarterly Journal of Studies on Alcohol.

22
Family Treatment in the Context of Individual Psychiatric Disorders

OBJECTIVES

- To be aware of family interaction patterns associated with individual psychiatric disorders
- To know the indications for, and techniques of, family intervention in combination with other treatment methods in specific psychiatric disorders

INTRODUCTION

The purpose of this chapter is not to discuss in great detail each of the diagnostic entities as exemplified by an individual patient. (This information is available in standard textbooks of psychiatry.) Rather, we will indicate those specific issues that are of particular interest to the family therapist in relation to a few selected psychiatric (DSM-III-R, Axis I)[1] disorders. For each psychiatric condition discussed, guidelines for family intervention are suggested, along with useful treatment strategies and techniques, and assessment of their relative effectiveness.

At times treatment will be largely focused on the obvious and explicit psychiatric symptoms of the identified patient (as in the acute phase of major depressive disorder). When the identified patient has a specific major psychiatric diagnosis, treatment of the individual may be relatively conventional. For example, antipsychotic medications will probably be used to treat the positive symptoms of schizophrenia.

324

However, in most instances treatment will be indicated for both the specific symptoms of the individual family member and the family problems and interactions that are concomitant to these conditions. Some of the family problems may be related to the etiology of the individual illness, some may be secondary to it, others may adversely affect the future course of the illness, while others may not be connected at all. For example, if schizophrenia has developed in a spouse early in the marriage, the therapist's attention must be directed to treatment of the mental illness *as well as* to the nature of the marital interaction, including its possible role in exacerbating the illness. If there is a major psychiatric disorder in one of the family members, attention must be paid to the families ability to cope with the illness, as well as to the manifestations of the disorder that may be symptomatic of, or interferring with, the attempts to deal with the family's other problems in living.

In summary, a major theme of this text is that family interventions for many psychiatric disorders will be just one component of a multimodality prescription. But that intervention may be crucial to success.

THE FAMILY MODEL AND INDIVIDUAL DIAGNOSIS

Labeling is used by people in all lines of work as a shorthand method for classifying information and communicating to others. In medicine, psychiatry, and related fields, the traditional focus of healing and treatment has been on disease and disorder. For some family therapists, any kind of labeling of the individual is anathema, as it locates the problems in the individual while ignoring the role of family members and other environmental conditions and stimuli. We believe, however, that with increasing evidence for the multiple causes of many psychiatric syndromes, including genetic, neurochemical, individual, and environmental, attention must be paid to both individual diagnosis and family interactions (see Chapter 7 for a fuller discussion of this issue). In this chapter we discuss a few syndromes described in the American Psychiatric Association's *Diagnostic and Statistical Manual of Mental Disorders, Revised Edition,* (DSM-III - R, Second Draft, 1986)[1] and ICD-9.

Some of the innovative features of the DSM-III-R include not only the course, age and onset, essential clinical features, degree of incapacity, differential diagnosis, and predisposing factors of each disorder, but also the sex ratio and familial pattern. The system is multiaxial as follows:

Axis I: Clinical Syndromes and V Codes (see below).
Axis II: Developmental Disorders and Personality Disorders.
Axis III: Physical Disorders and Conditions.

Axis IV: Severity of Psychosocial Stresses.
Axis V: Global Assessment of Functioning.

The system is devised to categorize the pathology of the individual patient, with only a relatively minor attention to the environmental factors in the individual's condition, including the family factors. Those individuals who do not have a diagnosable condition from symptom pattern or personality traits but who complain of discomfort due to family stressors are classified under the rubric of "Conditions Not Attributable to a Mental Disorder That Are a Focus of Attention or Treatment." These are the V codes referred to on Axis I (above).

The subcategories of "Conditions Not Attributable to a Mental Disorder..." include (but are not limited) to the following:

1. *Marital problem:* This category may be used when a focus of attention or treatment is a marital problem that is apparently not due to a mental disorder.

2. *Parent–child problem:* This category may be used when a focus of attention or treatment is a parent–child problem that is apparently not due to a mental disorder of the individual (parent or child) who is be evaluated.

3. *Other interpersonal problems:* This category may be used when a focus of attention or treatment is an interpersonal problem (other than marital or parent–child) that is apparently not due to a mental disorder of the individual who is being evaluated. Examples may include difficulties with coworkers or with romantic partners.

In some instances, one of these conditions will be noted because, following a thorough evaluation, no mental disorder is found in the present in any of the family members. In other instances, the scope of the diagnostic evaluation was not such as to adequately determine the presence or absence of a mental disorder, but there is a need to note the reason or the contact with the mental health care system. With further information, the presence of a mental disorder may become apparent. Finally, an individual may have a mental disorder, but the focus of attention or treatment is for a condition that is not due to the mental disorder. For example, an individual with bipolar affective disorder may have marital problems that do not seem directly related to the manifestations of the affective disorder but are the principle focus of treatment.

In addition to the above mentioned V codes that involve interpersonal difficulties that come to the family therapist, there are many situations in which a family comes for help in which one or more members do have diagnosable conditions. Likewise, there are situations in which an individual is evaluated and found to have a particular mental disorder and there is need for family/marital evaluation. The focus of this chapter is on those individual mental disorders that often indicate the need for assessment of the family and possible marital/family intervention at some time in the course of the mental disorder.

A recent survey[3] of family therapists indicates that they see the DSM-III diagnosis of the individual as useful, but incomplete for assessment and treatment planning. DSM-III-R almost totally ignores the relational context (meaning "the family") of the individual who has the symptoms. From a family therapist's point of view it is imperative that DSM-III-R be amended to include needed family contextual information.[2,3] It has been suggested that this be done by inclusion of an axis that documents positive and negative aspects of the relational context in which the identified patient lives. This could be accomplished by narrative social context formulations, global ratings of the family context, or a categorical or dimensionalized assessment of the family. Future clinical and research effort is needed to generate the most helpful procedures in this regard.

SCHIZOPHRENIC DISORDERS

From the early days of the family movement, family therapists have had a fascination with schizophrenics and their families. It is precisely in this area, relating to the most serious and obvious of mental illnesses and family interaction, that in the last ten years the family approach has changed dramatically.

Early family theorists were interested in the family's role in the *etiology* of schizophrenia. These writers emphasized concepts such as the schizophrenogenic mother,[4] faulty boundary setting, and family interactions such as "double bind,"[5,6] "pseudomutuality,"[7] and "schism and skew."[8] In contrast, current conceptualizations have been influenced by subsequent research concerning the multicausal factors in the etiology of schizophrenia. Schizophrenia is now understood to be a strongly familial disorder; the familial aggregation of schizophrenics appear to result largely from genetic factors.[9] A vulnerability/stress model of schizophrenic episodes[10] emphasizes individual deficits (e.g., information-processing deficits, autonomic reactivity anomalies, social competence and coping limitations) in combination with stressors (life events, family environmental stress) in the causation of psychotic episodes (see Figure 22-1).

Early family therapists were enthusiastic about the new approach, and the development of family treatment approaches was based on very little sophisticated research. Subsequently, there has been a growing body of research data both concerning interactions of families (including those of schizophrenics) and family therapy outcome. In 1962, a team of British investigators reported that patients who returned to live with their families following psychiatric hospitalization were more prone to rehospitalization than were those patients who went to boarding homes and hostels upon discharge.[11] In order to further these interesting leads, this group developed a semi-structured interview to quantify the family en-

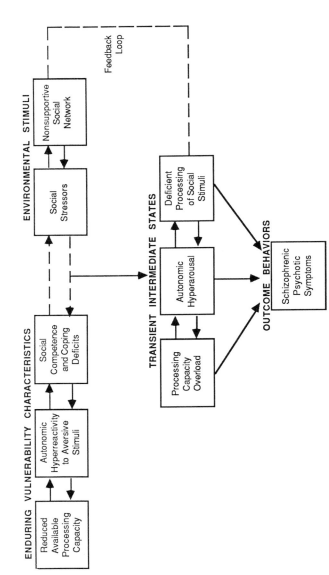

Figure 22-1. A tentative, interactive vulnerability/stress model for the development of schizophrenic psychotic episodes. From Nuechterlein K and Dawson M: A heuristic vulnerability/stress model of schizophrenic episodes. Schiz Bull 10:300-312, 1984. With permission.

vironment to which the patient would return. This instrument, the Camberwell Family Interview (CFI) provides measures of what these researchers have termed "*expressed emotion*" (EE), which is primarily an index of the family's criticism of, and overinvolvement with, the identified patient. In subsequent years, it has been found both with British and American samples that the percentage of patients in families with high expressed emotion who relapse, or are rehospitalized, is significantly higher than the percentage in the low EE homes. Although bypassing the question of etiology, this work is elegant in its simplicity and directness in showing that expressed emotion as manifested mainly in *hostility* expressed by family members toward the schizophrenic patient and *overinvolvement* by family members (i.e., spending more than 35 hours a week in face-to-face contact) does relate to resumption of symptomatology and rehospitalization.

This work has led to another element that is quite different in the current scene, and this is the *specificity* of family therapeutic approaches concerning schizophrenia (as opposed to the earlier work, which was nonspecific and like that applied to patients and families across diagnostic groups). In fact, early family therapists had an aversion to diagnoses of individual patients (in part because of their enthusiasm for emphasizing the role of the family system in creating an identified patient). With this orientation, there was an aversion to talking about specialized family therapy approaches to any and most diagnostic groups. However, influenced by the Brown research, the next logical step was to put together treatment packages with the specific goals of reducing familial hostility and overinvolvement. Such an investigation would not only provide data on a potential intervention strategy, but also provide experimental evidence that EE indeed has some causal relationship to the course of the illness. In the last few years, this work has been carried on in the United States[12,13] and in England.[14] This therapeutic approach has been used with chronic schizophrenics on an outpatient basis[12] and with more acutely disturbed schizophrenics in brief therapy immediately following hospitalization.[15] The major goals and strategies and techniques of these related groups of researchers are listed in Table 22-1.

A further major factor is the way family therapy is currently conceived as only part of the intervention package for schizophrenia, with attention to other aspects of that treatment and the timing of the family intervention. This is in contrast to the earlier approaches, which emphasized the paramount role of family therapy as described by family therapy advocates. McFarlane and Beels[16] point out that the family therapist must be extremely flexible and creative in approaching the schizophrenic and his family over the course of the illness. Wynne[17] emphasizes that family intervention can be a useful part of the treatment of schizophrenia in different forms at several different phases of the illness. During crisis periods when the patient is psychotic and may need hospitalization, contact is not only helpful to the family but beneficial for later collaboration with treat-

Table 22-1
Models of Intervention for Families With a Schizophrenic Member

Treatment Parameters	Model		
	Falloon	Hogarty	Leff
Mediating Goals			
Increase knowledge about schizophrenia	xxx	xxx	xx
Reduce family guilt	x	x	x
Explicit reduction of EE	-	-	xxx
Implicit reduction of EE	x	x	x
Improve communication skills	xxx	x	x
Improve problem solving skills	xxx	x	x
Strategies and Techniques			
Psychoeducation	xxx	xxx	xxx
Communication Training	xxx	-	x
Training in problem solving	xxx	xx	x
Contingency contracting	xx	-	-
Setting limits on unacceptable behavior	x	xx	x
Social skills training	x	-	-
Setting appropriate family boundaries	-	xx	x
Clarifying patient responsibilities	x	xx	-
Systems interventions	-	x	x
Dynamic strategies (e.g., interpretations)	-	-	x

ment personnel. The family therapist should take a positive, interested, un-demanding and *uninterpretive* stance toward the family during this phase. The acute psychosis may last for several weeks (or months), during which hospitaliza-tion may proceed, with use of neuroleptic medication. Many suggest that conjoint family meetings with the patient during this period are contraindicated as being too stimulating for the patient. Wynne counsels that family meetings with the patient should not be automatically ruled out, and in some cases brief meetings followed by more extensive ones may be helpful. During the subsequent subacute phase when symptoms are subsiding, the family's feelings (e.g., guilt, anger, wor-ry) are more likely to emerge. In the subchronic phase, (three to nine months) florid symptoms give way and expose negative symptoms such as lack of initia-tive and apathy in the patient. The families at this point need information and support in dealing with the chronic condition. The psychoeducational approach (see below) can be instituted at this phase, consisting of educational workshops with other families, family support groups, etc.

Psychoeducational Family Intervention

As an example of a well-formulated family intervention package, we summarize here the psychoeducational family program for families with a chronic schizophrenic member articulated by Anderson and colleagues.[13] The overall goals of the program are (1) to decrease the patient's vulnerability to environmental stimuli through maintenance medication, and (2) to stabilize the family environment by increasing their knowledge of the illness and supporting and mobilizing their coping strategies. These goals are approached through a four-phase process that spans several years.

Phase I begins during hospitalization of the identified patient (or just shortly after discharge in family sessions without the patient who is presumed to be too sick and/or agitated to be present). The focus of these sessions is on the families experience of the illness, including an exploration of their thoughts about the causes of the illness and the burdens that it places on them. The family therapist serves as an ombudsman for the family in dealing with the hospital ward, and the families strengths and commitment to helping the patient are encouraged and mobilized without making premature interventions that might alienate the family. The family therapist negotiates some realistic goals with the family and elicits a commitment to therapy for at least a year's duration.

Phase II consists of a day-long workshop with the family and similar families in which the treatment team provides basic information about the illness, its causes and course. In order to further the aims of future changes in family behavior toward the identified patient, it is emphasized that schizophrenia is a cognitive and perceptual disturbance, with likely genetic and biological causes, with a hypersensitivity to stimulation, including that coming from the family environment. Families are encouraged to reduce stimulation surrounding the patient by setting limits on emotional, involved behaviors, providing a low-keyed environment with structure, with little expectation on the patient for social and vocational performance.

When the acute phase of the illness has subsided, *Phase III* begins, which involves six months to a year of family sessions with the patient present for the sessions. The focus during these sessions is appropriate family boundaries and patient responsibility. Needed space and "time outs" are emphasized, and "mind reading" and over-responding to every symptom are discouraged. The marital/parental coalition is supported, and both patient and family are encouraged to make ties outside in the local neighborhood and community. The patient is encouraged by the treatment team to make a slow, low-key resumption of personal responsibility.

Once it is thought that the patient and family have achieved their maximum capacity for effective daily functioning, Phase IV begins with the option of either periodic maintenance sessions or more intensive family therapy on family interaction issues (e.g., marital conflict, sibling dysfunction, etc.).

In terms of the five basic strategies of family intervention as outlined in Chapter 12, the Anderson approach emphasizes conveying of information necessary for the best attitude to problem-solving around the illness in Phase I and II, followed by family communicational and problem-solving strategies in Phase III. Phase IV is either maintenance, using the strategies already mentioned, or more extensive use of strategies for restructuring family systems behaviors.

The Anderson psychoeducational approach is extremely well-thought out, thorough, and phased over the acute and more chronic phases of the illness, a plan that is extremely reasonable for a life-time serious illness such as schizophrenia. However, the approach demands much time and resources from the local mental health community, and this is in most cases not a possible approach. It is likely that the spirit of the approach will be used in local settings with modifications made by budgetary necessity (e.g., group approaches, fewer sessions). In addition, there is research that suggests even brief family intervention, either during the hospitalization[18] or immediately following hospitalization[15] may also be beneficial to the families of schizophrenics.

Paradoxical Intervention

We should not conclude this section without contrasting the psychoeducational approach with the creative work of Palizzoli and her colleagues[19] in using paradoxical approaches with schizophrenics and their families. In 12 sessions, once-a-month family treatment of one-year duration, this group approaches the family as a team and delivers injunctions, which are intended to disrupt and change nodal transaction patterns, thought to keep the patient in a particular symptomatic role. For example, overinvolved parents of a schizophrenic are told to go out once a week without letting their child know where they are. The assumption that the parental system is lacking in intimacy and the child is not being allowed to separate the intervention promotes positive change for all family members. While this approach is most exciting, it needs research verification of its effectiveness and delineation of which particular groups of schizophrenics and their families for which it is most effective.

MOOD DISORDERS

The association between marital/family conflict and mood disorders such as mania and depression can be conceived in a number of possible ways.

Marital/family stressors may elicit or precipitate depressive symptoms in a biologically vulnerable individual; marital/family stress or the lack of a sufficiently supportive intimate relationship may potentiate the effects of other environmental stressors; depressive symptoms may trigger maladaptive behaviors and negative responses from family members, thus acting to elicit marital/family conflict; or sub-clinical depression or characterological traits, behavior patterns, etc., may potentiate marital/family discord which, in turn, tends to trigger the onset of a depressive episode.[20,21]

Among some endogenous depressives, social dysfunction appears not to antedate onset of depressive symptoms. Instead, certain chronic forms of personality change and social maladjustment appear to develop over the course of repeated depressive episodes.[20,22] However, for a subset of depressed (primary affective disorder) patients, the chronic baseline impairment of social functioning is antecedent to, or coextensive with, the expression of the depressive symptoms. In a longitudinal study of depressed women,[23] clinically recovered depressives continued to experience problems functioning in their parental and spousal roles several months after recovery from the depressive symptoms. Moreover, the differential benefits of an interpersonally oriented psychotherapy over drugs alone in a sample of depressed women were shown to be specifically in the area of *social functioning*, manifest only in long-term outcome at six and eight month follow-up, and only several months after patients experienced relief from the depressive symptoms.[24,25] Hence, the presence of depressive symptoms is not a necessary precondition to marital/familial distress in these patients, but interpersonal dysfunction is viewed as one of several components of a depressive personality disorder and a relatively constant background to the affective episodes. There is a growing body of literature on the marital interaction between a depressed spouse and his/her mate.[26] The depressive's tendency to be aversive to others in social situations[27] is associated with his/her tendency to receive aversive responses from others[28]; the depressed individual tends to give and receive aversive stimulation at higher rates than evidences by other members of the family.[29] Similarly, there is some evidence that a depressed partner and his mate tend to engage in negative (aversive) exchanges more frequently than do non-distressed, "normal" couples.[30-32] Furthermore, "distressed" couples are more reactive to recent events, positive or negative, than are their non-distressed counterpart.[33]

Treatment Guidelines

The temporal and functional relationships between depression and aspects of marital/family interaction have important implications for the design and implementation of marital/family treatment of depressive disorders. In cases of depression, marital/family conflict is often reported as the primary precipitant in episodes of clinical depression. In such cases, marital or family therapy would be indicated for treatment of the interpersonal problems, often directed to (1) reducing the frequency of aversive communications between partners, and (2) inducing more frequent mutual reinforcement, as well as modification of distorted cognitive and perceptual responses to the behavior of the partner.[33] Antidepressant medication can be combined with these therapies for symptom relief without risk of compromising their effectiveness.[34] In cases where marital or family conflict appears not to be a contributing factor in the depressive episode, the identified patient should be treated with appropriate medication and then reevaluated for psychotherapy. The addition of short-term supportive marital and/or family therapies may be useful in helping to engage the patient in the recommended medication regimen.

With cases of endogenous depression, the stress of intimate relations with the depressed patient and the negative impact of the patient's symptoms on other members of the family[35] suggest the need for a bi-phasic program of marital or family intervention. During the initial phase, psychopharmacological treatments are begun and short-term supportive marital or family therapy is introduced to ameliorate the family's negative reactions to the symptoms (thus reducing secondary stress reactions) and to educate the patient and family to the nature of the disorder, the recommended treatment, and strategies for coping with residual symptoms and possible relapse. The family can be helpful (directly to the patient and indirectly in maintaining its own homeostasis) by recognizing symptoms (especially hypomania), by monitoring the patient's mood, by being aware of early signs of medication toxicity such as nausea, vomiting, diarrhea, ataxia, and dysarthria, and by encouraging medication compliance. Family therapy has the objective of helping the family develop new patterns necessary as a result of the patient's changes in role and function stemming from both the illness and the medication.

It is only after the florid symptoms have cleared and the patient and family have reached a plateau or relatively stable stage of adjustment that a second phase of therapy can be initiated with the family. Efforts to modify maladaptive communication patterns and problem-solving strategies, deal with resistances and effect structural changes are best reserved for this second phase of intervention with the family.

Case Illustration

One of the authors (IDG) recently treated a couple, both of whom suffered from recurrent depressive disorder. Mr. A. was a 46-year-old lawyer and his wife, Dr. A., was a 45-year-old physician. They had three children, ages 12, 9, and 6. The couple was referred for marital treatment (as a last resort) because of dissatisfaction with the marriage, so that divorce was seen as the only solution. Over the last year there had been an intensification of fighting (and mutual blaming) between the couple that had dated back to the beginning of the marriage some 20 years earlier. The areas of conflict focused on money and childrearing. Dr. A.'s need for control of the relationship was evident in financial and parenting issues, while Mr. A. was attempting unsuccessfully to combat her domination. To accomplish this, he would criticize his wife's attempts in both areas. For example, she would discipline the children; he would say she should not have been so tough on them. When she did not discipline them, he would proclaim that she was negligent.

Their past history revealed that both had been brought up in Europe in what they described as chaotic households, with parents who were also fighting more than their peers' parents. Each of them had a parent who had experienced depressive episodes. The history of past treatment attempts revealed that both husband and wife had had separate, classical psychoanalyses, which they described as "helpful but not sufficient to end the marital fighting." Diagnosis for both was Major Depressive Disorder, Recurrent Type.

When family treatment started, both were so depressed, manifesting symptoms of loss of interest and pleasure, low self-esteem, and lack of energy, that treatment sessions were centered around mutual blaming. Three sessions led to no improvement. At that point, antidepressant medication was instituted. After six weeks, they both experienced considerable improvement in mood and activity level.

This change afforded the therapist with two tactical advantages. Most obvious was the fact that with the mood improvement in cognitive set, the couple could now conceivably begin to deal with behavioral interactions that might build a viable relationship. Secondly, the therapist was now viewed as an expert who could prescribe tasks (e.g., taking the right medication) that were effective, and thus was in a position to prescribe interpersonal tasks to change the previously described negative feedback systems such as Dr. A.'s control, Mr. A.'s criticism, and their resulting morass of further depression and lowered self-esteem. At this point, the therapist took advantge of this position by guiding the couple to interpersonal changes that led to further marital improvement.

This case is an illustration of our experience that, whenever possible, when treating an initial or recurrent, acute depressive disorder in one or several members of a family unit, a combination of chemotherapy and family therapy was the most efficacious treatment strategy.

ANXIETY DISORDERS

The syndrome of agoraphobia, a type of anxiety disorder, is defined as a generalized fear of leaving home.[1] There are a variety of theories to explain this disorder, including good evidence that biological causes play an important role in its etiology. For the family therapist, this condition represents an interpersonal problem. There may be a mutually reinforcing system in which the dependent person is kept dependent by the significant other, usually the spouse, to cover up that individual's anger and dependence. The symptom bearer finds a symbolic, dysfunctional way of communicating with and controlling the spouse (e.g., a wife who refuses to leave the house, and thus forces her husband to stay home and take care of her).

Marital therapy (or behavior therapy) in combination with medication is the treatment of choice.[36] Individual behavior modification is not nearly as effective as family behavior modification because it tends to overlook the reinforcing nature of the interpersonal interaction.[37]

While there is little research on the interaction of general anxiety and the marital relationship, or investigation of the relative benefits of individual and marital treatment in this situation, there is some growing information on the relationship of agoraphobia and its treatment to the marital dyad.

Is the symptom of agoraphobia in a spouse related to the personality of the other spouse or the marital interaction? The answer seems to be complicated. In one study[38] the husbands of agoraphobic women could not be distinguished from the husbands of normal matched controls.

Does the removal of the agoraphobia in one spouse have systems effects on the marital relationship or on the adjustment of the other spouse? Again, the answer is probably not simple. In a behavioral treatment study of women with agoraphobia, there was no evidence of symptoms arising in the nonagoraphobic spouse.[39] On the other hand, in a study of the marital interaction of 36 married agoraphobic women treated by Hafner[40] over a period of three years, seven of the husbands displayed abnormal jealousy that adversely influenced the wife's response to treatment. Improvement in the wives was associated with increased jealousy in the husbands. In a more recent study of the husbands of 26 agoraphobic women, before and after intensive in vivo exposure treatment of the wives for agoraphobia, Hafner[41] found that most husbands had experienced transitory negative reactions including anxiety and depression. These negative reactions were often coincident with large, rapid improvements in the most severely disturbed patients. Hafner suggested that negative effects were most likely in those men who were hostile, critical, and unsupportive of their wives and who had adapted to their wives disability as part of a sex role stereotyped view of marriage.

This complicated picture suggests that in some situations, the wife can be successfully treated individually with behavioral interventions with no need for marital intervention. On the other hand, in some situations, especially where the male is hostile and has some investment in the wife's symptom picture, involving the spouse in the treatment may be quite necessary.

The addition of the spouse as a co-therapist in the behavioral treatment of the spouse with the phobia may enhance the treatment effect for nonsystems reasons. For example, Munby and Johnston[42] followed 66 agoraphobic patients 5–9 years after their involvement in a behavioral treatment. Patients who had a home-based program utilizing the husband as a co-therapist fared somewhat better than those not involving the husband. The authors suggest that this is because the patient and spouse learned to deal with the agoraphobic problem themselves with less need for further professional intervention.

PSYCHOACTIVE SUBSTANCE USE DISORDERS

Alcohol Dependence and Abuse

"Alcoholism isn't a spectator sport. Eventually the whole family gets to play."[43] Alcohol abuse may be a way of dealing with conflicts that cannot be expressed directly with family members, and it allows the alcoholic to express feelings (for example, anger) that cannot be expressed to family members without drinking. When the family member is drinking, a position of one-upmanship or control over the nonaffected family members is assumed. It is thus a way of sending a relationship-defining message while at the same time denying the message.[44]

It has not been demonstrated that family therapy alone is effective in changing the long-term course of the chronic, fixed alcoholic, but it may be useful in helping the family to adjust to the identified patient's alcohol abuse.

A family approach to alcoholism consists of attaining sobriety and changing the family dynamics and structure.[45] The main and first task is to cool off the high degree of reactivity to the alcoholic and to increase the emotional distance in the family system. To attain sobriety, Antabuse or Alcoholics Anonymous (or both) may be utilized. Family therapy is not possible while there is frequent disruptive drunkenness. The next phase of therapy is helping the nonalcoholic spouse to become detached from his or her emotional reactivity to the drinking. At this stage the spouse's distance may exacerbate the identified patient's emotional communication; thus there is a need for both AA or Al-Anon and conjoint family sessions to establish a new homeostasis, or when indicated to initiate sex therapy.

Not all patients with alcoholism follow a chronic course. An intermittent increase in drinking is often a response to a problem within the family. In these cases alcoholism can be appropriately treated with family therapy.

Case Illustration

In the A. family, the identified patient was Ms. A., a 36-year-old, white, single, Catholic, filing clerk. Ms. A. was hospitalized on the medical service because of acute gastritis secondary to a prolonged bout of alcohol intoxication. History revealed that she had a 20-year history of alcohol abuse. Medical staff noted that the alcohol abuse was now complicated by alcohol withdrawal symptoms and poor treatment compliance. Drinking episodes began at 14 when the patient began to drink (like her father) in order to "calm her nerves." Recent episodes seem related to either quarrels with her mother or around the anniversary of her father's death some 10 years ago. It was noteworthy that the mother had lost her job some 20 years ago and since then has been homebound. She and her daughter were in a continual struggle for control, with the patient exerting the mother to become more involved in life and socializing, while the mother was encouraging the patient to stop drinking and get a job. A maternal aunt was supporting both the identified patient and the mother.

Our understanding of the case was that the alcohol abuse was serving to deflect away from change on either part of the mother or patient toward more independent functioning. Patient diagnosis was Alcohol Abuse Disorder. Treatment goals were oriented around changing the family system to break up the symbiosis to allow the mother to socialize with her peers, and to allow the patient to become more independent and work more consistently. The treatment prescribed was family therapy, Alcoholics Anonymous, and Al-Anon.

Care must be taken that the nonaffected spouse does not prompt the alcoholic patient's drinking.[46,47] The spouse is the supplier and the victim simultaneously. For example, in the D. family, the wife was the identified patient with an alcohol problem. Husband and wife came to treatment complaining that they never went out together. After months of therapy the husband took his wife to a *wine-testing* festival. The script involves a continual reenactment of provocation, misbehavior, remorse, and atonement.

Are women alcoholics different from alcoholic men? There have been very few systematic studies of family treatment for the woman alcoholic. A review by Dinaburg and associates has pointed out that among the studies that have reported some success for family therapy for alcoholic women, none were controlled, and there were no post-treatment follow-ups.[48] That group reported a case with a 9-year follow-up. The data suggested that marital therapy, as the only intervention is not efficacious for treating women alcoholics and their families.

In contrast to the generally accepted speculation that alcoholism may result from cultural, environmental, and psychological influences, new epidemiologic evidence suggests that in addition to environmental factors, there is a strong genetic component to this disease.[49]

Substance Abuse

There is a difference between chronic use of drugs that cause physical dependence, such as barbiturates, cocaine and heroin, and casual use of nonaddicting agents, such as marijuana and LSD. The former category has been thought to be extremely resistive to family therapy intervention.

Clearly the most systematic and thorough attempt to use family intervention is the work of Stanton and Todd[50] with male heroin addicts. Their work is exceptional for the rigorousness of their methodology. By randomly assigning male heroin addicts (under age 36) to either (1) paid family therapy, (2) unpaid family therapy, (3) paid family movie (a placebo condition), or (4) individual counseling plus methadone, they show the superiority of family intervention. As interesting was the nature of family intervention used.

For this sample, the typical family structure was a very close and dependent mother–son dyad with a distant, excluded father. In approximately 80 percent of the cases, there was a parent with a drinking problem. A structural, and at times strategic, family therapy was used in an average of 10 family sessions. Thus, the major techniques of intervention included joining and accomodating to the system, restructuring boundaries, enactment, unbalancing the system, assigning tasks and homework to consolidate changes made during the session, and use of paradoxical interventions. The therapist kept the sessions focused on drug use until stable improvement had been achieved.

An overall strategy was to alter the repetitive interactional patterns that were seen as maintaining the drug taking. In practical terms, the most basic restructuring move was getting the parents to work together in relating to the addict, lest the triadic conflictual pattern persist and treatment fail. In the typical situation of a mother–son overinvolvement, a common technique was to get the father to take charge of the son. Family crises were common, and the general treatment strategy was to contain them within the family, and thus avoid spillover such as hospitalization, increasing medications, or extruding the addict from the home precipitously.

It was not uncommon for parental crises to emerge during the treatment, especially marital problems or heavy drinking by one parent. The general strategy was to keep the parents working together and not to separate until the IP's addiction was under control. Thus, the focus was on the parents as a parental system rather than a marital system during the first phases of treatment. Once the IP was stabilized and drug-free for some time, the intervention could focus on the marital pair.

Such drug users are sometimes removed from their sociocultural milieu, and family therapy is often not possible until the patient is detoxified. After that, many cases of cocaine and heroin addiction are chronic, i.e., will exacerbate chronically and therefore *require* family intervention. Some facilities are treating the nonaddicted drug user (even those, for example, with occasional mixed use of alcohol, marijuana, amphetamines, and psychedelics) by using family therapy as a primary form of treatment. This is based on the rationale that the drug use is a symptom of disturbed functioning and communication within the family.[51,52]

There are excellent critical reviews of studies related to the use of family therapy for drug abuse[53-56] and of studies of family treatment applied to drug problems.[57]

PERSONALITY DISORDERS

A common situation arises when a marital couple enters therapy with complaints about one or both person's basic character structure. Only later may the problem come to be seen as arising from a change in the family phase or from an acute crisis in the family, such as the loss of a job. Restructuring personality is extremely difficult by any method, but it may be possible to help the family system master its life-cycle tasks or to live with the character styles of the marital partners.

Patients with histrionic personality disorder are often excitable, unstable, overly reactive, self-dramatizing, seductive, and attention seeking. Such patients may marry obsessive-compulsive spouses, seeing in them strength, reliability, and firmness, whereas, at times, the spouses' real characteristics are those of rigidity and coldness. There are usually marked sexual problems between such couples.

Obsessive-compulsive marital partners are often attracted by what they take to be the other partner's sociability and spontaneity, only to later perceive that this same behavior is childish and non-goal-directed. The obsessive-compulsive husband increasingly withdraws at the same time that the histrionic wife becomes more flamboyant in her actions. Drug or alcohol abuse is often found in this relationship.

Other examples of couples with related personality styles are listed in Chapter 8 in our Table of Family Typologies.

ORGANIC MENTAL DISORDERS

Organic mental disorders that are especially common are those associated with presenile or senile brain disease or with chronic atherosclerotic brain disease. In addition, there are a variety of other chronic brain syndromes—for example, Alzheimer's Disease or cerebral vascular accidents—that incapacitate patients and create problems for their spouses and children.

Chronic *dementias* may create a great deal of havoc in the family. There is often much guilt (if the identified patient is hospitalized) and anger (if he or she is kept at home) felt by relatives. A family therapist in such situations must help the family face reality in coping with change and in making the necessary alterations in its structure and function. There may need to be greater contact with the extended family, relatives, or other members of the kinship system. A common problem is that guilt and anger are displaced. For example, when father has a stroke, a lot of old feelings of anger and resentment may be stirred up in the son. The sugges-

then say, "It's not that I don't want to spend the money; it's my wife who doesn't want to spend it." Alternatively the decision to bring an impaired parent into a nuclear family stirs up a great deal of feelings. When the disabled parent comes into the home and changes the family homeostasis, the task of the family therapist is to help the family to cope with these changes; in this situation the family should attempt change and not try to even up old scores.

As a last caveat, it should be noted that not all problems that appear to be due to family causes actually are. The family therapist should constantly be aware of the potential of organic disorders causing behavioral symptoms that at first glance seem to be causally related to change in the family.

Case Illustration

Mrs. R., a 60-year-old white, female, executive secretary presented for a diagnostic evaluation because of memory loss. She gave a three-year history of progressive inability to do her work because she was forgetting things, could not follow complicated tasks, and was "irritable on the job" (a marked change from her previous premorbid personality as a quiet, careful worker). Once Mrs. R. quit her job, her 65-year-old husband also quit his in order to "take care of her." Her functioning, however, continued to decline, and she developed a 20-pound weight loss, visual hallucinations, increasing forgetfulness, paranoia, and confusion. Antidepressants in low doses did not alleviate the syndrome. Three consultations (two with neurologists and one with an internist) suggested that the patient had senile dementia (due to vascular causes) and suggested a nursing home for placement.

The primary difficulty in implementing this placement was that Mr. R. saw his wife as having a temporary illness and could not accept her being placed away from home (and from him). He also was beginning to show signs of an early organic brain disorder.

The treatment suggested was marital therapy, with the objective of assisting the husband to return to work and to help him place his wife in a more appropriate facility, i.e., the nursing home.

The L. family consisted of father, age 40, mother, age 36, and son, age 7. After 10 years of reasonably happy married life, the mother became disenchanted and decided she wanted a divorce. A bitter struggle ensued between the parents. Several months following this struggle, the son began to have difficulty in school and developed temper tantrums. He became more and more of a problem to handle.

Based on the family difficulties, family therapy was suggested. Six months of family therapy resulted in worsening symptoms in the son, although the parents' separation became smoother. At this point the son became disoriented and had greater difficulty with schoolwork. A neurological consultant discovered signs of organic change. A full diagnostic evaluation revealed that the son had a brain tumor.

EATING DISORDERS

Eating disorders, including both anorexia nervosa and bulimia, have a typical onset in adolescence or early adult life, predominantly in females, and with seeming increasing frequency in our culture. Most clinicians argue for an integrated, multimodal treatment.[58,59] The family therapy work of Minuchin and colleagues[60] suggests that family therapy may be useful either alone or adjunctive to other treatments (e.g., hospitalization, medication behavioral programs) for the disorder. According to Halmi,[61] there is no typical family constellation when the identified patient has anorexia nervosa or bulimia. Because of this, she suggests an individualized approach when utilizing the family model. Different subsystems of the family may have to be seen (in contrast to always seeing the whole family) in planning strategies of intervention.

DISORDERS USUALLY FIRST EVIDENT IN INFANCY OR CHILDHOOD

Pervasive Developmental Disorder: Autistic Disorder

There is a heterogeneous group of disorders that includes what previously was called "childhood schizophrenia." When the disorder is severe and the child has few communicative skills, interactional therapies yield poor results. Controlled studies of family therapy with this group are scant. There has been very little evidence supporting the notion that the family may be the causal agent for this disorder. Having an autistic child makes it difficult for a family to function effectively. Family therapy by itself has not been shown to be effective treatment for this disorder.

Attention-Deficit Hyperactivity Disorder

Attention deficit syndrome is characterized by hyperactivity, short attention span, restlessness, distractibility, and impulsiveness. It is often associated with Axis II Developmental disorders in arithmetic, reading, language, etc., the so-called learning disabilities. In moderate to severe cases, medication and tutoring can be used to modify the symptoms. In all cases, behavioral interventions in the classroom and in the home (e.g., structuring) should be used to help the child to limit stimuli and control himself or herself. Consultation with the family is often "lifesaving" in cooling a family crisis (or long-term turmoil). Family intervention is necessary to provide psychoeducation about attention-deficit disorder (*the appropriate pattern is that parents blame each other and/or the child for what is primarily a physiologic disorder*) and instruction in behavioral techniques may be quite useful.

Mental Retardation

The term "mental retardation" comprises a variety of etiological possiblities, but in most instances there are secondary family problems.

In addition to the real problem of social development and functioning of the identified patient due to his or her possibly damaged biological equipment, there are the associated, often maladaptive, family reactions. The family feels a sense of antipathy, a sense of guilt, often social isolation, and actual anxiety about caring for the child's usual health needs.[62] Family members may make the mentally retarded child a scapegoat to cover up unresolved conflicts between mother and father or between parents and children.[63] Help must be focused on both the identified patient's specific needs and on the family's attitudes and behavior.

A high percentage of children who originally are diagnosed as mentally retarded turn out on closer examination to have interpersonal, familial, or cultural deprivation as the etiologic factor for their "mental retardation," rather than any specific organic or constitutional factors. This suggests some obvious family involvements both in the precipitation of this "disorder" and in its amelioration.

Conduct Disorders

The problem of delinquency appears to be an extremely complex one, involving social and cultural factors that have to be taken into account in any overall evaluation.

The parent of the same sex as the identified patient may be absent or inadequate. Parental limit-setting is either too lenient, too harsh, or extremely inconsistent. A "negative identity" and "bad-me" self-image may exist in many of these individuals.

The delinquent behavior is thought to be conditioned by parental covert expectations or overt approval. The child may get implicit cues to act in antisocial ways, together with explicit prohibitions against such activity. The unspoken message is, "Do it, but don't get caught!" The identified patient acts out the unconscious needs of the parents, who cannot tolerate such actions in their own behavior.[64]

Criminal behavior in adults may be residues of such earlier factors. In either juvenile delinquency or adult criminality, careful evaluation must be made to ascertain the extent to which patterns are acute or chronic, associated with stress or not, and acceptable to the individual or not. With respect to the possible use of family therapy, the involvement and interest of the family members in the antisocial individual needs to be ascertained. Such evaluation should aim to differentiate those instances in which family therapy would be helpful from those in which it might be fruitless.

In the area of juvenile delinquency, family therapists have attempted to direct their intervention toward ameliorating the defects mentioned above. Analogous attempts would be instituted in the case of adult criminality.

Minuchin's[65] focus is on helping the family to delay gratification by discussing their decisions before acting on them. The therapist attempts to define and strengthen the role structure of the family. Environmental manipulation is a major technique. The therapist must be extremely active in the therapy, especially in helping to reduce blaming. The identified patient often resists the work of family therapy, and the therapist must counter his self-destructive maneuvers.[66]

Family therapy is the treatment of choice for some conduct disorders of adolescence. Acting-out adolescents are less likely to form therapeutic alliances in individual therapy. With family therapy, blame may not be as focused on the offending adolescent, and it often shifts the responsibility for change onto all members of the family.

Anxiety Disorders of Childhood

This diagnostic category includes separation anxiety disorder, avoidant disorder, and overanxious disorder.

A recent survey of child psychiatrists in the United States indicates that family and individual therapy, often in combination, are the most frequently used interventions with childhood anxiety.[67] Behavioral techniques in both family and individual treatment are especially useful.

School phobias are ideal situations for family therapy. Commonly, when mother and child find it difficult to separate, there is an underlying marital problem. With all types of phobias, treatment of the individual by behavior modification should be considered, possibly using the parent as a co-therapist who assists with the behavioral exercises.

Mood Disorders

Although mood disorders have been discussed earlier in the chapter, one caveat must be mentioned. Recent research has demonstrated depressive as well as bipolar disorders may start in childhood or in adolescence. The clinical point is that both patient and family will deny their existence and focus mostly on the secondary family problems.

Just as in certain infections, it is not the direct destruction of the cell by the virus, but the response of the host that is responsible for producing the disease. So too, in psychiatry, there are certain behaviors that by themselves are not pathogenic, but the response of the family system that creates what we now call "pathology."

SUGGESTIONS FOR FURTHER READINGS

Patterson GR: **Coercive Family Process.** Eugene, OR: Castalia Publishing Co, 1982.
> *A book that can get quite technical about data analysis, but is nevertheless rewarding to the clinician who wants a feel for the interaction patterns in the family with a delinquent pre-adolescent, with concomitant recommendations for family intervention.*

Anderson C, Reiss D, and Hogarty G: **Schizophrenia and the Family.** New York: Guilford Press, 1986.
> *This is a detailed guide for implementing the psychoeducational approach to families with a schizophrenic member; an approach that is well thought out and researched.*

Clarkin JC, Haas G, and Glick ID (Eds): **Affective Disorder and the Family.** New York: Guilford Press, in press.
> *Chapters describe marital and family treatments for families with a depressed or bipolar patient.*

Goldstein M (Ed): **New Developments in Interventions with Families of Schizophrenics.** San Francisco: Jossey-Bass, 1981.
> *Includes chapters on the most important developments in the use of family intervention, along with other treatments for schizophrenia.*

Paolino T and McCrady B: **The Alcoholic Marriage: Alternative Perspectives.** New York: Grune & Stratton, 1977.
> *Systems therapy approaches to the alcoholic marriage.*

Stanton MD and Todd T: **The Family Therapy of Drug Abuse and Addiction.** New York: Guilford Press, 1982.
> *A rich, clinical description of the Addicts and Families Program in Philadelphia.*

Lansky MR: **Family Therapy and Major Psychopathology.** New York: Grune & Stratton, 1981.
> *This is the best textbook discussing the family model and schizophrenia, af-*

fective disorder, personality disorder, alcohol abuse disorder, organic brain disorder, and eating disorder.

REFERENCES

1. American Psychiatric Association: Diagnostic and Statistical Manual of Mental Disorder, Third Edition, Revised. Washington, D.C.: American Psychiatric Association, 1987

2. Wynne LC: A preliminary proposal for strengthening the multiaxial approach to DSM-III: Possible family-oriented revisions. Prepared for the American Psychiatric Association Workshop on DSM-III on Interim Appraisal. Washington, DC, October 14, 1983

3. Frances A, Clarkin J, and Perry S: Differential therapeutics in psychiatry: The art and science of treatment selection. New York: Brunner/Mazel, 1984

4. Fromm-Reichmann F: Notes on the development of schizophrenia by psychoanalytic psychotherapy. Psychiatry 11:267-277, 1948

5. Bateson G, Jackson DD, Haley J, et al.: Towards a theory of schizophrenia. Behav Sci 1:251-264, 1956

6. Bateson G, Jackson DD, Haley J, et al.: A note on the double bind—1962. Fam Process 2:154-161, 1963

7. Wynne LC, Ryckoff I, Day J, et al.: Pseudo-mutuality in the family relations of schizophrenics. In Bell NW and Vogel FF (Eds): A Modern Introduction to the Family. Glencoe, IL: Free Press, 1960, pp 573-594

8. Fleck S: Family dynamics and origin of schizophrenia. Psychosomatic Med 22:333-344, 1960

9. Kendler KS and Gruenberg AM: An independent analysis of the Copenhagen sample of the Danish adoption study of schizophrenia, VI. The pattern of psychiatric illness as defined by DSM-III in adoptees and relatives. Arch Gen Psychiatry 41:555-564, 1984

10. Nuechterlein KH and Dawson ME: Information processing and attentional functioning in the development course of schizophrenic disorders. Schiz Bull 10:160-203, 1984

11. Brown GW, Monck EM, Carstairs GM, and Wing JK: The influence of family life on the course of schizophrenic illness. Br J Prev Soc Med 16:55, 1962

12. Falloon IRH, Boyd JL, McGill CW, Razani J, Moss HB, and Gilderman AM: Family management in the prevention of exacerbations of schizophrenia: A controlled study. N Engl J Med 306:1437-1440, 1982

13. Anderson CM, Reiss DJ, and Hogarty GE: Schizophrenia and the family. New York: Guilford Press, 1986

14. Leff JP, Kuipers L, Berkowitz R, Eberlein-Vries R, and Sturgeon D: A controlled trial of social intervention in the families of schizophrenic patients. Br J Psychiatry 141:121-134, 1982

15. Goldstein MJ, Rodnick EH, Evans JR, May PR, and Steinberg M: Drug and family therapy in the aftercare treatment of acute schizophrenia. Arch Gen Psychiatry 35:1169-1177, 1978

16. McFarlane WR and Beels C: A decision tree model for integrating family therapies for schizophrenia. In McFarlane WR (Ed): Family Therapy in Schizophrenia. New York: Guilford Press, 1983, pp 325-335

17. Wynne LC: A phase-oriented approach to treatment with schizophrenics and their families. In McFarlane WR (Ed): Family Therapy in Schizophrenia. New York: Guilford Press, 1983, pp 251-265

18. Glick ID, Clarkin JF, Spencer JH, Haas GL, Lewis AB, Peyser J, Demane N, Good-Ellis M, Harris E, and Lestelle V: A controlled evaluation of inpatient family intervention. Arch Gen Psychiatry 42:882-886, 1985

19. Selvini Palizzoli M, Boscolo L, Cecchin G, and Prata G: Paradox and Counterparadox: A New Model in the Therapy of the Family Schizophrenic Transaction. New York: Jason Aronson, 1978

20. Akiskal HS, Bitar AH, Puzantian VR, Rosenthal TL, and Walker PW: The nosological status of neurotic depressions: A prospective three- to four-year follow-up examination in light of the primary-secondary and the unipolar-bipolar dichotomies. Arch Gen Psychiatry 35:756-766, 1978

21. Akiskal HS, Hirschfeld MA, and Yerevanian BI: The relationship of personality to affective disorders: A critical review. Arch Gen Psychiatry 40:801-810, 1983

22. Cassano GB, Maggini C, and Akiskal HS: Short-term subchronic and chronic sequelae of affective disorders. Psychiatric Clin North Am 6(1):55-67, 1983

23. Weissman MM and Paykel ES: The Depressed Woman: A Study of Social Relationships. Chicago: University of Chicago Press, 1974

24. DiMascio A, Weissman MM, Prusoff BA, Neu C, Swilling M, and Klerman GL: Differential symptom reduction by drugs and psychotherapy in acute depression. Arch Gen Psychiatry 36:1450-1456, 1979

25. Klerman GL, DiMascio A, Weissman M, Prusoff B, and Paykel ES: Treatment of depression by drugs and psychotherapy. Am J Psychiatry 131:186-191, 1974

26. Haas G, Clarkin JF, and Glick ID: Marital and family treatment of depression. In Beckham E and Leber W (Eds): Handbook of Depression: Treatment, Assessment and Research. Homewood, IL: Dorsey Press, 1985, pp 151-183

27. Coyne JC: Depression and the response of others. J Abnormal Psychology 85:186-193, 1976

28. Jacobson NS and Moore D: Spouses as observers of the events in their relationship. J Consult Clin Psychology 49:269-277, 1981

29. Reid JB: Reciprocity in family interaction. Unpublished doctoral dissertation. University of Oregon, 1967

30. Birchler GR and Webb L: A social learning formulation of discriminating interaction behaviors in happy and unhappy marriages. Paper presented at the annual meeting of the Southwest Psychological Association, Houston, TX, April 1975

31. Weiss RL, Hops H, and Patterson GR: A framework for conceptualizing marital conflict, a technology for altering it, some data from evaluating it. In Hamerlynck LA, Handy LC, and Mash EJ (Eds): Behavior Change: Methodology, Concepts and Practice. Champaign, IL: Research Press, 1973, pp 309-342

32. Wills TA, Weiss RL, and Patterson GR: A behavioral analysis of the determinants of marital satisfaction. J Consult Clin Psychology 42:802-811, 1974

33. Jacobson NS, Follette WC, and McDonald DW: Reactivity to positive and negative behavior in distressed and nondistressed married couples. J Consult Clin Psychology 50:706-714, 1982

34. Rounsaville BJ, Klerman GL, and Weissman MM: Do psychotherapy and pharmacotherapy for depression conflict? Arch Gen Psychiatry 38:24-29, 1981

35. Targum SD, Dibble ED, Davenport YB, and Gershon ES: The FAttitudes Questionnaire: Patients' and spouses' reviews of bipolar illness. Arch Gen Psychiatry 38:562-568, 1981

36. Zitrin CM, Klein DF, and Woerner MG: Behavior therapy, supportive psychotherapy, imipramine, and phobias. Arch Gen Psychiatry 35:307-316, 1978

37. Hafner RJ: The husbands of agoraphobic women and their influence on treatment outcome. Br J Psychiatry 131:289-294-1977

38. Buglass D, Clarke J, Henderson AS, Kreitman N, and Presley AS: A study of agoraphobic housewives. Psychological Med 7(1):73-86, 1977

39. Cobb JP, Mathews AM, Childs-Clarke A, and Blowers CM: The spouse as cotherapist in the treatment of agoraphobia. Br J Psychiatry 144:282-287, 1984

40. Hafner RJ: Agoraphobic women married to abnormally jealous men. Br J Med Psychology 52:99-104, 1979

41. Hafner RJ: Predicting the effects on husbands of behavior therapy for wives' agoraphobia. Behav Res Ther 22(3):217-226, 1984

42. Munby M and Johnston DW: Agoraphobia: The long-term follow-up of behavioral treatment. Br J Psychiatry 137:418-427, 1980

43. Rebeta-Burditt J: The Cracker Factory. New York: MacMillan, 1970

44. Gorad S, McCourt W, and Cobb J: The communications approach in alcoholism. Q J Studies on Alcohol 32:651-668, 1971

45. Berenson D: A family approach to alcoholism. Psychiatric Opinion 13:33-38, 1976

46. Deniker P, DeSaugy D, and Ropert M: The alcoholic and his wife. Comp Psychiatry 5:374-384, 1964

47. Rae J: The influence of the wives on the treatment outcome of alcoholics: A followup study at two years. Br J Psychiatry 120:601-613. 1972

48. Dinaburg D, Glick ID, and Feigenbaum E: Marital therapy of woman alcoholics. J Studies on Alcohol 38:1247-1258, 1977

49. Rutstein D and Beech R: Genetics and addiction to alcohol (editorial). N Engl J Med 298:1140-1141, 1978

50. Stanton MD and Todd TC: The Family Therapy of Drug Abuse and Addiction. New York: Guilford Press, 1982

51. Ganger R and Shugart G: The heroin addict's pseudoassertive behavior and family dynamics. Social Casework 57:643-649, 1966

52. Rosenberg C: The young addict and his family. Br J Psychiatry 118:469-470, 1971

53. Harbin HT and Maziar HM: The families of drug abusers: A literature review. Fam Process 14:411-431, 1975

54. Klagsbrun M and Davis DI: Substance abuse and family interaction. Fam Process 16:149-173, 1977

55. Seldin NE: The family of the addict: A review of the literature. Int J Addict 7:97-107, 1972

56. Stanton MD: Drugs and the family: A review of the literature. Marriage Family Rev 2(2):1-10, 1979

57. Stanton MD: Family treatment of drug problems: A review. In DuPont RI, Goldstein A, and O'Donnell J (Eds): Handbook on Drug Abuse. Washington, DC: National Institute on Alcohol, Drug Abuse and Mental Health Administration, Department of Health, Education and Welfare: and Office of Drug Abuse Policy, Executive Office of the President, 1979, pp 133-150

58. Maloney MJ and Klykylo WM: An overview of anorexia nervosa, bulimia and obesity in children and adolescents. J Am Acad Child Psychiatry 22:99, 1983

59. Yager J and Strober M: Family aspects of eating disorders. In Hales RE and Frances AJ (Eds): Psychiatry Update: Annual Review Volume 4. Washington, DC: American Psychiatric Press, 1985, pp 481-502

60. Minuchin S, Rosman B, and Baker L: Psychosomatic Families. Cambridge, MA: Harvard University Press, 1978

61. Halmi K: Personal communication

62. Adams M: Social aspects of the medical care for the mentally retarded. N Engl J Med 286:635-638, 1972

63. Vogel EF and Bell NW: The emotionally disturbed child as the family

scapegoat. In Bell NW and Vogel ED (Eds): A Modern Introduction to the Family. Glencoe, IL: Free Press, 1960, pp 382-397

64. Szurek S: Some lessons from efforts at psychotherapy with parents. Am J Psychiatry 109:291-295, 1952

65. Minuchin S, Auerswald E, King C, et al.: The study and treatment of families that produce multiple acting-out boys. Am J Orthopsychiatry 34:125-134, 1964

66. Minuchin S and Montalvo B: Techniques for working with disorganized low socioeconomic families. Am J Orthopsychiatry 37:880-887, 1967

67. American Academy of Child Psychiatry: Child psychiatry: A plan for the coming decades. Washington, DC: American Academy of Child Psychiatry, 1983

Indians and Squaws, Caughnawaga near Montreal by Cornelius Krieghoff. Courtesy of the Confederation Centre Art Gallery and Museum, Charlottetown, Prince Edward Island, Canada.

23
Family Treatment in the Context of Other Special Problems

OBJECTIVES

- To be able to utilize the family model in the context of such family issues as violence, incest, suicidal behavior, and psychiatric illness

INTRODUCTION

The last chapter described the family model in situations in which the family has a member with a diagnosable psychiatric disorder. There are other situations in which the family has one or more members involved in "behaviors" that are very disruptive to family functioning, such as suicidal behaviors, incest, and aggression. In addition, there are characteristic reactions to acute and chronic diagnosable mental and medical illness. We have separated out these problems for discussion here for a variety of reasons, but mostly because they so clearly involve the whole family, and because a behavior like "aggression" cuts across traditional diagnostic lines.

From the family perspective, these behaviors serve as mechanisms to maintain homeostasis (as well as sometimes serving to focus on the IP as the one who is "sick" or to blame). For example, sometimes the only way one spouse knows how to handle "brow beating" is to explode, or threaten suicide or homicide. We have discussed this concept (more fully) earlier in our discussion of the solution being worse than the problem.

352

DOMESTIC VIOLENCE AND INCEST
with Jonathan Pesner, Ph.D.

Domestic violence may be broadly defined as the use of *physical force* to inflict injury on an individual or the use of *psychological coercion* to control someone's actions or will. Domestic violence occurs in many forms (such as spouse abuse, child abuse and incest, elder abuse, or violence between siblings). We will focus on the problems of wife battering and incest. Violence is also discussed in Chapter 28.

Wife Battering

It has been roughly estimated that at least 50 percent of all families in the United States experience some form of violence against women.[1] While some may argue that pushing and slapping do not constitute violent acts when they occur between family members, it has been amply documented that such minor forms of violence form a part of the broader cycle of violence in families that too often leads to serious injury and even death.[2]

Homicide statistics illustrate the true severity of the problem. *Approximately 20 to 50 percent of all homicides in this country occur within the family.* Female victims of homicide are more often killed by a spouse, while the majority of male victims are killed by someone outside the family. About 40 percent of all female homicide victims are killed by their husbands, but only 10 percent of male victims were killed by their wives.[3] Thus, men are more likely to commit homicide, and many female victims are married to their assailants.

Violence begets violence as well. Over 60 percent of battering men came from families where they either witnessed or suffered physical abuse. Wife-beating is often accompanied by the physical abuse of the children. In one study, over 50 percent of wife beaters also physically abused their children while a smaller percentage of abused women admitted to abusing their children.[4] There are also effects on unborn children. Of the 80 families studied by Gelles,[1] one fourth of the women were pregnant when they were battered, and it is estimated that a tenth of all miscarriages are induced by husbands beating their pregnant wives.[5]

Spouse abuse is not limited to a particular social class or ethnic group, although the highest reported incidence is among the economically disadvantaged. Lower income people are more likely to rely on public agencies, including the police, for help. Middle and upper class families can preserve their privacy and anonymity through access to personal physicians, therapists, and attorneys.[6]

In this nascent period of public awareness and professional concern, the problem of wife abuse has continued to stir controversy among clinicians about the nature and efficacy of different treatment approaches. Issues such as therapist confidentiality and duty to warn intended victims of violence are central to a therapeutic paradigm when domestic violence is involved. Occasionally, other questions arise concerning child welfare and custody, work compensation, and disability claims that confound the content and course of therapy. It is often difficult to balance the conflicting demands of legal, social, and individual family structures and to reconcile them within a simple therapeutic perspective. As a result, the problem of domestic violence has challenged the dominant view that therapists can function in isolation from the larger social and legal context and constraints that affect their clients' lives. In turn, the therapist treating a violent family must inevitably examine his or her own values about prevailing social and legal institutions, as well as his or her underlying beliefs about the roots of inter-personal violence and its relationship to contemporary family structures.

Numerous authors have documented the social and historical sanctions of wife-beating.[7] It is interesting to note that the term "rule of thumb" originated from a late 18th century law in the United States according a husband the right to hit his wife so long as "he . . . (use) a switch no bigger than his thumb."[8] Although wife-beating is no longer legally sanctioned, current attitudes and, in many states, criminal justice procedures support turning a blind eye toward marital violence. Nonetheless, the implicit acceptance of violence against women and the myth of the inviolable privacy of the family unit are two beliefs that are slowly eroding as women's groups, the mental health community, and the legal profession coordinate their attempts to alleviate the problem of wife abuse.

Assessment

In many violent marriages, there appears to be a predictable cycle of violence, with three phases that vary in length and intensity.[2] The first or tension building phase may be marked by constant arguing or the escalation of conflict. It may last from days to years, and frequently leads to a battering episode. This second phase, the violent incident, often results in police intervention, the woman's voluntary departure from the home, or in her hospitalization. The final or conciliation phase finds the battering man typically remorseful, contrite, and begging for forgiveness. He may buy his wife gifts, promise her it will never happen again, and in some cases, may seek treatment on his own.

Why do men batter, and why does the battered wife stay with the perpetrator? Is battering an individual act or under the control of the spouse or family system? Bandura's social learning model[9] argues that violence is a learned response to stress and reinforced by the reduction in stress following a battering incident. Men are typically socialized from a very early age to inhibit their emotions and to act out physically instead of verbally. When a male child is raised in an abusive family, the likelihood increases that he will grow up to be a violent adult. Not only is Bandura's social learning model a powerful theoretical tool for describing socialized male violence, but it has been translated into a group treatment approach for battering men that is widely used by therapists across the country.[10] Data[11] indicate that battering men are strong externalizers, projecting blame and responsibility for problems or conflict usually onto their spouses. Pathological jealousy characterizes many of these men and is often a leading emotional precipitant to violence. Underlying this jealousy are deep-seated feelings of inferiority, insecurity around intimacy, social isolation, and general low self-esteem that may predispose the batterer to periods of depression. The impulsive nature of many of these men further accounts for their inability to control or appropriately express their anger. Alcohol and drug abuse is common, as is their tendency to hold stereotypical and demeaning attitudes toward women. Perhaps the most unifying characteristic is a history of violence, as children and in other intimate adult relationships.

Many abused women do leave their marriages for a brief time, but they invariably return because of their economic and emotional dependence on their husbands and, in some cases, because of continuing threats of violence from their husbands if they don't return. Like battering men, abused women tend to subscribe to traditional sex roles and values. They, too, have often experienced abuse as children. Many suffer from chronically low self-esteem and adhere to prevailing myths that they are somehow responsible for the beatings and the batterer's actions.

Systemic models of battering take as their point of departure not the violence itself but the interactional patterns of a dysfunctional family system that may precipitate an explosive conflict. A major focus of these approaches to wife abuse is the identification of relatively characteristic transactional patterns of couples in which wife abuse is prevalent. These may include family enmeshment or the absence of individuation, sex-role polarization, and violence as a mediator of proximity or distance.[12] Elbow[11] describes four abuse syndromes that bind the abuser and abused in a complementary need system. Homeostasis of the system is maintained by patterns of externalization and internalization. An example of this can be found in the common situation in which a batterer rationalizes or projects blame for his violence to avoid the loss of self-esteem while his wife accepts the blame to prevent her from feeling helpless.The homeostatic function of violence is also elaborated by Hoffman's[13] systemic view of battering. To compensate for his feelings of inadequacy, the abusive man resorts to violence in order to reequilibrate the relationship with his wife who, in contrast, sees herself as over-adequate. Weitzman and Dreen[14] view the battering relationship as a locked complementary system with rigid unilateral control and little or no room for negotiation. Any move toward symmetry or equality threatens the balance, and violence is then utilized to force a return to the status quo.

Advocates of family systems approaches to wife battering have been readily criticized, often by feminist researchers and clinicians, on a number of grounds.

Bograd has brought together these criticisms in a systematic review of approaches to domestic violence.[12] Violence, in her view, is not simply the result of other systemic problems, but also exerts a threatening and organizing influence on the marital system.The existing research indicates little evidence or support for the common assumption that women provoke violence from their mate.[7] Whether or not a woman provokes anger in her husband is a different issue from how much control she has over her husband's actions.

Therapy

Cook and Cook[15] have outlined a comprehensive treatment approach based on the following components:

1. Assessment of the problem and extensive history-taking.
2. An explicit protection plan.
3. A written agreement to be nonviolent.
4. Differentiation of roles.
5. Identification of coalitions and triangles.
6. Identification of conflict themes and sequences.
7. Facilitation of alternative patterns of communication and behavior.

The severity and lethality of violence is usually initially assessed, and if there appears to be an imminent or continuing danger of violence, the therapist might recommend separation of the couple or even more drastic steps to protect the woman, such as shelter placement or restraining orders.

Incest

Child sexual abuse in general, and incest in particular, is a problem of tremendous frequency, more than used to be expected by conventional wisdom, and of serious moment to the development of the child and the viability of the family. Since child sexual abuse is the product of a problematic family system, and all family members share in the development and maintenance of the problem, effective treatment can involve a systemic approach.[16]

Incest can be conceptualized as a boundary disturbance in a family's relationship to the community, between the generations, and boundary diffusion in the family in general.

The I. family sought help following discovery of an incestuous relationship between the father and the 14-year-old daughter. The mother sought help for the family to find out "whether Max is a sex maniac and ought to be put away or whether he's just plain rotten and ought to be put in jail and divorced."

Evaluation revealed that the wife and husband had not been getting along for many years. Recently the wife had begun to leave home after supper, telling her husband and daughter that she might be working all night, and cautioning them not to "get in trouble." The husband and daughter had then begun mutual petting prior to bedtime, which had progressed to intercourse.

Larson and Maddock[17] have formulated a typology of the incest family that can be used for differential treatment planning. The typology is based upon the four basic functions in the interpersonal exchange processes that are served by the incest behavior: affectional, erotic, aggressive, or rageful processes.

In the affectional type, the incest behavior serves affectional-exchange needs between two or more family members of different generations. These misdirected fathers engage in quasi-courtship behaviors with their daughters in order to develop closeness and express affection. Outpatient family therapy with an emphasis on appropriate differentiation of each family member is often helpful to these families who have strengths to call upon.

The second type of family eroticizes many interaction patterns. The erotic "game" in these families may include both parents and many of the children. Treatment needs to be directive in order to change the erotic interaction patterns. Group therapy with peers may be useful, as well as marital therapy for the perpetrator and spouse. When proper sexual boundaries have been established, family therapy may be useful in promoting more appropriate ways of expressing nurturance and intimacy in the family.

"Aggression based" incest families express sexualized aggression as a way of dealing with other frustrations and possibly anger toward other family members. For example, in order to "punish" his wife for her lack of affection, an enraged father may engage in angry and even violent sex with his daughter. Treatment may require highly controlled living situations, such as psychiatric inpatient, sheltered residence or foster care home settings. Marital therapy with a focus on conflict management and resolution, and family therapy focused on conflict resolution and problem solving, may be helpful.

The rage-based incest family involves a perpetrator who expresses anger, but not the overt aggression discussed above. Such families must be carefully assessed for propensity to violence and other pathological behaviors. Individual and group treatment, often in an inpatient setting, may be needed to explore the perpetrator's extensive conflicts. These families often dissolve, and often child protection agency assistance is needed, and the children are often raised by surrogate families.

What percentage of incest allegations are false? They are "rare" according to most experts except in contested custody disputes. Usually fathers are the targets and the allegation is used by mothers to prevent contact of fathers with children (and/or with her). This issue is also discussed from the point of view of the Pediatrician in Chapter 28.

THE SUICIDAL PATIENT AND FAMILY
with Gretchen Haas, Ph.D.

The suicidal patient remains a major unresolved public health problem. Our model is based on a family point of view, which assumes that often the seriously suicidal act (either complete or incomplete) is an attempt to resolve a family crisis.

We present a step-by-step management plan for the assessment and treatment of such patients and their families. Such families most often present to the family therapist in crisis, and we begin at that point.

Acute Management

Recognizing that the state-of-the-art of predicting the risk of suicide is *virtually impossible*, we, nevertheless, as a first step make an immediate judgment of risk. We dichotomize into the seemingly simplistic categories of "definitely will try" versus "probably will not try." In our experience, best predictors of those that will try are a past history of a life-threatening suicidal act (e.g., one that requires hospitalization in an intensive care unit) or a suicide of a close family member.

The former category—patients that "definitely will try"—we believe, should be managed with "one-to-one" family observation or hospitalization pending collection of further information from other members of the family. The latter group do not require such observation. Both groups next need a more extended evaluation.

Evaluating the Family

Once we've made the decision of whether or not to use maximal suicidal precautions, the next step is to obtain a family history. Some families ask why should they be involved? At our hospital, by way of inducing and maintaining a patient in treatment, our routine practice is to require (if indicated to achieve efficacy) that families be involved in treatment. If they do not participate, they are told that we will consider discharge of the identified patient back to his or her family.

The next step is to evaluate the role of the identified patient in the family problem. Although the suicidal act is often impulsive, *in other situations suicide attempts are often premeditated acts that are attempts to resolve mounting family conflict.*

A final step in evaluation involves making a differential diagnosis. Unlike many of our family colleagues who make the assumption that the primary (if not the only) cause of the suicidal act is a family problem, we assume that other causes can exist. We look for a major psychiatric disorder, such as schizophrenia or depressive disorder. For example, we've had the experience of seemingly restructuring and restabilizing a family after a suicide attempt only to discover (several years later) that the identified patient had a recurrent depressive disorder associated with suicidal ideation and largely unrelated to family problems, which in large part caused the suicidal behavior.

Involving the Family

The next step is to involve the family in the treatment. As we mentioned earlier, the family often attempts to "dump" the patient on the hospital (or family therapist) "door step" as a solution to the family crisis. At this point the therapist has leverage; we therefore inform the family that the patient cannot be treated without their involvement. They are told that if the family doesn't agree to participate in treatment, the patient will be discharged back to the family "regardless of the consequences." This statement is used as a tactic to involve the family rather than (as they may view it) as "ignoring the patient." The rationale is that we believe that effectiveness of treatment for the identified patient and the family is seriously impaired by lack of family involvement. Furthermore, if we collude with the family to allow uninvolvement, we find (as indicated in our follow-up studies of these patients) that they are readmitted over and over again.

The next step is "joining the family." This is a tactic by which we convey to the family that, "we're on your side."

Treating the Family

It has been our experience that *the suicidal ideation gradually decreases as the family problem is addressed*. Therefore, at this stage the task is to treat the family problem rather than to focus exclusively on the suicidal "identified patient." We believe the suicidal act may be a way to "wake up the family." It is an attempt to find a new option or solution to the family problem. The therapist stresses throughout this phase that although the focus of treatment began with the suicidal act, this is, essentially, a symptom of a larger problem. Thus, it is emphasized that dealing with the other family problems is the way to most effectively change the problem in the long run.

There is a continuing struggle here between the family's need to keep the identified patient in the suicidal role versus their feelings of wanting to help the patient, (and thereby move him out of that role). In our experience—especially with the family of the hospitalized patient—family forces may be extremely powerful in forcing the patient to the act of suicide as a family solution. At the same time, family members feel guilty and, in part, want to help, but are at a loss to find a new solution. This is the crucial part of the therapy.

The techniques we use in this phase of treatment are the conventional family techniques described in the rest of this book. An interesting approach has been presented by Coleman[18]—an enactment technique in which the therapist asks the patient to dress as if he were a corpse and the family has a mock funeral in the therapist's office. Obviously, the dynamics of the suicidal act can be clearly elucidated, and with structural techniques new options can be developed.

Discharging the Patient

Once the family has reached a new equilibrium in which the family problem has been reframed and redefined, the patient can be discharged back to the family for continued family therapy in the community using the more traditional family therapy techniques.

The following is a case example:

Ms. R. was a 16-year-old adolescent high school student admitted to the psychiatric inpatient service for her first suicide attempt, in which she ingested a "handful" of sleeping pills and told her parents she was going to sleep forever. The parents realized the threat and rushed her to the local emergency room, from which she was transferred to the psychiatric inpatient service. In the first evaluation session with the primary therapist, she let it be known that she had been sexually molested by her father since age 8. It had started with nongenital fondling, and had advanced to regular episodes of caressing and genital stimulation. Her mother, she thought, was totally unaware of this behavior. The suicide attempt stemmed from her low self-esteem and feelings of being trapped, despite good school performance and an age-appropriate relationship with a teenage boyfriend that was beginning to develop.

In individual sessions with the mother, age 45, and father, age 47, a stockbroker, the therapist confronted both parents with the situation. The mother was shocked, totally unaware of the situation, and became alternatively rageful and depressed over the ensuing weeks. The father was likewise shocked that his daughter had revealed their behavior and seemed surprised that the suicidal gesture was related. He confessed to the accuracy of what the daughter was saying, and pleaded for help with his daughter and his relationship with his wife.

Following several weeks of hospitalization and individual and family therapy sessions, the daughter was discharged much improved. Family therapy sessions, which also included the patient's 17-year-old brother, were used to acknowledge but not dwell on the past, and plan for firmer family boundaries in the future. Upon discharge, the patient continued in individual therapy, and the parents began a productive but painful period of marital therapy in which they reviewed the past and renewed their own intimate relationship.

FAMILY RESPONSES TO MENTAL ILLNESS
OF A FAMILY MEMBER

Families of the Acutely Ill

Families have been shown to experience a patterned sequence of responses to the occurrence of mental illness in an identified patient.[19] These stages are as follows:

1. *Beginning uneasiness:* The family does not know what to expect.
2. *Need for reassurance:* The family hopes that everything will be all right.
3. *Denial and minimizing:* The family denies that anything is wrong and minimizes the patient's difficulties.
4. *Anger and blame:* The family begins to see the extent of the problem and each member lays blame on the others or on the hospital staff.
5. *Guilt, shame, and grief:* Each member perceives his or her role and feels guilt and shame.
6. *Confusion in the changed family:* The family adopts new roles with resultant confusion.
7. *Acceptance of reality:* The family adapts to a new homeostatis.

In treating families in which an identified patient has a psychiatric illness, the therapist needs to be aware of these stages in order to make effective treatment plans. For example, to ensure that the identified patient with a manic-depressive illness takes his lithium medication as regularly as an individual with diabetes mellitus takes insulin, one needs to know how the family feels about the illness and its treatment.

FAMILIES OF THE CHRONICALLY ILL
with John A.Talbott, M.D.

Thirty percent of the patients discharged from mental hospitals are rehospitalized during the first year following discharge. Sixty percent of all admissions to state hospitals are readmissions. For many patients, rehospitalization occurs more than once and, indeed, becomes a way of life. One implication of these facts is that, for many patients, the family has become more involved in their long-term outcome.

We now know much more than we did five years ago regarding families of the mentally ill. We know, for instance, that of one million admissions to state, country and general hospitals, 3000 are married and one-half of the remainder live at home—meaning that 70 percent of the seriously ill have families who can or will be involved after discharge.[20] In addition, we know that of the mentally ill elderly, more are cared for at home than in institutions, and that institutionalization is sought only when the elderly person's burden on the family becomes overwhelming.[21]

The work of several British investigators on "expressed emotion" (EE) of family members as it effects the course of schizophrenic illness continued during the past five years to show how critical this variable was. EE remained the best single predictor of relapse in schizophrenics, although medication and infrequent contact with the family also protected schizophrenics from relapse. The worst prognosis occurred in those individuals with high EE families on no medication, with frequent contact; and the best outcomes occurred in those with low EE families and who were on drugs.[22]

In addition, we now know much more about the expressed needs of families of the mentally ill,[23-25] who want:

- information about mental illness, symptoms, and etiology
- help in handling their sick relative's behavior
- knowledge of resources
- respite care and services
- economic relief
- crisis care
- rehabilitation services
- reduction of anxiety

Families are most distressed by bizarre and abnormal or instrusive and disturbing behavior, and poor task functioning. They indicate the mentally ill person at home causes serious disruption to their family life (e.g., to siblings, marriages, social and personal life); excessive burden; as well as the emotional burdens of stress, anxiety, resentment, grief, and depression.[26] Those families who cope more effectively with their mentally ill relatives are characterized by greater acceptance, less "pushiness," avoidance of rigid statements, patience, better ability to "listen," lack of fear, and a positive attitude.[27] Although symptoms are not affected by familial expectations, performance is, at least in terms of activities of everyday living.[28]

Families seem critical to the patient's ability to survive in the community; with early rehospitalization directly related to low family symptom tolerance.[29] With repeated admissions, families become less willing to help[30] and subsequent hospitalizations of their relatives become related less to the families' symptom tolerance than to their dislike of the patient.[29]

Both families and mental health professionals now seem to agree that the emphasis of intervention with families of the chronically ill should be on educational approaches rather than traditional family therapy.[25] During the past five years the burgeoning of programs and descriptions of techniques of such psychoeducation is nothing short of amazing. While some programs are directed primarily at one effect, such as communication,[31] survival skills,[29] or attitudinal change,[32] some directed at families alone[34] and others to just the patient,[35] and some take place at home[36] and others in clinic settings,[37] all have certain common characteristics:[38-41]

- education about the disease and its treatment
- improvement in communications
- structured problem solving
- development of outside resources
- increasing structure and decreasing disorganization
- sharing the experience of living with a mentally ill relative
- concern for the healthy members' lives
- reinforcement of family boundaries
- anticipation and handling of stressful situations
- attempting to avoid relapse
- emphasis on biological etiology and avoidance of blaming the family

In the light of the research mentioned above showing that high expressed emotion in relatives is related to increased relapse, several groups have formulated programs that are aimed at directly decreasing the criticism, overinvolvement and hostility felt to be so critical to outcome.[34,42,43] Preliminary results on the effectiveness of these psychoeducational approaches are encouraging e.g., a relapse rate nine times greater in the controls receiving individual treatment,[36] no relapses verses 48 percent among controls at six months,[38] 7 percent relapses versus 57 percent in controls at 9 months, and two-year results of 3.63 days in the hospital after the program versus 83.26 days in the two years prior.[41]

Meanwhile, a remarkable change has taken place among the families of the seriously and chronically mentally ill, who have organized together, shared their common experiences, sought educational information, and destigmatized their views of themselves. As a result, beginning with the American Schizophrenic Association, which stressed orthomolecular therapy, parent groups have formed throughout the country, and in 1979, met and formed the National Alliance for the Mentally Ill (NAMI), which currently has 200 chapters. The groups are remarkably similar, seeking to end the "blame the family" trend in psychiatry, as well as to educate themselves, to support one another, to increase research efforts, and to advocate for a more efficient and effective service delivery system.[44-46] Families also are concerned that they, who know what has worked and not worked, are frequently not consulted by professionals during treatment planning.[47] Families point out that their views are frequently different from those of their ill relatives; for example, they tend to think that hospitalization and conservatorship are too difficult, discharge is too abrupt, the system is too permissive, and patients are allowed to refuse their medication too easily.[48] It has frequently been pointed out that one reason why the mentally ill have been placed in community care less successfully than the mentally retarded is because of the stigma felt by their relatives.[49]

In addition to the individual interventions mentioned above, families have demonstrated that their willingness to keep mentally ill relatives at home is much greater if certain system's changes are made, such as providing fiscal support, respite services, a sound social services program that reduces the family burden, and a true community care system.[50] Finally, while most programs have described their interaction with families in general terms, it is clear that further work needs to be devoted to what specific coping strategies work with the chronically ill, and what attitudes and behaviors are most useful.[51,52]

SUGGESTIONS FOR FURTHER READINGS

Latham TL: Violence in the family: An attempt to apply contemporary theories of non-violent action and conflict resolution skills. J Family Therapy 8:125-137, 1986.
   Excellent overview of the issue of violence in the family and its managment.

Treating Incest: A Multimodal Systems Perspective. J Psychotherapy and the Family 2:1986.
   An entire issue devoted to the topic of incest and the family.

REFERENCES

1. Gelles RJ: The Violent Home: A Study of Physical Aggression Between Husbands and Wives. Beverly HIlls: Sage Publications, 1974
2. Walker L: The Battered Woman. New York: Harper & Row, 1979
3. Dobash RE and Dobash RP: Wives: The appropriate victims of marital violence. Victimology 2:426-442, 1977/1978
4. Gayford JJ: Wife-battering: A preliminary survey of 100 cases. Br Med J 1:194-197, 1975
5. Gayford JJ: Research on battered wives. Res Soc Health J 95:288-289, 1975
6. Levinger G: Sources of marital dissatisfaction among applicants for divorce. Am J Orthopsychiatry 36:803-807, 1966
7. Schecter S: Woman and Male Violence. Boston: South End Press, 1982
8. Martin D: Battered Wives. San Francisco: Glide Publications, 1976
9. Bandura A: Aggression: A Social Learning Analysis. Englewood Cliffs, NJ: Prentice Hall, 1973

10. Sonkin DJ, Martin D, and Walker L: The male batterer: A treatment approach. New York: Springer, 1985

11. Elbow M: Theoretical considerations of violent marriages. Soc Casework 63:515-526, 1977

12. Bograd M: Family systems approaches to wife battering. Am J Orthopsychiatry 4:558-567, 1984

13. Hoffman L: Foundations of Family Therapy. New York: Basic Books, 1981

14. Weitzman J and Dreen K: Wife beating: A view of the marital dyad. Soc Casework 63:259-265, 1982

15. Cook DR and Frantz-Cook A: A systemic treatment approach to wife-battering. J Mar Fam Ther 10:83-93, 1984

16. Figley CR: Editorial note. In Trepper T and Barrett M (Eds): Treating incest: A multimodal systems perspective. J Psychother Family 2(2):1-3, 1986

17. Larson N and Maddock JW: Structural and functional variables in incest family systems: Implications for assessment and treatment. sychotherapy and the Family 2:27-44, 1986

18. Coleman SB: Brief therapeutic strategies to deal with severe death anxiety. In Gurman AS (Ed): Questions and Answers in the Practice of Family Therapy. New York: Brunner/Mazel, 1981, pp 450-455

19. Rabkin J: Public attitudes toward mental illness: A review of the literature. Schiz Bull 10:9-33, 1974

20. Goldman HH: The post-hospital mental patient and family therapy: Prospects and populations. J Marriage Family Ther, October 1980, pp 449-452

21. Kulys R: The family in the institutionalization of the elderly. J Soc Issues 37:145-157, 1981

22. Vaughn CE and Leff JP: The influence of family and social factors in the course of psychiatric illness. Br J Psychiatry 129:125-137, 1976

23. Hatfield A: The family as partner in the treatment of mental illness. Hosp Comm Psychiat 30:338-340, 1979

24. Lamb HR and Oliphant E: Schizophrenia through the eyes of families. Hosp Comm Psychiat 29:803-806, 1978

25. Hatfield AB: What families want of family therapists. Unpublished paper.

26. Hatfield AB: Psychological costs of schizophrenia to the family. Social Work 23:355-359, 1978

27. Hatfield AB: Coping effectiveness in families of the mentally ill: An exploratory study. J Psychiat Treat Eval 3:11-19, 1981

28. Greenley JR: Family expectation, post-hospital adjustment and the societal reaction perspective on mental illness. J Health Soc Behav 20:217-222, 1979

29. Greenley JR: Family symptom tolerances and rehospitalization experiences of psychiatric patients. In Simmons R (Ed): Research in Chronic Mental Health. Greenwich, CT: JAI Press, 1978, pp 357-386

30. Morris R: Integration of therapeutic and community services: Cure plus care

for the mentally disabled. Int J Mental Health 6:9-26, 1977/1978

31. Miller TW: A model for training schizophrenics and families to communicate more effectively. Hosp Comm Psychiat 32:870-871, 1981

32. Anderson CM, Hogarty C, and Reiss DJ: The psychoeducational family treatment of schizophrenia. ND 12:79-94, 1981

33. Dincin J, Selleck V, and Streicher S: Restructuring parental attitudes—working with parents of the adult mentally ill. Schiz Bull 4:597-608, 1978

34. Berkowitz R, Kuipers L, Ebelein-Vries R, and Leff J: Lowering expressed emotions in relatives of schizophrenics. ND 12:27-48, 1981

35. Falloon IRH, Boyd JL, McGill CW, Strang JS, and Moss HB: Family management training in the community care of schizophrenia. ND 12:61-77, 1981

36. Boyd JL, McGill CW, and Falloon IRH: Family participation in the community rehabilitation of schizophrenics. Hosp Comm Psychiat 32:629-632, 1981

37. Anderson CM, Hogarty GE, and Reiss DJ: Family treatment of adult schizophrenic patients. A psycho-educational approach. Schiz Bull 6:490-505, 1980

38. Goldstein MJ and Kopeikin HS: Short and long-term effects of combining drug and family therapy. ND 12:5-26, 1981

39. Atwood N and Williams MED: Group support for the families of the mentally ill. Schiz Bull 4:415-425, 1978

40. Thornton JF, Plum E, Seeman MN, and Littman SK: Schizophrenia: Group support for relatives. Can J P 26:341-344, 1981

41. Shenoy RS, Shires BW, and White MS: Using a sciz-anon group in the treatment of chronic ambulatory schizophrenics. Hosp Comm Psychiat 32:421, 1981

42. Leff JP: Developments in family treatment of schizophrenia. Psychiat Q 51:216-232, 1979

43. Snyder KS and Liberman RP: Family assessment and intervention with schizophrenics at risk for relapse. ND 12:49-60, 1981

44. Beels CC: Social networks, the family and the schizophrenic patient. Schiz Bull 4:512-521, 1978

45. Hatfield AB: Families as advocates for the mentally ill: A growing movement. Hosp Comm Psychiat 32:641-642, 1981

46. Terkelsen KG: No proof that families cause mental illness. FAMI Newsletter 2(3), March 1982

47. Hibler M: The problem as seen by the patient's family. Hosp Comm Psychiat 29:32-33, 1978

48. Buck M: Personal communication

49. Boggs EM: Contrasts in deinstitutionalization. Hosp Comm Psychiat 32:591, 1981

50. Segal SP: Community care and deinstitutionalization. SW 37:521-527, 1979
51. Kanter J and Lin A: Facilitating a therapeutic milieu in the families of schizophrenia. Psychiat 43:106-119, 1980
52. Kanter J: Coping strategies for relatives of the mentally ill. Unpublished paper.

Work and Rest by Jean Charlot, private collection.

24
Family Intervention and the Psychiatric Hospital System

OBJECTIVES

- To understand the role of the family in the psychiatric hospitalization of one of its members
- To be able to treat such a family with the goal of preventing rehospitalization and of reaching the highest functional level for the identified patient and family
- To become aware of family approaches and alternatives to hospitalization

INTRODUCTION

Family work on an inpatient unit has gone on throughout most of the history of inpatient work. Unfortunately, in some cases, the regard, and help, given families has reflected prevailing theories of *individual* patient psychopathology as well as the capacity of hospitals to "adopt" patients. Shorter lengths of stay[1] and a now developed literature on *hospital* and *family* theory and practice, have combined to inform us of: (1) the *limits* of hospital practice; and (2) *the importance of including, and allying with, families* for the effective short *and* long-term care of the hospitalized psychiatric patient.

370

This chapter focuses on the new model (or orientation) of the evaluation and treatment of families on a short-term (weeks, not months or years) psychiatric unit.[2] Models of approach are empirically, rather than theoretically, based. General guidelines for inpatient family work are provided, and specific approaches for specific diagnostic disorders are elaborated. Table 24-1 contrasts the individually-oriented model with the family-oriented model as they are utilized in a hospital setting.[3]

BACKGROUND

Psychiatric residents, psychology interns, and social work students currently in training may not realize it, but not that many years ago the family with a member in a psychiatric hospital was seen as, at best, purveyors of background information to the social worker and as payers of the bills. At worse, they were seen as malignant, pathogenic individuals who had played a major role in causing the patient's symptoms and who tended to make nuisances of themselves by interfering with the patient's treatment by the hospital staff.

The staff acted *in loco parentis* and often inappropriately blamed the family for the patient's symptoms. The family was frequently not allowed to visit during the early part of the hospitalization. The psychiatric hospital was associated with much fear and stigma, and, in many cases, families were only too happy to stay away. Prior to the availability of effective somatic treatments, hospital stays were much longer and already fragile family ties were broken. At the time of discharge, the hospital staff members would tend to remove the patient from the family setting because they viewed the family as an adversary.

In other cultures, families are sometimes considered a vital part of the psychiatric hospitalization of any of their members.[4] Because of a scarcity of trained professionals, families are needed in the hospital to care for the needs of the identified patient. They, in fact, often stay with the patient in or near the hospital. The assumption in other cultures is that the patient is an integral part of the family network, and it is unthinkable that the patient would return anywhere else but to the family.[5]

Over the last 15 years, there has been an increasing use of family intervention in inpatient settings,[6] but not without problems. In an article published in 1977, Anderson outlined some of the difficulties, many of which still remain to some degree.[7]

Regrettably, however, the family therapy literature is not particularly helpful to those working on inpatient units; such concepts as "defining the family as the patient" tend to alienate both the medical staff of an institution and the already overwhelmingly guilt-rid-

Table 24-1

Family Therapy in Individually Oriented Hospitals and Family-Oriented Treatment in the Hospital: A Comparison

Issue	Individually Oriented Hospitals	Family Oriented Hospitals
Locus of pathology	In the neurobiological system or psychodynamics of the individual	Dysfunctional individual behavior related to dysfunction in family interactions as well as individual neurobiological and psychodynamic factors—a biopsychosocial model
Locus of change and healing	In the biosystem or the intrapsychic system of the individual	In the individual within the family as a significant piece of the individual's ecology
Diagnosis	DSM-III-R, axes I, II, III	DSM-III-R, axes IV and V, and characterization of family interactions in relation to the symptoms or complaints
Role of the staff	To care for and to provide therapy for the patient	To facilitate changes in the family through family interaction or through planned interactions with the patient
Visits	During visiting hours, informal	Visits are a part of the treatment. Those people who visit are a part of the treatment plan
Role of family therapy	A modality to work on those aspects of the patient's problem which seem to be related to family functioning	The orienting therapy of the overall treatment program
Discharge planning	Related to the condition of the individual and higher ability to function outside the hospital	Related to the condition of the family and its ability to provide safety and continued growth for members

den families. The polarized approaches of family therapists, who generally operate on a "system" model, which overemphasizes interactional variables, and of psychiatrists, who generally operate on a "medical" model, which overemphasizes individual variables, disregard the complex and complementary interplay of biological, psychodynamic, and interactional factors. . . . A collaborative relationship between families and the hospital staff could be developed by the establishment of treatment contacts and by combining these two models, thus accepting the patient's illness as the focus while recognizing the importance of family variables.

This quote states extremely well the problem of integrating theories of etiology and pathogenesis from both environmental and biological data. This is a problem shared alike by patient, family, and hospital staff. Some advances have been made since 1977. The research on expressed emotion in the family environments of schizophrenics with subsequent family intervention research with this population[8,9] (see Chapter 22) have put biological etiological causes in perspective, along with environmental influences that can shape the course of the illness, thus focusing treatment intervention strategies. In addition, research designs that include pharmacotherapy in various doses plus family intervention[10] recognize and provide data on the importance of therapeutic attack on the biological and social front simultaneously.

FUNCTION OF THE PSYCHIATRIC HOSPITAL VIS-A-VIS THE FAMILY

Brief psychiatric hospitalization, which is now the norm in this country (and internationally), serves the function of providing a safe and controlled environment in which to treat acute symptoms of depression, suicidal ideation, alcoholism, severe personality disorder, and psychotic thought and behavior.[2] In addition, the hospitalization serves major functions for the family of the patient. By hospitalization, the identified patient is temporarily removed from the family environment when it seems no longer possible to contain the situation by other means. In acute family crises, hospitalization may be a means of decreasing behavioral eruptions. They may offer substantial relief to a desperate family that is headed for serious deterioration. This enforced separation is undertaken with the goal of evaluating and changing the conditions so as to improve the family's patterns of interaction.[11]

Hospitalization can also serve the function of dramatically symbolizing the problems and bringing them to a point that calls out for attention and resolution. This permits observation, evaluation, and discussion during the hospitalization of family interaction patterns around the patient, and permits establishment of a motivation for seeking marital and family treatment after the patient's return to a better functioning family setting. It may also set the stage for overt (as opposed to previous covert) consideration of separation in deadlocked marital or parent-child interactions.

FAMILY INFLUENCES ON THE HOSPITALIZATION PROCESS

While not trying to imply that the family interactions are a major, or sole, cause of the serious individual symptoms, it seems clear that the hospitalization of the family member can serve important functions for the family system.

1. The family is in a crisis and the hospitalization can be an attempt to solve the crisis.[12-14] In this connection, some couples have described the outcome of a psychotic episode and their attempts to cope with it as a strongly positive experience for them.[15]
2. The family extrudes the identified patient from the family in an attempt to solve the crisis.

> The M. family consisted of mother, boyfriend, and two teenage daughters. The eldest daughter had anorexia nervosa. The other sibling was functioning well in high school. The mother had long-standing chronic paranoid schizophrenia and was extremely dependent on her own mother. She had been divorced about ten years previously and had finally found a boyfriend.
>
> After the mother formed a relationship with her boyfriend and was seriously considering marriage, she began to argue with the elder daughter more frequently. The daughter began eating less and became paranoid. The mother then contacted a pediatrician, stating that the daughter was seriously ill and needed hospitalization. The mother reported she was unable to take care of the identified patient's demands because she was fearful of losing her boyfriend *since doing so would prevent her from spending time with him.* The pediatrician hospitalized the daughter.
>
> This case illustrated how one family member can extrude another member from the family in order to take care of his or her own needs. The mother was afraid of losing her boyfriend, and therefore restructured the family by having the identified patient hospitalized.

3. The family uses the hospital to get treatment for a member other than the identified patient. The hospitalized member is not necessarily the only "sick" one (or at times, not even the "sickest" one) in the family.[16] A family approach allows for the observation and evalution of all significant others, with appropriate treatment (including medication) for the group

and for the nonpatient individuals who may require it. Therapists concentrating on the treatment of one individual may entirely overlook even gross, florid psychological disturbance in a close relative. When therapists view their role as that of assisting a family unit, this sort of blind spot is less likely to occur.

4. The family uses the hospital as a resource to regain a "lost" member. For example, a father who drinks and is never home is finally convinced to go into a hospital because of his drinking. The family's motivation is to have him back as a functioning father and spouse; but the family may also need to keep him "sick" for its own needs and homeostasis.

5. The hospital is used as a neutral arena to change long-standing maladaptive patterns of family functioning. An example is the family with an alcoholic member, for whom hospitalization of the identified patient will sometimes allow for change of an underlying family pattern. Of course, for this to happen, the hospital staff must plan the appropriate family interventions—simply separating the identified patient and the family is necessary, but usually not sufficient for change.

6. If the identified patient has a chronic progressive or deteriorating condition like, for example, childhood schizophrenia, then the family may use the hospital as a respite to relieve family burdens.

If these assumptions about the needs of the family around the hospitalization are correct, then it follows that *in such cases the treatment program is inadequate unless it includes the family and its goals.*

THE PROCESS OF FAMILY TREATMENT
BY THE HOSPITAL TEAM

The process of family intervention by the hospital team involves steps similar to those in doing outpatient family treatment—involving the family assessment, defining the problem, setting goals, treatment, and referral for assistance following discharge. However, the context of hospitalization is unusual in the extent of pathology of one member, the seriousness of the event, and the crisis for the family, all of which require special mention and attention. Treatment, of course, should be individualized and fitted to the needs of the particular family.

Although all the necessary research has not yet been done, preliminary work suggests that there are differential indications for different types of family interviews. As a rule of thumb, family psychoeducational techniques are most indicated for families in which one member has a schizophrenic disorder or affective disorder, and psychodynamic techniques are more indicated for patients with personality disorder.

Involving the Family

Contact with the family should start very early, *preferably prior to hospitalization*, when the family is trying to arrange admission, or certainly by the time of the actual admission. Many hospital personnel have had the experience of beginning discharge planning late in the course of hospitalization, only to discover at that time that the family, implicitly or explicitly, resists having the patient at home. It usually has to be pointed out to the family that hospital treatment of the identified patient involves (or requires) treatment of all family members. This also may be made a condition of admission. A family representative may be appointed to be the central communicating link with the primary therapist in the hospital (see below).

Evaluating the Family

Evaluation of the family should involve the presence of the identified patient unless he or she is so psychotic that this is impossible or too disturbing to the patient. The evaluation will follow the general outline as that given in Chapter 7, but with particular emphasis on the immediate events, including family interactions and changes, leading up to the hospitalization. The evaluation should be constructed in such a way as to provide information as to whether further family intervention is needed during hospitalization, and, if so, the potential focus of that intervention, much like brief focal intervention discussed in Chapter 16.

Negotiating Goals of Family Intervention

Keeping in mind that the hospitalization is brief and time-limited, the therapist must quickly focus on the general goals and those most specific to the individual family and begin to negotiate these with the family either toward the end of the evaluation session or in the next session. This negotiation with the family must be done with confidence, delicacy, firmness, and with empathy, as the families are frequently upset about the condition of their loved one, may see no need for the hospitalization, may see no need for their participation in therapy as the patient is the only sick one, or may be hostile to the hospital for not quickly "curing" their family member.

Education about the illness in order to reduce family guilt over creating the condition, and information about the length of hospitalization and expectation for change will reduce anxiety. Realistic expectations for change may reduce unrealistic expectation of cure and subsequent disappointment and devaluing of the hospital and its staff. Education about needed family assistance will help in discharge treatment compliance. Sessions that can vary in length from 30 minutes to

1 hour can be scheduled on a daily, bi-weekly, or weekly basis, depending upon need and/or anticipated discharge date.

COMMON GOALS AND TECHNIQUES

There are six overriding goals that dictate the focus of family intervention when one family member is an inpatient. These goals set the course of the work with each family so that the aim and thrust of the intervention are clearly defined from the beginning of the hospitalization. While our own inpatient family intervention research[17] has been with two major diagnostic groups—schizophrenic spectrum patients and major affective disorders—the goals are not so specific to the diagnostic groups as much as they are specific to the serious problems presented to the family by a member in crisis and hospitalized for major pathology.

Such a family, whatever the diagnosis, is presented with multiple tasks: (1) forming a conceptual understanding of the patient's illness, (2) deciding about the family's responsibility for the illness, (3) making some alliance with hospital treatment staff while trying to ascertain if the staff blame them for the condition of their family member, (4) beginning to conceptualize the possible future course of the illness and adjusting any previous images and expectations of the ill member in light of the nature of the illness, (5) deciding on what future course of treatment following discharge from the hospital will be needed for the patient, and (6) making some decisions as to what living arrangements will be most beneficial for the family member once he or she is discharged. These tasks faced by the family are enormous, especially on first hospitalization of the patient, and without specific, organized attention from the therapeutic staff, are often faced without professional help despite the fact that the patient (family) is paying enormous fees for the hospitalization.

The six goals of inpatient family intervention are designed to meet the needs of the family as delineated above in a systematic fashion. It is our hypothesis that, if these family needs are addressed, the family can be a major asset in the recovery of the identified patient. If these needs of the family are not met, the family may react with hostility, chaos, and become an irritant to the patient, possibly leading to future exacerbation of symptoms, rather than becoming an asset to the patient in the crucial post-hospitalization phase. The six treatment goals with their corresponding treatment strategies and techniques are as follows.

Goal 1: Acceptance by the family of the reality of the illness, and developing understanding of the current episode.

This goal, while so obvious, is the cornerstone of the other goals, as the

family must begin to achieve some acceptance/understanding of the seriousness of
the episode that caused the hospitalization, otherwise their conception of the
patient in terms of setting future goals and their acceptance of needed future
treatment following hospitalization will be compromised.   Family therapists
can choose from a number of techniques to accomplish this goal. They can actively engage the family and patient and form a working alliance by recognizing
and expressing the burden of stress experienced by the whole family. They can
explore each family member's perception and articulation of the illness. While
therapists may not agree with the family member's understanding of the illness,
they can identify with and empathize with the family's previous attempts to deal
with the illness. In order to reduce inordinant feelings of responsibility for the illness, the therapist can provide the family with factual information about the illness, and (in the case of schizophrenia and major affective illness) articulate the
biological, genetic causes of the illness as seen today. Once the family has some
trust in the therapist and realizes that the therapist is not attempting to blame the
family for the current episode, the therapist can begin to explore with the family
the emergence and development of psychotic symptoms in the current episode, so
as to begin to identify stresses both external and internal to the family. As further
steps, the therapist can educate the family about the course of symptoms, including likely early signs, progression, and development in the future.

Goal 2: Identification with the family of precipitating stresses relevant to the current episode.

Once the family has in some fashion, even tentatively, accepted the reality of
the illness, the next step is to identify possible precipitating stressors that might
have been operating in the present episode, so fresh in the family's mind. This acceptance incorporates into the family's daily life the abstract notion that stress can
influence the patient who is vulnerable because of major psychiatric illness. Only
when this link between theory and life situation is made in the family's mind will
progress be likely to occur.

Strategies and techniques to achieve this goal are mainly educative, cognitive, and problem solving in nature. The therapist can encourage the family to
think about recent stresses, both in and outside the family environment, that may
have contributed to the patient's regression. In addition, the therapist and family
can rank the stresses in order to clarify which ones were potentially more important, and thus focus the brief intervention accordingly. In the best of situations, the
family comes to some growing consensus about the most important recent stresses.

Goal 3: Identification of likely future stressors, both within and outside the family environment, that will impinge on the identified patient.

Goals 1 and 2 are concerned in great detail with the immediate and remote past: the recent upset with psychosis, and stressors that might have contributed to this eruption. Once these goals have been accomplished to some extent, there is a natural pull on the part of the family and therapist to begin consideration of the immediate future. In fact, in some cases the pull to focus on the future (e.g., discharge) comes too early in the hospitalization and signals defensive denial, which must be met with refocusing on Goals 1 and 2 before proceeding to Goals 3 and 6.

Goal 4: Elucidation of the family's interaction patterns that produce stress on the identified patient.

Telling the family that they probably put stress on the patient is accepted intellectually and vaguely at best, but more persuasively when in the immediacy of the moment the family is shown that what they are doing right now is leading to the patient's symptoms (e.g., talking crazy or getting up to pace about the room). Then learning takes place.

While the previous goals are approached by cognitive and educative strategies, this attempt to point out stress on the patient in current family interaction more closely approximates systems or more traditional family therapy. After pointing out when such an interaction occurs in the session (e.g., "Every time you criticize him as you did just now he seems to put his head down and murmur something that sounds like nonsense under his breath"), the notion of blaming the family and thus incurring resistance and hostility can be softened by doing one of several things. The therapist can teach the family members that the current family interaction is not the cause of the disorder, but is likely to trigger current symptoms. In addition, the therapist can empathize with the family regarding their feelings of frustration and anger toward the patient's behavior, which lead them to criticize the patient, and let them know they need to find (with your help) better ways to try to influence the patient.

Goal 5: Planning strategies for managing and/or minimizing future stresses.

By the middle or toward the end of hospitalization there is often some relief in family members that the past is over. However, the therapist must remind them that what happened in the past could happen in the future, and that planning is needed now to ensure that history does not repeat. Role playing is an excellent technique at this stage.

The therapist can invite and initiate discussion of the possible return of symptoms and the family means of coping with them. There must be discussion about expectations the family has regarding the patient's future level of functioning, with realistic lowering of such expectations in some cases and, in some, stimulating hope in the family. The therapist can also help the family anticipate any potential stress related to the patient's re-entry into the community, including re-entry into employment, education, job, etc.

Goal 6: Acceptance of the need for continued treatment following discharge from the hospital.

This goal, which is central to preventing relapse and rehospitalization, comes full circle to the first goal of reducing denial of the illness/problem complex once the immediate symptoms are reduced. For families who have seen their patient go through numerous hospitalizations, there is no problem in anticipating the future possibility of rehospitalization, but they may be so discouraged and burdened that they need support and encouragement. For families going through a first break and first hospitalization, there is more danger of utter denial of the future possibility of psychotic episodes, and thus more chance of denying the need for aftercare.

The therapist can use strategies of visualizing with the family possible replays in the future of what just happened leading up to the present hospitalization. How would they perform differently the next time? What are the early signs that something is going wrong? Who would they contact? Further education provided by the therapist about typical courses of the condition may further emphasize the need for aftercare.

Not every family will need work on all goals, and some families will be so damaged and defective that only a few basic goals can be approached. However, most cases fit into this general schema.

PARTICULAR DECISIONS

Timing

Contact with the family should start in the decision-making process leading to hospitalization. Family therapists disagree about when in the psychotic process to begin family sessions with the patient present. Some believe that family therapy with the patient present should begin only when the active symptoms begin to diminish, because they disorganize under the family stress.[18] This seems reasonable, although it is our experience that this can be used as a rationalization to put off family treatment, and many patients even in a psychotic state become more coherent during family sessions that are well-planned and focused by the therapist.

Our preference is to begin family work from the outset of hospitalization and titrate the involvement of the identified patient. Our rationale is based on the notion that joining the family during the time when the identified patient is most disturbed allows the family to perceive the therapist as an ally in solving a family problem, rather than an individual problem (namely the loss of control), as empathic (i.e., experiencing what they are experiencing), and setting the stage to find coping mechanisms that will bear fruit later on in the course of hospitalization.

Staffing

Who should do the family therapy? The primary hospital therapist is the one in the best position to do the family therapy, because he or she has the best overall grasp of the case. The advantages of one therapist doing both the individual and the family therapy far outweigh the disadvantages. Time constraints may not always make this possible, however, and alternative solutions may have to be devised.

Family therapy has been carried out by all members of the hospital treatment team. Nurses, at visiting or other scheduled times, can meet with the patient and family. Occupational and recreational therapists can utilize family treatment. They can prescribe activities for the family, such as preparing a meal together or going on a picnic together. These professionals have crucial roles in changing long-standing behavior patterns in the family system.

The hospital milieu is especially advantageous for observing and pointing out family interaction patterns. For example, if an adolescent child is paranoid about the nursing staff, it may be demonstrated to him that this is similar to the way he reacts to his mother. Accurate, on-the-spot observation of the family may reveal that a patient has some good reasons for his or her symptom.*

How can the need for maximal communication among staff members be reconciled with the need for confidentiality between the patient and the therapist? Communication between staff seems crucial for effective treatment. The family should be told that the therapist will use all the material that is available in both the individual and family contacts to help the family function better. (This issue has been discussed in greater detail in other parts of this book.)

How about a co-therapist? Some therapists believe that family therapy in a hospital setting is the most difficult kind of psychotherapy. They recommend that every family therapist have a co-therapist to share the emotional strains of such therapy. Co-therapy in a hospital setting may be more practical than in a private office practice.

---

*Family diagnosis and therapy in the context of rehabilitation therapy, psychology, social work, and psychiatric nursing are described in Chapter 29.

There should be one member of the family designated as the *family represen-tative*. One member of the ward staff can be assigned as liaison to the family and should be available to the family at times mutually convenient, such as on nights and weekends. The assignment of roles is crucial in situations in which there are "factions at war" within the family.

TYPES OF INPATIENT FAMILY INTERVENTIONS

A variety of family therapy techniques are available for use in the hospital setting. These include:

1. Individual family therapy.
2. Multiple family-group therapy and conjoint couples group.[19]
3. Family psychoeducational workshops (also known as family survival skills workshops or family support groups).[20]
4. Family role-play and family sculpture—both role playing and family sculpture are nonverbal techniques that are often more helpful than cognitive techniques when treating a hospitalized (often nonverbal) sample of patients. We ask families to role-play the system when the identified patient is "on" medication and how it changes "off" medication.

It is rare for family treatment to be the primary therapy for hospitalized patients. Usually for psychotic patients it is prescribed along with medication and other rehabilitative therapies. For nonpsychotic patients it is usually part of a treatment package consisting of individual therapy, rehabilitation therapy, and other interventions.

In the W. family, a 17-year-old boy was admitted after having been extremely agitated and disoriented at home, refusing to eat or sleep. The working diagnosis was schizophrenic disorder. In the hospital he continued to be wary, eating only when his mother ate with him and avoiding participation in the activities involving other patients. The staff had decided to administer neuroleptic medication. They sat down with the boy and his mother and explained their observations and concerns. They then described the drug and the effects they hoped it would have. They also discussed side effects and remedies for these, and focused specifically on how the boy and his mother would be able to evaluate the effectivness of the drug. Specifically, if the boy were to find out that he could think more clearly and understand what is going on around him, then the medicine would be working and he could then help the staff decide what will be the best dose.

The boy hesitated, and his mother had some questions. Finally, however, she told the boy that she thought he should try it, and he agreed. Two days later he said that he felt better and wanted to stop the medication. The staff told him that there had not really been enough time to evaluate it, and they spoke again with him and his mother. Again she told the boy that she wanted him to take the medication. Again he agreed to do so. A week later he said he felt better but wondered if an increased dose would help him sleep better. In another conference with his mother a new dosage schedule was arranged.

The boy and his mother had a difficult kind of relationship through this experience. His mother had been consulted as a parent, and her competence to evaluate and help her son was underscored. The boy, on the other hand, had a new experience of negotiating with his mother. Decisions were not made for him, but he was included along with his mother in an active decision-making process. As the hospitalization progressed he felt freer to ask questions of both his mother and the staff, and the answers helped to clarify the confusion of his psychotic state. In this way the neuroleptic and the contextual experiences may have worked synergistically.

It is important to note that family intervention in a hospital setting is hard work. That is, it is not accepted easily (by either patient or family). The "counter-transferential" behavior emanating from the family is often intense, while the benefits are often not seen until well after the patient is discharged. It also requires good communication, socialization and control skills by the family therapist, and is very time-consuming to boot.

A WORKING MODEL OF INPATIENT FAMILY INTERVENTION

The GAP Committee on the Family[21] has summarized very succinctly the new family model:

Hospitalization should be viewed in most cases as an event in the history of the family, an event that can be devastating or valuable depending upon the skills and orientation of the therapeutic team. When hospitalization is viewed in this way, it becomes central to understand the role of the patient in the family system and to support the family as well as the patient. The hospital becomes an important therapeutic adjunct not only for severely dysfunctional individuals and their families, but also for families who are stuck in modes of relating that appear to interfere with the development and movement of individual members. For these families, hospitalization aims to disrupt the family set; this disruption can be used to help the family system to change in more functional ways.

Family-oriented programs can be implemented within existing hospital resources, though there is a general trend toward adapting and revising hospital environments to include family members in patient care. (This trend is also noted in other specialties, such as "rooming in" in obstetric and pediatric units.) Effective programs involve the staff, from admission clerks on up, in building an alliance with the family. Stewart describes this as "the engagement of the family with the institution in a relationship that achieves mutual

Table 24-2

Inpatient Family Intervention*

Definition: Inpatient family intervention (IFI) is work with the patient and his or her family together in one or more family sessions. It is aimed at favorably affecting the *patient's* course of illness and course of treatment through increased understanding of the illness and decreased stress on the patient. It has been carried out by inpatient social workers, first-year psychiatry residents, or both together as co-therapists.

Description:

I. *Assumptions*

    1. IFI does *not* assume that the etiology of the major psychotic disorders lies in family functioning or communication.

    2. It *does* assume that the *present-day* functioning of a family with which the patient is living or is in frequent contact can be a major source of stress or support.

II. *Aims*

    1. IFI aims to help the family to understand, live with, and deal with the patient and his or her illness; to develop the most appropriate possible ways of addressing the problems presented by the illness and its effects on the patient; to understand and support both the necessary hospital treatment and long-range treatment plans.

    2. It aims to help the patient to understand his or her family's actions and re-actions and to develop the most appropriate possible intrafamily behavior on his or her part, in order to decrease his or her vulnerability to family stress and decrease the likelihood that his or her behavior will provoke it.

III. *Strategy and Techniques*

  A. *Evaluation*

    1. Evaluation is accomplished in one or more initial sessions with the family, with the patient present when conditions permit. Information gained from other sources is also used.

    2. The patient's illness and its potential course are evaluated.

    3. The present effect and the possible future effect on the family are determined.

    4. The family's effect on the patient is evaluated, with particular reference to the stress caused by expressed emotion and criticism.

    5. Family structure and interaction and the present point in the family life cycle are evaluated in order to determine whether particular aspects of the patient's role in the family are contributing to exacerbations of illness or to the maintenance of illness and/or impairment.

  B. *Techniques*

    1. The family and patient are usually seen together.

    2. Early in the hospitalization an attempt is made to form an alliance with the family that gives them a sense of support and understanding.

    3. *Psychoeducation:* (a) The family is provided with information about the illness, its likely course and its treatment; questions are answered. (b) The idea that stress from and in the family can cause exacerbation of the illness is discussed. (c) The ways in which conflicts and stress arise within each family are discussed, and a problem-solving approach is taken in planning ways to decrease such stress in the future. (d) The ways in which the illness and the patient's impaired functioning have burdened the family are discussed and plans made to decrease such burden.

4. In some cases, the initial evaluation of subsequent sessions suggests that there are particular resistances due to aspects of family structure or family dynamics that interfere with the accomplishment of (2) and (3) above. If it is judged necessary and possible, there may be attempts in one or a series of family sessions to explore such resistances and make changes in family dynamics. Such attempts may use some traditional family therapy techniques. Such families may be encouraged to seek family therapy after the patient's discharge.

*The material in this section has been taken in part from a study, *Inpatient Family Intervention: A Controlled Study*, funded in part by an NIMH Grant (MH#34466) and was drafted by Drs. J. Spencer and I. Glick.

understanding and support and establishes clarity, acceptance, and commitment to mutually agreed upon goals for the treatment of the hospitalized patient."[22] This active reaching out is different from a commitment to change-oriented family treatment. Involvement of the family (as we are describing) makes possible the avoidance of staff overidentification with the patient against the family, as well as reducing the stigma of psychiatric hospitalization and increasing system-wide motivation for aftercare.

Many different types of staff/family interaction are possible and helpful. One may separate the tasks of alliance building, formal family therapy sessions geared to change, and staff and family interaction around medications, visits, and so forth, which can also have a therapeutic function. An example of an innovative, well functioning family-oriented approach in an inpatient setting can be found in Table 24-2.

GUIDELINES FOR INPATIENT FAMILY INTERVENTION

The guidelines for recommending family therapy in a hospital setting are similar to those for outpatient settings. Moreover, if the family is present and available, we believe it is more efficacious to utilize family evaluation and often some form of family intervention.[23] Similarly, patients who are visited by family tend *not* to elope, suggesting a kind of family protection against elopement.

A careful distinction has to be made between evaluation versus family treatment given the brief length of stay of most hospitals in the world. As a rule of thumb, each family unit should be evaluated, then educated to and induced into family treatment. The treatment should, whenever possible, be started in the hospital, but most goals commonly will be accomplished in the post-hospital phase.

Prototypic situations that call for some form of family intervention during hospitalization include the following:

• A suicidal and depressed adolescent living in the parental home is hospitalized following a car accident. There is some suspicion that the father is alcoholic and the parents are not aware of the adolescent's depression nor day-to-day functioning.

- A 22-year-old male college student is hospitalized following an acute psychotic episode in the fall of his first year at school away from home. Family sessions are indicated with the parents to educate them about the unexpected illness, to help them and the patient evaluate their mutual expectations for his performance, and to encourage follow-up psychiatric care, which the son has never needed in the past.
- A 39-year-old divorced woman living with her two children, ages 11 and 13, is hospitalized following a suicide attempt during a paranoid break in which she stabbed herself in the abdomen in the presence of the children. Family sessions with the children are needed to assist the mother, now in a denial phase, to communicate with the children about her illness episode and talk about the future.
- A 23-year-old female with a history of schizophrenia, who lives with her parents, is hospitalized following an exacerbation of symptoms occasioned by her younger sisters leaving for college and going off her own medication. The parents are suspected of high "expressed emotion" (they are critical of their daughter, and mother is constantly with her day and night), and family treatment is started during the hospitalization as a role induction into proper aftercare, with medication and possible family intervention following discharge.

The indications can be conceptualized as coming from the patient, from the family, and from the interaction between the family and the illness for which the patient is hospitalized. Patient-related criteria would include current living condition (e.g., living with spouse or family of origin), life cycle issues (e.g., patient is young adult trying to separate, or older adult living with and very dependent upon family of origin). Family criteria include current family conflict that appears to contribute to patient's difficulties, or significant psychiatric illness in one or more other members of the family. Criteria related to the interaction of family and the patient's illness on deficit behavior around the illness (e.g., family denial of illness, danger that patient will physically harm someone, family not supporting the vulnerable patient, family not supportive of treatment for patient's illness).

As to contraindications, for some patients (unfortunately we do not know for whom), family therapy may make them worse. Our speculation is that these patients are males now called "negative schizophrenics." It should be noted that even though family intervention may be indicated during the hospitalization, there are many situations in which that does not seem to be needed, nor the treatment of choice upon discharge from the hospital. When the patient is living alone, but needs the family support during hospitalization, often individual treatment is recommended upon discharge. When the individual patient is striving with some success for independence from parents, individual treatment may seem the best. If the parents are severely conflictful—with this problem coming to the forefront as the patient individuates—marital treatment may be recommended for them.

RESULTS

The only controlled study of family intervention in an inpatient setting is a study by Glick et al.,[17] in which inpatient family intervention (with a heavy family psychoeducational component) is being compared to standard hospitalization without family intervention for patients with schizophrenic disorders and affective disorders. The sample includes 169 patients and their families for whom family intervention is indicated, and who are randomized to one of the two treatment conditions. Both conditions are conducted with the use of treatment manuals. Assessments are made at admission, discharge, and 6 and 18 months postadmission, using patient and family measures on multiple dimensions from the vantage points of patient, family, and independent accessors.

Preliminary results suggest that, for families, the family intervention is more efficacious than the comparison treatment. From the point of view of diagnosis, family intervention is more efficacious for female schizophrenics with poor prehospital functioning and for patients and families with affective disorders (especially patients with bipolar disorders), but does not seem efficacious for acute schizophrenics. (It is helpful for the families of females with chronic schizophrenia). In a like vein, clinical experience suggests that the specific interventions of psychoeducational groups can help the demoralized family of the chronic patient to reestablish itself as a viable unit and lessen the burden of shame, guilt, despair, and isolation.[24]

OTHER TYPES OF FAMILY INVOLVEMENT AS AN ALTERNATIVE TO PSYCHIATRIC HOSPITALIZATION

At times of family crisis, psychiatric hospitalization of a family member is one solution. With the gradual shift of psychiatric services out of the hospital and into the community, other alternatives have emerged. Schizophrenic patients, in some cases, can be kept out of hospitals altogether by sending the treatment team to see them in their homes.[25,26] Day hospitalization with a focus on family treatment is another alternative to psychiatric hospital admission.[27] Day hospitals also have moved toward utilizing family therapy as a primary method of treatment. The population of such settings is chronic, and difficulties with family relationships are a major problem.

In the L. family there were two brothers, A. and M. The father had died and the mother was the grieving widow. One son lived by himself, managing marginally, while the other son came to a day hospital for management of his schizophrenia.

Treatment at the day hospital was oriented around helping him to obtain volunteer work. Whenever the volunteer counselor and his therapist at the day hospital came close to finding a job placement for him, they noticed that the patient would start screaming, become paranoid, and collapse on the street. Further investigation of these symptoms revealed that on the nights before the patient was to go to his appointments, his mother would, in painstakingly minute detail, describe her anxiety about not knowing his whereabouts, and how her heart would not pump as a result. She told him that she would not want to stop him from leaving but at the same time needed to know that he was safe in the day hospital, rather than at some volunteer job where she could not call him.

This case is typical of many chronic patients whose level of function is marginal. Any change in that level is often perceived as a threat by the family.

Often a change in the balance of family forces precipitates the request for hospitalization, and understanding the shift can result in strategies to prevent extrusion of the identified patient. Although hospitalization can be avoided, continued family work is needed to change behavior patterns that exacerbate the identified patient's condition.

READING FOR THE FAMILY

Over the past decade, a number of excellent books have been written for families with a mentally ill member. They include books by Wasow[28] and Bernheim et al.[29] The recent book by Korpell[30] uses a more traditional, individually oriented model and is therefore not recommended by us.

SUMMARY

As Lansky has pointed out, "family therapy began in the spirit of revolt, hostile to traditional ways of doing things and to established methods: to psychoanalysis, to medicine, to professional affiliations, and to the usual way hospitals were run and sick people were seen. Revolutionary zeal led to an overemphasis on the adaptational aspects of the disturbed behavior of "identified patients" for their entire family system. This emphasis had its unfortunate side. Family therapists seeking recognition and independence from medical models came close to abandoning the very patients who most needed the family approach, that is to say the very disturbed, for whom simplistic methods will not work. We have moved to a more integrative phase in the last five years. Family therapists are more likely to have the sophistication to see the value of educational aspects in the treatment of psychosis in the family context, the importance of narcissistic vulnerability in intimate relationships, and the use of special techniques derived for specific psychopathological predicaments and stages in family development."[31]

SUGGESTIONS FOR FURTHER READINGS

Group for the Advancement of Psychiatry: **The Family, The Patient and The Psychiatric Hospital: Toward a New Model**. New York: Brunner/Mazel, 1985.
   A well-thought out statement by the committee on the family.

REFERENCES

1. Glick ID and Hargreaves WA: Psychiatric Hospital Treatment for the 1980s: A Controlled Study of Short Versus Long Hospitalization. Lexington, MA: Lexington Press, 1979
2. Glick ID, Klar HM, and Braff DL: Guidelines for hospitalization of chronic psychiatric patient. Hosp Comm Psychiatry 35:934-936, 1984
3. Group for the Advancement of Psychiatry: The Family, the Patient, and the Psychiatric Hospital: Toward a New Model. New York: Brunner/Mazel, 1985, p.24
4. Bell J and Bell E: Family participation in hospital care for children. Children 17:154-157, 1970
5. Bhatti RS, Janakiramaiah N, and Channabasavanna SM: Family psychiatric ward treatment in India. Fam Proc 19:193-200, 1980
6. Harbin HT: Families and hospitals: Collusion or cooperation? Am J Psychiatry 135:1496-1499, 1978
7. Anderson CM: Family intervention with severely disturbed inpatients. Arch Gen Psychiatry 34:697-702, 1977
8. Falloon IRH, Boyd J, McGill C et al.: Family management training in the community care of schizophrenia. In Goldstein MJ (Ed): New Developments in Interventions with Families of Schizophrenia. San Francisco: Jossey-Bass, 1981, pp 61-77
9. Falloon IRH: Communication and problem solving skills training with relapsing schizophrenics and their families. In Lansky MR (Ed): Family Therapy and Major Psychopathology. New York: Grune & Stratton, 1981, pp 35-56
10. Goldstein MJ, Rodnick EH, Evans JR, May RA, and Steinberg MR: Drug and family therapy in the aftercare of acute schizophrenics. Arch Gen Psychiatry 35:1169-1177, 1978

11. Rabiner E, Malminski H, and Gralnick A: Conjoint family therapy in the inpatient setting. In Gralnick A (Ed): The Psychiatric Hospital as a Therapeutic Instrument. New York: Brunner/Mazel, 1969, pp. 160-177
12. Sampson H, Messinger S, and Towne RD: The mental hospital and family adaptations. Psychiatric Q 36:704-719, 1962
13. Sampson H, Messinger S, and Towne RD: The mental hospital and family adaptations. Psychiatric Q 36:704-719, 1962
14. Langsley D and Kaplan D: The Treatment of Families in Crisis. New York: Grune & Stratton, 1968
15. Dupont R, Ryder R, and Grunebaum H: Unexpected results of psychosis in marriage. Am J Psychiatry 128:735-739, 1971
16. Bursten B: Family dynamics, the sick role, and medical hospital admissions. Fam Proc 4:206-216, 1965
17. Glick ID, Clarkin JF, Spencer JH, et al.: A controlled evaluation of inpatient family intervention. Arch Gen Psychiatry 42:882-886, 1985
18. Guttman H: A contraindication for family therapy: The prepsychotic or postpsychotic young adult and his parents. Arch Gen Psychiatry 29:352-355, 1973
19. Davenport YB: Treatment of the married bipolar patient in conjoint couples psychotherapy groups. In Lansky MR (Ed): Family Therapy and Major Psychopathology. New York: Grune & Stratton, 1981, pp 123-143
20. Anderson CM, Hogarty GE, and Reiss DJ: Family treatment of adult schizophrenic patients: A psychoeducational approach. Schiz Bull 6:490-505, 1980
21. Group for the Advancement of Psychiatry: The Family, the Patient, and the Psychiatric Hospital: Toward a New Model. New York: Brunner/Mazel, 1985, pp. 27-29
22. Stewart RP: Building an alliance between the families of patients and the hospital: Model and process. NAPPH Journal 12:63-68, 1982
23. Gould E and Glick ID: The effects of family presence and family therapy on outcome of hospitalized schizophrenic patients. Fam Process 16:503-510, 1977
24. McLean C and Grunebaum H: Parent's response to chronically psychotic children. Paper presented at the American Psychiatric Association Meeting, Toronto, 1982
25. Pasamanick B, Scarpitti F, and Dinitz S: Schizophrenics in the Community. New York: Appleton-Century-Crofts, 1967
26. Davis A, Dinitz S, and Pasamanick B: The prevention of hospitalization in schizophrenia: Five years after an experimental program. Am J Orthopsychiatry 42:375-388, 1972
27. Zwerling I and Mendelsohn M: Initial family reactions to day hospitalization. Fam Process 4:50-63, 1965

28. Wasow M: Coping with Schizophrenia: A survival manual for patients, relatives and friends. Palo Alto: Science and Behavior Books, 1982

29. Bernheim K, Lewine R, and Beale C: The Caring Family: Living with Chronic Mental Illness. New York: Random House, 1982

30. Korpell H: How You Can Help: A Guide for Families of Psychiatric Hospital Patients. Washington, DC: American Psychiatric Press, 1984

31. Lansky MR: Book review. Am J Psychiatry 141:6, 1984, p.818

Section VII

Guidelines for Recommending Family Treatment

The question we are most frequently asked is, what are the guidelines—i.e., indications and contraindications—for this treatment? Now that we have discussed what family therapy is, how to do it, and to whom, we can discuss these issues. In Chapter 25 we describe our version of a *decision tree* for differential diagnosis and therapeutics, and in Chapter 26 we deal with complicated situations and their guidelines. In the former, we describe (1) when to do evaluation and (2) the different therapies, including the choices of type, length, and modality. All of these guidelines are, however, modified by such factors as the ethnicity of the family, gender issues involving *both* family and therapist, as well as the economic status of the family (usually meaning the money and time the family can spend on treatment). These latter considerations are addressed in Chapter 27.

Family Group by Philip Levine, 1966. Courtesy of Julius and Florence Myers Collection.

25

Indications and the Family Therapy Decision Tree

OBJECTIVES

- To understand the concept of the "clinical decision tree" in differential treatment planning
- To utilize the general indications, contraindications, and enabling factors for family and marital treatment

INTRODUCTION

Some family therapists believe that their field offers the best hope for many types of interpersonal distress. They tend to believe that it should be the exclusive method used and that it should never be used in combinations. Others, however, utilize family therapy as only one type among many and feel that it is "not a panacea, a substitute for all other approaches, or even appropriate in all cases as a totally self-contained service."[1]

Since the l960s, as the family field has evolved, more therapists have shifted to the latter view. Enough well-controlled outcome studies, which might guide us, have not been carried out, however; nor is there the needed empirical evidence on the spontaneous rate of change for families and patients who come for treatment with family and marital problems.[2,3] In formulating guidelines for family therapy, research data are included where available, but otherwise the recommendations are based on clinical experience (see Chapter 31).

In the past decade there have been a number of major changes in the delivery of mental health services (e.g., a shift from inpatient to outpatient and community work), new scientific discoveries (e.g., new psychopharmacologic agents, studies of effectiveness of family therapy compared to other therapies), and social changes (e.g., more one-parent families). The clinician needs an appreciation of those that affect the guidelines for utilization of family therapy.

THE FAMILY THERAPY DECISION TREE

The final recommendation of a particular kind of family treatment is the result of a sequence of clinical decisions. In presenting our material, we have followed a decision tree[4] that is presumably analogous to the sequential process in the clinician's mind as he or she evaluates the family.

Step I.   Is a family evaluation indicated? Our bias is that family treatment would never be recommended except after a family evaluation.

Step II.   Based on the results of the family evaluation, one must proceed to differential therapeutics: is the optimal treatment family therapy or a common alternative (e.g., individual therapy, hospital treatment)?

Step III.   If family/marital therapy is indicated, how can this treatment format be further specified in terms of intensity (crisis versus noncrisis treatment), duration (brief versus open-ended), focus (sex versus marital), subsystems involved (marital versus family), or as part of a sequence of various treatment modalities?

Step IV.   Is a particular methodology (e.g., systems, dynamic) of family intervention most indicated?

STEP I: IS FAMILY/MARITAL EVALUATION INDICATED?

Family evaluation as described in Section III is done to determine how the family influences, and is influenced by, the behavior and symptoms of its individual members, and to gather the data necessary to decide whether family treatment is possible and indicated.

Indications

The following are the indications for conducting a family evaluation:

1. In certain cases, family/marital evaluation is almost always essential in understanding the presenting situation and recommending appropriate treatment. For example:

   - A child or adolescent is the presenting patient
   - The presenting problem is sexual difficulty or dissatisfaction
   - The presenting issue is a family or marital problem serious enough to jeopardize the relationship, job stability, health, or parenting ability of the couple (e.g., child neglect or abuse, disruptive extramarital affairs, spouse battering, preoccupation with problems at work)
   - There has been a recent clear stress and emotional disruption to the family caused by family crisis (illness, injury, job loss, death) or a family milestone (graduation, marriage, birth)
   - The family/marital pair or individual defines the problem as a family issue, and there is motivation for family evaluation

2. Whenever psychiatric hospitalization is being considered, a family evaluation is usually indicated for one or more of the following reasons:

   - History-gathering
   - Clarification of how the family interaction is influenced by and has influenced the course of illness
   - To negotiate the treatment plan with the whole family (i.e., is hospitalization necessary or can the family manage with outpatient help? If hospitalization is necessary, what part will the family play?)

3. The following are less powerful but nonetheless common and important indications for family evaluation:

   - More than one family member is simultaneously in psychiatric treatment
   - Improvement in the individual patient is correlated with symptom formation in another family member or deterioration in their relationship
   - Individual or group treatment has been tried and is failing or has failed and (a) the patient is much more involved with family problems; or (b) the patient has difficulty dealing with family issues unless they are demonstrated directly in the room; or (c) the transference to the therapist is too intense or actualized and can be brought back to realistic propor-

tions by including family members; or (d) family cooperation seems necessary to allow the individual to change

- Although the patient presents with symptoms that are not immediately related to family issues, the therapist decided during the individual evaluation that the primary or secondary gain of the symptoms is an important expression of family systems pathology (e.g., a wife's worsening agoraphobia when husband works overtime)

Relative Contraindications for Family Evaluation

- One or more of the family members strongly prefer or insist upon the privacy of an individual evaluation (e.g., because of a "valid" family secret)
- It appears that the individuation of one or more family members would be compromised by family evaluation, e.g., one might not want to include the family of a young adult who has recently left home for the first time
- Family is breaking up with little or no desire for reconciliation
- The presenting problem is clearly the result of repetitive intrapsychic conflicts that recur in many of the individual's relationships and seem more amenable to individual intervention
- The family has a history of sabotaging treatment alliances
- The patient won't trust a therapist who has also seen his or her family
- There exists a fixed family prejudice against psychiatric intervention and other approaches may be preferred (e.g., use of clergy or social workers)
- Extreme schizoid or paranoid pathology

Many treatment facilities are structured in such a way as to unwittingly *preclude* the serious consideration of conducting a family evaluation when a prospective patient seeks assistance. While family clinics, by their name and reputation, attract those who see themselves as having family problems, most clinics are organized to deal with individuals (not family or marital units) who seek help. In such contexts, the secretaries, for example, ask on the first phone call for the name of the patient and a description of the individual's problems. They routinely given an appointment time to the individual, not the family. There may be no format for a family chart. Likewise, private practitioners often have reputations as primarily marital-family therapists or individual therapists. If care is not given to the initial steps in the help-seeking sequence, the decision to do or not to do a family evaluation can be made inadvertently either by the therapist or by the actions of the patient and his/her family, thus reducing a professional decision to acting out of biases.

STEP II: DIFFERENTIAL THERAPEUTICS

This section illustrates a model of differential treatment planning. We specify those factors discovered in individual and family evaluation that are most crucial in guiding the clinician to select family treatment as opposed to individual, marital, sex, or hospital treatment. Whenever clinicians recommend a specific treatment modality, they have consciously or intuitively matched patients' needs with their own experience of, or fantasies about, various treatments. The following guidelines are meant to broaden this perspective with research data and a summary of general clinical opinion. The process of choosing a therapy will become increasingly precise as the results of accumulating outcome research indicate the specific characteristics of patients who succeed or fail in each treatment modality.

The Choice of Family/Marital versus Individual Therapy

The basic theoretical premise of family and marital therapy is that individual symptoms can be viewed as interpersonal in etiology and/or current maintenance and can be changed by altering the family system. Perhaps one of the most fundamental and common therapy decisions is whether to direct the treatment to the family or to focus on the symptomatic individual. It is not surprising that, in a questionnaire of family therapists,[5] 83 percent were interested in the decision of how to combine individual and family therapies.

It will be noticed that our criteria (Table 25-1) depend more on the characteristics of the family and how the members function than on the particular diagnosis or problem area presented by the identified patient(s). The choice of family therapy, as in most psychiatric treatment, is not determined in any simple or reliable way by patients' problems or diagnoses. The problem is a final common pathway for multiple causes and influences that may or may not include a preponderance of family contribution. The topography of a problem (describing the problem in detail) tells one less how to change it than a functional analysis of the problem (i.e., how much the family in this particular case is maintaining or exacerbating the problem). For these reasons, we have not organized our indications around particular diagnoses. Nonetheless, there are areas in which limited research has shown the usefulness of family therapy for specific symptom constellations such as: schizophrenia;[6,7] marital therapy when one spouse is manic-depressive;[8] alcoholism;[9] adolescents with anorexia;[10] divorce;[11] asthma;[12] (see Chapter 22).

Table 25-1
Relative Selection Criteria for Treatment Format:
Family/Marital versus Individual

Family/Marital	Individual
Relative Indications	*Relative Indications*
1. Family/marital problems are presented as such, without either spouse or any family member designated as the identified patient; symptoms are predominantly within the marital relationship.	1. The patient's symptoms or character is based on firmly structured intrapsychic conflict that causes repetitive life patterns more or less transcending the particulars of the current interpersonal situation (e.g., family, job relationships).
2. Family presents with current structured difficulties in intrafamilial relationships with each person contributing collusively or openly to the reciprocal interaction problems.	2. Adolescent, young adult who is striving for autonomy.
3. Family has fixed and severe deficits in perception and communication: (a) projective identification so that each member blames the other for all problems; (b) family using paranoid/schizoid functioning: boundaries vague and fluctuating, parts of self readily projected onto other family members, trading of ego functions; (c) a relentless fixity of distance maintained by pseudomutual and pseudohostile mechanisms; (d) collective cognitive chaos and erratic distancing; (e) amorphous, vague, undirected forms of communication that are pervasive.	3. Psychiatric problem is of such private and/or embarrassing matter that it needs the privacy of individual treatment, at least for the beginning phase.
4. Adolescent acting-out behavior (e.g., promiscuity, drug abuse, delinquency, perversion, vandalism, violent behavior).	

5. Another form of treatment is stalemated or has failed (e.g., the patient has been unable to utilize intrapsychic mode of individual therapy or uses most of sessions to discuss family problems).
6. Improvement of one family member has led to symptoms or signs of deterioration in another.
7. Reduction of secondary gain in one or more family members is a major goal.
8. More than one person needs treatment, and resources are available for only one treatment.

Enabling Factors

1. Motivation is strongest to be seen as a couple or family, or an individual patient will accept no other format.
2. No family member has psychopathology of such proportions that family therapy would be prevented (e.g., extreme agitation, mania, paranoia, severe distrust, dangerous hostility, or acute schizophrenia).
3. Crucial members of a defined functional social system are available for family treatment.

Relative Contraindications

1. The presenting problem of the individual does not have a significant etiology in or effect upon the family system.
2. Marital problems, if present, are chronic and ego-syntonic.

Enabling Factors

1. Comfortable in dyadic situations; able to handle the potential intimacy of the individual treatment setting.
2. Financial and temporal resources needed for individual treatment.

Relative Contraindications

1. Only issue of real importance is a family problem.
2. Patient regresses in individual therapy relationships.

3. Defensive misuse of family therapy to deny individual responsibility for major personality or character illness.

4. Massive but minimally relevant or unworkable parental pathology that indicates symptomatic child or adolescent should be treated alone.

5. Individuation of one or more family members requires that they have their own and separate treatment.

6. Family treatment has stalemated or failed and has resolved what crises it can, and one or more individual members require additional individual treatment.

7. There is a need for another modality of treatment prior to family therapy (e.g., detoxification, medication, individual sessions to establish trust).

8. Motivation to be seen alone (e.g., adolescents who state emphatically that they have personal problems for which they want individual help).

The Choice of Marital versus Sex Therapy

Marital conflict may be caused by sex problems or may cause sexual dysfunction, and very commonly there is an interaction between the two. The clinician must decide whether or not to include sex therapy as a modality, and, if so, in what priority. Masters and Johnson[13] and Kaplan and Sager[14] have contributed significantly to clarifying appropriate indications for sex therapy and are the principal sources of the criteria in Table 25-2. It is extremely important that the therapist rule out the rare physical causes of sexual dysfunction before treating with psychotherapy in any form.

Although no controlled comparative studies are available to demonstrate the relative usefulness of sex therapy, some of the dramatically successful results

Table 25-2
Criteria for Sex and Marital Therapy

Sex Therapy	Marital Therapy
The marital problem is clearly focused on sexual dysfunction.	Sexuality not an issue, or it is one of many issues in marital dysfunction.
Enabling Factors	
Willingness and ability to carry out the sexual functioning tasks that would be assigned by therapist.	Anger and resistance too intense to carry out extra-session tasks around sexual functioning.
Strong attachment to marital partner; both partners interested in reversing the sexual dysfunction.	Couple not committed to each other; there are covert and/or overt behaviors to dissolve the marriage.

documented by Masters and Johnson[13] and by Kaplan[15] justify serious consideration of this modality when sexual problems are present.

The most clear-cut symptoms amenable to brief sex therapy and their respective "cure" rates are: (a) vaginismis, 100 percent; (b) premature ejaculation, 98
percent; (c) ejaculatory incompetence, 82 percent; (d) organismic dysfunction in
the female, 83 percent; (e) secondary impotence, 70-80 percent; (f) primary impotence, 55 percent. However, these results are somewhat biased in that Masters
and Johnson and Kaplan (appropriately) use screening criteria to exclude those
cases that are least likely to comply with and to benefit from the treatment.
Therefore, not all patients with these sexual complaints will average these impressive results. Because sex therapy is typically brief (5-15 sessions), it does not
preclude further family/marital therapy, whether or not the sexual problems are
resolved.

The criteria in Table 25-2 will help the therapist to choose between sex
therapy and marital therapy.

Family Crisis Therapy versus Hospitalization

Langsley and his colleagues[16,17] have shown, in an extensive, partially controlled comparative study of 300 patients followed for 18 months, that a family
crisis therapy approach is generally superior to hospitalization of the acutely
decompensating individual. His groups, which were matched and randomly assigned to either crisis outpatient family work or hospitalization, demonstrated that
the group receiving the family/crisis approach achieved greater social produc-
tivity, lost two-thirds fewer days of functioning, and cost one-sixth as much to
treat. This often quoted study has more recently been partially replicated by Rittenhouse.[18]

Table 25-3
Criteria for Family Crisis Therapy and Hospitalization

Family Crisis Therapy	Hospitalization
The risk of destructiveness to self or others is within assumable limits.	The patient is too dangerous to keep out of the hospital.
Level of family disruption relatively low.	Necessary to provide a transition and space for individuation of one or more family members.
Need to preserve job and family relationships.	Presence of psychotic person has harmful effects on family or society.
	Thorough evaluation requires 24-hour observation and medical facilities.
	Patient gets worse when with family.

Enabling Factors

Family intact, available, and motivated.	Family highly resistant, not available, or intact enough to carry on treatment and manage patient.
Availability of crisis team.	

This approach is probably suitable for many, but not all, families and requires the availability of a family crisis team. Assuming that this treatment modality is available, the criteria in Table 25-3 are useful for making the choice.

Should Family/Marital Treatment Be Combined with Other Treatments?

In complicated diagnostic situations, multiple diagnoses are an acceptable method for stating and at least temporarily resolving a quandary. Multiple treatment recommendations are less commonly justified or cost effective, and very often the clinician must make one "best" choice even if several seem reasonable and satisfy selection criteria. It is particularly difficult to select a specific treatment for those patients with overwhelmingly good or bad prognoses. The prognostic variable may make the patient appear a wonderful candidate for every treatment modality or, on the other hand, unable to benefit from anything at all.

In some situations, a given therapy is not self-contained and exhaustive, and more than one treatment, performed either sequentially or simultaneously, will be necessary to provide adequate care. Here differential therapeutics informs the process of selecting the proper combination and/or ordering of treatments. Many clinicians would not sharply differentiate marital, family, and sex therapy, and we have done so only to provide guidelines for the sequencing of these interventions.

A common indication for sequenced treatment occurs when the first chosen treatment has received a fair clinical trial and is not sufficiently successful. We will mention only a few of the many other typical instances when sequential treatments are useful.

Often family therapy is one component of a comprehensive treatment plan that includes other modalities. The treatment of patients with schizophrenia is a prominent example. Since having an identified patient with schizophrenia has long-term effects on the family, many have shifted to a therapeutic management with a focus around the family as a unit.[18] Somatic treatments by themselves do not cure problems of living. They can control specific psychophysiological symptoms and behaviors, but alone they will not improve or alter the preexisting family relationships, ways of coping with stress, and other pre-illness behavior. While family treatment seems helpful in these matters[19-21] further thought and research must be directed to when such family intervention is not helpful, such as possibly with late adolescent, early adult schizophrenic males,[22] or when the goal should be to remove the schizophrenic from the household.[23]

A family may present with an issue that clearly calls for family therapy. As the presenting problems resolve, it sometimes becomes clear that one or more family members will also require, or at that point be able to profit from, individual treatment.[24] On the other hand, if, during individual treatment, most of the transference is concentrated in the current relatedness to family members, including them in the treatment may be indicated. Many couples who would benefit from sex therapy are not ready for it and may require individual or marital treatment as a preparation. On the other hand, a good result in sex therapy may unmask further problems requiring marital or other treatment. The most common occasion for simultaneous treatment is probably combined family and individual therapy carried out at the same time by the same or by different therapists.

STEP III: THE DURATION AND INTENSITY OF FAMILY/MARITAL THERAPY

Presuming that (on the basis of evaluation and differential therapeutics) family therapy is indicated, what shall be its duration and intensity? To address this question, we have outlined criteria for family crisis intervention, and for short- and long-term family therapy.

The Choice of Family Crisis Therapy

Family crisis therapy is an intense (as often as daily) family intervention performed during a time of crisis and for a brief duration (usually under a month) to help prevent the imminent decompensation of family relationships or of one or more of the family members and, it is hoped, to reestablish the family equilibrium at a level equal to, or higher than, before the crisis.

This modality is indicated when there is an immediate crisis in the family causing severe and urgent family or individual symptoms or grief that could result in hospitalization or risk to life, limb, sanity, or the family's ability to continue as a unit. The crisis may be triggered by a stress that is:

1. Developmental—child born, child goes to school, marriage, caring for extended family, aging and retirement, wife goes back to work, teenage acting out, etc.
2. Accidental—injury, sickness, death, job loss, etc.
3. Interpersonal—an affair, bitter argument, etc.

The Choice of Brief Family Therapy

Most research investigations of family and marital therapy involve treatment that is brief, i.e., one to 20 sessions. Furthermore, most of the positive results of open-ended therapy are achieved in less than five months.[2] On the other hand, there are only a few reported investigations of therapies that are explicitly time-limited.[25-27] Obviously, the available resources and the goals of the treatment limit the length of the treatment. Criteria drawn from the research and clinical literature indicating a usefulness of family therapy of brief duration (usually under six months, with once-weekly sessions) with a time limit set either at the beginning of treatment or negotiated as it progresses are given in Chapter 14.

Long-Term Family Therapy

Long-term family therapy is a treatment without time limit when short-term intervention is inadequate or goals for the family are more ambitious.

Indications are:

1. Directly from evaluation:

   - Multi-problem family is inherently unstable and will require long-term external support and integration
   - Family is highly motivated for treatment, but problems are complex and not reducible to a manageable, short-term focus
   - Family is not highly motivated for treatment and will require induction period to establish adequate therapeutic alliance
   - Problems are likely to be chronic and not amenable to brief intervention (e.g., intense marital difficulties with mutual projection, fusion, long-standing disagreement)

- Short-term therapy was not sufficient in the past

2. As referral from brief or crisis therapy:

  - Brief therapy was not complete enough nor sufficiently successful; family is motivated to continue work; there is some hope for success
  - Family is especially receptive and responsive to family work and has enough problems to warrant continued treatment and has sufficient resources

Contraindications are:

  - When it appears that extended therapy encourages a family to avoid focusing on problems or to delay therapeutic change

STEP IV: SELECTION OF A PARTICULAR FAMILY/MARITAL THERAPY ORIENTATION

We have described in Chapter 10 the predominant schools or orientations to family therapy. There are, of course, techniques common to and overlapping in all these approaches, and techniques unique to each. Gurman[28] has provided an excellent critical comparison of the prevalent schools, without, however, suggesting when to apply the techniques differentially. Table 31-2 clearly illustrates the reason—the lack of data which would establish efficacy. We suspect that there is a large overlap between the behavioral and the systems techniques and that these approaches are most prominent in briefer treatments and in work with the severely disturbed. Dynamic approaches are probably best suited, because of the more demanding patient enabling factors, for more extensive work with less severely disturbed individuals, couples, and families. It remains for future research to specify which techniques of family treatment are most optimal for specific family types, with which enabling factors, and with what problem areas.[6]

SUGGESTIONS FOR FURTHER READINGS

Frances A, Clarkin JF, and Perry S: **Differential Therapeutics in Psychiatry: The Art and Science of Treatment Selection**. New York: Brunner/Mazel, 1984.
   A review of existing information on treatment planning that puts the selection of family therapy in perspective.

REFERENCES

1. Group for the Advancement of Psychiatry: The field of family therapy. Report No. 78. New York: Group for the Advancement of Psychiatry, 1978, p 543

2. Gurman AS and Kniskern DP: Research on marital and family therapy: Progress, perspective and prospect.In Garfield SL and Bergin AE (Eds): Handbook of Psychotherapy and Behavior Change: An Empirical Analysis (2nd Ed). New York: Wiley, 1978, pp 817-901

3. DeWitt KN: The effectiveness of family therapy. Arch Gen Psychiatry 35:549-561, 1978

4. Clarkin JF, Frances AJ, and Glick ID: The decision to treat a family: Selection criteria and enabling factors. In Wolberg LR and Aronson MS (Eds): Group and Family Therapy 1981. New York: Brunner/Mazel, 1981, pp 149-167

5. Wachtel EF and Wachtel PL: Family Dynamics in Individual Psychotherapy. New York: Guilford Press, 1986

6. Falloon IRH, Boyd JL, McGill CW, Razani J, Moss HB, and Gilderman AM: Family management in the prevention of exacerbations of schizophrenia. N Engl J Med 306:1437-1440, 1982

7. Leff J, Kuipers L, Berkowitz R, Eberlein-Vries R, and Sturgeon D: A controlled trial of social intervention in the families of schizophrenia patients. Br J Psychiatry 141:121-134, 1982

8. Davenport YB, Ebert MH, Adland ML, and Goodwin FK: Couples group therapy as an adjunct to lithium maintenance of the manic patient. Am J Orthopsychiatry 47(3):495-502, 1977

9. Stanton MD: Drugs and the family. A review of the literature. Marriage Family Rev 2 (2), 1979

10. Minuchin S, Rosman B, and Baker L: Psychosomatic Families. Cambridge MA: Harvard University Press, 1978

11. Kaslow FW: Divorce and divorce therapy. In Gurman AS and Kniskern DP (Eds): Handbook of Family Therapy. New York: Brunner/Mazel, 1981, pp 662-696

12. Minuchin S, Baker L, Rosman B, Liebman R, Milman L, and Todd T: A conceptual model of psychosomatic illness in children. Arch Gen Psychiatry 32:1031-1038, 1975

13. Masters EH and Johnson VE: Human Sexual Inadequacy. Boston: Little, Brown, 1970

14. Sager CJ: Sexual dysfunctions and marital discord. In Kaplan HS (Ed): The New Sex Therapy. New York: Brunner/Mazel, 1974, pp 501-518

15. Kaplan HS: Disorders of sexual desire. New York: Simon & Schuster, 1979

16. Langsley DG, Pittman FS, Machotka P, and Flomenhaft K: Family crisis therapy: Results and implications. Family Process 7:145-158, 1968

17. Langsley DG, Machotka P and Flomenhaft K: Avoiding mental hospital admission: A follow-up study. Am J Psychiatry, 1971, 127, pp. 1391-1394

18. Rittenhouse J: Endurance of effect: Family unit treatment compared to identified patient treatment. Proceedings, 78th Annual Convention of the American Psychological Association, 1970, pp 535-536

19. Glick ID, Clarkin JF, Spencer JH, Haas GL, Lewis AB, Peyser J, DeMane N, Good-Ellis M, Harris E, and Lestelle V: A controlled evaluation of inpatient family intervention. Arch Gen Psychiatry 142:1484-1486, 1985

20. Anderson CM, Hogarty GE, and Reiss DJ: Family treatment of adult schizophrenic patients: A psycho-educational approach. Schiz Bull 6:490-505, 1980

21. Beels CC: Family and social management of schizophrenia. Schiz Bull 1:97-118, 1975

22. Goldstein MJ, Rodnick EH, Evans JR, et al.: Drug therapy and family therapy in the aftercare treatment of acute schizophrenia. Arch Gen Psychiatry 35:1169-1177, 1978

23. Mosher LR and Gunderson JG: Group, family, milieu, and community support systems treatment for schizophrenia. In Bellak L (Ed): Disorders of the Schizophrenic Syndrome. New York: Basic Books, 1979, pp 399-452

24. Wynne L: Some indications and contraindications for exploratory family therapy In Boszormenyi-Nagy I and Framo J (Eds): Intensive Family Therapy. New York: Harper and Row, 1965, pp 289-322

25. Kinston W and Bentovim A: Brief focal family therapy when the child is the referred patient: II. Methodology and results. J Child Psychol Psychiatry 19:119-143, 1977

26. Wattie B: Evaluating short-term casework in a family agency. Social Casework 54:609-616, 1973

27. Weakland J, Fisch R, Watzlawick P, and Bodin A: Brief therapy: Focused problem resolution. Fam Process 13:141-168, 1974

28. Gurman AS: Contemporary marital therapies: A critique and comparative analysis of psychoanalytic, behavioral and systems therapy approaches. In Paolino TJ and McCrady BS (Eds): Marriage and Marital Therapy. New York: Brunner/Mazel, 1978, pp 445-566

Family Group by Agnese Udinotti. Courtesy of the artist.

26

Complicated Situations and Their Guidelines

OBJECTIVES

- To list the common clinical situations in which family intervention is often recommended
- To examine complex clinical situations in which family treatment may be contraindicated
- To understand the general and specific situations for which family treatment is usually recommended, including situations in which there is an identified patient
- To be aware of the changing criteria for recommending family treatment

INTRODUCTION

Now that we have reviewed the decision tree for marital or family treatment, we will cover some of the same ground by examining the situations in which treatment is often recommended (the so-called "indications") and sometimes not recommended (the relative contraindications). We use the modifier "relative" to make the point that these are less contraindications in the classical sense but more "therapy with scaled down, more realistic goals." The previous chapter is more schematic, while this one is more clinically focused. This chapter is by necessity somewhat repetitive with chapters on specific disorders, and age issues like children, adolescents, etc., and should be read in conjunction with those sections.

412

SITUATIONS IN WHICH FAMILY THERAPY IS OFTEN RECOMMENDED

Family treatment is often advised when either the therapist conceptualizes, or the family indicates, that the family system currently is involved to a significant degree in some type of psychosocial problem. Family treatment is appropriate for those situations in which the family's ability to perform its basic functions is inadequate. (These functions have been discussed in Chapters 3 and 4.)

Family treatment has been recommended for problems at all stages of the family life cycle and for "identified patients" (or clients) with all types of difficulties (correctional,[1] medical,[2-4] and educational). For example, school psychologists have moved increasingly toward using family therapy for "behavior problems" and for "poor performance," i.e., learning disorders. It has also been used for situations in which there are obvious conflicts between a family member and the community.

Family treatment is currently an accepted part of the treatment regimens for affective disorder and for schizophrenia (see Chapter 22). The psychosocial management of schizophrenia has, for some patients, shifted away from individual, psychoanalytic psychotherapy toward "psychotherapeutic management with a focus around the family."[5] To reiterate, now in the context of "guidelines," having an identified patient with schizophrenia has long-term effects on the family.[6] Somatic treatments by themselves do not cure problems of living. They can control specific psychophysiological symptoms and behaviors, but alone they will not improve or alter the preexisting family relationships, ways of coping with stress, and other preillness behavior. For these issues family intervention is indicated.

Marital Conflict and Dissatisfaction

There is one area in which a growing body of research has produced consistent results—the treatment of marital difficulties. For a number of years it has been a prevalent clinical opinion that marital therapy is the treatment of choice for marital difficulties.[7,8] Hurvitz[9] has written of the dangers of doing individual therapy with only one spouse in such a situation. In a recent review of marital therapy research results, Gurman and Kniskern[10] have summarized data indicating that conjoint marital therapy is *superior* to conjoint plus individual therapy, concurrent therapy, and individual therapy. Another criterion for differential therapeutics is the comparative deterioration (meaning "worsening," not lessening of positive effects over time) effects of various modalities of treatment. This approaches the question of treatment choice from the negative side, i.e., what treatment does the most harm. A survey of Gurman and Kniskern[11] found that the rate of deterioration for conjoint, group, and concurrent-collaborative marital therapies is half that of individual therapy of marital problems.

While marital conflict and dissatisfaction seem to lend themselves especially well to conjoint marital treatment, it is surprising to see how often such problems are still dealt with by means of individual treatment for one of the marital partners, with relatively little attention paid to the impact of the individual treatment on the marital system as a whole. The field of marital counseling[12-14] some time ago accepted the need to see the marital couple together in such instances, and this trend toward marital therapy appears to be growing, as results from outcome studies are being reported.[10] It is believed to be more efficient in terms of time and cost to treat a couple or a whole family rather than only an individual member, especially since the role of the identified patient in multiproblem families often shifts from one member to another.

Sexual Problems

In recent years conjoint treatment for sexual problems has shown increasing promise[15,16] (see Chapter 18). Common sexual problems have often proven intractable to individual treatment. When these same problems are viewed in an interactional framework and treated with both partners present, using a combination of sex therapy and marital therapy, surprisingly effective and rapid results have often been obtained.

The Child as the Identified Patient

When a child is the identified patient, it has long been the practice of child guidance clinics to involve at least one of the parents, usually in collateral treatment in which the patient and parent are both in individual treatment but with different therapists. This at least represents token recognition of the importance of the family, both in the difficulty and in its resolution.

A more thoroughgoing approach than this, however, seems indicated in these cases, with evaluation of the possible role of the child as the "symptom bearer" of more general family problems (often unresolved marital issues). Usually the marital partners are seen as a couple for a major part of the treatment. The "identified patient" may benefit from some individual attention addressed to the child's particular symptoms and psychosocial difficulties. A common sequence of events is for the entire family to start out in treatment together, and then for various individual dyads and triads to be separated out for special attention after an interval of time. Of these, the marital dyad is unquestionably the most important. Some family therapists suggest that whenever there is a symptomatic child who is prepubescent, family treatment is indicated, unless there are specific contraindications.

Over the past ten years, there have been marked changes in the field of child psychiatry. Many institutions are shifting from an individual psychoanalytic focus to a family systems approach.[17] An increasing range of childhood disorders is now being treated with family therapy.[18] For example, school phobias are now being treated with family therapy plus an antidepressant.

The cause of child psychopathology is an unresolved issue. "Historical and evolutionary studies reflect evidence to support familial as well as intrinsic factors within the child as responsible for child psychopathology."[19-21] Another issue centers on the concept of the relative importance of the completion of "developmental tasks." Child psychiatrists believe that successful completion of developmental tasks is crucial to the functioning of the individual and the family. Family therapists have taken the position that what is important is the here-and-now. By implication less attention is paid to the family's past history and the individual's growth and developmental patterns (concepts that are, of course, central to the individual psychotherapy model). Most family therapists primarily see adult patients and work with children using the family therapy model. The family model suggests that even if one does explore past issues of "growth and development," it does not change family patterns and behavior and therefore is a "useless exercise." Child psychiatrists disagree, and argue that only by exploring the past can such changes take place. Until controlled studies are done, the relative efficacy of either approach remains unclear. The authors would recommend using both approaches to help to change family behavior and allow for, among other things, optimal growth and development of the children.

An even better reason for the use of family therapy is that a number of prospective followup studies of children have indicated "that individually-oriented-play therapy or individual psychotherapy for child behavior problems are not related to outcome."[22] Alternative models of intervention are needed. The family treatment model is an attractive, but as yet systematically untested candidate.

It is interesting that there is a marked discontinuity between child and adult psychopathology. With or without treatment many childhood psychiatric disorders are self-limiting. Children who are very impaired show dramatic improvement as adults, and only 13 percent of the children who were treated as children were rated more disturbed than controlled in adult life.[22,23]

The Adolescent as the Identified Patient

With the adolescent as the identified patient, focus on the family is still indicated, especially while the adolescent is living at home, not yet having established psychosocial autonomy. A good deal of attention must often be focused on the marital partnership. The adolescent will often benefit from individual attention, as well as from the encouragement of peer group relationships. Presumably the more emancipated (capable of independent living) the adolescent, the less need there is for conjoint family sessions and the more emphasis there is on individual and peer group sessions.

In treating a family with an adolescent "authority problem," inclusion of the entire family group can dilute the adolescent's feelings about the therapist as authority figure. (These issues are also discussed in different contexts in Chapters 22 and 29.)

A difference of opinion relates to the treatment of adolescents involved in symbiotic, mutually destructive parent-child relationships. Some therapists take the view that this is an indication for family treatment in order to facilitate the weaning of the teenager.[24] Other therapists believe it is difficult to help further separation and individuation in family treatment, which brings all members together and may therefore involve them even more in each other's lives. They would, instead, recommend that such adolescents receive individual or group treatment to demonstrate concretely their individuation and promote their growth outside the family, and that perhaps the parents be seen together to solidify their attachment to each other and their ability to tolerate the loss of their child. There seems to be some growing consensus that family therapy is most indicated when the symptomatic adolescent is exhibiting acting-out behavior. Individuals are often seen who are unequipped to deal with symbolic psychological processes and are not able to benefit from insight-oriented individual modes of treatment. These people, however, may often be more amenable to a family system, action-oriented modality which, for them, seems to be more understandable and practical.

Other Intimate Interpersonal Systems

Other intimate interpersonal systems, less formally organized and sanctioned than marriages and families, may lend themselves successfully to conjoint interventions. *Couples who are involved significantly with each other, whether or not they are married or living together, or are heterosexual or homosexual, have been effectively treated.* The goal is to help the partners explore relevant issues and—if the relationship is premarital—the doubts and anticipations prior to the marriage.[25]

Mr. K. and Ms. L. consulted a family therapist after they had been dating for about six months. The reason for referral was that although they both expressed the desire to get married, they had some doubts as to whether the relationship could work. Both had been married previously. It turned out that Mr. K. was an orphan and had been raised by a series of family members. He had joined the army and retired at the age of 40. He had been out for about a year, and divorced for about two years, when he met Ms. L. He expressed a strong need to be with her all the time.

Ms. L. had been raised by a smothering mother, and her first husband had depended on her a great deal. She expressed a strong need to "find myself." She wanted to get a better grasp on her identity. Although she wanted a relationship with a man like Mr. K. (reliable, strong, and a good sexual partner), she also wanted time on her own.

The therapist provided the opportunity for the couple to explore these issues and the ramifications of their marrying. After ten sessions the couple decided not to get married but worked out an arrangement in which Mr. K. would spend three days a week with Ms. L. at her apartment. A two-year follow-up of this arrangement showed that it had worked out "just fine," according to both of them.

All too often people get married during the infatuation phase, when love is indeed "blind." This is that rare example in which a couple was able to realistically explore its own needs and each partner's personality (rather than what appears to be in the other partner's fantasy). Then, based on past patterns, the couple anticipated the future and worked out a realistic solution.

There has also been an increased emphasis on family therapy for families without problems or psychopathology. Here the focus is on "personal growth" defined as helping a couple or family to realize maximum potential in terms of functioning and feelings.

MORE COMPLEX SITUATIONS IN WHICH FAMILY THERAPY IS SOMETIMES RECOMMENDED. "THE RELATIVE CONTRAINDICATIONS"

Some situations require special sensitivity and experience, and not all family therapists will feel comfortable working with such cases. To date there are no outcome studies to document which types of situations are least responsive to family intervention, and many of these areas must still be considered experimental. The authors have modified items from Ackerman,[26] as follows.

Families in the Process of Breaking Up

If the family is irrevocably committed to dissolution—for example, if the actual process of divorce is going on—family therapy can often be helpful in permitting the breakup to occur in the most positive manner possible, with the fewest "raw edges" of unresolved feelings. Divorce therapy can lead to a less painful experience for each family members.[27] If the family members do not care about one another, they usually will fail in any form of family therapy.

Inexperienced therapists, however, may be overly pessimistic (or overly optimistic) about the changes that can be brought about in famiies. Marital couples or families may begin therapy by talking about breaking up and may appear more chaotic in the early sessions than they will later. Many families start treatment by emphasizing their worst aspects, and during a first interview the therapist may feel that the situation is hopeless.

After the family is known better, the therapist usually can see positive assets that the family may have been minimizing initially and that the therapist may have been overlooking. The fact that the family members come for treatment should in itself be taken as an indication that they are potentially seeking help for their difficulties. If the marital partners were determined to break up or divorce and if this were not a conflicted or difficult issue for them, they would see a divorce lawyer, rather than seek family therapy.

Many family therapists claim that they do not take sides on the issue of whether a marital couple should separate. They believe, rather, that their role is to help the couple clarify their own feelings about this question and also to give the couple an opportunity to think about other solutions to their marital difficulties. (Often, marital partners have separation and divorce as a hidden agenda and may delay facing it until the therapist opens up the topic for discussion.) It will often prove useful to clarify the fact that everyone in the couple's family may be hurting and has been struggling, although relatively unsuccessfully, to find ways to ease their pain and disappointment.

Other therapists feel that divorce is not a solution to marital problems because the spouses often remarry partners much like the previous one and continue in the same patterns. A few marital partners divorce and remarry each other several times. Everyone is familiar with marriages in which the spouses can neither live stably together nor stay apart. In such instances therapists might take a stand against useless divorce and instead actively encourage attempts to improve the current marriage.

Psychopathology in One Family Member Making Family Therapy Ineffective

Dishonesty or manipulation of the therapy for secondary gain would constitute a serious handicap to effective treatment. A family member may have a history of chronic stealing or lying. If this occurs in a child or appears to be more of a symptomatic response to a family situation than an integral part of a chronic character pattern, family therapy would be indicated.

If one family member is extremely paranoid, manic, or agitated, medication might be initiated for behavior too disruptive to control, prior to the onset of family therapy. Once the identified patient's conduct becomes more appropriate, family therapy can proceed.[28] Another possibility is to work with all family members except the one whose behavior is too disruptive and prevents therapy from succeeding—but this is clearly a second choice. Others (a minority) have argued that acute symptoms are often reflections of a family crisis, for which family therapy is particularly well suited.

Denial of Family Difficulties by the Family as a Whole

There are some families whose whole way of life is oriented around denial of difficulties. Such a family makes family therapy extremely problematic, but not impossible given the situation in which some other motivation can be developed to allow therapy to continue.

Organic Disease in One Member of the Family

Although no amount of family therapy can change the course of an organic disease, the family may be helped to live more comfortably with the secondary consequences of the illness. What might be changed are the reactions of the patient and family to the symptoms and dysfunction.

Risks for Consequences of Treatment Worse than Benefits

Family members may be concerned that treatment will leave them in a worse state than when they began. These possibilities should be explored at the outset and at all other appropriate points in treatment. The therapist should involve the family members in considering possible consequences of therapy and whether they wish to continue or abandon treatment.

In the T. family the identified patient was the son, R., who had been stealing cars. Mr. and Mrs. T., both suburban, upper-middle-class parents, were bewildered by their son's behavior. In the first interview they presented themselves as having an ideal relationship and being deeply in love. Their son, R., however, suggested that the two of them were not getting along. Further inquiry revealed that whenever the mother and father had an argument, the son would divert attention from their problems by getting into trouble with the law. In this family the mother and father actually had serious problems in their relationship. Exploration during family therapy led to threats of divorce by both spouses. This and other possible outcomes were aired with the family members, and they decided to discontinue therapy.

Another situation that illustrates the need to clarify treatment goals is the "doll's house marriage," a type of marriage in which there is an extremely unequal relationship. One spouse's incompetence is required or encouraged by the other. These marriages are extremely fragile and crisis prone and often break down with changes in the family situation (e.g., the birth of a child). Although family treatment is problematic and the results uncertain, the therapy has a greater chance of success if it basically respects the unequal framework and works to reestablish the equilibrium existing prior to the crisis.[29] This example highlights the need for clarifying the goals of treatment and for being satisfied with realistic and attainable objectives.

Identified Patient with a Fixed Physical Dependence on Alcohol, Barbiturates, Heroin, or Other Drugs

Family therapy may not be successful as the primary mode of treatment in preventing or treating physical dependence on drugs. It may be of help in the early stages, before the pattern becomes well fixed, when behavior is symptomatic of other concerns, or even later in aiding the family members to understand the condition and avoid nonuseful interventions and responses.

In the abuse of drugs in which physical dependence is not found, family therapy may have a more important role to play. Family therapy may be necessary to induce the user to discontinue the drugs when their use is a result of family psychopathology. This may be especially true for the adolescent drug user.

Existence of an Important, Valid Family Secret

Valid family secrets may exist that cannot be brought out in the open and that preclude the possibility of the family's doing any constructive work. Infidelity, bigamy, incest, homosexuality, and criminality may be issues that one partner refuses to discuss in conjoint sessions, and these may, in certain instances, interfere with the session's achieving beneficial results. Often, though, the anticipated consequences of revealing secrets is exaggerated, or the "secret" is already known to the other partner. The revealing of secrets may lead to major changes in the family organization, and these changes need to be anticipated.

Cultural, Religious, or Economic Prejudices

Unyielding, inflexible cultural, religious, or economic prejudices against any sort of outside intervention in the family system would certainly also make family therapy difficult. In these cases other alternatives can be offered, such as working with a clergyman or a community worker, with the family therapist acting as a consultant.

Necessities of Other Modalities of Psychiatric Treatment

Other modalities of treatment should also be considered. In some cases one would want to wait until the identified patient has established a relationship with the therapist; this is especially true of adolescents. A psychotic patient who is paranoid might not be able to tolerate family therapy until he or she has been reconstituted through the use of anti-psychotic drugs; such a patient before then would be too suspicious of the therapist to benefit from treatment.[26]

The Availability and the Type of Therapist

Many therapists find themselves uncomfortable doing family work and should not force themselves to undertake it. If the therapist encounters significant "countertransference" problems in working with a particular family, this, too, would be a contraindication. Therapists would be well advised to avoid treating families with whom they have strong emotional ties.

The age, sex, and race of the therapist in relation to the type of family are in the authors' experiences usually not crucial factors in treatment. Much more important are his other personal and therapeutic qualities.

The therapist must be active and directive, and must set limits in order to practice family therapy.[26] Allowing the identified patient or other family members to control the therapy will usually doom it to failure.

The preceding sections describe several situations in which the therapist and family should carefully consider the possibility of benefiting from treatment. In spite of one or more complicating issues, this would be the factor most important in deciding whether or not to utilize family therapy.

CONCLUSION

Family therapy is an approach rather than a single technique. It is a group of therapeutic interventions, all focusing on the family, but directed toward a variety of specific therapeutic techniques. Therefore the relative importance of the particular guideline depends in large part to what extent the therapist uses the family model; that is, if the therapist treats all problems with family therapy, then the guideline is not important. Conversely, when different problems are treated in different ways, then the guideline is all important.

Until the last five to ten years, indications and contraindications for family therapy have been based on ingenious hunches as to treatment efficacy in a specific situation and on clinical experience (a term defined by some as "making the same mistake for 30 years").

More recently there has been some controlled outcome data that define situations in which family or marital therapy might be the treatment of choice (see Chapter 31). These situations include:[10]

1. Marital therapy for a marital problem
2. Marital therapy for sexual dysfunction

3. Family therapy for certain childhood and adolescent behavior problems
4. Family therapy for eating disorders
5. Family therapy for the "chronic" patient (i.e., those in need of long-term continuing care and rehabilitation)

Any final authoritative pronouncement as to when to suggest family therapy should be withheld until more controlled data are available comparing family therapy with other types of treatment.

REFERENCES

1. Bard M and Berkowitz B: A community psychology consultation program in police family crisis intervention: Preliminary impressions. Int J Social Psychiatry 15:209-215, 1969
2. Jackson DD: Family practice: A comprehensive medical approach. Compr Psychiatry 7:338-344, 1966
3. MacNamara M: Family stress before and after renal homotransplantation. Social Work 14:89-98, 1969
4. Kellner R: Family Ill Health: An Investigation in General Practice. Springfield, IL: Charles C. Thomas, 1963
5. May PA: Schizophrenia: Overview of treatment methods. In Freedman AM, Kaplan HI, and Sadock BJ (Eds): Comprehensive Textbook of Psychiatry (2nd Ed). Baltimore: Williams & Wilkins, 1975, pp 923-938
6. Segal SP: Community care and deinstitutionalization: Implications for family policy. Social Work (in press)
7. Greene BL, Lee RR, and Lustig N: Treatment of marital disharmony where one spouse has a primary affective disorder (manic-depressive illness): I. General overview—100 couples. J Marr Fam Couns 1:39-50, 1975
8. Avallone S, Aron R, Starr P, and Breetz S: How therapists assign families to treatment modalities: The development of the treatment method choice set. Am J Orthopschiat 43:767-773, 1973
9. Hurvitz N: Marital problems following psychotherapy with one spouse. J Consult Psychology 31:38-47, 1967
10. Gurman AS and Kniskern DP: Research on marital and family therapy. In Garfield SL and Bergin AE (Eds): Handbook of Psychotherapy and Behavior Change: An Empirical Analysis (2nd Ed). New York: Wiley, 1978, pp 817-901
11. Gurman AS and Kniskern DP: Deterioration in marital and family therapy: Empirical, clinical and conceptual issues. Fam Process 17:3-20, 1978
12. Ard BN and Ard CC (Eds): Handbook of Marriage Counseling. Palo Alto, CA: Science and Behavior Books, 1969

13. Klemer RH: Counseling in Marital and Sexual Problems. Baltimore: Williams & Wilkins, 1965

14. Vincent CD (Ed): Readings in Marriage Counseling. New York: Crowell, 1957

15. Masters W and Johnson V: Human Sexual Inadequacy. Boston: Little, Brown, 1970

16. Kaplan HS: The New Sex Therapy. New York: Brunner/Mazel, 1974

17. Hollander L: Rethinking child and family treatment. In Sankar DV (Ed): Mental Health in Children. Westbury, NY: PJD Publications, 1975, pp 297-304

18. Schomer J: Family therapy. In Wolman B (Ed): Handbook of Treatment of Mental Disorders in Childhood and Adolescence. Englewood Cliffs, NJ: Prentice-Hall, 1977, pp 91-101

19. Brodie HKH: Comment. In Brady JP and Brodie HKH (Eds): Controversy in Psychiatry. Philadelphia: Saunders, 1978, pp 758-759

20. Sussex JN: An evolutionary perspective on child psychopathology. In Brady JP and Brodie HKH (Eds): Controversy in Psychiatry. Philadelphia: Saunders, 1978, pp 744-757

21. Anthony EJ: Yes, no, and neither: The views from Freud to Laing. In Brady JP and Brodie HKH (Eds): Controversy in Psychiatry. Philadelphia: Saunders, 1978, pp 725-743

22. Vaillant GE: Book Review. Am J Psychiatry 137(3) 387, 1980

23. Cass LK and Thomas CB: Childhood Pathology and Later Adjustment: The Question of Prediction. New York: Wiley-Interscience, 1979

24. Haley J: Leaving Home: The Therapy of Disturbed Young People. New York: McGraw-Hill, 1980

25. Gross A: Marriage counseling for unwed couples. New York Times, Magazine Section, April 24, 1977, pp 52-68

26. Ackerman NW: Family therapy. In Arieti S (Ed): American Handbook of Psychiatry (Vol. III). New York: Basic Books, 1966, pp 201-212

27. Toomin M: Structured separation with counseling: A therapeutic approach for couples in conflict. Fam Process 11:299-310, 1972

28. Guttman H: A contraindication for family therapy: The prepsychotic or postpsychotic young adult and his parents. Arch Gen Psychiatry 29:352-355, 1973

29. Pittman F and Flomenhaft K: Treating the Doll's House marriage. Fam Process 9:143-155, 1970

The Family by S. V. Ivanov, Russian State Museum.

27

Family Treatment as it is Influenced by Cultural, Ethnic, Gender, Social, and Economic Issues

OBJECTIVES

- To understand families of differing cultures, ethnic origins, socioeconomic status, and life styles
- To generate principles for accommodating therapeutically to such families
- To be aware of how stereotypes about gender and other biases can influence therapy with families

WORKING WITH FAMILIES OF DIFFERENT CULTURES AND ETHNIC ORIGINS

In the course of their teaching efforts, the authors are often asked how one works with a German family, a wealthy family, a black family, a single-parent family, and so on. In each of these situations, there may be differences in marital patterns and childrearing roles, and different ways of coping with each life stage. Most families, however, have the same basic framework, the same general life course, and the same essential need to establish some structured ways of coping with their tasks.

426

The Therapist-Family Fit

Should the therapist be of the same race and culture as the family in treatment? It is probably true that the closer the therapist is to the family in terms of race, ethnic background, social class, and value system, the greater the potential for mutual understanding and sensitivity. A background similar to that of a specific family does not guarantee, however, the therapist's successful treatment of that family. The therapist will still need to check all presumptions with family. It would be ill advised for the therapist to imagine that he or she can avoid the process of getting to know the family because of similar backgrounds. For one thing, families of a particular culture or race should not be stereotyped. Families that require treatment have often been found to function aberrantly for their particular cultural or racial group; while the therapist may have particular blind spots that are related to sociocultural factors. The therapist must be aware of these attitudes, since they may impede rather than facilitate working with families with similar characteristics. Also it would not be unusual for families to have negative attitudes toward working with a therapist of a similar background. Some individuals seem to prefer therapists from a different background. There is never a perfect fit between family and therapist, but racial and cultural differences should not be an absolute contraindication to their working together.

In different cultures the role of therapist means different things. In some cultures the therapist is often a stranger to the family, an outsider whom the family members are suspicious of. They may feel sensitive about their failure in taking care of a family member within their own extended family organization. This is to be contrasted with families in other cultures who at the first sign of family trouble go for help.

Guidelines for Understanding Various Family Patterns Within Different Cultures

The following is a brief itemization and summation of some of the ways in which families of different cultures can vary.[1]

1. *Role*. How are family members perceived in terms of their roles? The role of father, teacher, or doctor may be quite different in one culture from that of another in terms of power and authority.
2. *Interpersonal relationship and reciprocity.* How does the family handle interpersonal relationships and reciprocity? In some cultures there may be a strong sense of interpersonal reliance and mutual obligation within the family unit, whereas in other cultures the trend may be toward independence, with each person doing "his own thing."

3. *Propriety*. Cultural standards of right and wrong are important components of family functioning. Families of some cultures have a defined set of acceptable behavior, while families of other cultures may rely on a more pragmatic and flexible style of behavior. Overt public shaming of "wrongdoers," together with internalized guilt, is not an unusual form of chastisement in some cultures.

4. *Time and relationships*. In traditional cultures there are extended family clans, organization, and records that institutionally reinforce the feeling of family continuity over a period of centuries; in more modern cultures it is not uncommon to find that lower-class families are more present-oriented than the future-oriented middle- and upper-class families of the same culture.

5. *Symptoms*. The identified patient's culture, race, and class may have an influence on his or her symptoms. In some middle-socioeconomic class families feelings are supposed to be controlled, whereas in many upper-class families feelings can be expressed at will. In lower socioeconomic class families physical symptoms may be more acceptable than psychological ones.

   Sometimes cultural issues masquerade as symptoms, when in fact they are not the problem. For example, in the J. family, mother (a Catholic) and father (a Jew) fought about which religion to raise the children. The real issue was non-communication and nuclear family loyalty between the spouses.

6. *Models of mental illness*. In different cultures families will conceptualize mental problems in different ways. In some cultures psychological problems and symptoms are more stigmatizing.

There may be differences that create strains between generations in the same family. These are accentuated when families migrate, as when black families move from the rural South to the urban North. These families are often more comfortable in discussing their difficulties in their own style than they are in the manner of the predominant culture. Even though cultural issues play an important role, they may not be the sole cause of the problem.

Therapy

According to Spiegel,[2] the therapist must (first) address the three basic questions which will be on the mind of any family.

1. What is family therapy?
2. Why should we get involved?
3. Who is this person? (meaning the therapist)

The key point is that the questions must be addressed in the context of the answers specific to each ethnic group. We view the procedure as a kind of psychoeducation technique to get the family started in therapy.

The next step is *evaluation*, in which cultural beliefs about health concepts and practices, family life styles, as well as cultural values of the family, are explained. This boils down to an attempt to understand behavior in a cultural context, not just "resistance." Next, one must determine to what degree is the family aiming to assimilate, or melt into the mainstream, or remain separate or unable to make an integration. Following this assessment, treatment can "begin." Spiegel recommends that (first) cultural issues must be addressed (by constant questioning) and explaining, then the deeper family dynamics become available for exploration.

He uses the term *culture broker* to describe the therapist's role in reducing the family conflicts that maintain symptoms, and as an educational approach designed to achieve compromise. If this technique does not work, then deeper dynamics should be approached by a variety of eclectic choices from other techniques.

The therapist does not have to become an expert in every culture in order to be effective, but he should understand and respect cultural norms. Many treatment principles cut across different cultures. The therapist should remember that what is therapeutic in his or her culture may not be appropriate for the family in its own culture. A good example of this is in sex therapy, in which many therapists have extremely liberal values and feel fairly comfortable dealing with sexual matters. When they try to translate some of their concepts and techniques to a conservative family, there is great difficulty. The therapist must be sensitive to the values of other cultures and not impose the values of his or her culture on the therapy.

The Japanese K. family consisted of a mother, father, son, and younger daughter. The identified patient was the daughter, a 23-year old sophomore college student who had lost 40 pounds. Her diagnosis was anorexia nervosa.

The parents (as typical of their culture) favored the older son. The father worked as a food inspector and the mother prided herself on being an excellent cook. The therapist speculated that the area in which the daughter could have some leverage on the family was by starving herself to death. This caused the family to lose face. The parents' relationship had deteriorated over the years, with a lessening of intimacy.

Treatment strategy was oriented around bringing father and mother closer in a manner that would enable them to feel comfortable as individuals and also be compatible with their culture. The eldest son was used as an ally to change some of the parents' behavior in order to decrease the identified patient's symptoms. He would suggest to the parents that they give his sister more freedom. But on the other hand, he was fearful of yielding his favored position, for he believed that if his sister got more power, he would have a more difficult time with his parents.

The family believed that the cause of her not eating was physical. The therapist never directly challenged this belief, but suggested that if its cause was physical and if they wanted their daughter to eat more, the husband should work with his wife in preparing the meals. The aim was to increase parental intimacy and at the same time decrease the emotional distance between parents and children. Differentness in the family was also attended to—the daughter continued to attend Buddhist services with the parents once a week, but for the remainder of the time the parents were encouraged to allow her to pursue her own type of life-style at the liberal university she was attending.

McGoldrick and Pearce[3] have written an excellent and detailed book describing the understanding and treatment of families from different ethnic origins, e.g., the Italian family, the Hispanic family, etc. The interested reader should refer to this reference as the case arises. Likewise, interpretations should be utilized when language barriers are impeding therapy. The "interpreter" then becomes part of the family system.

GENDER ISSUES

Over the last decade, there has been an increased focus on gender issues in family theory and therapy. We list here a number of crucial points for the family therapist.[4]

1. In conceptualizing the family functioning for a systemic point of view, many therapists erroneously assume that all family pathology emanates from the parents. This could result in seeing women, e.g., the mother, as "the enemy." Thus women are penalized for their central role in family life.
2. As we discussed in Chapter 2, the therapist must be aware of the major changes in the socio-demographics of family life and how they have affected marriage, childrearing, work, and marital change problems. The increase in domestic violence and inadequate resources for childrearing in some cultures points to the need for a critical examination of power issues in families and the need to understand families in their context.
3. In therapy, therapists must be aware of their "sexist" biases. Each family must work out what is best for them, not what is best for the therapist. And needless to say, male members of a family may suffer from sexist biases of female therapists.

Finally, as Pittman[5] has written,

A non-sexist approach to the gender issues in family therapy is similar to the approaches suggested by students of ethnicity—respect for ethnicity involves the initial acceptance of cultural differences, polite exploration of those differences, and the most subtle explanations of how a given ethnic group's customs differ from the larger culture. The therapist, in Monica McGoldrick's term, is a "culture broker," helping families sort out what traditional values they wish to retain and which they can discard. Non-sexist family therapists are "gender brokers," performing the same function with gender roles and values.

WORKING WITH WEALTHY FAMILIES

In upper-class families, marital coalitions may be less well structured than in middle class families. There may be a considerable lack of emotional cohesiveness that is oddly reminiscent of the traditional stereotype of the lower-socioeconomic class family. Parenting may be intermittent, inconsistent, and largely managed by people other than the parents. This, again, is similar to the pattern of some low-income families. Offspring in these families may evidence an inability to formulate life goals and may seem to drift aimlessly. A family therapist for such families must be sensitive to their particular patterns, which include their tendency to escape difficulties through the use of money and their ability to bribe the therapist with high fees while treating him like a servant.

WORKING WITH POVERTY FAMILIES

Special modifications of family therapy have been suggested for the needs of poor families. A meaningful balance must be struck between dealing with reality issues (food, clothing, housing, interacting with the public agencies) and internal family issues. Too often the former areas have been neglected, based on the assumption that the family was capable of coping with its basic survival needs or that such matters did not properly belong in the province of family therapy.[6-8]

Many such families cannot come in for treatment during regular working hours, and the routine schedules of therapists and agencies should be more flexible to accommodate their needs. Emphasis should be directed to concrete problem-solving activities and behavorial rehearsals (rather than insight and intellectual understanding), current issues (rather than past history), and day-to-day realities (rather than fantasies) from session to session. The therapist often will have to go to the family rather than the family going to the therapist.

A number of clinicians believe that family therapy is *the treatment modality of choice* for poverty families, i.e., lower socioeconomic class families. It offers a medium for using such therapeutic techniques as role-playing, role-reversal, and advocacy-mediation. The rationale is that individuals in such families lack a capacity for self-observation, for reporting accurately or to work with another person in a trusting relationship. Based on this rationale, therapy is organized focusing on concrete tasks, teaching patients to observe themselves and helping them to share communication. Although true of all families, it must be emphasized here that there is an assumption that behavior in such families is multi-determined (that is, there are psychological, social, biological, and genetic factors, and educational and cultural values and orientations that are important determinants for family and individual behavior.)

SUGGESTIONS FOR FURTHER READINGS

McGoldrick M and Pearce J: **Ethnicity and Family Therapy**. New York: Guilford Press, 1982.
   One of the few books that explores this topic.

Pilalis J and Anderton J: Feminism and family therapy—a possible meeting point. J Family Ther 8:99-114, 1986.
   An excellent article relating feminism and family therapy.

REFERENCES

1. Shon S: Material presented at Grand Rounds, Langley Porter Neuropsychiatric Institute, October 25, 1977
2. Spiegel JP: Ethnic issues in family therapy. AFTA Newsletter, Winter 1984, pp 1-3
3. McGoldrick M and Pearce J: Ethnicity and Family Therapy. New York: Guilford Press, 1982
4. Communication to the family therapy community. Family Therapy Networker 9:17, 1985
5. Pittman F: Gender myths, when does gender become pathology? Family Therapy Networker 9:24-33, 1985
6. McKinney J: Adapting family therapy to multideficit families. Social Casework 51:237-333, 1970
7. Mannino F and Shore M: Ecologically oriented family interaction. Fam Process 11:499-504, 1972
8. Adams P: Functions of the lower-class parital family. Am J Psychiatry 130:200-203, 1973

Section VIII

The Family Model and Other Fields

The family plays an important role in the development of some and management of most *medical* and *surgical* illness. Now that we have effective treatments, issues of compliance have been crucially related to family interaction effects; i.e., whether or not the identified patient takes insulin is often related to how he or she is getting along with the family. These issues are discussed in Chapter 28, while similar issues are discussed for the mental health professions as they relate to psychiatric illness (Chapter 29). Finally, the role of the family in such diverse and seemingly unrelated (to the family) fields as architecture and law are discussed in Chapter 30.

Family, origami by Rachel Glick, 1979.

28
The Family and Medicine/Surgery

OBJECTIVES

- To enable the professionals in related medical fields to adapt the family model to their particular needs
- To enable the family therapist to understand the needs of medical fields and work collaboratively in using the family model

INTRODUCTION

The 1974 Nathan B. Ackerman Memorial Conference held in Venezuela had as its theme "The Growing Edge of Family Therapy." The theme was selected because, during the last decade, there had been an increasing adaptation of the family model in a variety of fields seemingly unrelated to the family. These fields included (but were not limited to) medicine and its subspecialties, the legal profession, and various mental health disciplines. This trend has intensified and the authors present a summary of recent material concerning the adaptation of the family model as utilized in other disciplines. Since these sections are targeted both for a specific set of readers (e.g., a surgeon or a lawyer), as well as for the family therapist, there is, by necessity, some overlap with other sections of the book.

THE FAMILY MODEL & FAMILY MEDICINE
with Sanford R.Weimer, M.D.
and Robert S.Hoffman, M.D.

Knowledge of family systems dynamics is necessary to the practicing physician. Sometimes that fund of knowledge and the skill to interview effectively are a matter of life and death. Like psychiatric illness, medical illness in a family is a family affair. In fact, health care is increasingly seen as a community problem. Psychological dysfunction in a family can cause symptoms, possibly even diseases, that bring patients to physicians.[1,2] Certainly dysfunction in a family can exacerbate chronic illness in a family member.[3,4] Understanding family dynamics, knowing how to get information about family dysfunction and areas of successful functioning, and knowing how to intervene skillfully are powerful, cost effective tools for every physician.[5-7] These issues are more important as families enroll in HMOs or large "managed care" packages.

The following cases illustrate the need for taking a good family history:

In the D. family, Mrs. D. was the identified patient by virtue of the fact that she had had seven episodes of diabetic acidosis in the last six months. Medication and dietary control had not decreased the frequency of these episodes. After the seventh episode, an offhand remark of Mrs. D.'s unmarried daughter who lived at home—that "these episodes always seem to occur after a weekend when the family is all together"—prompted the physician to call in the entire family.

It was discovered that Sunday was feast day in this Italian family and that the mother prepared a large meal, sampling all the dishes. An important part of the disintegrating relationship with her husband was preparing and eating large meals, and he felt this maintained his shaky status within his family. The diabetic acidosis seemed directly related to the mother's going off her diet on Sundays.

Management included a preliminary meeting with the entire family to clarify the situation. Separate meetings with the couple were then arranged. The physician encouraged the family to work out its own solutions. Mrs. D.'s married daughter began to prepare meals in her home rather than in the mother's. The elder son moved out of the house. An eight-month followup revealed no subsequent episodes of acidosis, and Mr. and Mrs. D.'s relationship improved.

Mr. R. was a 34 -year-old man with chronic fatigue, insomnia, and malaise. He complained that his irritability was causing marital problems. The family physician in this case was stumped after a complete medical and neurological workup ruled out illness secondary to hypertension. A negative dextroamphetamine sulfate trial was of no help, and an ENT consultation was unproductive. The patient turned out to have Obstructive Sleep Apnea. The clue to the correct diagnosis (of this potentially fatal condition) came after a family meeting. His wife reported that her husband had had excessive loud snoring and rest-lessness over the past year. She even thought that she had noticed "he had stopped breath-ing momentarily while sleeping." Based on this information, an appropriate diagnosis and treatment plan was begun. His energy level increased with more sleep, and the marital problems stopped.

This is not a new discovery. A remarkable book on illness in families written in 1945 by an internist *turned psychiatrist* has timely advice:[8] "The time is now ripe for a coordinated attack on the problems of family adjustment in relation to the maintenance of health and the treatment of illness." Even then, he decried "the many opportunities for enhancing the value of medical treatment . . . now being lost through overlooking the importance of the family unit."

The relationship between the family system, the variety of physical com-plaints possible in family members, and interaction between the family and the medical care delivery system is an immensely rich domain of practice and re-search.[9-12] Although one issue merges into another and no case presents a pure ex-ample of a given generic problem, this chapter can offer clinical insights and recommendations for intervention in commonly seen situations. For heuristic reasons, the chapter will distinguish several selected patterns of family dysfunc-tion that are important to the medical and surgical practitioner. Nevertheless, it is important to bear in mind that real life families offer infinite complexity and that the degree of family dysfunction, the degree of seriousness and acuity of illness, as well as the opportunity to intervene, vary along a continuum with no natural boundaries.

Our basic assumption is that the family is a system whose members satisfy physical, psychological, and social needs in interaction with each other and the society external to the family. When the system malfunctions because members of the family are unable to satisfy these needs, individuals become distressed and may express their distress as a *somatic complaint*.

The Somatizing Family

Every physician in practice will periodically meet both persons and families chronically dysfunctional. Their lives are turbulent and unhappy, and taking care of them is troubling. In some of these families, the physiological issues are insig-nificant, the somatic complaints serving as a ticket of entry into the health care system.[1,5,13] The system becomes the arena where conflict and manipulation are played out. The clinician's job is to recognize the origins of the complaint and in-tervene to improve family functioning, thereby reducing distress and reversing symptoms.[14]

Chronic Illness in a Family

When a family member has an illness in which physiologic disorders are prominent, the illness may be exacerbated in two important ways. In those illnesses where malfunctioning organ systems have rich autonomic innervation or sensitivity to the neuroendocrine system, family stress and conflict can aggravate the disease process, leading to increased morbidity and higher utilization of medical care.[11] Chronic illness frequently requires a strict adherence to doctor's orders, nutritional adjustments, and elimination of certain stresses. In a dysfunctional family, illness and the adaptations necessary to control it may become part of the family psychosocial dysfunction, with consequent non-compliance, poor physiologic control, and even outright sabotage. The outcomes may be disastrous.[3] Moreover, the onset of somatic illness is correlated with life changes directly related to family functioning—for example, the death of a spouse, divorce or separation, a jail term or even marriage itself.[15]

Serious Illness in the High Functioning Family

Finally, there are families that function at an effective level for years until some traumatic injury or highly symbolic illness such as cancer, impairs the family equilibrium, and coping mechanisms break down. These families, too, can present maladaptive behavior that exceeds the limits of the medical team. All of these varieties of family dynamics present "opportunities for enhancing the value of the medical treatment."

In short, when patients present complaints out of proportion to the physical illness, or communications break down, for example, the treating clinician must consider whether the problem relates to distress in the family. Is the problem one of channeling somatized complaints into a more efficient verbal channel? Has the serious illness or injury to a key family member forced a change in roles or communication patterns that interferes with appropriate medical care in a previously well functioning family? Is family interaction supporting behavior that sabotages good medical care? Is the family of the patient fundamentally dysfunctional or only transiently so in the face of overwhelming stress?

Somatic Complaint as a Ticket of Entry

Mrs. J., a 25-year-old mother of two had visited the clinic frequently with complaints of chest pain, headache, and lassitude. Frequent visits to the ER and clinic revealed no evidence of physical illness. All the while, Mrs. J. dropped hints to the doctors about her "wayward" husband, who allegedly was "catting around" and neglecting his family. After several visits in a few months' time, without result, the medical staff asked the family therapist for a consultation, "to determine whether to support her pastor's advice to accept her lot in life or help her get rid of the SOB." The patient, on interview, was evasive. When asked if her husband might come in for a conjoint interview, she stated that he wasn't interested (indeed he had never been seen). When pressed, she agreed to invite him. When asked how she would approach him, she said, "The doctor wants to see you to tell you how to treat me better." Patient and therapist finally agreed that that was hardly an invitation. When the husband did arrive, it turned out that he was eager to talk, and equally distressed about their failing marriage. In brief, things had been good until they returned to the area where the in-laws were living. She had been spending increasing time with her parents, where he felt belittled and criticized. In her family, emotions were hidden and, in his, freely expressed. Caught in a bind he couldn't resolve, he was reduced to feeling impotent and encircled in this extended family, complicated by his wife's sick role status. In desperation, he had begun an affair with another woman "to prove he could have a healthy relationship with someone." The key event in the interview came as he began to ventilate his pent up pain and discouragement. Suddenly, as it appeared that there were two sides to this unhappy story, Mrs. J. clutched her chest with a deep sigh. Mr. J. ceased talking; his face took on a worried, solicitous expression, and he moved to comfort his wife . . .

It is not every day that one sees such an interaction reproduce the essential family drama in the office, but this case illustrates the role of the symptom in the family economy as it controls communication and allocates power. It also highlights the need to observe the whole system before forming a hypothesis.

The case illustrates what some have called the latent function of the clinic.[16] The identified patient used her symptom as a ticket of entry to the clinic, unconsciously drawing staff into a collusion with her to define her husband as the cause of her distress. Her symptom and her sick role served to control her husband and avoid dealing with conflict over relations with the extended family, sex, and other unexpressed but unfulfilled expectations between them. In a study of high utilizing families, in a general practice clinic, the investigators found marked behavioral and structural differences between high and low utilizing families.[17] The high utilizing families perceived themselves as less expressive, more achievement oriented, more highly organized, and more concerned with control. The children perceived themselves as less independent and the families more concerned with religious and moral issues than the other families. The families reported themselves as atypically beset with illness recently, less satisfied with their doctors, and higher consumers of tranquilizers. The families were less social than their counterparts, doing less together and with other families, opening a void often filled with involvement in the health care delivery system.[16] The pattern of related findings implies a system that responds rigidly to stress.

Similarly, with the growth of liaison and consultation psychiatry, it has become evident that an important part of such consultations should be evaluation and management of the family and their input into the problem of the identified patient.

In the X. family, Mr. X. was a diamond merchant; his wife was a stockbroker. They were both in their sixties and had been married 20 years or so. Mr. X. had long-standing hypertension. As the wife's career developed and their children moved out of the house, the couple became distant, and communication markedly decreased. Mr. X. became more and more despondent, finding that his business no longer interested him the way it had when he was younger.

Just prior to hospitalization, he called his wife to talk about how "blue" he was feeling; she told him she could not talk to him because she had a conference. Soon afterward he swallowed 100 antihypertensive pills, then again called his wife and the police. He was brought into the intensive care unit of a general hospital. The psychiatric consultant focused on the hypertension and the acute episodes, but did not involve the identified patient's wife. Mrs. X. was "too busy" with her job to come to the hospital. Mr. X. was discharged after three days, only to make another suicide attempt two months later.

At this time the family therapist, working with the staff of the consultation service, had the wife come in for a joint interview. During this session, Mr. and Mrs. X. were able to lay out their difficulties for the first time and decided to enter marital therapy in which they could pursue a realistic plan to bring them closer.

The key lessons to be learned are:

1. Physicians should be alert when repeat visits to clinic do not lead to diagnosis.
2. The patient will generally have a ticket of entry to the clinic to engage the doctor's interest and obscure the family problem behind it.
3. The symptoms usually have meaning and function in a dysfunctional family.
4. Whenever possible, see all family members, rather than relying on the patient or intermediary, which can lead to premature conclusion.

Impact of Family Dysfunction on Chronic Illness

When serious chronic illness occurs in an already dysfunctional family, the consequences can be catastrophic to life. Several mechanisms occur commonly in dysfunctional families. The family system may reinforce the patient's ambivalence about following the medical regimen. In one epileptic middle-aged man, there was a history of frequent "breakthrough" seizures with occasionally complicating injury. Interviewed with his wife in the neurology clinic, his own reluctance to accept his sick role, and the need for regular anticonvulsants, were supported by the wife, who used his illness to foster an unrelenting depressive state and dependency in which she maintained control. Often this effect is unseen (like a hidden planet) until the other family members are brought into the interview.

Family compliance with sound medical advice is crucial in the care of the chronically ill. Gaining the compliance is sometimes a frustrating task, without knowledge of family systems.

Mrs. H. was a 67-year-old woman in a downhill week-long course of congestive heart failure. She refused hospital admission, agreeing only to return to clinic, daily. Her meek diminutive husband wheeled her about in a wheelchair. Clinic staff were panicked that her clinical state was rapidly deteriorating, but she adamantly refused admission. The psychiatric consultant interviewed her briefly, confirming the medical staff impression that she was virtually unreachable. She was mildly paranoid, slightly confused, and belligerent. However, no one had thought to interview the husband, let alone bring him in. The consultant spoke with him briefly. The husband was fearful she would die, agreed with the doctors that she needed hospitalization, but was thoroughly intimidated. The consultant told the husband to accompany him back into the room and at the appropriate moment, with the psychiatrist's backing, he would demand compliance. As he began his approach, she blustered. He began to cave in when the consultant said sharply to her, "Be quiet, you're not being fair to him!" Surprised, she stopped talking. The husband, with the consultant's encouragement, said as forcefully as he could, "You must come into the hospital, dear!" She then turned meek and agreed. Visiting her the next morning on the ward, the consultant found her breathing easier, less confused, and grateful. Her husband sat beaming at the bedside. The key lessons to be learned are:

1. Family members, often ignored, hold the key to successful outcomes.
2. Family ties are powerful forces and can break an impasse when properly mobilized for compliance.
3. A life-saving family intervention can sometimes take as little as 20 minutes for assessment and intervention.

Minuchin described an elegant example of the mechanism of interaction between stressful communication and impaired physiologic control.[16] A series of "brittle" diabetic youngsters were being followed unsuccessfully in a pediatric treatment system. The patients did well in the hospital setting but got out of diabetic control at home and were frequently admitted in a ketoacidotic state. Study of the family systems revealed in some instances that the child was caught in a dysfunctional family role. The parents were unable to express conflict and disagreement directly between them and used the child as an indirect medium of communication, a kind of triangulation. This led, in the child, to unbearable stress. In an elegant experiment, the three members of the triangle were interviewed while measuring serum-free fatty acids, which when elevated is a marker of distress and itself can interfere with diabetic control. First the parents were interviewed separately, with the child out of sight but able to hear the conversation. As the interviewer led them to conflicted material, the free fatty acid levels went up in all members. When the child entered the room the conversation switched to focus on the child. When this occurred as a diversion from the prior conflicted conversation, the child's level continued to rise and the parent's levels fell back toward normal. The management of the family with a chronically ill child has been the subject of other reports, as well.[3,4,18-23]

Another mechanism of dysfunction involves a family member *using the physician (or other health care providers) in a pathological interaction.* Often the intent is to undermine the patient's relationship with the doctor, who may be seen as an emotional threat to the dysfunctional family ecology. In one instance, which recalled the saviour/persecutor/victim triangle,[24] a woman brought her moribund and semicomatose husband to the ER of a big city university hospital. She told a story of poor care in a rural hospital and flattered the young house staff with her confidence that they would find the problem and cure her husband. The staff launched into a megaworkup, buying into the trap. As information began to accumulate, it turned out that the patient was in an end stage of disseminated cancer, and in fact, the prior hospital had done a credible job in diagnosing the problem. When the staff approached the woman with the news, she erupted in an angry, critical attack on the doctors, and prepared to move her husband to the next hospital. This woman was suffering from a pathological grief reaction that was hidden when the doctors accepted her story at face value.

Serious Illness in the Normal Family

Serious illness in a member of a family can evoke unexpected reactions in the patient and other family members. Cancer is an important example because of its powerful impact on families, putting all of the issues of chronic, relapsing illness in high relief. The patient, of course, has to deal with issues of disability, pain, disfigurement, sometimes stigma, and often death. An extensive review of family process and cancer[25] with a full bibliography reviews the issues and problems from diagnosis, to adaptation, and finally to dying and bereavement. It is clear from experience published in the literature and corroborated by hands-on clinical experience, that patients and families do better when caregivers are attuned to family issues and intervene when necessary.

One family presented many of the important issues and was sophisticated enough to seek help early and articulate many of the issues.

Mr. Q. was a 50-year-old economist with a promising corporate career when he was diagnosed with lung cancer on a routine physical. He was at that time up for a major promotion. Married for nearly thirty years, he and his wife had two adult children. While Mr. Q. had many of the typical individual responses of an acute grief reaction, what follows will emphasize family oriented issues. His first worry was of being blamed. Life-long smokers, both he and his wife felt guilty and ashamed, particularly since the rest of the family had been urging them to quit for years. They feared the angry "I told you so's" that never came. Thus they kept the news initially from others. They were terrified, moreover, that someone would emotionally break down, because as his son was later to confirm in a family meeting, "Dad is the emotional center of the family." Mrs. Q. tried to stay upbeat and played "cheerleader" while actually near breakdown herself. The couple vacillated over allowing their grief to show and maintaining a positive attitude. It is crucial at this stage to foster good family communication, which is central to the needed emotional support. Cancer patients in particular and many chronic patients in general become fearful and desperate, often squandering family resources, emotional and financial, on quack promises of cure.

A family meeting including both children, husband and wife, and the son-in-law was revealing. Mr. Q. had described his son-in-law as an inarticulate, unintelligent, unmotivated sort who was holding the daughter back. His attitude had clearly cut off some of his emotional support. In the meeting the son-in-law revealed a charming sense of humor and a remarkable ability to see through some of the family myths that blocked communication. The family in general complained that Dad kept too much to himself, denying them a chance to be supportive, and raising their anxiety because they were uncertain about what was going on and what he was feeling. The case illustrates the importance of direct observation of the family, particularly in interactions with each other.

The imminence of the threat to his life injected a quality of urgency into old issues. In a family meeting, the son-in-law blurted out the cause of much of the daughter's distress. She sought approval from Dad and never got it. Mrs. Q. continued smoking for many months, despite the morale-breaking effect it had on her husband, who had stopped and now worried extra about her. Finally it emerged that she, like some other patients, viewed smoking as a pre-conscious suicidal act. She did not want to face life without him, so she kept smoking in hopes of shortening her own life.

What is unusual about this family is the sophistication that led to direct consultation with a family therapist. Most of these patients and their families will be seen by generalists, surgeons, or internists. It is crucial to maximize patient compliance, quality of life, and maintenance of a viable support system, that the physician pay attention to these kinds of issues or get a specialist involved.

Trauma and the Family

Dealing with families of trauma victims is especially challenging. Even in normally functioning families, trauma will sometimes evoke pathological interactions. These interactions can add risk to family members and involve medical staff, which impairs their ability to function efficiently and retards adaptation. In contrast to chronic illness, there is little time to digest the news, the grief is immediate, and the involvement with the unfamiliar world of the ICU is intense and overwhelming to families.

Case Example

Marty was a troubled teenager lying in a bed in the ICU. Mom stood hovering over him, face contorted in grief. Her sister Ida stood helplessly at her side, trying awkwardly to comfort her. At the foot of the bed was Dad. Waiting outside was Dad's new wife of five years. Mom and Dad had divorced some seven years ago, when Marty was twelve after six years of increasingly nasty fights. When the family broke up, Mom and Marty had clung to each other at first; Marty in terror of losing his Dad and what little semblance of stability life had had, Mom in loneliness and shame over her failed marriage.

For the past two years, Marty had been showing increasing signs of independence. Mom was having trouble letting her first born go. On the day of his accident, he showed up on a motorcycle, explicitly forbidden by mother, bought with money he had been saving from a small inheritance to purchase a car for the commute to college. Angry words exploded between them, "I never want to see you again!" she screamed. He stalked out. Her next view of him was lying in a hospital bed, attached to a respirator.

Marty was a prototypic patient, young, with serious trauma received in an active sporting type accident. Artificial life supports and intensive biochemical manipulations maintain the verisimilitude of hope and life. The medical team is heavily identified with the patient, who is nearly the same age as many of them. Unable to make a decision to stop, the team passes the decision onto the family (the decision should rest to a large extent with the family). This is never an easy decision to make. But clearly, Marty's mother was in no position to make an unaided decision if anyone had taken the time to assess her state of mind. She had been spending all of her waking hours at her son's bedside, at times so intrusive and demanding that she interfered with routine care. She was sleeping little and suffering from frequent crying spells. She was neglecting herself and her other children and obligations during the several weeks of stormy ICU care. Although remarried and part of a supportive new family system, she felt totally alone at this crisis, watching her only tie to the lost paradise of her younger days, broken and silent on the ICU bed. In her crisis of guilt and loss, she cut herself off from others and was near breakdown, until her sister demanded help. She showed no sign of anticipatory grief reaction in that she could not or would not discuss her son's condition and only stated magical ideas like "a mother's love will restore Marty."

What follows is a step by step guide to the essentials of family management written especially for trauma families, but applicable in principle to any family situation in health care.

Information Flow

For nonfamily therapist physicians, the most important aspect of information flow concerning the family is simply not to forget them. The family needs to know what is happening to the patient and the physician needs to know:

1. Something about recent events that led to the presenting problem that might have some bearing on etiology or course
2. Any revealed facts that might influence therapeutic decisions such as drug or alcohol use or recent conflict
3. Strengths and vulnerabilities of the patient and others in the family that have relevance for the current stress
4. Evidence of hidden agendas that might involve staff in some family behavior pattern that adds unnecessary emotional costs to care of the patient and family
5. Evidence of suicidality in the patient or other family members
6. Family expectations and preconceived ideas about diagnosis, treatment, or prognosis

From the first interactions with family members, following certain principles will aid efficiency and avoid pitfalls. Many obvious points get lost in the chaos of the earliest moments. For example, often omitted but an important starting point in establishing favorable attitudes is introductions. The physician should introduce himself or herself and ask the same of family members. That breaks any potential hostile distancing and begins formation of an alliance. Clearly, this is best done with as complete an assembly of family members as possible. Following this, the physician might offer a brief statement about the clinical situation and the treatment plan. All of this can be done in 3-5 minutes. Any longer statement will distress the family and fail to get the information across. The family is in a state of anxiety that shortens attention span and decreases their ability to assimilate new information. That means that the physician may need to repeat information without irritation and frustration. It is crucial in establishing rapport early on to ask questions of the family. A brief outline of questions that should be part of the initial contact follows. It is not a rigid table, but rather a set of interactions that form a model for interaction; the order may change depending on the family's reaction.

Pitfall: Physicians who are uneasy with the task of meeting with family members, either because of the family's emotional displays or simply lack of confidence in dealing with a group, will often resort to the lecture modality. Families will believe the doctor seems more concerned with displaying his knowledge than providing usable information and emotional support.

Initial Interview Outline

1. After introductions and a brief statement of the clinical situation, the physician asks an open question, inviting family participation in a dialogue: "Do you have any questions?" Initial reponses to such an invita-

tion can be enlightening. Signs of disorganization or family conflict may emerge. On one occasion a patient with a known seizure disorder was admitted after two seizures for reestablishment of control. There were no complications. His wife was noted to ask in the emergency room "Is he going to die?"

Pitfall: A tightly structured interview completely controlled by the doctor will miss significant information.

2. A question about the family's specific concerns should follow. Many members of families have concerns that are irrational and distressing, and easily alleviated if discovered. Anxious people worry about the most unpredictable things. Fears of cancer, disfigurement, contagion, and stigma come up to plague people when least expected.

3. If the family's questions don't reveal implicitly that the situation is clearly understood, as "This bleeding in the brain, is it likely to . . . ?" or reveal the appropriate logical sequence ("Does it mean he will have brain damage?"), the physician may have to have family members repeat what they have heard. To avoid potentially offending someone, the doctor takes the burden on himself or herself: "I want to be sure I'm doing a good job of explaining things. Can you tell me what you've understood from what I've said?"

Pitfall: The physician may reassure about concerns not there, raising new ones or blocking rapport.

4. Ideally, the physician should break off contact after the first meeting with a promise for further contact. Giving a fixed meeting time depending on the situation or if any significant change occurs will reduce family anxiety and their need to interrupt busy staff. It is useful to have the family designate a spokesperson for quick communication in instances when all the family is unavailable or time is short.

Uncertainty and ambiguity are great compounding threats when a family member is sick or injured. Anything that can be done to reduce such uncertainty will reduce the chances of anxious family interfering with normal care procedures, support fragile members of family, and maintain the kind of rapport and alliance that avoids lawsuits in indignant, ignored families. Sometimes it is necessary to appoint a family spokesman, whether this is done by the family or with influence by the doctor depends on the family's style. A strong independent minded group will obviously do better if not rigidly controlled by outside authorities.

Pitfall: With uncertainty the rule in fast evolving trauma or critical illness situations, compounding the problem with conflicting reports by different team members, with rapid switches in optimism and pessimism communicated to family members, will undermine their confidence and heighten their anxiety. There is no substitute for an authoritative spokesperson for the medical side who is fully informed and able to communicate in simple clear language.

Three cardinal rules will help avoid misfortune in communication:
1. Encourage the family members to talk. Always allocate some time in a meeting for response; if necessary abbreviate the report and encourage a response. Listen carefully for misunderstandings, flooding anxiety, building resentment.
2. Avoid premature reassurance. We will have need to give reassurance, news that others will want to hear. Many a professional has been trapped by this temptation with later loss in crucially needed credibility.
3. Avoid the use of jargon. Nothing distances the doctor from the family quite like fancy terms. The goal is to inform at the level family members can understand, not to deliver an elegant medical lecture. Make it brief and simple.

In the natural course of events there are three processes that families may have to confront:

1. *Decision making*—to prolong life artificially, to call it quits, to allow dangerous tests or procedures. All of these decisions must be made under duress at times, and the support of the medical team is crucial. What is difficult at times is that the team may not be neutral. For many reasons the team may lose objectivity, as in Marty's case. Attitudes toward the family, positive or negative, investment in a procedure, identification with the patient. The latter is illustrated over and over in the ICU. Use of a consultant is often critical.
2. *Establishment of a routine*—during the uncertain period of vigil, marked by fear and disruption of normal routines, the family may need help in establishing a supportive routine. Uncertain about how much time to spend in the hospital, sometimes neglecting self or dependents, it may be useful to help families structure their time. It is often of great utility to enlist family help in nursing care routines or to assign tasks to sort out financial and social service problems. The mother of Marty in the case example had exhausted herself and left small children at home so she could stand vigil in the hospital.
3. *Anticipatory grief*—when death or serious disability are imminent possibilities, many patients and families will experience a fantasied rehearsal

of the grim outcome. This is a normal phenomenon and like any normal grief reaction serves the purpose of adjusting to losses. It is important that people who experience these thoughts be told that they are normal, even anticipate that they might have such thoughts before they mention them. Otherwise, people might experience guilt and panic over such normal thoughts.

Sometimes well meaning staff will try to obstruct family members seeing the deceased or injured person. The decision to see the patient should be left up to adults in the family. Staff should follow the families' lead in this. Many people recount how important it was to see the reality in order to have peace after the grieving process. On one occasion a mother of a young woman injured in a hit and run auto accident came straight from the airport to the hospital. She was obstructed by some well meaning friends who happened to be on the hospital staff, and a tortured mother full of anguish and doubts began to break down uncontrollably until a senior staff person intervened and took the mother to the bedside. After a few moments of tears, she composed herself and proceeded to begin notifying other family members by phone. Likewise, for some people seeing the lost relative in death, if they so desire, leads to a cleaner, speedier grief process and return to equilibrium.

Knowing the expectable sources of stress on the family can lead the team to make allowances or interventions that are tailor-made to ease family distress. Such strategies are preventive in nature. They prevent unnecessary psychopathology, unnecessary disruptions in hospital tasks, and avoid preventable lawsuits. The stresses follow from changes in relationships, environment and financial burdens. A spouse or parent or child loses a fundamental source of gratification and support for self-esteem in the loss of the patient as a functioning individual. Sudden changes in role may take place—e.g., a normally dependent individual may have to fend for himself suddenly, or even take responsibility for difficult decisions. Unexpectedly thrust into a new environment, where someone else is in charge, filled with unfamiliar machinery and unfamiliar customs, can be a disorienting experience for families. Forced dependency on the doctors and nurses, dependent for information and direction, may be unsettling.

Observing the family for signs of failure to cope is something every physician can do. Brief inquiry may determine who is having trouble sleeping, nightmares, or appetite changes, which may signal an impending stress syndrome.[33] In the family meeting, the physician can make a note of family members who express ambivalent feelings about the patients, those who have difficulty expressing verbally any of their emotional reactions, people who are overly dependent (like the daughter of one CCU patient who in a hysterical outburst said she felt like she was dying), or family members who seem to be isolative, either through nonattendance or nonverbal behavior in meetings.

Family members may have ambivalent feelings toward the patient. Like the explosion between Marty and his mother, there may have been a recent conflict that symbolizes a longer existing state of conflict, which may even play a role in the pathogenesis of the recent emergency. People who care for invalids over long periods of time may develop resentments and death wishes toward the patient that are intolerable to the conscious mind. The tension of repressing such feelings may erupt under the stress of acute illness. One daughter of an invalid, epileptic, elderly lady, expressed a heavy load of guilt over recently lowering her mother's dose of dilantin "because she seemed so sleepy." The onset of symptoms of a CVA terrified the daughter that she had somehow caused the stroke. One father who was a relatively weak figure in the family, warring with his wife for the last several years, had been isolated from the rest of the family. When his son came into the ICU after a car wreck, he continued to be excluded from the family support system by his embittered wife. He became increasingly depressed, as he felt useless and ostracized, and he began drinking heavily while experiencing frightening suicidal thoughts.

Thus it becomes apparent that anticipating pathological emotional states and identifying family members or whole families at risk can be important and at times life-saving. Early in gathering information, it is useful to take history on prior experiences with family catastrophe. How did people deal with stress, what troubles came up? The family may even know who in the family is at risk. On the other hand, the family may carry a myth of so-and-so as vulnerable in order to divert attention from other more feared family pathology. A profile of strengths and weaknesses in the family coping system is useful to have.

Information about such psychological emergencies paralleling somatic emergencies is readily available in family meetings for briefing and emotional stocktaking. Interventions can be set up that can selectively call on the abilities and availability of the physicians, the nursing staff, social work staff, and in the most difficult situations, the psychiatric consultation/liaison staff.

THE FAMILY MODEL AND SURGERY
with Alvin I. Glasgold, M.D.

Although the principles of working with the surgical patient and their families are similar to those described in the previous section dealing with medical patients, there are a number of important variants on the themes.

When the opportunity is available to plan for a surgical experience (and in most cases it is), it is important to consider not only the effect of the procedure on the patient, but also the effect on the family. In addition, the family usually plays a significant role during the pre- and postoperative period. The patient should be encouraged to bring a family member to the preoperative planning consultation.

Although this may take up somewhat more time or require an additional visit, in the long run it will be worthwhile and an effective use of time, particularly for the surgeon.

Too frequently the patient finds himself or herself in the middle of an adversary situation: The surgeon proposing a procedure and the family questioning whether that is the best alternative or whether other opinions should be sought. The patient is not only distraught by a threatening illness, but also by a controversy as to making the appropriate decision to combat this illness. His or her ability to understand and communicate the rationale of the decision may be lacking.

As a matter of fact, Marzuk[1] in discussing the issue of paternalism in medicine, has pointed out that,

> Refusal may be the result of direct or displaced anger toward the physician. The physician may unwittingly fall prey to complex family dynamics. One physician noticed that the wife of a patient with lung cancer continually berated her husband for his smoking and nagged about their children, his job, and family finances. In subsequent discussion, the physician learned that the patient's refusal to undergo a test represented a displacement of his anger toward his wife onto the physician.

This case is an excellent example of how the surgeon becomes part of the family dynamics. And our bias is that rather than ignore the family, thoughtfully working with the family increases the chances of successful outcome.

When the family is included in the preoperative discussion, they become part of the team working for the patient's benefit. They understand the problem, and their questions can be more intelligently answered directly by the surgeon. The objective is to help them to be supportive of the patient's decision, and helpful in both the anticipation of the procedure and during the postoperative period. This can minimize the adversary position (vis-a-vis the surgeon and the family) and reduce that aspect of stress for the patient. The surgeon often gets caught in the middle of a family fight. They can become part of the recuperative or rehabilitative process and smooth the transition from the hospital to the home and outside environment.

Patients with chronic illness may be physically changed so that they may have long rehabilitative processes. During this process the family may take over some of the responsibility of the health care team. This may shorten the hospital stay or decrease the number of postoperative visits to a health care facility, thus allowing the patient to spend more time at home and in a more comfortable and familiar environment.

The following case is an example of the importance of involving the family:

J.G., who had undergone laryngectomy for a carcinoma of the larynx, had temporarily been handicapped by the loss of voice: His job required him to communicate by phone. His postoperative course was smooth, and he did learn esophageal speech. Although his voice was good at home, it produced problems in phone conversation, particularly with people who did not know him. Prior to surgery he was extremely outgoing and the center of attention at social situations. Following surgery, the limitations on his speaking ability caused significant personality changes. Although cured of his disease, he was depressed. Preoperative counseling as to the anticipated limitations did alleviate some of the problems. His wife, who had not worked in many years, returned to work; this reduced some of the financial burden and allowed him to take a different job, which was not as dependent on his speaking ability. His family support assisted him in the speech rehabilitation process, and he was encouraged to participate, which brought him out of his reclusiveness. With the cooperation and encouragement of his family, he eventually made a very satisfactory adjustment to his new situation.

The cosmetic surgical patient presents a very interesting and challenging problem. Although there is no physical illness involved, this patient and just as commonly, the family, is disturbed by a physical appearance. This can translate into social and emotional problems. There may be complex factors involving the patient's self-perception. Many of these may be related to the family structure. A parent may have been inattentive or nonsupporting. Sibling jealousy, particularly if there is a more attractive or better achieving sibling, is a factor.

It is necessary for the surgeon to know the motives of the patient and the family requesting cosmetic correction, as well as to fully explore the anticipated result. The results should include a realistic expectation on the part of the patient as to the physical changes possible and to the gain expected from this change.

The family relationship may be very important in producing a satisfactory result. The family may not be sympathetic to the patient's desire for cosmetic change. This can make the anticipated surgical experience one of anxiety and tension for the patient. Following surgery the family is the initial exposure to society. Their reaction to the patient's appearance can be most significant. For example, they must understand that there can be some early bruising or swelling, and that the anticipated result takes some time. During this period the patient needs support and encouragement. The following is a case in which involving the family would have helped.

In the R. family, a 22-year-old daughter living at home and working as a secretary, consulted for rhinoplasty. She stated she felt unattractive. Her major negative feeling was her nose, which she felt was too large and had a bump. She stated that her family did not care whether she had surgery and would not be interested in the consultation. At the the second preoperative visit, the patient viewed a drawing of the anticipated result, and felt these changes would be satisfactory and she would be happier.

Postoperatively, it was the surgeon's feelings that the expected changes were accomplished; furthermore, the result was such that the patient appeared much more attractive than expected. However, on each of the early postoperative visits the patient was apparently not pleased with the results. Finally, she confided that her relationship with her mother had never been good. She had never had parental approval, and her mother did not approve of her decision to have cosmetic surgery. Mother was extremely negative when the dressings were removed, and although the swelling and bruising were minimal, told her she looked awful, that she looked as if she had been beat up and disfigured. She continued to be negative and told the patient she looked better before surgery.

It was not until several months after surgery that this now very pretty young lady began feeling that she was more attractive and was happy she had undergone rhinoplasty. This was brought about by the positive response she began to get from her coworkers and by the attention she was now receiving from men. Eventually this young lady showed the typical social and emotional gains that usually accompany successful rhinoplasty. In her case, because of a lack of family support in the early postoperative period, this took much longer and really did not occur until substitute family approval was gained.

THE FAMILY MODEL AND PHYSICAL MEDICINE

The Effect of Illness on the Family

When one member of the family has had a cerebrovascular accident, loses a limb, or has another severe injury, there is a corresponding ripple effect on the rest of the family. This loss of function in the one member must be compensated for by other members. This creates changes in structure and roles. Common dysfunctional patterns include:

1. The family does not pick up the function of the ill member.
2. The family withdraws from the ill member. This is especially true if the identified patient is the mother or wife (rather than husband) for reasons we discussed in Chapter 23, regarding the relative's response to illness.
3. The other family members do not allow the ill member to return to previous levels of function. Reasons vary but may relate to family dynamics that existed prior to illness—for example, the member was too dominant, as in the "overpowering mother." The other family members may take revenge at this point by taking over the patient's role, just keeping the patient around, or getting rid of the patient—leaving him or her to "gather dust."

The Effect of the Rehabilitation on the Family[1]

After the identified patient has suffered the illness and there have been changes in the family that resulted from that illness, it is at this point that the interventions of the physical medicine team must involve the family in the rehabilitation of the identified patient.

Mrs. A., a 50-year-old black female, was the dominant member of her family. Husband and children cowered when she raged. She developed a cerebrovascular accident with a right hemiplegia. Husband and children threw themselves into filling her role and her function. They felt closer than they had in years. Although Mrs. A.'s rehabilitation went well in the hospital, at home it went badly. Mrs. A. was not allowed to do the things she learned to do in the hospital (activities of daily living), nor was she found to be as motivated by the team to do her exercises. Family members were continually losing her crutches, canes, and other adjunct rehabilitative devices. It was only after her physical therapist brought the family together to discuss the situation and had a preliminary 10-minute meeting in her home prior to her home visit that Mrs. A. was able to continue her recovery. The physical therapist's tactic was to maintain some of the new power with the father and children, and to encourage a closer relationship between Mrs. A. and her husband.

An ingenious technique for anticipating the difficulty of family patterns as a result of disability has been worked out by one group. A special unit has been built at the hospital in which the family can actually live. The family lives here for two or three days prior to the patient's leaving the hospital. At this point the problem areas are identified and family interventions are made. Follow-up contacts are made at periodic intervals to make sure that the rehabilitation as well as the family therapy continues.

THE FAMILY MODEL AND PEDIATRICS
with William A. Sammons, M.D.

The pediatrician plays an important role in the life of the family, but it can be enhanced (and our bias is that it can be even more meaningful) if the pediatrician understand the new family model. This is uniquely because the pediatrician sees the family prior to development of marital or family problems. Moreover, with the care of some of the common infectious diseases of childhood like measles and mumps, more and more pediatricians are now involved in a form of family therapy as part of "behavioral pediatrics." As such, the family therapist is consulted as indicated.

The pediatrician's first contact with the family is usually immediately postpartum (see below for the exception of "the premature child"). The focus is usually (and appropriately) on the medical health of the child rather than on the emotional health of the family. But our bias is that we believe it is necessary for the pediatrician to understand normal family structure and function (including the reaction to the addition of a new member) in order to understand the family's adaptation to the baby (that he is examining).

A functional family may become dysfunctional even during the first few months of a child's life.[1-3] Parents may delay doing anything about a problem that develops based on the notion that "children will outgrow" certain stages, or the family will get itself together. In any case, the new member has a significant effect on the family and vice versa.[4,5] The child must not be thought of as a "passive doll."

By three to six months the family's equilibrium should have been reestablished. By that time some sense of self-sufficiency and independence should be established for both infant and parents.[6] The first signs of instability or separation problems can manifest at that time.

I began to realize too late that having a child did not ruin our marriage, it was how we raised him. We both wanted to do such a good job. We spent time, we responded to Evan's every demand. By the time he was eighteen months old he was ruling our lives. He felt like he couldn't get along without us, and after a year we were afraid that he would feel abandoned if we went away for a weekend. Because I was the "mother," Frank blamed me for the fact that he had gotten to hate his son. I can see that there is much more to it, and that neither one of us realized that we needed time together and not just time with Evan.

I know that I got myself into this, although I basically was following what the breast feeding books and the LaLeche league said to do. But I have been up every night for the last twenty months nursing her so that she goes back to sleep. If I don't, then she just cries and I feel like I'm killing her. Then Joe doesn't sleep and he gets in an awful mood because he can't handle the pressure at work. We don't have a sex life any more. He's tired, I'm tired, and the last three times we have tried to make love she has started to cry. By this point the nursing has become a sexual issue, because she has more of a physical relationship with me than I have with my husband. In many ways I have sacrificed much of my marriage, and much of my family, in order to be a human pacifier. Some days I get so angry with myself and with her that I want to hit her. Of course she never knew that I didn't want to nurse her forever. It's ironic what the term *demand feeding* can become if you don't understand that the demand is for much more than just food.

After the issue of re-equilibrium following the birth of a child, the second major set of problems for the family arise in the area of establishing discipline and control (we have discussed this in Chapter 3, but the pediatrician is in a family-influencing role in dealing with queries from family members.) This is a sensitive and relatively uncharted area of child development. Suffice it to say that discipline should not be thought of as punishment. Discipline is built through praise and is best done by parental example. The primary goal of the pediatrician is to avoid the extremes of suggesting either no limits or overcontrol.

Because we both work, dinner time was the only "family time" that we had during the week. But every day all that happened was a big fight. The kids never wanted to eat anything, and I dreaded that time of day and I resented cooking for them after I had had a long day in the office. Obviously the kids wanted attention at that time, but we were focused on making them eat. Rather than trying to force them to eat or yelling at them for food throwing, we needed to concentrate on our prime goal. We wanted to spend time with them as well. As soon as we made that clear and I gave up worrying so much about exactly what they ate, dinner was more enjoyable. We also had a lot less angry flareups over other things and Jim and I were more relaxed at 9 PM so we enjoyed our time together more.

I had tried yelling. I had tried hitting him. I tried having his father discipline him when he got home. Distraction only made it all worse. It seemed that all of the behaviors that I wanted to get rid of he was simply using over and over again as a way to get my attention. I may have been mad, but he certainly had my attention focused on him, regardless of who was around or what I was doing. Then everything started to get worse. He wouldn't eat, and I was begging him to try something at ten at night. He was hitting more when he was angry—which was all the time becuase I was saying "no" all of the time. He would create unbelievable scenes at the grocery store. Then I started giving him only one warning, and if he broke it I put him in his crib by himself with nothing to play with. He spent alot of time alone for three days, but now he is a great kid. It has made a huge difference to our marriage. We were spending so much energy trying to contain Kevin that we never could concentrate on our problems. I still don't know whether we can work things out, but one of the reasons we were trying to save the marriage, Kevin, was one of the reasons why we needed to be in therapy to start with.

What needs to be emphasized is that the infant or child is not totally helpless, i.e., is exerting influence on the family system. The two-month-old may be physically dependent, but he is not physically helpless. The child makes decisions in the same way as the parents.[1,7]

An important maneuver that pediatricians have found helpful is to help the family reestablish a daily schedule. Although many women seem to recover quickly from the physiologic and endocrine changes involved in giving birth, many couples have understandable difficulty dealing with the elusive feeling of "getting it right" in the first few months, or even years, working out their relationship with the child. There is stress put on a relationship when there is no predictable daily schedule. Someone has to take care of a task related to a child such as feeding it in the middle of the night. Sleep loss can cause irritability and, unless these tasks are mutually agreed upon by parents, this may create a major problem for the parents. What we are emphasizing here is that these problems often come to the pediatrician's office as repeated questions about working out a schedule. The "family model" pediatrician emphasizes that there must be compromises that involve *all individuals*. When the common problems that the pediatrician sees become severe and persistent (such as the parents complaining that either they or the child is not sleeping or they have feeding problems or discipline crises), this may be the point for family therapy referral.

Premature Infants: A New Definition of Normality

Premature infants and their families represent a special and difficult group of patients for the pediatrician. Approximately 10 percent of all births are premature, but they represent a much higher percentage of referrals for therapy and developmental evaluation because they all have been labeled as "high risks." At the same time, more than 80 percent will be developmentally normal at three to five years of age. Therefore, the pediatrician must be aware of the self-fulling prophecy that if the baby is premature, then the child will be a problem.

On the other hand, the families of such infants do have a higher instance of child abuse and divorce.[8,9] These families do go through a different beginning.[10] The parents do not have normal psychological growth and preparation for a full term pregnancy. They are grieving over the fantasy child they never had—the healthy full-term infant. Simultaneously, they are encouraged to "bond" and to try to care for the small, sick, fragile looking infant who is visually and emotionally unappealing. Many parents often say they cannot tell where the support machinery ends and the child begins. These children appear to be socially unresponsive so the parents seem to feel even worse when they get home.

Repeated evaluations for minor differences from "normal" need to be avoided in order for these familes to establish normal relationships. At the same time the pediatrician should be aware of problems in the family as they develop. Referrals for family treatment should be made if the pediatrician cannot handle the family interaction and changes around the growth and development of the premature infant.

THE FAMILY MODEL AND CHILD ABUSE
with Harvey S. Kaplan, M.D.

Parent-induced child abuse is one of the major clinical problems of childhood.[1] Child maltreatment occurs in families representative of all social classes and ethnic groups, although there is a bias toward the identification and reporting of child abuse in lower socioeconomic families. Neglect can rival poverty in its harmful effect on children's health and developmental potential, and is more difficult for society to respond to.

The spectrum of child abuse includes physical abuse in the form of the battered-child syndrome[3] of infancy and early childhood, poor maternal "bonding" during infancy resulting in the failure-to-thrive syndrome, child and adolescent sexual abuse including incest, and the unworthy or scapegoated child who is the end product of rejection and emotional abuse (these issues are also discussed in Chapter 23). Abuse in early childhood is the most damaging. Serious injury and death is associated with trauma involving the nervous system and vital organ systems of the chest and abdomen.[4] This can result from direct trauma as well as severe shaking. Infants are especially vulnerable to the effects of severe shaking, which can cause intracranial bleeding.[5] The presence of retinal hemorrhages suggest this type of abuse. The child who survives may have sensory, motor, or intellectual deficits. Burns and chemical poisoning are also seen sadly and not infrequently as an ongoing pattern of sadistic injury. Recognizable patterns of surface injury (e.g., bruises, bite marks) that differ from expected accidental childhood injuries are becoming increasingly familiar to the practitioner. Munchausen syndrome by proxy[6] is a more subtle form of child abuse, where the parent (usually the mother) fabricates a history or induces factitious symptoms in the child (fever, bleeding, vomiting, diarrhea, electrolyte imbalance) to express their own need for attention and help. Atonement for a self-perceived "sin" may cause the parent to symbolically "sacrifice" the child.[7]

A nonnurturing or physically dangerous and threatening family environment focuses the child's energies on survival strategies and may leave little margin for emotional and psychological development. Personality and behavioral traits seen in abused children include lack of self-esteem, fear of failure, pseudomaturity, and indiscriminate and shallow relationships with peers and adults.[8] Reflecting the violence of their childhood, abused children themselves develop aggressive ¬d violent tendenices, may abuse their own siblings,[9] and may perpetuate a violent and self-destructive life style when they grow up. The school-age child may show behavioral and learning problems that reflect past or present abuse. Child sexual abuse and intrafamilial incest, once considered rare and isolated to a small sector of society, is now recognized as an extremely common form of abuse and prevalent throughout "normal" appearing society. The child may be victimized by a "trusted" adult and coerced into keeping the abuse hidden.[10] Family therapists, and medical and school personnel may be the first to uncover the abuse, either through voluntary revelation of the "secret" or by recognizing "masked presentations"[11] such as psychosomatic symptoms, unusual or vague physical complaints, behavior disorders, school truency, and adolescent pregnancy. Medical evidence of abuse of the pre-pubertal child can be difficutl to discover, but is strongly suggested by identifying sexually transmitted infections[12] or physical abnormality if present. Reporting of suspected child sexual abuse is legally mandated, as well as a documented first step toward therapy and the cessation of the abuse.

Factors that may identify parents as high risk for being abusive include history of abuse in their own childhood, a strong belief in the value of harsh physical punishment, social isolation, low self-esteem, and inability to experience pleasure. Abusive mothers may share behavioral characteristics with depressed patients, but they use harsh authoritarian childrearing practices more often.[13] Inquiry about the status of their child in a group of mothers who attempted suicide revealed a strong risk of child abuse in 29 percent of cases.[14] Abusive parents expect performance or behavior control from their children that is totally inconsistent with their child's age ability. Severe punishment follows the failure of the child to meet these unrealistic expectations. Study of the mother-infant dyad by the use of videotaped sessions showed abusive mothers to be insensitive to the moods and signals of their children.[15] Physical abuse or failure to thrive may be a dramatic example of a lack of mutual atonement. The child as well as the parent may continue the behavior that maintains the maltreatment. There may be emotional role reversal of the normal parent-child relationship, where the young child seeks to pacify or interpret and meet the needs of the parent, in essence to "parent" the parent. Although the parenting style may be abusive and emotionally destructive, such parents are acutely sensitive to criticism of their abilities and often resent or reject outside efforts to change them. This reflects their own childhood experience of having been treated as "no good and worthless."

It has been suggested that there should be a shared professional responsibility for detection, case management, and treatment of child abuse[16] because the needs and rights of the parents may be in direct conflict with those of the child. Support services for the family to assist in childrearing include in-home friends to parents, homemakers, day care, respite care, public health nurses, and 24-hour telephone parental stress hotlines. Such services may be difficult to provide if there is a lack of evidence to warrent intervention in the home situation.[17] Many workers in the child abuse field now feel that such efforts at treatment of abusive parents, including attempts to engage them in ongoing therapy, were initially overly optimistic. Longer term studies show that large population of abusive parents refuse treatment or don't significantly improve over time with therapy. The children if not seriously battered continue to suffer emotional rejection or excessive physical punishment. The concept of "shared parenting" has been offered to bridge the gap between the helping facilities and the parents.[18] Where the parents are reachable, the children and parents can be helped and improved with a family-oriented approach, as was shown in a study designed to measure improvement in developmental milestones.[19] Treatment and family rehabilitation in intrafamilial forms of child sexual abuse has been strikingly more successful.[20]

Use of a family stress checklist has aided in identifying "high risk" parents in the prenatal period who are suitable for preventative services.[21] Recent studies disclaim the association of abuse with prematurity, low birth weight, or single-parent status, but show a slight association with young maternal age.[22]

The family therapist who does treat an abusive parent should be aware that the primary step is to allow the parent to develop a trusting relationship with someone before a specific behavioral change can be expected. This is called the "reparenting process" and is a nurturing phase that must precede any form of psychotherapy.

Of note, Goodwin and coworkers have described three cases of Cinderella Syndrome, i.e., children who simulate neglect. They alleged that their adoptive mothers dressed them in rags, made them do all the chores, and favored their step-siblings. Underlying these false accusations of abuse was a history that included (1) actual abuse of the child in a previous placement, (2) early loss of a mothering figure, and (3) emotional abuse in the adoptive home. Professionals involved in child protection need to recognize this syndrome, because intensive family therapy and temporary placement of the child outside the home are required in all cases. The child's false accusation of abuse is a cry for help and should not be dismissed as a manipulative fabrication.

THE FAMILY MODEL AND GENETIC COUNSELING
with Ellen Bloch, M.S., & Helen M. Blau, Ph.D.

Genetic counseling involves communication between counselor and family concerning problems associated with the occurrence of a genetic disease.[1] The genetic counselor provides a diagnosis if possible, information about the disorder, and understanding of choices and options available to the family, and support in the form of referrals and scheduled revisits. Contrary to popular notions, genetic counseling attempts to be nondirective, offering families information about alternatives rather than advice.

With the rapid explosion of knowledge about genetic diseases, there has been an increased need for genetic counseling. This increase is directly related to the development of procedures that allow the diagnosis of many genetic conditions prenatally. Amniocentesis, chorionic villi sampling and sophisticated ultrasound imaging all provide in utero diagnoses of many birth defects. Furthermore, advances in screening tests now help to identify many pregnancies at risk for prenatally diagnosable birth defects among specific ethnic groups in which incidence of these disorders is increased, for example, Tay Sachs disease and sickle cell anemia in Jewish and black populations, respectively. It is also rapidly becoming part of standard prenatal care to offer maternal serum alpha fetoprotein screening to the entire pregnant population to reveal the pregnancies at greater risk for neural tube and other birth defects.

It is not only in prenatal diagnosis that the impact of genetic advances is felt. After birth, DNA studies, gene mapping, and research in gene therapy have opened new doors to diagnosis and possible treatment of genetic disorders in affected individuals. In some cases gene carriers can now be identified for disorders before they manifest any symptom (e.g., Huntington's Chorea). Decisions about whether or not to pursue such studies and what to do with the information acquired are problematic issues for genetic counseling. Does an individual have a right to privacy when the genetic information obtained profoundly affects the lives of mates and other family members?

What makes genetic counseling different from other types of medical care is that the information provided often leads to unique problems for families. The family who comes in for genetic counseling often has a member with a hereditary disease that is of a chronic nature. Such chronic disease can be a tremendous burden to all family members. The discovery of a genetic disease in a family member creates very real financial and emotional burdens that compound preexisting family problems. Parents often feel guilty because of the nature of genetic disease, which is, that it is inherited even when they had no previous knowledge of their carrier status. Such guilt and blame can greatly affect parental interactions. In the experience of genetic counselors, parents with good relationships can withstand such chronic stress, but already strained marriages may suffer further. The genetic information may be denied, distorted, or magnified to suit the family's emotional needs; the genetic data become ammunition in the ongoing conflict. Mourning the loss of a normal child is a healthy grief response, and often precedes acceptance of the handicapped child. Overconcern with genetic facts, however, or lack of emotion or silence on the part of one member of a couple are symptomatic of deeper problems within the marriage and signal the need for family therapy.

In addition to parental problems, the family therapist or counselor should be aware of the special plight of healthy siblings. They may be affected by financial deprivation, since caring for a family member with a chronic illness is expensive. They often suffer from emotional neglect, since the family focus may rest with the handicapped child. Even if a severely handicapped child is placed in an institution outside of the home (an option that is often not available), healthy siblings may be plagued with guilt, feeling that they caused the disease in this sibling by the normal competitive desire to get rid of him or her a feeling that is not uncommon from time to time in children of normal families. Furthermore siblings may experience a fear that if they fall short of perfection they, too, will be disposed of.

Family therapy is indicated for many families who experience genetic counseling. In therapy, attempts to reduce guilt and blame should be made, and better means of coping should be explored. Genetic counselors should be encouraged to continue working with these troubled families to the extent they feel it appropriate; if further family therapy is indicated, the genetic counselor should make a referral (see Chapter 19).

SUGGESTIONS FOR FURTHER READINGS

Jonsen A, Siegler M, and Winslade W: **Clinical Ethics**. New York: Macmillan, 1982.
   Excellent text with important implications for the family therapy clinician.

Lask B: Physical illness and the family. In Bentovim A, Barnes G, and Cooklin A (Eds): **Family Therapy. Vol. 1**. London: Academic Press, 1982.

Black D: Handicap and family therapy.In Bentovim A, Barnes GG, and Cooklin A (Eds): **Family Therapy: Complementary Frameworks of Theory and Practice, Vol. 2**. New York: Grune & Stratton, 1982, pp 417-440.

Lask B: Physical illness and the famly. In Bentovim A, Barnes GG, and Cooklin A (Eds): **Family Therapy: Complementary Frameworks of Theory and Practice, Vol. 2**. New York: Grune & Stratton, 1982, pp 441-464.

Lask B: Family therapy in pediatric settings. In Bentovim A, Barnes GG, and Cooklin A (Eds): **Family Therapy: Complementary Frameworks of Theory and Practice, Vol. 2**. New York: Grune & Stratton, 1982, pp 465-478.

REFERENCES

Family Model and Family Medicine

1. Kellner R: Family Ill Health: An Investigation in General Practice. Springfield, IL: Charles C. Thomas, 1963, pp 79
2. Kasl SW, Evans AS, and Niederman JSC: Psychosocial risk factors in the development of infectious mononucleosis. Psychosom Med 41:445-446, 1979
3. Frey,III, J: A family systems approach to illness and maintaining behaviors in chronically ill adolescents. Fam Process 23:(2)251-260, 1984
4. Ferrari M, Matthews WS, and Barabas G: The family and the child with epilepsy. Fam Process 22:1,1983
5. Minuchin S, Baker L, Rosman BL, et al.: A conceptual model of psychosomatic illness in children. In Chess S and Thomas A (Eds): Annual Progress in Child Psychiatry and Child Development. New York: Brunner/Mazel, 1976
6. Kraft AM: Psychiatry: A Concise Textbook for Primary Care Practice. New York: Arco Publishing, 1977
7. Ransom DC and Vandervoort HE: The development of family medicine: Problematic trends. JAMA 225:1098-1102, 1973
8. Richardson HB: Patients have families, Commonwealth Fund, New York,

1945. Book Reviewed, Weimer SR, Am J Family Therapy, Vol. 9, No. 3, Fall 1981, pp 93-95

9. Weakland JH: Family somatics, a neglected edge. Fam Process 16(3):263, 1977

10. Meissner WE: Family process and psychosomatic disease. Int J Psychiatry in Med. 5:411-430, 1974

11. Grolnick L: A family perspective of psychosomatic factors in illness: A review of the literature. Fam Process 11:457-486, 1972

12. Block J: Parents of schizophrenic, neurotic, asthmatic, and congenitally ill children. Arch Gen Psychiatry 20:659-674, 1969

13. Dingle JH, Bidger GF, and Jordan WS Jr.: Illness in the Home: A Study of 25,000 Illnesses in a Group of Cleveland Families. Cleveland: Press of Western Reserve University, 1964

14. Buck CW and Laughton KB: Family patterns of illness: The effect of psychoneuroses in the parent upon illness in the child. Acta Psychiatrica Neurologica Scand 34:165, 1959

15. Holmes TS and Holmes TH: Short-term intrusion into the life-style routine. J Psychosom Res 14:121-132, 1970

16. Shuval JT: Social Functions of Medical Practice. San Francisco: Jossey-Bass, 1970

17. Weimer MD, Sanford R, Hatcher C, and Gould E: Family characteristics in high and low health care utilization. General Hospital Psychiatry 5:55-61, 1983

18. Minuchin S, Rosman BL, and Baker L: Psychosomatic Families. Cambridge, MA: Harvard University Press, 1978

19. Liebman R, Minuchin S, and Baker L: The use of structural family therapy in the treatment of intractable asthma. Am J Psychiatry 131:535-540, 1974

20. Barcai A: Family therapy and treatment of anorexia nervosa. Am J Psychiatry 128:286-290, 1971

21. Bruch H: Family transaction and eating disorders. Compr Psychiatry 12:238-248, 1971

22. Crisp A and Toms D: Primary anorexia nervosa, or a weight phobia in the male: Report of 13 cases. Br Med J 1334-337, 1972

23. Liebman R, Minuchin S, Baker L, et al.: Chronic asthma: A new approach to treatment. In McMillan MF and Henao S (Eds): Child Psychiatry. Treatment and Research. New York: Brunner/Mazel, 1977, pp 153-171

24. Liebman R, Minuchin S, Baker L, et al.: The treatment of anorexia nervosa. Current Psychiatric Therapies 15:51-57, 1975

25. Northhouse L: The impact of cancer on the family: An overview. Inter J Psychiatry 4:3, 1984

The Family Model and Surgery

1. Marzuk PM: Sounding board. The right kind of paternalism. N Engl J Med 313:1474-1476, 1985

Family Model and Physical Medicine

1. Peck RB: Physical medicine and family dynamics: The dialectics of rehabilitation. Fam Process 13:469-480, 1974

Family Model and Pediatrics

1. Als H: Social interaction: Dynamic matrix for developing behavioral organization. New Directions Child Develop 4:21, 1979
2. Seligman HR: Helplessness: On Development, Depression and Death. New York: WH Freeman & Co., 1975
3. Spitz RA and Cobliner WG: The First Years of Life. New York: International Universities Press, 1965
4. Wolff PH: The Causes, Controls and Organization of Behaviors in the Newborn Infant. New York: International Universities Press, 1965
5. Brazelton TB: Neonatal behavior assessment scale. In Clinics in Developmental Medicine No. 50, William Heineman Medical Books, 1973
6. Goldberg S: Social competence in infancy. A model of parent-infant interaction. Merrill-Palmer Q 23:163, 1977
7. Stern DN: The goal and structure of mother-infant play. J Am Acad Child Psychiatry 13:402, 1974
8. Sameroff A and Chandler MJ: Reproductive risk and the continuum of caretaking causality. In Horowitz FD (Ed): Review of Child Development Research, Vol. 4. Chicago: The University of Chicago Press, 1975
9. DeVito B and Goldberg S: The effects of newborn medical status on early parent-infant interaction. In Fields TM (Ed): Infants Born at Risk. New York: Spectrum, 1979
10. Field TM: Visual and cardiac responses to animate and inanimate faces by young term and preterm infants. Child Develop 50:188, 1979

The Family Model and Child Abuse

1. Wolock I and Horowitz B: Child maltreatment as a social problem: The neglect of neglect. Am J Orthopschiatry 54(4):530-543, 1984
2. Fontana VJ: The maltreatment syndrome of childhood. Pediatr Ann 13(10):7-36-44, 1984

3. Kempe CH, Silverman FN, Steele BF, et al.: The battered child syndrome. In Henry Kempe Memorial Research Special Issue, Child Abuse & Neglect 9(2):143-154, 1985

4. Ellerstein NS (Ed): Child Abuse and Neglect: A Medical Reference. New York: John Wiley & Sons, 1981

5. Frank Y, Zimmerman R, and Leeds NM: Neurological manifestations in abused children who have been shaken. Dev Med Child Neurol 27(3):312-6, 1985

6. Guandolo VL: Munchausen syndrome by proxy: An outpatient challenge. Pediatrics 75(3):526-30, 1985

7. Money J, Annecillo C, and Huthison JW: Forensic and family psychiatry in abuse dwarfism: Munchausen's syndrome by proxy, atonement and addiction to abuse. J Sex Marital Ther 11(1):30-40, 1985

8. Lamphear VS: The impact of maltreatment on children's psychosocial adjustment: A review of the research. Child Abuse & Neglect 9(2):251-63, 1985

9. Green AH: Child abuse by siblings. Child Abuse & Neglect 8(3):311-17, 1984

10. Summit R: Sexual abuse of children: A clinical spectrum. Am J Orthopsychiatry 48:1978

11. Hunter RS, Kilstrom N, and Loda F: Sexually abused children: Identifying masked presentations in a medical setting. Child Abuse & Neglect 9(1):17-25, 1985

12. Sgroi SM: "Kids with Clap": Gonorrhea as an indicator of child sexual assault. Victimology 2(2)251-67, 1977

13. Susman EJ, Trickett PK, Iannotti RJ, Hollenbeck BE and Zahn-Waxler C: Child-rearing patterns in depressed, abusive and normal mothers. Am J Orthopsychiatry 55 (2):237-51, 1985

14. Hawton K, Roberts J, and Goodwin G: The risk of child abuse among mothers who attempt suicide. Br J Psychiatry 146:486-9, 1985

15. Fontana VJ and Robison E: Observing child abuse. J Pediatrics 105(4):655-60, 1984

16. Kovitz KE, Dougan P, Riese R, and Brummitt JR: Multidisciplinary team functioning. Child Abuse & Neglect 8(3):353-60, 1984

17. Maddin BJ and Hansen I: The services provided during a child abuse and/or neglect case investigation and the barriers that exist to service provision. Child Abuse & Neglect 9(2):175-82, 1985

18. Gabinet L: Child abuse treatment failures reveal need for redefinition of the problem. Child Abuse & Neglect 7:395-402, 1983

19. Meyers PA, Brandner A, and Templin KH: Developmental milestones in abused children and their improvements with a family-oriented approach to the treatment of child abuse. Child Abuse & Neglect 9(2):245-50, 1985

20. Giarretto H: Humanistic treatment of father-daughter incest. In Helfer RE and Kempe CH: Child Abuse and Neglect: The Family and the Community. Cambridge, MA: Ballinger Publishing Co., 1976, pp 143-58

21. Murphy S, Okrow B, and Nicola RM: Prenatal prediction of child abuse and neglect: A prospective study. Child Abuse & Neglect 9(2):225-235, 1985

22. Leventhal JM, Egerter SA, and Murphy JM: Reassessment of the relationship of perinatal risk factors and child abuse. Am J Dis Childhood 138:1034-39, 1984

The Family Model and Genetic Counseling

1. Kessler S (Ed): Genetic Counseling Psychological Dimensions. New York: Academic Press, 1979

Gypsy Family. Photograph by Jack Reed Royce, 1973.

29
Family Intervention and the Mental Health Professions

OBJECTIVES

- To enable the professionals in the mental health disciplines to adapt the family model to their particular needs
- To enable the family therapist to understand the needs of the other disciplines and work collaboratively in using the family model

INTRODUCTION

In addition to medicine and surgery, the family model has had a major impact in the mental health disciplines of rehabilitation therapy, social work, psychology and, for obvious reasons, child psychiatry. Of course, the model has also had major impact on the field of psychiatry, and these are touched on throughout this text. As we have emphasized, the impact has varied from department to department and from one region/country to another. Suffice to say, the biological model seems more compatible (has provided an easier reception) than the individual, psychodynamic model.

468

THE FAMILY MODEL AND THE
REHABILITATION THERAPIST
with Susan Williams, M.B.A., O.T.R.,
Susanne Currie, O.T.R.,
and Susan Haiman, M.P.S., O.T.R.

The field of rehabilitation therapy has been gradually expanding from a primary focus on rehabilitation within an inpatient setting to include rehabilitation in the community. The rehabilitation therapist's function in both settings is to return the identified patient to a maximum level of functioning within the community.

Currently rehabilitation therapists work in a variety of settings, including traditional inpatient settings, as well as day treatment centers, community mental health centers, and, to an increasing extent, private practices where rehabilitation therapists provide therapy or consultation (or both) to various therapists doing psychotherapy, to extended care facilities, and to various private therapeutic facilities.

Although rehabilitation therapy has traditionally been practiced with the focus on both the individual and that individual's role in a group setting, there has been little emphasis on the family as one specific group configuration. Concurrent with the emergence of the family therapy movement, rehabilitation therapists have placed greater emphasis on the functioning of the identified patient in the context of the family. It is becoming patently clear that the identified patient is dysfunctional not only because of a psychiatric disability but also because of forces in the family.

The Family and the Rehabilitation Process

When the identified patient has a disturbance in functional capacity (for example, vocational or avocational impairment), an assumption is made that the functional capacity of the identified patient depends, in part, on the emotional climate of the family. For example, in the traditional empty-nest syndrome, the mother may not want the children to leave home and be employed because that would mean she is left alone with the father. She may, therefore, prevent their functioning. In another example, the identified patient may be abusing drugs or alcohol. This problem may be indicative of one person acting out the tension and lack of communication among the family members. One of the initial tasks of the rehabilitation therapist is to uncover the problems of the identified patient as they are understood within the family constellation.

Finally, exacerbation of psychotic symptoms in the identified patient may indicate an increase in the degree of emotional intensity expressed in the family.

This high degree of emotionality often occurs around the patient's ability to assume expected levels of function in daily tasks and occupational roles. The family's response may well inhibit productive independent function.

Rehabilitation Assessment

There are a variety of rehabilitation-oriented assessment procedures in which the task is to determine how the identified patient functions within the family context.

For some families it is useful to interview the patient and the family, with an emphasis on past functioning in relationship to family dynamics, interactional patterns among members, and family methods of coping with stress. For many families, however, an interview reflects the established "persona" of the family and may not accurately convey family roles and lines of authority. Task-oriented and projective family interactional techniques may be more revealing and ultimately more useful to the family. For example, the family may be asked to cook a meal together. In a situation like this, the therapist can observe interactional patterns in a "hands-on" way and eliminate the discrepancies of verbal reporting. The therapist notes both how the individual functions and how this functioning is influenced by the family.

For some families more projective-expressive techniques may be useful in the initial assessment. Art therapy has been extremely helpful in encouraging nonverbal communication and expression. The family members may be asked to respond to one another nonverbally through making lines and symbols on the same piece of paper. It is not difficult to see how this task might also clarify interactional patterns and lines of authority in the family. In another assessment procedure, family members may be asked to cut shapes out of construction paper to represent themselves and each family member. These are then placed on another piece of paper to reflect the closeness/distance dimension in the family. From this exercise, both the therapist and the family gain a fairly clear graphic depiction of the family dynamics from the point of view of each family member.

Techniques and Effect of Rehabilitation on the Family

Once the family problems are identified, tasks can be set up under the guidance of the rehabilitation therapist to correct the deficiences. Problems can be corrected on the spot. For example, a father who does every task for his son can be helped to allow his son to do more for himself. If the identified patient is in a hospital setting, the notion of family "visits" can be changed to make the family's participation in various activities mandatory.

Often the family can more accurately assess its own problems through tasks rather than through verbal interventions. Many families are performance, rather than verbally, oriented (perhaps because of limitations in verbal comprehension and concept formation). The idea of tasks makes more sense to them. A family-activity planning session can focus around various tasks in which the whole family might be involved and should include both leisure-time and house-maintenance activities. Other tasks for a family planning session might include:

1. Planning for family vacation: what will each member pack; who will be responsible for the packing; who will share in what preparatory task; and so on
2. Planning a family picnic or household festivity.
3. Delegating weekly chores for various family members.
4. Preparing and participating in a family meal.

One therapeutic setting has a "family activity night" as part of the clinic's adolescent program. These activities have been found to be useful in assessing family dynamics, pointing out "here and now" behavior, assessing the power within the family system, and evaluating each individual member's capacities for decision making and reality testing in relation to activities of daily living. These activities are especially useful for motivating the family members to do things together and for getting them to listen to, and communicate with, one another. Other treatment techniques involve more psychotherapeutically oriented interventions. An art project involving the drawing of a family situation may lead to understanding how the father, for example, may be handling a situation in ways similar to his own father. Often the graphic portrayal, or acting out, of situations may reinforce associations that verbal discussion may not.

The increasing involvement of rehabilitation therapists in day treatment settings provides an opportunity for the fostering of closer community ties and close monitoring of family functioning. Rehabilitation therapists can work with patients daily around tasks geared to return the patient to full community functioning. Rehabilitation therapists in private practice are also focusing more on work with families and the often important role played by the identified patient within the family setting. Regardless of setting, the rehabilitation therapist is able to provide assessment, treatment, and consultation regarding the functional status of clients in relation to the family.

Psychoeducation and Families

The most exciting new work in the field is implementation of psychoeducational techniques in work with families. Although this is discussed in Chapter 22, let us summarize here for the rehabilitation therapist. This trend in psychiatric treatment delivery combines didactic instruction with principles of rehabilitation and learning theory to reach families through the use of their cognitive and adaptive capacities. The psychoeducation model is useful in helping to better understand the patients' illness and the families' roles in preventing relapse. It is also useful in educating both patients and families as to what rehabilitation is.

Workshops have been developed to teach families about schizophrenia. The segment of that day-long workshop that deals with rehabilitation makes several important points.

1. The role of rehabilitation programs in the long-term treatment of the patient is defined.
2. The importance of taking gradual, manageable steps toward realistic goals for the patient is underscored.
3. Attention is directed toward the patient's assets and his ability to engage in meaningful activity despite his or her illness.

Along with highlighting these issues, families are given the opportunity to engage in an activity which, in an abbreviated fashion, introduces them to the type of session that might occur in rehabilitation programs using social skills training.

Another variation of psychoeducation philosophy involves the rehabilitation specialist in helping families to identify literature regarding specific psychiatric illnesses. This enables families to read and process essential, relevant information independently. Such an approach not only helps families gain a sense of mastery, but also communicates inherent respect for families' ability to utilize their cognitive, intellectual capacities. The development of mental health resource libraries that can be used by patients and their families is an evolving method of addressing the growing need for education around coping with mental illness.

THE FAMILY MODEL AND SOCIAL WORK
with Susan Matorin, A.C.S.W.

The centrality of the family has been a cornerstone of social work philosophy and practice throughout the history of the profession's development. This legacy is apparent in hundreds of existing family service agencies and settlement houses.

In addition to offering traditional family, conjoint, and individual counseling services, such settings provide parental counseling, advocacy assistance, homemaker and day care services, and a myriad of other programs. The underlying theme is that of preserving the integrity of the family and decreasing stresses that mar the fabric of family life.

The social work profession has transferred a family focus to a range of other practice settings—medical and psychiatric hospitals, probation offices, schools, and more recently employee assistance programs. Initially, despite a family orientation and philosophy, in practice, clients (as they were called) were most often seen individually. Multiple family members were divided among practitioners within one agency, or among several agencies. This was particularly so in the 1950s in child guidance settings. The development of family therapy models and methods has paved the way for new practice vistas, so that social workers in a variety of settings are now trained to apply such models of care and modify them to address a range of problems.

In the early 1960s, Virginia Satir directed attention to family communication patterns, clarifying disturbed ones and exploring areas of family growth. More recently, planned short-term treatment models, family treatment via home visiting in urban ghettos, and family work with different ethnic groups are but several newer areas of practice. Since much of earlier theory was based on research with middle-class families, there remains the need for research both in the area of treatment outcome and efficacy in general, and more particularly with multi-problem lower income families.

The major change that has occurred in the field is that over the last decade, the model of practice has shifted from (primarily) a psychoanalytic model to a family model with a special focus on psychoeducation. This issue is discussed in Chapter 1, and is reflective of changes in model occurring across the board in psychiatry.

THE FAMILY MODEL AND PSYCHIATRIC NURSING
with Beth Harris, R.N., M.A., C.S.

Psychiatric nurses work in a variety of settings, among them community outreach programs, HMOs, emergency rooms, and inpatient psychiatric units. With the advanced education and experience, nurses may assume, as part of their overall responsibility, the role of family therapist or co-therapist. At times when the nurse is not the therapist, her relationship with the family takes a different focus and involves different interactions and interventions. This section focuses on the nurse's involvement with the family as a nurse and not as a family therapist, and since most nurses work in an inpatient psychiatric setting, that is the focus of this discussion.

The first task is assessing the patient's current functioning and the family's ability to help the patient recover. During the assessment, the nurse strives to understand the ways in which the patient and family interact and rely upon one another in their daily lives. In the process, both the nurse and the family develop a clearer picture of the patient's abilities and of the family's capacity to help the patient.

Since the nurse is often the professional who has the most contact with both patient and family, it is essential that she welcome the family as part of the treatment team. This is best accomplished by acknowledging the enormous stresses families withstand prior to the decision to seek professional help, and by recognizing that the family knows the patient best, has worked with him or her the hardest, and will ultimately provide most of the patient's care. Another task during the first contact with the family is to orient the family to the hospital, making sure they know what to expect in the first few days of treatment and how to contact the other members of the treatment team. After this initial contact, and throughout the patient's treatment, the nurse keeps the family abreast of the patient's progress. In some hospitals, the family is given orientation and progress reports in weekly nurse-led meetings that are usually called family support groups or multi-family groups. In other places, contact with families is less formal and becomes a part of the nurse's everyday dealings with patients and families during the family's visits.

During the course of the patient's treatment, the nurse's interventions are aimed at helping the patient reduce symptoms and regain competence in as many areas as possible. To achieve this, the nurse spends most of her time working with the patient, educating him about his illness and treatment, administering medications and other somatic treatments, setting limits on unacceptable behaviors, and teaching the patient more effective ways of coping. As she does so, the nurse is often observed by the family and serves as a role model in areas where the family has difficulty—limit-setting, making requests, expressing feelings, and so on. As the nurse develops a plan of care for the patient, she shows the family how to problem-solve around activities of daily living such as showering, meals, and grooming. This process can help the family develop a realistic sense of the small, slow steps the patient must take in his or her progress toward the goal of self-care.

Just as the nurse educates patients about their illness and treatment, she must also teach the family or reinforce what has been taught by other professionals. This is especially important when it comes to medication. Since the nurse dispenses medication in most health care settings, she is often the professional who the patient and family most strongly associate with medications. Because medications are one of the most powerfully effective treatments we have for mental illness, it is essential that patients and family understand them. When families know how the medications work, what they can be expected to do, and how side effects are managed, they can be a powerful ally in assuring the patient's compliance. The nurse often provides the patient and family with this information by teaching medication classes or leading medication groups.

As part of their role as educator, nurses often lead families to other resourses for support or information such as books or other materials written for the layman, and local self-help groups.

It was mentioned earlier that nurses serve as role models for families in their interactions with patients. In many health care settings, nurses also intervene more directly, helping family members frame their interactions with patients so that their communications are clear, direct, and specific. Similarly, if the family needs help to problem-solve more effectively, the nurse can intervene in disputes as they arise, helping the patient and family to identify the problem, discuss alternative solutions, and choose the best one to act on. In all these efforts, the nurse works in concert with the entire treatment team (including the patient and family) toward a set of goals agreed upon by all.

THE FAMILY MODEL AND CLINICAL PSYCHOLOGY

Clinical psychologists are experts in the assessment, diagnosis, and treatment of emotional disorders, both those that are classifiable via DSM-III-R criteria, and those that do not neatly fit into such a classification. Trained to attend to the interface between the individual's behavior and the environmental context, the family model is congruent with a psychological orientation. This is borne out by the large number of psychologists who have contributed substantially to the theoretical, assessment, research, and clinical development of the family field.

At the present time experience in the theory and practice of family intervention is a commonplace in the training of a clinical psychologist. Most students have one or several graduate courses in family theory and intervention, and most receive supervised clinical experience in family therapy in internship placements. A majority of clinical psychologists utilize family intervention in hospital, clinic, and private practice settings.

Every psychologist in clinical practice, whether it be in a hospital, outpatient clinic, or private practice, should be attuned to the systems effects of every patient. Basic knowledge about the influence of marital interaction, family, extended family, community, and job systems upon individual pathology and recovery is necessary for the assessment of any patient. While not all psychologists will elect to become expert in family therapy, all must utilize the basics of systems pathology in the assessment of individuals, and use this knowledge in the differential treatment assignment and triage of some patients to family intervention.

THE FAMILY MODEL AND CHILD PSYCHIATRY
with John Patten, M.D.

It would seem obvious that family therapy would be a useful modality in the treatment of the problems and disorders of children. Children are usually brought to professionals for help by parents. The child's family is often involved with and affected by the problem. They are concerned, usually motivated, and may have their own theories about the causes expressed in terms of some family dysfunction. It is common for parents to blame themselves for the problem.

However, child psychology and psychiatry have been principally shaped by theories of the individual, the developmental cycle and of the psychoanalytical model. These theories might have a similar point of view as family systems theory as to the families role in "causing" the problem, but when it comes to therapeutic intervention, then the different theories lead to very different approaches. Psychoanalytic thinking views individual psychotherapy with the child as the primary modality. The parents are not involved because of transference issues, but they may be put in a separate therapy for themselves, individual or couple. Family systems thinkers believe that family treatment involving the child and various family members is the optimal way to produce change.

Evaluation

One thing there is a consensus on is that any evaluation of a child must include a family evaluation. But what constitutes a family evaluation means different things to different people. A family therapist would interview all family members and significant others at the same time. He or she would believe that procedure would give the most information about the child's "and families" problems; that a child psychiatrist, who interviewed the parents and child separately, and excluded siblings, was getting less information and not doing a family evaluation. Many good mental health professionals who work with children intuitively work with families. However, we believe that family therapy theory and the family therapist's clinical skills do have a much bigger place than they have been given in the child psychiatry field. Treating a 15-year-old school avoider in individual psychotherapy won't produce change if the child psychiatrist missed the family evaluation and didn't pick up that the 6-year-old younger sister is being abused by a parent. Conversely, as child psychiatry has a lot to offer the family therapy field—e.g., treating a 15-year-old "school avoider" with family therapy won't help if the family therapist misses his severe learning disability.

All children require careful medical, neurological, and developmental evaluations by professionals qualified to do so. To assume that a symptom has an "interactional basis" or that it is acting "as a metaphor for the systems problem" is premature and unprofessional.

Young Children in a Family Session

Many family therapists get confused and distracted by young children in a session. "They don't sit still, they just play," is a common criticism. Children's play and drawings can add much information to a family session. Keep some toys in the office. At different stages of a family therapy, excluding younger children may be appropriate, just as seeing sibling sub-system or the parental subsystem may be. Children and adolescents have delicately balanced internal psychological forces, which are in constant interaction with the external forces of the family.

Where, and how to intervene, should come out of a careful evaluation of all these factors.

Other "Significant People" in a Child's World

Teachers, pediatricians, clergy and neighbors—any of these may be very significant and should be consulted with if they are part of the system.

Infants and Young Children

Many therapists prefer to involve everyone in the household, including infants (and perhaps even pets), during the evaluation period in order to observe how family members relate to one another. Helpful observations may be gathered, such as differences in how parents relate to each other with and without the infant present, how one parent holds an infant, and what the role of the other parent is. After the initial evaluation is completed, the therapist must decide whether the continued inclusion of an infant or relatively nonverbal child tends to aid or disrupt the work of therapy.

Many family therapists would probably agree that infants and children should be included at least once for diagnostic purposes. Certainly much can be gained from having children present for many of the sessions, if for no other reason than that they often tend to be more open and direct than adults and will say what they think.

Treatment

When *young children* are present, the parents are expected to exert appropriate behavioral control over them. If not, the therapist helps the parent to accomplish the task. The therapist explains the "rules of the house," including behavioral limits and freedom of communication. The therapist must decide who should handle requests to go to the toilet and water fountain. The therapist may wish to provide material for play, such as toys, paper, and crayons.

Bell,[1] writing about the general process of therapy, has offered some pertinent guidelines concerning children in therapy sessions. He first meets with parents, alone in order to explain the basis of family therapy. Then he meets with children and parents together for orientation. He explains that the children have a voice in what is said and that the parents are expected to listen and not to talk while the children are talking. He calls this the "parent-child phase." He then moves into the parent phase, during which the problems of the parents are explored. During this time, the children, as they gain trust in the therapist, are usually more active. In the next phase, the identified patient is more active in the family in a more constructive way. Most so-called *forbidden topics* usually have already been heard by the children and, in this, Bell's experience with children in therapy concurs with ours.

Adolescents will be crucially involved in the family unit's concerns and interactions and often represent the "identified patient." They should be included in the sessions so that intergenerational conflicts and inadequate communication can be dealt with. One of the primary tasks of the late adolescent, however, is to achieve increasing psychosocial autonomy from his or her family of origin. If such adolescents are consistently included in all family sessions, there is a structural reinforcement of their being involved in all of the family's interactions. In addition, there may be little recognition of those specific interactions of the husband-wife pair that do not, and should not, involve their children. Thus it may be useful to have some sessions with only the husband and wife. Other sessions may be devoted to seeing an adolescent alone for the special purpose of reinforcing or increasing autonomy. Conjoint sessions, however, may also be successfully used to explore issues of differentness and separation.

When a marital relationship has ruptured to the extent that treatment cannot be accomplished without the inclusion of the adolescent children, the children may serve as buffers, neutralizers, or reality testers until such time as the couple is able to resume functioning as a dyad.

Careful recognition must be given to the readiness and ability of both the adolescent and his or her family to separate. Although individual autonomous functioning is seen as a desirable goal, there will be situations in which the therapist must be realistic with respect to the family's ability to tolerate an abrupt separation, as well as to the autonomous potential of adolescents suffering from brain damage, chronic schizophrenia, or severe characterological difficulties.

Systematic studies on outcome of treatment for children have been rare. Kinston and Bentovim have requested outcome of brief focal family therapy for children and adolescents. Of their first 29 cases, 22 engaged in therapy; the referred child improved in 19 of these cases. Eleven of the engaged families improved.[2]

Turf Issues

When the child is a focus of intervention, both the fields of family therapy and child psychiatry/psychology have turf claims on the situation. Child psychology and psychiatry have been historically shaped by theories of the individual, the individual developmental cycle, and the psychoanalytic model. McDermott[3] could say in 1974 that there was an undeclared war between child psychiatry and family. At this writing it would appear that the war is over, the dust is settling, and there is accomodation on both sides. Family therapists are beginning to see that individual diagnosis is important, that not all of the variance of individual pathology and symptomatology is under the control of the family system, and that there are some instances where family therapy is not the primary mode of intervention. On the other side, child psychiatrists are beginning to recognize the influence of the family system on the maintenance and exacerbation of child pathology, and recommend family intervention when family factors are assessed as salient.

SUGGESTIONS FOR FURTHER READINGS

Black D: Child guidance clinics. In Bentovim A, Barnes GG, and Cooklin A (Eds): **Family Therapy: Complementary Frameworks of Theory and Practice, Vol. 2.** New York: Grune & Stratton, 1982, pp 479-496.

Lieberman S and Cooklin A: Family therapy and general psychiatry: Some issues. In Bentovim A, Barnes GG, and Cooklin A (Eds): **Family Therapy: Complementary Frameworks of Theory and Practice, Vol.2.** New York: Grune & Stratton, 1982, pp 515-526.

Bentovim A: A family therapy approach to making decisions in child care cases In Bentovim A, Barnes GG, and Cooklin A (Eds): **Family Therapy: Complementary Frameworks of Theory and Practice, Vol. 2.** New York: Grune & Stratton, 1982, pp 527-543.

REFERENCES

The Family Model and the Rehabilitation Therapist

1. Andreasen NC: Negative symptoms in schizophrenia. Arch Gen Psychiatry 39:784-788, 1982
2. Fine SB: Psychiatric treatment and rehabilitation: What's in a name? J National Assoc Private Psychiatric Hosp 11:8-13, 1980
3. Lamb HR: An educational model for teaching living skills to long term patients. Hosp Comm Psychiatry 27:875-877, 1976
4. Michaelson A, Nitzberg L, and Rubinton P: Mental health resources library: A consumer guide to literature. Psychiatric Hosp 15:133-140, 1984

The Family Model and Social Work

1. Manor O (Ed): Family Work in Action—A Handbook for Social Workers. London: Tavistock Publications, 1984, pp 192

The Family Model and Psychiatric Nursing

1. Falvo DR: The family in patient education. In Effective Patient Education: A Guide to Increased Compliance. Rockville, MD: Aspen Publications, 1985
2. Clements IW and Buchanan DM: Family Therapy: A Nursing Perspective. New York: John Wiley & Sons, 1982

The Family Model and Child Psychiatry

1. Bell JE: Family group therapy. Public Health Monograph No. 64. Washington, DC: Department of Health, Education and Welfare, Public Health Service, 1961
2. Bentovim A and Kinston W: Brief focal therapy when the child is the referred patient—II. Methodology and results. J Child Psychology & Psychiatry 19:119-143, 1978
3. McDermott JF and Char WF: The undeclared war between child and family therapy. Am Acad Child Psychiatry 13:422-435, 1975

The Family of Charles IV Detail by Goya, 1800. Courtesy of the Prado Museum, Madrid

30
The Family and Other Fields

OBJECTIVES

- To enable professionals in architecture, law, education, and other institutions to adapt the family model to their particular needs
- To enable the family therapist to understand the needs of these fields and work collaboratively in using the family model

ARCHITECTURE AND DESIGN
with Earl Pope, Architect

According to some architects the field of architecture has been overly dominated by technical, aesthetic, and economic considerations, rather than by the needs of the families. How can the architect quickly and effectively become aware of and understand family needs so that optimal design can be achieved despite this limitation? It is obvious that each architect will have to develop a method for doing fairly rapid family evaluation, based not only on the principles that we discussed earlier (Sections II & III) but also on principles especially adapted to architectural needs. The architect would need to go through a series of steps including:

1. Meeting the whole family, rather than only one member
2. Attempting to understand the family needs and how the family functions

482

3. Delineating objectives for the design, but only after understanding the problem

An example of such a procedure would be the following:

The family consisted of Mrs. S. and her two teenage sons who lived in a low-income apartment with very limited space. Mrs. S. told the architect, who was conducting a program on family space planning and furnishing for the neighborhood community center, that her older son never brought his friends home. Furthermore, he never wanted to stay around the house, thereby hindering all communication with her. The architect met with the family and discovered that the son was an excellent athlete who had won many trophies for his achievements in sports. The apartment they were housed in was designed in such a way that the son was living in a small room, shared by a younger brother, where he had very little space for himself. The architect sensed the need for the son to feel better about his room and home to make it more his place, so that he would feel comfortable in bringing his friends there and would spend more time there himself. One small part of the solution was to provide a shelf in the son's small room that would run around the entire room at door height and that would have enough space for him to display his trophies. His change in the relation to his home was startling.

This is obviously an oversimplification of a complex set of events. It does highlight, however, the points that we discussed above.

Family patterns of dining (Chapter 9) become an important area for architects to consider. Dining space might be set up not only for eating but also to maximize family communication.

When low- and moderate-income housing standards are used, minimum spatial requirements (such as HUD Minimum Property Standards) often become the maximum, leaving little opportunity for families to adapt their living space to their members' needs. Also, many housing programs are designed for small families (two children at the most), rather than for a variety of family sizes. The result is that the specific problems of larger families are not dealt with, such as the need for multiple study areas and privacy for parents as well as children.

Middle-income families have a similar problem. Most speculative housing (the most common type of middle-income housing by far) is stereotyped in form—three bedrooms and a family room, with the living room and the dining room reserved for ceremonial use only. The middle-income family often, by convention or by design of the developer, lives in a large square foot area theoretically, but its living pattern is confined to a small square foot area not unlike a low-to-moderate-income family (the family room and three bedrooms).

Finally, there are issues beyond personal space. The family must also relate to the community. If the family's personal environment is satisfactory but it feels alienated from its community and neighbors, all parties will suffer. Does our environment suggest communications other than a casual nod in the elevator? Are there places to meet, to talk, to exchange ideas, or to develop an identity with a neighborhood? Are we threatened and vulnerable, or do we look forward to seeing our neighbors during a casual communal encounter?

In a like vein, in designing multiple-occupancy dwellings, the needs of the families should not get lost in the overriding needs of the community. For example, a principle that many architects follow is to house families without children on the upper floors, whereas families with children (who need to be close to other children in playgrounds) are housed on the lower floors.

These are only a few of many examples that can be cited. For a full discussion of the subject see references.[1-4]

LAW AND THE JUDICIAL SYSTEM
with Gail Saliterman, Ph.D., J.D.

Every family therapist should recognize that the American legal system depends on the idea that the adversarial process is the best way to get at the truth. When applied to the family, this "fact finding" process can be enormously destructive. Thus, while courts are supposed to help resolve conflicts, they frequently cannot do so without touching on and permanently affecting the interactions and relationships of all the parties involved: husband, wife, their children, and even the therapist. Family members, in short, can use and even abuse the law and its enforcement by the courts in order to hurt each other. A therapist, to be effective, must be aware of this potential to use the law to promote conflict as well as cooperation.

The family therapist's involvement in the legal system generally takes one of three forms: first, the court, an attorney, or a family member may ask the therapist to evaluate the family. Second, the family therapist may serve as a mediator before or in conjunction with a court hearing. Third, the family may want to utilize a family therapist to help resolve the new problems posed by the dissolution of the family. This is particularly likely if the family employed the therapist prior to the breakdown of relations that led one or more members of the family to resort to an attorney or the court. Each of these roles demands a different perspective on the family. Therefore, the family therapist who fulfills one role cannot and should not attempt to perform any other role.

The Family Evaluation

An attorney or judge may ask a family therapist for an evaluation of the family, or of a particular family member. The attorney for one spouse in a custody fight may, for example, be seeking someone who can evaluate the family and testify on behalf of that attorney's client in support of the client's claim that he or she is the better parent. No family therapist who has been treating (or who wants to treat) a particular family, can also work for an attorney representing one member of that family. Even if all parties consent, the family therapist should avoid being put in a position of having to divulge information gathered in the confidence of the therapeutic session. *Family therapy, in short, should not be confused with family evaluation.* Any family therapist confronted by a request from an attorney or judge to testify or otherwise prepare evidence concerning a family with whom the therapist has been working should advise the attorney or the court to retain an independent therapist to conduct an evaluation of that family.

Aside from the obvious conflicts of interest, by its very nature, family therapy rarely lends itself to an evaluation of the independent worth or the disabilities of a particular family member. The family therapist considers not only the identified patient, if one exists, but the capacity of the entire family system to deal with the need of each member, particularly the needs of the children. Family therapy, in other words, dictates intervention and treatment based on the needs of all concerned. An attorney, in contrast, seeks individually oriented reports that favor his or her client's interests.

Even if the court, rather than a particular family member's attorney, orders a family system report, the family therapist will almost inevitably find one or more members of the family objecting to the admission of the family evaluation into evidence. Moreover, even if no one objects to the report, the therapeutic advantages of the family sessions will almost certainly be lost if any family member harbors the slightest concern that what is being said in therapy might end up being revealed to others.

On the other hand, courts and attorneys are, with increasing frequency, seeking family evaluations from therapists who have never treated the particular family in question. The Uniform Marriage and Divorce Act, promuligated in 1979 and adopted in whole or in part by most states, explicitly encourages every judge handling a divorce proceeding to seek the advice of professional personnel when appropriate. The Act further provides that such advice must be "in writing and made available by the court to counsel upon request."[1]

The therapist who is retained to provide professional guidance to a court or an attorney regarding a family must be able to prepare an evaluation after relatively brief and few encounters with a family riddled with conflict and pain. The task, therefore, requires great perceptivity and enormous detachment. Such reports are rarely sought when the parties are able to settle their disagreements themselves.

In many states either party can ask the court to strike the family system evaluation from the record if it is not favorable. Other states provide that either side is free to seek another, possibly more favorable report, if he or she feels the report is detrimental. Whenever this occurs, the therapists preparing these reports must each be ready to defend his or her conclusions from attack by the attorney representing the disadvantaged party. Specifically, each therapist will be asked to testify at a court hearing and to prepare for cross-examination from the opposing counsel. In drafting a family evaluation report, the therapist should, therefore, outline all the options available for the court and provide clear, precise, and meaningful reasons for each proposal.

Mediation

For the past decade, precisely because of the expense, trauma, and devisiveness associated with the dissolution of the family, many courts and attorneys have encouraged the development of a non-judicial technique for dispute resolution called mediation. In California since 1980, for example, judges are required to order mediation of any custody dispute prior to a court hearing. The purpose of this law is to make everyone attempt to resolve their differences without a contested court hearing.

In some states, the mediators tend to be attorneys. In many jurisdictions, however, therapists, social workers, and counselors of all descriptions are becoming involved in family dispute mediation. Cornblatt[2] reports that one directory of family mediation services lists 406 different mediators or mediation groups. Connecticut has gone even further and is experimenting with an interdisciplinary approach to mediation. The mediator is a mental health professional who has access to a mediating attorney. The attorney can be called in at appropriate times to provide legal information, describe options, and draft a separation agreement, which the parties take to independent legal counsel for review. It is, however, the mental health professional who conducts the mediation.

If called to serve as a mediator, a family therapist must recognize that the confidentiality of any communications in the mediation is not protected despite any claims by the mediation program to the contrary. Further, some mediation programs provide that the mediator's recommendations will be conveyed directly to the court. If so, the mediator is always subject to cross-examination regarding his or her recommendations. Even if the mediation program does not require any report to the court, the family therapist should realize that, if mediation fails, the mediator may well be called to court as a witness by one party's attorney and asked to testify about what was said in the mediation sessions and about any recommendations the mediator would make. Basically, both the therapist and the family members need to be aware of the parameters governing the therapist's role as mediator. Within these limitations, however, the mediation process is frequently an excellent way for the parties to avoid the costs and unfairness associated with most contested family court hearings. The family therapist cannot forget, however, that the threat of a contested hearing permeates the entire process by which out-of-court settlements are generally attained.[3]

Family Therapy

Most frequently, however, the family therapist will begin or continue to serve to provide therapeutic counseling to the family as it proceeds through the dissolution proceedings. For the therapist who has been working with the intact family, the family's involvement with the courts and attorneys will raise a whole host of new issues. The most salient ones involve confidentiality, separation and divorce counseling, and the rights of the children. Each of these are discussed, in turn, below.

Confidentiality and Privilege

A situation may arise as a result of the formal dissolution proceedings in which one spouse wants to compel the other to testify about material that came up during the family therapy in order to gain a personal advantage. The rules of evidence specifically prohibit testimony regarding "interspousal communications" without the consent of the non-testifying spouse. If, for example, the wife seeks to gain custody of the children and the husband has admitted during therapy that he secretly consumes large quantities of alcohol, the husband can object to the court receiving any information from the therapist about the husband's drinking as evidence in the custody hearing. This objection would be valid, even if the couple had separated, as long as the information came to light in treatment while they were still living together.

Such information would not be privileged, however, if it came up after the spouses were formally separated or divorced. This would be the case even if the couple was in therapy in the hope of reconciling. A therapist who is working with a separated, but not yet divorced couple needs, therefore, to make certain that the couple is aware of this possibility.

The family therapist should also realize that confidential information may come to be used against the interests of one family member if either side or the court asks the therapist to take the best interest of the child into account. Under those circumstances, without divulging the confidential communication, the therapist will inevitably rely on information obtained in therapy to conclude that one of his or her clients would be a less effective parent.

Some family therapists believe they should use their power to consider the best interests of the child as a way to force the parents to decide an issue. In cases in which the spouses cannot agree on a custody issue, a therapist could, for example, inform the family that he or she will go to court and testify to the facts that suggest that the child should be placed in foster care. Such a threat generally arises from a conviction that if one spouse "wins" in court on the custody issue, as inevitably happens, the child ends up feeling torn and guilty. In such cases, the custody decision may prove detrimental to the child's future growth and development.

On the other hand, many are critical of the therapist who assumes an aggressive, interventionist role. First, such a role can threaten the therapeutic process. Second, while it is important for the therapist to encourage parents to settle their custody battles outside of court, it may be disingenuous for the therapist to recommend foster care when one or either parent can provide satisfactory care. However resolved, the example demonstrates the power that the therapist has in the ajudication of custody disputes.

By and large, contemporary thinking emphasizes the advantages of the child's maintaining meaningful relationships with both parents during and after dissolution.[4] The need to minimize the negative psychological effects of parental separation on children is well documented.[5] The family therapist who recognizes the importance for the child of positive relationships with both parents can do more to minimize the destructive side of the adversarial system than can any other of the participants.

Separation and Divorce Counseling

Even an attorney who is unusually sensitive to family situations is obligated to suppress his or her broader concerns in the interest of obtaining the outcome that is best for that particular client. The competent attorney must therefore utilize any tactical device that best serves this purpose. Given this adversarial context, the family therapist should be prepared for an escalation of differences between the parties. This escalation may well be counterproductive to the goals of family therapy. An attorney may advise the wealthier spouse, frequently the husband, to make the wife feel that he will give her as little as possible. He may even lead her to believe that he is willing to abandon all visitation and custody rights regarding the children. This, of course, is not what he intends to do. He wants to share custody and wants to provide adequately for the children, but he will use the threat of abandonment in order to force his wife to compromise. She, of course, is worried that he might actually intend not to support her and the children. She may feel threatened. At the very least, her lesser income puts her at a disadvantage in negotiations. The family therapist must understand that the different rules and goals that dictate the role of the dissolution attorney frequently exacerbates the very family tensions the therapist seeks to minimize.

The family therapist can help the family members cope with the negative impact of the adversarial system by focusing everyone's attention on the process of change in family interaction. Another tact, consistent with the goals of family therapy, might be to ask the family members what they feel would be in the best interest of the child or children. Obviously, the "best interests of the child" depend on who is conceiving that interest. This, however, is the point the therapist wants the family to recognize.

The therapist may also have to confront the problem of an excessive beneficence on the part of one spouse. Occasionally, a spouse, because of an exaggerated sense of guilt, will make a decision about the disposition of a child or of family assets that is inappropriate or excessive. A guilty husband with a new lover might, for example, offer $2,000 a month in alimony and child support, although he only makes $3,000 a month. His wife, also a professional earning a substantial salary, should fairly receive only $1,000 a month. In the long run the generosity could be counterproductive to the best interests of the family, as that spouse's guilt turns to anger and he or she reopens what seemed to be settled issues.

A therapist may recommend a trial separation. If so, the couple involved needs to be cognizant of the fact that such a separation, even for a trial period, can disadvantage the spouse who relinquishes custody of the children when more permanent custody arrangements are litigated. Similarly, whatever financial arrangements are instituted during the trial separation may well serve as a precedent for the post-divorce arrangements. Community property—be it a bank account, house or car—becomes an issue as soon as the couple begins to think about separation. The first one to take possession of any joint funds may well end up with them, if only because they are frequently quickly spent. This issue is particularly important, since women, with the repeal of special alimony laws, often end up with little capital or other means of support. Any unemployed woman thinking about divorce must consider what income will be available to her until she can support herself. The community property assets may be her only resource.

As a result, the therapist should suggest that the couple meet with an attorney prior to any separation, either separately or together. If the couple meets with an attorney together, that attorney will be precluded, by law, from acting as an attorney for either partner in the future because of the possible violations of the attorney-client confidences. On the other hand, the attorney the couple sees together must fairly lay out all the various alternatives and their consequences for each party. Thus, the joint visit can serve to instruct the couple in the realities of modern-day divorce; furthermore, the couple's emotional reactions to the visit will give each spouse a taste of what the actual divorce proceeding is likely to involve.

It is useful for a therapist to establish independent relationships with a range of attorneys who are willing to provide such joint legal counseling. The therapist might even suggest an attorney participate in a particular family session to help resolve some of the questions being asked. Insofar as the attorney does not serve in an adversarial role but is retained solely to provide relevant information and legal feedback, the attorney's role is congruent with therapeutic goals.

Children's Rights

Perhaps the single most important area of concern for the family therapy is new trends in children's rights. Each year over one million children experience the divorce of their parents.[6] Whenever the state is involved in an action involving families, it can be assumed that the children's interests and the parents' interests are not identical. Ideally, family therapists can work for the good of the total family unit at the same time that they are protecting the expectations of the individual members, including the children.

As the therapist tries to take the whole family's interest into account and to act in its best interest, irreconcilable differences may arise. If this occurs, and the couple needs to retain separate legal counsel to protect each spouse's separate interest, it is likely that their children should have independent legal representation as well. In such cases, the family therapist may find that the therapeutic goals of each party can no longer be appropriately treated in the family therapy context and the sessions should be terminated.

Custody

Historically, in our Western culture, the father had the exclusive right to custody of the children. This doctrine changed in the late 19th and early 20th centuries so that, until very recently, all courts presumed that the mother should be the custodial parent. In the last 15 years, however, the twin notions that neither parent can be presumed to be "best" and that joint custody is preferable took firm hold. A recent New York State study recommends, for example, a "no fault" custody order that gives parents joint custody over their children. The rationale behind these developments was that fathers should not be excluded from parenting and that joint custody is least disruptive for the children. Clearly, custody practices change over time. Even now, in the late 1980s, there seems to be a swinging of the pendulum away from joint custody on the grounds that "it lacks the stability children need."

For the therapist, the absence of clear rules regarding custody means that couples must see the importance of coming to an agreement regarding their children, even though they may not be able to resolve their property disagreements.

Adoption and Foster Home Placement

The areas of adoption and foster home placement are closely related. A common situation in marital therapy is the couple's belief that the solution to their problem is to adopt a child. (This myth is discussed in Chapter 4.) Even if this is an appropriate move, the family therapist may be asked by the placement agency to evaluate the parents' suitability for adoption. In this area, just as in a dissolution proceeding, the therapist must recognize that family therapy is different from family evaluation. Each needs a separate therapist. Furthermore, the family therapist can only provide information on a couple's functioning; so the evaluation of the suitability of the couple for adoption must be left for others to make.

Conversely, couples (or their parents or other agencies) who are having difficulty with one or more children sometimes believe that the solution to their problem may be to give the child (or children) up for adoption. This view is the opposite of the myth that "everything will be all right if we have a child." In these instances the therapist should first carefully evaluate the family situation and, if possible, engage in a trial period of family therapy before coming to the conclusion that placement outside of the home offers the best alternative. Even when it appears reasonable for the child to be placed, and even after the parents agree on adoption after dealing with their ambivalent feelings, it is not uncommon for the natural parents to later want to have the child back. In this situation, experience indicates that it is better for the child that the placement decision is irrevocable.

In the M. case the identified patient was Mrs. M., 31 years old. Her husband was 35 years old. They had a 5-year-old daughter and 3-year-old son. The patient gave a 10-year history of periodic major depressions and inability to function. While in these episodes, the patient was unable to take care of the children. During the course of the marriage, the husband became more and more involved in his work and spent less time with both the wife and children. When Mrs. M. was symptomatic, neither parent cared for or disciplined the children. Because of school problems with one of the children, the parents were brought to the attention of legal authorities, who suggested that the children would need foster care placement.

The family therapist handling the M. case had to decide whether the children should be placed in a foster home or if the family could be pulled together. This meant that the therapist had to decide each spouse's functional capacity as a parent and his or her willingness to work to create a functional family.

Foster home placement may be used as a temporary solution. The family therapist and the lawyer should realize that once a child is placed in foster care, it is usually temporary. Perhaps the best interest of the child is served when there is permanent placement in a foster situation and the rights of the natural parents are terminated. The foster family should adopt the child rather than serve as a temporary way station.

In summary, there are three options of child care available to the parents. The first is to have the child stay with them. The second is to separate the child from the home (permanently and irrevocably) and move toward adoption on the grounds that the couple is not functional. The third is the middle-ground position of foster care with the notion that this is temporary and the child will return to the natural parents once they are more functional. The role of the family therapist should be to encourage and facilitate the discussion of these issues with recognition of the strongly ambivalent feelings that will inevitably be presented, so as to help the family move toward a decision.

Conclusion

Representatives of the legal and judicial systems seek to use the family therapist as the expert on various issues that confront families in trouble. In fact, there is usually no set of empirical data to help a therapist formulate an expert opinion. What is frequently substituted instead, unfortunately, are the personal opinions and prejudices of the family therapist, which other social systems dealing with the family accept all too readily. In reality, the problems to be resolved by both the courts and the therapists raise crucial but frequently ambiguous, thorny, and even insolvable questions. Lawyers, judges, and case workers want to shift the burden of making these Solomon-like decisions to the "family expert." A therapist is well-advised to accept such an assignment with caution and to recognize his or her role as expert may confuse and contaminate the basic therapeutic goal of helping a family and its members to arrive at decisions that are best for them.

At the same time, the family therapist's training and neutrality vis-a-vis a family in trouble permit him or her frequently to play a very important role in resolving disputes that cannot be left unattended. The independent family evaluation that more and more courts require is the best example. New developments in the law suggest a yet more expanded role for the family therapist. At present, for example, the task of interviewing the child involved in the custody dispute is almost always left to the judge. Such interviews rarely consist of more than a short meeting in chambers and probably have little reliability. This function of obtaining the child's input would almost certainly be better performed by a therapist, albeit not the same family therapist who has been counselling the family.

THE SCHOOL SYSTEM
with Audrey J. Clarkin, Ph.D.

Elementary and secondary schools are the first institutions in the lives of children and their families open to public observation and intervention. It is the first time that society has a powerful opportunity to systematically reinforce positive growth and development begun in the family and community, and to compensate for underdevelopment and correct maldevelopment. School places two sets of demands on the child: to acquire knowledge and to develop social skills. For better or worse, people carry imprints of their school experiences throughout life.

In describing the dramatic changes in today's family structures as they affect the school-family coalition, numbers may speak louder than words. In 60 percent of the married couples with children under 18, both parents are working for pay. Approximately 22 million children under 13 years of age have working mothers. Estimates of the number of "latch key" children who spend at least three hours a day in self or sibling care, range from two to seven million. The number of one parent households increased by 200 perecnt from 1960 to 1985.

The implication of these trends for education is enormous. Traditional methods of relating to students' families need to be reevaluated and modified to meet the challenges of today's society. For many children, school represents the most secure and predictable aspect of their lives; six hours a day, five days a week. Some children see more of their teacher than they do of their parents.

The question can be asked, why should the school psychologist/social worker deal with the family? One knows the opposing arguments. For schools to get involved with parents can be time consuming, energy draining, and staff can be intimidated by the parent/taxpayers unrealistic demands and expectations. On the positive side, parents are the primary adult models for their children. They consciously (or unconsciously) communicate values, and they foster both social and learning skills, thereby influencing their children's attitudes. Legally responsible for their offspring, parents can be resources for the school as partners for behavior change.

One need not elaborate on the fact that children with problems often have hostile, uncooperative parents. Often the parents themselves experienced school failure or blame the school (to assuage their own disappointment), or are involved in family conflict that transcends the school. Despite the misperceptions of teachers and parents, *the need does exist for family and school to establish mutual goals*, and the child's progress will depend on the consistency exerted to achieve those goals.

The role of the psychologist in the school system is diverse and depends upon the particular school, its unique needs, the foresight of its leaders, and the creativity of the school psychologist. Expertise with human systems (the school system, the family system, the peer system among children) enables the psychologist to intervene in multiple ways: i.e., secondary prevention with families and their children having recognized problems; preventive programs with teachers, children, and their families; and training for teachers to attune them to the assessment of youngsters with potential psychiatric difficulties.

In the usual or traditional role, the psychologist is involved with secondary prevention, that is, a child has a problem that requires attention assessment via interview and/or testing, on-the-spot counseling, consultation with the family, and possible referral for professional help. In a prevention role, the psychologist works with the school system to intervene before there is an acute problem.

The three common approaches by the school psychologist to involving the family include: (1) direct contact with the parents to explore a family situation that is affecting the youngster's learning or emotional states, (2) eliciting the parents' cooperation in changing the negative behavior of the child within the school setting, and (3) working directly with the child to explore and resolve family conflict. Although a school psychologist does not engage in long-term family therapy, nevertheless, because children move over time through several grade levels within a building, there often can be multiple contacts and an understanding of family dynamics. This fact places the school psychologist in a pivotal role in uniting home and school resources for the welfare of the child.

Classroom observation, teacher contact, and student counseling provide the psychologist with a day-to-day appreciation of the child's functioning in school that can then be communicated to the family. The family, in turn, often reveals the stresses within the home that impede the child's progress, both academic and emotional, and the psychologist serves as a link between the two systems. This link is strengthened by family meetings with and without the child, and when indicated, three-way meetings with student, teacher, and family. When family problems intensify and extend beyond the boundaries of school, the psychologist will recommend outside professional help, but even then contact is often maintained between the family therapist and the school psychologist. In all of these interventions, understanding and utilizing the family systems model may be very helpful.

Family Theory and Institutions

Some writers see many similarities in the structure and functioning of institutions and families. Because all members of any corporation come from and usually have families, many of their own interactional patterns, rules, and multi-belief constellations may be translated into their work situation. Sometimes it is easy to see the "father," "mother," "grandfather," "youngest-child" equivalents operating in the board room and daily life of an institution.

Family theory may in the future provide some fascinating insights into how these structures operate adaptively or nonadaptively. Collaboration between sociologists, management consultants, and family therapists may provide an even broader foundation in helping to understand our cultural environment and institutions.

SUGGESTIONS FOR FURTHER READINGS

Committee on the Family of the Group for the Advancement of Psychiatry: **New Trends in Child Custody Determinations**. New York: Harcourt Brace Jovanovich, 1980.

The best single reference describing the issues of the family and models in child custody problems. Also useful as a guideline even when custody is not a problem.

REFERENCES

Architecture and Design

1. Hall ET: The Hidden Dimension. New York: Doubleday/Anchor, 1969
2. Neutra R: Survival Through Design. New York: Oxford University Press, 1969
3. Newman O: Defensible Space: Crime Prevention Through Urban Design. New York: Macmillan, 1972
4. Sommer R: Tight Spaces: Hard Architecture and How to Humanize It. Englewood Cliffs, NJ: Prentice-Hall, 1974

Law and the Judicial System

1. The Uniform Marriage and Divorce Act, Section 404, 9A, U.L.A. 203, 1979
2. Cornblatt AJ: Matrimonial mediation. J Family Law 23:99-109, 1984-5
3. Mnookin R and Kornhauser L: Bargaining in the shadow of the law: The case of divorce. Yale Law J, 88:950, 1979
4. Wallerstein J and Kelly J: Surviving the Breakup: How Children and Parents Cope with Divorce. New York: Basic Books, 1980
5. Hess R and Camera G: Post-divorce family relationships as mediating factors in the consequences of divorce for children. J Social Issues 35:79, 1979
6. National Center for Health Statistics, Bureau of the Census: Advance Report of Final Divorce Statistics, 1981, 32 Monthly Vital Statistics Report, at 1-2, January 17, 1984

Section IX

Research and Training

In many ways, the most important part of this text is in this section. To understand our ideas about the family model, the student must be aware of the data upon which our notions are based. Accordingly, Chapter 31 reviews the latest data on outcome of treatment, and describes a method for the beginner to evaluate the literature. Chapter 32 reviews the process of therapy, i.e., the data on what is known about *how* it works. We conclude this section with our suggestions for training family therapists both in free-standing family institutes and in settings in which it is part of another program, such as psychiatric residencies, and psychology and social work training programs, etc.

Family Meal by Johann-Mongels Culverhouse. Courtesy of Hammer Gallery, New York.

31

Results: Research on the Outcome of Family Therapy

OBJECTIVES

- To become familiar with the scientific criteria for family psychotherapy research
- To be able to critically review modern studies on outcome of family therapy
- To be able to compare the outcomes of family therapy with other therapies and nontreatment conditions
- To help the reader formulate clinical generalizations from existing process and outcome family therapy data

INTRODUCTION

This chapter provides an overview of the results of family therapy outcome data that is available currently. In addition, we present several studies in some detail to give the reader a fuller sense of the kinds of designs, problems, and results found in family therapy research and types of criteria used to judge the quality of a research project. Finally, we will draw clinical generalizations from this existing research data base.

OVERVIEW OF PSYCHOTHERAPY
OUTCOME RESEARCH

The quality and quantity of psychotherapy research has grown tremendously in the last 15 years. It is informative to compare well known reviews of this research as they occurred across the years. In their early (1970) thorough and thoughtful review of therapy research, Meltzoff and Kornreich[1] summarized the then known information on design, measurement of change, and the effects of method, schools of therapy, patient and therapist variables, and duration and frequency of treatment on the outcome of therapy. By 1975, there was enough comparative psychotherapy research for Luborsky, Singer, and Luborsky[2] to do a "box score" on which therapies seemed best for which conditions, but they concluded that, "there were so many ties, all had run and all had won." Most recently, Smith, Glass, and Miller[3] have done what they call a meta-analysis of some 475 outcome studies that meet certain criteria. By using a statistical technique called "effect size," they were able to combine the studies and generate generalizations from the research to that data, which can be summarized as follows:

1. Overall, psychotherapy is effective, with the average treated patient better off than 80 percent of those who need therapy, but who remain untreated.
2. Well-controlled comparisons of different approaches to therapy yielded no reliable differences in effectiveness of behavioral and verbal therapies. Thus, there was little evidence of differential effectiveness among the different therapies.

These results were met with mixed enthusiasm. While it was encouraging to find that treated patients were better than nontreated ones, other results were disappointing. It was discouraging to see that most of the research in psychotherapy, when amassed in one place as done by these authors, was done on relatively healthy individuals, by behaviorists. In addition, summarizing the data this way gave little information for differential treatment planning, namely, which treatment should be received by what patient for what specific conditions.

OVERVIEW OF FAMILY THERAPY OUTCOME RESEARCH

In one of the earliest systematic reviews of marital and family therapy research, Wells, Dilkes, and Trivelli[4] found 14 studies. By the time of Gurman and Kniskern's 1978 review,[5] there were almost 200 family and marital therapy research studies, although many were uncontrolled. Using a scoring system based on some 14 criteria for adequacy of design, these reviewers found that in compara-

Table 31-1
Summary of Gross Improvement Rates in Nonbehavioral
Marital and Family Therapy

Treatment type and Setting	Number Studies Reviewed	Total *N*	Improved (percent)	Little or No Change (percent)	Worse (percent)
Marital Therapy					
Individual	7	406	48	45	7
Conjoint (marital Rx)	8	261	70	29	1
Conjoint group	15	397	66	30	4
Concurrent	6	464	63	35	2
Total	36	1528	61	35	4
Family Therapy					
Outpatient	26	897	76	23	1
Day hospital	3	194	59	37	4
Inpatient	10	341	78	22	0
Total	39	1414	75	24	1
Grand Total	75	2942	68 (1988/2942)	3 (883/2942)	2 (71/2942)

(From Gurman AS and Kniskern DP: Deterioration in marital and family therapy. Fam Process 17:3-20, 1978. With permission.)

tive studies of marital and family therapy nearly half (21 of 46 studies) were of good or very good design, and 82 percent of them had been done since 1970.

Numerous reviews[6-8] of the family therapy outcome and process research seem to point to the following general conclusions (Table 31-1):

1. Family treatment is more effective than no treatment. This is manifest in studies that contrast family and marital treatment to no-treatment control groups. The rates of improvement from marital and family treatment are about 66 percent, approximately the rates found in most therapy outcome studies of individual therapies also.

2. While many patients benefit from family therapy, some patients (estimated at from 5 to 10 percent) worsen or suffer negative effects from family intervention. This deterioration rate is lower than that estimated from individual therapies.

3. There are a few areas in which some evidence suggests that family/-marital therapy may be the preferred treatment intervention strategy. To say that in these instances family therapy is the *treatment of choice* may be putting the case too strongly, but comparative outcome studies do favor the family/marital treatment format in the following situations: (a) marital treatment for marital problems/conflict; (b) conjoint sex therapy for sexual dysfunctions that involve the interaction context; (c) family

therapy for the treatment of childhood and adolescent acting out such as aggressiveness[9] and adolescent soft juvenile delinquency.[10] Other situations in which evidence indicates that the family marital format is effective, but for which further comparative research is needed, include family treatment of asthma and anorexia,[11] adult drug addiction,[12] marital treatment when one spouse is depressed,[13] and adjunctive treatment when an adolescent or young adult is schizophrenic.[14]

4. While the various schools of family intervention (e.g., structural, systems, behavioral, etc.) often claim or imply superiority, there is very little controlled research on the strategies while holding the format of treatment constant (see Table 31-2). This approach would probably yield little differential information even if done. Rather, the field is going to manualization of therapies with precise specification of techniques, and when these are applied, often in usefully eclectic mixtures, results are forthcoming.

COMPARISONS OF OUTCOME OF FAMILY THERAPY WITH OTHER PSYCHOTHERAPIES

Evidence is accumulating that would indicate that individual therapy for a marital problem results in positive change in about 50 percent of the cases.[15,16] This compares to the figure of about 66 percent positive change resulting from marital therapy. For the first time marital therapists are now in a good position to assert that marital therapy may be not only as efficacious as individual therapy but rather may be even *better*. (Further research is necessary to clarify this finding, but at least the question of the comparative efficacy of those two kinds of psychotherapy has been raised.) Marital therapy also appears to have approximately one-half the deterioration rate (5 to 6 percent unimproved or worse) as compared with individual therapy (about 11 percent).

Tables 31-3 and 31-4 suggest that family therapy appears to be superior to individual psychotherapy "when one member of a family unit or dyadic relationship asks for treatment with problems involving family living."[15] Although these data are preliminary and must be taken with caution, in every study that has compared family therapy with other types of treatment, the former has been shown to be equal or superior to the other therapy.

Controlled Studies of Outcome

Only within the 1970s have there been controlled studies of family therapy. Are they consistent with the trends suggested in the preceding two sections? Tables 31-5 and 31-6 indicate that family therapy is better than other treatment options (usually no treatment) in 10 out of 15 comparisons.

Table 31-2

Overall Estimates of the Effectiveness of Various Marital and Family Therapies for Specific Disorders and Problems

Type of Therapy	Adult Disorders					Child/Adolescent Disorders			Marital Problems	
	1	2	3	4	5	6	7	8	9	10
Behavioral	2[a]	2[b]	1	3[c]	0	3[d]	3[d]	0	3	1[e]
Bowen FST	0	0	0	0	0	0	0	0	0	0
Contextual	0	0	0	0	0	0	0	0	0	0
Functional	0	0	0	0	0	2	0	0	0	0
Humanistic[f]	0	0	0	0	0	0	0	0	0	0
McMaster PCSTF	0	0	0	0	1	1	1	1	0	0
Milan Systemic	0	0	0	0	0	1	1	1	1	0
MRI Interactional	0	0	0	0	0	0	1	1	1	0
Multigenerational: Other[g]	0	0	0	0	0	0	0	0	1	0
Psychoeducational	3	0	1	0	0	0	0	0	0	0
Psychodynamic-Eclectic	0	2[h]	0	0	1	0	1	1	2	1
Strategic	1	2[i]	0	0	1	0	0	0	0	0
Structural	0	2[i]	0	0	2	0	0	0	0	0
Symbolic-Experiential	0	0	0	0	0	0	0	0	0	0
Triadic	0	0	0	0	0	0	0	0	1	0

KEY: **1** = schizophrenia; **2** = substance abuse; **3** = affective disorders; **4** = anxiety disorders; **5** = psychosomatic disorders; **6** = juvenile delinquency; **7** = conduct disorders; **8** =mixed disorders; **9** = marital discord; **10** = divorce adjustment.

NOTES: **3** = effectiveness established; **2** = effectiveness probable; **1** = effectiveness uncertain; **0** = effectiveness untested.

a = behavioral family management; b = alcohol abuse; c = spouse-assisted exposure therapy; d = parent management training; e = divorce mediation; f = Satir (1967); g = based on Framo (1976) and Williamson (1981, 1982a, and 1982b); h = conjoint couples groups for alcoholism; i = integrative structural/straregic therapy (Stanton, et al. 1982).

From Gurman AS and Kniskern DP: Research on the process and outcome of marital and family therapy. In Garfield S and Bergin A (Eds): Handbook of Psychotherapy and Behavior Change (3rd Ed). New York: Wiley, 1986.

Therapist Factors in Outcome

There seems to be some validity to the notion that the more experienced the therapist, the better the outcome. In addition, not only knowledge and special technical competence but warmth and empathy on the part of the therapist will help the family members to *stay* in treatment. (This, of course, leaves unanswered the issue of efficacy of treatment.)

PREDICTION OF PROCESS AND OUTCOME

Prediction of treatment process and outcome are still extremely difficult to make. This has not, however, deterred some senior clinicians from making them. The normative responses of the family to conjoint family therapy have been described: "Most families who accept conjoint family therapy when it is offered, and even families who might be considered unsuitable for therapy for various reasons, will enter into and participate in treatment."[16] Most family members will not initiate a move to drop out of therapy. It is difficult to predict in advance which families will be easy to treat and which will be difficult and what resistance will occur during treatment. It appears that an experienced therapist has a good chance of anticipating the members' common resistance that "only others in the family have troubles."

It was also found that "one can conclude that conjoint family therapy is rarely harmful to members of the treated family." Predictions of the effectiveness of family therapy made to the family were uniformly underestimated by the therapist. (The same thing is done in clinical medical practice when the therapist tells the family that he may not be able to help them or help them only to a limited degree.)[17]

LIMITATIONS OF FAMILY THERAPY

It is obvious that not all problems are due to defects in the family. There are many families in which overall family structure and function are relatively healthy but, nevertheless, one member has a problem.

Mrs. B., a 46-year-old, came with her husband and four children seeking therapy. She told the story of both parents dying in a plane crash when she was a year old. Throughout her life she was raised by a series of adoptive parents and relatives. At each point of the comings and goings in the family—for example, an adoptive father being drafted into the

Table 31-3

Outcomes of Comparative Studies of Marital Therapy*

Author	Treatments Compared (Setting)[a]	Outcome Criteria (Source)[b]	Outcome (Design Quality)
Beck and Jones (1973)	Short-term; open-ended; conjoint; individual (FSC)	Overall change (P,T); overall change (P,T)	No difference; conjoint superior[c]
Burton and Kaplan (1968)	Group; individual individual; concurrent (OPC)	Global self-change (P); global self-change (P)	Group superior; concurrent superior (poor)
Cookerly (1973)	Group and "interview" concurrent, conjoint, and Individual (OPC)	Marital status (O); quality of outcome status (J)	Conjoint and conjoint group superior (poor)
Cookerly (1974, 1976)[d]	Concurrent, conjoint, and group (OPC)	Individual, personal-social, and marital adjustment (P)	Concurrent superior on individual pathology; conjoint and conjoint group superior on marital; no difference in social (good)
Cookerly (1976)[e]	Group and "interview" concurrent, conjoint, and Individual (OPC)	Marital, social, and personal adjustment (P)	Conjoint and conjoint group superior in marital adjustment (poor)
Cookerly (1976)[f]	Group and "interview" concurrent, conjoint, and individual (OPC)	Divorce rate 1 to 3 years post-therapy (O); marital status satisfaction (P)	Lowest divorce rates and most satisfaction in conjoint (37%) and conjoint group (40%) (poor)
Corder et al. (1972)	Conjoint group; individual group (IP)	Alcohol spouse's drinking (6-month follow-up)	Conjoint group superior (fair)
Davenport et al. (1975)	Group; individual; community care (MF)	Rehospitalization (O); marital status (O); social functioning (P)	Group superior (fair)

Study	Treatment	Outcome measures	Results
Freeman et al. (1969)	Conjoint; group; individual[g] (OPC)	Marital relationship; division of responsibility (P, T)	No differences (poor)
Friedman (1975)	Conjoint; drug therapy (OPC)	Depression of identification point (P, J); family role performance and marital relationship(P)	Marital therapy superior for marital relationship; drug superior for depressive symptoms (good)
Graham (1968)	Conjoint; conjoint and individual (CC)	Positive references to spouse (J); reconciliation (O); interpersonal dominance and affiliation (P)	Conjoint superior (good)
Hepworth and Smith (1972)	Individual; conjoint and individual[h](FSC)	Achievements of goals (J)	No difference (poor)
Hickman and Baldwin (1970)	Conjoint; programmed communication training (CC)	Reconciliation (O); marital relationship (P)	Conjoint superior (very good)
Macon (1975)	Conjoint; conjoint group (FSC)	Communication (P); self-esteem (P); problem-solving skill (P); spouse-image (P)	No difference (fair)
Matanovich (1970)	Encounter group tapes; Individual and conjoint (CC)	Reconciliation (O); interpersonal dominance and affiliation (P); rating of helpfulness (P)	No difference on any criteria (very good)
Mayadas and Duehn (1977)	Communication modeling(CM); CM plus video feedback (CMV); verbal counseling (VC) (OPC)	Five problematic communication behaviors (O)	CMV>CM>VC (very good)

Table 31-3 *continued*
Outcomes of Comparative Studies of Marital Therapy*

Author	Treatments Compared (Setting)[a]	Outcome Criteria (Source)[b]	Outcome (Design Quality)
Mezydlo et al. (1973)	Parish pastoral counseling; "office priests; lay therapists (all conjoint)(catholic FSC)	Target complaints (P)	Office outcome>lay>parish (poor)
Pierce (1973)	Communication training; group (OPC)	Communication skill and self-exploration (J)	Communication training superior (fair)
Reid and Shyne (1969)	Conjoint; individual brief; open-ended (FSC)	Presenting problem (T,J) Presenting problem (T,J)	No difference; brief superior on some dimensions (good)
Smith (1967)	Conjoint group; individual group (IP)	Alcohol spouse's drinking (H,W,T)	Conjoint group superior (fair)
Swan (1972)	Communication training; eclectic conjoint (CC)	Level of conflict (J)	No differences (good)
Valle and Marinelli (1975)	Communication training; group (PP)	Facilitative skill (J); marital relationship (P); individual functioning (P)	Communication training superior (fair)
Wattie (1973)	Short-term; open-ended (FSC)	Marital congruence (P); global change (P,T,J)	Short-term superior on husband change only (good)
Wells et al. (1975b)	Communication training; conjoint[i] (FSC)	Marital adjustment (P); dyadic empathy and warmth (P)	No difference at termination; conjoint superior at 3-month follow-up (fair)
Ziegler (1973)	Long group; intensive group (OPC)	CPI and omnibus personality inventory (P)	No clear difference; long had more intense change, intensive, wider range of changes (good)

Summary		
Conjoint	Individual	Group
Conjoint superior 16	Individual superior 2	Group superior 15
Tie 10	Tie 5	Tie 8
Others superior 0	Others superior 12	Others superior 2
Conjoint superior 4	Individual superior 1	Group superior 0
Tie 2	Tie 1	Tie 6
Individual superior 0	Group superior 9	Conjoint superior 0
Conjoint and group (combined) superior		31
Tie		11
All other superior		2

Note: Comparative studies of behavior therapy are reported elsewhere in this chapter.

[a] FSC = family service center or family counseling centers; OPC = outpatient clinic; CC = conciliation court; PP = private practice; MF = medical facilities; IP = inpatient.

[b] P = patient; T = therapist; J = judge or trained observer; O = objective indices not based on behavioral observation.

[c] This major national census study examined comparative treatment modalities as at most a secondary (and probably a tertiary) goal; thus the standards of experimental research are probably not appropriately applied here; hence, we have omitted a design quality rating.

[d] The author's 1974 report included data only on MMPI changes; his 1976 report included these data plus the other criteria noted. Both reports used the same sample and are therefore combined here.

[e] "Outcome" was actually based on client's "immediate attitudes" toward the helpfulness of sessions and was based on postsession responses for each therapy session over a 4-month period.

[f] All of Cookerly's studies, two of which (1973, 1974) had been previously reported, were reported in his 1976 paper.

[g] Although these were the predominant forms, an indeterminable number of study patients were involved in an indeterminable mixture of treatments.

[h] Although the authors describe this study as one comparing individual and conjoint therapy, it is in fact one of individual versus conjoint *plus* individual therapy; in the "conjoint" condition, averaging 26 sessions per case, 41 percent (11 sessions) were held with wives alone, 31 percent (eight sessions) with husbands alone, and only 28 percent (seven sessions) conjointly.

[i] Actually, due to clinical necessity, several of the conjoint couples also receive some communication training, although not in groups; although the initial intent was for the conjoint condition to be "behaviorally oriented" (Wells et al., 1975b, p. 1), this treatment clearly emerged as quite eclectic.

Reprinted with permission from Gurman AS and Kniskern DP: Research on marital and family therapy: Progress, perspective and prospect. In Garfield SL and Bergin AE (Eds): Handbook of Psychotherapy and Behavior Change: An Empirical Analysis (2nd Ed). New York: Wiley, 1978. Copyright 1978 by John Wiley & Sons, Inc.

Table 31-4
Comparative Studies of Family Therapy Outcome

Author	Treatments Compared (Setting)[a]	Outcome Criteria (Source)[b]	Outcome (Design Quality)
Abroms et al. (1971)	Family;[c] individual (IP)	Identified patient symptoms at discharge (S)	Family improved 86%; individual improved 81% (poor)
Alexander and Parsons (1973[0])	Family behavioral-system; client-centered family; eclectic-dynamic family (OPC)	Identified patient recidivism at 18 months (O)	Behavioral systems = 26% recidivism; client-centered = 47% eclectic-dynamic = 73% (good)
Bernal and Margolin (1976)	Behavioral parent counseling (BT) Client-centered parent counseling (CG)(OPC)	1. Child's verbal abuse (O) 2. Deviant child behavior (O) 3. Targeted child behavior (Par) 4. Parental attitudes toward child (Par) 5. Satisfaction with therapy (Par)	No differences within or between groups on criteria 1 and 2; no difference between groups on 3; but both showed change; partial superiority for CC on 4; BT superior on 5 (good)
Budman and Shapiro (1976)	Individual;[d] family[d] Individual terminators;[e] Family terminators[e] (OPC)	Identified patient functioning at 4½-month follow-up (Par,P) Identified patient functioning at 4½-month follow-up (Par,P)	No difference in reported functioning Individual terminators were more positive in reports of patient functioning[f] (poor)
Dezen and Borstein (1975)	E_1 = probation with family therapy E_2 = probation services as usual (OPC)	Identified patient recidivism at 6 months (O) Identified patient symptomatology (Par) Parental overinvolvement (Par) Report of parental behavior (C)	Family probation superior on symptom measure only (fair)
Evans et al. (1971)	Conjoint;[g] individual (IP)	Identified patient symptomatology (S) Return to work (O)	Conjoint superior to individual on both measures (poor)

Study	Treatment conditions	Measures	Results
Ewing (1975)	Crisis intervention; psychodynamic child guidance (OPC)	Patient functioning (M)	Crisis equal to child guidance in one-tenth treatment time (poor)
Finol (1973)	Guided videotaped feedback; guided audiotaped feedback;	Positive and negative comments toward patient (O)	Videotape superior to audiotape on one measure and to discussion on one measure (good)
Gould and Glick (1976)	Conjoint family; conjoint and multiple family (family unavailable); no family therapy (family available)(IP)	Severity of illness (S); psychiatric function (S); role function (IP, Family); employment (S,O)	On all measures, conjoint>conjoint and multiple>no family therapy (family unavailable)>no family therapy (family unavailable)(fair)
Hendricks (1971)	Multifamily group counseling (MFG) Standard inpatient treatment (IP Addiction Treatment Center)	Continued discharge (outpatient) status at 1-year follow-up (O)	41% of MFG patients remained outpts. versus 21% for standard addiction treatment (fair)
Jansma (1971)	Conjoint family; multiple family (OPC)	Family adjustment (Family); family congruence (Family); family satisfaction (Family); marital satisfaction (par)	Multiple superior to conjoint on 7 out of 9 measures (good)

Table 31-4 *continued*
Comparative Studies of Family Therapy Outcome

Author	Treatments Compared (Setting)[a]	Outcome Criteria (Source)[b]	Outcome (Design Quality)
Johnson (1971)	Conjoint family; nonfamily treatment (OPC)	Patterns of communication (O)	Conjoint superior to individual on 8 out of 9 measures (good)
Klein et al.[h] (1975)	E_1 = family behavioral-system; E_2 = client-centered family groups; E_3 = eclectic-dynamic family (OPC)	Sibling court contracts in 3 years (O)	Behavioral-systems = 20% client-centered = 59% eclectic-dynamic = 63% (good)
Langsley et al. (1969)	E_1 = family crisis intervention (Home); E_2 = hospital treatment as usual	Rates of rehospitalization (O) Social adjustment inventory (Family)	Family superior to hospital in length and frequency of readmissions; no difference on adjustment (good)
Love et al.[j] (1972)	Family-oriented videotape feedback of interaction; individual child psychotherapy; parent counseling (OPC)	Identified patient school interaction ratings (J); grades (O)	Feedback = parent counseling individual therapy on grades; all treatments improved interaction (good)
Pittman et al. (1968)	E_1 = conjoint family crisis intervention E_2 = individual long term (OPC)	Return to work (O)	Conjoint superior to individual (poor)

Study	Treatment (Patient type)	Outcome measures	Results
Rittenhouse (1970)	Family therapy (home); hospital treatment (IP)	Overall improvement (P); identified patient readmissions (O); family pathology (F); community functioning (S.O.)	Family superior to hospital on patient improvement and readmissions; no difference on family or community (good)
Sigal et al. (1976)	Psychodynamically oriented conjoint; early terminators from conjoint treatment (OPC)	Identified patient presenting symptomatology at 4 years from termination (Family); Identified patient new problems (Family); level of family functioning (Family)	Early terminator had fewer new problems; no differences on other measures[k] (fair)
Stanton and Todd (1976)	Structural family therapy; standard methadone treatment (OPC)	IP heroin use (O); IP work and school adjustment(F)	Family therapy superior to usual heroin addiction treatment (very good)
Trankina (1975)	Traditional child guidance; crisis family therapy (OPC)	Family satisfaction and adjustment (par); family life quality (Par); child behavior (par); overall improvement (S, Par)	Crisis therapy superior on criteria 4, with fewer dropouts and in less time (fair)

Table 31-4 *continued*

Comparative Studies of Family Therapy Outcome

Author	Treatments Compared (Setting)[a]	Outcome Criteria (Source)[b]	Outcome (Design Quality)
Wellisch et al. (1976)	Conjoint family; individual problem oriented (IP)	Rehospitalization (Family); Identified patient return to work or school (Family); Family interaction (J)	Conjoint superior on all measures except family interaction (good)

[a] OPC = outpatient clinic; IP = inpatient.

[b] S = staff; Fam = family; O = objective indices; J = judge or trained observer; Par = Parents; P = patient; S.O. = significant other; C = children; M = mother.

[c] Inpatient families were treated with a variety of individual, group and conjoint family therapy.

[d] Patients or families attending four or more sessions of therapy.

[e] Terminators are those patients or families who attended from 1 to 3 sessions.

[f] Family terminators reported two identified patients had deteriorated; no reports of deterioration in individual terminators.

[g] Treatment as usual in this setting included individual sessions in all cases and often included medication and ECT.

[h] Data is based on follow-up of siblings of identified patients reported on in previous study (Alexander & Parsons, 1973).

[i] Treatment as usual included individual and group psychotherapy, milieu therapy, and medication.

[j] Some of these subjects reported in Kaswan and Love (1969).

[k] There was a strong trend for long-term treatment families to report better family functioning.

Reprinted with permission from Gurman AS and Kniskern DP: Research on marital and family therapy:Progress, perspective and prospect. In Garfield SL and Bergin AF (Eds): Handbook of Psychotherapy and Behavior Change: An Empirical Analysis (2nd Ed). New York: Wiley, 1978. Copyright 1978 by John Wiley & Sons, Inc.

army—she would become very depressed, tearful, and angry, blaming other family members for their various deficiencies.

Family therapy was sought at this time because the family was having trouble living with Mrs. B. in her depressed state—a problem that had been present for 30 years. The task of the family therapist was to see what could be changed. It turned out that the precipitant was the oldest daughter going away to college. So the family therapist helped the identified patient and the rest of the family cope with the derivatives of the mother's classical separation experience (loss of the parents at an early age as it now affected the family structure). The family therapist could *not* change the fact that the identified patient would have a strong and dysfunctional reaction to loss.

The family therapist commonly assumes that when a family comes for help with a specific problem, the cause is generally found in system problems of a more serious nature. Therefore it follows that the treatment strategy is to treat the system. The assumption is that treating the system will cause the symptom to change. Treating the system and even changing the system to function better does *not* necessarily mean that all symptoms in the family will show improvement. In practice there are symptoms that will be left untreated.

What are the variables that limit change in families? To the extent that families or couples have not been able to cope with and master previous stages of development, they may have limitations in coping with a current phase. Other limiting factors include the degree of rigidity of chronic character traits and styles of couples, as well as biological, physical, and social variables.

NEGATIVE EFFECTS OF FAMILY THERAPY

If a treatment—any treatment—induces beneficial results, it must also be capable of producing harmful effects.[18] Although not a great deal has been written about this subject in family therapy literature, most experienced clinicians would agree that family therapy can, to an unknown extent, induce negative effects.

Table 31-7 points out five categories of negative effects, as follows. First, exacerbation of presenting symptoms: In most cases there is a phase of family therapy in which problems may worsen. Second, appearance of new symptoms: This is common (but not universal) in family therapy. What usually happens is that a new symptom occurs in a family member other than the identified patient. Third, patient abuse or misuse of therapy: Most commonly one family member tries to use the family therapy for "one-upmanship." Father might say, "Dr. So-and-So said that I seemed to have the best judgment in the family," and then proceed to blast his spouse and children. Other times families refuse to terminate therapy even though the therapist believes they are capable of functioning without it. Fourth, the family's overreaching itself: Some therapists believe that "anything

Table 31-5
Controlled Studies of Marital Therapy Outcome

Author	Treatment(s); (Treatment Length);[a] Setting[b]	Outcome Criteria (Source)[c]	Results (Design Quality)
Alkire and Brunse (1974)	Videotape feedback in ongoing groups (short); VA-OPC	Self-concept (P); marital casualties (divorce, separation separation, suicide (P)	More casualties and more *decreased* self-concept in treated group (good)
Cadogan (1973)	Conjoint group (moderate); OPC	1. Drinking behavior (P) 2. Marital communication (P) 3. Acceptance and trust (P)	Treatment>control on criterion 1, not on 2 and 3 (very good)
Cardillo (1971)	Conjoint communication training (short); OPC	1. Self-concept (P) 2. Interpersonal perception method (P) 3. Helpfulness of therapy (P)	Treatment>control on all measures (very good)
Cassidy (1973)	Conjoint communication training (short); PP	1. Communication (P) 2. Target behaviors (P) 3. Attitude toward spouse (P)	Treatment>control on all measures (very good)
Christensen (1974)	Conjoint communication training (short); OPC	1. Self-esteem (P) 2. Decision making (J) 3. Choice fulfillment (P)	Treatment>control on some measures of criterion 1, and 2; no difference on 3 (very good)

Friedman (1975)	Conjoint (moderate); OPC	1. Two psychiatric rating scales (J) 2. Global change (J) 3. Symptom ratings (P) 4. Family role performance (P) 5. Marital relationship (P)	Treatment>control on most measures (very good)
Graham (1968)	Conjoint; conjoint plus individual (short); CC	1. Reconciliations (O) 2. Positive references to spouse (O) 3. Dominance and affiliation (P)	Conjoint>control on criterion 1 only; conjoint plus individual = control on all criteria (good)
Griffin (1967)	Individual (short); FSC (wives)	1. Perception of self (P) 2. Perception of spouse (P)	Treatment>control on both measures (good)
Hickman and Baldwin	Conjoint; programmed communication training (short) CC	1. Reconciliation (O) 2. Attitude toward marriage (P)	Conjoint>control on both criteria; programmed = control (very good)
Matanovich (1970)	Encounter tapes[d] (moderate); conjoint plus individual (short); CC	1. Reconciliation (O) 2. Dominance and affiliation (P)	Encounter tapes>control on criterion 1; conjoint plus individual = control on both criteria (very good)

Table 31-5 *continued*
Controlled Studies of Marital Therapy Outcome

Author	Treatment(s); (Treatment Length);[a] Setting[b]	Outcome Criteria (Source)[c]	Results (Design Quality)
Pierce (1973)	Communication training; conjoint group (long); OPC	1. Communication skill (J) 2. Self-exploration (J)	Treatment I>control on both criteria; treatment II = control on both criteria (fair)

Summary

Conjoint>control	3		
No difference	0		
Conjoint<control	0		
Group>control	1		
No difference	1		
Group<control	1		
Individual>control		Conjoint plus individual	1	0
No difference		>control	0	
Individual<control		No difference	0	2
Communication training >control		Conjoint plus individual	5	0
No difference		<control	1	
Communication training <control	0	Total	1	
Treatment<control	1	Treatment>control		10
		No difference		4

[a] Short = 1 to 10 sessions; moderate = 11 to 20 sessions; long = 21 or more sessions.

[b] CC = conciliation court; FSC = family service or counseling center; OPC = outpatient clinic; PP = private practice; VA = veterans administration.

[c] J = trained judge or interviewer; O = objective records; P = patient.

[d] Although this treatment was carried out in a group setting, the report emphasizes within-dyad encounters instead of group process; so that in the summary the study us classified as communication training, not group therapy.

Reprinted with permission from Gurman AS and Kniskern DP: Research on marital and family therapy: Progress, perspective and prospect. In Garfield SL and Bergin AF (Eds): Handbook of Psychotherapy and Behavior Change: An Empirical Analysis (2nd Ed). New York: Wiley, 1978. Copyright 1978 by John Wiley & Sons, Inc.

is possible" and encourage families to attempt tasks and try for goals that clearly are beyond their reach. Such attempts are destructive and should be avoided. Fifth, disillusionment with the therapy or the therapist, or both: The family may try family therapy as a last resort. When the therapy does not produce beneficial change (at least in the family's terms), the family may be worse than at the start, since the members have lost their last hope.

The precise incidence of negative effects resulting from family therapy is not known, but it probably occurs in 5 to 10 percent of all cases (see Table 31-8).

What happens if the outcome of marital treatment is separation or divorce? One might automatically assume that such an outcome is deleterious and that marital and family therapy should be designed to hold the families together. On reflection, experience seems to indicate otherwise. Marital therapy allows the partners to examine whether or not it is to their advantage to stay together, and it gives them permission to separate if that is what they need to do.

In the A. family the couple were in their thirties. He was a dentist, she a housewife who had previously been a teacher. She came from a family in which her father had been a chronic "runaround," and she married her husband because he appeared to be reliable and stable. He came from a family in which the mother was dull and masochistic, and he married his wife because she seemed exciting and interesting.

The couple came to therapy after five years of marriage when it was "discovered that the husband was having extramarital affairs." (He had left several notes from girl friends around.) Exploration of the situation revealed that soon after marriage Mrs. A. had become slowly and imperceptibly disillusioned with her husband when she found that he was very insecure about himself, was very unreliable, and characteristically "lied and cheated." Dr. A. perceived after several years that his wife was not as exciting as he had thought and would not fulfill the role he had envisioned for her—that is, being the "slave" to a professional husband.

The therapy allowed the couple to examine some of the original premises on which they had gotten together and they found them faulty. The process of therapy, and not the therapist's values, gave them the necessary permission to separate.

DEFECTION AND PREMATURE TERMINATION OF FAMILY TREATMENT

In one study about 30 percent of all the families referred for family treatment failed to appear for the first session (defected) and another 30 percent terminated in the first three sessions, leaving about 40 perecnt who continued.[19] The main reason families gave for termination was a lack of activity on the part of the therapist, whereas defectors in general had a "change of heart" and denied that a problem existed. The motivation of the husband appeared to play a crucial role—

Table 31-6

Controlled Studies of Family Therapy Outcome

Author	Treatment(s) (Treatment Length);[a] Setting[b]	Outcome Criteria (Source)[c]	Results (Design Quality)
Alexander and Parsons (1973)	Behavioral-systems; (short); client-centered (short); eclectic-dynamic (moderate); OPC	Identified patient recidivism at 18 months (O)	Behavioral system superior to control; client-centered and eclectic-dynamic = control (good)
Beal and Duckro (1977)	Conjoint (short); juvenile court	Termination of court hearing or referral to noncourt agencies versus appearance before court (O)	17% of treated IPs appeared in court versus 35% of untreated cases ($p<.05$)(fair)
Garrigan and Bambrick (1975)	Conjoint (short); school	1. Family adjustment (P) 2. Behavior symptoms (teach) 3. IP self-concept (P) 4. Family relationships (P)	Treatment superior to control on family adjustment only (good)
Garrigan and Bambrick (1977)	Conjoint (short); school for emotionally disturbed children and adolescents	1. Family adjustment (Par) 2. Marital facilitative conditions (F) 3. IP self-concept (P) 4. Family members' state-trait anxiety (F) 5. IP symptoms (Par)	Treatment superior to control on Par rating of family adjustment, on two out of four facilitative condi-tions and on IP symptoms; no difference on criteria 3 and 4 (very good)

Study	Treatment (design)	Measures	Results
Jansma (1971)	Multiple (?); conjoint (?) OPC	1. Family adjustment (F,T) 2. Family congruence (F,T) 3. Family satisfaction (F,T) 4. Marital adjustment (F,T)	Multiple superior to control on eight out of nine measures; conjoint family superior to control on one out of nine measures (?)
Katz et al. (1975)	Conjoint (short); OPC	Family interaction (J)	Treatment superior to control on appropriate topic changes; no difference in speech clarity or humor (very good)
Klein et al.[d] (1975)	Behavioral-system (short); client-centered (short); eclectic-dynamic (moderate); OPC	Sibling recidivism at 3 years (O)	Behavior-systems superior to control; client-centered and eclectic-dynamic = control (good)
Knight (1974)	Parent effectiveness training (short); OPC	1. Frequency of enuresis (Par) 2. Anxiety (Par) 3. Interpersonal distance (F)	No significant positive effects, some deterioration in female identified patients and parents (?)
Reiter and Kilmann (1975)	Mothers' groups (short); OPC	1. Marital integration (Par) 2. Verbal interchanges (J) 3. Child symptoms (Par) 4. Family congruence (Par)	Treatment superior to control on measures 1 to 3 (very good)

Table 31-6 *continued*

Controlled Studies of Family Therapy Outcome

Author	Treatment(s) (Treatment Length);[a] Setting[b]	Outcome Criteria (Source)[c]	Results (Design Quality)
Stanton and Todd (1976)	Conjoint (moderate); OPC	Identified patient heroin use (O); identified patient work and school adjustment (F)	Therapy superior to attention placebo and no treatment group on both measures (very good)
Stover and Guerney (1967)	Filial therapy (mothers groups) (short); OPC	1. Mothers' reflective and directive statements (J) 2. Child's playroom behavior (J)	Treatment superior to control on measure 1; no difference on measure 2 (very good)

Summary

Adult/family IP>control		2
No difference		1
Adult/family IP<control		0

Child/adolescent IP therapy>control	6	
No difference	6	
Child/adolescent IP therapy<control	1	
Total		
Family therapy>control	8	
No difference	7	
Family therapy<control	1	

[a] Short = 1 to 10 sessions; moderate = 11 to 20 sessions; long = 21 or more sessions.

[b] OPC = outpatient clinic.

[c] O = objective records; P = patient; Par = parents; F = family; Teach = teachers; J = trained judge; T = therapist.

[d] Same families as reported in Alexander and Parsons (1973).

Reprinted with permission from Gurman AS and Kniskern DP: Research on marital and family therapy: Progress, perspective and prospect. In Garfield SL and Bergin AF (Eds): Handbook of Psychotherapy and Behavior Change: An Empirical Analysis (2nd Ed). New York, Wiley, 1978. Copyright 1978 by John Wiley & Sons, Inc.

the more motivated he was, the more likely the family was to continue treatment. (See Chapter 13, "The Course of Treatment.")

PATIENT AND FAMILY SATISFACTION

There is a major difference between patient satisfaction, family and "significant other" satisfaction, and outcome of treatment as judged by the therapist. Sometimes all three correlate. In many cases, however, they do not. Often what the patient feels is an improvement is actually a regression by the family. Similarly, what the therapist considers an improvement is considered by both family and patient as a change for the worse. The following case vignette will serve these points:

The K. family, consisting of mother, father, and three children ranging between 15 and 25 years, had come for treatment following the death of one of the teenage siblings due to leukemia. Some of the problems included the father's drinking and difficulties in communication between the mother and father and between the children and father. A long course of family therapy resulted in marked improvement in all of these areas. The mother and the children considered it a very successful outcome. The father consistently maintained that nothing had been accomplished: he could not remember changes made in the family as a result of the therapy and therefore felt that nothing had been done in therapy.

CLINICAL IMPLICATIONS OF DATA FROM FAMILY THERAPY OUTCOME STUDIES

Using conclusions from the Gurman and Kniskern reviews, important implications for family therapists can be formulated.[5,8] The following is a list of their conclusions with the authors' appended implications:

1. Individual therapy for marital problems is a very ineffective treatment strategy and one that appears to produce more negative effects than alternative approaches.

   Implication: Traditional clinical lore has always been that individual therapy was the treatment of choice in marital problems. For the first time recent research has questioned this assumption. It may be that marital therapy is not only as good as individual therapy, but it may even be better. We recommend that the family therapist use the option of individual or marital therapy depending on his or her understanding of the needs of the case (see Chapter 17).

Table 31-7
What Constitutes a Negative Effect?

Exacerbation of Presenting Symptoms	Appearance of New Symptoms	Patient's Abuse or Misuse of Therapy	Patient "Overreaching" Self	Disillusionment with Therapy or Therapist
"Worsening," increase in severity, pathology, etc.	1. *Generally* may be observed when (a) psychic disturbance is manifested in a less socially acceptable form than previously; (b) symptom substitution occurs when a symptom that had fulfilled an imperative need is blocked	1. Substitution of intellectualized insights for other obsessional thoughts	1. Two forms: (a) undertaking life tasks (marriage, graduate school, etc.) that require resources beyond those of patient; (b) undertaking life tasks prematurely	1. May appear variously as (a) wasting of patient's resources (time, skill, money) that might have been better expended elsewhere; (b) hardening of attitudes toward other sources of help; (c) loss of confidence in therapist, possibly extending to any human relationship; (d) general loss of hope (all the more severe for initial raising of hopes that may have occurred at onset of therapy.
2. *Generally* may take form of or be accompanied by (a) exacerbation of suffering; (b) decompensation; (c) harsher superego or more rigid personality structure	2. *Specific* examples: (a) erosion of solid interpersonal relationships; (b) decreased ability to experience pleasure; (c) severe or fatal	2. Utilization of therapy to rationalize feelings of superiority or expressions of hostility toward other people	2. May be related to (a) intense wishes to please therapist; (b) unculcation of inachievable middle-class "ideals"; (c) increased "irrational" ideas	
3. *Specific* examples of symptom exacerbation: (a) depressive breakdown; (b) severe regression; (c) des-		3. Therapy becomes an end in itself; a substitute for action		
		4. Fear of "intellectualiza-		

3. May result in any or all of the following (a) excessive strain on patient's psychological resources; (b) failure at task; (c)guilt; (d) self-contempt

tion" prevents patients from examing their ethical and philosophical commitments

5. Participation in more radical therapies encourages belief in irrational in order to avoid painful confrontation with realities of life

6. Sustained dependency on therapy or therapist

psychosomatic reactions; (d)with drawal; (e) rage; (f) dissociation; (g) drug/alcohol abuse; (h) criminal behavior; (i) suicide; (j) psychotic breaks

tructive acting-out; (d) increased anxiety; (e) increased hostility; (f) increased self-downing; (g) increased behavioral shirking; (h) increased inhibition; (i) paranoia; (j) fixing of obsessional symptoms; (k) exaggeration of somatic difficulties; (l) extension of phobias; (m) increased guilt; (n) increased confusion; (o) lowered self-confidence; (p) lowered self-esteem; (q) diminished capacity for delay and impulse control

Reprinted with permission from Hadley SW and Strupp HH: Contemporary views of negative effects in psychotherapy. Arch Gen Psychiatry 33:1298-1299, 1976. Copyright 1976 by the American Medical Association.

Table 31-8

Summary of Reported Deterioration Rates in Studies of Nonbehavioral Marital and Family Therapy[9]

Therapy Type or Setting	Number Studies Reporting Improvement Rates	Number Studies with "worse" Category	Number Studies Reporting Deterioration	Percent Studies with "Worse" Category Reporting Deterioration	Deterioration Rate Across Studies with "worse" Category (percent)
		Marital Therapy			
Conjoint	8	3(37%)	1	22	2.7 (2/72)
Individual	7	5(71%)	4	80	11.6 (27/233)
Group	15	7(47%)	4	57	16.6 (17/102)
Concurrent/Collaborative	6	4(67%)	1	25	3.3 (11/332)
Total	36	19(53%)	10	53	7.7 (57/739)

Inpatient	10	2(20%)	0	0	0 (0/17)
Outpatient	26	13(50%)	4	29	2.1 (10/477)
Day Hospital	3	2(67%)	1	50	7.3 (7/96)
Total	39	17(44%)	5	29	2.8 (17/580)
Grand Total	75	36(48%)	15	42	5.4

Reprinted with permission from Gurman AS and Kniskern DP: Research on marital and family therapy: Progress, perspective and prospect. In Garfield SL and Bergin AF (Eds): Handbook of Psychotherapy and Behavior Change: An Empirical Analysis (2nd Ed). New York: Wiley, 1978. Copyright 1978 by John Wiley & Sons, Inc.

2. Couples benefit most from treatment when both spouses are involved in the therapy, especially when they are seen conjointly.

   Implication: Both partners should be involved in conjoint therapy.

3. Family therapy appears to be at least as effective and possibly more effective than individual therapy for a wide variety of problems, including both "individual" difficulties as well as more obvious family conflicts.

   Implication: For some problems individual therapy might be the treatment of choice, whereas for others family therapy would be preferable. In the absence of research data to use as guidelines for treatment, the choice between these approaches probably should "continue to reflect the biases and training of the individual practitioners."

4. For certain clinical goals and problems—for example, decreasing hospitalization rates for some chronic and acute inpatients, treating anorexia nervosa, many childhood problem behaviors, some forms of juvenile delinquency and sexual dysfunction—systems therapies may offer the treatments of choice. Specific effective treatment programs and strategies exist for some of these problems and should be taught in any training program in marital and family therapy.

   Implication: Since the results of family treatment for these conditions are encouraging, such strategies should be taught in any training program pending further definitive outcome results.

5. Short-term and time-limited therapies appear to be at least as effective as treatment of longer duration; moreover, most of the positive results of open-ended therapy were achieved in less than five months.

   Implication: Family therapy appears to move more rapidly than individual psychotherapy. This may be due to the fact that it is more action oriented, more geared to the present than the past, more geared to problem solving than to "insight," deals more with transactional issues with all family members present, and is based on more direct observations of behavior and interaction than a report from only one member of the family. Some of the changes, however, take considerably longer than five months to manifest themselves. (The transcript in Chapter 35 illustrates such a case.)

6. Several marital and family "enrichment" programs appear to have promise as useful preventative strategies in family living.

Implication: Although the data are not yet in, the range of family therapy is rapidly expanding. Family therapists should probably remain cautious about claims of efficacy at this point.

7. The more members of the family involved in the family therapy, the better the outcome seems to be. This is especially true when the child is the identified patient.

> *Implication:* For the symptom to change, the situation should change.[20] Evaluative measures should include not only the presence or absence of "better behavior" but also evaluation of whether or not the *system* in which the behavior took place also was changed. The more family members involved, the better the outcome seems to be. This may require some major changes in clinical practices—for example, inpatient services, child psychiatry services, and so on. Family therapy is the most economical treatment in time and money for multi-problem families.

8. Therapist relationship skills have major impact on the outcome of marital family treatment regardless of the "school" or orientation of the clinician. Training programs must focus on both conceptual-technical skills and relationships skills for beginning family therapists.

> *Implications:* Family therapy relies on the therapist's cognitive and technical skills, but there should also be an emphasis in any training program on what kind of person the family therapist is. The kind of experience the family has with the therapist as a person will affect outcome

DESIGN STRATEGIES

There are a number of different ways to design a study that will yield information about the effectiveness of a particular type of psychotherapy. The APA Commission on Psychotherapies[21] conceived of research designs as proceeding from lower level I types of design (e.g., one-shot case study) through higher levels to level V (e.g., multivariate designs), which are increasingly complex, reduce confounding of variables, and increase the level of knowledge obtained from the research effort. While the interested reader is referred elsewhere for more detail,[20] a short description of these major designs is in order for the beginning family therapist.

In the one-shot case study (level I) a group of patients is investigated following some period of intervention. At level II, the one-group pre-test/post-test design involves the measurement before, during, and after treatment on one group of patients who undergo the treatment in question. Level III designs, so-called intensive designs or extended baseline *A-B* designs, use the patients as their own controls in that the symptom or behavior to be changed is measured on each patient over an extended baseline period, then during and following treatment. *A* refers to the period prior to treatment, and *B* refers to the intervention period. Single case designs where one patient is followed through a baseline period, during treatment, and sometimes following the intervention (*A-B-A* design) are a variant of this approach. Pre-test/post-test control group designs (level IV) provide a control group that allows one to make inferences that the effects of time or maturation in the patient(s) cannot account for differences that appear in the experimental and control groups. Patients are assessed not only prior to, and immediately following, the intervention, but also at follow-up periods (e.g., 6 and 12 months following the termination of the treatment) so as to check on the duration or even possible enhancement of treatment effects showing at discharge. The most complex and sophisticated level V design, the multivariate design, involves the simultaneous investigation of a number of variables, e.g., patient, treatment, and outcome variables in such a way as to measure the effect of each variable alone and in interaction with the other variables. The so-called factorial designs are a type of multivariate design. In this design, two or more dimensions are varied in two or more ways. For example, if family treatment with the patient present is compared with family treatment with the patient absent (two variations of family treatment) is investigated with two diagnostic groups (schizophrenia and affective disorder), that would be a factorial design.

CRITERIA FOR SCIENTIFIC INVESTIGATION OF PSYCHOTHERAPIES

It is useful here to consider the scientific criteria that are applied to any psychotherapy outcome study. Most of these criteria apply to the higher level (levels IV and V) mentioned above. The state of the art has certainly advanced in the last 20 years, and the informed clinician should know how to judge journal reports of such investigations. Listed here are the criteria that would apply to any such investigation, whatever the format of treatment or the strategies and therapeutic interventions.

1. Assignment to treatment condition by random assignment, matching, etc.
2. Measurement of the status of the patient/family on foci of the intervention before and after treatment.
3. Matching of treatment and control groups on major independent variables such as therapists' experience and competence level, enthusiasm and

belief in the treatment they are administering, equal amounts of time in therapy, etc.

4. Assessment of patients not only at the end of treatment, but also at follow-up period (often 6 months, and/or 12 months) in order to assess the durability of the treatment effects.

5. Description of the therapeutic techniques and strategies in sufficient detail (i.e., often some form of treatment manual) in order to teach therapists the techniques and rate to see if the treatment as described is being delivered.

6. Assessment instruments carefully selected in order to: assess individual and family change; assess those areas targeted by the two treatments as foci for change either as mediating or final results; judge change from the multiple perspectives of patient, family, therapist, independent observer; assessment of both positive and negative outcomes.

7. Statistical analysis that would assess group differences with mean scores, percentage of patients/families clinically improved in both groups, etc.

8. Data on any possible other concurrent treatment.

STUDY ILLUSTRATION

As an illustration of a well-designed (though not perfect) outcome study involving the family therapy format, we describe the controlled research by Falloon et al.[14] on the influence of family management intervention in the prevention of exacerbations with schizophrenics. The reader can apply the criteria for scientific investigation of psychotherapies mentioned above to this design and make judgments about its areas of strength and weakness.

Patients between the ages of 18 and 45 years of age, carefully diagnosed as schizophrenic with the semi-structured interview called the *Present State Examination*, who resided or were in close contact with their biological parents, were the subjects of the treatment investigation. Most patients came from households that were rated as high in expressed emotion, that is having critical attitude and behavior and overinvolvement with the patient, as measured on the Camberwell Family Interview. Through random assignment, 20 patients were assigned to family intervention and 19 were assigned to a contrasting form of intervention, individual therapy.

Patients in either family intervention or individual intervention were seen on the same schedule: weekly during the first three months, biweekly for the next six months, and monthly through the remaining months of the total year of treatment. Three therapists each saw six family intervention patients and six individual therapy patients. The family intervention sessions were held in the patient's home, while the individual sessions were held in the clinic. In addition to the psychosocial interventions, all patients in both groups were seen on a monthly basis for optimum maintenance on neuroleptic medication. The psychiatrist who saw the patients in this capacity were blind to which psychosocial intervention the patients were receiving.

The family intervention is described as having as its goal the reduction of environmental stress by training patients and their parents to utilize more effective problem solving. Psychoeducational strategies were used in the first two sessions to instruct patient and family about the nature (biological and genetic causes with deemphasis on the etiological role of the family interaction) and course of schizophrenia, reinforcing the need for medication, and emphasizing the potential of the family in assisting in the potential good course of the illness. In subsequent sessions, behavior techniques of rehearsal, modeling, feedback, and social reinforcement were used to teach, shape, and enhance problem-solving skills of the family. In this manner, families were taught to effectively express positive and negative feelings, clearly state requests for behavioral change, and engage in reciprocal conversation.

In the individual supportive psychotherapy, the patient met individually in the clinic with their therapist, and the goal was education about the nature, course, and treatment of schizophrenia, and assistance in efforts to cope with the problems of everyday living.

Outcome measures, administered by raters blind to the treatment condition, included the following: a rating of clinical exacerbation (recrudescence of florid symptoms of schizophrenia of at least one week duration or requiring a major change in medication or hospitalization), ratings of target symptoms on a monthly basis, a rating of symptom remission based on the *Present State Examination* given at the nine-month point, and a tally of community tenure (number of days in a psychiatric hospital and number of hospitalizations).

Before reviewing the results of the study, the adequacy of design and possible flaws that may limit the validity of the results should be noted. Relatively speaking, this is a highly sophisticated therapy comparison outcome study. Patients carefully diagnosed by a reliable method were randomly assigned to one of two treatments. The two treatments were carefully described, and described in enough concrete detail so that others could replicate the method. The therapists were all experienced clinicians, so that if a treatment does not work one cannot (idealistically) fault the skill of the therapists. The number of sessions in each of the two treatments is matched. Treatment other than the contrasting psychosocial interventions—chemotherapy in this case—is carefully monitored so as not to be a factor favoring either group. Outcome measures were done by raters blind to treatment assignment, and the outcomes involve behaviors (e.g., number of rehospitalizations) that are reliably measured and clinically meaningful.

However, all psychotherapy designs involve compromises, and there are some circumstances here that make one pause. The three experienced therapists who treated patients in both conditions were the three major investigators and authors, and may have been biased to show that the family therapy was the most effective. In addition, the family therapy was done in the family's home, manifesting concern and effort on the therapist's part (so as to avoid possible cancellations the authors state) while the individual treatment was in the clinic. One wonders if the clinic patients did have more cancellations, and if the family treatment per se was important, or meeting in the home was the most important variable. While the outcome measures show superiority in individual functioning for patients in the family group, none of the outcome measures tap the family functioning per se, which was the target of the family intervention. The study would have been more convincing if the mediating goals of the family intervention (e.g., family problem solving skills) were measured and shown to improve, along with the final goals (e.g., patient functioning).

The results were encouraging. At nine-month follow-up the family treatment was superior to the individual treatment in preventing major symptomatic exacerbations. Only one patient (6 percent) in the family treatment group had suffered a clinical relapse, as compared to eight such patients (44 percent) in the individual treatment group.

SUMMARY

Although outcome research still has not exactly elucidated indications and contraindications for family treatment, the clinician has a much better idea now than ten years ago of when to do what. This chapter should be reviewed with the next chapter (on process) and with the section on guidelines. Needless to say, even then, the outcome data along with clinical experience and the features of each case will determine appropriate interventions.

A final reason for continuing the push for treatment assessment is that the public is demanding proof of efficacy of all psychotherapies.[22] Efficacy is being measured against treatments that have been shown to work, most prominently psychopharmacology. We believe the implication for the family therapist is that the day may not be far off when third party payers will reimburse only those treatments demonstrating efficacy.

SUGGESTIONS FOR FURTHER READINGS

Gurman A and Kniskern D: Research on the process and outcome of marital and family therapy. In Garfield S and Bergin A (Eds): **Handbook of Psychotherapy and Behavior Change (3rd Ed)**. New York: Wiley, 1986.

A recent review of the experimental literature.

REFERENCES

1. Meltzoff J and Kornreich M: Research in psychotherapy. New York: Atherton Press, 1970
2. Luborsky L, Singer B, and Luborsky L: Comparative studies of psychotherapy. Is it true that "everyone has won and all must have prizes"?Arch Gen Psychiatry 132:995-1008, 1975
3. Smith ML, Glass GV, and Miller TI: The Benefits of Psychotherapy. Baltimore: Johns Hopkins University Press, 1980
4. Wells RA, Dilkes T, and Trivelli N: The results of family therapy: A critical review of the literature. Family Process 7:189-207, 1972
5. Gurman AS and Kniskern D: Research on marital and family therapy: Progress, perspective and prospect. In Garfield S and Bergin A (Eds): Handbook of Psychotherapy and Behavior Change (2nd Ed). New York: Wiley, 1978, pp 817-901
6. Todd TC and Stanton MD: Research on marital and family therapy: Answers, issues and recommendations for the future. In Wolman BB and Stricker G (Eds): Handbook of family and marital therapy. New York: Plenum, 1983
7. Beach SR and O'Leary KD: The current status of outcome research in marital therapy. In L'Abate L (Ed): Handbook of Family Psychology and Psychotherapy. Dorsey: Homewood, IL: 1984
8. Gurman AS, Kniskern DP, and Pinsof WM: Research on the process and outcome of marital and family therapy. In Garfield SL and Bergin AE (Eds): Handbook of Psychotherapy and Behavior Change (3rd Ed). New York: Wiley, 1986, pp 565-624
9. Patterson GR: Coercive Family Process. Eugene, OR: Castalia Publishing Co., 1982
10. Alexander J and Parsons B: Short-term behavioral intervention with delinquent families: Impact on family process and recidivism. J Abnormal Psychology 81:219-225, 1973
11. Minuchin S, Rosman BO, and Baker L: Psychosomatic Families. Cambridge, MA: Harvard University Press, 1978
12. Stanton MD and Todd TC: The Family Therapy of Drug Abuse and Addiction. New York: Guilford Press, 1982
13. Davenport YB: Treatment of the married bipolar patient in conjoint couples psychotherapy groups. In Lansky MR (Ed): Family Therapy and Major Psychopathology. New York: Grune & Stratton, 1981, pp 123-143
14. Falloon IRH, Boyd JL, McGill CW, Razani J, Moss HB, and Gilderman AM: Family management in the prevention of exacerbations of schizophrenia. N Engl J Medicine 306:1437-1440, 1982
15. Gurman AS: Contemporary marital therapies: A critique and comparative analysis of psychoanalytic, behavioral and systems theory approaches. In

Paolino T and McCrady B (Eds): Marriage and Marital Therapy: Psychoanalytic, Behavioral and Systems Theory Perspectives. New York: Brunner/Mazel, 1978, pp 445-566

16. Rakoff VM, Sigal JJ, and Epstein NB: Predictions of therapeutic process and progress in conjoint family therapy. Arch Gen Psychiatry 32:1013-1017, 1975

17. Siegler M: Pascal's wager and the hanging of the crepe. N Engl J Med 293:853-857, 1975

18. Hadley SW and Strupp HH: Contemporary views of negative effects in psychotherapy. Arch Gen Psychiatry 33:1291-1302, 1976

19. Shapiro R and Budman S: Defection, termination and continuation in family and individual therapy. Fam Process 12:55-67, 1973

20. Haley J: Communication and therapy: Blocking metaphors. Am J Psychiatry 25:214-227, 1971

21. APA Commission on Psychotherapies: Psychotherapy Research: Methodological and Efficacy Issues. Washington, DC: American Psychiatric Association, 1982

22. Marshall E: Psychotherapy faces test of worth. Science 207:35-36, January 4, 1980

Untitled photograph by Ken Heyman. Courtesy Ken Heyman, private collection.

32

Research on the
Process of Family Therapy

OBJECTIVES

- To acquaint the clinician with the methodology of family process research
- To be able to critically review modern studies of family process research
- To suggest areas for further investigation

INTRODUCTION

Research on family processes, both cross-sectional (at one point in time) and more importantly longitudinal, is crucial to the understanding of how families function, (both) functional and dysfunctional, and, thus, to how to plan intervention strategies with those family systems in distress.

ASSESSMENT METHODOLOGY

Traditional assessment has focused on measuring an individual's behavior, including thoughts, attitudes, conflicts, emotional reactions, etc. Family and marital theory focuses not just on the individual, but on the interactional behavior between individuals, so the field was driven to develop new terminology (Chapter

538

l) to describe such behaviors, and, in addition, new methodology for operationalizing and measuring interactional behaviors. We briefly describe some of the methodologies for measuring interactions, especially those that have been used in the process studies to be reviewed in this chapter. For more information on these technologies, extensive reviews are available.[1]

Self-report

In many ways the easiest and least costly way to gather information on couples' or families' interactions is through self-report, either asking the individuals to report on their interactions, or their perception of spouses' behaviors, or to keep an ongoing diary or record of family interactions. The ease of gathering the data is matched by the problems, e.g., low correlations between self-report and actually observed behavior of the family.[2] However, the practicality of using self-report instruments sometimes outweighs their weaknesses, and they can still provide useful information for research hypothesis generation or clinical interventions. The most useful self-report instruments for the clinician are reviewed in Chapter 9.

Observation and Behavioral Coding

There are a number of coding systems that have been developed to yield reliable coding of a couple's or family's interaction, audiotaped either in the home or laboratory situations. The Marital Interaction Coding System (MICS)[2] can be applied to preplanned conflicts presented by the experimenter's or patient's attempts to resolve their own conflicts. It has been found that 29 codes provide an adequate coverage of dyadic problem-solving behaviors. These 29 codes are reduced to three summary scores: positive social reinforcement, negative social reinforcement, and problem-solving behaviors.

Observation of the family *as they interact in their own home* environment and coding of this behavior by a trained observer is a direct way to measure interactions. Patterson used this approach in observing the interaction of families with delinquent adolescents, and developed a reliable coding schema, the Family Interaction Coding System[3] for the interactional sequences. It was designed to describe aggressive behaviors and the antecedents and consequences associated with them. Behaviors are coded into 29 categories such as approval, attention, disapproval, humiliate, ignore, negativism, etc.

Family Tasks

The Revealed Differences Task[4] has been used in numerous studies of marital and family interaction. The marital partners or family members are asked to discuss differences after having made individual evaluations or decisions on predetermined topics. Others[5] have modified this procedure so that spouses are asked to resolve concealed differences (that is, while unaware they had been given conflicting prior information).

The SIMFAM[6] is another frequently used laboratory task. Spouses or families play a game similar to shuffleboard in which the rewards are given out under complete control of the experimenter.

Communication deviance (CD), that is communication between family members that is vague, illogical, confusing, has been operationally defined and measured in families containing a schizophrenic member.[7,8] A projective test, the TAT, is given to the parents together, and their conjoint production (a story about the picture on the TAT card) is scored for communication style. More recently, Lewis, Rodnick, and Goldstein[9] have used an audiotaped five-minute segment of a family discussion on a focused topic to score for CD.

CROSS-SECTIONAL STUDIES

Marital Conflict

We summarize here, based upon several recent reviews[10,11] the research data on interactional behaviors that statistically differentiate nondistressed from distressed married couples. We have discussed this issue in the clinical context (in Chapter 5) of how to distinguish functional from nonfunctional families.

AFFECT

Nondistressed couples show more positive cues of affect (empathic smiles; warm, tender voice; attention); more social reinforcement (e.g., approval, agreement); more reconciling acts (e.g., changing the subject, using humor, accepting the other's ideas); more supportive behaviors (e.g., self-confidence; outcome and process agreement). In contrast, distressed couples show more negative affect; more coercive acts (e.g., using an outsider to get the other to agree); more negative social reinforcement (e.g., put down, disagree, criticize); more defensive behavior (e.g., process and outcome disagreement).

STATUS

Nondistressed couples change more easily between acceptance and rejection of mutual control in the interaction; have a higher ratio of instructions, suggestions, or requests that actually modify behavior of a spouse relative to the number of attempts to so modify spouse's behavior. In contrast, distressed couples are characterized by status and power struggles.

PROBLEM SOLVING

Nondistressed couples show more problem-solving acts (e.g., compromise); more cognitive acts (e.g., seek information, give information); show almost no coercive acts (e.g., demand compensation, induce guilt); and develop a more neutral problem discussion. Distressed couples are more negative in problem solving tasks; engage in much longer conflict scenes.

The findings above are hardly surprising. Couples who describe themselves as in conflict or seek assistance in clinics for conflict emit negative behaviors that anyone would describe as conflictual, negative, and distressing. The next step would be to investigate the genesis or development of such behaviors over time, and the interactional sequences that seem to elicit such negative behaviors. Such an approach might lead us to understand why such distress occurs.

Depression

Social learning theorists suggest that the quality of marital/family relations is determined by the ratio of positive to negative exchanges.[12,13] The depressive individual's tendency to be aversive to others in social situations is associated with his or her tendency to receive aversive responses from others.[12] The depressed individual tends to give and receive aversive stimulation at higher rates than evidenced by other members of the family.[14] Similarly, a depressed partner and his mate tend to engage in negative (aversive) exchanges more frequently than do nondistressed couples.[15,16] Furthermore, distressed couples are more reactive to recent events, positive or negative, than are their distressed counterparts.[17]

In a study of the interaction patterns between depressed individuals and their spouses, Hooley[18] classified spouses as high or low EE on the basis of the Camberwell Family Interview. Subsequently, couples were videotaped during a 10 minute face-to-face interaction. Compared with low EE spouses, high EE spouses were more negative and less positive in verbal and nonverbal behaviors directed at their depressed partners. They made more critical remarks, disagreed with their partners more frequently, and were less likely to accept what their mate said to them. The depressed mates of high EE spouses exhibited low frequencies of self-disclosure and high levels of neutral nonverbal behavior.

Depressed married women display less problem-solving behavior than their spouses; both spouses show less self-disclosure; the couple express less facilitative behavior, and depression reduces aversive behavior in the spouse.[19]

Interaction between depressed female inpatients and their spouses changes during the course of hospitalization.[20] In initial sessions the patient was heavily influenced by joint discussion with the spouse, but by the last session there was a more equal balance of power.

Others[21] have studied the interaction between couples seeking marital treatment, including a subset in which one spouse showed a clinically significant unipolar depression. Sequential conversations were recorded and scored using an interaction category system. Couples with a depressed partner exhibited negative and asymmetrical communication with expression of dysphoric and uncomfortable feelings. The depressed spouses spoke negatively regarding themselves and positively in regard to their spouses. In contrast, the nondepressed spouses rarely spoke of themselves, but evaluated their depressed spouses negatively. Since all the patients in this study had marital conflict, there is no representation of those without marital difficulty. However, Kowalik and Gotlib[22] compared the interactions of depressed and nondepressed outpatients, and nondepressed, non-psychiatric controls and their spouses in an interactional task. The results suggest that depressed psychiatric outpatients' interactions with their spouses are characterized by negativity, which was not evident in the nondepressed patient and control couples. The level of negative intent and the lack of positive intent seems characteristic of the pairs in which there is a depressed member.

In a similar vein, in another study[23] it was found that couples with a depressed spouse experienced each other as more negative, hostile, mistrusting and detached; as less agreeable, nurturant, and affiliative than did nondepressed couples.

In addition to studies of the interaction between a depressed adult and spouse, there are a few studies of the interaction between a depressed parent and family. In one study,[24] children of mothers who were depressed, displayed significantly more irritable affect than did controls. The fathers and children reduced irritated and sarcastic behavior immediately following a mother's displays of dysphoric affect along with a suppression of caring behavior.

Adolescent Delinquent Behavior and Family Interaction

In a series of investigations using home observation and coding of behavior by trained observers, Patterson and colleagues[25] have described the typical interaction patterns in the families of adolescents who exhibit delinquent behavior. This work is outstanding for its attention to technical detail (e.g., reliable coding, statistical analysis) and deserves careful reading and study by anyone interested in doing family interactional research. By careful observation and coding of the interactions in the home of families with a delinquent child (e.g., court referred social aggressors, stealers, etc.), they were able to describe probabilities of certain events given the presence of certain other events. For example, what is the likelihood of the child's whine followed by a mother's hug? Most important for understanding the delinquent behavior of a young adolescent, what is the likelihood of such behavior given certain preceding parental behaviors? Data supporting a "coercion" theory of antisocial behavior emerged. By sequential analysis, it was found that the aggressive response of the child was maintained by the positive and negative reinforcements given by the parents.

There has been much written in the family literature about circular causality, which helps explain the behavior of families much better than linear causality. However, there is very little if any research on the actual circular feedback loops in family behavior, other than that by Patterson and his co-workers.

Schizophrenia

Since certain kinds of family behavior (overinvolvement, criticality) called "expressed emotion" have been found to correlate with future relapse of the index schizophrenic,[26] there have been some research attempts to explore the construct validity of the EE concept. In the classic studies, EE was measured by the Camberwell Family Interview (CFI), a semi-structured interview with one family member in which the person reports on his attitudes and behaviors toward the patient. The first question that arises is if a family member scores high on EE in the interview, does he in fact behave that way (overinvolved, critical) in actual interaction with the patient? If so, what other behaviors of family members and patients are correlated with this? For example, do the sicker patients stimulate more EE behavior from parents?

Preliminary data does suggest that high EE relatives on the CFI do behave in like fashion in actual interaction with the patient. For example, a measure of Doane's affective style in a family discussion task correlates with similar attitudes on the CFI.[27] High EE parents on the CFI use more critical remarks in a direct interaction task.

Tarrier et al.[28] used a measure of skin conductance as a biological marker of arousal in high and low EE families. They found that while both groups showed high arousal when the patient was not physically present, when the patient entered the room, the low EE relatives habituated, whereas the high EE relatives continued in their high arousal state.

There is some evidence that the EE concept is too global and can be broken down into meaningful subgroups. In a recent study,[29] schizophrenic patients from high and low EE homes showed identical symptomatology and social adjustment scores. But when the high EE group was subdivided, patients from emotionally overinvolved families showed poorer premorbid adjustment and greater residual symptomatology at discharge than did patients from critical families.

Leff[30] originally found that high or low EE of relatives was not correlated with characteristics of the patients (e.g., severe symptomatology, premorbid status). In contrast, Miklowitz[27,31] found that patients with a poor premorbid adjustment were significantly more likely to come from families where the mothers emotionally displayed overinvolvement attitudes than those whose mothers were highly critical on the CFI.

Cross-sectional Data: Summary Comment

Cross-sectional data yield correlations of variables, such as family interactions correlated with certain kinds of symptoms. But this correlational material is limited in the causal understanding relationship between the variables. Just because hostile interactions, for example, are correlated with marital dissatisfaction does not demonstrate that one causes the other, nor does it indicate which preceeds the other over time. Hence, longitudinal studies, which are more expensive of time and money, are needed to explicate such issues.

LONGITUDINAL STUDIES

Depression

There is a growing body of data to suggest that depression and marital/familial stress and conflict are related over time. Paykel et al.[32] found a sixfold increase in the risk of developing a clinical depression in the six months following a stressful life event. Marital conflict was the most common event reported preceding the onset of the depression. In a survey of over 3,000 adults, Ilfeld[33] likewise found depressive symptoms related to stress, especially stress in parenting and marital relations.

Henderson[34] found an association between week social bonds and neurotic behaviors including depression in an epidemiological study of a random sample in Australia. In subsequent longitudinal studies[35,36] he found the association between weak social bonds and neurotic behavior related to three variables: social bonds as a protection against the development of symptoms, individuals who because of disquieting moods drive away potentially supportive others, and the presence of a personality that leads to both the development of symptoms and inability to form mutually satisfying interpersonal relations.

In a study of women living in London, Brown and Harris[37] found that an intimate, confiding relationship with a man, often a spouse, was a buffer against the development of depression. This finding has been replicated in a study[38] of depressed women compared to a matched group without a history of depression. Weissman and Paykel[39] studied depressed women and matched normal neighbors in a New England Italian working-class neighborhood through a depressive episode during treatment and following recovery. While withdrawing somewhat from extended family, during the acute depression these women showed friction and tension with their mates and children. The marriages were characterized at this time by hostile communication, dependency, and diminished sexual satisfaction. Depressed women with relatively good marriages withdraw from the spouse, while those with poor marriages blame the spouse for the depression. As the woman recovers from the depressive symptoms, the interpersonal relations improve at a slower pace. Residual impairments in family relations remain with inhibited communication, friction, and argumentative behavior.

Schizophrenia

Doane et al.[40] followed a cohort of 65 nonpsychotically disturbed adolescents and their families in a prospective design. At the time of the first five-year follow-up, a measure of parental communication deviance (CD) obtained from scoring Thematic Apperception Test data (TAT), predicted schizophrenia spectrum disorders in the adolescents. When a measure of affective style (obtained with a modified Strodbeck interaction task given to all family members) was added to the CD measure as a predictor, a high degree of precise prediction was obtained. For example, only when parents exhibited both high CD and negative affective style did the offspring manifest schizophrenic spectrum disorders upon five-year follow-up.

Wynne[41] is prospectively studying a group of 4, 7, and 10 year-old male children of parents diagnosed from Schizophrenia by DSM-III criteria, with a contrasting group of children of parents who have suffered from unipolar, bipolar, and neurotic depressions. Such a comparative design will be helpful in sorting out which (if any) family interaction variables are specific to schizophrenia or affective disorder as opposed to being common to several diagnoses. Preliminary results[42] indicate at three-year follow-up that an index of parental communication deviance is correlated with a measure of poor psychosocial competence in the offspring.

CLINICAL GUIDELINES DRAWN
FROM PROCESS RESEARCH

The clinically oriented family therapist may wonder what family process research has to do with family therapy. What are the practical clinical guidelines that can be gleaned from the current body of family interaction research?

First of all, family process research puts some cherished family therapy hypotheses to the test, and the results are often more complicated than our armchair theories. For example, as indicated in the section on agoraphobia, it would seem that fears in one spouse do not always serve a systems function. In many cases, when the symptom bearer becomes better, the marital system is improved rather than adversely affected, as theory would suggest. This means that one can-not assume that all symptoms in one individual are under the control of the inter-action system. It may mean that marital therapy is indicated in some situations where there is an agoraphobia in one spouse, and in other situations marital therapy is not needed.

Secondly, family interaction research helps specify the interactions that are crucial to the presence of certain symptoms. This specificity may lead to more focused family intervention, either for the individual family clinician or for future family research. For example, expressed emotion, communication deviance, and affective style play a role in the course of schizophrenia; coercive behaviors are instrumental in adolescent delinquent behaviors; negative interaction and poor problem-solving skills are associated with marital discord. Family and marital in-tervention packages can be constructed so as to intervene with specific toxic aspects of the family environment that have been elucidated by cross-sectional and longitudinal data.

SUGGESTIONS FOR FURTHER READINGS

Jacob T (Ed): **Family Interaction and Psychopathology**. New York: Plenum, 1987.
A recent, up-to-date and thorough review.

Barnes GG: Pattern and intervention: Research findings and the development of family therapy theory. In Bentovim, A, Barnes GG, and Cooklin A (Eds): **Family Therapy, Complementary Frameworks of Theory and Practice, Vol.1.** New York: Grune & Stratton, 1982, pp 131-155.

REFERENCES

1. Weiss R and Margolin G: Assessment of marital conflict and accord. In Ciminero A, Calhoun K, and Adams H (Eds): Handbook of Behavioral As-sessment. New York: Wiley, 1977, pp 555-602
2. Hops H, Wills TA, Patterson GR, and Weiss RL: Marital Interaction Coding System. Eugene, OR: University of Oregon and Oregon Research Institute, 1971. (Order from ASIS/NAPS, c/o Microfiche Publications, 305 East 46th Street, New York, NY 10017.)
3 Patterson GR: Some procedures for assessing changes in marital interaction patterns. Oregon Res Instit Bull 17(7), 1976
4. Strodbeck FL: Husband-wife interaction over revealed differences. Am Sociological Rev 16:468-473, 1951

5. Olson DHL and Ryder RG: Inventory of marital conflicts. J Marr Fam 3:443-448, 1970

6. Olson DH and Straus MA: A diagnostic tool for marital and family therapy: The SIMFAM technique. The Family Coordinator 21:251-258, 1972

7. Singer MT and Wynne LC: Principles for scoring communication defects and deviances in parents of schizophrenics: Rorschach and TAT scoring manuals. Psychiatry 29:260-288, 1966

8. Wynne L, Singer M, Bartko J, and Toohey M: Schizophrenics and their families. Recent research on parental communication. In Tanner JM (Ed): Developments in Psychiatric Research. London: Hadden & Staughton, 1977, pp 254-286

9 Lewis J, Rodnick E, and Goldstein M: Intrafamilial interactive behavior, parental communication deviance, and risk for schizophrenia. J Abnor Psychology, 90:448-457, 1981

10. Schaap C: A comparison of the interaction of distressed and nondistressed married couples in a laboratory situation: Literature survey, methodological issues, and an empirical investigation. In Hahlweg K and Jacobson NS (Eds): Marital Interaction: Analysis and Modification. New York: Guilford Press, 1984, pp 133-158

11. Jacobson NS: Behavioral marital therapy. In Gurman AS and Kniskern DP (Eds): Handbook of Family Therapy. New York: Brunner/Mazel, 1981, pp 556-591

12. Jacobson NS and Moore D: Spouses as observers of the events in their relationship. J Consult Clin Psychology 49:269-277, 1981

13. Weiss RL, Hops H, and Patterson GR: A framework for conceptualizing marital conflict, a technology for altering it, some data for evaluating it. In Hamerlynck LA, Hand LF, and Mash EJ (Eds): Behavior Change: Methodology, Concepts and Practice. Champaign, IL: Research Press, 1973

14. Reid JB: Reciprocity in Family Interaction. Unpublished doctoral dissertation. University of Oregon, 1967

15. Birchler GR and Webb L: A social learning formulation of discriminating interaction behaviors in happy and unhappy marriages. Paper presented at the Annual Meeting of the Southwest Psychological Association, Houston, April 1975

16 Wills TA, Weiss RL, and Patterson GR: A behavioral analysis of the determinants of marital satisfaction. J Consult Clin Psychology 42:802-811, 1974

17. Jacobson NS, Follette WC, and McDonald DW: Reactivity to positive and negative behavior in distressed and non-distressed married couples. J Consult Clin Psychology 50:706-714, 1982

18. Hooley J: Expressed emotion and depression: Interactions between patients and high versus low EE spouses. J Abnorm Psychology 95:237-246, 1986

19. Biglan A, Hops H, Sherman L, Friedman LS, Arthur J, and Ostee V: Problem-

solving interactions of depressed women and their spouses. Behav Ther 16:431-451, 1985

20. Merikangas KR, Ranelli CJ and Kupfer DJ: Marital interaction in hospitalized depressed patients. J Nerv Ment Dis 167:689-695, 1979

21. Hautzinger M, Linden M, and Hoffman N: Distressed couples with and without a depressed partner: An analysis of their verbal interaction. J Behav Ther Exp Psychiatry 13:307-314, 1982

22. Kowalik D and Gotlib IH: Depression and marital interaction: Concordance between intent and perception of communications. Unpublished manuscript, University of Western Ontario, 1985

23. Kahn J, Coyne JC, and Margolin G: Depression and marital conflict: The social construction of despair. J Social Personal Relationships, in press

24. Biglan A, Hops H, and Sherman L: Coercive family processes and maternal depression. In Peters RD and McMahon RJ (Eds): Marriages and Families: Behavioral Systems Approaches. New York: Brunner/Mazel (in press)

25. Patterson GR: Coercive Family Process. Eugene, OR: Castalia Publishing Co., 1982

26. Leff J and Vaughn C: Expressed Emotion in Families. New York: Guilford Press, 1985

27. Miklowitz D: Familial and symptomatic characteristics of schizophrenics living in high and low expressed emotion home environments. Unpublished master's thesis, University of California at Los Angeles, 1981

28. Tarrier N, Vaughn C, Lader, M et al.: Bodily reactions to people and events in schizophrenia. Arch Gen Psychiatry 36:311-315, 1979

29. Miklowitz D, Goldstein M, and Falloon I: Premorbid and symptomatic characteristics of schizophrenics from families with high and low levels of expressed emotion. J Abnorm Psychology 92:359-367, 1983

30. Leff JP: Schizophrenia and sensitivity to the family environment. Schiz Bull 2:565-574, 1976

31. Goldstein M and Doane J: Family factors in the onset, course and treatment of schizophrenic spectrum disorders: An update on current research. J Nerv Ment Dis 170:692-700, 1982

32. Paykel ES, Myers JK, Dienelt MN, Klerman GL, Lindenthal JJ, and Pepper MP: Life events and depression: A controlled study. Arch Gen Psychiatry 21:753-760, 1969

33. Ilfeld FW: Current social stressors and symptoms of depression. Am J Psychiatry 134:161-166, 1977

34. Henderson AS, Duncan-Jones P, Byrne DG, Scott R, and Adcock S: Psychiatric disorders in Canberra: A standardized study of prevelance. Act Psychiatrica Scan 60:355-374, 1979

35. Henderson AS, Duncan-Jones P, Scott R, and Adcock S: Social relationships,

adversity and neuroses: A study of associations in a general population sample. Br J Psychiatry 136:574-583, 1980

36. Henderson AS, Byrne DG, and Duncan-Jones P: Neurosis and the social environment. Sydney, Australia: Academic Press, 1981

37. Brown GW and Harris TO: Social Origins of Depression: A Study of Psychiatric Disorder in Women. London: Tavistock, 1978

38. Roy A: Vulnerability factors and depression in women. Br J Psychiatry 133:106-110, 1978

39. Weissman M and Paykel E: The Depressed Woman: A Study of Social Relationships. Chicago: University of Chicago Press, 1974

40. Doane JA, West KL, Goldstein MJ, et al.: Parental communication deviance and affective style. Arch Gen Psychiatry 38:679-685, 1981

41. Wynne LC: The University of Rochester Child and Family Study: 1972-1980—Overview of research plan. In Watt NF, Anthony J, Wynne LC, et al.(Eds): Children at Risk for Schizophrenia. New York: Cambridge University Press, 1984, pp 335-347

42. Jones JE, Wynne LC, Al-Khayyal M, et al.: Predicting current school competence of high-risk children with a cross-situation measure of parental communication deviance. In Watt NF, Anthony J, Wynne LC, et al.(Eds): Children at Risk for Schizophrenia. New York: Cambridge University Press, 1984, pp 393-398

Family, drawing by Jonathan Glick.

33
Training in
Family Intervention

with Stuart Sugarman, M.D.

OBJECTIVES

- To specify family therapy training objectives
- To specify an optimal family therapy training program
- To describe models and techniques of family supervision
- To describe a procedure for evaluating trainees
- To describe a continuing education program for the family therapist
- To describe political/contextual issues in psychiatry residency training programs

INTRODUCTION

Parallel to the diverse models (or schools) of family therapy, there are a number of models of family training. The setting in which training occurs (e.g., inpatient, outpatient, family clinic, school) and the range of pathologies and family problems that are treated in the family therapy format are important considerations, too. *And the level of mastery desired is also crucial: Some desire training to become a specialist, while others need to know it as one among other interventions.*

552

WHO SHOULD BE TRAINED? AT WHAT LEVEL OF EXPERTISE?

Historically, there has seemed to be an enthusiastic assumption in the family field that almost anyone can be taught to treat families—professionals and non-professionals alike—with traditional professional roles ignored, if not disdained.[1] Family therapy training is being offered to mental health professionals, such as psychiatrists, psychologists, psychiatric social workers and nurses, and marriage and family counselors. Professionals and trainees in other fields that involve working with families in distress have sought, and been offered family therapy training courses. This group includes primary-case physicians, pediatricians, obstetricians and gynecologists, marriage and divorce counselors for the courts, ministers, probation officers, welfare case workers, teachers, and architects. The family model is now being taught in many law schools as a required part of family law courses. With the spread of community psychiatry concepts and the increasing use of paraprofessional personnel in a variety of helping roles, family therapy training for housewives, college students, neighborhood leaders (or "ombudsmen"), and indigenous persons is a reality.

Only time and the accumulation of data will answer how broad a range of trainees can learn and effectively use what range of therapeutic skills. The experienced supervisor knows that every trainee is quite different, and that there is a range of innate talent, life experience, empathic skills, and flair for the family method that each brings to the supervisory venture. While there are certain basic skills that can be learned by most trainees, sophistication about people and a repertoire of creative ways to help them change seem less teachable and are probably not within the reach of all trainees.

It is our orientation that family therapy is not the treatment of choice for all conditions; it is a central treatment, but only one among many methods of intervention. This has two corollary points in terms of training. Those clinicians who wish to specialize in family therapy should have, in addition, training in other formats of intervention such as group and individual. Secondly, all mental health professionals, who have major responsibility for triage of patients, should have a basic grounding in family theory and techniques so they can effectively evaluate families when needed and refer appropriately.

TRAINING OBJECTIVES

The final product of the training is the demonstrated skill of the trainee in the art of family treatment. The training process will be most successful, we believe, if it constantly focuses on the skills that the therapist in training needs and must gradually begin to demonstrate. *The role of the supervisor is to create an atmosphere in which these skills can be defined, described, demonstrated, and put into effective operation with families in need.*

A first distinction must be made between training a clinician versus training a researcher/teacher. The Ph.D. programs in family therapy have focused on all three goals, the freestanding institutes tend toward the clinician and sometimes "teacher" missions, while many other family therapy programs (including M.A. in family therapy and psychiatry residency programs, to name a few) focus on training the clinician. Within the latter mission, one can ask: Is the goal to teach the clinician about family therapy, to do family therapy, or to be a family therapist? Most particularly, residency programs have leaned toward at least the first (*about*) and some of the second (to do family therapy).

As family therapy strategies and techniques are delineated, it becomes possible for family therapy supervisors to define specific learning objectives for the trainees. This is most clearly represented in the work of Cleghorn and Levin[2] and Tomm and Wright.[3] In this approach an attempt is made to systematically isolate and describe critical functions performed by the family therapist, such as engagement, problem identification, facilitation of change, and termination. Various therapist competencies are related to each function—i.e., skills or clusters of skills that the therapist possesses and executes. One can further define in smaller and more detailed ways the multiple skills, both conceptual and executive, that are needed. The skills taught can extend across the various schools, e.g., dynamic, behavioral, structural-systems, experiential. Table 33-1 is an illustrative summary of the various skills that have been isolated.

The cognitive, conceptual skills are taught in a seminar format. The executive skills can be modeled either live or on videotape by experienced family therapists, role-played by the trainees, and eventually executed in supervised work with families. The directness and simplicity of the approach makes it appealing, especially for beginning family therapists. A version of this approach has been used extensively to train paraprofessionals.[4]

ELEMENTS OF TRAINING

As we discussed above, family therapy training varies depending on the context (i.e., part of a broader psychotherapy program or specifically a family therapy degree/institute program) and the goals of training. We feel that the elements described in this section will differ in emphasis and priority from program to program. However, our remarks are directed specifically at psychiatry residency programs. Even within them, not all the elements are currently available in each program. However, we feel it is an ideal worth aiming toward.

Before embarking on speciality training in family therapy, a person would

Table 33-1

Perceptual/Conceptual and Executive Skills as Conceptualized in a Competency-Based Family Therapy Training Program

Perceptual Conceptual Skills	Executive Skills
Perceive the individual's problems and potential for change in the context of the whole family as a system.	Evaluate the individual's problems through conjoint interview and assessment.
Perceive the therapist's role as helping the family mobilize its own assets to solve problems around symptoms, etc.	Communicate to family members their assets, and stimulate their own active problem solving.
Perceive the family's unique and idiosyncratic use of language and communication.	Use and adapt the family's preferred modes of communication.
Recognize the value of explicit expectations and goals of treatment.	Make explicit with the family the goals and expected length of therapy.
Use information around problematic events in the family to generate tentative hypotheses about the presenting problem.	Follow inquiry about the interpersonal context of problem behavior with verbalization of one's emerging understanding of the problems. Obtain feedback from the family.
Sort out remarks about the past that are relevant to current problems.	Ask for further detail on historical data that are relevant to current problems.
Be alert to data about problems in the immediate interactions of family members in the session.	Allow or stimulate interaction between family members.
Generate hypotheses about the association or interpersonal sequences and problematic behaviors.	Verbalize and validate associations of antecedent behaviors and events, and problem behaviors.
Perceive the power of the structural relationship between people.	Introduce change by restructuring family interaction.
Visualize possible adaptive interaction patterns potentially available to the family.	Stimulate new adaptive behavioral sequences.

Summarized from Tomm K and Wright L: Training in family therapy: Perceptual, conceptual and executive skills. Family Process 18:227-250, 1979.

ideally have had experience with several prerequisites. It would be helpful if such individuals already knew about individual personality development, psychopathology, and psychotherapy. It would also be helpful if they understood group dynamics and had experience in group therapy. A knowledge of the family system itself—its development over time as well as its "disorders"—would obviously be germane, as would some knowledge of larger societal systems and the mutual interaction of these with family systems.

Ideally, the student of family therapy would start the learning process at the same time that he/she is learning group and especially individual psychotherapy. If not, ideas about pathology and therapy become based on an individual unit and it is difficult (some would argue impossible) to make the conceptual shift to "systems" thinking. It is similar to the situation of learning languages. It is much easier for a child to learn French and English at the same time in a bilingual family, than to learn one language early and have to acquire the other as an adolescent or adult.

Many family therapy training programs offer essentially three types of experiences: seminars, clinical work, and supervision. The following outline will indicate some of the elements of a fairly complete family therapy training program. Not all elements will be available in any one program, nor need they necessarily be available. The emphasis and priorities may be quite different from one program to another.

Basic Seminars

Some of these basic seminars would be discussion groups with assigned readings in relevant literature. Others would make liberal use of videotapes or film (or both) to illustrate didactic points with case material.

1. The Family As a Social Institution
   The history and concept of marriage and the family
   Cross-cultural family studies
   Contemporary American marriage and family patterns
   Theories of family structure and function
   The family and other social institutions
2. Theories of Family Pathology
   Theories of family pathology
   Variables in family pathology
   Models of family process and family pathology
   Process and longitudinal research on family pathology
3. Techniques of Family Evaluation and Study
   Structured family interviews
   Self-report instruments

Family interactional assessment tasks
Family projective tests
Cross-sectional and longitudinal research designs
4. Techniques of Family Intervention
Historical survey of family therapy development
Levels of intervention
Models of intervention: prevention, service, treatment, rehabilitation
Types of family therapy
Marital and sex therapy
Goals, strategies, techniques and values of the family therapist
Stages of family intervention
Family therapy outcome research
5. The Larger Clinical Context
Appropriate clinical referral
Modality selection criteria
Combining family therapy and other types of psychotherapy
Combining family therapy and medications
Co-therapy administrative issues: insurance forms, medical records, etc.

Clinical Work

There is no substitute for actually working with a family and attempting to understand what is happening with them, although simulated families and videotapes may be quite helpful at times during the training experience.

A stepwise series of increasingly graded exercises in responsibility for clinical work is pedagogically useful. Specifically, the trainee first observes a supervisor working with a family, usually in a continuous case. The next step is for the trainee to work with an experienced cotherapist. Finally, the trainee is allowed to work with a family alone.

The following types of experiences might be included:

- Intake and evaluation in inpatient and outpatient settings
- Crisis and brief treatment
- Extended family treatment
- Treatment with families having a member with a major psychiatric diagnosis (e.g., Schizophrenia, Major Affective Disorder)
- Marital and sex therapy
- Family consultation to community agencies
- Training in family therapy supervision
- Home visits

Supervision

FORMATS

Supervision would be designed in a variety of formats to enable the trainee to have the benefit of examining clinical experience in some organized way and integrating it with theoretical concepts. These formats might include the following: individual supervision, group supervision, intake conferences, treatment review, and family consultation seminar.

MODELS AND TECHNIQUES

Although the literature on alternative approaches to family therapy supervision is in its infancy, it is possible to identify and describe different models.[5] It seems only natural that the method of psychotherapy supervision would often resemble and closely parallel the model of therapy being taught.

The skills of the dynamically oriented family therapist are taught in a supervisory session characterized by reflection, exploration of the therapists' feelings about various family members, and formulation of a dynamic understanding of the patients and the family. In the systems model, the neophyte learns to change the current repetitive interchanges between individuals in the family by receiving and carrying out tasks given by the supervisor in live supervision via telephone contact or discussion during a break in a session.[1,6] The existential family supervisor can teach the new therapist skills of empathy and recognition of emotional experience by role-playing the family with the trainee,[7] and thus explore the therapist's own countertransference feelings.

In general, family supervision has been unique in its emphasis on live supervision as the trainee is in therapeutic contact with the family. This live contact of supervisor with trainee-family interaction can take place via co-therapy with the supervisor, with the supervisor behind a one-way mirror and a telephone hook-up between supervisor and trainee.[1] Modeling of the therapy by experts is done in demonstration sessions or on videotape, with verbatim transcripts, and by role playing.

Techniques to Further Self-knowledge

The distinction has been drawn by reviewers[8] and supervisors[1] between techniques to teach specific therapy skills and techniques to assist the therapist in his or her own growth and self-knowledge. Certainly, both must be important, and the balance between the two is a matter of degree and emphasis that should be thought out in the training of therapists at different levels of experience and in different settings. Important there is the fact that techniques, some of which are unique to family therapy supervision, have been developed to assist trainees in self-awareness, especially in their current and historical relationships to their families of origin.

Family photographs and home movies[9,10] are utilized as aids to enable family members, including trainees, to achieve more awareness about themselves in the context of their own family group. Family sculpting, i.e., choreographing critical family experiences in space without words, has been used as a training technique.[11] Bowen and his colleagues[12] have put much emphasis on the exploration of the trainee's relationship to his or her own *family of origin* in the supervisory process. The trainee is coached by the supervisor to make current contacts with the family of origin via letters and visits in order to experience and understand such phenomena as fusion, triangulation, etc., and to gradually achieve emotional distance from the process. Or the families of the trainees can be explored via genograms, with the theoretical framework bond on "invisible loyalties" with family system concepts and countertransference issues discussed.[13] Others[14] have suggested use of a multiple-family marathons for training therapists.

Self-awareness and personal psychotherapy need to be distinguished. Our view is that all trainees that plan to do therapy need to increase their self-awareness, but that psychotherapy—although always helpful—should not be mandatory except for those few trainees who are felt to have significant personal obstacles to practicing therapy themselves. It is interesting to note that informal surveys of family therapists show that most who have had personal therapy have had individual (rather than family!) therapy. Our view is that an experience of family therapy could be helpful (in addition to being at times necessary) in having the trainee experience and understand the therapeutic process from the other side.

EVALUATION OF TRAINING

Evaluation, both program evaluation and that of the individual trainee, is an essential component of any training program. Since family therapy has only recently emerged from its infancy, evaluation of training in this field is still rudimentary. Periodic, systematic evaluation of the teachers and the program seems desirable, as do meetings of the faculty and students for the purposes of criticism and feedback. Trainee evaluation can be done by viewing (and rating) videotapes comparing sessions done early in the program and those done toward the end of a training module. A useful trainee evaluation form is included for possible utilization (Figure 33-l).

CONTINUING EDUCATION

Some trainees might find it particularly valuable to use source material for more extended study in the clinical application of family therapy principles. For such students the authors make the following recommendations to supplement the suggestions for further reading already given in each chapter.

It is always useful to observe other therapists actually doing therapy, and a number of films are available. There are organizations that rent and sell actual clinical interviews of experienced family therapists, starting with Ackerman. It is useful to view interviews, as there is much in the therapy process that is not reducible to words such as style, nonverbal communication, micro-transactions, and gestalt therapeutic interaction. Both Haley/Hoffman[15] and Papp[16] have put together interesting books that contain transcripts with experienced family therapists. Discussions between the therapists and the authors in which the therapists are asked to explain the rationale for their interventions are included. Some books that describe the family approach of a particular therapist or school are also recommended for comparison. Satir,[17] Ackerman,[18] Minuchin,[19] Bowen,[20] Haley,[21] the M.R.I. approach[22] and the Systemic Approach[23] are classic examples.

A more extensive and systematic annotated bibliograpy of the field can be found in Glick, Weber, Rubinstein, and Patten[24] covering 1950-1979. Olson and colleagues[25] have covered the period from 1980-1983. There are also computer data bases that have been developed over the last few years that are available from any sophisticated medical/psychology library. Furthermore, a number of publishing houses (e.g., Guilford, Aspen, Brunner/Mazel and Grune & Stratton) have extensive collections of books and volumes on family therapy that have become available over the last decade. There are scholarly articles and research publications in family therapy journals and in journals of other disciplines such as psychiatry, clinical psychology, marriage and family counseling, sociology, nursing, and social work that are of interest to the family therapist. The trainee who wishes further experience can follow up with any of the current multitude of one-day to one-month workshops/conferences that are available all over the country. Furthermore, there are free standing institutes in many countries that offer more organized postgraduate curriculums.

CRITICAL CONTEXTUAL ISSUES

There are a series of contextual issues, some of which have been alluded to earlier in this chapter, that determine the viability of family therapy training within a given psychiatry residency program. Although family therapy training is required, the explosion of psychiatric knowledge increases competition for scarce

TRAINEE EVALUATION FORM FOR FAMILY THERAPY

Trainee: _____

Supervisor: _____

Dates of Supervising Period: _____

Type of therapy supervised:
(e.g. Individual Family Therapy, or Multifamily Therapy, etc.) _____

Frequency of Therapy: _____

Frequency of Supervision:
(e.g., each week for 1 hour in a group of 4, etc.) _____

The numbering system permits five choices. They can be defined as follows:
(5) Far exceeds reasonable expectations. Only a few trainees will merit this.
(4) Usually exceeds reasonable expectations, but is not really outstanding.
(3) Always meets reasonable expectations, but occasionally exceeds them. Most will merit this rating.
(2) In general meets reasonable expectations but occasionally falls short.
(1) Often falls short of reasonable expectations.
(0) Insufficient knowledge to make a judgment or not relevant.

Figure 33-1. Trainee Evaluation Form for Family Therapy Trainees. (Adapted from Payne Whitney Psychiatric Clinic's Resident Evaluation Form and from Family Trainee Evaluation Form, developed by Constantine LL: Designed experience: A multiple goal-directed training program in family therapy. Fam Proc 15:373-387, 1976. Reprinted with permission of Family Process, Inc.)

I. Overall Rating

II. Clinical Work

These descriptions represent the current thinking on the criteria for sucessful completion of our (Cornell University Medical College) training program in each of five areas of competence. In each area the first description applies to completion of the first year and the second description to completion of the entire program.

  A. Basic Knowledge

      1.Has acquired a basic fund of knowledge about how family systems work and can demonstrate an ability to make conceptual links between his or her own experiences, the experiences of others, and this kind of knowledge. Understands and can make use of basic family-systems concepts: process and structure, psycho-politics, dimensional analysis of process, boundary and entry phenomena.

      2. Has added to a basic fund of knowledge and integrated more elaborate and specialized concepts of how family systems function. Is familiar with more than one theoretical framework for understanding and affecting family systems. Can develop an idiographic (working) theory of a particular family and understands the uses of idiographic and nomothetic (general) theories of family.

  B. Generation and Use of Information:

      1. Has demonstrated an ability to take in, and make use of, information about the self and his or her professional behavior and performance, including openness to both approval and disapproval.

      2. Has developed skill in selecting and delivering feedback to others: understands factors of style, modality, timing, and context that affect a person's ability to take in and utilize feedback. Can participate productively in mutual peer reviews and supervision of his or her family work.

  C. Interpersonal Flexibility:

      1. Can identify salient aspects of his or her interpersonal style, especially preferences for particular psychopolitical positions and maneuvers and is aware of his or her tendencies toward stuck arrangements.

      2. Has taken specific steps to increase his or her interpersonal flexibility and has demonstrated increased psychopolitical flexibility in both therapy and peer group contexts.

Figure 33-1 (continued)

D. Self-Awareness and Use of Self:
  1. Has increased awareness of ways in which his or her self and personal family history are a part of present work as a therapist and other interpersonal process. Can relate seminar experiences and family-system concepts to personal family experience. Has been able to share and make use of personal history in the learning process. Has revealed a capacity for change in some significant area.
  2. Has demonstrated increased awareness of his or her self and immediate experience of self and can use this information in the therapy situation. Has made use of personal experience and family history in therapy and learning processes. Is evolving an effective personal style of therapy that includes a presentation of self or style of entry compatible with being a therapist — that is, conducive to alliance formation, not excessively aggressive, critical, etc. Has gained insight into how his or her psychopolitical patterns originated and how these are played out in the present, especially family and interpersonal contexts that tend to lead to replay of old patterns.
E. Inverviewing and Intervention:
  1. Has acquired a basic knowledge of the interview process and salient issues in initial interviews, including the interviewer's and family's anxiety, the entry process, the information of alliances, etc. Knows some of the strategic moves he or she should be able to make to gather information about the workings of a family system and to bring about change. Has developed skill as an observer of process and can organize his or her observations, in a meaningful and useful way.
  2. Has demonstrated an ability to conduct family interviews and to execute effectively therapeutic manipulations in live situations. Can evaluate a real family system and develop an idiographic theory or map of the family. Has shown an ability to plan evaluation and therapy strategically, making use of both idiographic and nomothetic theories to devise focused interventions. Has used a variety of tools and techniques of evaluation and intervention.

Figure 33-1 (continued)

III. *Supervisory Relationship*
    A. Ability to accept and utilize criticism   0 1 2 3 4 5
    B. Capacity to learn from supervisor   0 1 2 3 4 5
    C. Establishment of collaborative relationship   0 1 2 3 4 5

IV. Are there any questions about this trainee's integrity or emotional stability? This question is extremely important. YES _____ NO_____

V. *Special Areas*
Comment on special talents, nature, and degree of character interference with learning or administration.

VI. *Additional Comments and Suggestions*
VII. *Trainee's Response to Evaluation*
    Include areas in which disagreement occurred.
Trainee's Signature _____ Date _____
[This indicates that this evaluation was seen by the trainee and discussed with that person.]

Supervisor's Signature _____ Date _____

Figure 33-1 (continued)

resident time, and the current biologic focus of American psychiatry has resulted in decreased emphasis for all types of psychotherapy. Within a given program, the views of the residency committee are crucial. Those committees that view family therapy training as central tend to augment the amount of time devoted to family therapy training in a particular program. Over years, however, the feedback of residents (both in terms of their interest and their evaluation of current training) tends to augment/decrease the focus on family training. There are a series of controversial issues concerning the specifics of integrating family training into residencies that have been explicated in detail by one of the authors.[26] These include controversies about the definition of the field, elective versus required teaching, curriculum context, and when, where, and who should teach family therapy in this training context. The interested reader is referred to this source.

CONCLUSION

At the end of a family therapy training program, the trainee's education is actually just beginning. In a rapidly changing field such as family therapy, an individual must begin a program of lifelong self-education based on a continual awareness of the literature and course work, and on the need to evaluate his or her own work, to entertain new ideas, and to discard old ones. As obvious as this may seem, it is the inculcation of these principles that identifies the inspired and skillful clinician, teacher, or researcher.

SUGGESTIONS FOR FURTHER READINGS

Clarkin JF and Glick I: Supervision of family therapy. In Blumenfield M (Ed): Applied Supervision in Psychotherapy. New York: Grune and Stratton, 1982.

Clarkin JF: Family and marital therapy. In Sachs MH, Sledge WH, and Rubinton P (Eds): **Core Readings in Psychiatry: An Annotated Guide to the Literature**. New York: Praeger, 1984.

Sugarman S: Integrating family therapy training into psychiatric residency training programs and policy issues and alternatives. Fam Proc 23:23-32, 1984.
  The best up-to-date discussion of some of the major issues involved in family therapy training.

REFERENCES

1. Haley J: Problem-Solving Therapy. San Francisco:Jossey-Bass, 1976

2. Cleghorn JM and Levin S: Training family therapists by setting learning objectives. Am J Orthopsychiatry 43:439-446, 1973

3. Tomm KM and Wright LM: Training in family therapy: Perceptual, conceptual and executive skills. Fam Proc 18:227-250, 1979

4. Flomenhaft K and Carter R: Family therapy training: Program and outcome. Fam Proc 16:211-218, 1977

5. Clarkin JF and Glick ID: Supervision of family therapy. In Blumenfield M (Ed): Applied Supervision in Psychotherapy. New York:Grune & Stratton, 1982, pp 87-106

6. Montalvo B: Aspects of live supervision. Fam Proc 12:343-359, 1973

7. Bockus F: Couple Therapy. New York: Jason Aronson, 1980

8. Liddle HA and Halpin RJ: Family therapy training and supervision literature: A comparative review. J Marr Fam Counsel 4:77-98, 1978

9. Anderson C and Malloy E: Family photographs in treatment and training. Fam Proc 15:259-264, 1976

10. Kaslow F and Friedman J: Utilization of family photos and movies in family therapy. J Marr Fam Counsel 3:19-25, 1977

11. Papp P: Family choreography. In Guerin P (Ed): Family Therapy. New York: Gardner Press, 1976, pp 465-479

12. Guerin P and Fogarty T: Study your own family. In Ferber A, Mendelsohn M, and Napier A (Eds): The Book of Family Therapy. New York: Science House, 1972

13. Boszormenyi-Nagy I and Spark G: Invisible Loyalties. New York: Harper and Row, 1975

14. Goldenberg I, Stier S, and Preston T: The use of a multiple family marathon as a teaching device. J Marr Fam Counsel 1:343-349, 1975

15. Haley J and Hoffman L: Techniques of Family Therapy. New York: Basic Books, 1967

16. Papp P: The family who had all the answers. In Papp P (Ed): Family Therapy: Full Length Case Studies. New York: Gardner Press, 1977, pp 143-165

17. Satir V: Conjoint Family Therapy: A Guide to Theory and Technique. Palo Alto, CA: Science & Behavior Books, 1967

18. Ackerman NW: Treating the Troubled Family. New York: Basic Books, 1966

19. Minuchin S: Families and Family Therapy. Cambridge, MA: Harvard University Press, 1974

20. Bowen M: Family Therapy in Clinical Practice. New York: Jason Aronson, 1978

21. Haley J and Hoffman L: Techniques of Family Therapy. New York: Basic Books, 1967

22. Boden AM: The interactional view: Family therapy approaches of the mental research institute. In Gurman AS and Kniskern DP (Eds): Handbook of Family Therapy. New York: Brunner/Mazel, 1981, pp 267-309

23. Selvini-Palazolli M, Cecchin G, Prata G, et al.: Paradox and Counterparadox. A New Model in the Therapy of the Family Schizophrenic Transaction. New York: Jason Aronson, 1978

24. Glick ID, Weber D, Rubinstein D, and Patten J: Family Therapy and Research: An Annotated Bibliography of Articles, Books, Videotapes and Films Published 1950-1979 (2nd Ed). New York: Grune & Stratton, 1982

25. Olson DH and Markoff R (Eds): Inventory of Marriage and Family Literature, Volume 9. Beverly Hills, CA: Sage Publications, 1983

26. Sugarman S: Integrating family therapy training into psychiatry residency programs: Policy issues and alternatives. Fam Proc 23:23-32, 1984

Section X

Finishing Touches

There are several important issues that need to be discussed that don't fit neatly into our previous sections. They include a consideration of the ethical issues inherent in practicing family therapy, a related topic—informed consent—and a review of the meanings implicit in the issue of *who* in the family *pays* for therapy. We close, appropriately, with a discussion of professional issues, i.e., standards, humanistic qualities needed, and the question of whose responsibility it is for change.

As a final touch, we think it is important to illustrate some of the more important didactic concepts that we have presented throughout the text. Accordingly, Chapter 35 presents excerpts from an actual case example illustrating the process of treatment of a family over 16 months, including a ten-year follow-up.

Shiva and Parvati (?) Veined sandstone, Baphuon Style, Late 11th Century A.D., Khmei.
Courtesy of Asian Art Museum of San Francisco, the Avery Brundage Collection.

34
Ethical, Financial, and Professional Issues in Family Therapy

OBJECTIVES

- To be aware of the professional issues inherent in family therapy practice
- To be aware of the ethical issues as one practices family therapy
- To be able to utilize informed consent procedures
- To be aware of the family implications of "who pays the bill"

ETHICAL ISSUES INHERENT IN FAMILY THERAPY

A number of authors have enumerated the ethical issues that are involved in doing family therapy, some of which overlap with ethical issues of psychotherapy in general and others that seem unique to the family method.[1,2] For openers, let us realize that when the therapist takes a family perspective, it implies an ethical decision.

There are three important ethical issues in family therapy: (1) whose interests should the family therapist serve, (2) what position should the family therapist take regarding secrets, and (3) what position to take regarding harmful effects of one member on another in the family.

Commonly in most clinical situations, the interests of each member of the family are not the same. Boszormenyi-Nagy and Spark[3] emphasize the contractual obligations and accountability between persons in the multigenerations of a family. The family therapist in this view is uniquely attuned to the well-being of each of the family members (who will be affected by the treatment process) via their deep-rooted relatedness over time and through many generations. Relational ethics is concerned with the balance of equitable fairness between people. To gauge the balance of fairness in the here-and-now, and across time and generations, one (both the family members and the family therapist) must consider both one's own interests and the interests of each of the family members. The basic issue is one of *equitability,* i.e., everyone is entitled to have his or her welfare and interests considered in a way that is fair to the related interests of other family members. In essence, the therapist "chooses sides" and often will be the advocate for the weakest person in the system, e.g., the identified patient or a child.[4]

In family therapy it may not be clear as to who the patient is. The symptomatic family member is often thought by the family to be the patient, but the family therapist reframes the situation by designating the whole family system as the patient. The point for the family therapist is to be aware of the ethical issue in implying that non-symptomatic family members are patients, when they originally did not see themselves as such or explicitly contract for treatment. It is a given of the modality.

Because family therapy often involves meetings with all or most of the family members present, the family therapist may be in the position of urging certain non-symptomatic individuals to attend sessions against their wishes. This may involve urging both resistant adults and minors to attend. This situation may become particularly troublesome if a previously non-symptomatic individual comes to family therapy and develops symptoms.

There may be times when it is difficult to decide whether a therapeutic action or suggestion may be helpful for one individual, but not helpful or even temporarily harmful to another individual. In their concern for the healthy functioning of the system as a whole, therapists may inadvertently ignore what is best for one individual. An ethical issue is "who" should make the decision. Should it be the therapist or should it be the family? And how much information should they be given on the pros and cons of modalities. Our bias is to negotiate and give the family all the relevant information so that they can make the most informed decision possible.

Some strategies and techniques of family intervention, e.g., paradoxical injunctions, are seen by many as manipulative of the patient(s) and therefore unethical by their nature. One can only shudder to think of a scenario in which a patient is told (paradoxically) that it is a wonder he or she is not more depressed.

Instead of using the "paradox" to cheer up (that is, disobey the therapist), the depressed person feels more demoralized and suicides. Perhaps this is less an ethical issue than knowing when certain issues are contraindicated. Again, it is the responsibility of the therapist to be aware of the risks and benefits of each intervention.

In Chapter 15 we discussed "family secrets." Let us return to that issue in the context of ethical concerns. By the nature of the work, the family therapist is often privy to both secrets and to potentially, and actually harmful, effects of one family member upon other members. This ranges from incest, to physical abuse of spouse or child, to harmful sequelae of divorce on children and spouses, to harmful effects of depression in a parent upon the children via the impact of the depression on the parenting skills and behavior. For example, clinicians are legally obliged to protect identified third parties from dangers posed by patients. A number of courts have held that this situation is one in which a breach of confidentiality is necessary. Gutheil[5] gives the clinical example of a patient who seriously threatened a parent during therapy. The situation was used to inform the parent in a therapeutic and conflict-diffusing way.

INFORMED CONSENT

Similar to other psychotherapy formats, family therapy does not require informed consent from the family before initiating treatment. Our bias is to inform the family of possible outcomes of treatment both good and "bad," including the possible deterioration of one or more family members during the treatment. It seems quite appropriate and necessary that the therapist clearly state and negotiate the treatment goals with the family so they can make an informed judgment about their desire to embark upon the therapy. The negotiation should be done both at the onset and throughout the therapy.

The family members should also be informed in general as to the fact that individual secrets may become the business of the therapy and that individual privacy may be questioned.

More importantly, we agree with Gutheil et al.[5] that the sharing of uncertainty through the informed consent procedure can be a focal point in building a therapeutic alliance. They point out that, "Increasingly, patients and families who experience tragic disappointment in their expectations . . . attempt to assuage their grief, helplessness, and despair by blaming . . . the physicians." This sharing can be done by understanding the origins of the fantasies of *certainty*, empathizing with unrealistic wishes, and by weaning the family from the fantasy of certainty.

FINANCIAL ISSUES

Who pays the bill is relatively simple in individual treatment with adult patients, but in marital and family work the issue is more complicated. The ethical issues of who pays the bill become especially tense in marital treatment of spouses in conflict. For example, if both spouses have insurance coverage from their respective employers, whose insurance should be used? This becomes most delicate when the spouses have conflicting views of the matter for any number of reasons, e.g., "I don't want my secretary seeing the insurance forms," "Using my insurance makes me the patient," etc. As with many concrete issues of conflict, the family therapist should approach the matter with a sense of fairness and making clear that there is a system problem by having each spouse pay one half of the bill.

PROFESSIONAL ISSUES

In order to protect the public from untrained, incompetent, and/or unethical family therapists and family intervention, there must be a clear delineation of the competencies needed to do family therapy. In addition, ways of teaching and assessing the presence (or absence) of these competencies must be developed. Competencies of family therapists and the methods of training to achieve them, are discussed further in Chapter 33.

Some of the qualities that we think are important for the family therapist, in addition to those required to do other therapies include:

- Tolerance of family fighting
- Comfortableness with family secrets
- Ability to adapt to different technical models or mix different "schools" together in a treatment package
- Interest in "cultural" issues
- Ability to be active and directive

In addition, we have a strong bias that in the training of family therapists, there should be attention paid to the humanistic qualities of *integrity, respect,* and *compassion* for patients and their families. Our point is that although assessment of such qualities is difficult, guidelines for a standardized approach to assessment are now available and can be used by training programs. Similarly, Lask,[6] in discussing the *responsibility for change* has made an impassioned plea for a better balance between the role of the therapist and the role of the family. He writes,

Family therapists seem to go to extraordinary lengths in their attempts to help their clients, taking on the most apparently unhelpable families, working at any hours that families demand, using wonderfully impressive high technology equipment and large numbers of people behind one-way screens to provide teams, supervisors, and even "choruses". The term resistance has become a dirty word; to say a family is impossible is a heresy! We are expected to devise strategies to help families overcome their natural disinclination to change, however strong that may be.

We agree. Our bias is that for successful long-term outcome, both family and therapist(s) must play a part. We may, for example, recognize a family's need to be cared for, or an inability to make decisions, but it is not our responsibility to take over in these respects, but rather to help the family recognize its difficulties and start seeking solutions. While therapists may decide to accept responsibility for providing a setting, establishing and maintaining a therapeutic alliance, and offering observations and suggestions, those who take considerably greater responsibility for change are diluting what energy and motivation the family might have, as well as being likely candidates for burnout.

SUGGESTIONS FOR FURTHER READINGS

Wendorf DJ and Wendorf RJ: A systemic view of family therapy ethics. (Commentary by Boszormenyi-Nagy I and rejoinder by Wendorf DJ and Wendorf RJ). Fam Proc 24:443-460, 1985.

> *Informative discussion of family therapy ethics including a commentary by Boszormenyi-Nagy.*

REFERENCES

1. Morrison JK, Layton D, and Newman J: Ethical conflict in decision making. In Hansen JC and L'Abate L (Eds): Values, Ethics, Legalities and the Family Therapist. Rockville, MD: Aspen Systems, 1982
2. Bodin AM: Family therapy. In Karasu RB (Ed): The Psychiatric Therapies. Washington, DC: American Psychiatric Association, 1984, pp 441-481
3. Boszormenyi-Nagy I and Spark G: Invisible Loyalties: Reciprocity in Intergenerational Family Therapy. New York: Harper and Row, 1973
4. Boszormenyi-Nagy I and Ulrich K: Contextual family therapy. In Gurman A and Kniskern D (Eds): Handbook of Family Therapy. New York: Brunner/Mazel, 1981, pp 159-186
5. Gutheil TG, Bursztajn H, and Brodsky A: Malpractice prevention through the sharing of uncertainty, informed consent and the therapeutic alliance. N Engl J Med 311:49-51, 1984
6. Lask B: Whose responsibility? J Fam Ther 8:205-206, 1986

Holy Family with Saint Joan by Anthony Van Dyck. Courtesy of the Collection of the
Phoenix Art Museum.

577

35

A Case Transcript of a Family Treated Over a Sixteen-Month Period

OBJECTIVES

- To give examples of types of processes that occur during the course of the family treatment
- To give examples of the kinds of interventions that the therapist can make
- To discuss the rationales behind these interventions

INTRODUCTION

Many trainees find an actual case transcript useful in helping to bring to life the didactic concepts discussed earlier. In this chapter we present excerpts from actual family diagnostic and treatment sessions that lasted once a week for 16 months; also included is a 10-year follow-up.

An introduction to each segment, then the transcript, and finally comments will be presented. The transcript is from a movie made by one of the authors and is available for use in conjunction with this chapter.[1] It can also be compared to transcripts of parts of cases published by other family therapists.[2,3] Furthermore,

578

there is a book devoted to 11 excellent, full-length case studies of family therapy done by experienced therapists with a step-by-step account of their thoughts about the cases and their reasons for what they did.[4] In a like vein others have described their cases in depth, alternating transcript with explanation, session by session.[5]

BACKGROUND INFORMATION ABOUT THE FAMILY

This transcript is based on treatment of a family over a 16-month period. It demonstrates family techniques (including videotape playbacks) and problems that arise during therapy, and gives an overview of the course of a family treatment from beginning to end.

The family includes Mr. S., age 50, a minister; Mrs. S., age 48, a housewife who also plays the organ at her husband's church; a daughter, age 18, who is away attending college; and the identified patient, the 25-year-old son, Bill. Bill is an unemployed college dropout with a history of two prior acute schizophrenic episodes, the first one at age 16. Following his third decompensation, he was treated as an inpatient in a university hospital. After his discharge from the hospital, the primary treatment was family therapy. Two aspects of the case, which was managed in the early 1960s, illustrate how the field has progressed in the interim. First, antipsychotic medication was not used following discharge; the use of such medication for the treatment of schizophrenia was more controversial than it is today. Second, more psychoeducation would be given to the patient and family, especially in the beginning of the family therapy, concerning schizophrenia, its causes, symptoms, prognosis, and responsiveness to stress, including that in the home environment. However, many of the mediating goals (clarification of family patterns of interaction, improved family communication, keeping the son out of the marital difficulties, improving the marital coalition) and techniques of family intervention would be the same today.

These sessions demonstrate treatment techniques used in working with a family in which the identified patient has a psychotic illness. The treatment involves a family that is in the empty-nest phase of development, in which the offspring have reached chronological adulthood.

The transcript that follows highlights segments from certain sessions during the course of this therapy.

SEGMENT 1: ONSET OF THE TREATMENT

Segment 1: Introduction

In the initial session, communication from individual family members is directed mostly to the therapist, rather than among themselves. This may be related to the fact that the family often attempts to force the therapist to be the judge. The therapist goes along with this in the first session, using the rationale of the side-taking function (Chapter 12) and serving as a role model for the father and son in dealing with the mother. Other family therapists might use the style of encouraging members to talk to one another. This would be a matter of the therapist's choice.

Segment 1: Transcript

Therapist: In our initial consultation we ended up talking about what we would do for the future in terms of treatment for the family, Bill in particular. After reviewing the entire case and my discussion with all of you, it is my feeling that Bill's problems are very much related to the problems of the family, and, to best treat him, we should treat the entire family as a unit in family therapy. That is, we would meet every week for 50 minutes. I think from 3:40 to 4:30 every Wednesday, if that's okay with you.

Mr. S: Well, it is. It would suit us if we could meet a little earlier—we have engagements—she and I both on Wednesday nights; but *(pauses)* we're going to work with you at the time that you best feel.

Therapist: Okay. We've had a couple of family sessions now, and the only rule I am going to set is that we all meet together. I'll be working with you— sometimes very much involved in one discussion, other times I'll let you carry it—you're the family and you have to make the decisions. And the main thing I'll be trying to do is to make sure that everybody gets a chance to talk. What we're working for is better understanding and communication, as well as the goals that you talked about last week. Do you recall them—what you wanted to get out of treatment?

Mr. S: Well I don't know if I recall just how we stated them, but I believe we said that, first of all, we wanted to help Bill to get into his problems and disturbances and then . . .

Therapist: Help Bill *into* his problems, did you say?

Mr. S: To get into his problems. I mean discover what the basic difficulties are, and I think probably we said something about helping him with the drinking problem, which may be due to these difficulties; and, if I remember right, we were going to try to improve the entire family situation.

Therapist: Uh-huh. And Bill, you also had some specific goals you wanted. Do you know what they were?

Bill: (looking down at the floor and not at the therapist) Well, I just wanted to relieve my mind a little bit somehow. During the last few days and all of today I've been thinking that's really the worst thing there is now that I'm getting all these meanings out of things and I just somehow know maybe that I don't read things right. I used to do this even . . . just two or three years ago back at school; I'd just get off on some of these things, *(referring to his paranoid thoughts)* and . . . *(pauses)*

Therapist: One of the things, one of the goals you had, was to work on some of these thoughts and meanings. You also wanted to do something very concrete, as I recall.

Bill: Yeah, so I can get over this and maybe live.

Therapist: Live, meaning what? You said you wanted to get out . . .

Bill: Get out and go to work, and ...

Therapist: Right, get out and work. Okay, that's what we decided and that's what we ought to aim toward: to get you out of the home and to get you working.

Mrs. S (to therapist): We're willing to work with you to achieve these goals.

Segment 1: Comment

In Segment 1 we see that the therapist: (1) conveys the idea to the family that the problems of the identified patient have something to do with the entire family; (2) establishes rapport with the family; (3) explains the goals of treatment; (4) begins to point out the interaction processes involving the identified patient and the other members of the family (e.g., the comment about "helping" Bill, the identified patient, to get "into" his problems); and (5) begins to establish ground rules for treatment (such as that the family members all meet together and that they all have a chance to talk).

In the initial session one observes both the family and the identified patient and notices that the patient is paranoid. He covers his face with his hands because he fears other people are talking about him and laughing at him. It is also revealed that he drinks when he begins to become delusional. At present, he is sleeping in the same bed with his parents, because they claim they are worried about his behavioral problems (when, in fact, they fear intimacy with each other).

SEGMENT 2: HISTORY TAKING (3 Weeks Later)
Segment 2: Introduction

Segment 2 illustrates techniques of obtaining a family history (Chapter 6). There are two main objectives: (1) to obtain factual historical material and (2) to clarify patterns of family interaction.

This segment also shows the effects of the interaction between the parents on the identified patient. While the parents fight, the patient holds his head and leans back in his chair. Mrs. S.'s role and the patterns of family interaction in general are beginning to change; the son is beginning to take a prominent role in the family's communication patterns.

Segment 2: Transcript

Therapist: All right, from Bill's comment earlier . . . he commented on a demand. Apparently there was some demand, though . . .

Mrs. S: Uh-huh. No, there was *not* a demand. In fact, I think I'm going to say this right now before Bill, although I don't want to worry him with it. We had tried to hold back from demanding, if you want to call it *demanding;* it wouldn't be *demanding,* ah . . . frankly, I think we've held back too much by trying to keep down any religious pressure that may be caused by his being a preacher's son. Sometimes I think we have held back too much and sometimes I think we've hurt Bill by holding back. . . . *(Family begins arguing and Bill holds his head and leans back against his chair)*

Therapist: This is a real . . . this is a real loaded. . . .

Mrs. S: If you wanted to go to Sunday school, you went. If you wanted to go to church, you went.

Bill: I never missed.

Mrs. S: No, you never missed but . . .

Bill: . . . except when I was going to college.

Therapist: Hold it a second. This sounds like a real loaded issue *(laughter),* something we're going to come to once we get a little more history—that of the question of your going into the ministry or even going to Sunday school. We'll get to that. *(This issue is later discussed at another session.)* Now, let's see, you were talking about a problem in the marriage. how did you finally work it out?

Mrs. S: Well, now, doctor. There wasn't . . . really wasn't . . . a problem except naturally. . . . They were going to sort of complain, which is natural.

Therapist: Uh-huh.

Mrs. S: I know they expected me to be so-and-so, and I just wasn't going to do it.

Therapist: You say "they," who are you . . .

Mrs. S: Preacher's wife or no preacher's wife.

Therapist: . . . whom are you referring to?

Mrs. S: The people, church members, I wasn't going to do it.

Therapist (to Mr. S): How did you feel about that? It was your . . .

Mrs. S: You know. I mean, I wasn't desperate . . . I was . . .

Therapist: It was his congregation, right?

Mrs. S: . . . the little things that are asked of you behind the scenes. Frankly, if they bother you, I think you ought to say what you think.

Therapist: Well, how did you feel about that and what did you finally do about it?

Mr. S: Well, I don't know if I exactly get into what she's saying . . .

Mrs. S: Well, I mean that's a little . . . I mean it wasn't a problem. It was just that he was talking about us talking together about my role as a preacher's wife.

Mr. S: Well, actually . . .

Mrs. S: And he wouldn't dare complain to his members. . .

Mr. S: Ah, we didn't discuss it. . .

Therapist: Wait a minute. Your're both talking at one time.

Mr. S: We didn't discuss her role as a minister's wife a great deal. I had told her from the very beginning (and have continued to do so through the years) that she should just do what she wants to do without feeling obligated to the congregation because they're not . . . they're not paying her salary; they only pay mine. I work, although she does play the organ at the church on a voluntary basis.

Therapist: I think I'd like to pause a minute to go back to get a little history, so we have some kind of foundation on which to talk. I'm kind of an outsider, and I'd like to go back a little bit since we're all here in kind of family. Do you think you can tell me how it was that the two of you met?

Mr. S: Well, actually our families lived in the same community for a time when we were growing up. Of course, I'm nine years older than she is. My father was a Baptist minister in the community and her father was a Methodist minister, and, of course, I noticed her as a little girl, but not with any ideas that we'd ever meet. Some years later, however, we did meet when I went to the town where she and her family were then living. I started to court her, and then I went off to school in Texas but would come back occasionally to see her. Things kept moving along and in one form or another we became engaged.

Therapist: What was that form?

Mr. S: Well, I suppose when we were engaged there was some uncertainties about our relationship. Another man came into the picture and she was considerably undecided. I think . . . maybe she wasn't entirely settled when we married. Of course, I took the position that a plain heart never won a fair lady and pursued the thing until I got her.

Therapist (To Mrs. S): "Fair Lady," how did you feel about . . .

Mrs. S: Well, I taught with this other man, and, since we lived in the same boarding house, we were thrown together very closely. And if I had wanted to marry him, I—and this is not bragging, it's just facts—I could have married him several times, but I did not. I want that understood. I wasn't planning to marry him, although he certainly had a good personality and was a nice person. We were both teachers in the school, but I got together with him because my husband was going to school in another state and coming home very little. If you live in the same boarding house with a person, you will most likely be together some; you can't help it—even if it is only at meals. And it did cause some conflict, yes, in my relationship with my future husband. But, even if I had wanted to marry this other man, I would have held back. At that time, I didn't think it was right to break engagements . . . I feel very differently now. I am older now; and I have thought things over. I think about young people these days; if they are engaged and find that they are not in love enough to marry then they should break the engagement, rather than marry that person and not live congenially. But at that time . . .

Bill: So you feel like you should have broken the engagement?

Mrs. S: No, I am not saying that, I am not saying . . .

Therapist: Excuse me, if you don't mind my talking. You thought she was saying that . . .

Mrs. S: I'm not saying that . . .

Bill: . . . that she should have broken the engagement with Daddy.

Segment 2: Comment

In this segment we see some indication of the difficulties existing between the husband and wife. (See Chapters 3 and 5 for a discussion of these issues). The mastering of certain family tasks (especially those of developing and maintaining a marital and parental coalition and those of rearing and enculturating the offspring) is a source of contention between the spouses that apparently has never before been discussed. Mrs. S.'s unresolved feelings about her own role as a minister's wife, as well as that of a parent, seem to be related to her statements that perhaps she and her husband did not provide enough religious grounding for the identified patient. The therapist senses that this is an important issue, but one that may be too explosive to discuss this early in the therapy.

A core problem is the relationship between the parents. There is a major disturbance in the marital coalition, which is being worked out through the son. The parents are using the son's problems as a means of holding their marriage together.

SEGMENT 3: EARLY-MIDDLE STAGE OF TREATMENT (2 Months Later)

Segment 3: Introduction

The family has been in treatment for two months. The inappropriateness of the son's sleeping in the parental bedroom has been discussed, and the son has now moved back to his own room. The next objective was to get the son out of the parents' home and into a work situation. Encouraging increased parental communication led to a major shift in the family system. Bill eventually moved 200 miles away from the family and began working.

In this segment Bill begins to see his symptoms as foreign rather than as part of him.

Segment 3: Transcript

Bill: I saw the vocational therapist today. . . . And I always had difficulty not being able to read into people what I think they're thinking and this and that . . . you know. In a way he has sort of a pensive look and I kinda read into him that he's thinking, you know, that, ah, "Heavens, he's really gonna have a hard time finding a job." *(Laughs)* You know, he had a . . ., but I have a tendency to read a great deal into what people are thinking, and this and that and the other thing. I mean, you know, just like I told you . . .

Therapist: What did he say?

Bill: Oh, he didn't say that, ah, but . . .

Therapist: I assumed that . . .

Bill: No, no I asked him—he looked, you know, rather pensive, ah, a little bit thoughtful and somber. He's very nice, very somber and all, and sort of kindly and I don't know ; and I just got the impression that he might think, you know . . . but he said that . . . we talked in terms of short-range plans and long-range plans and the idea of having maybe a short-term job.

Segment 3: Comment

This short segment highlights the crucial shift in the family; that of the son moving out of the home and getting a job. The therapist lets the identified patient do the talking and is there only to support him in case he (or the family) back-slides by trying to sabotage his job plans.

SEGMENT 4: MIDDLE STAGE OF TREATMENT (Eight Months Later)

Segment 4: Introduction

It is now eight months into therapy. The family has accepted the central no-tion of family therapy; that is, the problems of the identified patient are related to the problems of the family. Bill's symptoms have decreased as other problems in the family have been brought to the fore. At this point core issues involving the in-timate relationship between the couple can again be approached.

In this segment the marital couple are seen alone. The decision to do this was made only after a great deal of preliminary groundwork, the most important of which was separating the son from the parents and establishing rapport with the parents to reassure them that therapy would not make their relationship worse.

The couple, who have not been away in ten years, is talking about taking a vacation together. Mrs. S. says that she does not want to be alone with her husband because it will mean that they may have to have sexual relations. It has taken eight months for this subject to be brought up, albeit in disguised form.

Segment 4: Transcript

Mrs. S: Disgusted, just disgusted! And I have felt that, just disgusted. And that's all there is to it, just absolutely disgusted with the whole thing. And I thought many times that he was positively acting childish, and I mean it, child-ish. Because we are plenty old enough not to get sexually frustrated and not to get all upset because of one point.

Mr. S: We're not into . . .

Mrs. S: Yes, it is important. I don't think it ought to *frustrate* people.

Therapist: I don't think frustration is the issue here; the issue is can the two of you . . .

Mrs. S: Well, he's said he's gotten frustrated.

Therapist: He also said that he wants to be close to you.

Mrs. S: Well, he's got to show up a little better himself, and I'm not blaming him.

Therapist: The two of you both have to make the effort.

Mrs S: The two, yeah, I know it's the two.

Therapist: The two of you have to work at it. And if he's going to show some feeling toward you . . .

Bill who has been outside, enters

Bill: Do you want to see me at all today?

Therapist: Yes, we do, and I'll be with you in just a second. You can wait outside.

Bill: Fine, I'll be right here. *(leaves)*

Therapist: It's got to work both ways, and I think this is very crucial to all three of you. And I think you have to try it. Even if you don't want to, you've got to.

Mrs. S: I'll just have to close my mind, and that's that.

Therapist: Well, I don't think you do because I think you have indicated in these sessions . . .

Mrs. S: I'll just have to close my mind.

Therapist: You have indicated that you have a great many positive feelings for him.

Mrs. S: Hmmmm. I do have great concern for him. If I didn't, I'd have left him . . .

Therapist: Right.

Mrs. S: Yes.

Therapist: So I think you know that this can be tried. And you've got some time to think it over now. What did you decide about the vacation?

Mr. S: We'd decided to go but then she changed her mind. Later, with persuasion and consideration, she decided to go. We had planned to go Friday, but she was afraid that today's session would get her too upset and she would not want to go after all.

Therapist: Has everybody survived so far? Are you all . . .

Mrs S: We're going to take you along.

Therapist (bantering): I could use a trip to Florida. *(Laughter)*

Mrs. S: Not because you're a doctor but just to have somebody else along. It might be good if we did have someone else along . . .

Therapist: I think it's a good decision for just you two to go.

Therapist (authoritatively): Look, go away, go to FLorida, have a good time. As your doctor, I strongly recommend that you try this.

Mrs. S: Well, frankly, I'll have to close my mind to any sexual overtures: I mean that.

Therapist: Well, try to enjoy being with one another.

Mrs. S: All right. I'll just have to close my mind and be a . . .

Therapist: Let's have Bill come in and let's . . .

Mrs. S: . . . be a machine

Therapist: Let's continue to discuss the same thing we've been talking about.

Mrs. S: Be a machine.

Therapist: I don't think you'll be such a machine if you truly love him. Allow for the intimacy to develop between you.

Bill enters

Bill: Well, have you said anything relevant about me?

Mrs. S: Have you seen Mr. Byron *(the vacational therapist)?*

Bill: No.

Therapist: Will anybody answer his question?

Bill: Has there been any discussion having to do with me?

Mr. S: Ah . . .

Mrs. S: Mainly with us.

Mr. S: The discussion was about us. We feel our relationship can be improved and that you have done a great deal on your part already. What we need to do is to . . .

Bill: As I came down the hall, heard vaguely something about how I could slide back or something like that. Did you say that? I could just vaguely hear something. *(Puts his hands to his head)*

Mrs S: We said that we wanted you to feel better, and that if we did better, you would feel better.

Therapist: Well, I also said the opposite, though.

Bill: What's that?

Mr. S: That if we didn't do better, you could slip back. That's what he said.

Bill: Is that what he said?

Mrs. S: And feel worse.

Bill: I thought I heard you say something like that.

Therapist: Well, I think you know that.

Bill: Yeah, yeah, I know, that's not surprising. Well, was anything else relevant said about me?

Therapist: What do you have to say about yourself that would be relevant. *(Laughter)*

Bill: I don't know. I just feel that somebody is always talking about me when I'm not around. I'm always, always . . .

Mr. S: Always what?

Bill: I'm just always suspicious toward people who are talking when I'm not around.

Mrs. S: You're not talked about as much as you used to be. You're not quite the center of the conversation as you used to be, because, for one thing, you're feeling better.

Bill: Well, I wasn't feeling good yesterday, nor do I today. I'm just really tired out. I worked 11½ hours yesterday and I am really exhausted. And I have been hyperventilating, too, a whole lot of the last two days. Boy, that hyperventilation can really . . . *(Long pause)*

Mr. S: It's an out-of-condition body.

Bill: I have felt very dizzy all day and, yeah, just bad, just that I feel tired, that my face is hot and so on.

Therapist: Your complaints are the complaints of a hard-working man. . . .

Segment 4: Comment

At each point the therapist has to make critical decisions as to whether to intervene at all, and if so, in what way. The therapist must decide as best he can, during the onrush of the session, what the main themes and goals seem to be and how best to deal with them. Important issues recur continually. The experienced therapist does not worry that something important has been missed; there will always be another opportunity to deal with it later.

Since this was the first time in ten years that this couple was going away alone together, it was clearly an important item for them. Some therapists would have dealt with the vacation issue differently. Individual stylistic and attitudinal factors will specifically influence the manner in which the therapist intervenes and responds to a particular situation. Another therapist, for example, might have accepted the wife's offer to go with her on the couple's vacation in the hope of eliciting a reaction from the husband.

The other crucial intervention comes at the end of the segment when the therapist encourages the concept of Bill's working *in spite* of his symptoms. This is done in front of the parents, who in the past would have reinforced his dependency on them.

SEGMENT 5: VIDEO PLAYBACK
(10 Months Later)

Segment 5: Introduction

This segment illustrates how cognitive and verbal changes can occur as a result of behavioral changes. There has been a major shift in the family configuration. The family members are now able to talk about how "we weren't much of a family," the identified patient describes how he sent out "double messages," and they all talk about the ways in which their actions affect each other. The focus has also shifted from the identified patient to Mr. and Mrs. S., espeically the latter. Bill is not absolutely quiet, as in the first segment, or hostile and negativistic, as in the second segment, but is showing more emotion, is better in touch with reality, and is experiencing more anxiety.

In this segment videotape playback is used with moderate success to try to break through the mother's denial and projection. Bill is commenting on what he observed during the playback of the previous session.

Segment 5: Transcript

Bill: What I want to do is to read out of it what is there.

Therapist: Well, what feeling was there?

Mrs. S: You've been suspicious for all these years, and if . . .

Therapist: Well, one other thing that was there was what Bill just said. . . . You said that your mother was what?

Bill: Oh, since the start she just sort of moved in and sort of took over; it seemed like she was protecting my . . .

Therapist: Right. We had said this about a month ago that she seemed to be *(Turning to Mrs. S)* Remember I told you a month or two ago that I thought you looked like the center of the family and had taken over . . .

Mrs S: I sure hope, I sure wish I hadn't been.

Therapist: You had said, "No, I'm not, I can't be." And here you are now as an independent observer looking up on the TV screen. Now watch the next session. See whether you can see who's running things.

Mrs. S: Okay, but wait. . . . You said something about me being the front of it. I didn't want to be the front.

Bill: Well, in the first one she wasn't so much as in that session.

Mrs. S: And I still mean it, too.

Therapist: Well, I think you are less now than you used to be, but let's see this videotape of the third session . . .

Mrs. S: Or, maybe if we had more participation . . . but I won't say on my husband's part . . . I wouldn't have talked in front of him.

Therapist: Right, I agree.

Mrs. S: Okay.

Therapist: Your husband agreed on that too. He said if he would have done more. . . . Let's see the third one.

Mrs. S: Okay.

Videotape of earlier session, focusing on history taking, begins.

Therapist: Well, there appears to have been a lack of communication concerning the decision to have a child.

Mrs. S: Well, frankly, I was just very happy during pregnancy, and I just took it a day at a time. I just never really thought about having a baby.

Therapist: Your pregnancy was very good as far as you saw it.

Mrs. S: Yes, I felt very good, I felt real good during pregnancy when maybe some other mothers were nauseated and sick and . . .

Mr. S: I'm not asking the questions, I guess, but I just wondered what she meant by the . . . what she meant when she felt physically good. I don't remember your feeling so good.

Tape is stopped

Therapist (to Bill): Well, as you see from the videotape, I think it bothers you when your parents disagree. That's why you try to remove yourself by pushing your chair away from your parents and staring off in the other direction. Notice how you look away and frown when we discuss your mother's pregnancy.

Tape resumes:

Mr. S: Mentally happy, or what?

Mrs. S: Well, physically and mentally happy. I thought I was happy.

Therapist (to Mr. S): Why do you ask that?

Mr. S: Well, I just wanted to know if by that time she had felt more settled and that our home was being established. I do recall that she had told me once or twice that she wanted to have a child because she felt it would help our relationship.   *(Mr. S. places his hand on his son's shoulder).*

Therapist: Were you angry about being pregnant?

Mrs. S: Angry? Did I say angry? I may have been angry.

Therapist: I asked if you were angry.

Mrs. S: Naturally when you're pregnant, you're going to . . . you have to be more settled because certainly it makes . . . gives a marriage more seriousness.

Therapist: Can you be more specific on what you mean by *settled?*

Bill (interrupting): That she and Daddy were going to break up; that's what it sounds like.

Therapist: You think it sounds a little. . . . Was there some question of breaking up in those first two years?

Mr. S: Well, I don't know if there was any more doubt than there has been from the start.

Therapist: The beginning, in the beginning, what was the question?

Mr. S (hesitates); When we married she just didn't seem to be quite certain. She didn't even seem certain after we married.

Videotape ends

Therapist: I think that's it. That was an interesting segment.

Bill: Well, one thing, I did act quite differently. Like I said, I looked like I don't know . . . I acted like a four-year-old child.

Mr. S: Well, the discussion we were having could make you feel like that.

Therapist: Hmmm. Exactly.

Bill: Well, that's what the doctor said.

Therapist: Do you follow that point?

Mrs. S: You mean make Bill feel like a little child . . .

Therapist: Yes.

Bill: Oh, the discussion about the pregnancy and the relationship being unsettled. Once you get pregnant that kind of seals it, you know, that kind of settles it. That could have been . . . I can't . . . I don't remember what made me act like that. I didn't remember having been that childish, the way I was acting.

Therapist: Well, you see. I think that session pointed out what's been happening for a long time. That's what's bothering you about your relationship with your parents and you show it. And you're not even aware you're doing it.

Bill: Yeah, uh-huh.

Therapist (to Mr. S): Did you see that? You were talking. The discussion was on your breaking up, and Bill looked away horrified.

Mr. S: You know, he sure was.

Bill: I was not sure all that was going on. I really was, wasn't I? And that was very different from the other two. I mean, in the other two I was more fiddling with my eyebrow and so on, but I looked quite different in that one, very different. I was really, I was turning one way and the other and had my head covering my face and things like that, that I did not do in the first two.

Mr. S: Well, it would seem to me that probably his feelings there . . .

Bill: The topic of my mother's pregnancy was very difficult to discuss.

Mr. S: . . . were the feelings he had from, say way back, because he was able to observe that we weren't able to understand much about the relationship between us?

Bill: And from the time I knew how you felt about the pregnancy.

Mr. S: Well, I mean, beyond that, as you were growing . . .

Mrs. S: That may have had something to do with it, but the way Bill was looking was a carryover from the way he was looking the first time we ever came.

Bill: No. It's dramatically different. Very different.

Mrs. S: You say it was different. Okay. I'll let you off. I didn't notice it, and I'll just sit and listen.

Bill: Very different. The first time, yeah, I mean, both times were what the doctor would call strange behavior; but the third time that we just finished with was just all, I mean, it was just all so different. Very different. The other two I did at least sit up, but I kept fooling with my eyebrow and I was saying different things, too—the doctor says sending out different messages. The third time I wasn't really consciously sending out any message. I don't think, unless it was just all on the problem like I was in the other tape. But it was different behavior, and it had a different meaning to it. Evidently I still can't recall at the time thinking . . . yes, yes, I can. I think that way even now. It brings all sorts of ideas to mind about, I mean, just the way I was moving, the way I act even now.

Mr. S (laughs and hesitates): I acknowledge and confess to one thing. That looked like there wasn't much family relationship there, but I'm sure we don't act like that all the time. It is evident, however, that our behavior affected Bill.

Therapist: Well, it not only affected Bill, it affected all . . .

Mr. S: Yeah. Affected all of us.

Therapist (to Mrs. S): Did you see that? What did you see there? *(referring to her dominance and her husband's passivity)*

Mrs. S: Ah, I want to comment first on one thing. *(To Mr. S)* You're looking so hard . . .

Mr. S: Looking so hard to?

Mrs. S: Looking so hard to be able to say what you just said.

Mr. S: You mean I'm looking hard to . . .

Mrs. S: And that's discouraging. You're looking so hard for what you just said.

Mr. S: Well, it is hard to say.

Mrs. S: I said you're looking for, ah, you're trying to be on the negative so much and to me it's disgusting. I don't like it.

Mr. S: Well, now, wait a minute.

Mrs. S: I mean, he's trying to see the negative points and he always has.

Bill: That's pretty negative saying that.

Therapist: It's the changes in your behavior that we're looking for.

Mrs. S: It's negative: trying to look for the negative. Everybody wasn't negative.

Therapist: If you all feel better about yourselves as individuals and as a family, then some positive changes have occurred as a result of these sessions.

Segment 5: Comment

In this segment the therapist tries to identify the patterns that have changed in order to maintain the gains after therapy has stopped. He is active in challenging the mother's denial of problems. Families often focus on the past in order to avoid changes. For this reason the therapist focuses on the present and the positive changes that have occurred.

SEGMENT 6: END STAGE OF TREATMENT (16 Months Later)

Segment 6: Introduction

This is the last session, and it must be compared to earlier sessions. There is now a mood of tranquility in the whole family. Nobody is acutely ill at this point. A nest equilibrium has been established. The couple is getting along reasonably well; they are more intimate and are having sexual relations regulary. The identified patient is adjusting well to his job and to living apart from his parents. There is considerable improvement from 16 months previously.

Segment 6: Transcript

Therapist (to family): You're doing pretty well, and *(to Bill)* you're doing pretty well.

Bill: Pretty good. I said, I'll tell you, it's really hard, I mean to imagine back when I was doing so darn much worse. I mean it's hard now, you know, to even imagine, so I am doing pretty good, I mean, compared to what I was doing, I'm doing just marvelously, I mean. I was just very . . . I don't know, the whole world just seems different altogether. But you're bound to run into a few snags if you are out of it as long as I was. And I pretty much was out of it. In fact I never, I don't know, I never really grew up at all, say like even when I was 14 or 15, and whether you just, whether you call it being extremely sheltered or what, it was that, and I don't know what else. I just was, I just don't know—shut in, maybe. I found out so many things just in the last eight months that I just didn't dream of, I mean, you know, that I just didn't have any idea that it was that way, you know, that things were that way. I just didn't get out in the world much, say from the time I was back in high school on, from the time I was maybe 14 or so.

Mr. S: I don't recall that we sheltered . . . tried to keep you from getting out or anything like that. In fact we've been wanting you to get out.

Long silence

Therapist (to Mr. S): I think we now realize that there was resistance on both sides over the issue of separating.

Segment 6: Comment

Although this segment is very brief, it does highlight the change in equilibrium. Whereas previously Mrs. S. had been controlling, dominating, and hostile, now she is very quiet. Mr. S. expresses his feelings and thoughts more readily. He also is able to tell his son that he wants him to get out from under the family's wings. Mr. and Mrs. S. are now much better able to communicate and have a greater inner contentment, as shown by the longer periods of comfortable silence. The identified patient also explains that things were working out for him. He does not have the same anxiety and somatic complaints that he demonstrated in the earlier sessions.

EPILOGUE (10 Years Later)

The family was contacted by telephone at 5 and 10 years following onset of treatment.
The relationship between Mr. and Mrs. S. had continued to get progressively better. They felt more comfortable with each other and were able to be more intimate. Mr. S. continued to be more active, both as a husband and as a father. (This had been a problem prior to treatment.) Mrs. S. was not as fearful or depressed about Bill's behavior or about her marital relations. She had worked for a year, stopped when they moved, and then did not go back to work. She described her role as "helping my husband," a family task she had previously resented. She described their relationship as "no two people could be closer." Husband confirmed this, as did the son (who had been quite critical of their relationship prior to his illness).

The identified patient had a 10-year history of working episodically for about three-quarters of the time. He had lost three of four jobs, probably related to his inability to do complex tasks. He had worked in his present job (as a teacher's aid) for three years and was receiving excellent evaluations. When he lived in a smaller town, he described his relationships with people "as more than adequate." Since moving to a large city in order to get better employment he had had fewer contacts with others, however, and described this as a "problem." He continued to be episodically symptomatic. He had minimal paranoid symptoms and mildly incapacitating obsessive-compulsive and phobic symptoms. He had two brief hospitalizations, one for two days and one for seven days, and was treated with phenothiazines in low doses during this time. He has never regularly taken medication over a sustained period of time.

At the 10-year follow-up all three family members were very enthusiastic about the family treatment. They felt that the therapist had not put the blame on any one family member. Mrs. S. said that the therapy was "a blessing." Bill said that therapy had helped him to improve greatly, and he felt as if it had "resurrec-ted" him to improve greatly, and he felt as if it had "resurrected" him.

SUGGESTIONS FOR FURTHER READINGS

Napier A and Whitaker C: **The Family Crucible**. New York: Harper and Row, 1978.

> *A very readable description of the whole treatment of a family by two expert therapists.*

Papp P (Ed): **Family Therapy: Full Length Case Studies**. New York: Gardner Press, 1977.

REFERENCES

1. Glick ID and Marshall GJ: Family Therapy: An Introduction. Videotape and 16mm black and white sound film, 43 min.
2. Minuchin S: Families and Family Therapy. Cambridge, MA: Harvard University Press, 1974
3. Haley J and Hoffman L: Techniques of Family Therapy. New York: Basic Books, 1967
4. Papp P: Family Therapy. Full Length Case Studies. New York: Gardner, 1977
5. Napier AY and Whitaker CA: The Family Crucible. New York: Harper & Row, 1978

Author Index

Subject Index

Mother-headed single parent family,
86-87. *See also* Single-parent
family
Mourning, 196
MPCI, 162, 164
Multi-generational family model, 27-
28
Mythic time, 14-15

NAMI, 363
Nathan B. Ackerman Memorial Con-
ference of 1974, 436
National Alliance for the Mentally Ill
(NAMI), 363
Negative effects of family therapy,
515, 519, 524-527
Newborn, adaptation of family to,
455-457
New family forms. *See* Cohabitation;
Companionate marriage; Gay
male couple; Lesbian couple;
Multi-generational family
model; Remarried family
units
Nonmonogamy in gay male couple,
305-306
Nuclear family, history of, 25-28
Nursing, psychiatric, 473-475

Objectives for training in family intervention, 553-554, 555
Object relations point of view,
functioning family and, 75
Obsessive-compulsive marital partner,
340
Onset of treatment, case transcript of,
579-583
Open-coupled style of gay males, 305
Organic mental disorders, 340-341,
419. *See also* Psychiatric disorder in individual member
of family

Outcome of family therapy. *See*
Research, on outcome of
family therapy

Paradoxical technique, 203-204
schizophrenia and, 332
Parental coalition, 110-112
in functional family, 68-69
Parental deprivation, 69
Parents. *See also* Childbearing;
Childrearing; Lesbian parent;
Parental coalition
of family therapy participant, tests
for, 164
at high risk for child abuse, 459
Participant in family therapy, 225-226,
237-238
caretaker as, 239
compared with other psychosocial
therapy formats, 17
for divorce, 291
evaluation process, 122-123
young children, 477
extended family and significant
others as, 238
pet as, 239-240
remarried family unit as, 294
Passion in long-term relationship,
266(*f*)
Past disappointments and hurts, 106
Pediatrics, family model and, 454-457
Personality disorder, 340. *See also*
Psychiatric disorder in individual member of family
Pervasive developmental disorder, 342
Pet as participant in treatment, 239-
240
Phobia, 268
Physical medicine and family model,
453-454
Physician
career-oriented family life of. *See*
Physicians and their families
family model for. *See* Family